INSTRUCTOR'S MANUAL

to accompany

FUNDAMENTALS OF MANAGEMENT

Ninth Edition

James H. Donnelly, Jr.
James L. Gibson
John M. Ivancevich

Prepared by

Barbara A. Gorski
University of Saint Thomas—St. Paul, MN

Irwin B. Kroot
Technology Skills Development Center—City of New York

IRWIN
Chicago • Bogotá • Boston • Buenos Aires • Caracas
London • Madrid • Mexico City • Sydney • Toronto

ISBN 0–256–15116–4

1 2 3 4 5 6 7 8 9 0 P 1 0 9 8 7 6 5 4

INSTRUCTIONAL SUPPORT SYSTEM: AN INTRODUCTION

With the publication of the ninth edition of *Fundamentals of Management,* we continue our efforts to provide a full integrated supplement package that provides instructional support for both the instructor and student. We have continued, and improved upon, the excellent framework for the *Instructional Support System.* Our goal with the revision and update of those supplements has been to make the supplements for this edition even more useful and helpful.

Here is a brief overview of the seven teaching/learning aids that comprise the *Instructional Support System:*

1.   *Instructor's Manual*—The manual has been improved with easier access to materials. The manual's segments are described in more detail later in this preface.

2.   *Lecture Resource Manual*—This guide provides additional lecture resource materials that supplement the *Fundamentals of Management* text.

3.   *Transparencies*—The set of transparencies are multicolored reproductions of the textbook's tables and figures and selected transparencies from the *Lecture Resource Manual* which are especially useful as teaching aids for your class lectures. These multicolored transparencies are provided free to adopters upon request. Additional transparency masters are included in the *Instructor's Manual.*

4.   *Test Bank*—The Test Bank contains a variety of test questions such as true/false, multiple choice, and essay questions. The questions are grouped by topic according to the text outline. Also included with each test question is the text page number on which the correct answer (or discussion) may be found. Correct answers are provided. See the preface of the *Text Bank* for information about improvements in layout and easier access.

5.   Irwin's Computerized Testing Software—This advanced-feature test generator allows you to add and edit questions; save and reload tests; create up to 99 different versions of each test; attach graphics to questions; import and export ASCII files; and select questions based on type, level of difficulty, or keyword. *Fundamentals of Management* questions are categorized by chapter, type i.e., multiple choice, true-false, or essay) and by level of difficulty (i.e., easy, medium, or difficult).

     TeleTest—TeleTest is an in-house testing service designed to provide adopters of *Fundamentals of Management* with another testing alternative. Upon your request, representatives will provide you with a TeleTest bank and order form for this title. After consulting the TeleTest bank and choosing the questions (either Random question selection, Sequential question selection or a Combination of both), call our tollfree number or mail the order form to the TeleTest for your customized exam.

HOW TO USE THE INSTRUCTOR'S MANUAL

This ninth edition *Instructor's Manual* has been improved to provide a comprehensive set of teaching aids that are tied directly to the text. The manual is comprised of the following elements:

COURSE SYLLABI

The suggested syllabi provides you with a selection of three course plans with each plan designed to accommodate a ten-week quarter or 1 5-week semester:

1. Plan A: Course requirements are comprised of three examinations and a business simulation.
2. Plan B: Course requirements are comprised of three examinations and a research paper (a list of 80 possible topics are included as part of the syllabi).
3. Plan C: Course requirements are comprised of three examinations and completion of the seven-part series "Create A Company."

In addition, course objectives, course requirements (along with grading weights for each requirement) and class format are also provided.

INSTRUCTOR'S MATERIALS FOR EACH TEXT CHAPTER

Each set includes numerous features:

1. **Learning Objectives** for the chapter.

2. **Chapter Synopses**, which provide a capsule summary of the chapter's approach to the topics and an overview of the primary concepts discussed.

3. **Teaching Tips**
   1. *Lecture Ideas*—interesting ideas on approaching the text material that can increase student understanding of the chapter material.
   2. *Project/Exercise Ideas*—interesting individual/group project ideas that enhance student's understanding and enjoyment of the major concepts/topics in the text. Including many ideas for guest speakers.

4. **Chapter Lecture Outline Notes**, comprise a detailed comprehensive outline of the chapter material. These notes are the most detailed ever produced for *Fundamentals of Management*. Rest assured that every major topic and point made in the chapter is contained in these outlines. The outlines are easily detachable for your use during your lectures. Many instructors lecture directly from the outlines, making additional notes in the margins.

5. **Answers to the Chapter's Discussion and Review Questions**
    Responses to these questions have been expanded and often provide insights for leading the classroom discussion as students explore their own understanding of the text material.

6. **Additional Discussion Questions**
    Some of these additional questions are issue and thought-related; however, more were developed to directly test students' knowledge of the text material. Answers and discussion facilitation information are provided. As mentioned in the *Test Bank*, many of these questions would also serve as excellent Essay Questions on exams.

7. **End of Chapter Cases**
    This segment includes a capsule summary of the chapter's application cases and answers to the questions for analysis.

ANALYSIS OF COMPREHENSIVE CASES

This segment offers advice on how to effectively use cases as teaching aids and provides analyses of the text's three comprehensive cases. Also included are responses to all questions for analysis.

EXPERIENTIAL EXERCISES IN MANAGEMENT

This section offers advice on the use of experiential exercises in teaching management. The section provides suggestions for conducting the exercises, answer keys when needed, and some questions to ask participants during post-exercise class discussion.

RECOMMENDED VIDEOS

This section highlights available videos which are particularly useful as a supplement to the text material. All recommended videos are listed in the Video Resource Guide with complete information provided. This edition of the *Instructor's Manual* includes over 100 new titles and short reviews. These newly included items are indicated with an asterisk.

TRANSPARENCIES

In addition to the separate color transparencies available, additional transparencies for each chapter are included in this manual.

RESEARCH PAPER TOPICS

This expanded listing of research paper topics is grouped by chapter for easier reference and accompany the information within that chapter. However, many topics are applicable for term-long research papers.

We hope that you find this *Instructor's Manual*—and *Fundamentals of Management Instructional Support System*—be most useful to you in teaching students the art and science of management in business today. We would very much appreciate any comments, criticisms, and suggestions for improvement.

As a final note, we would like to thank the people who helped us bring this book to you. They supplied endless hours of computer and human support. Mark Borovansky, Amy Kroot, Kerstin Rohde and Bridget Zimmer—we appreciate each of you. We dedicate our efforts to the memories of Lois Gorski and Edith Rice, and to the health of our family and friends.

Barbara A. Gorski
Irwin B. Kroot

CONTENTS

SECTION I

COURSE SYLLABI

INSTRUCTOR NAME
CLASS LOCATION

OFFICE HOURS
OFFICE LOCATION
PHONE

TEXTS

Fundamentals of Management, Daniel, Gibson, Ivancevich (Richard D. Irwin, 1993)

COURSE OBJECTIVES

The effective management of work of employees within organizations is the backbone of industrialized societies. It is the manager who must make decisions about the use of human resources, materials, technology, and capital. The course will attempt to portray a realistic picture of what the manager's job involves and how it has changed over the years. It will point out the skills that managers must apply to achieve crucial goals and performance standards. This picture will not provide perfect answers to every managerial situation, issue, or problem. However, it will show that managing within organizations is a mixture of artful and scientifically based decision-making judgments, application of skills, and the performance of various roles.

Among the objectives which will serve as the focal point of the course are the following:

1. To gain a basic understanding of management principles including planning, organizing, and controlling.
2. To gain a basic understanding of concepts for managing people including human resources, motivation, leading, and communications.
3. To improve the students ability to examine managerial issues and problems and develop feasible alternatives that can result in better decision making.
4. To create within the student an ability to uncover variables or factors that result in problems and issues. The way variables fit together is an important insight into managing.
5. To develop an awareness of multiple approaches that can be used to resolve managerial issues and problems in becoming a practicing manager.
6. To understand the impact of the world economy in which business operates.

INSERT APPROPRIATE PLAN DESCRIPTION

PLAN A

COURSE REQUIREMENTS

The final course grade is comprised of the following elements:

Exam #1	25%
Exam #2	25%
Final Exam	25%
Simulation	25%
TOTAL	100%

EXAMS:

Three exams will be used to test your knowledge of the subject matter. The tests will be straightforward, covering the lectures and the reading assignments.

IMPORTANT DATES

> : Bus Simulation Report #1 due
> : Bus Simulation Report #2 due
> : Bus Simulation Report #3 due
> : Bus Simulation Report #4 due
> : Exam #1
> : Exam #2
> : Final Exam

CLASS FORMAT

The class format is primarily lecture with an emphasis on class discussion. Students are expected to be prepared to discuss class assignments by keeping up with assigned readings.

COURSE SCHEDULE (PLAN A)
15-WEEK SEMESTER

Week	Class	Topic	Reading Assignment
1	1	Managers and the Evolution of Management	C1
	2	Managers and Their Environment	C2
	3	Introduce Simulation	MG
2	4	Managing in a Global Environment	C3
	5	Corporate Social Responsibility and Ethics	C4
	6	Foundations of Managing Work and Organizations	R5-10
3	7*	Management Decision Making: Types & Process	C5
	8	Mgt Decision Making: Individual versus Group Decision Making	
	9	The Planning Function: Elements & Importance of Planning	C6
4	10	Objectives, Resources, & Implementation of Plans	
	11	The Strategic Planning Process	C7
	12	Strategic and Operational Planning	
5	13#	Organizing: Specialization & Delegating Authority	C8
	14	Organizing: Departmentalization & Dimensions of Structure	
	15	Organization Design: The Universalistic Approach	C9
6	16	Contingency Organization Design	
	17	The Controlling Function	C10
	18	Exam #1	
7	19@	Foundations of Managing People	R11-16
	20	Motivation: Content & Process Theories	C11
	21	Motivation Strategies	
8	22	Work Groups: Formation & Type	C12
	23	Work Group Development, Characteristic and Consequences	
	24	Leading: Trait and Personal-Behavioral Theories	C13
9	25!	Situational and Transformational Theories and Effectiveness Factors	
	26	The Communications Process	C14
	27	HRM: Employment Activity & Training	C15
10	28	HRM: Wage & Salary Management, Benefits & Services, and Labor Relations	
	29	Organizational Change, Development and Innovation	C16
	30	A Model for Managing Organizational Change	
11	31	Exam #2	
	32	Foundations of Managing People and Organizations	R17-19
	33	P/OM: Transformation Process and Quality Concern	C17
12	34	P/OM: Quality Factors & TQM	
	35	Production Planning: Linear Programming	C18
	36	Production Planning: PERT	
13	37	Inventory Planning and Controlling: Types, Purposes, & EOQ	C18
	38	Inventory Planning and Controlling: MRP and JIT	
	39	Decision Support Systems: MIS & DSS	C19
14	40	DSS: Organization and Design	
	41	Entrepreneurship	C20
	42	Management Careers	C21
15	43	Review of Comprehensive Cases	
	44	Exam Review	
	45	Final Exam	

C: Chapter
R: Review Upcoming Chapters and
    Read Comprehensive Case
MG: Management Game Simulation

* Business Simulation Report #1 due
# Business Simulation Report #2 due
@ Business Simulation Report #3 due
! Business Simulation Report #4 due

COURSE SCHEDULE (PLAN A)
10-WEEK QUARTER

Week	Class	Topic	Reading Assignment
1	1	Managers and the Evolution of Management	C1
	2	Managers and Their Environment	C2
	3	Introduce Simulation	MG
2	4*	Managing in a Global Environment	C3
	5	Corporate Social Responsibility and Ethics	C4
	6	Foundations of Managing Work and Organizations	R5-10
3	7	Management Decision Making	C5
	8	The Planning Function	C6
	9	Strategic Planning	C7
4	10#	The Organizing Function	C8
	11	The Organization Design	C9
	12	The Controlling Function	C10
5	13	Exam #1	
	14	Foundations of Managing People	R11-16
	15	Motivation	C11
6	16@	Managing Work Groups	C12
	17	Leading People and Organizations	C13
	18	The Communications Process and Negotiations	C14
7	19	Human Resource Management	C15
	20	Organizational Change, Development and Innovation	C16
	21	Exam #2	
8	22!	Managing Production & Operations	C17
	23	Production/Operations Management	
	24	Production Planning	
9	25	Inventory Planning and Controlling	C18
	26	Decision Support Systems	C19
	27	Entrepreneurship	C20
10	28	Management Careers	C21
	29	Review of Comprehensive Cases Exam Review	
	30	Final Exam	

C: Chapter
R: Review Upcoming Chapters and
    Read Comprehensive Case
MG: Management Game Simulation

* Business Simulation Report #1 due
# Business Simulation Report #2 due
@ Business Simulation Report #3 due
! Business Simulation Report #4 due

PLAN B

COURSE REQUIREMENTS

The final course grade is comprised of the following elements:

Exam #1	25%
Exam #2	25%
Final Exam	25%
Research Paper	25%
TOTAL	100%

EXAMS:

Three exams will be used to test your knowledge of the subject matter. The tests will be straightforward, covering the lectures and the reading assignments.

RESEARCH PAPER

The research paper assignment entails preparing a paper that examines a pertinent management topic or issue. A list of potential topics is attached; however, topics are not limited to those on the list. On _____, all students must submit a research paper topic statement, a double-spaced typed statement that specifies your paper topic. The paper must be at least _____ pages in length. The final paper is due on _____.

IMPORTANT DATES

> : Research Paper Topic Statement Due
> : Exam #1
> : Exam #2
> : Research Paper Due
> : Final Exam

CLASS FORMAT

The class format is primarily lecture with an emphasis on class discussion. Students are expected to be prepared to discuss class assignments by keeping up with assigned readings.

COURSE SCHEDULE (PLAN B)
15-WEEK SEMESTER

Week	Class	Topic	Reading Assignment
1	1	Managers and the Evolution of Management	C1
	2	Managers and Their Environment	C2
	3	Introduce Simulation	MG
2	4	Managing in a Global Environment	C3
	5	Corporate Social Responsibility and Ethics	C4
	6	Foundations of Managing Work and Organizations	R5-10
3	7	Management Decision Making: Types & Process	C5
	8	Mgt Decision Making: Individual versus Group Decision Making	
	9	The Planning Function: Elements & Importance of Planning	C6
4	10*	Objectives, Resources, & Implementation of Plans	
	11	The Strategic Planning Process	C7
	12	Strategic and Operational Planning	
5	13	Organizing: Specialization & Delegating Authority	C8
	14	Organizing: Departmentalization & Dimensions of Structure	
	15	Organization Design: The Universalistic Approach	C9
6	16	Contingency Organization Design	
	17	The Controlling Function	C10
	18	Exam #1	
7	19	Foundations of Managing People	R11-16
	20	Motivation: Content & Process Theories	C11
	21	Motivation Strategies	
8	22	Work Groups: Formation & Type	C12
	23	Work Group Development, Characteristic and Consequences	
	24	Leading: Trait and Personal-Behavioral Theories	C13
9	25	Situational and Transformational Theories and Effectiveness Factors	
	26	The Communications Process	C14
	27	HRM: Employment Activity & Training	C15
10	28	HRM: Wage & Salary Management, Benefits & Services, and Labor Relations	
	29	Organizational Change, Development and Innovation	C16
	30	A Model for Managing Organizational Change	
11	31	Exam #2	
	32	Foundations of Managing People and Organizations	R17-19
	33	P/OM: Transformation Process and Quality Concern	C17
12	34	P/OM: Quality Factors & TQC	
	35	Production Planning: Linear Programming	C18
	36	Production Planning: PERT	
13	37#	Inventory Planning and Controlling: Types, Purposes, & EOQ	C18
	38	Inventory Planning and Controlling: MRP and JIT	
	39	Decision Support Systems: MIS & DSS	C19
14	40	DSS: Organization and Design	
	41	Entrepreneurship	C20
	42	Management Careers	C21
15	43	Review of Comprehensive Cases	
	44	Exam Review	
	45	Final Exam	

C: Chapter
R: Review Upcoming Chapters and
   Read Comprehensive Case

* Research Paper Topic Statement Due
   # Research Paper Due

COURSE SCHEDULE (PLAN B)
10-WEEK QUARTER

Week	Class	Topic	Reading Assignment
1	1	Managers and the Evolution of Management	C1
	2	Managers and Their Environment	C2
	3	Introduce Simulation	MG
2	4	Managing in a Global Environment	C3
	5	Corporate Social Responsibility and Ethics	C4
	6	Foundations of Managing Work and Organizations	R5-10
3	7*	Management Decision Making	C5
	8	The Planning Function	C6
	9	Strategic Planning	C7
4	10	The Organizing Function	C8
	11	The Organization Design	C9
	12	The Controlling Function	C10
5	13	Exam #1	
	14	Foundations of Managing People	R11-16
	15	Motivation	C11
6	16	Managing Work Groups	C12
	17	Leading People and Organizations	C13
	18	The Communications Process and Negotiations	C14
7	19	Human Resource Management	C15
	20	Organizational Change, Development and Innovation	C16
	21	Exam #2	
8	22	Managing Production & Operations	C17
	23	Production/Operations Management	
	24#	Production Planning	
9	25	Inventory Planning and Controlling	C18
	26	Decision Support Systems	C19
	27	Entrepreneurship	C20
10	28	Management Careers	C21
	29	Review of Comprehensive Cases Exam Review	
	30	Final Exam	

C: Chapter
R: Review Upcoming Chapters and
   Read Comprehensive Case

* Research Paper Topic Statement Due
# Research Paper Due

PLAN C

COURSE REQUIREMENTS

The final course grade is comprised of the following elements:

Exam #1	25%
Exam #2	25%
Final Exam	25%
CAC Reports	25%
TOTAL	100%

EXAMS:

Three exams will be used to test your knowledge of the subject matter. The tests will be straightforward, covering the lectures and the reading assignments.

"CREATE A COMPANY" PROJECT

"Create A Company" is a six-part exercise which is designed to provide you with a more in-depth understanding of the managerial functions of planning, organizing, and controlling through the mock creation of your own business. Working on a group basis, each student group will select an industry of interest, and create and manage a company through seven activities:

1. Developing a strategic plan for your business
2. Designing the business' organizational structure
3. Developing a control system and human resources function for your business
4. Addressing key production/operations issues in your company
5. Developing a plan for expanding your business' activities into a foreign market
6. Addressing several managerial career issues that will affect your company. A written report is required for activities 1, 2, 3, 5, and 6. More details requiring report content will be provided later along with guidelines concerning each activity. Each report will contribute five percent toward your final grade.

IMPORTANT DATES

```
            : CAC report #1 due
            : CAC report #2 due
            : CAC report #3 due
            : Exam #1
            : Exam #2
            : CAC report #4 due
            : CAC report #5 due
            : Final Exam
```

CLASS FORMAT

The class format is primarily lecture with an emphasis on class discussion. Students are expected to be prepared to discuss class assignments by keeping up with assigned readings.

INSTRUCTOR

The six "Create A Company" exercises are provided in the Study Guide.

COURSE SCHEDULE (PLAN C)
15-WEEK SEMESTER

Week	Class	Topic	Reading Assignment
1	1	Managers and the Evolution of Management	C1
	2	Managers and Their Environment	C2
	3	Introduce Simulation	MG
2	4	Managing in a Global Environment	C3
	5	Corporate Social Responsibility and Ethics	C4
	6	Foundations of Managing Work and Organizations	R5-10
3	7	Management Decision Making: Types & Process	C5
	8	Mgt Decision Making: Individual versus Group Decision Making	
	9	The Planning Function: Elements & Importance of Planning	C6
4	10*	Objectives, Resources, & Implementation of Plans	
	11	The Strategic Planning Process	C7
	12	Strategic and Operational Planning	
5	13	Organizing: Specialization & Delegating Authority	C8
	14	Organizing: Departmentalization & Dimensions of Structure	
	15	Organization Design: The Universalistic Approach	C9
6	16*	Contingency Organization Design	
	17	The Controlling Function	C10
	18	Exam #1	
7	19	Foundations of Managing People	R11-16
	20	Motivation: Content & Process Theories	C11
	21	Motivation Strategies	
8	22	Work Groups: Formation & Type	C12
	23	Work Group Development,Characteristic and Consequences	
	24	Leading: Trait and Personal-Behavioral Theories	C13
9	25	Situational and Transformational Theories and Effectiveness Factors	
	26	The Communications Process	C14
	27	HRM: Employment Activity & Training	C15
10	28*	HRM: Wage & Salary Management, Benefits & Services, and Labor Relations	
	29	Organizational Change, Development and Innovation	C16
	30	A Model for Managing Organizational Change	
11	31	Exam #2	
	32	Foundations of Managing People and Organizations	R17-19
	33	P/OM: Transformation Process and Quality Concern	C17
12	34	P/OM: Quality Factors & TQC	
	35	Production Planning: Linear Programming	C18
	36	Production Planning: PERT	
13	37	Inventory Planning and Controlling: Types, Purposes, & EOQ	C18
	38	Inventory Planning and Controlling: MRP and JIT	
	39	Decision Support Systems: MIS & DSS	C19
14	40	DSS: Organization and Design	
	41*	Entrepreneurship	C20
	42	Management Careers	C21
15	43 *	Review of Comprehensive Cases	
	44	Exam Review	
	45	Final Exam	

C: Chapter   * CAC Reports Due
R: Review Upcoming Chapters and
   Read Comprehensive Case

COURSE SCHEDULE (PLAN C)
10-WEEK QUARTER

Week	Class	Topic	Reading Assignment
1	1	Managers and the Evolution of Management	C1
	2	Managers and Their Environment	C2
	3	Introduce Simulation	MG
2	4	Managing in a Global Environment	C3
	5	Corporate Social Responsibility and Ethics	C4
	6	Foundations of Managing Work and Organizations	R5-10
3	7*	Management Decision Making	C5
	8	The Planning Function	C6
	9	Strategic Planning	C7
4	10*	The Organizing Function	C8
	11	The Organization Design	C9
	12	The Controlling Function	C10
5	13	Exam #1	
	14	Foundations of Managing People	R11-16
	15	Motivation	C11
6	16	Managing Work Groups	C12
	17*	Leading People and Organizations	C13
	18	The Communications Process and Negotiations	C14
7	19	Human Resource Management	C15
	20	Organizational Change, Development and Innovation	C16
	21	Exam #2	
8	22	Managing Production & Operations	C17
	23	Production/Operations Management	
	24	Production Planning	
9	25	Inventory Planning and Controlling	C18
	26	Decision Support Systems	C19
	27*	Entrepreneurship	C20
10	28	Management Careers	C21
	29	Review of Comprehensive Cases	
		Exam Review	
	30	Final Exam	

C: Chapter
R: Review Upcoming Chapters and
   Read Comprehensive Case

* CAC Reports Due

CHAPTER OUTLINE
FOR USE IN A PROCESS-ORIENTED INTRODUCTORY MANAGEMENT COURSE

Using *Fundamentals of Management*, 9/e, in a course organized around the traditional management processes or functions of planning, organizing, and controlling can easily be accomplished by using the following presentation of the material:

PART I. Management and the Environment
1. Managers and the Evolution of Management
2. Managers and their Environment
3. Managing in a Global Environment
4. Social and Ethical Responsibilities of Management

PART II. Managing Work & Organizations: Planning, Organizing, Controlling
5. Management Decision Making
6. The Planning Function
7. Strategic Planning
8. The Organizing Function
9. Organization Design
10. The Controlling Function

PART III. Managing People in Organizations
11. Motivation
12. Managing Work Groups
13. Leading People in Organizations
14. Communication and Negotiation
15. Human Resource Management
16. Organization Change, Development, and Innovation

PART IV. Managing People in Organizations
17. Production and Operations Management
18. Production and Inventory Planning and Control
19. Managing Information for Decision Making

PART V. Special Management Topics
20. Entrepreneurship
21. Management Careers

SECTION II

INSTRUCTOR'S MATERIALS

1 MANAGERS AND THE EVOLUTION OF MANAGEMENT

LEARNING OBJECTIVES

After completing Chapter 1, students should be able to:

Define   the terms manager and management.

Describe   the evolution of management as a field of study and how the three established approaches to management provide the foundations for practicing management.

Discuss   why the study of management can be important to almost anyone.

Compare   the tools and techniques used by management scientists.

Identify   the human relations and the behavioral sciences approaches.

CHAPTER SYNOPSIS

This introductory chapter provides a discussion of the global economy, a brief conceptual definition of management, an explanation of the importance of studying the field of management, an overview of management's evolution as a field of study, and a brief look at the three major tasks that comprise the work of management.

The chapter presents management as the coordination of specialized efforts of individuals to achieve results that aren't possible by one individual working alone. The importance of studying management is emphasized by stressing the points that: 1) management plays a prominent role in international competition; 2) managers serve the critical function of guiding and directing the organizations upon which society depends; and 3)many people who aren't trained to be managers often find themselves in management jobs.

The major portion of the chapter addresses the evolution of management as a field of study by summarizing the key characteristics of the three established approaches to management which have emerged since the early 1900s: the **Classical Approach**, the **Behavioral Approach**, and the **Management Science Approach**.

The Classical Approach to management is an outgrowth of the work of two schools: Scientific Management (the management of work) and Classical Organization Theory (the management of organizations). Scientific Management is addressed by discussing its assumptions and its three major contributions (work management, simplification, and scheduling) in terms of key Scientific Management theorists and their work. Frederick Taylor's efforts in finding the best way to perform work, and his four principles of managing work, are discussed. The efforts and perspectives of Frank and Lillian Gilbreth (in the area of work simplification), Henry Gantt (work scheduling), and Harrington Emerson (work efficiency) are highlighted. Classical Organization Theory is addressed by discussing the management principles of Henri Fayol (whose principles were presented as guidelines to thinking in 1929) and James Mooney (who offered his principles as natural laws in 1931).

The Behavioral Approach, covering the issues and fundamentals of managing people, involves two schools of thought: the **Human Relations Approach** and the **Behavioral Science Approach.** The Human Relations Approach is addressed by focusing on the **Hawthorne studies** (which were a major force in awakening managers to the influence of the individual's psychological and sociological dimensions on the job and organizational performance). The Hawthorne studies' four phases, contributions, and shortcomings are explained. Concerning the Behavioral Science Approach, the authors define behavioral science, discuss concerns which led to the emergence of the approach, and explain the interdisciplinary makeup of the approach.

The discussion of the **Management Science Approach** includes the historical development of management science and production and operations management, the relationship between these two areas, the characteristics of management science, and the role of mathematical models and the types used in P/OM.

Two recent attempts (the **Systems Approach** and the **Contingency Approach**) to integrate the three earlier management approaches are also profiled. The chapter then summarizes with the three major functions of the modern manager—managing work and organizations, managing people, and managing production and operations. These three tasks serve as the focal points for three of the book's sections.

TEACHING TIPS

LECTURE & DISCUSSION IDEAS

1. It is useful to launch the introductory lecture by emphasizing the pervasiveness of the management function both in business and in all areas of society. The importance of management and the functions which it encompasses become more evident when the concept is related to diverse occupations (e.g., secretary, pro football quarterback, surgeon, school teacher, U.S. president). It becomes readily evident that all these occupations involve management and that effective or ineffective management can substantially impact the performance and well-being of others.

2. From this opening discussion, the general concept of management should emerge. As the text definition is amplified, you may want to introduce other definitions of management such as: management as decision making, management as a change agent, management as an economic resource. The objective should be to emphasize the necessity for a field definition so that the course does not broaden to "Universe 101."

3. It is useful to discuss fully the framework for the study of management presented in Figure 1-4 which illustrates the author's approach to the study of management as well as the book's format. As noted, the primary tasks of managing work and

organizations, people, and production/operations are the focal points for three of the book's five sections. Section 2 focuses on the fundamentals of managing work and organizations by addressing the various facets of planning, organizing, and controlling. The book's third section, the foundations of managing people, concentrates on behavioral research and its contributions to our knowledge of leading, motivating, group dynamics, communication, and organizational change. The fourth section, the foundations of managing production and operations, concentrates on concepts and tools useful in planning and controlling production and operations. (The book's first section discusses the managerial environment, global issues and their impact on management, and the increasingly important consideration of ethics and social responsibility. The final section addresses issues of entrepreneurship and management careers.)

4.   A note about the Gilbreths: your students may be more familiar with the Gilbreths than they realize. Ask them if they've ever seen *Cheaper by the Dozen* on late-night television. The highly popular 1950 film (and its sequel, *Belles on their Toes*) is the story of the Gilbreth family. Clifton Webb and Myrna Loy played the Gilbreths.

PROJECT / EXERCISE IDEAS

1.   Increasingly in the last five years, articles have been published in major business publications (e.g., *The Wall Street Journal, Business Week, Fortune*) that focus on the major challenges facing top-level business managers today. As a research assignment, your students could collect several articles on this topic and discuss their content in class, drawing upon the similar and contrasting opinions expressed by business leaders concerning today's major managerial challenges.

2.   A broad range of professional management and management-related periodicals is listed at the end of Chapter 1. Students can select one or more journals from each of the three categories indicated in the list (topical discussions, theory and research, or practical applications) and report back on the general topics of articles presented during the past year and the general approaches taken to management issues in each. Alternatively, students can select a broad general topic (such as management in the "new" Eastern Europe or management among high-tech firms) and compare and contrast the information presented in one periodical from each of the three categories of periodicals.

3.   One way to encourage a more thorough evaluation of the strengths and shortcomings of the Classical Approach is to conduct a class debate on the issue. Select two groups (each composed of up to five students) with one group arguing the merits of the Classical Approach (or Scientific Management) and the other group arguing its shortcomings. The groups should first conduct research to develop and substantiate their positions. This exercise is particularly effective in discussing the merits and shortcomings of Scientific Management.

4.   One way to enhance your students' understanding of management science models is to assign them the task of obtaining a research article which uses a model to solve a particular problem and prepare a report on the study and its findings. This project can

provide students with a better understanding of how models are applied in organizations. *Interfaces* and *Decision Sciences* are two academic journals which frequently carry studies on management science models.

LECTURE OUTLINE NOTES

I. Chapter Introduction

   A. A new **global economy** is emerging
       1. The competitive edge in the global economy comes from harnessing the rich and diverse human resource in organizations.
       2. New and proven management tools are critical for effective management.
   B. The U.S. is at a crossroads because of the increase in international competitiveness.
       1. Traditional management approaches are proving inadequate.
   C. **Management** is the process undertaken by one or more individuals to coordinate the activities of others to achieve results not achievable by one individual acting alone.

II. **Why Study Management?**

   A. Because managers guide and direct the organizations that provide goods and services upon which society depends. In doing so, managers serve a critical function.
   B. Because individuals who aren't trained as managers often find themselves in managerial positions. Studying management better equips individuals to handle managerial responsibilities.
   C. Because the future success of the U.S., Canada, Japan, France, Germany, or any industrialized nation in the global village lies in managing productivity, being able to cope with environmental changes, and properly managing the workforce.

III. **The Evolution of Management as a Field of Study**

   A. Contributors to the evolution of management consist of three groups:
       1. Practicing managers who describe their own experiences and generalize principles from those experiences which they believe can be applied in similar situations.
       2. Social and behavioral scientists who study management as a social phenomenon using scientific methods.
       3. Engineers, sociologists, psychologists, anthropologists, lawyers, economists, accountants, mathematicians, political scientists, and philosophers who represent a middle ground between the perspectives of management as practice and management as science to studying management.

18

B.   There are three well-established approaches to management thought: the **Classical Approach**, the **Behavioral Approach**, and the **Management Science** approach.
1.   These approaches provide different ways of looking at management tasks. Although they are discussed in order of their development in history, no one has replaced the other. They are all used today as appropriate.
C.   Two recent attempts to integrate the three established approaches are the **Systems Approach** and the **Contingency Approach**.
D.   Managers can make a difference in organizations of all sizes.
1.   The study of management shows what managers do right to create opportunities for employees, judge performance accurately, and encourage optimum productivity.
2.   The study of management also points out the errors that managers make.
3.   We can use these lessons to find the management ideas with continuing value for practitioners in the 21st century.

IV. **Foundations of Managing Work and Organizations**

A.   **The Classical Approach**
1.   Emerged in the early 1900s. It includes two schools:
a.   **Scientific Management**
1)   Theorists (primarily engineers) focused on increasing the efficiency of work.
2)   Believed the most efficient—the best—way to do a job could be determined through analysis of data, and urged managers to observe actual work performance and collect objective data.
b.   **Classical Organization Theory**
1)   Theorists (primarily practicing managers) believed organizations could be effectively managed via principles and practices stressing productivity and efficiency.

B.   **The Management of Work (Scientific Management)**
1.   Major contributions
a.   **Work management**—Frederick Taylor (the "father" of Scientific Management) was the major contributor.
1)   As a supervisor at Midvale Steel Company, he became interested in ways to improve lathe work. His goal was to provide scientifically based standards for defining a fair day's work.
2)   He developed the four principles of managing work:
a)   Develop a science for each element of a man's work which replaces the old rule-of-thumb method.
b)   Scientifically select, train and develop the worker.
c)   Cooperate with the workers to ensure the job is done in accordance with the science that has been

19

developed.

        d)   Equally divide work and responsibility between management and workers. (Previously, workers handled almost all of the work and most of the responsibility).

  b. **Principles of work simplification**

      1)   Taylor followers, Frank and Lillian Gilbreth, increased the productivity of bricklayers by 200 percent by studying their movements (for example, bending, reaching, stooping), eliminating inefficient movements, combining others, and simplifying the work. Reduced the number of motions involved in laying a brick from 18 to 4½.

  c. **Principles of work scheduling**

      1)   Engineer Henry Gantt, a close Taylor associate, developed the Gantt chart which shows the relationship between work planned and completed on one axis and time elapsed on the other. The Gantt chart is still commonly used in industry for scheduling activities.

      2)   He expanded Scientific Management analysis to include the work of managers.

  d. **Principles of efficiency**

      1)   Harrington Emerson established principles for accomplishing the efficient use of resources. Managers should:

          a)   Use scientific, objective, and factual analysis.

          b)   Define the aims of the undertaking.

          c)   Relate each part to the whole.

          d)   Provide standardized procedures and methods.

          e)   Reward individuals for successful task execution.

2. Significant and lasting contributions

  a. Identification of management's responsibilities for managing work.

      1)   **planning**

      2)   **organizing**

      3)   **leading and influencing**

      4)   **controlling**

C. **The Management of Organizations (Classical Organization Theory)**

1. The two lasting contributions by theorists (practicing managers):

  a. **Principles of management**

      1)   Henri Fayol sought principles to facilitate the "soundness and good working order" of the firm.

      2)   Principles of managing organizations—Fayol's 14 principles to guide managers' thinking in managing organizations (shown in Table 1-1 of the textbook).

          a)   However, Fayol said that the moral character of a manager determines the quality the manager's decisions.

   b. **Principles of organization**

     1) James D. Mooney viewed management as the art of directing and inspiring other people.

       a) Organization is the technique of relating specific duties or functions in a coordinating whole.

       b) The primary purpose of management is to devise an appropriate organization.

       c) Natural laws of organization exist.

V. **Foundations of Managing People in Organizations**

 A. Theories have been developed to challenge the fundamentals of the classical approach. These have followed two branches:

   1. **Human relations**—became popular in the 1940s and early 1950s.

   2. **Behavioral science**—emerged in the early 1950s and today is emphasized in much of the management literature. (See Figure 1-1 for a summary of the influence of each of the two branches in managing people.)

 B. A report by the American Association of Collegiate Schools of Business emphasizes the need for "people skills" among managers in the 21st century.

   1. Communications, decision-making, leadership, motivation, and conflict resolution are all key skills.

 C. **The Human Relations Approach**

   1. Human Relations writers brought to management's attention the important role of the individual in determining organizational success or failure.

   2. Accepted the major premises of the Classical Approach but believed they should be modified due to differences in individual behavior and the influence of work groups on individuals (and *vice versa*).

   3. Focused on the job's social environment.

   4. Development of this approach was spurred by the **Hawthorne studies**—conducted by Harvard University industrial psychologists at the Chicago Hawthorne plant of Western Electric from 1924–1927. The findings of the study were a major force in alerting management to the importance of the individual's psychological dimensions in the workplace. Researchers originally sought to study the relationship between productivity and physical working conditions. The studies included four phases:

     a) **Illumination experiments**—conducted to determine the effects of changes in illumination on productivity.

       1) A work group was split into two separate groups: an experimental group, exposed to varying lighting levels, and a control group which worked under a constant lighting level.

       2) Results showed that when light intensity was increased in the experimental group, both groups increased production. When light intensity was decreased in the experimental group, production in both groups still

increased until light intensity in the experimental group was reduced to that of moonlight, at which point the production in the experimental group declined.

      3)   Researchers' conclusion—illumination had little or no effect on the two groups' productivity.

  b)   **Relay assembly room test experiment**—conducted to determine effect of changes in working conditions on productivity.

      1)   In one phase, a group worked in isolation and changes (in such factors as room temperature and refreshments) were made in working conditions, with little effect on productivity.

      2)   In another phase, a group of women workers was isolated and given a special monetary group incentive. Productivity increased.

      3)   Researchers' conclusion—changes in job conditions had little effect on productivity.

  c)   **Employee interviews**—workers were interviewed throughout the plant to determine attitudes. At that point, the then-puzzled researchers premised that the human element in the work environment more significantly influenced productivity than the job's technical and physical aspects.

      1)   Researchers' conclusion—the work group as a whole determines production output of individual members by enforcing a norm which constitutes a "fair day's work."

  d)   **Bank wiring observation room experiment** - done to test the conclusion reached at the end of the Employee Interview project.

      1)   Nine men assembled terminal banks for telephone exchanges under a group piecework incentive pay plan. Researchers hypothesized that the group would maximize its output to maximize pay.

      2)   Results showed that the group's daily output did not exceed a level determined by the group to be a "fair day's work." No relationship was found between productivity and intelligence, dexterity, or other individual skills or attributes.

      3)   Researchers' conclusion—group acceptance and security were more important in determining a member's output than pay was.

5.   Critique of the Hawthorne studies

  a)   The studies have been criticized for a lack of scientific objectivity and for research bias.

  b)   However, the studies have made a major contribution — they have generated much interest in human problems in the workplace, have led to questioning the assumptions of early management writers, and have provided a major catalyst for future research of human behavior in organizations.

  c)   The studies triggered revised assumptions about human nature, and attacks on the "dehumanizing" aspects of the Scientific Management approach and bureaucratic organizations.

D. The **Behavioral Science Approach**

1. Emerged in the early 1950s with the establishment of the Foundation for Research on Human Behavior.

2. Defined as the study of observable and verifiable human behavior in organizations, using scientific procedures. It focuses on human behavior, and draws primarily from psychology, sociology, and anthropology.

3. Behavioral scientists believed that:

   a) Conceptualizing management as planning, organizing, leading and controlling leads to descriptions, not analysis and understanding, of what managers do.

   b) The Classical Approach's "Economic Man" and the human relationists' "social man" were oversimplifications.

4. The behavioral sciences are interdisciplinary, composed of:

   a) **Psychology**—the study of human behavior. Particularly involves social psychology (behavior as it relates to other individuals) and organizational psychology (behavior and attitudes in organizations).

   b) **Sociology**—the study of human behavior in groups (especially small groups). Sociology looks at both emergent, informal groups and formal organizations, focusing on bureaucratic behavior and structural relationships.

   c) **Anthropology**—the study of learned behaviors and other behaviors encompassing culture. An understanding of this area is increasingly important in the global arena, in particular to multinational corporations.

VI. **Foundations of Managing Production and Operations**

A. The central function of the **Management Science Approach** is to provide managers with quantitative bases for decisions regarding operations under their control. It is defined as "the science devoted to describing, understanding, and predicting the behavior of complicated systems of men and machines operating in natural environments."

B. **Development of Management Science**

1. Management Science has been in existence for approximately 50 years.

2. The terms **Management Science** and **Operations Research** are synonymous.

3. The activities of management scientists have emphasized the mathematical modeling of systems.

4. Characteristics of the tools and techniques of Management Science:

   a) A primary focus on **decision making**—principal end results have direct implications for management action.

   b) Appraisal rests on **economic effectiveness criteria**—the worth of feasible actions is based on financial measures (for example, costs or rates of return).

   c) Reliance on **formal mathematical models**.

23

        d)   **Dependence on computers**—due to the complexity of mathematical models, the volume of data, and/or the number of computations necessary to implement the model.

    5.   Figure 1-2 shows the use of many of these tools in planning and controlling production and operations.

C.   **Production/Operations Management**

    1.   Production and operations management encompasses managing:

        a.   **Production**—the manufacturing technology and flow of materials in a manufacturing plant.

        b.   **Operations**—refers to the goods or services-producing activity in any organization. Similar to production management but focuses on a wider class of problems, and includes organizations with technologies quite different from manufacturing.

    2.   P/OM's foundation is management science.

    3.   **The Role of Mathematical Models**

        a.   Managers cannot conduct *bona fide* scientific experiments to, for instance, determine the inventory level that minimizes carrying and ordering costs, because of real world practicalities. However, mathematical models enable managers to experiment with possible solutions without interrupting the ongoing system. With models, managers can simulate the behavior of the real system.

        b.   A **mathematical model** is a simplified representation of the relevant aspects of an actual system or process. An accurate model forces the manager to systematically consider the variables in the problem and the relationships among the variables.

        c.   Some useful P/OM models include:

            1)   **Allocation models**—focus on determining the most effective allocation of limited resources to achieve a given objective (e.g. allocating production time across three products to maximize the profit objective).

            2)   **Network models**—used for planning and controlling simple and complex projects.

                a)   **PERT (Program Evaluation and Review Technique) models**—provide a method for planning and controlling nonrepetitive projects.

            3)   **Inventory models**—provide answers to two questions: how much, and when? These models enable the manager to determine the **EOQ (Economic Order Quantity)** and the optimum reorder point.

VII. **Attempts to Integrate the Three Approaches**

    A.   There have been attempts within the past 30 years to integrate the three approaches to management. Two of these are:

        1.   **Systems Approach**

            a.   Views organizations as a total system composed of a group of interrelated parts with a single purpose.

b. Actions by one part affect all others. Consequently, managers must adopt a broad perspective to their jobs, viewing the organization as a dynamic whole when solving problems.

c. Figure 1-3 shows that input, transformation, and output processes are strongly interdependent and are influenced by feedback and control mechanisms.

d. The objectives of the individual parts of an organization must be compromised to meet the objectives of the whole.

2. **Contingency Approach**

a. Argues that there is no one best way to manage. The best management approach depends on the situation.

b. Seeks to match different situations with different management methods. Increasingly popular in the last 20 years and supported by some research results.

c. Has become more relevant in the global environment because of:
1) increased globalization.
2) demands for ethical and socially responsible leadership.
3) changing demographics and skill requirements of the workforce.
4) new organizational structures that emphasize speed in reacting to environmental changes.
5) changing needs, preferences, and desires of employees.

d. The student of management preparing for the 21st century must learn multiple ways to compete, innovate, create, motivate, and lead.

VIII. **The Three Tasks of World Class Managers**

A. All modern managers in any country in the world face three tasks:
1. **Managing work and organizations**
2. **Managing people**
3. **Managing production and operations**

B. These three fundamental tasks must be learned and practiced in a world that is globalizing, where there is demand and competition for better quality production and services, where the workforce is becoming increasingly culturally diverse, and where the public insists on ethical and socially responsible decisions.

C. See Figures 1-4 and 1-5 for conceptual illustrations of how management tasks, functions, and the three approaches to management interrelate.

D. The three managerial tasks are focal points for the textbook's three major sections (see Figure 1-6).

1. **Question:** *Have you ever managed anything—for example, as part of a job, or in a social or civic organization? If so, did you perform the management functions of planning, organizing, leading and controlling without being aware of it? Discuss your managerial experience and relate it to the functions of management.*

Answer: The purpose of this question is to spur student thinking about their own managerial experiences, and in particular to realize that often they've performed managerial functions (usually in everyday, nonbusiness situations) without realizing it. Students can discuss their roles in those organizations in terms of planning, organizing, leading and influencing, and controlling.

2. **Question:** *One writer has stated: "People who don't manage are either too young, too old, or found in institutions for the incompetent." What is this writer trying to say? Do you agree? Why?*

Answer: Students' interpretation of this comment will vary; however, the writer's probable message is that almost everyone is a manager but that truly being a manager requires numerous abilities including experience, intelligence, logic, and the ability to make decisions.

3. **Question:** *Are managers really needed in organizations? There are some who believe that managers and what they add is no longer of much value to organizations or society. What do you believe?*

Answer: This question arises in many organizations today, as the processes of "downsizing", "right-sizing", and flattening of organizational structures occur. Students can refer to the work of Frederick Taylor, who promoted recognition of the nearly equal division of work and responsibility between management and workers; and they can discuss the traits of managers who effectively incorporate management tools and techniques to guide and improve their organizations.

4. **Question:** *Why is it likely that a contingency approach to managing people, information, or change is needed in a rapidly globalizing and interconnected world?*

Answer: The question as posed provides an opportunity to review the basic tenet of the Contingency Approach—that managers must find different ways to plan, organize, lead, and control, and that the appropriate ways depend on the specific situation(s) encountered. The five factors enumerated on page 21 of the textbook all contribute to the prominence of the Contingency Approach; as information becomes more readily available at ever-increasing speeds, geopolitical boundaries change, and economies become more interconnected, dogmatic approaches to management issues become less and less relevant.

5. **Question:** *What are the advantages of having an ethnically diverse work force in a globalizing world?*

Answer: Through this question, students have an opportunity to explore the cultural issues faced in international, national, and even local commerce today. An ethnically diverse workforce, in which staff have different cultural backgrounds and languages, can provide access to customers who might otherwise be unapproachable or uninterested. Students may also move into a discussion of the unique challenges to managers in culturally diverse environment, a topic which is further discussed in Chapter 13 of the textbook.

6. **Question:** *Over 70 years have passed since the Hawthorne Studies were conducted, and the "dehumanizing" aspects of various forms of managing still exist according to some critics. What are some of the "dehumanizing" aspects of management that you are familiar with and can identify? Has the claim of "dehumanization" been exaggerated?*

Answer: Different student work experiences will provide different responses to this question. Those who have worked in rigidly controlled manufacturing or service environments, regardless of the country in which they worked, may provide extreme examples of attempts to increase productivity solely through control of the physical working conditions. A discussion of the role of labor unions and of coordinating bodies in centralized economies may also result.

7. **Question:** *How would you determine whether Americans, Japanese, or Germans are better managers? Is it even worthwhile to discuss which country has better managers? Why?*

Answer: Much discussion has occurred in the past decade over the relative strengths of business in the United States, Japan, and Germany. This discussion has taken place in the professional business arena, the political arena, the news media, and even in popular literature and film (e.g. *Rising Sun* by Michael Crichton). Comparisons of business leaders and management styles in each country are instructive in helping managers today to better understand the dynamics of the global economy. However, despite the fact that managers worldwide have the same basic responsibilities (planning, organizing, leading and influencing, and coordinating; managing work and organizations, people, and production and operations) the specific strategies they employ may be largely influenced or even determined by the culture(s) in which they operate. It is therefore difficult to say which country's managers are "better". The discussion is useful, though, in that looking at the general differences among managers from country to country reinforces the necessity of the Contingency Approach to management today.

8.	Question:	*Are there significant differences in what is referred to as scientific management and management science? Explain.*
	Answer:	They are very different. Scientific management refers to the practices introduced by Frederick W. Taylor to accomplish the management job, by using scientific procedures to find the one best way to do a job. It also includes the work of the Gilbreths, Henry Gantt, and others who were influenced by Taylor.

Management science, on the other hand, is an approach to management that includes a body of research and literature characterized by its use of mathematical and statistical techniques to build models for the solution of production and operations problems. The aim of management science is to provide managers with quantitative bases for decisions. Management science includes tools and techniques for Production and Operations Management (P/OM).

Unlike scientific management, management science does not attempt to find a single solution to improve productivity. Rather, it employs a range of tools and techniques to assist managers in their ongoing decision-making processes, as they attempt to increase productivity.

9.	Question:	*Talk to a few managers and ask them what is the most rewarding aspect of their job. What is the most frustrating aspect of their job?*
	Answer:	This question is designed to help students broaden their perspective on the challenges and rewards faced by managers on a day-to-day basis. Students can be encouraged to explore the degree to which managers' rewards and frustrations center around the work and organizations they manage, the people they manage, and the production and operations they manage.

10.	Question:	*What were the last three purchases you made? How much competition was there for your dollars?*
	Answer:	Students should be able to easily recall their last three purchases, whether they included candy bars, clothing, or a stereo. Have them describe the vast choices and how they came to purchase the single items they chose. Decisions might have been based on taste preference, brand preference (why?), amount of money available to spend, etc. The main idea is that there is almost infinite competition for their dollars, however many (or few) dollars they have to spend.

END OF CHAPTER CASES

CASE 1-1: GOYA FOODS: COMPETITION AND JOB CREATION

CASE SUMMARY: This case chronicles the success and new challenges of the largest

Hispanic-owned company in the United States—Goya Foods. Prudencio Unanue, who had lived in both Spain and Puerto Rico, moved to New York in 1915 and worked odd jobs in the food industry. Although he did not formally study management, he carefully observed the managers in the firms for which he worked. He also noticed that foods of Spain and Puerto Rico were difficult to find and purchase in New York. In 1936, he and his wife started Goya Foods to fill that niche. By 1992, Goya had annual revenues of $452 million and more than 1800 employees, selling more than 840 products.

Goya has kept up with its changing market over time, adding products familiar to the Hispanics of Central American and Mexican descent. Today, large corporations are stepping into the Hispanic food market and challenging Goya's dominance. Goya's challenge will be to remain successful in the face of this new competition.

ANSWERS TO QUESTIONS FOR ANALYSIS:

1. **Question:** *Could Prudencio Unanue have started Goya Foods in a planned communist economy such as North Korea? Why?*

   Answer: As a private individual, Mr. Unanue could not have legally started such a venture in a planned communist economy. He would have had to gain approval from the government, convincing them of the value of filling the ethnic food niche he noticed. He would also have had to work very closely with the government to assure continual access to the imported foodstuffs which are the staple of his business. Finally, the cultural, ethnic, and geographic origin demographics of North Korea and other communist countries are generally less diverse than those of the United States; Mr. Unanue might well not have found the kind of unexploited niche he perceived in New York in the 1930's. Overall, it would be unlikely that he could have started such a venture in a planned communist economy.

2. **Question:** *Why is the observation of others sometimes an effective way for people to learn how to operate as a manager?*

   Answer: Managing involves both quantitative and qualitative skills. The quantitative skills can certainly be learned through formal study, but the qualitative skills require a more hands-on approach to acquire. Observation of the qualitative skills of others can be very instructive.
   As the textbook explains, Henri Fayol believed that the moral character of managers determines the quality of their decisions. Also as discussed in the chapter, the ability to use information technology, speedy decision-making, strategic alliances, a combination of individualism and teamwork, and a melding of the skills of an increasingly diverse workforce provides the competitive edge in the global economy. While aspects of these abilities can be learned from texts or developed on one's own, the most efficient mechanism for their acquisition is often to observe those who have themselves already learned to manage well. Management is an occupational area which readily lends itself to mentoring as a learning strategy.

29

3. **Question:** *What activities of managers was Mr. Unanue not able to learn by observing managers doing their jobs?*

    Answer: Mr. Unanue could not learn the specifics of management science tools simply from observing other managers (although the modelling tools of management science were largely developed sometime after the startup of Goya Foods). He also could not learn what the thought processes were behind the choices made by managers in their planning, organizing, leading and influencing, and controlling processes through simple observation alone. Instead, he would have had to discuss the reasons for their choices with them, to learn the principles which guided them.

ADDITIONAL QUESTIONS AND ANSWERS

1. **Question:** *Why is there no "one best way" to manage?*
    Answer: There is no universal approach because every managerial situation is unique to some degree in its characteristics, problems, and demands on the manager. Thus, applying a single approach to widely varying situations is bound to be problematic. The manager must adapt his or her approach to the situation, not *vice versa*.

2. **Question:** *Why did three distinct approaches to management arise in the development of the management discipline?*

    Answer: There is more than one approach to management because there are a variety of problems with which managers must deal. For instance, it can be argued that each approach emerged in response to emerging needs, and as a response to the approach that preceded it. The Classical Approach was developed in the absence of formal management theory, in response to the need to develop ways to increase worker productivity. The Behavioral Approach followed, in response to the need to deal with problems of worker dissatisfaction and low motivation, many of which arose from implementation of the Classical Approach. And the Management Science Approach was developed in response to solving increasingly complex production and operations problems which could not be solved using the Classical or Behavioral Approaches alone.

3. **Question:** *Is management a profession?*
    Answer: Management is a profession in the sense that it is an occupation that involves serving others, in which effectiveness requires an understanding of and adherence to certain principles and guidelines. However, it is not a profession defined as a field of expert knowledge that requires licensing, graduate study and certification.

4.   **Question:**   *In your opinion, what characteristics must an individual possess to effectively apply the Contingency Approach to management?*

        Answer: Students' opinions will differ; they may cite such characteristics as perceptiveness (the ability to perceive subtle changes in situations which require adjustments in a manager's approach to a problem), intelligence, self-confidence (the belief in one's ability to employ versatile approaches to manage effectively), and the ability to deal successfully with change and to adapt. Managers who are uncomfortable with change may not be particularly perceptive to situations which require alterations in their management approach, and may therefore tend to feel uncomfortable in employing the Contingency Approach.

5.   **Question:**   *Employees in many organizations believed during the 1960s, 1970s, and 1980s that by giving their employer their long-term loyalty, they would in return receive long-term security and steady employment. In the 1990s, though, layoffs and restructurings are commonplace. What are the implications for managers?*

        Answer: People skills are paramount in management in the 1990s, for many reasons. One reason for the prominence of the Contingency Approach today is the changing needs, preferences, and desires of employees for job security, participation, ownership, and personal fulfillment. As employees' perceptions of job security are threatened, and indeed as employees see their co-workers laid off or involuntarily redeployed, maintaining morale can be highly problematic. The ability of managers to lead, inspire, and motivate the people who remain in the organization takes on increasing importance; in the absence of effective management of the human resource, all the interlinked management tasks (managing work and organization, managing people, and managing production and operations) are likely to falter.

6.   **Question:**   *Distinguish between the Systems Approach and the Contingency Approach to management.*

        Answer: The Systems Approach views an organization as a total system composed of a group of interrelated departments contributing to a single purpose. This approach emphasizes the need for managers to adopt a broad perspective to their jobs, and to realize that the effects wrought by a managerial decision can touch many (if not all) aspects of the organization. The Contingency Approach emphasizes that there is no "one best way" to manage; rather, effective management depends on the particular situation.

7.   **Question:**   *In your opinion, which of the three tasks of modern managers — managing work and organizations, managing people, and managing production and operations—is the most challenging? Explain.*

        Answer: This question is designed to spur students to think about the relative demands of each major task. Opinions will of course differ, and discussion should focus on why the task cited as most challenging is so demanding.

8. **Question:** *A supervisor comments: "I don't understand why we are spending so much time discussing these definitions of management. As far as I'm concerned, management is what my boss says it is." Do you agree? Why or why not?*

   Answer: This statement is an often-heard complaint by supervisors. It has considerable merit as, above all, workers (including supervisors,) who work in a hierarchical structure view their jobs and tasks according to their superiors' expectations. On the other hand, supervisors often have management responsibilities in any or all of the four major areas of planning, organizing, leading and influencing, and controlling. Supervisors who cannot take on these activities as required, and managers who are arbitrary and capricious in their viewpoints of the roles of managers, leave their organizations in a precarious position.

9. **Question:** *Can the ability to manage be learned?*

   Answer: This question typically spurs student discussion, as opinions always significantly differ. It can be argued that some aspects of management, such as organizing activities and planning resource allocations, can be learned through training. But can the ability to lead and motivate be learned? Can the entrepreneurial ability to see what others don't see be learned?

10. **Question:** *Describe the role models you use when thinking about the role of managers.*

    Answer: This question is designed to encourage students to think about the individuals who serve as their managerial role models. In answering this question, students should focus on identifying the characteristics of their role models that exemplify excellent managerial characteristics.

2 MANAGERS AND THEIR ENVIRONMENTS

LEARNING OBJECTIVES

After completing Chapter 2, students should be able to:

Define an organization and its environment in terms of a system.

Describe the internal environment in which a manager must function.

Discuss how a more culturally diverse workforce is becoming a reality in American organizations.

Compare the three basic skills necessary for effective managerial performance.

Identify the various roles managers in organizations must perform.

CHAPTER SYNOPSIS

The chapter addresses managers and their environments by focusing on the external environment and the internal environment of organizations.

The chapter discusses the organization's **external environment** in terms of the **direct forces** which directly influence an organization (customers, competitors, suppliers, and human resources) and the **indirect forces** (technology, the economy, political, legal and regulatory action, culture and social values, and the international component) which indirectly affect organizations. Examples are provided for each component. Particular emphasis in the discussion of the direct human resources force is paid to the increase in diversity in the workforce as we enter the 21st century, and to the implications for managers as they attempt to create effective work units and motivational programs. In studying this section, students acquire an overall understanding of the makeup and potential impacts of these forces and management's responsibilities in dealing with them.

The organization's **internal environment** is discussed by focusing on four topics: 1) the three managerial levels (operations, technical, and strategic); 2) the relationship of the type of manager (top, middle, and first-level) to the three managerial levels; 3) the technical, human and conceptual skills of managers; and 4) the ten managerial roles which managers assume in their daily work, broadly categorized as **interpersonal**, **informational**, and **decisional** roles. The chapter's **Management in Action** points out the interrelationship between downsizing and diminution of company loyalty, and discusses a predicted change in organizations from the supervisor-subordinate type of hierarchy to a more horizontal arrangement in which "coordinators" work alongside, or perhaps replace, traditional managers. The **Management Focus** segments discuss the attitudes, needs, and wants of employees belonging to various groups in diverse organizations; environmentally sound principles of social responsibility; and Coca-Cola's track record in developing new markets around the world.

TEACHING TIPS

LECTURE & DISCUSSION IDEAS

1. An effective way to clarify the systems theory of organizations, the ten managerial roles, and the direct and indirect forces of the external environment is to apply concepts to a particular example. Use a manufacturing business (e.g., General Motors, a local manufacturing company), and a service organization (e.g., the local municipal hospital, the university). Select a nationally prominent manager with whom students are familiar (e.g., Bill Clinton, John Sculley) and place the ten managerial roles in the context of the particular manager. Select a visible industry (e.g., automobile, computer, construction industries) and discuss the direct and indirect forces in the context of the selected industry.

2. Concerns about the earth's environment have been prominent in society for many years, but businesses have typically lagged behind social views of the importance of environmentalism. Have students debate the value of environmentally sound practices in a manufacturing industry from a cost-benefit perspective.

PROJECT / EXERCISE IDEAS

1. As a group exercise, have your students (working in groups of four to five members) interview a top-level executive to obtain a better understanding of the activities which comprise the job of a top-level manager. By interviewing an executive, students can gain insights into how the ten managerial roles apply in the executive's activities; which roles are predominant and most important to the executive's work and which are relatively minor; which managerial skills are most important and why; and whether the executive assumes other roles besides the ten presented in the text, and how those other roles can be defined.

2. In examining the impact of increasing diversity in organizations, an interesting exercise is to create an employee "timeline". Students can ask employees at organizational units to which they have access to line up in chronological order of employment, with those with the greatest longevity in the organization at one end of the line and the newest employees at the other end. In most organizations in the U.S. today, the "newer" end of the line is much more gender, race, disability, and age diverse than the "older" end. Long-term managers can then be interviewed to determine the impact of this shift on their own work styles and the challenges they face.

I. **Chapter Introduction**

    A.   Managers must deal with both the external environment and the internal environment.

        1.   **External Environment:** includes all outside forces which act on the organization.

        2.   **Internal Environment:** forces within the organization in which managers perform their functions.

II. **The External Environment**

    A.   The environment is composed of direct and indirect forces (see Figure 2-3, Direct and Indirect Forces of the Organization's External Environment).

        1.   For an organization to succeed, its managers must recognize the external forces, comprehend their interrelationships, and understand their real and potential impacts, to minimize their negative and maximize their positive effects.

    B.   Direct forces exert an immediate and direct influence on the organization. The primary forces are:

        1.   **Customers**—perhaps the most vital force to an organization.

            a.   Organizations typically respond to customer forces in the external environment by conducting research that focuses on present and potential customers. The goal is to identify present customers' degree of satisfaction with the organization's product/ services and any changing customer preferences.

                1)   Current customers are emphasized because keeping a current customer costs about 1/5 as much as finding a new one.

                2)   Research on potential customers focuses on demographics and other factors to identify potential buyers.

            b.   Companies in the US are responding to customers' relatively new desire for better product and service quality.

        2.   **Competitors**—the companies against which an organization competes for customers and needed resources in the external environment.

            a. Competitors are:

                1)   **Intratype** competitors—companies that produce the same or similar products/services as the organization.

                2)   **Intertype** competitors—distinctly different and competing organizations (e.g., Prudential Insurance Co. competing with Smith Barney Shearson Investors).

            b.   Competition can be viewed as an ongoing process of moves and countermoves by an organization and its competitors; it may be fast-paced and difficult to predict.

            c.   **Competitor analysis**—is performed on an ongoing basis by an organization to understand its competitors.

1)   Much information from many sources (e.g., media, suppliers, wholesalers) is reviewed to identify a competitor's objectives, strategies, strengths and weaknesses.

2)   Growing numbers of companies are establishing competitor intelligence teams, small groups of employees who are assigned to obtain specific information on a competitor.

3.   **Suppliers**—provide an organization its resources—funds, energy, equipment, services, materials.

    a.   To reduce vulnerability to supplier problems (e.g., low quality, labor strikes), many organizations spread purchases across several suppliers so dependence on any one supplier is reduced.

    b.   Some companies have implemented **backward vertical integration** where they themselves manufacture at least some of the raw materials needed to produce the final product or service.

       1)   Costly to implement, but provides the company with more control over materials cost, quality, and delivery.

    c.   Some companies are **single sourcing**—relying on one supplier for a type of material or service. They risk greater dependence on one supplier in return for a long term relationship which can provide:

       1)   Higher supply quality which can occur when the organization works with the supplier to improve quality.

       2)   Greater consistency in supplies.

       3)   More flexible production scheduling because a buyer can more easily coordinate production schedules with fewer suppliers.

4.   **Human resources**—the people pool in the external environment from which an organization obtains its employees. Four trends pose major challenges for management:

    a. **A more culturally diverse workforce.**

       1)   Figure 2-2 shows eleven different factors that comprise diversity in the workplace, ranging from race and ethnicity and country of birth to skill level and experience.

       2)   Managers are faced with attempting to balance the wants, needs, and perceptions of an increasingly diverse workforce.

       3)   Managing this diversity requires managers to consider accommodating within reason significant individual and group differences.

          a)   The Management Focus, *What Diverse Employees Want*, shows some of the things employees in various groups want in their workplaces.

       4)   Language and communication, how to motivate people from different cultures and backgrounds, career planning,

and the types of training programs to implement are some of the changing issues and decisions created by the mix in the workforce.

    b.   **Women in the workforce**

        1)   Women will be nearly 50% of the workforce by the year 2000.

        2)   Women are beginning to be seen in high-paying, high-status jobs.

        3)   Organizations have a moral and legal obligation to hire, promote, and develop women.

        4)   Organizations will have to become more creative at identifying and supporting affordable child and elder care systems.

    c.   **The downsizing trend**

        1)   Between 1987 and 1992, nearly 5 million workers who had held their jobs for at least three years were dismissed.

        2)   Loyalty to the firm is diminishing, and being replaced by a Darwinian, "take control of your own destiny" approach by employees.

    d.   **An aging population**

        1)   The percentage of the US population under 35 is shrinking dramatically.

        2)   The median age of the workforce has increased from 28 years of age in 1970 to a projected 40 years of age in 2000.

        3)   The managerial challenges are how to keep older, experienced employees on the job (when more people are retiring sooner), and how to retrain older workers to start a second career.

C.   **Indirect forces**—can affect an organization via:

    1.   Exerting a direct influence on the organization, or an indirect influence on a direct force in the environment (e.g. the media reporting on a management decision).

    2.   Affecting the climate in which the organization must function (e.g., the economy may expand or decline requiring management responses).

    3.   **Technological forces**—developments in technology that can affect an organization by influencing the organization's use of knowledge and techniques in producing goods or services and/or the technological characteristics of the organization's goods/services.

        a.   Management must keep abreast of the latest technological developments by:

            1)   Maintaining close contacts with R&D organizations, research scientists, and anyone else involved in technological developments.

            2)   Updating the skills/knowledge of employees who are responsible for technology.

3) Creating competitor intelligence teams to work on competitors' work technology.

4) Developing their own technology advancements (an activity usually restricted to large companies).

4. **Economic forces**—changes in the economy that pose opportunities and/or threats for the organization.

   a. Management must monitor the economy for changes.

5. **Political, legal, and regulatory forces**—local, state, and federal laws, government regulations and political activities—all of which can greatly affect an organization and its climate.

   a. Provide both constraint and opportunity.

   b. Many organizations monitor governmental and legislative developments, to insure their own compliance and to lobby for their interests.

6. **Cultural and social forces**—changes in the U.S. social and cultural system that can affect an organization's actions and the demand for its products/services.

   a. Examples include environmentalism, a focus on healthy foods, and a shift to moderation in alcohol use.

7. **International forces**—apply to U.S. organizations when the organization:

   a. Relies on a foreign supplier.

   b. Competes with international companies in the U.S.

   c. Expands its products/services into foreign markets.

      1) In this case, the organization must learn to operate in an environment where many of the rules of business differ greatly from those in the U.S.

III. The Internal Environment

A. There are three managerial levels in the environment inside the organization (shown in Figure 2-4)

1. **Operations level**—managers focus on effectively performing what the organization produces (goods) or does (services).

   a. The manager's task—to best allocate resources to produce the desired output.

2. **Technical level**—managers coordinate operational level activities, and also determine the goods/services to produce.

   a. The managers' tasks—manage the operations function and serve as liaison between the company and users of the company's products.

3. **Strategic level**—managers set the organization's long range objectives and direction (how the organization will interact with its external environment).

   a. Managers may also seek to influence the environment through lobbying, advertising, or educational programs.

B. Types of managers and levels of management (see Figures 2-4 and 2-5):

1. **Top level** (strategic level).

2. **Middle level** (technical level).

3. **First-level** (operations level).
C. Management involves basic skills (shown in Figure 2-6)
    1. **Human skill**—the ability to work with, communicate with, and understand others.
        a. These are the essential activities of first-level supervisory jobs.
    2. **Technical Skill**—the ability to use specific knowledge, techniques, and resources in performing work.
        a. Most important to the effectiveness of middle managers.
    3. **Conceptual skill**—the ability to understand all of the organization's activities and interests, how they interrelate, and how the organization functions as a whole.
        a. Most crucial for top managers.
D. Managerial roles: Managers, especially upper-level executives, assume many roles in their daily work; Henry Mintzberg has identified 10 different role of top managers, in three overlapping groupings (see Figure 2-7):
    1. **Interpersonal roles**—these focus on the manager's interpersonal relationships.
        a. **Figurehead** role—involves symbolic/ceremonial duties (for example, a mayor presenting the key to the city to a celebrity).
        b. **Leadership role**—involves directing and coordinating subordinates' activities (leading, motivating, controlling).
        c. **Liaison** role—involves developing and maintaining interpersonal relationships within and outside the organization (for example, production supervisor interacting with sales managers).
    2. **Informational roles**—the manager acts in sending and receiving nonroutine information and building a network of interpersonal contacts.
        a. **Monitor** role—involves examining the environment to gather information which may affect the unit (for example, gathering information on a competitor's strategy).
        b. **Disseminator** role—the manager provides important information to subordinates that they might not ordinarily know about (for example, a president informing the sales force that a customer will soon declare bankruptcy).
        c. **Spokesperson** role—the manager represents his/her unit to other people internally (lobbying for a salary hike for subordinates) or externally (representing the firm on a public interest issue at a civic forum).
    3. **Decisional roles**—these involve managerial decision making (arguably the manager's most important function).
        a. **Entrepreneur** role—the manager devises new ideas, and plans and implements change to improve organizational performance (for example, a college dean planning changes to result in higher-quality education).
        b. **Disturbance handler** role—the manager makes quick decisions or takes corrective action in response to pressure beyond his/her control, with a goal of returning to stability (for example, a plant supervisor responding to a labor strike).

39

c.   **Resource allocator** role—The manager decides who will get what resources (for example, the U.S. President and Congress deciding whether to allocate more funds for defense or for social programs).

d.   **Negotiator** role—the manager bargains with units and individuals to obtain advantages for his/her unit (for example, a top manager negotiating with labor representatives).

4.   Managers at different levels spend different amounts of time in each role, and perform different activities. (Top managers, for example, may spend more time in the figurehead role and may have more interaction outside the organization.) But all managers perform roles in each of these groupings.

ANSWERS TO DISCUSSION AND REVIEW QUESTIONS

1.   **Question:**   *Why should managers be concerned that downsizing has had a negative impact on firm loyalty?*

      Answer: Competitiveness is key to survival in virtually every industry today. Effectiveness among teams and productivity on an individual-by-individual basis provide the basis for competitiveness. Among the direct forces discussed in the chapter, the attraction and retention of skilled, motivated individuals provides what is arguably the single most important internal resource for any organization. As downsizing and "rightsizing" continue, employees become fearful for their own economic security, and are perhaps less likely to make short-term sacrifices of time, money, or effort for the dwindling likelihood of long-term gain within their organization.

      Students may discuss their own experiences, or the experiences of others they know, with downsizing and economic dislocation, and discuss the impact on their own attitudes. They may also be encouraged to compare the climate of the 1990s with what they know of earlier decades in this century.

2.   **Question:**   *What demographic changes suggest that managers must become more effective in working with culturally diverse work groups?*

      Answer: According to the Bureau of Labor Statistics, the largest growth in the labor pool for the remainder of this century will occur among white females, hispanic males and females, and black females and males. The historic view of the workforce as monolithically male and white is rapidly becoming obsolete in all sectors of the US. As the older, more homogeneous workforce retires at increasingly earlier age, they are replaced by far more diverse employee populations.

Also, as society's understanding of the breadth of meaning of the term "culture" expands, managers must deal with differences in the many areas shown in Figure 2-2. Increased immigration, legislation such as the Americans with Disabilities Act and laws prohibiting discrimination on the basis of sexual orientation, the dramatic increase of women's participation in the workforce, and other demographic factors mean that managers are faced with an ever-increasing array of cultures in their organizations.

3. **Question:** *If you were trying to identify top managers at the school you attend, what titles would you look for? If you had to identify them based on what they do, what would you look for?*

    Answer: The school's top management would include the college/university president and vice presidents. (Middle managers include the deans of schools within the college, while first-level managers would be department chairpersons who coordinate the "line" employees, the instructors.) In terms of identifying top-level managers based on activities, such functions as interacting frequently with individuals in the organization's external environment and acting as an information disseminator and a spokesperson would be indicative.

4. **Question:** *Discuss human, technical, and conceptual skills in relation to a college instructor. What would be a good mix, in your opinion? Why?*

    Answer: In regard to an instructor, the human skill is the ability to understand students' instructional needs and how to effectively motivate them to want to learn. Technical skills would include the instructor's knowledge of the management material and the instructional tools (blackboard, overhead projector, textbook) and techniques (such as how to prepare an effective and cogent lecture, how to pose interesting and relevant questions to the class, how to effectively guide and not dominate class discussion). The conceptual skill relates to the knowledge of how all the components of a management class interrelate in facilitating effective learning (and how a change in one component affects the other components). However, students' perspectives of these skills in relation to an instructor may differ and often are enlightening.

5. **Question:** *In your opinion, can human and conceptual skills be taught, or are they inherent?*

    Answer: Many students are likely to regard these as inherent skills. However, they should be encouraged to see that through learning in classes such as management, studying case situations, readings, and personal awareness in the job, they can develop additional conceptual and human skills to those they have already learned through life experiences.

6. **Question:** *What are the differences between managers' jobs at the top, middle, and first-line levels at the college or university you attend? Use the total university or college as the basis for your analysis, with the institution's president or chancellor representing top management. As you identify the jobs of these different managers, is it accurate to state that they require different mixes of the three managerial skills? Explain.*

Answer: Figure 2-5 in the text shows the university president as the top manager, vice presidents and deans as middle managers, and department chairpersons as first-line managers. As shown in Figure 2-6, the mix of managerial skills changes the higher in the organization the manager advances. Emphasis on skills will change as one moves up the organizational hierarchy. Discussion might center on why the mix changes and how managers can develop their skills as they are promoted.

7. **Question:** *As the chapter notes, the direct forces in the external environment pose many challenges to organizations. Which challenge, in your view, is the most difficult for managers? Explain.*

Answer: Students should quickly recognize that customers pose the greatest challenge because they are the foundation of any organization's success. At the same time, in a free market situation, competition results in a fickle customer base to which there must be constant adaptation. A second viable answer is that human resources pose a considerable challenge because they are so vital to the company's operations but it is so hard to control the outcomes of this resource.

8. **Question:** *Some observers assert that the importance of each of the various forces in the external environment differs across types of industries. Do you agree? Discuss.*

Answer: External forces will indeed have different effects depending on whether an industry is labor-intensive, capital-intensive, or subject to rapid technological change, for example. The oil and housing industries are very subject to economic swings compared to the grocery industry. In this way, any two industries can be chosen and compared in terms of differential effects of forces in the environment.

9. **Question:** *If you were being interviewed for a position in a firm and were asked why businesses need to be aware of environmental forces, how would you respond?*

Answer: This question deals specifically with environmental *forces*, the external and internal forces impacting on an organization, as opposed to environmental *issues*, the ecological concerns that society is increasingly focused on. In responding, students can draw upon their understanding of the broad impacts of the forces that act on an organization from the outside, as well as those day-to-day forces within organizations in which managers perform their functions.

10.	Question:	*Some management observers assert that Mintzberg's typology of ten managerial roles is incomplete. What other roles do managers assume?*
	Answer:	Most students will make suggestions about roles, but upon close observation they should be able to see that they do fall into one or more of Mintzberg's categories of roles. One managerial role which Mintzberg has not discussed explicitly is that of long term strategic planning.

END OF CHAPTER CASES

CASE 2 - 1: MCDONALD'S TUNES INTO THE ENVIRONMENT

CASE SUMMARY: The McDonald's Corporation is the largest food service organization in the world. The case opens with a discussion of Ray Kroc's innovative marketing, his insistence on organization-wide uniformity and quality, and his belief that the customer is always right. It then focuses on several health, environmental, and customer taste concerns addressed by the corporation in the past 20 years:

—a reduction in fat content and a switch to the use of all-vegetable oil.

—a switch from paper to styrofoam in the 1970's, to save forests; and a phase-out of styrofoam in 1987 to avoid ozone depletion.

—a strategic alliance with the Environmental Defense Fund to reduce food source waste.

—introduction of salads, which now account for 9% of sales

—several attempts to introduce pizza, to compete in the fastest-growing segment of the fast food industry.

McDonald's is committed to responding effectively to environmental forces in all of the more than 60 countries in which it competes.

ANSWERS TO QUESTIONS FOR ANALYSIS:

1.	Question:	*Should McDonald's have responded to environmentalists who expressed concerns about the excessive use of paper products?*
	Answer:	Social and cultural forces, when ignored as indirect forces, may eventually become direct forces. By responding to the best information available at the time (in the 1970s) and switching to styrofoam use, McDonald's was demonstrating environmental responsibility to its customers and precluding such potential direct impacts as legislation or competition from organizations perceived by customers as being more responsive. Students can use this example to explore the notion that environmental forces will shift, and organizations must continually monitor them in order to remain responsive.

2. **Question:** *Some management experts consider McDonald's to be a firm that attempts to manage as much of their environment as possible. What do they mean?*

    Answer: As a major multinational corporation, McDonald's carefully monitors all the direct forces in its environment—customers, competitors, suppliers, and human resources. There is also a strong corporate emphasis on uniformity, with carefully researched variations to account for local tastes. Students can discuss their experiences and expectations of McDonald's stores they have visited in diverse geographic locations.

3. **Question:** *Do you think that McDonald's is correct in continually attempting to gain a foothold in the pizza market? Why?*

    Answer: Some debate on this issue is likely. The discussion can center around the value and uses of customer research and competitor analysis.

CASE 2-2: MANAGERS MAKING DECISIONS

CASE SUMMARY: Six short cases are presented. In each instance, there is no single correct solution to the case; students are encouraged to use what they've learned of managerial roles to determine one or more plausible responses. Some of the overlapping key managerial roles involved are listed for each case, along with several approaches. (Note that not all the approaches listed are actually recommended.) Students should debate the merits and drawbacks of the approaches they arrive at.

Case Situation 1: *Request for Leave of Absence*

Case Summary: A key employee requests a two-month child care leave of absence at a time when his presence is critical to the organization.

Managerial roles: Resource Allocator
Negotiator
Leadership
Disturbance handler

Approaches: —negotiate part-time work or work at home for the employee.
—bring in an outside consultant to coordinate the project.
—delay the start of the project.
—provide day-care on site.
—deny the employee his leave.

Case Situation 2: *Unpaid Debt/Bill of Top Customer*

Case Summary: A top customer in Spain has defaulted on a $4 million dollar overdue bill because of economic problems in his country.

Managerial roles: Liaison
Disturbance handler
Monitor

Approaches: —help the customer work with banks to restructure the debt.
—cut off the customer, and institute legal proceedings.

Case Situation 3:   *Teamwork*

Case Summary: A manager has an outstanding group of employees who cannot work effectively together.

Managerial roles: Negotiator
Leadership
Entrepreneur

Approaches: —discuss the problems directly with individual employees and with the group, pointing out the impacts of their behaviors on the organization.
—set behavioral contracts with formal behavioral expectations for each employee.
—refer problematic employees to the organization's Employee Assistance Program for counseling.
—fire problematic employees

Case Situation 4:   *Company Policy*

Case Summary: A valued employee's husband is unemployed, and might have to leave the area for a new job. The company can use employees with the husband's experience, but company policy forbids employing spouses. The wife's manager wishes to discuss changing company policy with the president.

Managerial roles: Monitor
Entrepreneur
Liaison

Approaches: —request a policy change. Document this and similar cases, and suggest controls such as spouses not working in the same division within the facility, or not working in direct or indirect reporting relationships with each other.
—enforce company policy as it stands.

Case Situation 5:   *Personal Time Management*

Case Summary: An employee is working very long hours, and yet is unable to keep up with his workload. His attitude and performance are deteriorating, and he wants to get back on track.

Managerial Roles: Resource allocator
Leadership
Negotiator

Approaches: —get additional support for the employee (i.e. *per diem* or intern workers).
—reallocate some of the employee's work.
—set up a realistic schedule of prioritized tasks with the employee.
—refer the employee for counseling at the Employee Assistance Program.
—tell the employee that unless his performance improves, he will be subject to a poor performance appraisal and possibly disciplinary procedures.

Case Situation 6:	*An Ethical Dilemma*
Case Summary:	An audit manager requires significantly more time than he and the senior partner originally estimated to complete the task. He is advised not to report the excess time, since the organization frowns on excessive hours.
Managerial Roles:	Disseminator (to managers, rather than subordinates) Resource allocator
Approaches:	—tell management about the excess hours; try to document as part of an ongoing problem —redo the work plan to cut down the time required —"bury" the extra hours

ADDITIONAL QUESTIONS AND ANSWERS

1. **Question:** *Describe and explain the primary distinctions between the job of top-level managers and first-level managers.*

   Answer: Top level managers are required to operate more at the strategic level of an organization, while first-level managers generally operate more at the operations level. Top management deals far more with the organization's external environment, often in a figurehead or spokesperson role; while first-line managers' responsibilities are generally focused on human and technical skills levels within the organization.

2. **Question:** *In accommodating the needs and wants of women in the workforce, would instituting a comprehensive day-care program be sufficient? Explain.*

   Answer: While women are often more directly concerned than men with child care issues, they are also looking for equality of opportunity and pay. Students may discuss such issues as the "glass ceiling," women's exclusion from some job titles and industries, mentoring programs, pay equity, and sexual harassment in the workplace, among others.

3. **Question:** *Discuss how the key managerial skills relate to the levels of management.*

   Answer: Top-level management requires conceptual skills more than do middle or lower-level management. Technical skill is more important at the middle level of management than other skills. First-level management requires human skills (because they directly supervise non-managerial workers) and technical skill because they must be knowledgeable in the line areas which they directly supervise. Figure 2-6 visually depicts the mix of managerial skills and how they vary across organizational levels.

4. **Question:** *Describe a business where the international aspect of the external environment significantly influences the firm's activities.*

Answer: The purpose of this question is to spur students' thoughts about the impact of the international component of the external environment on an actual firm. Students should consider how this element affects organizations and what organizational responses are typical in dealing with international competition.

5. **Question:** *Distinguish between intratype competition and intertype competition.*

Answer: Intratype competition occurs between organizations that are engaged in the same activities, such as IBM competing with Apple computers. Intertype competition occurs between different types of organizations such as the National Football League and universities competing for outstanding high school football players.

6. **Question:** *What managerial role(s) do you believe is(are) most essential to managerial success and organizational performance? Explain.*

Answer: Student opinion will, of course, differ; however, many students typically cite the entrepreneur role because it involves the development of new ideas and implementation of change. Both of these activities are critical to keeping the organization viable. Arguably, it is also the most difficult managerial role.

7. **Question:** *Of all the managerial skills, which one do you believe is the most difficult to acquire?*

Answer: It can be argued that technical skills are the most easily learned. Some students will likely argue that human skill cannot be learned but is rather an ability acquired through experience and use of particular personality characteristics. Conceptual skill is developed over time and requires overall experience in the organization and other similar organizations.

8. **Question:** *Distinguish between direct and indirect forces in the environment.*

Answer: Direct forces (customers, suppliers, competitors, and human resources) directly influence organizational performance. Indirect forces indirectly affect an organization, often by influencing a direct force or by influencing the climate in which the organization operates.

9. **Question:** *In your opinion, has the political, legal, and regulatory component of the external environment changed in recent years? If so, how?*

Answer: It can be argued that major change has occurred in the regulatory element. Government regulations in many areas such as environmentalism, occupational health and safety, and non-discrimination have substantially increased. These have served the public's interests in many instances but have also frequently resulted in substantial financial costs to business organizations.

10. **Question:** *Has the cultural and social component of the external environment changed? Explain.*

Answer: Students will likely assert that society has increased its expectations of business in regard to ethics and social responsibility. Have students cite examples to support their claims. This question is also addressed further in Chapter 4.

3 MANAGING IN A GLOBAL ENVIRONMENT

LEARNING OBJECTIVES

After completing Chapter 3, you should be able to:

Define   culture and the ways in which cultures can differ across nations.

Describe   the three primary issues that encompass an organization's decision to become a multinational company.

Discuss   the assumed benefits of economic alliances such as the European Community and the North American Free Trade Agreement.

Compare   the different ways of entering a foreign market.

Identify   the major challenges facing expatriate managers in their overseas assignments.

CHAPTER SYNOPSIS

This chapter addresses the highly relevant topic of the issues and processes of multinational management by focusing on six topics: why organizations do business internationally; international agreements and regional economic alliances; basic elements that comprise a company's decision to become an MNC; the different aspects of the multinational environment; management in a multinational corporation; and managing people in multinational corporations.

The chapter begins with a general discussion of the pervasiveness of international trade, and explores the opportunities and return on investment that global markets provide. The international GATT agreement is then described, along with several economic alliances (including the European Community, NAFTA, and the Association of South East Asian Nations). The chapter then defines the multinational company (**MNC**) and the recent growth in multinational activities. Three primary decisions involved in becoming an MNC are discussed: choice of markets, products or services, and entry strategy. Four major strategic entry options are discussed (sourcing, exporting, direct investment, and foreign activities, which include licensing and joint ventures).

The MNC managerial environment is addressed through four key factors (culture, economics, politics, and technology) which must be considered by management in planning and carrying out multinational activities. These factors are discussed in terms of potential differences between host countries and the U.S. The chapter also discusses the planning, organizing, leading, and controlling managerial functions in multinational companies and how they can differ from the functions in domestic firms. The chapter concludes with a discussion of criteria for selecting MNC managers and the question of placing nationals or expatriates in high—level management positions in subsidiaries abroad.

The chapter's **Management in Action** segment discusses Michael Porter's four "diamond" factors of competitive advantage in a global economy. The **Management Focus** segments explore the economic growth of the Pacific Rim countries and Japan's influence over its neighbors; the Foreign Corrupt Practices Act and the potential business liability to the United States for *not* making payoffs and bribes abroad; and price comparisons for various items in major cities outside the US.

TEACHING TIPS

LECTURE & DISCUSSION IDEAS

1. One way to generate a class discussion on the influence of culture and other aspects of a foreign nation on managing abroad is to ask your students who have traveled and lived abroad to discuss ways of life in other countries and how foreign cultures are similar to and different from those in the U.S.

2. As a way of furthering students' understanding of how a nation's culture significantly affects ways of doing business, have them think of and list every aspect or practice in American business which is at least partly influenced by America's culture. Their lists should be lengthy; one example is compensation which is more individual-based (e.g., piece rate in some companies and individual-based incentives) than in other countries. The Japanese, for instance, reject individual-based compensation because it focuses on the individual, which is degrading behavior in Japanese society. Other aspects of American business influenced by culture include attitudes toward profit, the length and timing of the work day (no tea time as in England or 2-3 hour afternoon breaks as in Mexico), and attitudes toward competition.

3. Many of the arguments against NAFTA, especially those put forward by environmental and labor groups, were very strong and persuasive, and many in the U.S. remain unconvinced that NAFTA is beneficial legislation. Students may be encouraged to research those arguments in detail, and to debate the best ways to implement NAFTA to avoid the predictions of its detractors.

PROJECT / EXERCISE IDEAS

1. As a group project, have your students identify a local multinational company, interview a high ranking manager, and prepare a written or oral report on the nature of the company's multinational operations. The report should address the reasons why the respective company established international activities, the problems and challenges the firm has encountered, and how it has dealt with them. Companies that utilize sourcing, exporting, foreign activities, and/or direct investment strategies should be represented across the group reports. If no local businesses are involved in international business, have students select a nationally prominent MNC (such as Coca-

Cola, McDonalds, Xerox, IBM) and present a report on the company's international activities based on library research.

2. If you have foreign-owned companies in your community managed by foreign managers, have your students interview a manager from these companies and prepare a report on the challenges and adjustments they've had to make as foreign managers in the U.S. supervising American employees. These managers can provide some interesting insights into the cultural differences between the U.S. and their own country and differences in the two countries' ways of managing and doing business.

LECTURE OUTLINE NOTES

I. Chapter Introduction
    A. The Global Business Era
        1. Americans consume goods from all over the world.
        2. U.S. firms are increasingly doing business abroad.
        3. International trade has grown sevenfold since 1970.
        4. More than 1/4 of the goods and services produced worldwide today cross national borders.
    B. Why do Business Internationally?
        1. Global markets provide substantial opportunities and higher return on investment.
            a. U.S. markets for some products are mature or declining.
            b. Foreign business may allow for use of excess manufacturing capability.
            c. International business reduces the risk of operating in only one geographic market.
    C. International Trade
        1. Sets the tone for business interactions, the creation of joint alliances, and the development of focused international strategy.
II. International Agreements and Economic Alliances
    A. **General Agreement on Tariff and Trade (GATT)**
        1. Established in 1947.
        2. Rules to govern and resolve conflicts in international trade.
        3. Has reduced tariffs on over 50,000 items.
        4. Current (Uruguay) round focused on stabilizing worldwide currencies and preventing stifling protection laws.
    B. Economic Alliances—Table 3-1 lists six major alliances
        1. **European Community (EC).**
            a. Established in 1958.
            b. Twelve member countries.
            c. Agreements include

          1)   elimination of trade barriers.

          2)   creation of uniform technical product standards.

          3)   creation of uniform financial regulations.

    d.   Maastricht Accord (1992) encouraged EC to develop a common central bank and monetary union, using the European Currency Unit (ECU), by 2000.

  2. **North American Free Trade Agreement (NAFTA)**

    a.   Economic alliance among the U.S., Mexico, and Canada.

    b.   Provides for the phased elimination of tariff and most nontariff barriers within 10 years.

    c.   Establishes free trade in agricultural products between the U.S. and Mexico within 15 years.

    d.   Opposed in 1993 by environmentalists because of lax environmental regulation and enforcement in Mexico, and by labor because of cheaper wage rates in Mexico.

  3. **Association of South East Asian Nations (ASEAN)**

    a.   Ratified in 1967 by Singapore, Thailand, Malaysia, Indonesia, and the Philippines; joined in 1984 by Brunei.

    b.   Includes preferential trading arrangements, coordinated development of industry, and a joint finance corporation, along with exchange rate agreements.

    c.   Lack of financial resources among member countries has meant slow progress and conflict.

III.   The Multinational Company

  A.   A **multinational company (MNC)** does business in two or more (typically many) countries.

    1.   MNCs are large and growing. Many U.S. MNCs (for example, Pfizer, Mobil Oil, Hoover) sell most of their output abroad. Many (for example, Coca-Cola, Xerox, Chrysler) earn over half their profits outside the U.S. (See Table 3-2 for the 25 U.S. companies with the largest non-U.S. sales, and Table 3-3 for a listing of the various types of MNCs).

    2.   The present growth rate of the world's 200 largest MNCs (most are American) is two or three times the growth rate of individual advanced nations.

  B.   **The MNC Decision**—the move to becoming an MNC essentially encompasses three decisions:

    1.   The international market to be served—i.e., potential market size and wealth, and ease of doing business in host country.

    2.   The products or services to be marketed—taking into account the needs, preferences and idiosyncracies of the consumers in the selected host country.

      a.   **Shot-In-the-dark method**—many companies select products/services to be marketed abroad by simply selecting one of their products/services that has done well at home and marketing it abroad.

      b.   **Phased Internationalization**—a more sophisticated approach based on product-market research in the prospective host country.

        1)   The company designs a product/service that fits consumers' needs. Tic Tacs and Bailey's Irish cream were created using this approach.

3.   The mode of entry into the international market—a firm can pursue one of four basic strategies for entering a foreign market (see Figure 3-1 for an illustration of these strategies.) Each strategy represents a progressively greater commitment to the international venture:

    a.   **Sourcing**—uses labor in countries where labors costs are low.

    b.   **Export**—selling a product in international markets, but with no international manufacturing facilities. Involves little or no change in organizational mission, objectives and strategies.

        1)   An agent may be used to perform some or all of the exporting tasks (promotion, collecting, revenues, making credit arrangements, and shipping the product).

        2)   See Table 3-4 for a list of the 20 largest U.S. exporters.

        3)   Utilized by smaller companies as well as large corporations because of the relative simplicity and low cost, relative to other strategies.

        4)   A challenge of exporting: the exporter has little control when an agent is used.

    c.   **Foreign activities**—involves joining with nationals in a foreign country to establish production and/or marketing facilities. Usually involves one of two arrangements:

        1)   **Licensing**—the firm grants to an outside company the right to produce and/or market the firm's product in another country, or to use the firm's intangible assets (e.g. patents or technology).

        2)   **Joint venture**—A business joins with local investors to create and operate a business in the host country, with each investor as a partner sharing the ownership of the new venture. Useful in countries with very different business and cultural environments from that of the firm's home country.

            a)   Advantages include less risk and lower cost than direct investment, and gains from pooling skills and resources with host country partner(s).

            b)   Disadvantages occur because of differences of joint ownership objectives and management styles. Because of this, over 40% of joint ventures fail, and most last only 3 to 4 years.

            c)   Careful partner selection should take these factors into account and partners should come to clear prior agreement concerning mechanisms for resolving disputes, and each partner's role in managing the venture.

    d.   **Direct Investment**—the firm produces its products abroad with no association with a host country investor. The strongest commitment and risk to multinational operations.

1) Advantages include partial to full control over production, marketing and other key functions; lower labor costs; avoidance of tariffs; and confidence-building with consumers and the host government.
2) Disadvantages include dealing with local economic market, political, and government problems; regulations; culture; business practices; and exit barriers.

IV. The Environment of the Multinational Manager
   A. Effective management requires consideration and understanding of potential differences in four elements:
      1. **Culture**—includes knowledge, beliefs, laws, morals, customs, values and other capabilities and habits that an individual learns as a member of society.
         a. Managers of MNCs must be culturally sensitive and adapt their managerial practices to the host country culture, with an awareness that:
            1) Cultures are learned.
            2) Cultures vary, especially between eastern and western countries.
               a) Different objectives and behaviors are prized.
            3) Cultures influence behavior.
         b. Culture determines the relative importance of individual needs and the ways needs are satisfied.
      2. **Economics**—a nation's economic stability, inflation rate, and currency stability are key considerations in multinational management.
         a. Nations are classified as **developed (DC)** or **less-developed (LDC) countries**. An LDC is less economically developed, has a low GNP, little industry, and underdeveloped educational, distribution, and communications systems. LDCs make up 80 percent of the world's population; only 25 percent of the world's international business occurs there. Because of nationalistic feelings and a desire to consolidate control of their economies, many LDCs have developed extensive government regulations that restrict MNC growth. However, recently the trend has shifted due to changing attitudes and rising direct investment:
            1) Direct investment in LDCs has doubled since the early 1960s as many MNCs believe the possible returns are worth the risks. However, potential problems still remain due to host country concerns over MNC exploitation of resources and threats to sovereignty.
      3. **Politics**—the three political factors that most influence an MNC's operations and performance are:
         a. Governmental attitudes toward imports and direct investment—governments can greatly help or hinder MNCs.
            1) They can provide incentives for establishing businesses in the host country (e.g., low-interest government loans, tax holidays, accelerated depreciation, capital grants).
            2) LDC governments often set requirements that seek to

54

obtain as much value as possible from the MNC while not compromising the country's sovereignty

    a)   A **fadeout**—the majority ownership of an MNC's facility is transferred to a host country investor within a set number of years.

    b)   India limits foreign ownership of a local facility to 40 percent and must approve the operation's production capacity and entry into new markets.

    c)   LDCs may require that an MNC hire a specified number of local citizens, and/or sell its technology to local businesses.

    d)   Restrictions may be placed on the amount of funds that can be transferred out of the country.

    e)   Government can require an export of equal or higher value for every item imported by a resident MNC.

  b.   Efficiency of government—many countries have inefficient bureaucracies which hinder MNC operations. In many European and Asian countries, legal systems are based on civil law which is greatly influenced by civil servants (bureaucrats).

  c.   Government stability—greatly impacts the MNC.

    1)   In highly unstable countries, an MNC may face:

        a)   **Expropriation**—the leaders in power seize MNC facilities without compensation.

        b)   **Nationalization**—the MNC is forced to sell its facilities to local buyers.

    2)   **Political risk**—unanticipated changes in the host country's political environment that affect MNC operations.

        a)   **Macro risk**—political changes that affect all MNCs in a host country.

        b)   **Micro risk**—affect certain industries or firms in a host country.

    3)   **Political risk analysis**—involves identifying and assessing the sources of risk, and the probabilities that adverse political change will occur in a host country. Risk analysis methods include:

        a)   Visiting the host country and interviewing government officials, business executives, and others.

        b)   Using a panel of experts on the host country to rate the political risk factors.

        c)   Using a political risk analysis program designed to meet the MNC's specific needs.

4.   **Technology**—managers must determine how the technological levels in foreign countries affect their operations and sources of raw materials, energy, and transportation.

V.   Management in a Multinational Corporation

  A.   The **planning function**—the planning function can be affected by many factors in the host country. (Table 3-6 presents some of the factors that can complicate the MNC manager's planning environment.)

    1.   MNC objectives cannot be the same as if it were operating only in the U.S., because of potential for conflict between corporate objectives and economic and political objectives of the host country.

          a.   The host country may have objectives (for example, a favorable balance of payments, an improved standard of living for citizens) which do not coincide with MNC corporate objectives.

          b.   A common point of conflict is often that some of the subsidiary's earnings are returned to MNC headquarters in the U.S., which can negatively impact the host country's balance of payments.

    2.   Civil servants often establish the conditions under which the MNC manager's planning function operates.

B.   The **organizing function**—an organizational structure for the MNC must be established that is adapted to local conditions in the host countries in which the MNC operates and which provides control over international operations.

    1.   The structure involves establishing an effective worldwide communication system for transmitting information throughout the organization.

    2.   MNCs usually use the three basic organizational structure designs:

          a.   **Product design**—a single unit is operationally responsible for a product or product line. Widely used by MNCs with diverse product lines marketed in geographically dispersed areas (for example, Unisys). (See Figure 3-2.)

          b.   **Geographic design**—all functional and operational responsibilities are grouped into specific geographical areas. Widely used by MNCs whose product lines aren't widely diversified (for example, International Telephone and Telegraph). Area managers have decentralized decision making. (See Figure 3-3.)

          c.   **Functional design**—managers at corporate headquarters have global responsibilities for such functions as marketing, production, and finance. Useful for MNCs with a very limited product line, because duplication of effort can be avoided. (See Figure 3-4.)

    3.   Many factors can influence organizational structure, including technology, level of managerial experience, and the degree to which management is home-country oriented, host-country oriented, or world-oriented.

C.   The **leading function**

    1.   Formal

          a.   Leaders in appointed or elected positions of authority; outlined in the MNC's organization chart.

    2.   Informal

          a.   Achieve influence because of special skills, expertise, or charisma

    3.   The most studied and yet least understood function.

    4.   How leadership is applied differs from country to country because of

cultural differences.

D. The **controlling function**—may not be used in some countries to the same degree as in the U.S. due to cultural differences. However, the same three basic conditions for effective control are required:

1. Establishing standards—overall corporate objectives and local conditions must be considered, often involving input from local managers so that standards don't conflict with culture.

2. Providing information to measure actual performance and appraise that performance against standards—problems can arise such as whether profits should be measured in home or local currency. Excessive and irrelevant information fed into the MNC communication system can also be a problem.

3. Corrective action—involves the key question of the degree to which authority should be decentralized. Usually, international managers take most actions with specific guidelines provided by corporate headquarters.

VI. Managing People in Multinational Corporations

A. Effectiveness in managing people can vary widely across countries because of differing cultures which influence individual needs, motivation bases, and reactions to leadership styles.

B. A primary issue for an MNC is whether to hire host-country citizens or transfer their own managers **(expatriates)** into management positions in the overseas facilities. (see Table 3-8.)

1. Using expatriates ensures that the facility has the necessary managerial skills; however the strategy is more costly than hiring locals.

2. Failure rates of expatriates is high (about 30 percent of all assignments fail).

   a. Problems occur with managers adjusting to the local culture and business environment.

   b. Some expatriates lack the special qualities needed for success—communication skills, flexibility, and ability to work with people from different backgrounds and culture.

   c. MNCs often inadequately prepare expatriates for their assignments.

C. Some MNCs are attempting to better prepare their expatriates by:

1. Carefully screening employees for expatriate assignments.

2. Encouraging expatriate managers to return home at least once per year.

D. Approximately 250,000 US citizens work as expatriates in MNC facilities abroad; more than 45 million US workers are employed by foreign organizations. (See Table 3-7.)

57

ANSWERS TO DISCUSSION AND REVIEW QUESTIONS

1. **Question:** *Discuss how culture could affect an employee's willingness to change.*

   Answer: Since cultures influence behavior, an employee's willingness to change may be directly influenced by the degree to which change is embraced by his or her culture. In societies such as the U.S., with a great deal of cultural diversity, individuals may be accustomed to other viewpoints, or may have reacted to the diversity around them by closing down their receptiveness to alternative views. Similarly, in more monolithic environments, individuals may resist or may actually seek out variety because of their relative lack of exposure to it. Students should be encouraged to discuss their own receptiveness to change.

2. **Question:** *How would a manager use Porter's "diamond" framework and analysis to evaluate the attractiveness of forming a joint venture in a country such as Costa Rica?*

   Answer: Porter's major contention is that managers must focus on gaining competitive advantage for their organizations, rather than simply increasing in size. Students should discuss the means by which they could analyze each of the four factors (firm strategy, structure and rivalry; demand conditions; factor conditions; and related and supporting industries) in Costa Rica for the specific type of business venture under consideration. The sources of information available and analytic processes employed in the evaluation should be considered in responding to this question.

3. **Question:** *Do you believe that you would be an effective expatriate manager? Explain why or why not.*

   Answer: This question is intended to allow students to identify the individual characteristics necessary for success in overseas management and to consider whether they "fit the bill" for such work.

4. **Question:** *Some managers are calling for the repeal of the Foreign Corrupt Practices Act, charging that the law greatly diminishes their competitiveness abroad. In your view, should the law be repealed? Discuss.*

   Answer: Students who support the Foreign Corrupt Practices Act will cite moral and ethical reasons for their support, and the potential damage bribery activities render to the image of the American business community abroad. Other students will argue that the act severely handicaps American MNCs in dealings with foreign governments. Given that bribery is considered a necessary and accepted practice in many countries, opponents of the FCPA argue that the image argument is illogical.

5. **Question:** *Why would an American firm be reluctant to establish a new plant in a country such as Saudi Arabia?*

   Answer: All the aspects discussed in the chapter—Porter's four "diamond" factors; economic alliances; the three MNC decisions; the four environmental factors; and issues in managing people in other cultures, come into play in answering this question. Students may discuss their understanding of cultural, political, economic, and other factors in conducting an analysis of the profitability of establishing such a plant.

6. **Question:** *Why might American managers prefer domestic versus global assignments? What are the advantages and disadvantages of each?*

   Answer: Students should identify several advantages and disadvantages to domestic versus global assignments in MNCs. The list should help students understand the complexity of managing in MNCs. Managing in a foreign environment involves coping with a great deal of change in almost every aspect of management, including the nature of subordinates (who are influenced by a culture usually quite different from the U.S.) and the nature of subordinate-supervisor relationships. It also requires adapting to different situations influenced by the host-government society's norms, laws, and other factors. The ability to not only adjust to such substantial change but to be effective in such an environment is essential. The magnitude of adjustment required makes global assignments highly challenging.

7. **Question:** *Suppose you were the CEO of a computer manufacturing company with plans to establish a production facility in Japan. You want to transfer some of your managers to the Japanese facility. What steps would you take to ensure that your expatriate managers are effective in their new assignments?*

   Answer: The success of such staffing depends a great deal on the cultural sensitivity of those managers. They and their families need to study the culture, the language, and the lifestyle, and make some visits to be sure they are enthusiastic about the move and feel they can adjust. The CEO should ensure that there is careful screening of these managers both initially and at this stage. Managers need some training in the way the Japanese do business, the on-the-job expectations of workers, and what kinds of leadership and communication styles will be most effective, without negating the "headquarters" knowledge and skills which they can bring to the venture.

8. **Question:** *Could economic alliances such as the EC and NAFTA result in greater trade protectionism against nations not included in the alliance? Explain.*

   Answer: This question gives rise to much speculation as to the economic impacts of such alliances. Students are encouraged to explore the nature of and differences among the major alliances, to examine the relative self-sufficiencies of the alliance members, and to discuss the impact of ongoing GATT negotiations on global trade.

9. **Question:** *Would the social responsibility aspects of managerial actions differ between domestic and international managers? Discuss.*

    Answer: They could, since in many foreign countries the public's expectations of corporate social responsibility are not as high as they are in the U.S. Moreover, most government regulations which require social responsibility activities (e.g., pollution abatement requirements, workplace safety) are much less stringent (and in many cases are nonexistent) in foreign nations. These factors would tend to reduce an MNC's responsible activities in foreign countries.

10. **Question:** *Of the economic, cultural, political, and technological factors in the international environment, which factor do you believe has the greatest impact upon MNC performance? Explain.*

    Answer: Students should recognize that the answer to this question is highly situational, and is contingent on the host country, the type of MNC operation, and the status of the four factors at any particular time. Probably the most common factor to have a major impact on MNC performance is the economic, because it is so volatile and uncontrollable.

END OF CHAPTER CASES

CASE 3-1: THE MAQUILADORAS

CASE SUMMARY: This case profiles what a Texas Governor has called "the best-kept industrial secret in the U.S.". The secret is more than 1,500 foreign owned and operated plants in the towns along the U.S.-Mexico border, where Mexican workers assemble parts imported from other countries into products. Once assembled, the products are shipped back to the foreign owners and operators of the plants, mostly U.S. companies. Many U.S. and Japanese corporations are establishing *maquiladoras* to reap the substantial benefits of exceptionally low labor costs (Mexican employees are paid less than $3 a day). For U.S. companies, there is no tariff on parts shipped to Mexico, as long as the assembled products are reimported into the U.S. Companies in the U.S. find the *maquiladoras* strategy to be a sound way to compete against Asian businesses that enjoy the advantage of very low labor costs in their own countries. Mexico, too, gains, in that the *maquiladoras* provide badly-needed employment opportunities. The output from these businesses ranks second only to oil as Mexico's top foreign exchange earner. However, there are problems. Managers from the U.S. must go through lengthy customs inspections on their commute each day. Electricity and telephone service in the Mexican towns is erratic. Turnover among the Mexican employees is very high. And Mexicans charge that the plants offer only low skill jobs, with little opportunity for advancement. Partly in response, international companies are building fully integrated manufacturing facilities, offering higher skill and wage jobs, in the interior of Mexico.

60

NAFTA may mean the end of the *maquiladoras*, with an elimination of tariffs, and the absence of duty drawbacks on third-country components in products shipped to the U.S. and Mexico. This case presents an excellent opportunity to debate the soundness of the *maquiladoras* strategy for U.S. companies, from the perspective of the corporations and employees.

ANSWERS TO QUESTIONS FOR ANALYSIS

1. **Question:** *Evaluate the impact of maquiladoras on the Mexican economy. What grade would you give them, A, B, C, D, or F? Why?*

   Answer: The *maquiladoras* clearly have a tremendous impact on the Mexican economy. Their "grade" can be debated among students, given the benefits to Mexico and the foreign operators, and the extremely rapid growth rate of the industry, along with the liabilities and future uncertainty of the plans.

2. **Question:** *Should American labor unions attempt to keep semi-skilled, relatively low wage jobs in the United States?*

   Answer: Students who followed the debates on NAFTA in late 1993 may have much to say in responding to this question. International competition for such jobs has grown enormously, and the answers to the issue raised here will of necessity include broad consideration of U.S. economic and industrial policies.

3. **Question:** *Do you think that NAFTA will eventually eliminate the maquiladoras industry? Why?*

   Answer: NAFTA provisions will certainly change the environment in which the *maquiladoras* operate, but whether or not they will be eliminated entirely will remain to be seen over the next several years. This question provides students an opportunity to research the specific legislative features and interpretations of NAFTA.

CASE 3-2: INVEST IN RUSSIA: WHY?

CASE SUMMARY: There are many good reasons to invest in the large, completely open market that is Russia today, including the high degree of satisfaction expressed by U.S. companies already doing business there. The major reason Americans are overall investing so little, though, is largely because Russian companies don't understand how to attract U.S. investors, and Americans don't know how best to benefit from Russian opportunities. Problems include Russia's high taxes and the uncertain future tax and regulation picture; the judicial inconsistencies faced when working with the Russian government; the lack of Russian understanding of the value of capital combined with the high "hurdle rate" (minimum return on investment) of American companies; and the difficult living conditions in Russia.

These problems have arisen during 70 years of Communist rule, isolated from market cultures. It is in Russia's interest to make changes, and many American companies are investing on a limited basis now, establishing a foothold for larger investment later. The relative absence of competition in Russia today makes the Russian market an attractive one for commercializing new products.

1.   Question: *Using Porter's "diamond" analysis, explain why a Western manager would consider entering the Russian market.*

   Answer: Porter emphasizes innovation and competitive advantage in entering a market. Students can discuss the positive aspects of Russia's firm strategy, structure, and rivalry (probably the weakest factor); demand conditions; factor conditions (probably the strongest factor); and related and supporting industries in assessing the competitive advantage to Western companies of entering the market.

2.   Question: *The case outlines some reasons why American companies in 1994 are not investing heavily in Russia. What are some other business reasons not presented?*

   Answer: Many factors may be cited by students, including a focus on trade with countries in North America and Europe; language barriers; Russia's relative lack of wealth among consumers; geographic distances; an increasing crime rate and influence of organized crime in Russia; cultural differences; spotty technology, communications, and transportation access; and economic instability.

3.   Question: *Why would McDonald's and Polaroid believe that early entry into Russia would provide a competitive advantage at a later point in time?*

   Answer: Students may discuss the opportunity to gain familiarity with the local cultures, the development of economic ties along with communication and transportation infrastructure links, the possibility of gaining political influence, the chance to establish high product visibility, and other factors.

ADDITIONAL QUESTIONS AND ANSWERS

1.   Question: *What features do you believe the United States has which might make it attractive to foreign multinationals?*

   Answer: Some factors that could be mentioned are a favorable attitude toward competition, stable government, relatively stable economy, relatively sound monetary system, favorable attitude toward direct investment, and relatively efficient governmental organizations.

2. **Question:** *Is it safe to say that most American business organizations would prefer to do business domestically? Why.*

Answer: Such is likely so. Doing business in the U.S. is relatively simpler than abroad because management is more familiar with the external environment and its demands. Doing business abroad can often introduce much uncertainty and complexity into the organization.

3. **Question:** *Why do you think companies continue to use the shot-in-the-dark method for establishing an international market, as opposed to adopting a phased internationalization approach?*

Answer: This question will stimulate discussion on the resources devoted to market research and product design allocated by various companies, as well as a consideration of business decisions made for political, vanity, or other less well- founded business reasons.

4. **Question:** *Discuss some of the reasons why a business might decide to do business abroad.*

Answer: There are five primary reasons: the desire for growth, competitive pressures, domestic environmental pressures, incentives offered by foreign countries, and opportunities for increased operating efficiencies.

5. **Question:** *Briefly identify the four basic strategies a firm can employ for entering a foreign market.*

Answer: The four strategies are: 1) sourcing, which involves using labor in countries with low labor costs; 2) exporting goods abroad, which is the simplest way to enter a foreign market, requiring little organizational change; 3) foreign activities, which involve joining with nationals in a foreign country to establish production and/or marketing facilities (joint ventures) or licensing agreements; and 4) direct investment, in which the firm produces its products abroad. Of the four strategies, direct investment is the strongest commitment to multinational operations.

6. **Question:** *Distinguish between licensing and joint venture arrangements which relate to the foreign activities strategy of entering foreign markets.*

Answer: Licensing involves a firm granting to an outside company the right to produce and/or market the firm's product in another country. When a firm enters into a joint venture, it joins a group of foreign investors to begin a business in a foreign nation with each group member sharing ownership.

7. **Question:** *Why do so many international joint ventures fail?*

Answer: The impact of cultural differences among business partners, and the need for mutually agreed-upon objectives, are key in developing the answers to this question. Differences not only in general business approaches but also language, regulatory requirements, political considerations, values, and a host of other factors may negatively affect joint ventures. Even successful joint ventures may later create enormous difficulties. For example, a partner with limited technology access may later use what it has learned in the joint venture to outcompete its former partner.

8. **Question:** *Discuss the impact of the Foreign Corrupt Practices Act on U.S. MNCs relative to their international competitors.*

    Answer: The act is claimed by many to place US MNCs at a distinct disadvantage because it prohibits American MNCs from bribing foreign government officials. In many countries, bribery is seen as an accepted and necessary business practice. Governments expect this benefit from companies and can make doing business quite difficult for those who don't provide bribes. In some countries, bribes are tax deductible as business expenses. Because of the FCPA, foreign competitors are free to offer bribes, while American companies are not.

9. **Question:** *Briefly describe the three basic organizational designs for MNC companies.*

    Answer: Students should describe the product, geographic, and functional designs and how they are used in MNCs. In discussing student responses, it is useful to have them consider the strengths and disadvantages of each structure relative to MNC operations.

10. **Question:** *Present a profile of an individual who, in your opinion, would perform effectively as a manager in a foreign country.*

    Answer: Student responses will likely differ. However, essential individual characteristics include: 1) flexibility—the ability to adapt to and be effective in an environment of considerable change; 2) ability to deal with ambiguity—because ambiguity is prevalent in managing in an unfamiliar environment; and 3) patience—which is essential for learning new ways in a new land and for becoming accustomed to and appreciating the differences in employees who are natives in that land.

4

SOCIAL AND ETHICAL RESPONSIBILITIES OF MANAGEMENT

LEARNING OBJECTIVES

After completing Chapter 4, students should be able to:

Define   social responsibility in terms that reflect your view of the role of corporations in society.

Describe   the manner in which managers' ethics affect their decisions regarding social responsibility.

Discuss   the purpose, process, and pitfalls of establishing an effective code of ethics.

Compare   arguments for and against a specific corporate action, based on your own ethical standards.

Identify   the various actions managers are taking to ensure that their organizations are ethical.

CHAPTER SYNOPSIS

This chapter addresses the issue of management's social and ethical responsibilities by focusing on four topics: the meaning of social responsibility, specific socially responsible activities, changing expectations for corporate performance, and managerial ethics. Noting that social responsibility has been defined in many ways, the chapter discusses the concept from three perspectives: social responsibility as (1) **social obligation** (wherein proponents believe that a company is socially responsible only when it pursues profits); (2) **social reaction** (wherein a company reacts to societal expectations); and (3) **social responsiveness** (which involves planned, preventive, and proactive—not reactive—socially responsible activities). Specific socially-responsible activities are discussed in terms of two prominent classifications: by activities, and by the beneficiaries of activities. The beneficiaries may be internal (customers, employees, shareholders) or external (specific groups or general society). The chapter presents an historical perspective of the evolution of society's demands for corporate social responsibility, focusing on three crises in 1870, 1930, and 1970. Managerial ethics is then addressed, along with the three bases often used in developing guidelines for ethical decision making: **egoism, altruism,** and **obligation** to a formal principle. The chapter concludes with a discussion of the corporation's role in managerial ethics.

The chapter's **Management In Action** segment gives three examples of companies participating in the "green revolution", entering the environment on the balance sheet. The **Management Focus** segments describe the "trade-not-aid" philosophy of The Body Shop, a socially responsible company with above average financial returns; examine the apprentice program and educational incentives at Detroit's Milford Fabricating Company; and discuss Nike's experience with corporate social responsibility programs, particularly with the US minority community.

LECTURE & DISCUSSION IDEAS

1. One effective way to spur student thought and discussion on the subjectivity of social responsibility and ethics is to describe a situation of questionable ethics or breach of social responsibility and have the students express and discuss their reactions to the situation. An incident relayed in the *Fortune* magazine article, "Industrial Espionage at the Harvard B-School," (September 6,1982, pp. 70-76) provides an excellent example. The situation: during a week-long computerized management simulation game, one team of Harvard MBA students stole confidential competitor information, enabling the team to win the game. In discussing the incident (and the school's response), it's useful to ask students: what would you have done?

2. In your discussion of managerial ethics, it's useful to pose the following question to students: "Should top management provide guidelines to its managers concerning ethics in decision making (given that the company is ultimately responsible for the decisions its managers make)? If so, how can top management do so (and is it possible to instill ethics in individuals)?"

3. Multinational corporations have a particularly challenging experience in setting corporate ethical standards, since business ethics are largely determined by local culture. Determine whether students in the class are native to or have lived in other cultures, and have them describe business or government practices regarding bribes, warranties, monopolies, collusion, or other practices in those societies which may differ from the standards in the U.S.

PROJECT / EXERCISE IDEAS

1. As a group project, have your students identify a local business that assumes a social responsiveness approach to social responsibility. The students should interview the company's CEO and prepare a written or oral report on the company's perspective and activities in the area of social responsibility. The report should focus on the company's past, present and planned activities, the nuts and bolts of its philosophy, and its benefits and costs. The report should also address how the company's perspective on social responsibility has evolved over the years.

2. How influential are special interest groups in affecting the activities of businesses in the area of social responsibility? One way to find out is to have students select a particular interest group and research and prepare a report on the group's activities and its impact on business. Students may opt to interview the members of a local interest group that has influenced or attempted to influence local and regional businesses. Some suggested interest groups: National Organization for Women, the Sierra Club, the NAACP, and Common Cause.

3. One way to illustrate the influential power of public opinion concerning a company's social responsibilities is to divide the class in groups and have each group select and research a past situation where public opinion influenced company/industry activities in the area of social responsibility. Students should address such elements of the situation as how public momentum concerning the respective area of social responsibility developed, how it influenced corporate activities, and the subsequent actions by companies and results. Some examples: minority recruitment and hiring; product safety in the areas of automobiles and medicines (and protective anti-tampering packaging of medicines). Have each group present a report on its research.

LECTURE OUTLINE NOTES

I. The Meanings of Social Responsibility.

    A.   Definitions of social responsibility are numerous and can be classified into three categories:

        1.   Social responsibility as **social obligation**—according to this view, a company is socially responsible when it pursues a profit within the constraints of law as imposed by society. Any behavior illegal or not in pursuit of profit is socially irresponsible.

            a.   Rationale for this perspective:

                1)   Management's sole responsibility is to serve the interests of the shareholders to whom they are accountable by managing to produce profits.

                2)   Socially responsible activities should be determined by law, public policy, and private individuals.

                3)   Management abuses its authority when it allocates profits to social improvement activities.

                    a)   Management is taxing shareholders by using profits for purposes that don't have immediate profitable return for shareholders, without input from the shareholders.

                    b)   Management is taking actions that affect society without being accountable to society.

                    c)   Managers are not trained to make noneconomic decisions.

                4)   These actions may be disadvantageous to society. This type of social spending by management may end up increasing the price of the company's goods and services. Customers and shareholders interests therefore aren't served.

        2.   Social responsibility as **social reaction**—defines social responsibility as an organization's reaction to society's expectations for business

behavior which extend beyond providing goods and services. The focus is on reacting to society's norms, values, and performance expectations.

    a.   A restrictive interpretation holds that social responsibility involves only voluntary reactions. That is, actions required by law or economic factors are not socially responsible behavior. Only voluntary, altruistic behavior is socially responsible in this view.

    b.   A broader interpretation views social responsibility as reactions that go beyond the law (typically reactions to expectations of specific groups such as consumerists, social activists, unions, etc.).

3.   Social responsibility as **social responsiveness**—views social responsibility as anticipatory and preventive rather than reactive and restorative behavior; that is, actions that go beyond social obligation and social reaction. The broadest meaning of social responsibility.

    a.   Advocates of this view cite three rationales:

        1)   Everything a business does has social consequences; thus as a major participant in society, businesses must be responsible for proactively dealing with society's major problems.

        2)   Businesses are possibly the best problem-solving organizations in a capitalist society—their alleged lack of training for social decision making is not an issue.

        3)   Management is not abusing its authority. Shareholders have rarely challenged their business' support of social causes; to the contrary, a company's social efforts are often supported by all of its constituencies.

B.   See Figure 4-1 for a continuum which depicts the three perspectives. Being socially reactive implies the firm's acceptance of social obligation as well. Being socially responsive requires social-obligation and social-reaction behavior.

II.   Specific Socially Responsible Activities

A.   Socially responsible activities can be classified in several ways. Two common classifications:

1.   **By activities:**

    a.   Product line—by manufacturing safe, reliable, high-quality products.

    b.   Marketing practices—being truthful and complete in advertising.

    c.   Employee education and training—educating employees and providing means for career advancement.

    d.   Environmental control—reducing pollutants.

    e.   Employee relations, benefits, and satisfaction with work—providing benefits such as day care.

    f.   Employment and advancement for minorities and women—hiring, and encouraging professional development.

    g.   Employee safety and health—providing a clean, safe, comfortable working environment.

h.   Corporate philanthropy—making donations to groups and causes in society.

2.   By the **beneficiaries** of each action:

a.   **Internal beneficiaries**—each group has an immediate stake in the organization. Corporate activities in response to each group may be classified as obligatory, reactive or responsive.

   1)   **Customers**
      a)   Examples include responding promptly to complaints, providing accurate product information and truthful advertising, and developing products responsive to customers' social concerns.

   2)   **Employees**—responsibilities can be minimally met by obeying laws relating to employee—employer relationships (for example, safety and working conditions, wage and hour provisions), or can be extended with fringe benefits (retirement, health, and other benefits).
      a)   Companies may also provide such employee services as training, career development, and counseling.
      b)   To meet family responsibilities, companies may offer flextime, childcare, and elder care.
      c)   Socially responsible employee activities may also benefit the employer, through increased attendance and productivity.
      d)   Trade-offs include longer work hours and higher stress levels for employees.

   3)   **Shareholders**—includes responsibilities to disclose use of corporate resources and results of those uses.
      a)   Stockholders have a legal, fundamental right to information about the organization, on which the stockholder can make a prudent investment decision.
      b)   Many argue that management's top responsibility is to shareholders.
      c)   However, evidence exists that indicates that firms that aggressively pursue socially responsible behavior are more profitable than those that don't. However, such evidence is controversial because many disagree on how social responsibility should be measured and how it relates to performance measures.
      d)   Today, more and more individual shareholders and investor groups are challenging management's actions through shareholder resolutions or outright battles for control.

b.   **External beneficiaries**—classified as:
   1)   **Specific**—clearly defined groups (for example, minorities and ethnic groups, women, the disabled, the aged)

69

seeking to redress historical grievances. Some groups have obtained laws that require organizations to support their efforts (for example, equal employment and affirmative action).

    a)   Corporate actions can be obligatory (in response to antidiscrimination laws), reactive (going beyond the letter of the law), or responsive (attempting to go to the heart of the causes, without prompting by law or direct pressure).

  2) **General**—elicits organizational efforts to solve or prevent general social problems (for example, solving or preventing environmental problems, and upgrading education, the arts, and community health through gifts and donations of executives' time).

    a)   Companies have much freedom in determining their level of involvement in this area of social responsibility.

III.   Changing Expectations for Corporate Performance

    A.   The prevailing mood today is that large organizations are not only *capable* of contributing to social progress but are *responsible* for doing so.

    B.   Contemporary expectations for corporate social responsibility seem to have evolved from three business crises:

      1.   Crisis of 1870—the industrialization of America and incorporation of businesses created major corporate powers who often abused power. Public outcry for legal redress led to laws on rate regulation, fair-trade practices, and labor. Landmark law—Sherman Act of 1890.

      2.   Crisis of 1930—in the early 1930s, corporations grew in size (via many mergers) and many Americans as stockholders shared the wealth. However, the Great Depression occurred and many blamed business, believing that business had betrayed the country's faith. FDR and the New Deal substantially increased government's regulation of business activities, and asserted the responsibility of business to treat those with a direct stake in the corporation fairly.

      3.   Crisis of 1970

        a.   From 1950-1970, two economics evolved:

          1)   **Public economy**—run by the government; regularly intervenes in business practices (comprises one-fourth of the national social system).

          2)   **Private economy**—three-fourths of the social system (500 firms account for two-thirds of all manufacturing).

        b.   These two economies confront and accommodate each other.

        c.   In 1970s, new ideas spawned by the 1960s unrest (for example, consumerism, feminism, environmentalism) challenged the business-government relationship and made new demands on business' social responsibility.

    C.   Events of the 1980's and 1990's have reinforced the attitude that corporations must react to problems created by their own actions. Business must go beyond obligatory behavior and reactive behavior; business must demonstrate socially responsive behavior.

IV. Managerial Ethics

    A. **Ethics** refers to principles of behavior which distinguish between good, bad, right, and wrong.

    B. Codes of ethics enable individuals to make choices among alternative behaviors.

    C. The importance of ethics increases in proportion to the consequences of the outcome of a behavior.

    D. The role and state of ethics in U.S. business is an issue of growing concern, because:

        1. Business scandals have been widely publicized.

            a. More than 2/3 of the *Fortune* 500 companies have acted illegally in some fashion in the last fifteen years.

            b. According to one study, 40 percent of the manager respondents said they had compromised personal principles to meet a company demand.

        2. Companies are realizing that ethical misconduct by management can be very costly to the company and to society.

        3. Determining what is and isn't ethical is often difficult to do.

            a. Ethical decision-making may not be a choice between right and wrong, but rather "conflicts of right vs. right".

    E. Ethical standards—in making decisions, managers must weigh consequences for themselves, their company, and society. There are three bases for developing ethical guidelines for decision making (see Figure 4-2):

        1. Maximum personal benefits (egoism)—an egoistic manager makes decisions that maximize his or her personal benefit (salary, prestige, power).

        2. Maximum social benefit **(altruism)**—an altruistic manager makes decisions that provide greatest happiness for the greatest number.

        3. **Obligation to a formal principle**—an act's rightness or wrongness depends on principle, not consequences. Stands between the extremes of altruism and egoism.

            a. The viewpoint that actions can be judged by one particular principle is unacceptable to many who prefer a pluralistic approach where decision making considers several principles arranged in a hierarchy of importance. The advantage of a pluralistic approach is that the hierarchy provides the decision maker with a basis for evaluating decisions.

    F. The organization's role in ethical behavior

        1. Although a company is responsible for its managers' decisions, few companies have provided guidelines concerning ethics in decision making.

        2. Those that do often develop a corporate **code of ethics**.

            a. The code is usually developed by top management.

            b. It consists of a written statement of the company's values, beliefs and norms of ethical behavior. (See Figure 4-3 for an example from Johnson & Johnson).

c. Ideally, it should provide employees direction in dealing with ethical dilemmas, clarify the organization's position regarding areas of ethical uncertainty, and achieve and maintain overall ongoing conduct that the organization views as ethical.

d. Often ineffective because:

1) Codes tend to be legalistic, focusing on strict legalities and illegalities instead of tackling the more complex questions of ethics and values.

2) Codes tend to focus on conflicts of interest or infractions that affect profits rather than on actions that affect the community.

3) Codes tend not to allow flexibility to meet local customs and norms.

4) Codes often are not well implemented or enforced.

3. Many companies with effective codes:

a. Translate their values and beliefs into specific ethical standards of behavior.

b. Determine penalties for code violations, communicate them to employees, and implement them when violations occur.

c. Conduct ethics seminars for employees.

d. Set realistic performance objectives for employees to avoid the type of unreasonable performance pressure that can lead to unethical behavior.

e. Establish the position of ethics advocate who evaluates the organization's position and actions from an ethics perspective.

G. Figure 3-4, The Corporation's Social Responsibility and Managerial Ethics, shows a model which integrates social responsibility, expectations for corporate behavior, and ethics.

ANSWERS TO DISCUSSION AND REVIEW QUESTIONS

1. **Question:** *Describe the steps an organization could take to become more socially responsible. In your discussion, include some examples of how these steps would apply to other internal and external beneficiaries.*

    Answer: Students' response to this question should demonstrate their understanding of the categories of social responsibility, from social obligation to social responsiveness. Becoming more socially responsible may include taking on additional activities in categories not previously addressed by the organization.

The question also tests students' understanding of the populations that comprise internal and external beneficiaries, and the differences between specific and general external beneficiaries.

It is helpful to have students be as specific as possible in responding to this question, providing examples based on real or hypothetical organizations.

2. **Question:** *How can an organization, through its guidelines and actions, influence an individual manager to make ethical decisions? Provide some examples.*

    Answer: This question should stimulate discussion of corporate codes of ethics, their implementation (or lack thereof), and their overall effectiveness. The implementation strategies described in the chapter, particularly those involving effective sanctions, training, and ethics advocates, are especially important in insuring that organizational ethical standards are met by managers. It may be instructive to discuss the effectiveness or ineffectiveness of organizational responses to specific U.S. scandals of recent years (e.g. Drexel Burnham Lambert, Lincoln Savings and Loan, the Congressional House Bank scandal, the Tailhook scandal).

3. **Question:** *Which of the three meanings of social responsibility reflects your opinion? Explain.*

    Answer: This question is intended for students to identify, describe, and assess their own viewpoint concerning corporate social responsibility. In discussing responses, it is useful to encourage students to debate with each other, to defend their positions, and to explain why they don't support the others' perspectives.

4. **Question:** *Identify a situation where an organization might be socially responsible to one group of internal beneficiaries but not socially responsible to another group.*

    Answer: This question is intended to point out the idea that ethical decision-making is often not a choice between right and wrong, but rather a choice between right and right. For example, a small manufacturing plant's expensive pollution abatement processes beyond what the law requires may be socially responsive to its customers who live in the vicinity of the plant, while at the same time showing little social obligation to its shareholders (at least over the short term). A second example is a software company which expands the hours of its toll-free support lines, providing response at the social reaction or socially responsive level for its customers; in doing so, it may have to reduce or eliminate alternative work schedules for its support line employees.

5. **Question:** *What are the basic arguments for and against each of the three meanings of social responsibility?*

    Answer: Proponents of the social obligation view argue that social responsibility should be viewed as activities in pursuit of profit because non-profit activities may be disadvantageous to society. However, many disagree with this view of social responsibility, arguing that many activities in pursuit of profit are often excessive and can harm society's welfare. Proponents of the social reaction perspective argue that a business' social responsibility activities should be based on society's expectations because society is the best determinant of what activities should comprise corporate social responsibility. However, some argue that corporations should go beyond just reacting to society's expectations and should assume a more active role. Proponents of the social responsiveness approach to corporate social responsibility believe that businesses should be actively involved benefitting the general welfare of the society in which they operate, and take actions that go beyond meeting society's expectations. Opponents of this view believe that such an approach can be too costly for the company and that money can be better spent in other, more profitable pursuits.

6. **Question:** *The corporation is responsible to a wide range of interest groups, on both an internal and external basis. Should any one interest group (e.g., employees, shareholders, government, the general public) be given more priority? Why?*

   Answer: Student responses will vary according to their own ethics and opinions. Corporations' preferential treatment of one interest group over another will most likely reflect the personal ethics and opinions of its CEO or top management. Discussion could center on how such diversity may be beneficial for society in general. Also, students should come to realize that such decisions may require a trade-off between egoistic and altruistic choices.

7. **Question:** *Can you think of a situation you have been in where your attitude and views toward ethical behavior and/or social responsibility conflicted with those of your peers? Explain.*

   Answer: Everyone has experienced such instances at one point or another. Situations described by students may range from the relatively innocuous (badgering a substitute teacher, calling in sick to work and going to the beach) to the dramatically serious (a drunk driving accident, commission of a felony). Many of the situations described may lend themselves to the subjective nature of discussions of ethics and levels of social responsibility.

8. **Question:** *One manager's comment: "Since most foreign competitors do not follow or ever have strict codes of ethics, it is unfair to expect American companies to adhere to rigid standards. Rather, when operating overseas, American companies should have the right to discard domestic standards of ethical conduct." Do you agree?*

   Answer: This discussion question challenges not only students' personal views of ethics, but also their view of culture (as discussed in Chapter 3. Ethics are rooted in culture; should the culture of a U.S. based MNC operating outside the U.S. be that of the United States, or that of the

74

country in which it operates? Are ethics contextual for individuals, or are they absolute? It is unrealistic to expect class consensus in the discussion of this question.

9. **Question:** *In your opinion, what is the greatest challenge in developing an ethical environment within a business?*

    Answer: The conflict between meeting short term company objectives and maintaining truly ethical behavior often presents itself as a compromise to managers in their decision making. Given the internal and external pressures on managers, determining the appropriate outcome may be an enormous challenge. Managers need to be encouraged to consider ethics and social responsibility as important for the long term integrity and possibly the viability of the organization. It is often, however, a grey area in which judgment is called for because there are no clear answers. In such cases, if a manager's experience or the company's code of ethics does not clarify the issue, then he or she should be encouraged to consult with peers and superiors in the organization.

10. **Question:** *Much has been written of corporate responsibilities in achieving ethical standards of behavior in its relations with internal and external beneficiaries. However, little has been mentioned of these beneficiaries' responsibilities to the corporation. Do you believe they have any? Why or why not?*

    Answer: The issue of what responsibilities beneficiaries have to the corporation is sticky. It's now a matter of "what do I owe you?" instead of "what do you owe me?" Using the employee as an example, it might be argued that the business is owed a fair day's work for a fair day's pay. But defining "fair" is difficult. This question may help lead students to understand that "responsibility" is everyone's business and is at least a two way street. Students should examine the roles and responsibilities of each of the specific categories of beneficiaries.

END OF CHAPTER CASES

CASE 4-1: BUILDING ETHICS AT GENERAL DYNAMICS

CASE SUMMARY: This case chronicles efforts by General Dynamics to build a strong sense of ethical conduct at the company after the company was caught overbilling the federal government. General Dynamics' ethics program includes a written code of conduct, ethics awareness seminars conducted for all employees, ethics program directors who counsel employees on how to handle ethics dilemmas, a full-time corporate ethics director, and 30 ethics hotlines where employees can call for information and advice in handling ethics dilemmas on the job.

ANSWERS TO QUESTIONS FOR ANALYSIS

1. **Question:** *Do you feel General Dynamics took a reactive or proactive approach to developing an ethics program? Does the choice of approach influence a program's outcomes? Why or why not?*

   Answer: Given that the company was faced with either implementing an ethics program or losing the Navy's business, the approach to developing the program was decidedly reactive.

   Students may disagree on the importance of the approach to the outcome. While proactive programs may experience less direct pressure for quick results than reactive programs, the nature of the outcome is probably more dependent on commitment than on any other executive-level factor.

2. **Question:** *Evaluate the effect that implementation of the ethics program had on the various internal beneficiary groups. Were employee expectations regarding improvements in the quality of work life realistic? Discuss*

   Answer: The degree to which employee expectations were realistic is difficult to assess without further information about how employees viewed their own roles before an dafter implementation. However, this question can spur discussion of the degree to which a change in one component of corporate culture may or may not have far-ranging impacts on other aspects of the organization.

3. **Question:** *Based on your reading of this case, what recommendations would you provide to companies that do not currently have ethics programs in place? What further actions would you recommend that General Dynamics take?*

   Answer: In answering this question, students should discuss as specifically as possible what they believe succeeded and what they believe did not succeed with the program. Certainly, many features of the program provide a strong model for other companies to follow. General Dynamics would probably be well advised to examine the portions of the program applicable to the less-satisfied internal beneficiaries (employees, shareholders) and revise those portions as needed on an ongoing basis.

CASE 4-2: THE TRAINING DEBATE

CASE SUMMARY: This case presents a timely and controversial issue that is emerging in many companies: Does management have the right to put employees through training that is physically or psychologically uncomfortable and that in some cases seeks to alter their fundamental beliefs? The case provides several examples of such controversial training (e.g., programs at the Pecos Learning Center, training by the Church of Scientology, and a quite controversial and now defunct program at Pacific Bell). The case provides an excellent opportunity to debate the question of the limits of managerial influence over employees, in terms of managerial prerogatives and individual rights.

1.   **Question:**   *As a manager who supports unconventional training, what would be your arguments concerning the ethics of providing such training for your employees?*

      Answer: An advocate may argue that such training does not impinge on employee rights and individuality and is not harmful. Rather it is geared toward developing a more effective and profitable organization that produces returns for both the company and employees.

2.   **Question:**   *As a manager who opposes unconventional training, provide a response to the arguments you've developed for question 1.*

      Answer: Opponents would strongly disagree with the position that such training is not exploitative or intrusive. They may argue that an individual's commitment to the organization is to perform the job well. That obligation should not extend to training that they consider troublesome, intrusive, and that offensive to their individuality.

3.   **Question:**   *Which position would you personally take? Explain.*

      Answer: This question seeks students' personal opinion on the subject.

ADDITIONAL CHAPTER QUESTIONS AND ANSWERS

1.   **Question:**   *Can a business be too socially responsible? Explain.*

      Answer: No, so say some activists in areas of social responsibility. But a business can be too socially responsible if the business sacrifices itself in its zeal for social responsibility. For instance, consider a company that strives to reduce its industrial plant's pollution emissions to a minuscule level. The financial expense of meeting this goal could threaten the company's existence. Every business needs to balance its sense of social responsibility to the public with its sense of financial responsibility to itself.

2.   **Question:**   *Discuss a business' costs and benefits of being socially responsible.*

      Answer: A socially responsible business can incur financial costs (for instance, the extra expense of reducing the pollution levels of a manufacturing plant), the cost of time spent by management on social responsibility issues, and the more intangible costs of disgruntled stockholders who oppose the company's efforts (as stockholders indirectly pay for those efforts). The business receives the benefits of a strengthened image as a socially responsible and concerned company in the minds of the public and the satisfaction of contributing to solving social problems, and an avoidance of long range costs from damage lawsuits or from the added expense and tax burden of dealing with the impacts of those social problems. In some instances, businesses are able to market their social contributions effectively to build a stronger consumer base among customers for whom social responsibility issues are important.

3. **Question:** *In your own words, define social responsibility and managerial ethics.*

    Answer: The purpose of this question is to test students' understanding of these two difficult-to-define terms and to emphasize the ambiguous nature of these two concepts.

4. **Question:** *Briefly identify the internal and external beneficiaries of a company's socially responsible activities.*

    Answer: The internal beneficiaries are its customers, employees, and stockholders. The external beneficiaries are specific (such as interest groups seeking to redress historical grievances) and general (society as a whole, which benefits from corporate efforts to solve or prevent general social problems).

5. **Question:** *In your opinion, can the top management of a business instill ethics in the firm's middle and lower-level managers? If so, how? What are the limits of such an approach?*

    Answer: Student opinion may differ; however, it can be easily argued that top management can instill ethics (at least concerning business decision making). Such can be done via developing an organizational culture that values and reinforces ethical behavior. Top management, particularly the CEO, can also instill ethical behavior by setting a personal example, and by promulgating those standards via communication within the company and to the public. Top managers can, when appropriate, visibly reward ethical behavior which reinforces the behavior among managers. The primary limit to this approach is that managers' ethical behavior is not totally open to influence by top management. An individual's own ethical standards are an important and often independent influence on decision making.

6. **Question:** *Can you think of any instances where your attitudes and views toward ethical behavior and/or social responsibility could affect your decision whether or not to accept a certain job? Explain.*

    Answer: Student's should be urged to examine their own values in considering employment opportunities. For example, if you believe that tobacco products are harmful, how would you feel about accepting a job with Philip Morris? Students should discuss the idea that people are happier at work if their employer has personal philosophies similar to their own. A company's code of conduct may be a good foundation to compare philosophies.

7.   **Question:**   *Briefly identify the three bases for developing ethical guidelines for decision making.*

   Answer: The three bases are egoism (where the manager makes decisions that maximize his or her personal benefit), altruism (where decisions are based on realizing "the greatest good for the greatest number"), and obligation to a formal principle (where decisions are based on principle, not consequences).

8.   **Question:**   *Provide an overview of the evolution of contemporary expectations for corporate social responsibility.*

   Answer: Contemporary expectations evolved from three business crises. The crises of 1870 and 1930 both resulted in increased government regulation of business activities. From the Crisis of 1970, new ideas spawned by the 1960s unrest challenged the business-government relationship and made new demands on business' social responsibility.

9.   **Question:**   *Why is it so difficult for an industry to establish an effective code of ethics?*

   Answer: Ethics involves a personal interpretation of society's standards. Of course, personal interpretations will differ in the top management of the numerous large companies that comprise an industry. Establishing an effective code requires obtaining agreement from industry leaders, at least; this task is very difficult to accomplish.

10.   **Question:**   *Many management experts believe that ethics can be a particularly frustrating problem for young managers in their first jobs. Why?*

   Answer: An organization's ethical standards are rarely clearly communicated to young managers, often because they've never been explicitly established but instead reside rather ambiguously in the organization's culture. However, young managers new to business and inexperienced in decision making involving ethical questions particularly need guidance in how to deal with and resolve ethical dilemmas. They need to understand the business' definition of ethical business behavior. But such guidance is rarely provided.

5

MANAGEMENT DECISION MAKING

LEARNING OBJECTIVES

After completing Chapter 5, students should be able to:

Define   programmed and nonprogrammed decisions.

Describe how the types of decisions managers make are related to their levels in organizations.

Discuss the process of decision making.

Compare individual and group decision making.

Identify the major sources for locating problems that require management decisions.

CHAPTER SYNOPSIS

The chapter addresses managerial decision making by first distinguishing between the two general types of **decisions: programmed decisions** which involve routine problems and **nonprogrammed decisions** which are made in response to unique and unstructured problems. Examples are provided to clarify the two decision types, and their relationships to top, middle, and lower management levels is discussed.

The six-step process of decision making, which is most applicable to nonprogrammed decisions, is presented, and the three primary sources of problem identification (deviation from past performance and plans and outside criticism) are discussed. Three sources of difficulty in problem identification are also discussed - 1) an unrealistic perception of the problem situation; 2) defining problems in terms of solutions; and 3) identifying symptoms as problems. The problem types (**opportunity, crisis, and routine**) are discussed.

The chapter discusses the conditions of certainty, risk (and the use of objective and subjective probabilities under risk), and uncertainty as aspects of the evaluation of alternatives. Four types of decision makers are discussed which apply in conditions of uncertainty (**optimistic, pessimistic, regret minimizing, and insufficient reason decision makers**). The chapter also focuses on the reality of organizational decision making, including the probable lack of optimal decision-making conditions because while serving one objective, another objective is often short changed. Decision implementation stresses the need to consider others who are affected by the decision. The control and evaluation phase of decision making concerns the need to periodically measure the decision's results and to make changes when actual results fall short of planned results.

The chapter's final two sections focus on individual decision making. Included in this section is the impact on decision making of a decision maker's **values, personality, propensity for risk, and potential for dissonance** are discussed) and on individual versus group decision making. In this final segment, the pros and cons relative to group and individual decision making are presented, and three techniques for stimulating creativity are described: **Group brainstorming, the Delphi technique,** and **the nominal group technique.**

The **Management In Action** section lists a stream of decisions that Apple Computer recently made to return the company to its place of prominence as the industry innovator. These decisions included the introduction of new products and collaborative efforts with other organizations. The chapter's **Management Focus** sections look at how new styles of managerial decision making at AT&T are making a necessary difference; Honda's response to their recent ineffective decisions; and how women who are effective decision makers are moving up the corporate ladders.

TEACHING TIPS

LECTURE & DISCUSSION IDEAS

1. Ask students to identify a programmed decision they have already made that day. Ask for volunteers from the class to briefly explain a recent nonprogrammed decision they have made. Solicit from the students a definition of intuition. Encourage discussion among students about the role of intuition in both programmed and nonprogrammed decision making. If students indicate the importance of intuition in decision making, ask for methods to increase intuition in individuals. Assist the group in identifying the reasons intuition is not always seen as a legitimate decision-making tool. Determine is they agree with this thinking.

2. Peter Drucker, management specialist and author, speaks passionately about the need for managers to encourage errors among their staff, including when they are making decisions. He believes an organization that discourages error making is an organization that stifles growth, creativity and ownership. Engage your students in a discussion about the role of error making in organizations. If they believe error serve an important purpose, ask them to describe methods managers can use to encourage error making in their organizations.

3. There is tremendous information now available on the differentiated activities handled by the right and the left portions of the human brain. Some of your students may be aware of this research from some of their other classes. Some researchers believe that "right-brain dominant" individuals may be more creative; whereas, "left-brain dominant" individuals may be more logical and systematic. Ask your students to discuss how this may affect various individuals' approaches to decision making and if one approach is more useful than the others. Invite students to consider ways to increase the effectiveness of their none dominant approaches to decision making.

PROJECT / EXERCISE IDEAS

1. As a group assignment, have your students interview a CEO from a local business and prepare a written report on the executive's approach to decision making, specifically his or her self-described decision style, approach to decisions substantially affecting

the business (especially those involving high risk), and attitude toward risk and uncertainty. The report should also include the executive's comments on how his or her decision style has evolved over the years of acquired business experience.

2. As a self-assessment exercise, have your students identify three recent and important nonprogrammed decisions he or she has made. In a written report, the student should recount how each decision was made and apply what's been learned from the chapter material and evaluate the quality of each decision. Specifically, students should address ways in which the decision process used could be improved to produce a better decision. If a particular decision was successful, students should consider the factors that accounted for the decision's success.

3. If you'd like to explore the topic of creativity beyond the use of the creativity exercise, have your students as an individual or group assignment, prepare written reports on factors that have been studied in terms of influence on creativity—education, family upbringing, gender, age, and creative training. Just recently, creativity researchers are asserting that creativity skills can be learned, which is a far cry from the traditional belief that creativity is an innate, not acquired, talent. Concerning this issue, students could prepare a report on creativity training techniques currently used to train managers and employees to be creative. Much has been written on the subject in recent years.

LECTURE OUTLINE NOTES

I. **Types of Managerial Decisions**
    A. There are two general types:
        1. **Programmed decisions** - have a repetitive and routine solution, for example, the procedures used to clear the registers at the end of shifts.
            a. Are usually handled using rules, standard operating procedures, and specific policies.
        2. **Nonprogrammed decisions** - decisions for novel and unstructured problems, for example, decisions concerning the actions that should be taken by teachers and administrators when a school burns.
            a. Require more time and effort and involve more uncertainty than programmed decisions.
            b. Have traditionally been handled by general problem-solving processes, judgment, intuition, and creativity.
        3. Modern management techniques for nonprogrammed decisions are much less developed than for programmed decisions.
    B. Top management focuses on nonprogrammed decisions; middle management handles mostly programmed decisions, although, nonprogrammed decisions occasionally arise; and lower-level management handles programmed decisions almost exclusively (see Figure 5-1 which depicts these relationships).

82

II. The Process of Decision Making

A.   Decision making is the process of thought and deliberation that results in a decision and is the means to obtaining a response to a problem.

B.   The decision making process is sequential (Figure 5-2 presents the process which applies more to nonprogrammed than programmed decisions).

1.   **Identify and define the problem.**

   a.   Three conditions are problem indicators:

   i.   Deviation from past performance - a sudden change in an established pattern of performance, such as unexpected declines in annual state tourism rates

   ii.   Deviation from the plan - when results don't meet planned objectives, such as, the inability of a previously successful non-profit organization to raise expected levels of funding, indicates that some plan may be off course.

   iii.   Outside criticism - outsiders identify problems, such as consumers boycotting a product due to a company's environmental negligence.

   b.   Sources of difficulties in problem identification occur when managers have an unrealistic perception of the problem situation, define problems in terms of solutions, or identify symptoms as problems.

   c.   Types of problems are usually those of opportunity, crisis, or routine. Often managerial time devoted to the latter two types detracts from the time needed to maximize long-term opportunities.

2.   **Develop alternatives**, which are potential solutions to the problem. Each alternative's potential consequences should be considered.

3.   **Evaluate alternatives** by measuring and comparing each alternative relative to the decision maker's goals and objectives. The evaluation of alternatives must include the determination of:

   a.   **Conditions of certainty** - exist when each alternative's outcome is known.

   b.   **Conditions of risk** - occur when there is enough information to allow the use of probability in evaluating the alternatives.

   i.   **Objective probability** - reflects historical evidence (e.g., probability of obtaining either heads or tails on a coin toss is .50).

   ii.   **Subjective probability** - there is no historical evidence, but enough information is available to estimate a probability.

   iii.   With probabilities, the expected value of the decision is expected to be maximized..

   c.   **Conditions of uncertainty** - occurs when no information exists relevant to the possible alternatives. In this case, the decision maker's personality can affect alternative choice. The four decision maker types:

   i.   **Optimistic decision maker** - always acts as though

everything will come out to his/her benefit. Picks the choice that maximizes the maximum outcomes.

    ii. **Pessimistic decision maker** - acts as though the worst possible outcome will always occur. Estimates the worst outcomes associated with each alternative and selects the best of these worst outcomes .

    iii. **Regret minimizing decision maker** - wants to minimize the amount of dissonance experienced after the decision is made. Make decisions that have outcomes not too far removed from the best outcome possible under the circumstances.

    iv. **Insufficient reason decision maker** - assumes that all possible alternatives have an equal chance of occurring. Assigns equal probabilities to each alternative's outcome and then selects the alternative based on the maximum expected value.

4. **Choose an alternative**
   a. Done to solve a problem and achieve a predetermined objective.
   b. The decision is not an end in itself. Is only a means to an end.
   c. Rarely does one alternative achieve the desired objective without impacting another objective(s) positively or negatively. Sometimes, an organizational objective is achieved at the expense of a societal objective.
   d. Thus, optimal decisions are often impossible. So, rather than optimize, the decision maker is a satisfier, picking the alternative that meets a satisfactory standard.

5. **Implementing the decision**
   a. Involves putting the decision into action.
   b. Because implementation involves people, the test of a good decision is the behavior of people affected by the decision.
   c. A manager must transform decisions into behavior in the organization.

6. **Control and evaluation**
   a. Involves periodic measurement of results.
   b. Actual results are compared with planned results (the objective) and if deviations exist, changes are made.

III. Individual Decision Making

A. Four individual behavioral factors can have a significant impact on some or all of the decision making process:

1. **Values** - the guidelines you use when confronted with a situation in which a choice must be made.
   a. Acquired early in life; an essential part of your thoughts.

2. **Personality—traits**, such as attitudes and intelligence combine with situational and interactional variables to influence the decision-making process.

3. **Propensity for risk** - one's tendency to take risks in decision making. If you have a low aversion to risk, you will establish objectives, evaluate alternatives, and select alternatives differently than you **would if you were highly** risk aversive.

4. **Potential for dissonance** - a decision maker's potential for experiencing cognitive dissonance—anxiety felt when attitudes and beliefs are believed to be inconsistent after a decision is made. Causes doubts and second thoughts about the decision.

    a. Dissonance can be reduced by admitting a mistake has been made. However, most decision makers instead:

        i. Seek information that supports their decisions.

        ii. Selectively perceive and distort information in such a way to support their decision.

        iii. Adopt a less favorable view of the foregone alternatives. 4) Minimize the importance of the decision's negative aspects and exaggerate its positive aspects.

        iv. Dissonance potential is affected by personality, self-confidence, and the ability to be persuaded.

IV. Group decision making

A. Group decision making is prevalent in organizations, especially in nonprogrammed problems.

B. Individual versus group decision making

    1. More expertise and perspectives are provided in a group.

    2. With five or more members, groups usually are superior to individual decision making, majority vote and leader decisions.

    3. Groups are more effective than individuals with nonprogrammed decisions because these decisions benefit from pooled talent.

    4. Concerning each step of the decision process:

        a. Groups are probably better in setting objectives because of a greater knowledge pool.

        b. Individual efforts are required in identifying alternatives to obtain a broad search.

        c. Groups are better in evaluating alternatives (group's collective judgement).

        d. Groups usually accept more risk than individuals in selecting an alternative.

        e. Implementation rests with the individual manager.

C. However, groups pose disadvantages:

    1. More time is required to make a group decision.

    2. Often group discussion can be inhibited by:

        a. Pressure to conform.

        b. Influence of a dominant personality.

        c. Status incongruity—lower-status members are inhibited by higher-status members.

        d. Influence of those perceived to be expert in the problem area.

D. Three techniques are useful in stimulating a group's creativity:

    1. **Brainstorming** - implemented via a set of rules:

a.   State any ideas regardless of how extreme or outlandish.
b.   Approach each idea as belonging to the group and build upon the ideas of others.
c.   Generate, don't evaluate, ideas.

2.   **Delphi technique** - involves soliciting and comparing anonymous judgements on a problem/topic via a set of sequential questionnaires.
a.   Involves no face-to-face interaction between the judges (removing biasing effects).
b.   A questionnaire is sent to participants via mail, completed surveys are returned and responses summarized by analysts.
c.   Written summary is mailed to participants along with a second questionnaire for reassessment.
d.   Participants independently evaluate their earlier responses.
e.   Analysts typically go with tabulated results as the decision after the second or third round.

3.   **Nominal group technique**
a.   A group (7-10 members) sit around a table, but don't communicate.
b.   Each member writes ideas on a pad of paper.
c.   After five minutes, each member presents an idea in round robin fashion until all ideas are presented (a recorder writes all ideas on a chart before the group). During this there is no discussion among group members.
d.   Structured discussion occurs; each idea receives attention.
e.   After discussion, each member privately votes by ranking alternatives. The group decision is the mathematically pooled vote outcome.

4.   Both the Delphi and NGT methods of decision making are more effective than brainstorming, and they also differ in terms of:
a.   Participants remain anonymous in the Delphi technique and become acquainted in the NGT.
b.   NGT has participant face-to-face interaction; Delphi does not.
c.   Communication - written only provided from monitors to participants in the Delphi but face-to-face and verbal with the NGT.

ANSWERS TO DISCUSSION AND REVIEW QUESTIONS

1.   **Question:** *What is a decision?*
     Answer: They are an organizational mechanism through which an attempt is made to achieve a desired state of affairs. They are an organizational response to problems.

2. **Question:** *We make decisions daily. Describe in detail two programmed decisions you make each day. Why do you consider them to be programmed ? Were they ever nonprogrammed ? If so, discuss why.*

   Answer: Students will produce a variety of examples. The important points are that the decisions are repetitive and routine at present. If at one time a decision was not programmable, the reasons it is now considered programmed should be discussed. For example, when a student first began using a word processing package to complete their research papers, both the research process and the use of the computer was nonprogrammable decisions. After the student mastered both of these, the decisions regarding how to do research and how to word process are now programmable.

3. **Question:** *Describe a nonprogrammed decision that you recently made. Describe the circumstances surrounding the decision and state why you believe it was nonprogrammed. Did this belief influence your decision-making approach ? In what ways?*

   Answer: Students might identify more major decisions, such as whether or live on or off campus, what major to select, or where to complete an internship. The idea is that the decision is not routine and is not made often. Students might describe a more thorough analysis and thought process when supporting their view that it was a nonprogrammed decision.

4. **Question:** *Describe the organizational factors that could possible lead to decision paralysis, the inability to make decisions in a timely fashion. How could an organization avoid such situations?*

   Answer: The organizational culture could constrict or encourage resistance to change; a continual desire to wait until all data is available, which seldom occurs; and inability to operationalize the six steps of decision making; a greater concern for selecting the best decision-making method, than for making the decision. To overcome such tendencies, members could make routine during staff meetings or other decision-making times, the use of alternative generating methods, such as brainstorming; establish evaluation criteria that includes provide feedback about and rewards for effective decision making; designate particular individuals within the organization to be "watchdogs" and advocates for effective and timely decision making.

5. **Question:** *Select and describe a business situation where the Delphi Technique or NGT could be utilized effectively as part of the decision-making process.*

   Answer: The Delphi Method of decision making would be very effective when all members involved in the decision cannot be together at the same time or in the same location. This would be especially useful in organizations that has managers at various geographic locations. The Delphi Method would also be useful in organizations where individuals work various shifts, yet need to make a joint decision. The NGT Method would be beneficial when numerous alternatives need to be generated and/or there is no one right or better answer or decision. NGT would also work well when a decision simply needs to be made, but there does not need to be a tremendous amount of group support or "buy in" for the final decision.

6.   **Question:**   *Describe a business situation in which there is a strong, positive relationship existing between the number of alternatives generated and the quality of the decision itself.*

     Answer: Students may have only limited exposure to actual situations in organizations; thus, they might be helped by having them think about situations in their families or with their friends when the generation of many possible alternatives had a positive affect on the effectiveness of the decision. In business the process of identifying alternatives becomes more critical the decision being made is new for the company, affects more or different people than before, or is hoped to have greater longevity.

7.   **Question:**   *Describe a group decision-making situation in which you were involved. Did any problems develop? Describe them in detail. Was the decision reached by the group different from the one you would have made as an individual? Do you think that the group decision was better? Why?*

     Answer: A worthwhile example is the purchase of a family car. One parent or guardian influences certain aspects while the other parent or guardian influences others. In most cases, the student's choice would have been different from the one made but they usually admit that while the decision was not a good one for them personally, it was better for the family (group) as a whole. This is an often-cited benefit of a group decision. Other examples may be the selection of a college, purchase of a home, or a decision made by a social or fraternal organization of which the student is a member. This question is designed to encourage students to apply group concepts and characteristics they learned in the chapter. In discussing student responses, it is useful to identify factors that influence individual conformity to a group decision, even though the individual may disagree with the decision and the reasons why group decision in the cited examples were superior or inferior to the individual's decision.

8.   **Question:**   *Why are the management function of planning and the process of decision making so closely related ?*

     Answer: The two are closely related because both are influenced by many forces that are dynamic and evolutionary. Also, both require management thought, reflection, and a sequential approach to achieve desired results.

9.   **Question:**   *Think of a corporate executive who, you believe, is a good decision maker. What traits make this executive effective?*

     Answer: If students have already studied leadership, they may benefit from having them recall the traits theories and the characteristics identified. Encourage students to explore the differences in their reactions to

10. **Question:** *Describe a situation you have encountered where a decision made by an individual could have been better made by a group. Why do you feel this way?*

   Answer: Students may be able to identify situations in their own experiences with clubs of other student activity organizations when one individual made a decision which affected their entire group, but did not get the other group member's thoughts and suggests for alternative. Students may be able to easily recall the annoyance or resentment others felt.

END OF CHAPTER CASES

CASE 5-1: ONE MANAGER'S TOUGH DECISION

CASE SUMMARY: A district sales manager with Sigma Industries, Kimberly Brouchous, is faced with the difficult decision of needing to determine how to reduce her personnel expenses by a minimum of 10 percent. She currently has 10 sales staff members, all of whom have been with Sigma for over four years. She can either reduce staff, reduce their salaries by increasing the amount of sales needed to receive their commission, or a combination of both. Any of these three choices results in creating new difficulties.

She knows that one of her staff members, who had been with Sigma for 19 years, is planning to retire in approximately six months; however, if he leaves prior to that date he will lose benefits and receive a reduction in retirement payments. Kimberly also has been provided confidential information from a college friend who also works for Sigma, that her newest staff person has just requested a two-month medical leave and is receiving reimbursements of antidepressants. Kimberly has two weeks to make her decision.

ANSWERS TO QUESTIONS FOR ANALYSIS:

1. **Question:** *Is the decision that Kimberly has to make, a programmed or nonprogrammed one? Explain why.*

   Answer: This is a nonprogrammed decision because it is not routine. Kimberly cannot utilize a pre-established set of procedures or policies to determine her decision.

2. **Question:** *How do Kimberly's personal values and sense of ethical responsibility impact her decision?*

   Answer: Kimberly's personal values and ethics could have an impact in her decision in the following ways: she continued to listen to information from Tom, her friend from college, even though she was aware that the information was supposed to be confidential; she will be influenced by her values regarding the importance of relationships in the workplace; her own values regarding mental health and illness will influence her responses toward Brian, the employee requesting medical leave; whether she decides to attempt renegotiation with her superiors to locate the necessary reductions in other areas of the budget, and her manner in approaching that individual, if she choices is also affected by her values and sense of ethical responsibility.

3. **Question:** *Should Kimberly involve her salespeople in the decision making process? Why or why not?*

   Answer: Your students answer to these two questions may vary. Encourage them to consider the different approaches regarding generation of alternations and commitment to the final decision. Be certain to probe their thinking about what they would prefer if they were one of the employees and what they would prefer to do if they were Kimberly. Ask them to explore the differences in their responses, if they exit.

CASE 5-2: GROUP DECISION MAKING AT LONGLEY UNIVERSITY ————

CASE SUMMARY: Tom Madden, a professor in the College of Business Administration, finds himself rushing from one meeting to another, often wondering when he will have time to do the work created in all of these meetings. On this particular meeting he arrives 10 late to his faculty meeting, having just left another meeting across campus.

Upon his arrival he finds that the members are being asked to consider a proposal to establish a Latin American MBA program. Tom has not read the report, having only received it three days earlier. He and his colleagues seated next to him at the meeting, exchange a few brief comments about the proposal. The dean asks the proposal author to briefly explain the idea presented, and then the dean asks if there are any questions or comments.

Tom attempts to raise one question and is immediately confronted by the dean for questioning the efforts of the proposal writer, as well as the dean himself. Tom is then reprimanded for having been late to the meeting. At this point Tom decides not to continue with his question and the remainder of the room grows silent.

The dean thanks everyone for their total support of the proposal and leaves them with a word of praise for their ability to be for involved in their participative decision-making efforts.

ANSWERS TO QUESTIONS FOR ANALYSIS: ————

1. **Question:** *Analyze this case, and outline the factors that influenced the faculty decision in this case - either positively or negatively?*

   Answer: The factors influencing the faculty's decision are: the short period of time in which they were to have reviewed the proposal; the dean's support manner, which does not encourage dissent; the dean's manner in running the meeting--reprimanding Tom for attempting to raise a question; the apparent lack of information available concerning the feasibility of such an endeavor; the dean serving as the facilitator of the meeting and clearly having a vested interest in the outcome of the decision; the dean's inability or unwillingness to step back from the proposal; the faculty members' collective action of silence and the inability or unwillingness to challenge the dean on his decision making style.

2. **Question:** *Does this case indicates that shared decision making cannot be worthwhile and effective? How could it be made more effective in the College of Business Administration?*

   Answer: Your students may be tempted, or perhaps should even be encouraged, at this point to share their own examples of poorly run meetings and ineffective decision making. This additional generation of information can then be used to assist the students in exploring what factors or conditions would have needed to be present to turn the situations they were describing into more effective decision-making opportunities. To be effective, decision making must include some focus on each of the six steps explained in the text.

3. **Question:** *Do your believe that decision making of this type may be more worthwhile and effective in some types of organizations than in others. Discuss.*

   Answer: There are certain conditions and circumstances that inhibit or appropriately discourage the use of group decision making. In emergency situations or environments requiring immediate action, taking time to involve others or generate numerous alternatives could cost dearly, even in terms of human lives. Medical professionals, military personnel and police frequently find themselves in circumstances where immediate action is required. These individuals are typically well prepared for such conditions and have trained themselves to respond to situations, in which many of us would find ourselves needing to use nonprogrammable decision making methods, with protocol and well integrated conditioning.

   Organizations that have developed high levels of trust and cross-understanding of various organizational functions would preform well in group decision-making activities. All organizations could move more of their activities toward this and benefit greatly in terms of increased morale and commitment to the chosen alternative.

ADDITIONAL QUESTIONS AND ANSWERS

1.   **Question:**   *Briefly summarize the six steps which comprise the decision making process.*

        Answer: In the decision making process, the individual: 1) identifies and defines the problem; 2) develops alternative solutions to the problem; 3) evaluates alternative solutions (measuring and comparing the potential payoffs and possible consequences of each alternative); 4) selects an alternative; 5) implements the decision; and 6) evaluates and controls the solution by monitoring the decision's effects and making necessary adjustments.

2.   **Question:**   *Differentiate between conditions of risk and uncertainty.*

        Answer: Under a condition of risk, the decision maker can estimate the likelihood that the various states of nature (events beyond the decision maker's control) will occur. Under a condition of uncertainty, the likelihood of occurrence for each state of nature is not possible because of historical data concerning the probabilities for occurrence exists.

3.   **Question:**   *Would you rather make an individual decision or be involved in a group decision ?*

        Answer: This question is intended for students to explore their own preferences for individual or group decision-making processes. A follow-up question to students' responses: Why do you prefer individual or group decision making? What factors account for your preference?

4.   **Question:**   *Most experts in decision making processes believe that each individual possesses a decision style which is his or her own particular way of processing information and making decisions which is the result of learning and past experiences. Describe your own decision style. What are its strengths and weaknesses?*

        Answer: This self-assessment question is intended for students to identify and evaluate how they go about making decisions. They should identify their particular decision making process and any particular cognitive shortcuts they use.

5.   **Question:**   *Does the decision-making process involve the use of any principles of managing? Explain.*

        Answer: Many principles and functions of management are related to reaching decisions. Such principles are unity of command, authority, and span of control are needed especially when reaching emergency or quick decisions. An individual with authority must often specify a decision action and his or her subordinates (span) must react accordingly to achieve the goals of the quick decision. Without adherence to some principles of management, the process would flounder and not be made with confidence and understanding

6. **Question:** *What role does creativity play in the decision-making process?*
    Answer: This is a thought question designed for students to consider the concept of creativity and its impact on decision making. Have students in their own work define the concept and discuss its impact on each of the six steps in the decision process model.

7. **Question:** *What primary factor is not presented in the decision-making model?*
    Answer: Perhaps the primary factor is the accuracy of the information used in the decision-making model. Often in managerial decision making, the accuracy of information isn't given due attention.

8. **Question:** *Think of an informal group to which you belong. Does a status hierarchy exist in the group? On what is it based ?*
    Answer: Most students will respond that a status hierarchy does exist within their informal group as this group characteristic is often necessary for group performance. A status hierarchy can be based on one factor or several such as seniority of membership, ability relevant to the group, age, gender, and personality characteristics such as charisma.

9. **Question:** *Identify some businesses that operate under conditions of certainty. Describe the elements that are certain.*
    Answer: Generally businesses in stagnant industries will operate under conditions of certainty. Even then, changes are inevitable and conditions will become unstable and uncertain.

10. **Question:** *Differentiate between the three techniques for stimulating creativity in group decision making.*
    Answer: Brainstorming includes a strict set of rules to enhance idea generation without evaluation or ranking and inhibition. The Delphi Technique employs anonymous responses by way of written questionnaires without face to face encounter and feedback provided by monitoring staff. NGT participants are acquainted, meet collectively, and communicate directly.

6   *THE PLANNING FUNCTION*

LEARNING OBJECTIVES

After completing Chapter 6, students should be able to:

Define   the planning function in terms of managerial responsibilities and decisions.

Describe   the planning functions four principal elements.

Discuss   why the planning function must begin with the determination of objectives

Compare   arguments for and against the alternative means for implementing a plan.

Identify   the most useful forecasting technique for a particular set of circumstances.

CHAPTER SYNOPSIS

This chapter introduces a two-chapter description of the planning function by addressing six topics: 1) the planning function concept; 2) the importance of planning, and 3) objectives; 4) actions; 5) resources; and 6) implementation, with these final four being the elements of the formal organizational plan also called the outcome of the planning process. These four elements are discussed and related in what management does in the planning function.

The planning function is defined as all managerial activities that set objectives and the means for achieving them. The importance of planning is discussed in terms of the our key benefits which planning provides: 1) coordination of an organization's activities or efforts; 2) preparation for change; 3) development of performance standards; and 4) development of managers.

Concerning objectives, the chapter focuses on objective setting and ordering or prioritizing. The concept of strategic planning and functional or operational planning are introduced and the time differences between short, intermediate and long-term objectives are explained. The issue of conflict in determining objectives is discussed as is the task of measuring objectives. Measures for four types of organizational objectives are detailed. These four types of measurements ore profitability, marketing, productivity, and physical and financial objectives.

The chapter segment on courses of action centers on forecasting and four common forecasting techniques: **hunches, market surveys, time-series analysis, and econometric models**. The concepts of **variable budgets** and **moving budgets** are discussed in the chapter's discussion of budgeting resources.

The manager has three primary implementation tools, which are: **authority, persuasion,** and **policy**. The criteria for each of these implementation tool's effectiveness is also included.

The chapter concludes with a brief discussion of the key issues associated with the planning process. The chapter's **Management in Action** describes in detail the planning and the four objectives undertaken by Procter & Gamble to win customers in a highly competitive market. The **first Management Focus**, "The Risk/Reward Ratio" describes the success of the Lillian Vernon company from one woman advertizing to personalize purses and belts to the current company which boasts $160 million in annual sales. Emphasis is given to the need for entrepreneurs to be both risk takers and effective planners. The **second Management Focus**, "A Vision Leads to a Plan," highlights the success of one man's vision to develop in American's a relationship with gourmet coffee, much like that of the Italian's. Starbuck's was born. His continuously updated business plan documents his plans, objectives and strategies. "Planning for Quality at Ford," the **final Management Focus** discusses two planning efforts by Ford, the production of the world car, the Mondero, and the construction of the paint-finishing plant in Oakville, Canada. Both of these projects required complex planning to a degree not before undertaken by an automobile manufacturer.

TEACHING TIPS

LECTURE & DISCUSSION IDEAS

1. The descriptive nature of the chapter provides an opportunity to introduce several planning-related issues into your lecture which aren't discussed in the text, such as:
   a. The nature or organizational politics and their impact on objective setting and planning.
   b. The dynamics of conflict in organizational planning.
   c. The costs that planning and policy can incur for organizations.
   d. The increasing participation of lower-level managers and subordinates in organizational planning activities.
   e. How cultural differences in employees affect planning.

2. The forecasting and budgeting discussion can be augmented in class by introducing more recent developments in forecasting and budgeting.

3. A key issue relating to the planning function is managers' attitudes toward planning. Some research has shown that many managers dislike planning because of the time needed, the deliberate and reflective thinking necessary, and the dealing with ambiguity and conflict. Many managers also dislike planning because organizations don't always reward effective planning and because the results of planning typically aren't obvious for some time. Your could address this issue by asking students in your class who have worked as managers to describe their attitudes toward planning and their reasons for their thinking. For students who have not yet served as managers, they could reflect upon their own lack of planning in their academic and personal lives. What keeps them from being more effective planners? What systems or conditions would need to be present to increase their effective planning? Would these systems or conditions assist managers in organizational planning?

4.	The differences between variable and moving budgets could be further explained. An example of each budgeting approached could be detailed. The advantages and disadvantages of each method could be highlighted.

PROJECT / EXERCISE IDEAS

1.	For a closer examination of sales forecasting techniques and how business use them, the class can be divided into groups, each of which would be assigned a particular forecasting technique to research. Each group could present to the entire class their findings, explaining in detail how their particular forecasting method is used, and providing examples of uses by business, and assessing the techniques' advantages and shortcomings.

2.	According to recent reports, long-range planning is an increasingly popular activity in state governments. To what extend do city and county governments plan? Students can investigate this question by conducting research on municipal and county planning or by interviewing a county or city planner. A key question this activity can address: Do governmental planning processes differ from planning by businesses, and if so, in what ways?

3.	Invite a corporate manager from a local business to speak to your class on the company's planning process. The planner could provide insights into how corporate planning processes work in business, and specifically discuss the step-by=step planning procedures, how objectives are set, the bases used for prioritizing, and the degree of participation by lower-level managers in developing and implementing plans.

4.	A local business person who is responsible for forecasting the firm's sales could be invited to speak. The forecaster could provide insights into how techniques are used, the rationale for use of specific variables in forecasting sales, the problem of uncertainty which forecasting present, and how their particular company deals with these problems. This speaker could be an effective supplement to the students' research on sales forecasting techniques.

5.	Students could design a training program to be used in an organization to involve lower-level managers in the planning process. What material/information would need to be included? How would they excite managers to become involved when some may see this as simply more work to be done? What examples would students include to assist these operational and tactical managers in learning how to effectively plan?

6.	Students could develop a personal plan for their lives. Emphasis could be placed on the obtainment of their college education. Budgets could be included and students would need to defend their budgeting approach. Students could then present their plans to the entire class, who could serve as a board of directors to question individual on their plans and to coach each other to improve their effectiveness.

7.	A college or university administrative could be invited to class to discuss the planning function of her or his office. Many changes have taken place recently in the philosophies of many Career Planning and Placement Offices, which have resulted in the need to do more planning. This office may hold particular interest for students as they begin to focus more on their own career planning and development.

LECTURE OUTLINE NOTES

I. **The Focus of Planning**

    A.   Includes managerial activities which set objectives and appropriate means for achieving objective.

    B.   Assumes a future focus, specifying what the organization is to accomplish in the future, and prepares the organization for the future.

    C.   Results in a written plan which specifies predetermined courses of action.

    D.   Considered by many managers to be the primary management function.

II. **The Elements of Planning**

    A.   **Objectives**-specify future conditions aimed for, such as, achieving an eight percent increase in market share by the second quarter of 1995.

    B.   **Actions**-specific, preferred means to achieve objectives, such as, increasing market share by increasing amount of sales to current customers. Setting objectives and actions requires forecasting the future.

    C.   **Resources**-constraints on courses of action, for example, the personnel costs for increasing sales to current customers cannot be increased by more than 10% of the costs for the previous year. Budgeting identifies the funding sources and resources limitations.

    D.   **Implementation**-assigning and directing personnel to carry out the plan.

    E.   The elements are highly interrelated (see Figure 6-1, The Planning Function, which illustrates the interrelationships.

III. **The Importance of Planning**

    A.   The planning process can range from very simple to highly complex activities and occurs at all organizational levels.

    B.   The importance of planning is due in part to the benefits derived, which are:

        1.   **Coordinating efforts**-by setting objectives for the total organization and orchestrating the movement of separate portions of the organization towards these objectives;

        2.   **Preparing the organization for change**-by requiring contingency plans and thinking.

        3.   **Developing performance standards**-by identifying objectives and actions which can serve as standards for individual performance, for example, a manager's performance evaluation can be based on whether his or her unit met the production objective or by whether she or he performed as specified actions dictated.

        4.   **Developing managers**-by sharpening the participant's ability to deal with

abstract ideas and uncertainty, and to think systematically about the present and future.

IV. **Setting Objectives and Priorities** (see IIA. above)

    A.   This first step in the planning process involves:

        1.   **Prioritizing objectives**-given a set of objectives, ranking individual goals in order of importance.

        2.   **Establishing a time frame for objectives**-identifying which objectives are short-term, intermediate, and long-term.

           a.   **Short-term objectives**

             1)   can be accomplished in less than one year

             2)   at times, can be in opposition to other short-term, intermediate or long-term objectives. For example, commitment to a decrease in short-term operational costs could detract from a long-term commitment to improving quality or retaining customers.

             3)   along with intermediate goals must be met to achieve long-term goals or objectives.

           b.   **Intermediate objectives**-require one to five years to complete

           c.   **Long-term objectives**

             1)   extend beyond five years for completion

             2)   must be met to assure organizational survival.

           d.   **Strategic planning**

             1)   focuses on defining long-term objectives and the strategy to be used in that planning.

             2)   usually completed by upper level and top management.

           e.   **Functional or operation planning**-performed in an organization's individual units and focuses on intermediate and short-term objectives.

        3.   **Dealing with conflict among objectives**-the manager must contend with often conflicting expectations of the organization's interest groups, such as stockholders, employees, the public and government.

           a.   Studies suggest that the more successful firms place greatest emphasis on profit-seeking activities that maximize stockholders' wealth, in conjunction with other activities.

        4.   **Measuring Objectives**-determining how each goal should be measured and what should be measured in each area related to the goal.

           a.   Specific, measurable goals increase employee and organizational performance.

           b.   Among specific goals, difficult goals, if accepted by employees, result in better performance than easier goals.

           c.   An organization should establish objectives in at least eight areas:

             1)   market standing

             2)   innovation

             3)   productivity

             4)   physical and financial resources

    5) profitability
    6) management performance and responsibility
    7) worker performance and attitudes
    8) social responsibility

d. Several alternative measurements exist for four of these objectives (see table 6-1, Selected Measures of Objectives),

1) **Profitability objectives**-measures include:

a) **Profits to sales ratio**-figures taken from income and balance statements along. Recently emphasized as the most important profitability measure,

b) **Profits to total assets ratio**-figures taken from income <u>and</u> balance sheet; measures management's used of all resources regardless of origin.

c) **Profits to capital (net worth) ratio**-also taken from income <u>and</u> balance sheets; however, measures management's use of owner's contributions.

2) **Marketing objectives**-measure performance relating to products, market, distribution, and customer-service objectives.

a) Popular measures may include:
    i. **market share**
    ii. **sales volume**
    iii. **number of sales outlets**
    iv. **rate of new product development**
    v. **levels of customer satisfaction**

b) Focuses on prospects for long-run profitability. Viewed as a total quality indicator.

3) **Productivity objectives**-measured by ratios of output to input, for example ratios of **value added to sales and to profits. Value added** is the amount of value added to purchased materials due to the firm's collective efforts.

4) **Physical and financial objectives**-reflects the organization's capacity to acquire sufficient resources. Uses numerous accounting measures, for example, current, debt-to-equity ratios.

5) Objectives may also be measured by many other quantitative objectives, for example, innovation, social responsibility, employee attitudes, which are not as easily measured as the quantitative methods listed above.

B. See Table 6-2 for a detailed example of objective setting and measurement.

V. **Courses of Action**

A. Actions to implement plans are either **strategies**, which are actions with long-run organization-wide implications, or **tactics**, being actions with short-run, unit-side implications.

99

B. Actions and objectives are causally related, meaning the obtainment of the objectives is caused by the actions taken.

C. Action effects can be tested by **forecasting**, the process of using past and current information to predict future events. **Four major methods** of forecasting, which can be used, for instance, to predict sales volume are:

1. **Hunches**-forecasting future sales based on past sales, salespeople and customer comments, and instinct.

2. **Market survey**-estimating future sales by surveying customers using statistical sampling.

3. **Time-series analysis**-predicting future sales by studying past movement of sales over time which is affected by seasonal factors, cycles of business activity, and trends.

4. **Econometric models**-inputting past sales data and historical information on variable affecting sales, for example, price, competing products, etc. into a computer to derive a linear equation that expresses the historical relationships among the variables. This is the most sophisticated forecasting technique.

D. Forecasting is highly subjective; no technique entirely eliminates uncertainty.

VI. Budgeting Resources

A. Actions depend on the level of resources budgeted to meet plan objectives. **Budgeting** is the primary tool used for resource allocation (see Figure 6-2), The Budgeting Process).

1. The usefulness of financial budgets depends on the budget's flexibility to changing conditions.

2. There are two primary methods to provide this needed flexibility in the budgeting process:

   a. **Variable budgeting** computes financial scenarios if actual output, such as, product sales, deviates from planned output (see Table 6-3 for a sample budget. To be complete, changes in any one budgets when using variable budgeting, require adjustments in all supporting budgets.

   b. **Moving budgeting** involves preparing a budget for a fixed period, for example, one year, and updating the budget at fixed intervals, typically monthly. For instance, a budget prepared at the end of December for the next 12 months is updated monthly; a revised budget is developed at the end of January and projected for the next 12 months, February through next January.

      1) Moving budgets are advantageous because they demand systematic re-examination.

      2) However, they are a disadvantage to an organization because they are costly to maintain.

3. Budgeting has been **criticized** in that:

   a. Companies can tend to focus too much on the numbers, neglecting such critical variables as quality and service.

   b. Budgets encourage short-term moves, such as cutting prices too sharply to respond to an immediate decrease in sales, and discourage smart, long-term changes, such as increasing quality as a means of increasing sales.

    4.   To avoid these pitfalls, some companies follow these **guidelines** in developing budgets:

        a.   Plan first, budget later.

        b.   Budget for managers, not accountants.

        c.   Measure output, not input.

        d.   Design budgets to protect against turf wars.

VII.   Implementation of Plans

A.   Plan implement requires the use of resources and actions. See Figure 6-1 for an illustration of these interactions.

B.   Plans are usually implemented through people with the manager using **three tools of implementation:**

    1.   **Authority**-the manager's legitimate power gained through his or her position which provides the right to expect subordinates to carry out a responsible plan. Authority is often sufficient to obtain implementation of simple, status quo plans; complex plans often require more.

    2.   **Persuasion**-process of "selling" plans to subordinates who must implement them. Requires convincing individuals to accept plans on their own merits rather than on the manager's authority. Greater employee loyalty to an organization usually results in increased usefulness of persuasion.

    3.   **Policy**-developed to implement permanent plans. Usually written statements, reflecting objectives and actions for achieving objectives. Policies should be:

        a.   **Flexible** enough to accommodate change, yet **stable** enough to achieve a plan's sense or direction.

        b.   **Comprehensive** enough to cover any contingency.

        c.   A **coordinating** aspect for the various subunits whose actions are interrelated.

        d.   **Ethical.**

        e.   **Clearly written and logical.**

VIII.   Key Planning Issues

A.   **Benefits** to both large and small companies of formal planning include the ability to:

    1.   development more complete knowledge and understanding of environment.

    2.   choose from and implement a wider range of strategy options.

    3.   develop new products.

    4.   engage in cooperative agreements with other firms.

    5.   secure equity investments.

B.   Launching the planning process often means asking the right and fundamental questions (see Table 6-4 for a summary of **Key Planning Questions.**

1. **Question:** *Discuss the problems an organization would face if it failed to plan. Specifically, address the impact that failing to plan would have on employees, the organization's ability to compete effectively, and the organization's chances for long-run survival.*

Answer: Failure or inability to plan will have tremendous impact on the long-term survival and health of the organization. Some of the problems, which would be created are:

1) Managers and decision makers will be uncertain as to how best to use resources; 2) there will be frequent conflict regarding the actions being pursued; 3) there will be a lack of information about the organization's competitive environment; 4) fewer strategy options will be identified; 5) increased uncertainty about the best actions to be pursuing; 6) the organization may lag in developing new products or services; 7) the organization may encounter greater difficulty securing additional funding.

Specifically, employees may receive conflicting information regarding actions to be taken. Overall, the long-term survival of the organization is greatly reduce when planning does not occur.

2. **Question:** *A manager is overheard saying, "Plan? I never have time to plan. I live from day to day just trying to survive." Comment.*

Answer: This quotation draws attention to three critical points. First, managers engage in activities which are actually planning but may not be recognized as such. Secondly, this quote may really be an issue of descriptive versus prescriptive theory. If this individual is really not planning, than she or he is not really a manager as defined in this text. Lastly, this quote also highlights the fact that successful managers, those who are able to do more than merely survive, do effective and timely planning. The quoted manager has, in fact, articulated the distinction between effective and ineffective managerial work.

Students should be encouraged to reflect on their own lives and explore how much effective and timely planning they do. Are they taking the approach of this quoted manager or are they using effective planning technique and thus doing more than merely surviving?

3. **Question:** *Is it accurate to say that since it involves values judgements, planning is the implementation of the manager's value system? Why?*

Answer: This statement is true to the extent that a manager's values can substantially affect the prioritizing of objectives, assessment, selections

102

of actions and strategies, and implementation of the plan. However, many other factors also affect planning. When done effectively, planning is an integration of the thoughts and goals of many individuals in the organization. In fact, current literature illustrates that the more effective organizations strive to move planning to those individuals most effected by the plans and their outcomes. This allows for greater involvement and more accurate planning. This increase in employee responsibility results in increased levels of morale and a reduction in the possibility for a single individual to sway planning in a particular direction.

4. **Question:** *Describe the possible similarities and differences in the objectives set by nonprofit organizations and those set by for-profit organizations.*

   Answer: Both types of organizations must determine priority and time of objectives. Similar measurements may also be employed. Students may be tempted to think that a non-profit organization does not been to plan for or measure financial aspects of the organization. This question provides an excellent opportunity to discuss with students the necessity of non-profit organizations to measure and plan for their financial conditions. In addition, students should be encouraged to explore the role of funders in non-profit organizations and their similarity to customers in for-profit organizations.

   There are certainly differences in the kind of objectives established and the strategies designed for achieving those objectives between the two types of organizations. However, many studies are indicating that one of the major concerns in non-profits organizations today is their inability to effectively plan and to determine how to manage and measure their financial resources.

5. **Question:** *Describe a situation in which an organization you belonged to had to choose among several conflicting objectives. What was the basis for assigning a higher priority to one of the objectives over the others?*

   Answer: Students will have different examples from their own work histories. For students who have not worked outside of their homes, challenge them to think of conflicting objectives within their families. For example, the desire of everyone to take a family vacation needing to be balanced by the need to purchase a new car or pay tuition. Students may be able to reflect on conflict among their personal objectives. The need to work on weekends and the desire to study or go away with friends. These conflicts become especially real for students who may be receiving financial aid. They must maintain a certain grade point average and may also have to work so many hours a week on campus as part of their work-study position. Balancing both of these objectives may be very difficult.

6. **Question:** *How would the planning process differ between a small business and a large organization? Should the one place a stronger emphasis on planning than the others? Why or why not?*

    Answer: The process of planning is the same regardless of the size of the organization. Planning is planning. Students may suggest that the smaller organization may not need to be as detailed about planning since there are fewer employees and changes can be communicated more easily. However, smaller organizations may need to be involved in even more planning than larger organizations because they frequently have less financial cushion for errors than a larger organization may have at their disposal. This is not to suggest that larger organizations can be haphazard about their planning or their action strategies, just that other divisions within the organization may be able to "cover" for a temporary weakness in another area.

    The differences in planning between small and larger organizations is really in their level of involvement. In smaller organizations, all employees may be able to work simultaneously in the creation of the plans, whereas, the sheer numbers of employees within a larger organization may prohibit such hands-on, simultaneous planning. However, larger organizations are more likely to have resources available to do more extensive measurement of objectives and investigation of their competition and their customers.

7. **Question:** *Why is it important when forecasting events to utilize both qualitative (e.g., hunches, gut feeling, experiences) and quantitative (e.g., time series) methods? Are there occasions when one method is clearly superior to the other? Explain.*

    Answer: There is no one errorless, perfect method for forecasting. All reasonable means, which produce accurate information, should be employed. However, constraints of resources, such as time, money, personnel, or available knowledge, may force the selection of one alternative over another. When resources are constrained less sophisticated techniques should be used. However, managers need to guard against assuming the resources cannot or should not be allocated to engaging in quantitative forecasting methods. The greater the number of variables introduced, the more sophisticated the method required.

8. **Question:** *Several companies are experimenting with programs that shift most of the responsibility for planning to the lower levels of the organizations. Discuss possible advantages and disadvantages to be realized from such programs.*

    Answer: There are several advantages and disadvantages to moving planning to lower levels of the organization. The greater involvement employees have in creating the plans of the organization, the more committed they will feel toward accomplishing those plans. Involving the users of the plans in the planning process also provides the opportunities for these

104

same employees to assist in trouble-shooting and to improve systems, ensuring the accomplishment of the objectives.

Including lower-level employees in the planning process is initially a costly and timely endeavor. Employees must be trained in effective planning, for which time must be allocated. Also, until employees become familiar and comfortable with the planning, the process will be slower than if it were handled entirely by upper-level management. With experience, however, these disadvantages will be lessened, especially in light of the gains to be made for the organization.

9. **Question:** *Describe, through use of an example, how a lack of available resources could cause a change in an organization's ability to reach their planned objectives. In what stage of the planning process would this lack of resources most likely be noticed?*

    Answer: Lack of resources are most frequently noticed in the implementation stage of planning, however, this should not be the case if planning is done effectively. The availability of resources should be confirmed in the objective setting and strategy definition stages. If resources are determined to be unavailable actions should be taken to either secure the necessary resources or to redefine the objectives given the available resources.

    One resource which changes in organizations, often without the organization's ability to change the situation is the employees available to accomplish the work. Individuals may leave the organization who were critical to the completion of a particular objective, due either to their particular knowledge and skill levels or to their ability to motivate others with the appropriate knowledge and skills to complete the objective. Layoffs, right-sizing, and/or down-sizing has this same impact on the ability to accomplish certain objectives. This should be taken into consideration with adjustments to personnel are being considered. Either critical employees need to be retained or new staff members brought on.

    Another example of how unavailable resources can effect the organization's ability to reach their planned objectives would be the limiting of materials due to either natural disasters, increase in government safety or environmental regulations, or being out-purchased by a competitor.

10. **Question:** *Discuss how a bank manager could utilize authority and persuasion in motivating his or her staff to implement a plan to improve customer service.*

    Answer: The bank manager could utilize her or his authority by making increased customer service by all bank employees part of the evaluation system and thus connect employees' ability to improve in this area to future promotions and raises. In addition, the bank manager could use his or her persuasion to convince employees of the necessity for increasing customer service to ensure economic stability of the bank. Employees will respond more favorably if they feel a connection with the manager and/or the bank. This persuasion could be delivered in the form of personal encouraging, selling the idea to the entire staff, and/or demonstrating through personal example.

END OF CHAPTER CASES

CASE 6-1: PLANNING FOR CHANGE LEADS TO A CHANGE IN PLANNING—

CASE SUMMARY: This case discusses the changes Hewlett Packard Company has recently undergone to revive their market share in the computer industry. Although originally a decentralized organization, they seemed to follow their competitors and evolved into an extremely bureaucratic structure, thus, slowing decision-making and lengthening the product development cycle.

Although the original founders were both approaching 80 years of age and long retired from HP, they returned to revitalize the company. Due to the ability to effectively plan and aim for the future, the two founders took some risks in redirecting the company. The founders owned one quarter of HP's stock and were highly respected thus, they could create quick and significant change. They redesigned the organization to be much more decentralized and made changes in meeting the market needs. Steps HP's competitors were not able to achieve. The case illustrated the need for planning for change and changing organizational plans.

ANSWERS TO QUESTIONS FOR ANALYSIS:

1. **Question:** *Discuss how past successes could contribute to the inability of managers to successfully plan for the future.*

   Answer: Success can often create a sense of false security. Managers are often tempted to not engage themselves, their colleagues and their subordinates in the type of activities necessary to remain successful for the long run. Success sends the signal that all actions being taken are the correct ones. This is accurate for the present time. However, as conditions change in the market, the competitive environment, governmental regulations, etc., each manager must be diligent about remaining in front of the planning curve. Forecasting must continuously be done to ensure that necessary information is coming into the organization as planning continues. Old data about customers' needs and wants or the status of competitors will result in poor planning decisions.

2.	**Question:**	*Describe how William Hewlett's and David Packard's authority and persuasiveness influenced the planning process at Hewlett Packard.*

	Answer:	As the original founders of the organization, they were well respected for their early expertise, which had brought HP so far. In addition, between the two of them they owned one quarter of the stock. As a result of these two factors, William Hewlett and David Packard were able to use all three primary implementation tools for their planning: authority, persuasion and policy. They had the legitimate authority to create change through their planning processes, due to their ownership of the company and their roles as founders. They were also able to use persuasion since members of the corporation had high regard for both of the men. Hewlett and Packard were also able to create policies due to both their legitimate authority and the respect they received.

3.	**Question:**	*How was the use of the marketing strategy metaphor able to effectively guide the development of specific objectives and deployment of resources at HP?*

	Answer:	"Don't attack a well entrenched competitor. Early on, stake out your own hill and fortify," is a military metaphor which has guided HP's marketing strategy for many years. As such, HP uses techniques of creating new markets and developing their products to top levels of quality as a means to gain and maintain their market share. Specifically, they sometimes are able to use speed, which is enhanced by their decentralized structure, to beat their competitors to market; sometimes HP fortifies itself by investing heavily in new and alternative technology; and sometimes it simply buys market share, by acquiring other companies.

4.	**Question:**	*What is meant by the final statement in the case, "In order to plan for change, a company must effect a change of plan?"*

	Answer:	When most of the large companies of today began they did not have to cope with the rapid rate of change they are now encountering. Stability and slow, steady growth were the conditions in which most companies were able to function. However, the current business conditions are very different. Consumers are better educated and more demanding regarding quality, the global marketplace has shifted the competitive focus drastically, and the brisk rate of development of new technologies are requiring organization to change at break-neck speeds. Thus, an organization must include in their planning equation the need to undertake constant environmental forecasting and orchestrate change. Creating change now must be part of each organization's plan. Planning requires focusing on the future; the manager's responsibility is to ensure the organization is prepared to move into the future.

CASE 6-2: PROBLEM IDENTIFICATION IN A CONSUMER PRODUCTS FIRM——

CASE SUMMARY: This incident illustrates the complexity and potential for conflict which is inherent in planning the activities of functional organizations. The problems which each functional manager presents will be subsequently defended as having highest priority. Whether you wish to discuss planning politics is a matter of choice. The difficult question relates to priority setting and should be addressed in the discussion.

ANSWERS TO QUESTIONS FOR ANALYSIS: ———————————————————

1. **Question:** *In what order of priority would you place these problems?*

   Answer: The overall objective must be defined to respond to the necessity for setting priorities. In this instance, the firm's top management believed that it was on the verge of bankruptcy due to the combination of government-imposed restrictions and the inflationary bias. Consequently, it placed in priority those problems which threatened its survival. The firm needed cash. Top management decided to emphasize the problems of immediate concern—production, sales, and finance. Meeting government regulations and staff development were given low priority.

2. **Question:** *Is there any basis for interrelating the problems, or is each a separate unrelated problem? Explain.*

   Answer: The logical basis is to seek underlying causes. Thus, rising prices and wages account for the problems in engineering, finance, and sales. Other causes include obsolete machinery and credit practices.

3. **Question:** *Once problems are identified, what information is needed for subsequent planning decisions?*

   Answer: Planners should focus their information search on obtaining information that is directly relevant to the problem and resist the temptation to believe that ~the more, the better.~ Drowning in mounds of information is a common problem in the planning process. Relevant information is that which provides more insight into the problem's nature, costs, and consequences and is relevant to feasible alternative solutions.

ADDITIONAL QUESTIONS AND ANSWERS

1. **Question:** *Discuss the differences between the use of authority, persuasion, and policy as means of implementing plans. Give examples of when each would be most beneficial. What are the disadvantages to each of these methods?*

   Answer: Formal authority and the ability to use such to create change or implement plans have decreased as organizations have become more decentralized and decision-making and planning have been moved down the organization. When authority can be used to execute plans, steps must be taken to ensure that employees are aware of the need to implement certain plans and that their willingness and ability to do so will be reflected in their performance evaluations.

Persuasion is the act of convincing or selling others to accept or implement a plan due to the merits of the plan rather than the authority of the individual requesting such action.

Policies assist in the implementation of long-term or permanent plans. The use of policies helps to ensure some consistency among the execution of plans, as well as greater formalization of the plans. Question #9 below outlines the characteristics of effective policies.

The higher the level of involvement of the employee in establishing both the plans and their implementation, the greater the likelihood of successful implementation. Persuasion and involvement in policy creation provide the opportunity for increased dialogue and thus, greater engagement by the workers. However, the use of authority and the activation of pre-existing policies is typically a quicker method for implementing plans. The benefit of increased speed must be considered in light of potential lessened commitment by the employees when determining which implementation method to use. A combination of implementation tools is also possible.

2. **Question:** *Accelerating change in the external environment has resulted in an increasing emphasis on corporate planning in recent years. Has rapid change in the external environment affected planning in your own life ? Explain.*

   Answer: This question serves to encourage students to consider the importance of planning in their own lives and the impact which change in their environments can have on their own future and the need to plan.

3. **Question:** *Question: Why should objectives be specific and measurable?*

   Answer: If objectives are not specific, the planner has no rationale for selecting one strategy over another. If an objective is not measurable, it is impossible to determine if the objective has been achieved.

4. **Question:** *If pressed, most individuals would admit that they don't effectively plan. (To check your own planning ability, compare what you actually accomplished last week with what you planned to accomplish.) Why are most people not effective planners?*

   Answer: This question usually spurs an active class discussion once students admit that they're often ineffective planners. They may cite several reasons. Planning requires time which some individuals believe they don't have. It requires thinking about the future, directly dealing with uncertainty and often making difficult decisions. Difficult decision making and actively dealing with uncertainty are tasks which many people would rather avoid and deal with only when they must.

5. **Question:** *Summarize the four benefits which an organization can accrue from planning.*

Answer: Planning: 1) coordinates an organization's efforts through objective setting; 2) prepares the organization for change by requiring contingency thinking and the development of contingency plans; 3) sets objectives and actions which can serve as performance standards; and 4) develops managers by sharpening the participant's ability to deal with uncertainty and abstract ideas and to think systematically about the future and plan effectively.

6. **Question:** *Differentiate between long-run, intermediate, and short-run objectives.*

Answer: Long-run objectives have deadlines for accomplishment that extend beyond five years and must be met to ensure organizational survival. Intermediate objectives require one to five years. Short-term objectives are those to be accomplished within one year. Both short-term and intermediate objectives must be met if long-term objectives are to be attained.

7. **Question:** *Explain several factors that contribute to the presence of conflict between departments and divisions in the planning process.*

Answer: Students will likely suggest several factors. Of course, conflict is inherent because the end product of plans—objectives and strategy—largely determines how many resources each department will receive. Each party contends for his share of the resource pie and often competes for more. Another factor is represented in the second case presented at the end of the chapter. Research has consistently shown that managers perceive organizational problems (and answers) in terms of their own functional areas (e.g., marketing, finance, accounting, manufacturing). When individuals come together with such different perspectives and the tendency to view issues very differently, conflict is bound to occur.

8. **Question:** *Distinguish between variable and moving budgets.*

Answer: Variable budgeting computes financial scenarios if actual output deviates from planned output. Moving budgeting involves preparing a budget for a fixed period and updating the budget at fixed intervals. For example, a budget prepared at the end of December for the next 12 months is updated monthly (for example, initially at the end of January and extending through the next 12 months, February through next January).

9. **Question:** *What characteristics must a policy possess to be effective?*

Answer: The policy must be ethical, clearly written and logical, comprehensive enough to cover contingencies, provide for coordination of the various subunits whose actions are interrelated, and be flexible enough to accommodate necessary change but stable enough to maintain a sense of direction.

10. **Question:** *What are some of your instructor's policies in your management class ? Why do you think they have been established?*

   Answer: This question almost always spurs class discussion. Class policies can be discussed with respect to the major reasons for developing policy statements outlined in the text; consistency, direction, and to protect the reputation of the college (or university).

11. **Question:** *Is conflict within the planning process dysfunctional?*

   Answer: It all depends. Conflict helps in the sense that it spurs some individuals, such as those undecided on the question, to spend more time and effort considering the issues which are the source of conflict. Conflict is quite functional if the parties disagree not on organizational objectives but disagree on the means to achieve them. However, excessive conflict can encourage much politicking, backbiting, and other costly activities, and the real objectives of the planning process, such as developing effective objectives and strategies, can get lost in the battle.

7 STRATEGIC PLANNING

LEARNING OBJECTIVES

After completing Chapter 7, students should be able to:

Define strategic planning in terms of the direction it gives to the entire organization.

Describe how the mission and strategies of an organization should mesh.

Discuss why strategic planning has grown in importance in recent years.

Compare organizational objectives and operational objectives.

Identify appropriate strategies for each business type identified in a portfolio matrix.

CHAPTER SYNOPSIS

The second in a two-chapter section on planning, Chapter 7 focuses specifically on strategic planning. Strategic planning is presented in three sections: 1) an introduction to the concept and a brief review of conditions leading to the increasing use of strategic planning in organizations; 2) the strategic planning process; and 3) using the strategic planning process.

Concerning the first section, which focuses on the role of strategic planning in the organization and the reasons for its growing importance in organizations today, discusses the differences between the four phases of planning as described in Chapter 6 and the need for an overall organizational blueprint or strategic plan.

The second section, the strategic planning process, focuses on defining the elements of the process' end result, the strategic plan (see Figure 7-1). This second section also illustrates the need to integrate information from the environment in deciding on the organizational mission, objectives, strategies, and portfolio plan. The **organizational mission statement is** discussed in terms of its purpose, criteria for effectiveness, and the three key factors which should be considered in its development: 1) the organization's history; 2) distinctive competencies; and 3) the environment in which the organization operates. **Organizational objectives** are also defined in terms of purpose and requirements for effectiveness. The authors discuss **organizational strategy** in terms of its function and the four common types of **strategies: 1) market penetration; 2) market development; 3) product development; and 4) diversification.** Discussion of the final phase of the strategic planning process, the development of an **organizational portfolio plan,** focuses on explaining the Boston Consulting Group business portfolio matrix which is a popular approach to plan development.

The chapter's **Management in Action** profiles the activities of three CEOs in developing the organization's strategic plan and moving their particular company to higher levels of success. John H. Bryan, CEO of Sara Lee, understood the maturation of the American food industry and chose to diversity his company. At Blockbuster, CEO H. Wayne Huizenga decided to position his organization as an entertainment powerhouse and managed deals to broaden their role; thus, facing head on the concerns raised by expanding cable channels.

Nicholoden's Geraldine Laybourne expanded the tinny company's position in the market by reaching adults with favorite re-runs while their children slept and introducing paid advertising.

The **first Management Focus** segment looks at the organization's success being closely linked to the drive of top management and the ability of these individuals to have an organizational vision. General Electric's CEO, Jack Walsh, and his bold restructuring of GE to eliminate one-third of the employees and make the company more profitable is the subject of the **second Management Focus**. And the **final Management Focus** highlights how Borden examined their past mistakes and made significant adjustments.

TEACHING TIPS

LECTURE & DISCUSSION IDEAS

1. Students sometimes have difficulty in obtaining a firm conceptual grasp on the elements of a company's overall strategic plan and the planning process. You may want to begin with having students make comparisons between what organizations do and what families do. Ask students to describe what their family mission statement is and the steps taken toward achieving that mission. Most students probably have not considered their family in this manner and may need some prompting. Examples such as the significance of higher education and how monies were acquired for tuition may start them on this line of thinking. What was the family mission in terms of providing opportunities to learn skills and to develop attitudes necessary for success in adult life.

2. Another way to facilitate their understanding is to select a business noted for its strategic planning and refer to it for examples as your lecture proceeds through each component of strategic planning. A particularly good example, which has been used effectively in this regard is Philip Morris, a conglomerate which produces several products that are well known to students (e.g., numerous cigarettes such as Marlboro, Players, Virginia Slims, Benson & Hedges, and Merit; Miller Beer, and, until recently, 7-UP). An excellent source of information is a policy case on the company in *Cases in Strategic Management* by A. J. Strickland III and Arthur A. Thompson (Plano, Texas: Business Publications, Inc. 1982). Other articles on the company have appeared in recent issues of *Business Week, Fortune,* and *The Wall Street Journal.* Note that in the exercise on the BCG matrix in the *Study Guide,* students plot Philip Morris businesses in the BCG matrix.

3. When discussing business strategies, identify one or two local businesses that have a clear and highly visible strategy. Having students identify and critique the business' strategy is one way to enhance their understanding of the purpose and overall makeup of business strategy.

113

4.   A particularly important point to make in your treatment of strategic planning—and one that students often miss—is that the activity involves anticipating and dealing with continual change. As Peter Drucker asserts, all mission statements, objectives, and strategies eventually become obsolete, because environmental components (notably technological developments, competitors, customers, and public expectations) continually change. One way to impress this point upon your students is to cite examples of such change and the resulting impact on organizations. For example, concerning competitors, the entry of Japanese car makers into the U.S. auto market forever changed the nature of the industry's competition (and how American automakers view the industry). IBM's entry into home computers helped transform the home computer market (and posed substantial problems for smaller competitors). Concerning technological change, witness the impact of the development of the handheld calculator on the office products industry and the effects of IBM's ball font on the typewriter industry in the 1960s. As a part of this discussion, ask your students to cite other examples and to discuss the effects on related businesses.

PROJECT / EXERCISE IDEAS

1.   Have your students scan major business publications (e.g., *Fortune, Business Week, The Wall Street Journal*) and prepare a report on a business experiencing troubles related to mistakes in its strategic planning. This project can enlighten students concerning the types of planning mistakes which companies can make and the consequences of those mistakes.

2.   Have your students research the corporate planning process of a major diversified conglomerate (examples include ITT, Litton, Gulf and Western, Fuqua Industries and Northwest Industries). This project can educate students on how a highly complex firm conducts strategic planning across its many and distinct product and service lines. (A frequent student question is: What bring all the conglomerates' diverse activities together to serve one major purpose? This exercise can help them answer this question.)

3.   One way to further student understanding of the four strategies discussed in the chapter (market penetration, market development, diversification, and product development) is to have students, as an individual or group project, identify a company that pursues these strategies and prepare a written report on the company's strategy, its payoff to date, and the company's reasoning behind the strategy. The students should address whether the strategy is new or long-term, and if new, the reasons for the company's shift in strategic direction.

4.   Have a strategic planner from a large local business speak to your class on the nuts and bolts of his or her company's strategic planning process. The planner should address how the company develops a mission statement, organizational and operational objectives, strategies and policy. Other questions to pose: How often is the company's strategic plan revised? How much has the planning process contributed to the organization's performance?

5.　A city or county planner which was suggested as a class speaker for Chapter 5 is also applicable here as the planner can discuss the same strategic planning questions addressed by a strategic planner from private business.

6.　A member of your college or university's planning staff could also effectively speak to your class on the planning process used by your school. The politics of the planning process is a particularly relevant issue here as public colleges and universities depend on political institutions—the state and federal governments—for resources. The speaker could also discuss the dynamics of the school's budgeting process which is a key element of the planning function in colleges and universities.

7.　To emphasize product/market matrix, ask students to bring products from to class which illustrate each of the four quadrants. They may be amazed to discover, simply by reading labels, the extent to which various companies use they strategies to increase their market share and growth.

LECTURE OUTLINE NOTES

I.　An organization is guided by a larger framework or **blueprint** developed for the entire organization. Planning done by top management has the objective of achieving advantage over competitors. Strategic planning provides the **planning context** for all divisions and functions.

II.　**The Growth of Strategic Planning**

　　A.　Most organizations began in more stable times and were able to profit from steady, but rapidly growing markets.
　　B.　Since World War II, the external environment has **become more unstable**, uncertain, and fast-changing.
　　　　1.　Luck, wisdom, and intuition alone are no longer sufficient to guide organizations.
　　　　2.　More **organizations must use strategic planning**, which takes into consideration changing environments, because:
　　　　　　a.　markets are increasing global.
　　　　　　b.　technology has evolved at a rapid pace.
　　　　　　c.　new forms of distribution are present.
　　　　　　d.　services have grown.
　　　　　　e.　continuous inventions of new organizational forms.
　　　　3.　Strategic planning **includes review of:**
　　　　　　a.　market conditions.
　　　　　　b.　customer needs.
　　　　　　c.　competitive strengths and weaknesses.
　　　　　　d.　sociopolitical, legal and economic conditions.

        e.   technological developments.

        f.   availability of resources.

        g.   the total organization with input from all functional areas.

4.   Strategic planning **results in establishment of** (see Figure 7-1, The Strategic Planning Process):

      1.   organizational mission

      2.   objectives

      3.   strategies

      4.   portfolio plan.

III.   The Strategic Planning Process

The process produces a written plan composed for four components:

A.   **Mission Statement**

    1.   States the **organization's long-run vision** of what it is trying to become, the unique aim distinguishing it from other similar organizations.

    2.   Provides direction for the entire organization. Should be **periodically revised** because the present mission may:

        a.   Become irrelevant because the organization has expanded into new products, markets, and/or industries.

        b.   Remain relevant, but lose management's interest.

        c.   Become inappropriate due to environmental change.

    3.   In developing the statement, management must:

        a.   Ask (and answer), "What is our business?"

        b.   Consider three elements:

            1)   The **organization's history**—its past objectives, accomplishments, mistakes and policies.

            2)   The organization's **distinctive competencies**—what a company does best which provides a competitive advantage (for example, Coca-Cola's advertising, Toyota's manufacturing quality).

            3)   The **organization's external environment**—dictates opportunities, constraints, and threats which must be identified before a mission statement is developed.

    4.   An **effective mission statement:**

        a.   **Focuses on markets** (an external focus) not products (an internal focus)—focusing on client and customer needs rather than products or services offered.

        b.   Is **achievable and realistic.**

        c.   **Motivates employees** by providing a shared sense of purpose outside the activities performed within the organizations. d. Is specific, providing clear direction and guidelines for management (see Table 7-1 for examples of mission statements).

        d.   Is **specific.**

    5.   Every mission statement eventually becomes **obsolete.**

B.   **Organizational objectives**

    1.   The end points of the organization's mission, i.e., what the organization seeks through ongoing, long-run operations.

116

2. Effective organizational objectives must:
   a. Be capable of being **converted into specific action**.
   b. **Provide direction**, serving as the starting point for more specific, detailed objectives at the organization's lower levels--operational planning.
   c. **Establish** the organization's **long-run priorities**.
   d. **Serve as standards**, facilitating management control. (See Table 7-3 for examples of organizational objectives).

C. **Organizational strategies**
   1. The organization's grand design, i.e., its action plan for achieving its organizational objectives.
   2. Involves determining whether to concentrate on present customers or create new ones or both.
   3. Four strategies are commonly used (see the Product/Market Matrix, Figure 7-2):
      a. **Market penetration**—focuses on increasing current product/service use by present customers, for example, Coke launching a new ad campaign to boost product consumption by current Coke drinkers.
      b. **Market development**—focuses on finding new customers for present products/services, for example, an agency may increase outreach to inform individuals who have never used their services before of what the agency can provide for them.
      c. **Product development**—focuses on developing new products for present customers, for example, a laundry detergent manufacturer begins making and distributing a product to soften clothes which can be added to the dryer.
      d. **Diversification**—developing new products for new customers, for example, a manufacturer of sports safety equipment using their technology to manufacture and distribute braces for physically challenged individuals.
   4. Strategies should be chosen which are **consistent with the organization's mission and exploit distinctive competencies**.

D. **Organizational portfolio plan**
   1. The final stage of the strategic planning process wherein top management decides which of its businesses to build, maintain, or eliminate and/or which business to add to its operations.
   2. A popular method for developing the plan is the **BCG business portfolio matrix** created by the Boston Consulting Group. The approach involves four steps:
      a. Identify organization activities which meet the requirements of a **strategic business unit** (SBU):
         1) has a distinct mission
         2 has its own competitors
         3) stands as a single business or collection of related businesses
         4) can be planned for independently from the organization's other businesses

117

<blockquote>

    b.   Classify each SBU as a:

        1)   **Star**—a SBU with a high market share in a high-growth market. Requires large investment to support rapid growth, for example, a leading video cassette recorder manufacturer.

        2)   **Cash cow**—a SBU with a high market share in a low growth market. Produces substantial cash for the organization which can be used to support other SBUs or pay debt. Doesn't require large investment (for example, the leading bank in a low-growth community).

        3)   **Question mark**—a SBU with a low market share in a high-growth market. Strategic decision—build into a star (requires substantial funds) or phase down or eliminate.

        4)   **Dogs or Cash traps**—a SBU with a low market share in a low-growth market (for example, a Slavic language department in a university).
</blockquote>

    c.   Plot each SBU in the portfolio matrix (see the Figure 7-3). A SBU's matrix position depends on its industry's annual market growth rate and the SBU's relative market share (the SBU's market share compared to the market's top competitor).

    d.   Determine which of four alternatives to pursue for each SBU:

        1)   **Build**—invest in the SBU.

        2)   **Hold**—preserve market share. Effective for cash cows.

        3)   **Harvest**—increase short-term cash with little concern for actions' long-term impact. Appropriate for all SBU's except stars.

        4)   **Divest**—get rid of the SBU. Appropriate for question marks and cash traps.

    e.   SBUs change matrix positions overtime (for example, question marks may become stars, stars can become cash cows).

    f.   Major criticisms of the matrix:

        1)   BCG model assumes market growth is uncontrollable.

        2)   Assumptions about market share may be inaccurate, especially in international markets.

        3)   Assumes major source of SBU financing is internal.

        4)   The model does not take into account any interdependencies which may exist between SBUs.

        5)   Model based on the assumption that corporate strategy begins with a competitive position analysis.

  E.   The complete strategic plan facilitates development plans in each of organization's functional areas.

IV.   The Relationship Between the Strategic Plan and Operational Plans

  A.   All operational plans (for example, production, marketing, personnel, financial plans) are derived from and contribute to the accomplishment of the strategic plan (see Figures 7-4 and 7-5).

  B.   Individuals at the top levels of the organization are involved in broader planning; moving down the organizational chart increases the level of detail in the planning.

C.   Individuals at the tops levels of the organization engage in planning which covers a longer time span; moving down the organizational chart decreases the length of time to be taken to accomplish the plans made at that level.

ANSWERS TO DISCUSSION AND REVIEW QUESTIONS

1.   **Question:**   *Discuss the statement: "Why should companies bother to engage in long-term planning?" They have enough problems coping with planning for the short run. "*

       Answer: Managing principally for current cash flows, market share, and earnings tend to mortgage the firm's future. Long-range planning is a means of envisioning where the firm is to be in the future and working to achieve that vision. Long range planning tends to force the firm to be proactive and not be complacent. Change is inevitable. Long range planning helps insure future survival.

2.   **Question:**   *Explain why you agree or disagree with the following statements: a) Planning is the easiest where environmental change is minimal. b) Planning is most valuable where environmental change is great.*

       Answer: When environmental change is minimal, the planning function is less complex than when environmental change is great. Planning is necessary under either set of circumstances but is more necessary and valuable (as well as more difficult) when unstable conditions prevail. For most industries today, environmental change is much more commonplace than even a decade ago.

3.   **Question:**   *Describe how a company, through placing too much emphasis on achieving long-term objectives, could jeopardize its short-term profitability and other operating results. Use an existing company, as an example, in formulating your answer.*

       Answer: A company which places too much emphasis on achieving long-term objectives may overextend themselves betting on the future and may penalize short-term profitability to an extent that the company becomes vulnerable to takeover or other destructive actions. The Management Focus about Jack Walsh at GE and the one about Borden are both examples of this lack of balance taking place. In both scenarios, actions which were taken to overcome this problem are described.

119

4. **Question:**   *Discuss the potential problems an organization could encounter if its mission statement failed to provide a long-run vision of what the company is striving to become.*

    Answer: Since the mission statement provides the major coordinating structure of the organization, one which does not provide a long-run vision fails to equip employees with the necessary information to accomplish effective planning at their own level. A lack of a visionary mission statement allows individual greater likelihood of moving in their own direction without any coordination between and among units.

5. **Question:**   *Choose a company and describe its distinctive competencies. Do you believe that these competencies are capable of leading the company to a sustainable competitive advantage? Why or why not?*

    Answer: Students should be able to identify several companies that demonstrate distinctive competencies. They should realize the firm's competencies are what distinguishes it from other competitors. If firms are to sustain a competitive edge their competencies must be maintained over time. Otherwise, opportunities become illusions that are not attainable.

6. **Question:**   *This chapter states that an effective mission statement will focus on markets rather than products and be achievable, motivating, and specific. Select three of the actual mission statements presented in Figure 7-1 and value them based on these criteria.*

    Answer: Responses will vary depending on the statements selected. In discussing their evaluations, students should suggest ways to improve the statement being critiqued.

7. **Question:**   *What is the relationship between organizational mission, organizational objectives, and organizational strategies?*

    Answer: Organizational objectives define the organizational mission in operational terms; the objectives are the achievable, specific ways of actualizing the mission. Organizational strategies are the means to accomplish organizational objectives.

8. **Question:**   *Discuss how a company which manufactures and markets children's toys could pursue growth through utilization of the strategies presented in Figure 7-2.*

    Answer: A toy manufacturer has four methods for increasing their market share and growth. These are the same four strategies available to all organizations.

    1.   Market Penetration Strategies--With this strategy, the toy manufactures will strive to have their current customers purchase more of their products. Special techniques may be used such as discounting for increase in quantities purchased, increasing the number of distribution centers or distribution locations.

    2.   Market Development Strategies--The toy manufacturer will seek

to find customers who have never purchased from them before. In this case, the manufacturer could begin to advertize some of its current products for use by adults. As more people are beginning to recognize the healthfulness of play and relaxation a market could be created for adults engaging themselves with certain children's toys and games. Another new market would be to take some of their current products to other countries.

3.   Product Development Strategies--The manufacturer could develop new product lines, either by offering current products in different forms, such as various quality levels of bicycles, etc. or by developing entirely new products.

4.   Diversification--With this strategy the toy manufacturer will seek to develop new products for customers it is not currently serving. For example, if the manufacturer decided to pursue the adult market, in addition to advertizing some of their current children's toy for adults as suggested in Market Development above, the manufacturer could also development and market toys made especially for adults.

9.   **Question:**   *Do you believe each of the criticisms, related to use of the BCG Portfolio Model, are valid ones? Why or why not?*

     Answer: The major criticisms of the matrix are:

1.   BCG model assumes market growth is uncontrollable.

2.   Assumptions about market share may be inaccurate, especially in international markets.

3.   Assumes major source of SBU financing is internal.

4.   The model does not take into account any interdependencies which may exist between SBUs.

5.   Model based on the assumption that corporate strategy begins with a competitive position analysis.

Regarding item #1, the aspect of market growth which is controllable is to decide to slow growth. However, increases or maintenance of growth are sometimes outside of the control of the organization. In addition, decline in growth sometimes occurs when not desired. What have been some of the criticisms of this model in the past are becoming less so today. Organizations are becoming more sophisticated in acquiring information about competitors, even those abroad. Also organizations are becoming more aware of the need to be proactive rather than reactive and thus, greater caution will be used in applying this model to any single organization.

10.   **Question:**   *Explain, through use of some examples, how managers and employees at lower levels of an organization influence the development and implementation of the strategic plan.*

     Answer: When executed properly, planning results in all objectives in the organization being related to all other objectives within the organization regardless of level. This is due primarily to all objectives being means for accomplishing the mission of the organization.

For example, the mission of a non-profit organization may be to design and implement a dropout prevention program in high schools across the country. To accomplish this mission, certain areas of the organization are responsible for developing the tools and program to be offered to school. Another task within the organization is to recruit schools who are interested in implementing this program. In addition, funds must be secured from corporate donors or governmental funding sources to off-set the costs for the schools. In any one aspect of the organization fails to accomplish their objectives, all other areas of the organization will be negatively affected. If schools are located and funds obtained, but then there are no products or services to provide the schools, the mission of the organization, to keep students in school, cannot be achieved.

In addition, to best use resources of time, money, materials, personnel, and knowledge all individuals must be aiming their work in the same direction--to accomplish the mission of the organization--to keep students in school. If one area is focusing on objectives that are not in keeping with the mission, the mission of the organization is unlikely to be realized.

END OF CHAPTER CASES

CASE 7-1: ENCOURAGING DIVERSITY AS PART OF THE STRATEGIC PLANNING PROCESS

CASE SUMMARY: The Chemical Group of the Monsanto Corporation has taken a very proactive approach to diversity and sees the implementation of these efforts as strategies toward accomplishing their plan for increasing diversity. Managing diversity is seen as a long-term process and thus, a strategic action plan, called the Process for Diversity Management, is being implemented.

Monsanto has a three-part strategy aimed at: 1) increasing employee awareness of diversity-related issues; 2) establishing accountability as a measure of performance; and 3) changing the processes that support the ways in which people are managed.

ANSWERS TO QUESTIONS FOR ANALYSIS:

1. Question: *Why did Monsanto address diversity-related issues as part of its strategic planning process?*

   Answer: Monsanto is working from the assumption that diversity in the work place is going to continue to increase. With this increase, people will perceive less homogeneity, and if left unaddressed, barriers will be built which will inhibit effective relationships and therefore productivity will be decreased.

2. **Question:** *Assume you were hired to solve the problems related to employee turnover at Monsanto. What would you have done differently or in addition to the actions taken?*

   Answer: Students may provide a variety of answers to this question, including Monsanto should not have done anything. People should have the right to associate with whomever they want." Encourage students to explore what kinds of things they wish would have occurred when they were the new member to a group.

   Ask students to discuss the usefulness of pairing people together who are different from one another. What criteria would students offer in defining difference? Certainly gender and race will be mentioned. What about values, interests, abilities. Should this information should be made public or should only obvious, visible differences be included.

3. **Question:** *Choose three of the eight barriers present in the case. Explain why these barriers do, in fact, prevent employees from understanding diversity.*

   Answer: The eight barriers list in the text are:
   1. denial of issues
   2. lack of awareness of problems
   3. restrictions on bringing bad news up the organizational ladder
   4. a lack of trust about how others will perceive and respond to diversity issues
   5. the need to be in control of one's job
   6. a compulsion to fix "them" rather than "us"
   7. issues outside one' reality
   8. past, well-intended, diversity actions.

   Common through many of these barriers is the difficulty of seeing the world from someone else's sense of reality. Many individuals are so insulated in their own cultures, that they do not recognize that other people experience the same events and thoughts differently. There is also a believe of "when in Rome, do as the Romans do," which suggests that everyone should act in the ways most like the majority of individuals present. What is most challenging about this perspective, however, if that the demographics are changing at such rapid speed that the individuals now comfortable in the majority will soon find themselves in environments where they are no longer a part of the largest group present.

   Managing or celebrating issues of diversity has been one of the greatest challenges of our society. People remain very reticent about their

123

various levels of comfort with this issue. Thus, people continue to experience difficulty in discussing and exploring these issues with other.

4.   **Question:**   *In general, how can actions taken toward achieving diversity assist organizations in becoming more competitive?*

       Answer: Our markets have become more diverse due to increase technologies, transportation methods, and globalization. With this increase of diversity in our markets, each organization must be more secure in its ability to reach across lines which in the past were dividers. Increasing the diversity of our organizations, makes easier our task of understanding a more diverse customer pool.

                In addition, diversity comes in many forms, not simply differences in gender and race. Diversity is also reflected in people's values and interests. This increased perspective can assist in the organization making decisions about their product/market mix.

CASE 7-2: STRATEGIC PLANNING AT THE FAMILY STORE ──────────

CASE SUMMARY: This is a fictionalized version of an ongoing situation. It is not unlike those which are occurring all over the nation as income and population shifts impact on heretofore successful local or regional businesses. These organizations are here today because many years ago they offered the right product at the right time to a rapidly growing market. Many of Jacob's critical decisions were made without the benefit of strategic thinking or planning. They resulted in a momentum which has carried the chain to where it is today. However, today's management must turn to strategic planning.

ANSWERS TO QUESTIONS FOR ANALYSIS: ──────────────────────

1.   **Question:**   *Why is Jacob facing these problems? Were they inevitable? Discuss in detail.*

       Answer: The problems being faced, while not uncommon and certainly understandable, were not inevitable. They are present because the organization has continued to try to do better what it was already doing without consideration of whether it should continue to do so or not. This is common among small successful businesses which often operate on the belief that success can be continuously repeated.

2.   **Question:**   *Assume you are hired as a consultant by Jacob. What, if anything, could you do, to help him?*

       Answer: Jacob needs a thorough analysis of the social and economic trends that are expected to influence retail business in the 1980s in his market area. This can then be used as a basis for developing an organizational strategic plan based on a specific mission statement of direction which in turn is based on an analysis of the distinctive competencies of the organization. Surely the organization by virtue of its successful history in the region has some distinctive competencies. Many possibilities do exist. The business could be sold to a national organization, it could redirect its own efforts to shopping malls, etc., and it could enter other retail businesses.

ADDITIONAL QUESTIONS AND ANSWERS

1. **Question:** *Write a mission statement for an organization with which you are familiar.*

   Answer: In completing this involvement exercise, students should prepare a statement which explicitly considers the organization's environment, its history and its distinctive competence. The statement can range in length from one sentence to a full page.

2. **Question:** *Suppose Hugh Heffner, founder of Playboy Enterprises, Inc., asked you the question, "What is my business and what should it be ?" How would you respond?*

   Answer: This question illustrates the difficulty and necessity in addressing this issue when formulating a business ~ mission because the answer to this question either directly or indirectly guides the course of an organization's activities. In regard to the business of Playboy Enterprises, students may cite "entertainment," "a way of life or lifestyle," or a "frame of mind or way of thinking." Some students may argue that the Playboy mission is becoming obsolete due to the changing roles of men and women.

3. **Question:** *Summarize the criteria for effective organizational objectives.*

   Answer: Effective objectives should be: 1) capable of being converted into specific action; 2) provide direction; 3) establish the organization's long-run priorities; and 4) serve as standards which facilitate management control.

4. **Question:** *Differentiate between product development and market development strategies.*

   Answer: In pursuing a market development strategy, a firm attempts to find new customers for its present products or services usually by increasing its advertising/promotion or finding new uses for the product (e.g., Arm and Hammer baking soda). A firm which pursues a product development strategy focuses on attracting present customers with new products (such as R. J. Reynolds developing a low tar and nicotine version of its Winston's cigarettes).

5. **Question:** *Describe what you believe to be the distinctive competence of: 1) IBM; 2) Campbell's Soup Company; 3) McDonald's; 4) Levi Straus; 5) Ted Turner Broadcasting; and 6) Time magazine.*

Answer: This question typically spurs an interesting student discussion as students will differ in their opinions of each company's distinctive competence. Students should realize that distinctive competence is what a company does clearly better than its competitors. Discussion can also focus on the difficulties in establishing a distinctive competence (few companies have them) and whether all distinctive competencies are equal (no, given that distinctive competence is important only if the competence influences demand for the company's product/service).

6. **Question:** *In your opinion, what are the strengths and shortcomings of a diversification strategy?*

Answer: Diversification enables a business to spread its risk. Operating solely in one business can be risky if the respective product suddenly becomes obsolete or the business' external environment undergoes sudden change which adversely affects the form. Essentially, a one business organization has all its eggs in one basket. By operating in diverse markets, an organization's risk is spread. However, diversification can be financially expensive and increases organizational complexity. A diversifying firm must be sure that its management is not spread too thinly across its different businesses and has the skills to manage a multi-faceted corporation.

7. **Question:** *Given what you've learned about the BCG matrix, how would you classify the following businesses (e.g., as a star, cash cow, question mark, or dog)?: Apple Computers, Levi Straus, Sony, Kentucky Fried Chicken.*

Answer: This question will test students' understanding of the four business categories in the BCG matrix. Their responses will vary because specific information on relative market share and annual industry growth rate isn't provided. However, their general familiarity with the businesses should be sufficient for discussing each business' likely classification.

8. **Question:** *Provide examples of companies that have orchestrated a significant strategy turnaround. What factors accounted for their success?*

Answer: Students may cite several examples; any company that has, through strategic change, weathered a crisis or a severe financial or product demand downturn qualifies. This question is useful for encouraging students to consider the factors that contribute to successful achievement of major strategic change.

9. **Question:** *Explain what is meant by a "harvesting" strategy.*

Answer: When a corporation harvests a SBU, it increases the SBU's short-term cash flow with little concern for the long-term impact of its harvesting activities. These activities can include price cutting, reducing research and development of the product, and eventually reducing quality control standards. Once an SBU is harvested, it is then usually divested.

126

10. **Question:** *In your opinion, is a cash trap always a "problem" business?*

Answer: Not really. A business can have a low market share in a low-growth industry but still remain relatively profitable if production costs are low and the profit margin per unit sold is high. This exception has been cited as a major shortcoming of the BCG matrix's prescription for cash traps. As our methods of dealing with these issues have evolved, there has inevitably been some work done in this area which was not very refined or developed. This level of work created even greater discomfort for many individuals who are not even more uncertain about pursuing further learning in this area.

8   *THE ORGANIZING FUNCTION*

LEARNING OBJECTIVES

After completing Chapter 8, students should be able to:

Define   the organizing function in terms of required management decisions.

Describe   the effects of the span of control on the manager and the organization.

Discuss   the relationships between the planning and organizing functions.

Compare   two organizations using the dimensions of structure as the basis for the comparison.

Identify   the ways to describe differences among jobs.

CHAPTER SYNOPSIS

This is the first of a two-chapter section on organizing. This chapter have two major purposes: 1) to clarify the ways organizational structure differ along certain dimensions, and 2) to illustrate how managers make organization structures different by their decisions related to jobs and departments.

Regarding the activity of dividing tasks into jobs, chapter discussion emphasizes the activity's primary objective—determining the level of **labor specialization** which minimizes the cost per unit of output produced. The task of grouping jobs into departments is addressed by discussing the **internal operations oriented bases (process and functional)** and the **external focused bases (product, customer and geographical)**.

The chapter beings with a discussion on the dimensions of organizational structure, horizontal and vertical complexity, formalization, and centralization.

The chapter also presents the use of multiple bases in organizations, the issue of structurally fitting international activities into the business, and the criteria for selecting appropriate departmental bases. The section of **delegating authority** centers on **decentralization** and its advantages and potential problems. The section of **departmental size** concerns **span of control** relative to managerial work and organizational shape. Span of control is defined and the advantages and problems of narrow and wide spans of control, and criteria for selecting the degree of span of control are reviewed. In additional full explanation of **potential and actual relationships** is given.

The chapter's **Management in Action** focuses on changing organizational structures five different industries (Motorola, The First National Bank of Chicago, Rohm & Haas Bayaport, Lechmere Inc., and Volvo) and briefly explains how each has reorganized to better meet with organization's goals and more effectively involve the workers in defining the work and how best to accomplish it. The **first Management Focus** explains how LifeUSA and Wabash National have taken steps to involve their employees in the success of the organization. At

LifeUSA employee receive 10 percent of their compensation in stock options. At Wabash National employees are offered free classes in finance, etc. so they are better equipped to understand the economic health of the organization. The **second Management Focus** describes how Marlow Industries has decentralized and divided their quality control function, thus allowing these individuals to work more closely with a team and are able to determine ways to prevent defects rather than merely catching them at the end of the process. The **final Management Focus** examines the role of downsizing in creating a more effective structure. Many of the corporate giants of the 1980s who chose to reduce their workforce did so in an effort to increase profits through increases in efficiency. However, a decade later, may of these hopes for outcomes are not being seen at the rate anticipated.

TEACHING TIPS

LECTURE & DISCUSSION IDEAS

1. Have students recall a previous job they have held and ask them to describe it using the various terms included in the chapter. Be certain to have them describe the amount of specialization in their work and the work of others, how authority was handled, the size of departments, and whether the organization was structured with an internal (function or process) focus or and external (territories, product or customer) focus. Also students should discuss how formalized and complex their organizations were.

2. A useful point to make when discussing span of control is that the wrong span of control (i.e., a supervisor has too few or too many subordinates to supervise) can produce substantial problems. To illustrate this point, have your students recall from their past experiences, times when such a situation existed. What problems did they as subordinates experience? They'll likely cite the frustration of not receiving adequate guidance or the feeling of someone constantly hovering over their shoulder.

3. One interesting aspect of the organizing function is the predominant use of the organization chart to depict the organization's structure and reporting relationships. While emphasis is placed in this chart on the information which is available through the study of a firm's organizational chart, have students discuss what they can not ascertain from the organization chart. Encourage students to explore organization culture, placement in the market, economic health of the organization, informal lines of communication and authority as some possible important data not available from the organization chart.

4. One potentially major problem which the matrix design presents is role conflict and ambiguity experienced by members of the product development team because they each report to two supervisors. To illustrate this problem to students, ask them to consider if they've ever reported to two bosses. If they have, how did they feel about the situation? Did conflicts arise? How were they resolved?

1. An effective way to increase students' understanding of the different bases of departmentalization for businesses is to have them identify a company in the local community which is organized according to one of the bases discussed in the chapter. The students can obtain an organization chart from the company and interview a member of the organization for insights into the design's advantage and disadvantages. his project could be a group assignment with each group assigned a particular departmentalization base.

2. As the chapter notes, the decision to delegate authority is no easy matter. Often, the manager is reluctant to give up any part of his or her authority and often questions whether a subordinate manager has the ability and experience to effectively assume additional authority and responsibility. To illustrate these points, have your students, as an individual or group project, interview a manager who has made such decisions concerning delegation of authority. The students should ask the manager about the pros and cons of delegation, and to discuss experiences when delegation worked very well, when it did not, and the factors contributing to each outcome.

3. Interesting developments in job design are taking place in the auto industry which typically has subscribed to a highly specialized approach to production jobs. Workers in the General Motors-Toyota plant in Fremont, California, are assuming much more decision making authority and responsibility in their jobs. At GM's Saturn plant, job design changes and worker input into decisions at all plant levels has been termed revolutionary for the industry. As an individual or group assignment, have your students research interesting applications of job design (many examples exist in the management literature) and prepare a written report on one example of job design change, discussing the reasons for the change, and the implications for management and workers.

4. Have students investigating the increasing use of teams in the workplace. Local industries will be able to provide some information, as well as the management literature. In addition, have students identify some of the difficulties in having workers in teams.

5. Have students develop a training program that would assist workers in understanding how best to work in teams. Be certain they include information from the text and management literature which would assist workers in accepting the shift to teamwork.

6. There are many speakers who could provide your class with excellent insights regarding this organizing chapter. Some possible speakers could be:

   a. Top-level manager from a company structured along a particular departmentalization base to discuss the company's selection of the particular base, and the advantages and problems the structure has provided the company. You might want to ask the speaker to discuss how his or her company's organizational structure has evolved through the years. Why were the changes made? What impact has growth had on the company's structure?

b.   Invite the head of a company whose management philosophy is clearly decentralization or centralization of authority. The speaker could provide some excellent insights into the advantages and disadvantages of each philosophy.

c.   Invite a job engineer to discuss the art of determining the most effective degree of labor specialization for particular jobs. The speaker could discuss the factors involved in determining the "correct" degree of specialization. He or she could also likely tell some interesting stories concerning problems encountered when a particular job was under- or over-specialized.

d.   If a faculty member in your school's management department has conducted research in the job design area, he or she could provide an interesting overview of future directions in job design research and job design development in organizations.

7.   If you can locate a local business that uses or has used the matrix design, invite a representative who was or is involved in the matrix team to discuss how the team functions, its purpose, and the benefits the design has provided and problems it has posed for the company. The speaker could provide some interesting insights into the challenges which can arise when a new and quite different organizational form is introduced into an organization.

LECTURE OUTLINE NOTES

I.   The Organizing Function Overview

A.   Business historians will call the 1980s and 1990 the **era of "reorganization."**
B.   **Effects individual jobs and the way the jobs are grouped.**
    1.   Decisions about **specialization/division of labor and delegation of authority/centralization most effect individual jobs.**
    2.   Decisions about **departmental bases and size of departments most effect how jobs are grouped.**
C.   Serves **to achieve coordinated effort** through the **design of a task structure or specialization and authority relationships.**
    1.   **Design**—implies that management intentionally predetermines how work is done by employees.
    2.   **Structure**—the relatively stable aspects and relationships which forms the organization's framework; acts as a framework within which the organization functions.
        a.   Focuses on differentiation of positions, formulation of rules and procedures and prescriptions of authority.
        b.   Purpose of structure is to regulate or at least reduce uncertainty about the behavior of individuals.
    3.   The **function involves:**

      a.   **dividing overall tasks** into individual jobs.

      b.   **assigning authority**.

      c.   **aggregating individual jobs into departments** of specific bases.

      d.   **determining the best size** for each department.

II.   Dimensions of Organizational Structure

A.   The difficulty of defining and measuring the concepts of organizational structure have made the understanding of organizations very challenging.

B.   These dimensions vary independently. Important to realize not just that organizations are different along these dimension, but that these differences can affect performance. See Table 8-1 for summary of main points.

C.   Three commonly used methods of describe and analyze an organization are:

    1.   **Formalization**

      a.   The extent to which expectations regarding the means and ends of the work are **specified, written and enforced**.

      b.   May go beyond written information, such as the unwritten rules and procedures which every employee knows and obeys.

    2.   **Centralization**

      a.   Refers to the **location of the decision making and authority** within the hierarchy of the organization.

      b.   **Challenging to specify** in some organizations because:

         1.   differences of decision-making processes and authority of different positions within the same level of the organization

         2.   not all decisions are of equal importance

      c.   Organizations are identified as either **centralized**, which maintains most authority within limited areas of the organization, or **decentralized**, which involves more levels of the organization and employees.

    3.   **Complexity**

      a.   Refers to the number of distinctly different job titles or occupational groupings, and **the number of distinctly different units or departments**.

      b.   Relates to the **differences among units** and thus, frequently called **differentiation**.

         1.   **Horizontal Differentiation**-refers to the number of different jobs at the same level

         2.   **Vertical differentiation**-refers to the number of levels in the organization

III.   Division of Labor

A.   One of two organizational aspects (centralization or authority is the other) that most affects individual jobs.

B.   Concerns the extent to which **jobs are specialized**.

C.   Managers divide the total task of the organization into specific jobs having specified activities; perhaps the most important responsibility is to design jobs that **enable people to perform the right tasks at the right time**.

D.   Jobs can be **specialized both by method and application of the method**.

E. How jobs are divided and organized has **changed with time.**

  1. **Historically,** managers tended to divide jobs into rather **narrow specialties** because of the **advantages of division of labor.**

     a. Employees can be **quickly trained** for jobs that consist of few tasks.

     b. Employees can become **highly proficient** in performing tasks where they are limited. This proficiency can create better quality of output.

     c. Gains derived from narrow divisions of labor **can be calculated in economic terms:**

        1) If the relative increase in output exceed the relative increase in costs of performing the smaller job elements, increases from specialization results.

        2) However, at some point, the cost of specialization begin to outweigh the increased efficiency of specialization (See Figure 8-1).

     d. The traditional method of using narrow job design was first supported by Frederick W. Talyor, about 90 years ago, in this theory of Scientific Management.

  2. **Now** more jobs are being designed with the focus on **teams and teamwork,** which is explained in detail below (See III.F.4.).

F. **Specialization of Labor at the Job Level**

  1. Has been the traditional guideline when determining the content of individual jobs. Focus now shifted to teams doing work rather than individuals. This is described below (See III.F.4.).

  2. Specialization **measured in relative terms**--how one job compares with another. Organizations with highly specialized jobs are relatively formal, complex, and centralized compared to those that use less specialized jobs, such as team-based jobs.

  3. When comparing degree of specialization, there are **five aspects that differentiate jobs:**

     a. **Work Pace**-the more control the employee has over speed of work, the less specialized the job.

     b. **Job Repetitiveness**-the greater the number of different tasks an employee performs, the less specialized the job.

     c. **Skill Requirements**-the more skilled the employee must be, the less specialized the job.

     d. **Methods Specification**-the more latitude employee has in using various methods and tools, the less specialized the job.

     e. **Required Attention**-the more mental attention required, the less specialized the job.

  4. **Team Approach to Job Design**

     a. A relatively **new innovation** (See III.D.1. and III.F.1. above), which reflects increasing respect for the power of teams and teamwork for accomplishing goals.

     b. Teams consist of **five to 20 individuals** and team **members learn several jobs.**

     c. There are several **advantages** to the team method to job design.

133

1) This approach **provides more flexibility and quicker responses to market changes.**
2) Since the number of different jobs is reduced, the number of different **job classifications and work rules are reduced,** which results in greater flexibility to achieved higher levels of productivity and quality.
3) Allows workers to exercise relatively more discretion over pace and methods.
4) Reduces the amount of supervision needed.

   d. However, this method requires considerable more skilled employees.

   e. Not a perfect answer for all organization. Text gives example of Proctor and Gamble's challenge with teams.

IV. **Delegation of Authority**

A. One of two organizational aspects (division of labor or specialization is the other) that most affects individual jobs.

B. Includes two aspects. The right of the individual to:
1. **make decision without approval by higher management**
2. **to exact obedience from others.**

C. Refers specifically to making decisions, not to doing work.

D. **Managers decide how much authority should be delegated** to each job and worker.

E. Degree of delegated authority can be **relatively high or relatively low** with respect to both aspects of authority.

F. Organizations must choose the **appropriate balance** between centralizing and decentralizing or delegating authority.

G. **Advantages to delegating or decentralize authority** or why delegate authority
1. Relatively high delegation of authority **encourages the development of professional managers.**
   a. Allows managers to make significant decisions and gain skills which **advances the company.**
   b. Managers with broad decision-making power often make difficult decisions, and thus, are being trained for promotion.
   c. Advancement based on performance eliminates favoritism and personality conflicts.
2. High delegation of authority **can lead to a climate of internal competitiveness** since employees are compared with their peers.
   a. Internal competitiveness **can enhance overall organizational performance.**
   b. However, **internal competitive can also be destructive** if the success of one manager occurs at the expense of another.
3. Managers with relatively high authority can exercise **more autonomy.**
   a. This allows managers to be more creative and ingenious.
   b. Contribute to manager's desire to participate in problem solving.
   c. And allows the organization to respond to change.

H. There are **reasons not to delegate authority.**
   a. **Managers must be trained** to delegate authority and that can be costly

for the organization.

b. Managers are accustomed to making decisions and **may resist delegating authority to their subordinates.**

c. Managers **must have means of measuring the effectiveness** of delegated authority and thus, administrative costs are incurred when new or altered accounting and performance systems must be developed.

d. Decentralization or delegation of authority **may result in duplication of functions.**

I. **Delegation of Authority in International Settings**

1. Countries that were the **former Soviet Union are having difficulties** due to their previous experiences.

    a. Managers had emphasized short-term outcomes, such as efficiency and production.

    b. This creates barriers to pushing decision-making down the hierarchy.

2. A study in **England** shows that the **cost of duplication** within divisionalized organizations **led to increased centralization** of activities.

J. **Empowerment: Specialization and Delegation**

1. Has become a **cornerstone** in many organizations.

2. Involves designing jobs that are **relatively unspecialized and have considerable delegated authority.**

3. See Figure 8-1 for an illustration of the **relationship between , specialization of labor, and delegation or authority.** Empowerment increases in direct proportion with increased delegation of authority and decreasing job specialization.

4. **Empowerment cannot succeed in all organizations.**

5. Employee empowerment is **most likely to succeed** when the employees are able to develop a sense of ownership. This occurs when the organization:

    a. institutes a **cross-training program** to provide employees with skills to exercise additional responsibility and authority.

    b. **encourages and rewards innovative behavior.**

    c. **provides access to all pertinent information.**

    d. **supports employee decision making** even if doing so involves considerable risk.

V. **Department Bases**

A. One of two organizational aspects (size of departments being the other) most **effect how jobs are grouped.**

B. Jobs are groups together into department bases to provide for the **coordination of the jobs,** since the jobs must be performed in a specific manner and sequence.

C. The **larger the number of specialized job, the greater the need for effective coordination,** which is handled by a manager.

D. There are **five more widely used departmentalization bases. Functional and process refer to internal organizational activities; product, customer and geographic are external to the organization.**

1. **Functional Departmentalization**

a. Like product departmentalization emphasizes the internal operations of the organization.
b. Every organization undertakes **certain activities** or functions, which are necessary to create, produce and sell a product.
c. Each of **these activities could be organized as a specific department** and jobs combined accordingly.
d. Often found in relatively **small organizations** which provide a narrow range of products or services.
e. Also use as the basis in **divisions of large multiproduct organizations**.
f. **Manufacturing organizations are often structured** on a functional basis. (See Figure 8-3A)
g. Functional structures **provide greater efficiency** for an organization because each department consists of experts in a particular filed.
h. The **disadvantage** to functional structures is that **organizational goals may be sacrificed in favor of departmental goals** because individuals are working with other specialists and may encourage each other in their areas of expertise and interest.

2. **Process Departmentalization**
a. Like functional departmentalization, emphasizes the internal operations of the organization.
b. Typically this bases is used in **small firms with limited product lines.**
c. Processes refer to the **technical operations required**, which are performed by specialized trained in that particular operation.
d. Figure 8-3B illustrates an organizational chart of a manufacturing firm organized by process departmentalization. This is in contrast to Figure 8-3A which illustrates a functional structure.
e. **Advantages and disadvantages parallel those of function-based departments** and encourage skillful and efficient performance of activities.

3. **Product Departmentalization**
a. Like customer and geographic structures, product is external to the organization.
b. Often **used in larger, diversified companies** and is **preferred as a company increased the number of products marketed.**
c. All **jobs associated with producing or selling a product, product line or service are grouped together** under one manager.
d. Allows for **development of expertise** regarding all work, such as manufacturing, researching and distribution of a particular product line.
e. Concentration of authority, responsibility, and accountability in a product department allows top management to coordinate the activities of that particular product.
f. Figure 8-4A illustrates an organization structured by product departments.
g. Product-based organizations or "divisional organizations" has

136

been a **key aspect in developing modern capitalism.**
- h. Product-based structure **encourages initiative and autonomy** due to managers being given necessary resources to accomplish plans.
- i. However, this structure also **has the potential to create duplication or redundancy** because each division wants own research, marketing, etc.
- j. Technical and professional personnel are found throughout the organization at the division level.
- k. Some companies have also decentralized the quality assurance activities throughout the firm in this structure. The **Management Focus** illustrates this.

4. **Customer Departmentalization**
- a. Like product and geographic structures, customer departmentalization is external to the organization.
- b. In this structure **jobs are grouped by customers or clients.**
- c. Educational institutions are an example of this structure with their day, evening, weekend and extension programs. Other examples include department stores and the loan department of a commercial bank.
- d. The drive toward **increased customer satisfaction** has increased the popularity of this structure. These organizations are typically better able to satisfy customer-identified needs than those which base departments on non-customer factors.
- e. Customer-based organizations, as well as those organized by territory or product, **provide employees with latitude to act and make decisions** that respond to the needs of the local situation.
- f. This organization structure creates relatively nonspecialized jobs, provide more authority for decision-making and reduce reliance on rules and procedures.

5. **Geographical Departmentalization**
- a. Like product and customer structures, geographic departmentalization is **external to the organization.**
- b. With this structure, all **activities within a certain region are assigned to one manager.**
- c. Territorial departments are **advantages to organizations with widespread geographic dispersion;** physical separation makes centralized coordination difficult.
- d. Figure 8-4C illustrates a manufacturing organization structured by geographic departmentalization.
- e. Large multi-unit retail stores often use this structure.
- f. Two **advantages** to this structure are that:
  - 1) **managers can be assessed regarding their progress in a region.**
  - 2) this experience can **provide insights about how products and/or services are accepted in the field.**

6. **Multiple Departmental Bases**
- a. **Large corporations** use different bases at different levels.

b. Figure 8-5 illustrates how at each level different bases can exist both among within departments.
   1) Each product department or division will have all resources needed to act as an independent business unit.
   2) The departmental basis at the next level down is typically function.
   3) The next level is departmentalized by geography.

7. **Combined Bases for Departmentalization: The Matrix Organization**
   a. Attempts to **maximize the strengths** and **minimize the weaknesses of both the functional and product bases** by combining these two structures.
   b. Achieve the desired balance between function and product departmentalization by superimposing a horizontal structure of authority, influence and communication on the vertical structure.
   c. Figure 8-56 illustrates how personnel are assigned to both a functional department and a particular product or project.
   d. Thus, employees report to two managers. This **dual authority system** is the distinguishing characteristic of a matrix organization.
   e. This structure provides **advantages to organization which:**
      1) require **rapid change in two or more environments,** such as technology and markets.
      2) face uncertainties that **generate high information processing requirements.**
      3) must **deal with financial and human resources constraints.**
   f. Matrix organizations facilitate the utilization of **highly specialized staff and equipment,** which can be **shared** among units rather than needing duplication of resources.
   g. This design allows for **greater flexibility and quicker response in competitive conditions.**
   h. There is considerable diversity in the application of the matrix organization, yet the essential feature is the creation of overlapping authority and the existence of dual authority.

8. **Departmentalization in Multinational Corporations (MNCs)**
   a. The foreign activities are **extensions of the domestic business.**
   b. How the foreign activities are coordinated to achieve strategic outcomes involved issues similar to those of local activities.
   c. **Most prevalent** departmental basis is **territory.**
   d. MNCs with **diversified product lines** will find some advantages in the **product-based organization structure.**
      1) This structure assigns worldwide responsibility for a product to a single office and all units associated with that product report to that corporate product office.
      2) The basic product unit, termed a line of business (LOB) make decisions independently and succeeds or fails accordingly.
   e. MNCs with **very restrictive product lines** will use the **function approach.**

138

f. **Affected by the national culture.** Examples of Japanese versus Western approaches are discussed.

VI. **Span of Control**

A. The **determination of the number of jobs** to be included in a specific group.
1. Decision is concerned with determining the **volume of interpersonal relationships** a manager is able to handle.
2. Includes **both formally assigned subordinates,** as well as those who have **access to the manager,** for example in the capacity of committee chair.
3. The number of **potential interpersonal relationships increase geometrically** as the **number of subordinates increase arithmetically,** because managers contend with three types of potential relationships:
   a. **direct single relationships** occur between the manager and each subordinate individually; that is in a "one-to-one" setting.
   b. **direct group relationships** occur between the manager and each possible permutation of subordinates.
   c. **cross relationships** occur when subordinates interact with one another.
4. The **frequency and intensity** of the **actual relationships,** not the number of potential relationships, is what **determines the manager's span of control.**

B. **Actual Relationships** are used to determine optimum scan of control. Thus, three factors seem important:
1. **Required Contact**-generally the greater the inherent ambiguity existing in an individual's job, the greater need for supervision or required contact to avoid stress and conflict.
2. **Degree of Specialization**-the more specialized the and job, such as at lower levels in the organization, the greater the possible span of control. Managers can combine highly specialized and similar jobs into relatively large departments because employees may not need close supervision.
3. **Ability to Communicate**-the need to discuss job-related factors influences span of control. The greater the manager's ability to communicate concisely, the larger their potential span of control.

C. Span of Control and **Downsizing**
1. Figure 8-8 demonstrates how **increasing the span of control can reduce** the number of managerial levels and the number of managers.
2. Managers, especially those at middle levels, are reduced in larger proportions than non-managers during downsizing.
3. The final Management Focus discusses downsizing.
4. Downsizing is driven by the **belief that highly trained individuals, empowered with authority and competence, can manage themselves.**
5. Downsizing is **more widespread** now than ever before.
6. There have been **mixed outcomes:**
   a. **Positive** effects, such as **renewed commitment** by those who have benefitted and have been empowered, have been found.
   b. **Negative** effects, such as **increased stress** due to additional pressure due to larger numbers of subordinates, are also present.
7. For **downsizing** or flattening to have the most **significant impact:**

139

a.   managers and employees must **"add value"** to directives they receive, meaning individuals must take directives they receive and determine its full potential for adding to the organization's well-being and effectiveness.

b.   Other believe the success of downsizing depends upon the willingness and ability of employees to **provide quality service** and high performance, even **peak performance**, of their assigned duties.

c.   Others claim the single most important factor in determining success is the manager's ability to **comprehend the new relationship** between managers and non-managers; managers can no longer set themselves apart.

VII.   **Recap of Relationships Among Organizational Dimensions and Organizing Decisions**

A.   The final section of this chapter is a **useful review** in the form of lists of the various aspects of the organizing function.

B.   This section also clearly **illustrates the interconnectedness** of these aspects, for example as specialization increases what are the affects on span of control and authority.

ANSWERS TO DISCUSSION AND REVIEW QUESTIONS

1.   **Question:**   *What managerial and organizational purposes does the structure of an organization accomplish? What would be the evidence that would establish whether these purposes have been achieved?*

   Answer: The purpose of the organizing function is to achieve coordinated effort through the design of a structure of task and authority relationships. Thus, the structure of an organization assists in achieving the organization's goals and objectives. Measurement of goals and objectives, as described in the planning chapters, would provide evidence as to whether the structure of an organization is assisting in meeting the goals.

2.   **Question:**   *What would be the characteristics of firms that would have relatively complex, specialized, and formal organizational structures? What would be the characteristics of firms that would have relatively simple, generalized and informal organizational structures?*

   Answer: Organization that are relatively complex, specialized and formal are typically those that have diverse product lines and are more hierarchial or taller. Firms that are relatively simple, generalize and informal at typically flatter and more decentralized.

140

3. **Question:** *Explain the relationships between the four organizing decisions (division of labor, delegation of authority, departmental bases, and span of control) and the dimensions of organizational structure.*

   Answer: Organizational structure can be defined in terms of formalization, centralization and complexity. The relationships are illustrated in the chart on next page.

   Formalization is the result of high specialization or division of labor, centralization of authority, the use of functional/process departments and narrow spans of control.

   Increased centralization results from higher specialization or division of labor, greater centralization or less delegation of authority, greater use of functional or process departments, and narrower spans of control.

   Complexity, the third method to define organizational structure, is directly related to the dividing of work and creation of departments. Complexity increases with greater specialization or division of labor, centralization or minimal delegation of authority, decreased use of territorial, customer and product bases, and narrower spans of control.

ORGANIZING DECISIONS: → DIMENSIONS OF ORGANIZATION STRUCTURE:	High Level of Specialization Or Increased Division of Labor	Low Level of Specialization Or Decreased Division of Labor	Centralized Or Limited Delegation of Authority	Decentralized Or Expanded Delegation of Authority	Functional/ Process Departments	Territorial/ Customer/ Product Departments	Narrow Span of Control	Broad Span of Control
Formalization								
High	X		X		X		X	
Low		X		X		X		X
Centralization								
Centralized	X		X		X		X	
Decentralized		X		X		X		X
Complexity								
Greater	X		X		X		X	
Less		X		X		X		X

4. **Question:** *Identify the bases for the department in the college you attend or in the firm where you work. What alternative bases can you think of which might make a difference in the way the college or firm performs its work?*

   Answer: Answers to this question will vary considerably depending on the structure of you institution. To assist students in answering this question thoroughly, consider having copies of the organizational chart of the school available. An organizational chart of a well-known organization, such as a local fast food restaurant, could also be used. Encourage the students thinking by having them consider the organizational changes needed if the focus of the organization changed to be more customer driven, or if it were to expand geographically.

5. **Question:** *How does the culture of a country influence the way the organization in that country specializes jobs. For example does the Japanese culture encourage different levels of specialization than does the American culture?*

   Answer: Japanese firms typically have relatively narrow sets of business activities, unlike US firms. Thus, Japanese employees perform relatively fewer specialized jobs with relatively more homogeneous skills and experiences due to the fewer business specialties to be performed. A typical Japanese manufacturing job has less range than its US counterpart. Also the authority associated with each job is less, although the Japanese practice more participative management and thus workers have a say in matters that immediately affect their jobs. Middle managers are evaluated on their ability to initiate opportunities for workers to be involved. And Japanese firms more often are based on function and process. Japanese firms prefer to do business in few industries and create closer ties with their suppliers.

   These differences relate closely to the cultural differences in the two countries.

6. **Question:** *Explain the differences between potential and actual relationships among subordinates and managers and why actual, not potential relationships are important for assessing the appropriate span of control.*

   Answer: There are three types of potential relationships. These are 1) direct single relationships which occur between the manager and each subordinate individually; that is in a "one-to-one" setting; 2) direct group relationships occur between the manager and each possible permutation of subordinates; and 3) cross relationships which occur when subordinates interact with one another.

   More critical than potential relationships in determining a manager's appropriate span of control are his or her actual relationships, and specifically the frequency and intensity of these actual relationships. Thus, three factors seem important: 1) Required Contact-generally the greater the inherent ambiguity existing in an individual's job, the greater need for supervision or required contact to avoid stress and conflict; 2) Degree of Specialization-the more specialized and similar the job, such as at lower levels in the organization, the greater the possible span of control. Managers can combine highly specialized and similar jobs into relatively large departments because employees may not need close supervision; and 3) Ability to Communicate-the need to discuss job-related factors influences span of control. The greater the manager's ability to communicate concisely, the larger their potential span of control.

Thus, the intensity and frequency of relationships is far more significant in determining the "drain" on the manager and the appropriate span of control.

7. **Question:** *Obtain information about the spans of control among chairpersons of departments in the college you attend. Chances are, no two chairpeople have the same span of control. What account for these differences?*

   Answer: Once again, specific answers will vary greatly depending on the institution. In general, however, students should be encouraged to explore the factors with create differences among departments.

   Span of control is influenced by the actual relationships each chair has with members of his or her department, especially the frequency and intensity of these relationships. In addition, the formalization, authority for decision making and complexity of each department influences the span of control appropriate for each chair.

8. **Question:** *Using the same chairpersons as question 7, determine the degree of decentralization of authority for each by documenting the decisions which all chairperson can make without checking first with the dean. Then determine whether and why some chairperson have more authority compared to their peers.*

   Answer: This question allows students the opportunity to interview "real organizational members" and investigate an organization with which they are familiar.

   Differences in decentralization of authority probably will be explained in the terms of the text, such as the division of labor, the bases for structure and the individual's span of control. The explanation for the differences probably will also be explained in terms of the characteristics of the dean. As students report this information to the class, invite them to explore the issues of actual relationship, their intensity and frequency, and how these could be part of what the chair is explaining, although perhaps in different terms.

9. **Question:** *Explain the relationships among downsizing and the four organizing decisions and the dimensions of organizational structure.*

   Answer: The four organizing decisions:

   1. Division of Labor-Organizations with highly specialized jobs are relatively formal, complex, and centralized compared to those that use less specialized jobs, such as team-based jobs. Thus, downsized organizations, which are not as complex or centralizes will have a lower level of specialization or division of labor.

   2. Centralization of authority-Downsized organizations typically will be more decentralized because downsizing is driven by belief that highly trained individuals have the ability to make their own decisions effectively.

   3. Bases for departmentalization-Downsized organizations can still take many organizational "shapes" or design.

   4. Span of control-will be increased due to fewer middle managers.

   The Dimensions of Organization Structure:

   1. Formalization-is decreased as middle managers are removed; employees are given greater freedom in determining how to get work done.

   2. Centralization-is greatly decreased with downsizing.

   3. Complexity-is also decreased with downsizing since layers of the organization are often removed.

10. **Question:** *What is meant by employee empowerment and what is the relationship between , division of labor, and delegation of authority?*

   Answer: Employee empowerment involves designing jobs that are relatively unspecialized and having considerable delegated authority to decide job-related issues. The relationship between , division of labor and delegation of authority is shown in Figure 8-2. Empowerment increases in direct proportion with increased delegation of authority and decreasing job specialization.

END OF CHAPTER CASES

CASE 8-1: ORGANIZATION STRUCTURE OF SAXE REALTY COMPANY——————

CASE SUMMARY: This case summarizes the changes made in the organizational structure of Saxe Realty, a family owned and operated agency in San Francisco, whose growth has caused a mismatch between the firm's organization structure, management practices, and the requirements of a large firm. The realty has adopted a geographic-based structure with increased decentralization. Formal descriptions have been developed for all key management positions. The structure also provides for reporting channels from each branch associate to the chief executive officer.

1. **Question:** *Draw an organization chart that depicts the structure being implemented at Saxe.*

   Answer: The chart shown below illustrates the company's structure:

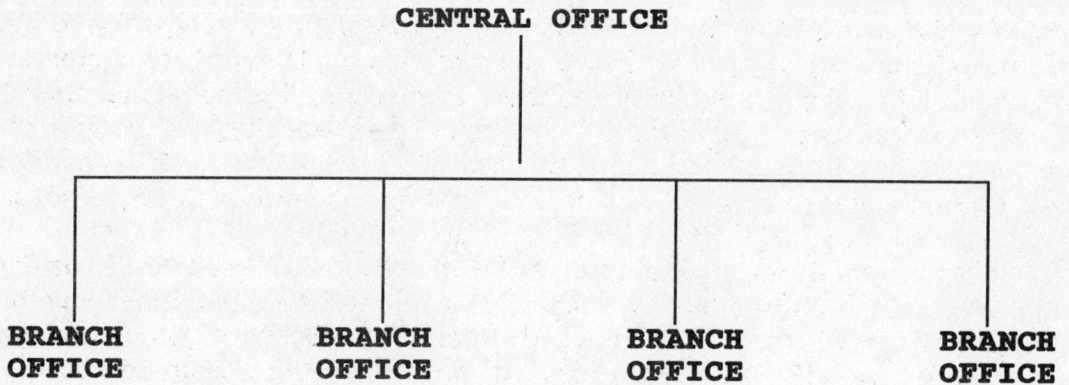

```
                    CENTRAL OFFICE
                          |
   ┌──────────────┬───────┴───────┬──────────────┐
 BRANCH        BRANCH          BRANCH          BRANCH
 OFFICE        OFFICE          OFFICE          OFFICE
```

   As the case notes, the company uses geography as the basis for departmentalization. The director of each branch office reports directly to the company CEO at the central office.

2. **Question:** *What alterative structures could Saxe have implemented, and what would be the advantages of each in comparison to the one Saxe did implement?*

   Answer: Several alternative structures are possible. For instance, Saxe could have implemented a functional-based structure which emphasizes the performance of each specialized operation. The company could have been structured according to customer time (e.g., consumer and commercial divisions). However, given the nature of the real estate business, the decision to use a geographic-based structure was a good one.

3. **Question:** *What are the relationships between the planning function and the organization function as depicted in the Saxe case?*

   Answer: The structural changes were the outcome of the planning function and were developed to meet the organization's planning objectives. The new structure also affects communications concerning planning objectives by establishing reporting channels for such communication from the branch offices to the CEO.

146

CASE 8-2: CHANGING THE ORGANIZATIONAL STRUCTURE OF A COLLEGE OF BUSINESS

CASE SUMMARY: This case presents students with the opportunity to explore the real implications of organizational change. The case itself is presented in the form of a memo from the Dean of the College of Business at Midwestern State University, in which he announces a recommended change in the college organizational structure.

He begins his memo by identifying reasons for considering a reorganization at this time. These reasons include: 1) a need to improve program quality so there is greater integration of the various functional areas of accounting, economics, finance, management, marketing and decision sciences; 2) a decline in the number of faculty; 3) changes in enrollment reflecting the shift from undergraduate to graduate students; 4) financial considerations; 5) a need for an increased emphasis on service; and 6) decreasing faculty turnover.

Next, the dean outlines the objectives of the reorganization. These are: 1) a desire to improve academic programs by assigning responsibilities for each graduate academic program to a specific academic unit. Under the proposed structure, the School of Accountancy will become responsible for the MS and Ph.D. programs, as well as the undergraduate program. The School of Management will include the MBA program and the Ph.D. in Business and will integrate the remaining undergraduate degree programs not taken by the School of Accounting or the Department of Economics. And the Department of Economics will assume responsibility for the MS and Ph.D. programs in Economics, as well as their undergraduate program.

The third part of the dean's memo is an enumeration of the sources of savings, which include 1) the decrease in the number of chairs or directors from the current six to the proposed three; 2) the significance of making this change at this time; 3) the possible elimination of one of the Associate Dean positions; 4) significant savings in the amount of faculty time devotes to various committees; 5) simplification of paper flow.

The dean highlights that the most significant changes will occur in the School of Management which will become responsible for the integration of previous functional areas. He recommends the additional of "Area Coordinators," to represent the areas currently not part of the School of Management.

The dean concludes his memo by outlining specific changes in staffing, particularly at the upper management level.

ANSWERS TO QUESTIONS FOR ANALYSIS:

1. **Question:** *Based on the information in the memorandum, draw the organization chart of the College of Business as it exists prior to reorganization.*

   Answer: See the chart below for this information.

2. **Question:** *How will the jobs of administrative personnel change as a result of the reorganization in terms of those factors which describe job specialization? How will the jobs of faculty members be changed in terms of specialization?*

Answer: The positions of the administrators (Associate Deans, Chairs, Directors) with become less specialized, and therefore administrators will have broader job tasks and more authority within their area. Faculty positions will also become less specialized as academic departments include both undergraduate and graduate areas, as well as their own research and service areas.

3. **Question:** *What happens to the Dean's span of control as a result of the reorganization? Will the new organization be more complex? more formal? more centralized?*

   Answer: The Dean's span of control will decrease because the actual relationship, both in terms of frequency and intensity will be reduced. The new organization will be less formal, since the means and the ends of each job will not be as specified; more decentralized, since decision-making will be moved down and throughout the hierarchy; and more complex vertically.

Dean of the College of Business

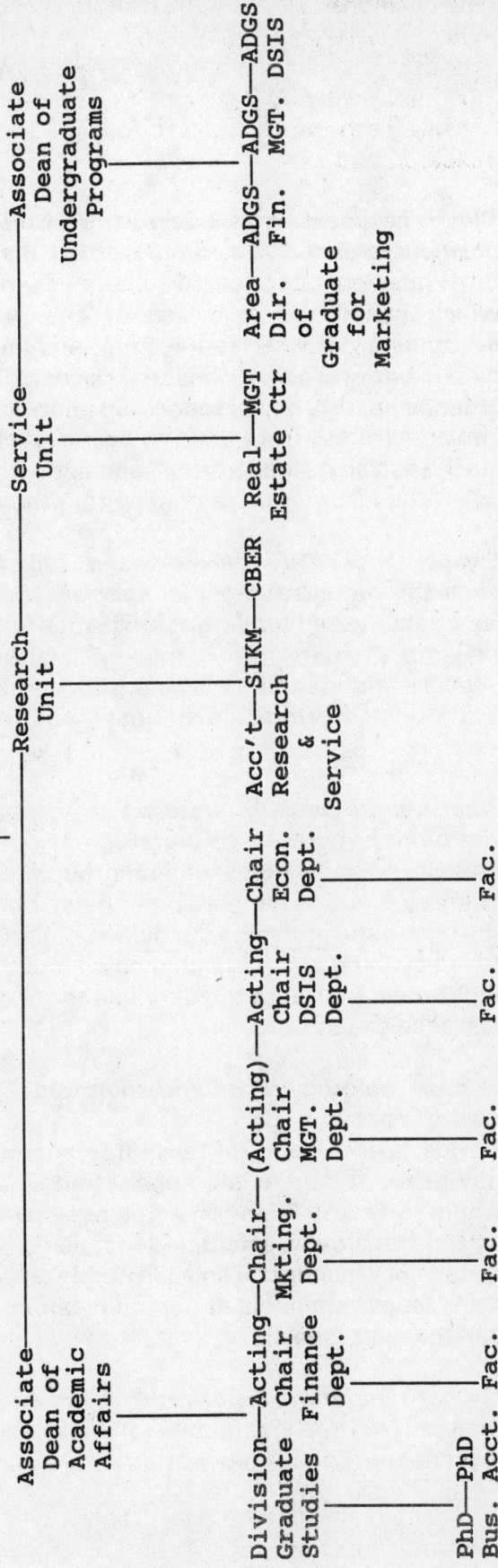

Associate Dean of Academic Affairs — Research Unit — Service Unit — Associate Dean of Undergraduate Programs

Research Unit:
Acc't — SIKM — CBER
Research & Service

Service Unit:
Real Estate Ctr — MGT Dir.
Graduate for Marketing

Associate Dean of Undergraduate Programs:
Area — ADGS — ADGS — ADGS
Fin. MGT. DSIS

Associate Dean of Academic Affairs:
Division Graduate Studies — Acting Chair Finance Dept. — Chair Mkting. Dept. — (Acting) Chair MGT. Dept. — Acting Chair DSIS Dept. — Chair Econ. Dept.

PhD — PhD Bus. Acct.

Fac.   Fac.   Fac.   Fac.   Fac.

1. **Question:** *Why is it necessary to create staff positions in organizations? Do these positions reduce the authority of line managers? Explain.*

   Answer: Staff positions are created to take advantage of specialized knowledge which cannot be expected of line managers. Specialties such as accounting, finance, engineering, and law cannot all be comprehended by any one individual; thus, the necessity arises for hiring specialists. In one sense, staff personnel do not diminish the authority of line personnel if staff are used in advisory capacities. But the influence of staff specialists can often supersede the influence of line managers when the issue or problem is within the realm of the staff's specialty.

2. **Question:** *Explain how a functional-based organization is most effective in obtaining the advantages of specialization of labor.*

   Answer: Functional-based departmentalization is based on grouping together individuals from the same specialization into one department. Specialization is the department's chief emphasis. Through interaction and a unified effort, substantial gains from specialization of labor are realized.

3. **Question:** *What are the primary purposes of organization structure?*

   Answer: The primary purpose of organization structure is to channel the work behavior of each individual and group toward objectives defined by the planning function. Accordingly, each job and department has specified objectives and prescribed activities. Communications, information flows, and decision making are channeled and distributed among the jobs and departments through the defined task and authority relationships which comprise the structure.

4. **Question:** *Discuss the advantages and shortcomings of a narrow span and wide span of control.*

   Answer: A wide span of control facilitates communication but in some cases, may result in inadequate supervision of employees because managers simply have too many subordinates to supervise. A narrow span of control can provide effective supervision but incurs greater management costs (more managers) and can create communication problems because of the longer channels of communication (due to the greater number of management levels).

5. **Question:** *In what type of business would a product structure be used?*

   Answer: Product structure is effective for businesses that produce a wide variety of products. Today, product structures are common in food, toiletries, and chemical industries. Philip Morris (maker of over 50 brands of cigarettes, Miller beer, and paper products) is a major corporation that's structured by product.

6. **Question:** *If you were managing a group of research and development professionals, would you use a wide or narrow span of control? Why?*

   Answer: A wide span of control should be used because the subordinates are highly skilled and do not require close supervision. However, before deciding upon the exact span of control, other factors should be considered, such as managerial ability, the nature of the subordinates' jobs, and the time available to do the job.

7. **Question:** *Why would large organizations like Eastman Kodak, Boise Cascade, and Gulf and Western tend to use multiple organizational structural forms ?*

   Answer: Large organizations tend to use multiple structural forms because they have widely different components (divisions, subsidiaries) each with different tasks, technologies, and structural needs. No single structural form effectively accommodates a very diverse organization.

8. **Question:** *Differentiate between horizontal and vertical complexity.*

   Answer: Horizontal complexity refers to the degree of complexity at one organizational level (for instance, the level of complexity in the finance and marketing departments). Vertical complexity refers to the number of managerial levels in a organization.

9. **Question:** *Describe the benefits to a matrix structure and identify some of the reasons some managers resist using this structure.*

   Answer: The matrix structure allows an organization to attempt to maximize the strengths and minimize the weaknesses of both the functional and product bases by combining the two structures. This structure allows for rapid change in two or markets, and allows for greater flexibility and quicker responses in competitive conditions. In addition, the matrix structure assists organizations which must deal with financial and human resources constraints by utilizing highly specialized staff and equipment by sharing them among departments.

   Some managers resist utilizing the matrix structure because the decision-making and resources get moved from their control to shared control throughout the organization. In addition, this structure can be more expensive as certain personnel functions, such as evaluations for each individual, must be handled by two sets of departments.

10. **Question:** *Explain the conditions which have caused organizations to rethink their structures and how they are organized.*

    Answer: Historically, managers tended to group jobs into divide jobs into rather narrow specialties because of the advantages of division of labor. This thinking was encouraged by Frederick Taylor as much as 90 years ago due to his findings that the ability of workers to develop areas of

151

expertise or specialization increased productivity. However, continued study of the fit between the worker and the work has lead to some variation of this thinking, although many industries continue to utilize Taylor's approach with great success.

The changing market due to globalization has caused management theorists and research to continue to explore the effectiveness of various approaches. What has become increasing clear over time is that there is no one right way in which to structure an organization or divide the work. What does appear to be an organizational constant at this point, is that individuals working in teams, which have been given the authority to define their own work approach, are the most productive and involve workers to such a level that increased worker satisfaction is being reported.

11. **Question:** *In your opinion, what problems could potentially arise with a matrix organization design?*

    Answer: The major problem which can arise is role conflict and role ambiguity among members of the product development team. This problem arises because each member has two bosses—a supervisor in the functional department from which the member was recruited to serve on the team and the manager of the product development team. Often, this violation of the unity of command principle can create confusion and conflict within each team member especially when two bosses place conflicting time demands and expectations on the individual.

12. **Question:** *Based on what you know about matrix design, what do you believe are the design's potential problems.*

    Answer: This question is intended to encourage students to think about problems that can arise with this rather complex design. Problems can include role conflict and ambiguity which members of the matrix team can experience because they report to two bosses, the tendency toward excessive participative decision making on the matrix team, and overemphasis on team processes to the exclusion of consideration of the external environment.

13. **Question:** *Why is the matrix organization design so popular in organizations with a technical and research orientation?*

    Answer: Because in these organizations, the need to bring specialists together to solve problems or complete tasks is great. By using a matrix design, management is able to bring together the needed expertise without totally disrupting the organization.

LEARNING OBJECTIVES

After completing Chapter 9, students should be able to:

Define   organization design in terms of the universalistic and contingency viewpoints.

Describe   the implications of technology, environmental uncertainty, and strategy for the design of organization structure.

Discuss   the fundamental differences between classical and neoclassical organization design.

Compare   the alternative arguments that conclude there is no one best organization design.

Identify   criticisms of the universalistic viewpoints by those who support the contingency viewpoint.

CHAPTER SYNOPSIS

This chapter addresses organization design by presenting the two primary perspectives of design theory: the **universalistic approach** ,which assumes there is one best way to design an organization; and the **contingency approach** which proposes that the best design depends on the particular situation.

Two universalistic designs are discussed: **Classical Organization Design** (widely used in the late 1800s) **and Neoclassical Organization Design**. Two forms of Classical Design, **Bureaucratic Organization Design and Classical School Organization Design**, are presented with attention focused on each perspective's major principles.

Neoclassical design, developed in response to the shortcomings of classical design, is discussed in terms of its key assumptions. The Contingency Approach, which supports that the best design depends on the situation, is addressed by focusing on three key variables which substantially influence organization design—**technology, the environment, and strategic choice**. Concerning the environment variable, three types of environments (**stable, changing, and turbulent**) are defined, sub-unit (departmental) design and sub-environments (specifically, the **product market, technical-economic, and scientific sub-environments**) are discussed. The chapter concludes with a look at the third influential contingency variable, strategic choice. Generic strategies, **cost leadership, differentiation, and focus** and Alfred Chandler's four-stage corporate growth process are outlined. Structures that best apply to these strategies/stages are presented. This final section's key message: organizational structure should follow strategy.

The **Management in Action**, which opens this chapter, explains the evolution of organizational designs to the present-day genesis of the virtual corporation. Named by Jan Hopeland of Digital Equipment Corporation, virtual corporations will focus on their core competencies and outsource the rest of their work. This design allows for more rapid response to opportunities and changing conditions than traditional large, capital intensive, vertically integrated corporations. Virtual organizations rely on the partnerships they create with their outsourcers.

The **first Management Focus** describes how General Motors, a classical, bureaucratic structure, has organized its subsidiary, Saturn with features of a neoclassical structure. Organized as a collection of small, self-directed units, Saturn employees are empowered with the authority to make all their own decisions. The result is a high-demand car and improved morale among employees. The **second Management Focus** provides four examples of how firms cope with uncertainty through their organizational structures. With innovative designs, employees are free to involve themselves with a wide variety of other employees and various aspects of the organization resulting in creative, timely products and improvements for the company. The **final Management Focus** highlights three companies who were 1992 Baldrige Award winners for the excellent quality management systems. The importance of involving customers and employees in quality improvement efforts is also mentioned.

TEACHING TIPS

LECTURE & DISCUSSION IDEAS

1. An effective way to generate class discussion on the Bureaucratic Design is to have students relate their experiences with a bureaucratic organization. They should focus on their positive and negative reactions to their encounter. A question for students to ponder: is some degree of bureaucracy needed in all organizations? How can management determine when bureaucracy becomes excessive? What are the signs?

2. Often in discussing technology as a contingency variable affecting organization design, students tend to underestimate its importance because they relate technology only to manufacturing firms. To expand their understanding of the technology concept, ask them to identify the technology of organizations besides manufacturing businesses such as an insurance company, hospital or university. Then, have them consider how these service technologies affect organizational structure.

PROJECT / EXERCISE IDEAS

1. An effective way to increase your student's understanding of the dynamics of the various organizational designs is to assign them the task of researching and preparing a report on a business which primarily uses a particular design approach e.g., bureaucracy, contingency design. You may want to assign students companies which are profiled frequently in common press articles and noted for their innovative and usually effective structures. Information sources about companies are *Fortune, Forbes, Business Week,* and *The Wall Street Journal.* In their written or oral reports, students should focus on explaining the company's design features, the factors contributing to the structure's development, and its strengths and shortcomings.

2. One way to enhance your students' understanding of the link between an organization's strategy and structure is to select an industry that's well covered in the management literature and have your students research the major competitors in the industry in terms of their differing strategies and structures. As a group assignment,

each group can present a written and/or oral report on a particular competitor, explaining the company's strategy and then discussing its structure, focusing on how the structure helps and hinders strategy implementation, and on past strategy and structure changes by the company. Class discussion can focus on comparing and contrasting the different companies' strategies and structures. (Suggested industries to use: the soft drink, automobile, tobacco, home appliance, computer, and petroleum industries.)

3.   Have students research further the findings of Weber, Woodward and Chandler, as well as the Hawthorne Studies. Students could then be asked to debate one another regarding the merits of these studies.

4.   You can supplement your discussion of bureaucracy by inviting an expert on the organizational form from your school's political science department. Another potential speaker could be a historian who could provide insights into Max Weber (the father of bureaucracy) and his Ideal Bureaucracy. These speakers could discuss early forms of bureaucracy, its substantial growth in the 1940s and 1950s, its advantages, shortcomings and its applications today in organizations.

5.   See Additional Question #10 for an idea on how to encourage students to compare and contrast differences in organizational structures.

LECTURE OUTLINE NOTES

I.   Designing organizational structures is a **difficult task** because:

   A.   There are **no clear-cut criteria** for choices.
   B.   Contemporary management theory provides general guidelines but they are **contradictory and contain limiting assumptions.**
   C.   **Contemporary organization design theory** contains two categories of thought (Universalistic Approach & Contingency)   (Table 9-1 summarizes the differences):

II.   **Universalistic Approach**-states that there is one "best way" to design an organization. However, there are two universalistic designs, which are quite different: Classical Design and Neoclassical Design.

   A.   **Classical Organization Design**—a natural extension of specialization of labor to the organizational level, i.e., the design of jobs determines the design of organizations. (See Figure 9-1 which depicts this assumption of Classical Organization Design).
      1.   Classically designed organizations are:
         a.   **highly complex**
         b.   **highly formalized**

   c. **centralized regarding authority**

2. Classical Organization Design was widely used in the **late 1800s,** when a primary social and managerial concern was efficient use of resources and maximum production.

3. During this time, **two sets of different, though compatible, perspectives** on Classical Organization Design emerged. Both Bureaucracy and Classical School designs **stress labor specialization and centralized authority** to design organizations that minimize the negative impact of jobholders.

  a. **Bureaucratic Organizational Design**

   1) Unlike the modern-day negative connotations which the term bureaucracy brings to mind (e.g., inefficiency, red tape, frustration), the "ideal bureaucracy" was promoted by many as superior in precision, stability, discipline, and reliability.

   2) It **de-emphasizes human idiosyncracies** in favor of mechanical predictability.

   3) Bureaucratic Design has **five key characteristics:**

    a) It has a **clear division of labor** with well defined, understood, and routine jobs.

    b) Each manager has a **clearly defined relationship** with other managers and sub-ordinates via a **formal hierarchy.**

    c) Behavior is guided by specific **rules, policies, and procedures.**

    d) Managers **minimize favoritism** via impersonal application of rules, policies, discipline, and rewards.

    e) Managers use **rigid and fair selection criteria** in hiring personnel.

   4) Proponent **Max Weber** asserted that a bureaucratic model is superior in any situation.

  b. **Classical School Organization Design**

   1) The approach refers to ideas expressed in the **early 1900s** and **stresses that design follow certain principles of organization.**

   2) The **key principles** are:

    a) **Division of labor**—highly specialized jobs.

    b) **Unity of direction**—jobs grouped according to function or process and grouped into departments.

    c) **Centralization of authority.**

    d) Jobholders must have **authority commensurate with responsibility.**

    e) **Unity of command**—each jobholder should report to only one supervisor.

B. **Neoclassical Organization Design**—characteristics are **opposite** to those of Classical Organization Design. **Developed in reaction to Classical Organization Design** (see Figure 9-2).

1. **Characteristics** of neoclassical organization designs are:
   a. **low complexity**
   b. **low formalization**
   c. **low centralization**
   d. **relatively wide spans of control**
   e. **heterogeneous departments**
2. **Support** for the Neoclassical Design is **based on two assumptions** (uniqueness of individuals and the demands of the situation):
   a. The **uniqueness of individuals** cannot be ignored.
      1) **Hawthorne studies** were the first to understand the importance and impact of individuals.
         a) Studies conducted at **Western Electric Plant, Hawthorne, Illinois**
         b) Found that workers were members of **friendship groups.**
            i. These groups defined the level of output considered fair and equitable.
            ii. These groups seemed to exert greater influence than managers, and with authority to back their influence.
      2) **Classical Design's Inherent Flaws**-appears to reward wrong behavior and fails to take into account consequences of human behavior in the workplace.
         a) Early study analyzed relationship between rules and job behavior and found that extensive use of rules, characteristic of highly complex, formal and centralized organizations (such as classically designed organizations), encourage workers to follow rules as through they were the ends rather than the means.
         b) Second study supported idea that rules define minimum level of expectations and discourages innovative behavior.
         c) Chris Argyris believes the Classical Design suppresses the development and growth of employees and is not congruent with the human needs:
            i. autonomy
            ii. self-expression
            iii. accomplishment
            iv. advancement
   b. **The Demands of the Situations**
      1) Classical Designs gained popularity when conditions were relatively stable; however, this gave way to instability and uncertainty. There were advances in:
         a) communication
         b) transportation
         c) manufacturing processes

d)   medicine

     2)   Organizations had to become more adaptable and flexible.

     3)   Rensis Likert, a leading advocate of the Neo-Classical Design, stated in contemporary society this design utilizes human and technical resources more fully.

III.   **Contingency Approach**-states that the **"best way"** to organize **depends upon the situation.**

     A.   Different organization designs **facilitate different purposes** and should be structured depending on whether is must be relatively:

          1.   **efficient and productive,** or

          2.   **adaptive and flexible.**

     B.   The critical issue becomes determining the circumstances which create the need to be efficient and productive or adaptive and flexible. Among the **circumstances or variables** which influence the design decision are:

          1.   **age of the organization**-older organizations tend to be more complex, formalized and centralized than younger ones.

          2.   **size of the organization**-tendency for large organizations to be designed more along the lines of Classical than Neo-Classical.

          3.   **form of ownership**

          4.   **technology**

          5.   **environmental uncertainty**

          6.   **strategic choice**

          7.   **member (employee) needs**

          8.   **current fashion**

     C.   The **three most apparent implications** for management are technology, environment, and strategic choice.

          1.   **Technology and Organization Design** - first variable affecting design

               a.   Defined as **"the types and patterns of activity, equipment and material, and knowledge or experience used to perform tasks."**

               b.   Can be either **machines or knowledge**

               c.   **Technology as a Contingency**

                    1)   **Affects the design of jobs** which in turn effects the design of organizations.

                    2)   The organization design is thus, contingent upon the state of the technology which management incorporates in the design of individual jobs.

                    3)   See Figure 9-3.

                    4)   **Joan Woodward** studied the relationship between technology and structure.

                        a)   **Classified technologies as unit, mass or process production.**

                            i.   Unit production refers to production to meet a customer's specific order.

                           ii.   Mass production refers to the production of large quantities, such as on an assembly line.

                          iii.   Process production refers to producing

materials or golds on the basis or weight or volume.

b) Found a **strong relationship between performance and both organizational design and technology.**

   i. Highest performing organizations with unit and process technologies used Neo-Classical Design and had jobs with low specialization, high depth and range, which were best organized in a structure with relatively low complexity, formalization, and centralization.

   ii. Highest performing organizations with mass production technologies used a Classical Design, since no latitude is needed on the part of the employees.

c) Woodward's research resulted in **principles that suggest how technology influences organizational design.**

   i. The more **complex the technology,** the **greater the number of managers and levels** of managers.

   ii. The more complex the technology, the **larger the number of clerical and administrative personnel.**

   iii. The **span of control** of first-line managers **increases from unit to mass production systems,** and then **decreases** from **mass to process production systems.**

d. **Flexible Manufacturing Technology (FMT)**

   1) Enables managers to use the **computer to integrate sections of the organization into a continuous operation.**

   2) This technology **increases the flexibility of manufacturing** through the ability to:

      a) transfer information, material and other resources throughout the organization

      b) design products quickly in consultation with others

      c) set up machines to manufacture only the needed quantity, thus, reduce the need for inventory.

   3) Major effect of FMT on structure is to **challenge the case for classical design in mass production firms.**

      a) FMT in mass production settings creates managerial problems similar to those in job order and process manufacturing settings.

      b) Major managerial problem is managing interdependent activities under rapidly changing conditions.

   4) FMT and other developments in manufacturing enables different parts of the company to become more

159

independent as they become more dependent on one another; this paradox emphasizes the importance of integrating the activities.

2. **Environment**-the second critical variable affecting organizational design.

    a. **Competitors, suppliers, customers, creditors, and the government** as some of the environmental factors which must be considered.

    b. Environmental **Types**

        1) **Stable**-where there is little unpredictable change.

        2) **Changing**-where shifts or adjustments in the competition's strategy, the market, personnel practices, technology, etc. create rather frequent but somewhat expected changes.

        3) **Turbulent**-where changes are unexpected and unpredictable.

    c. **Mechanistic and Organic Structures**

        1) **Mechanistic** structures have the same characteristics as **Classical Designs** and are **optimal in stable** environments; consequently jobs can be designed to include minimal depth and range, and maximum specialization.

        2) **Organic** structures have the characteristics of **Neo-Classical Designs** and are most suited to **turbulent environments**; thus, jobs must be designed to give employees considerable range and depth.

        3) **Relationships** between environment conditions and design is shown in **Figure 9-6**.

    d. **Designing Organizational Sub-Units**

        1) Departments which face **uncertain and turbulent** environments should follow **Neo-Classical Designs**.

            a) despecialized

            b) informal

            c) decentralized

        2) Departments which face **certain and predictable** environments should follow **Classical Designs**.

            a) specialized

            b) formalized

            c) centralized

        3) The contingency viewpoint is reflected: "the **internal functioning** of organizations must be **consistent** with the **organization task, technology, or external environment, and the needs of its members** if the organization is to be effective.

        4) Design the departments to **fit the demands of the department's sub-environments**, which may result in having a diverse range of organizational designs within the same organization.

            a) One sub-environment consists of the market for a company's products.

b)   The technical-economic sub-environment refers to the external sources of information and resources which are required for production.

c)   The third sub-environment is the scientific knowledge and know-how that firms relate to through their research and development departments.

5)   Designing the organization on a **department-by-department basis** can result in **considerable diversity** within one organization.

      a)   Departments designed along **Classical Lines** could **achieve interdepartmental coordination through rules, procedures and policy.**

      b)   Department designed along **Neo-Classical** guidelines could achieve coordinated **efforts only through cross-departmental teams and individuals.**

e.   **Creating External Networks** of Cooperative Relationships with Suppliers, Distributors, and Even Customers.

1)   Networks of relationships enable organizations to **achieve both efficiency and flexibility.**

2)   Network organizations have become pervasive, being referred to as the **models for 21st century organizations,** and have only just begun to be examined.

3)   Enables the principal organization to **rely upon smaller, closer to the market partner** to notice and respond to changes.

4)   The **exact form of a network varies.**

      a)   Relationships could be with:
           i.   Key suppliers
           ii.   Marketers and distributors
           iii.   Parent organization, who deals independently with product designers, suppliers, etc.

      b)   Decisions involve which function to buy, which to purchase, and how to manage relationships with partners.

      c)   Managers in network organizations have less environmental uncertainty , because much uncertainty has been subcontracted.

      d)   These structures are, in a sense, boundary-less organizations.

3.   **Strategy and Organization Design** - third variable affecting design

a.   Involves the **selection of missions and objectives,** and appropriate **courses of action** to achieve these objectives.

b.   **Figure 9-7** illustrates this relationship.

c.   Thus, specific **organization design should follow from a specified strategy,** Generic or Growth.

1) **Generic Strategies**-organizations can select one of three general strategies.
   a) **Cost leadership**
      i. Implies that the firm will outstrip its competition by being the **low cost producer.**
      ii. The firm will **emphasize efficiency and productivity.**
      iii. Thus, organization design must encourage efficiency and productivity, which the **Classical Design,** with its emphasis on complexity, formalization and centralization accomplished.
   b) **Differentiation**
      i. The second generic strategy
      ii. Involves the firm in **creating products that are unique.**
      iii. Requires **creativity, basic research skills, strong marketing, and a reputation for quality.**
      iv. Quality is one means a company can use to differentiate itself from its competition.
      v. Requires **flexible response to changing customer preferences and perceptions.**
      vi. Organizational structure which facilitates the strategy would tend toward **Neo-Classical characteristics,** such as low specialization, low formality, and decentralized authority.
   c) **Focus**
      i. The third generic strategy
      ii. Involves achieving **either cost leadership or differentiation or both in a particular segment of the market.**
      iii. Rather than competing throughout the market, the firm focuses on one segment.
      iv. Thus, the focus strategy implies a trade off between market share and responsibility.
      v. The design implies **a mix of both Classical and Neo-Classical** characteristics because the firm can attempt both cost leadership and differentiation.
2) **Growth Strategies**
   a) Chandler concluded that organization structures follow the growth strategies of firms and found that **growth strategies tended to follow certain patterns:**
      i. **Initial Stage**-the firms are typically involved

162

in a **single industry and perform a single function.**

ii. **First stage** of Growth is through **Volume Expansion** where **current customers purchase more of current product.**

iii. **Second stage is Geographic Expansion,** through which the firm continues as it had, but with larger geographic areas by means of **field units.**

iv. The **third growth stage is Vertical Integration** during which the firm either **buys or creates other functions.**

v. The **final growth stage, Product Diversification,** involves the firm in **new industries with through merger, acquisition or creation (product development).**

b) **As firm moves through these stages, organization structure must change.**

i. **Initially, Classical Design** is appropriate.

ii. As the firm moves **through** the steps of **geographic expansion and then product diversification,** concerns for **adaptability and flexibility increase.**

c) Some evidence indicates that the relationship between growth strategy and structure is **applicable in other countries.**

d) The idea that organization design should change to reflect the organization's strategic choice **implies a growth-oriented strategy.**

e) Also **implies managers** will **understand the need for changing the structure.**

f) The process approach to organization design is the orientation to change and the knowing.

g) The strategic choice approach assumes managers know that they should alter the organization design as they change the firm's strategy from volume expansion to product diversification.

ANSWERS TO DISCUSSION AND REVIEW QUESTIONS

1. **Question:** *Contrast the main arguments of universalistic and contingency approaches to organization design. Which of the two approaches is easier to implement in practice? Explain.*

   Answer: The two approaches essentially differ on one point: the Universalis Approach assumes there is one best way to design an organization regardless of the situation while the Contingency Approach assumes that the best way to design an organization depends on the situation. The Universalistic Approach is easier to implement because, though the particular design may be ineffective, there is only one type of design to implement. The major challenge which the Contingency Approach presents is determining the correct design to implement. One organization may incorporate several different designs if it assumes a contingency perspective.

2. **Question:** *Contrast the main features of the classical and neoclassical organization designs.*

   Answer: Classical Organization Design is a natural extension of labor specialization to the organizational level, i.e., classically designed jobs have high specialization, low depth and low scope. Organizations are thus highly complex, with high formalization and centralized authority. Organizational design characteristics follow the characteristics of classically designed jobs. Neoclassical Organization Design assumes that organizational structures should have low complexity, low formalization, and low centralization. Neo-classicists believe that this type of structure is an effective response to the uniqueness of individuals and the demands of situations.

3. **Question:** *Compare what you believe to be the popular meaning of the term "bureaucracy" with the meaning in management literature. Why do "bureaucracy" and "bureaucratic" have negative connotations ?*

   Answer: Typically the terms bureaucracy and bureaucratic connote an ineffective organization which is bogged down by regulations and red tape. Rules govern its operations to the point that it cannot quickly respond to environmental demands. In short, obeying the regulations is the bureaucracy s prime objective. Of course, this view does not apply to all bureaucracies; however, many people view bureaucracies in this way.

4. **Question:** *Explain why an organization with classical design characteristics is likely to be more efficient and productive but less flexible and adaptable than an organization with neoclassical design characteristics.*

   Answer: Classically designed organizations operate with much centralized control because of the high degree of formalization and centralization. Thus, top

164

management can more easily control the organization s activities which in many cases results in efficiency and productivity (given capable top management). However, these characteristics of Classical Design do not provide an organization with flexibility. Organizations structured along the Neoclassical approach have low formalization, centralization and complexity which afford greater adaptability. An organization is less restricted by regulations and procedures and decision-making authority is delegated to the lower management levels making the organization more capable of quickly reacting to environmental demands.

5. **Question:** *Compare two organizations that you know about, either through employment or membership, in terms of classical and neoclassical design characteristics. What explains the differences you find in the two organizations?*

   Answer: The question is intended for students to apply what they have learned about the Classical and Neoclassical design approaches in assessing the structure of an actual organization. Differences in design between the two organizations may be due to several factors including differences in the management philosophies of the two companies, and in the external environments, strategies, and technologies of the two companies.

6. **Question:** *What are the bases for the opinion that technology is an important contingency variable? Do you believe that technology is the primary factor to be considered when management designs a structure? Explain.*

   Answer: Technology is an important contingency variable because by influencing the design of jobs, technology influences the design of organizations. Joan Woodward s classic studies also illustrate the significant relationship between technology and organizational structure. Technology determines the process of an organization's work and thereby substantially influences how the organization is structured to perform its work.

7. **Question:** *What are the relevant sub-environments of business firms? of hospitals? of universities? What sub-units, or departments, exist in typical business firms, hospitals, and universities to deal with those sub-environments?*

   Answer: Departments must be designed to fit the demands of the department's sub-environments. One sub-environment consists of the market for a company's products; the technical-economic sub-environment refers to the external sources of information and resources which are required for production; the third sub-environment is the scientific knowledge and know-how that firms relate to through their research and development departments.

See diagram on next page.

TYPICAL SUB-UNITS OR DEPARTMENTS THAT EXIT
IN INDUSTRIES TO DEAL WITH VARIOUS SUB-ENVIRONMENTS

THREE TYPICAL SUB-ENVIRONMENTS

	Market Sub-environment	Technical/Economic Sub-environment	Scientific Knowledge Sub-Environment
INDUSTRIES:			
Business Firms	Marketing	Computer Support Accounting	Research & Development
Hospital	Admissions Community Education	Pharmacies, Medical Records, Accounting	Affiliated Universities, Laboratories, Experimental Therapies & Drugs
University	Public Relations, Admissions, Publications	Registrar, Payroll Financial Aid	Research & Publications, Library, Achieves

166

8.   **Question:**   *What are the bases for the opinion that environment is an important contingency variable? Do you believe that environment is a primary factor to be considered when management designs a structure? Explain.*

       Answer: A business organization is not an entity in and of itself. Rather a business organization is a mechanism or system for providing customers and members/employees with desired services and goods. As such, the organization must be able to respond to the changes in those desires. Some business organizations are providing goods and services that remain most consistent and stable over time. Other industries, such as technology research and development firms, are responding to customer and member needs which are changing very rapidly, and thus, these industries exist in turbulent environments.

                     Environment is a primary and critical factor to consider as an organization determines what structure will best meet their objectives. These objectives are met within a certain type of environment, from very static or stable to highly changeable or turbulent, and thus, the organization must function within those environments. Research has well documented that certain organizational designs work better in some types of environments.

9.   **Question:**   *What are the bases for the opinion that strategy is an important contingency variable? Do you believe that strategy is a primary factor to be considered when management designs a structure? Explain.*

       Answer: Proponents of this view assert that an organization must fulfill its strategy in order to meet long-term objectives upon which the organization's survival depends. Thus an organization's structure should serve to accommodate its strategy.

10.   **Question:**   *Develop an explanation of the important contingency variables that would integrate the technology, environmental, and strategy points of view.*

       Answer: The intent of this question is to spur students to apply the three perspectives in identifying important variables which affect organizational design.

END OF CHAPTER CASES

CASE 9-1: GENERAL MOTORS: ITS CHANGING ORGANIZATION DESIGN————
CASE SUMMARY: This case describes the organizational changes that have taken place at GM since World War II. The first change to the original structure moved the company to a divisional organizational structure consisting of five independent divisions-Chevrolet, Pontiac,

167

Oldsmobile, Buick, and Cadillac. Each of these divisions essentially competed against one another.

This divisional structure continued throughout the post-World War II period when Gm became the largest manufacturing organization in the world; however, the design began to impede progress and market response, in part due to the massive corporate support staff. When Roger Smith took over as CEO in 1981, he began to move the decision making down into the operating divisions and reduced the number of staff at corporate headquarters.

In 1984 he created two autonomous groups, BOC, which consists of Buick, Oldsmobile and Cadillac, and CPC, consisting of Chevrolet, Pontiac and GM of Canada. Roger Smith delegated each group complete authority to determine their own structure. BOC chose to organize around four autonomous product groups or strategic business units (SBUs), which would have complete authority to design, produce and sell cars. CPC, in contrast, organized around functional lines with centralized authority, with a matrix overlay to facilitate communication across functional lines.

In 1993, the new CEO Jack Smith (Roger Smith had been replace by Robert Stempel, Stempel was replaced by Jack Smith) had to respond to the continuation in the drop of GM's market share and thus, created a single operating division, North American Operations (NAO).

Currently, GM has returned to the original five divisions-Chevrolet, Pontiac, Oldsmobile, Buick and Cadillac-as marketing units. All other work, including production, product design and purchasing are done as one unit.

ANSWERS TO QUESTIONS FOR ANALYSIS:

1. **Question:** *Identify the environmental forces that have driven General Motors to change its organizational design.*

   Answer: The environmental forces which have driven GM in their past have included competitive forces from around the world, especially Asia and Europe. Additional environmental forces were expectations from their customers, tightening regulations regarding safety and lessening pollution. The environment for auto manufacturing and distribution went from being stable to turbulent and uncertain.

2. **Question:** *Have the changes in structure been in the appropriate direction? Have they been misguided? Explain your answer and your reasoning.*

   Answer: In some ways Roger Smith's plan of two autonomous groups reinforced duplication of effort. There had been five such areas of duplication and Roger Smith did bring those to only two potential areas. However, BOC and CPC, by having complete authority to shape themselves, maintained numerous aspects of the previous duplications. Jack Smith has taken centralization further reducing duplication. However, GM lost valuable time from Roger to Jack.

3.	Question:	*Discuss the possibility that redesigning the organizational structure is actually an irrelevant response to what ails General Motors.*

	Answer:	Some would suggest GM lost touch with customers and their changing expectations. Thus, GM really needed to reconsider the theory of their business as Peter Drucker would content. By asking: "Who are the customer?" "What do the customers value?" "What will they value in the future?" Next Gm needed to review and revise their mission statement. They may have let critical opportunities to make adjustments pass them by.

CASE 9-2: FEDERAL EXPRESS STRIVES FOR A LEAN ORGANIZATION———

CASE SUMMARY: This case discusses Federal Express strategic objective of maintaining a lean organizational structure. They have responded to this challenge by: developing an awareness campaign, communicating and sharing information with other firms, implementing a reward system for ideas, reviewing all personnel requests, examining applicability of self managed work groups, offering group incentives, applying scientific management, and hiring temporary employees when possible.

ANSWERS TO QUESTIONS FOR ANALYSIS: ———————————

1.	Question:	*What do you think of Federal Express's interpretation of the term "lean organization"? Does it seem that the company is practicing a modern-day version of managing by principles of organization? Explain.*

	Answer:	Students need to recognize that a lean organization is needed to remain flexible in such a dynamic environment, and profitable in such a competitive one. Students may feel that such principles of organization are being adhered to too rigidly at the expense of people considerations.

2.	Question:	*What are some of the potential outcomes associated with downsizing an organization? Are all these outcomes good for Federal Express?*

	Answer:	Downsizing affects the entire organization. Some potential outcomes are: shorter chain of command; wider span of control; more delegation of authority; changes in behavior of both employees and managers; and changes in levels of productivity and efficiency. Many of these changes could work for or against Federal Express depending on how they are handled.

3.	Question:	*What are the technological, environmental, and strategic forces influenced Federal Express's decision?*

	Answer:	The forces that influenced Federal Express decision included: increased automation, increasing competition, their commitment to avoid layoffs, fast industry growth, multinational operations, and economic pressures.

1. **Question:** *Briefly describe the key characteristics of Bureaucratic Design.*
   Answer: Bureaucratic Design has five major characteristics: 1) a clear division of labor and well-defined and routine jobs; 2) a formal organizational hierarchy wherein each manager has a clearly defined relationship with other managers and his or her subordinates; 3) behavior guided by specific rules, policies, and procedures; 4) minimal favoritism shown by managers due to impersonal application of rules, policies, discipline, and rewards; and 5) the use of rigid and fair selection criteria in hiring employees.

2. **Question:** *Briefly summarize the findings of the Woodward research. What three principles did her work produce?*
   Answer: In her study of British manufacturing firms, Woodward found that the highest performing unit and process production firms used Neoclassical Design while the highest performing mass production firms used the Classical Design structure. The three principles developed from the conclusions of her research are: 1) the more complex the technology, the greater number of managerial personnel and managerial levels; 2) the more complex the technology, the larger the number of administrative and clerical personnel; and 3) first-line managers span of control increases from unit production systems to mass production systems and then decreases from mass to process production systems.

3. **Question:** *What factors have hampered the progress of research in establishing definitive technology structure relationships?*
   Answer: Progress has been hindered by inconsistencies in research; namely, in defining and measuring the technology and structure concepts and in selecting the level of analysis (individual, group, or organizational).

4. **Question:** *Briefly describe the three generic strategies used by organizations.*
   Answer: The strategies are: 1) cost leadership wherein the firm stresses production efficiency and productivity to become the low price leader; 2) differentiation where the firm creates products perceived to be unique (due to brand image, product features, customer service, or some other factor); and 3) focus where the firm strives to attain cost leadership and/or differentiation in a market segment.

5. **Question:** *Classical organization theory proposed that stability and predictability are appropriate objectives of organization. Do these objectives conflict with creativity and innovativeness?*
   Answer: Stability and predictability are appropriate in stable environments and routine technology. If the organization is in an uncertain environment

and uses complex technology, then it should facilitate creativity through the creation of an organic structure.

6. **Question:** *Is it true that all organizations have some of the characteristics of bureaucracy? Moreover, can it be argued that bureaucracy is necessarily a poor form of organization?*

    Answer: All organizations are bureaucratic in the sense that bureaucracy is the rationalization of collective activities. The answer is not a yes or no, but of degree. A bureaucratic organization which approaches the ideal type may not be a "poor" organization if it is compatible with the demands of the environment and technology. This is a conclusion and prescription of contingency theory.

7. **Question:** *Briefly describe the four-stage process of growth strategies proposed by Alfred Chandler.*

    Answer: Chandler asserts that organization growth strategies develop via a four-stage process: 1) volume expansion—the firm makes and sells more of its products/services to customers; 2) geographic expansion—the firm's activities spread into new geographic areas; 3) vertical integration—the firm buys or creates other functions; and 4) product diversification—the firm moves into new industries via merger, acquisition, or creation. Chandler notes that as a firm moves through these growth strategies, its structure changes from a Classical to Neoclassical Organization Design.

8. **Question:** *Explain how a bank CEO could use the ideas of contingency theory to design the structure of the bank, including the designs of each of the major banking divisions such as commercial loans, installment loans, trust, and operations.*

    Answer: The question demonstrates how organization design can be applied at two levels. The overall organization level design may best be managed using classical principles because customers demand relatively homogeneous services and have little disposition to participate in the delivery of services. At the subunit level, however, the different units may have customers who require more or less diverse services and more or less participation in the delivery of services. A trust departments customers and needs is quite different from the installment loan department. The implication is that the trust department should reflect more neoclassical characteristics than the installment loan department.

9. **Question:** *Describe how the emergence of modern manufacturing technologies such as flexible manufacturing has altered the way technology is thought to relate to organizational structure.*

    Answer: The question is designed to get students to think about the paradox of FMT. The effect of FMT on organization structure is to challenge the use of classical designs in mass production firms. FMT emphasizes integrating activities and emerging neoclassical structures to achieve integration.

171

10. **Question:** *What organizational design is used at your university or college? What contingency factors must be considered? How has the school's structure changed over time? How is it different from other institutions of higher education in the area? If there are differences, what creates the differences in structure and design? Are they the most effective structure to be used?*

Answer: Answers to these questions will be determined by the actual circumstances at your school. Students may be encouraged to explore the differences more by creating comparison charts.

10 THE CONTROLLING FUNCTION

LEARNING OBJECTIVES

After completing Chapter 10, students should be able to:

Define   the controlling function in terms of the three features of effective control.

Describe   representative standards, information, and corrective action for general methods of control.

Discuss   the bases for distinguishing among preliminary, concurrent, and feedback control methods.

Compare   the control techniques designed to maintain quality of inputs with those designed to maintain quality of outputs.

Identify   the different standards that can be used to assess potential profitability of capital investments.

CHAPTER SYNOPSIS

This chapter addresses the controlling function, the third primary managerial function, by focusing on the functions and techniques of the three major types of control: preliminary, concurrent, and feedback.

Topic coverage begins with a definition of the controlling function as all managerial activities undertaken to ensure that actual results conform to planned results. Three conditions must exist for the controlling function to be effective: standards must exist, information indicating deviations between planned and actual results must be available, and corrective action must be possible.

Preliminary control is defined as managerial actions that increases the probability that actual results will compare favorable with planned results. The preliminary control of human resources (via effective selection and recruitment), materials (via statistical sampling), capital (using the payback method, rate of return on investment, and/or discounted rate of return techniques), and financial resources (via budgeting) are described.

Discussion of concurrent control focuses on its primary tool, the supervisor's daily direction of subordinates and the importance of communication in achieving effectiveness. Feedback control, focusing on historical outcomes as the basis for future actions, is addressed by discussing its four major forms financial statement analysis, standard cost analysis, quality control, and employee performance evaluation which is cited as the most important and difficult feedback control technique.

The chapter's **Management in Action** discusses re-engineering as the "radical redesign of business process (BPR) to achieve major gains in cost, service or time," which has gained tremendous following in international business communities, as well. Re-engineering does not simply speed the existing functions within a business, but that re-engineers the core system or process. In this particular synopsis, the company referred to, Barr & Stroud, were being negatively effected by perestroika and glasnost. But rather than allow their company to collapse, top management began undertaking radical change. To achieve their re-engineering goals, both management and employees had to understand fully that small incremental changes were not going to provide the needed response. Re-engineering actually changes former ways of doing business.

In the **first Management Focus** provides a short summary of Du Pont's recent need to attend to their employees' welfare. When efforts were made to increase profits, their previous excellent safety record began to shatter. Top management had to quickly shift their focus to reemphasizing principles that had guided Du Pont safety for many years. While these efforts may have initially been perceived to be contradictory, or at least not in compliance, with the new thrust for increasing profits, the end results were an increase in safety, as well as an increase in profits. Du Pont's strong commitment to employee welfare really paid off. In the **second Management Focus** provides insights as to how three executive women were able to balance their family priorities and their careers with assistance from their organizations. The role of governmental policies is also explored. The **final Management Focus** poignantly illustrates the role of control systems for recovery of information systems and records immediately following a disaster. Examples from the World Trade Center bombing are given to illustrate the role of companies specializing in these services and the need for all organizations to consider a disaster-recovery plan.

TEACHING TIPS

LECTURE & DISCUSSION IDEAS
1. An effective way to personalize the concept of control is to ask students to characterize the control system(s) they've experienced as members of an organization. Have the students consider the purposes of the control system(s), the mechanism(s) used, and effects.

2. Another way to bring the control concept "closer to home" for your students is to ask them to consider and describe the "control system" that they maintain in their own lives. (For example, what types of control do they employ concerning material purchases?)

3. Another question for students to ponder in the discussion of the three types of control: which type is most challenging to successfully implement and maintain? Have students substantiate their replies.

PROJECT / EXERCISE IDEAS
1. Have your students describe control systems that they have personally experienced (for instance in part-time jobs, in school, or in their own families). Discussion should focus on the characteristics of the control system and its perceived benefits and shortcomings. Did they feel stifled by the system? Why?

2. One way to extend your students' understanding of control systems at work in organizations is to divide the class into groups, and as a group assignment, have the students prepare a written or oral report on a control system in operation at a local

business. The report should include the system's major characteristics, the primary forms of preliminary, concurrent, and feedback control, and an overview of how the system has evolved through the years.

3.   To further student understanding of preliminary control of materials, have your students, as a group or individual project, interview a manager involved in quality control of incoming materials and prepare a written report on the nuts and bolts of statistical sampling as a mechanism of materials quality control. The manager can discuss how the technique is used by the company (how often, etc.) and also other techniques that are used to ensure acceptable quality of purchased materials.

4.   Invite a representative of a local company to speak on the same topic. You might want to invite a financial comptroller to describe the control function in the respective company's financial activities. A quality control inspector could also provide added insight into the nuts and bolts of establishing effective product quality control.

5.   Invite a standard cost analyst from a local business to talk to your class about how standard cost analysis is used by his or her respective company. The analyst can discuss how standard costs for direct labor, direct materials, and overhead are established, and how deviations are identified and corrective actions are taken. Ask the analyst to discuss past experiences when corrective actions were necessary and the complexities of allocating overhead costs per unit produced.

LECTURE OUTLINE NOTES

I.   **The Controlling Function**
   A.   Includes all activities the manager undertakes in attempting to **insure that actual results conform to planned results.**
   B.   Requires **three conditions:**
      1.   **Standards** must be **established.**
         a.   They are **criteria** against which **future, current, or past actions** are **compared.**
         b.   They must be **clear** and logically **relate to** the work unit's **objectives.**
      2.   **Information indicating deviations** between actual and standard results must be available.
         a.   Most easily acquired for activities with specific concrete results (for example, production output).
         b.   More difficult for less tangible output (for example, managerial work outcomes).
      3.   **Action** to correct deviations between actual and standard **must be possible.**
   C.   **Individuals responsible** for taking corrective action must have:

175

		a.	**ability to discover the need** for such action
		b.	**necessary authority.**
	D.		There are **three types of control**: preliminary, concurrent, and feedback. (See Figure 10-1 for an illustration of the controlling function.)

II. **Preliminary Control** - first type of control

    A.   Managerial **actions that increase the probability** that **actual results** will **compare** favorably **with planned results.**

        1.   Focuses on **preventing deviation** in **quality and quantity** of resources.

        2.   **Future focused.**

        3.   Often involves **implementing policies.** (Note: setting policies is part of the planning function.)

    B.   **Preliminary control of human resources.**

        1.   Achieved through **implementing effective personnel selection and placement procedures.**

            a.   **Staffing**—procedures designed to **obtain qualified managers.**

            b.   **Selection and placement**—procedures designed to **obtain qualified non-managers and operatives.**

            c.   Considered by many among the **most important task managers do.**

    C.   **Preliminary control of materials**

        1.   Actions taken to ensure that **purchased raw materials** (to be converted into a finished product) **meet quality standards.**

        2.   **Statistical sampling** is a frequently used tool.

            a.   Management **sets a maximum percentage level** (e.g., three percent) of defective items that is acceptable from the supplier.

            b.   Material is **inspected via a sample of materials** selected randomly from the shipment. **Percentage of defects is calculated** and if **exceeds maximum** allowable levels, the **shipment is typically rejected.**

            c.   **Errors** in sampling can result in accepting a lot containing more than the allowed percentage of defects or rejecting a lot that contains less than allowable amount.

            d.   **Deciding whether to accept or reject** materials based upon sampling, or whether to **take another sample** is based on straightforward, **pre-established instructions.**

    D.   **Preliminary control of capital**

        1.   Control of capital acquisitions reflects the need to **replace existing equipment or to expand the firm's productive capacity.** Acquisitions are in the **capital budget**, an intermediate and long-run planning document that details alternative sources and uses of funds.

        2.   The **control methods for screening investment proposals** each formulate a standard which must be met:

            a.   **Payback method**

                1)   **Simplest** and most widely used

                2)   Calculates the **number of years** needed for proposed capital acquisition to repay its original cost out of generated future cash earnings (years = original cost/annual additional after tax cash inflow; see example

calculation in the chapter).
3) **Shortcomings**
    a) **Does not** produce a **measurement of profitability**.
    b) **Does not** account for the **time value of money**.
b. **Rate of return on investment**
    1) A **measure of profitability** calculated by **dividing annual additional net income after taxes produced by the acquisition by the acquisition's original cost** (see example calculation in the chapter).
    2) Calculated return rate percentage is **compared to a standard**.
    3) **Easy to understand**.
    4) **Does not** account for the **time value of money**.
c. **Discounted rate of return**
    1) A **measure of profitability** which **accounts for time value of money**. Similar to the paycheck method, only cash inflows and outflows generated by the investment are considered.
    2) **Widely used** because it can be **applied to** virtually **any capital investment project**.
E. **Preliminary control of financial resources**

1. Involves **budgeting as principal means of controlling availability and cost of financial resources**.
2. **Important control goal is timing cash availability** to meet cash obligations, i.e., ensuring that cash is available during inventory buildup and used wisely when accumulated inventory is sold (see Figure 10-4 for a graph illustration of the cash and inventory relationship).
3. **Considers all cash inflows an investment will generate**, not just those to the payback point.
4. **Important financial ratios** are used in financial resources control: **current ratio, acid-test ration, inventory turnover, and average collection period**.

III. **Concurrent Control** - second type of control

A. **Monitors ongoing operations** to ensure objectives are pursued.
B. Consists primarily of **supervisors' actions that direct the work of subordinates**.
C. **Direction** refers to the acts of managers when they:
    1. **Instruct subordinates** in the proper day-to-day work methods and procedures.
    2. **Oversee subordinates' work** to ensure objectives are achieved.
D. Degree of supervision **depends on nature of** subordinates' **tasks**.
E. The primary function of first-level supervisors; the **activity's frequency decreases** as a manager **moves up the organizational hierarchy**.
F. Effective direction depends on **interpersonal communications** (directives must be responsible, intelligible, appropriately worded, and consistent with organizational goals).

IV. **Feedback Control** - third type of control

A. **Focuses on historical outcomes** as the bases **for correcting future** actions. Four widely used **methods:**

177

1. **Financial statement analysis**
   a. detailed analysis of the **firm's balance sheet, income statement, and sources-and-uses-of-funds statement** to determine firm's earnings power and ability to meet short- and long-term obligations.
   b. **Accounting system principle sources of information** to evaluate historical results.
2. **Several ratios** are used as analytical tools:
   a. **Current ratio**—ratio of **current assets to current liabilities.** Most often-used measure of liquidity (firm's ability to meet obligations as they come due).
   b. **Acid-test ratio**—ratio of **current assets, less inventories and prepaid expenses, to current liabilities.** More rigorous liquidity test.
   c. **Accounts receivable turnover**—ratio of **credit sales to average accounts receivable.** The higher the turnover, the more rapid the conversion of accounts receivable to cash.
   d. **Inventory turnover ratio of cost of goods sold to average inventory.** High ratio: possible seriously low inventory; low ratio: potential over investment in inventory (funds could be used more profitably elsewhere).
   e. **Ratio of net income before interest and taxes to interest expense indicates ability to meet long-term obligations.** High ratio preferred. If ratio is low and **NIBIT/IE** ratio is high, firm may not be taking advantage of debt as a source of funds. As a rule, a firm's proportion of debt should vary directly with stability of its earnings.
B. **Standard cost analysis**
   1. Major contribution of **scientific management era.**
   2. Provides a means for managers to **monitor costs with an aim toward ultimate reduction.**
   3. Analysis **compares actual costs** (e.g., manufacturing) **to predetermined costs** via establishment of a standard cost accounting system. In manufacturing, analysis involves:
      a. **Establishing standard costs** for direct labor, direct materials, and overhead per unit of output; i.e., a unit costs $10 for materials, $8 for labor, and $3 for overhead. Direct labor cost is comprised of standard usage of labor (for example, two hours per unit) times standard labor price ($4 an hour).
      b. Accounting system provides information enabling **comparison of actual** labor, materials, and overhead **cost per unit with standard costs.**
      c. **Deviations** (for example, an unfavorable labor variance when actual labor costs exceed standard) **are identified and corrective action is determined.**
C. **Management control of quality**
   1. Controlling quality is important **throughout** the product/service production **process.**
   2. Management **thinking** about the quality/productivity relationship has greatly **changed in the last 20 years.**

3. **Historically** quality has been viewed as a controlling activity **near the end of a product's manufacturing process.**
4. This **was a costly process** since all items were inspected and found defects **resulted in waste or rework.**
5. **Now** quality control is **built in as part of product development.**
6. Quality in **all aspects of the organization** is important, and **all employees** should be **involved** in bettering quality.
7. With this perspective:
   a. The **number of defects declines** which boosts output.
   b. Making it right the first time **reduces** many of the **rejects and reworking.**
   c. **Making employees responsible** for quality **eliminates** the need for **inspection.**
D. **Employee performance evaluation**
   1. The **most difficult and important** feedback control technique.
      a. Important because **people** are an **organization's most critical resource.**
      b. **Difficult** for several reasons:
         1) **Performance standards** are **seldom objective** and straightforward.
         2) **Involves** much **subjective judgment.**
         3) **Incentives tied to attainment of standards**, which **causes discontentment.**
         4) Need **various evaluation systems** throughout the organization.

ANSWERS TO DISCUSSION AND REVIEW QUESTIONS

1. **Question:** *Explain, utilizing an example, why the planning and control functions cannot exist without one another. Should the one function be given priority status over the other? Why or why not?*

   Answer: Planning includes determination of what standards or objectives are to be met. Essentially, the outcomes of planning, well done correctly, should dictate the controls to be utilized to measure if plans are being accomplished. An organization that plans without utilizing controls will have no method to measure or determine if plans are being accomplished; nor, will there ba a process for implementing corrective actions. Without plans, an organization would not know what to measure or what path to follow.

   On an individual level, as well as an organizational level, both plans and controls are essential. If a student plans to get a college degree but does not have means to determine or control/measure if the courses completed are adding to a degree (a transcript, the university catalog describing required courses for each major, accumulation of a grade point average), then the student will never be certain if or when a degree is completed. Similarly, students on the track team could implement control mechanisms, such as monitoring their long-distance running speed, but have no plans of how to improve their speed. The measuring alone is unlikely to assist the student in improving their speed. A plan must be in place, which includes hours of practice, meets, stretching and warm-up exercises, etc.

Given their symbiotic nature, both planning and controlling are equally important.

2. **Question:** *Standards are derived from objectives. How might the setting of inappropriate objectives lead to the setting of inappropriate standards? Illustrate, using an example.*

   Answer: Standards are the criteria for comparison of future, current, or past activities. Because standards are so tightly linked to objectives, effective standards must be clear, related, and measurable for best results. Otherwise, managerial actions may be inappropriate or lead to undesired performance. For example, the standard set for raw materials on an assembly line impacts the quality of finished products from the line.

3. **Question:** *Describe how managers at a bank could utilize preliminary control procedures. Would their efforts differ significantly from those of managers at a manufacturing company? Why or shy not?*

   Answer: Bank managers could use preliminary controls to ensure that new hires arrive with certain skills and abilities.
   A manager of a manufacturing firm would be involved with very different specific preliminary controlling efforts because the plans and standards of that organization are different than those of a bank. However, the process would be basically identical. For example, both managers could define the qualifications for new hire. Although each organization would require different skills and abilities, the process of defining those standards and hiring to meet their specific standards would be similar.

4. **Question:** *A lack of organizational control can lead to disastrous results. When could too strict adherence to organizational control mechanisms lead to disastrous results?*

   Answer: The question is intended to get students to understand that too much control, information, or detail can be damaging. Also, managers need to be sensitive to the degree of direction they provide subordinates.

5. **Question:** *Describe how the owner of a small bakery could utilize cost and quality control procedures to improve the operating performance of his/her business.*

   Answer: The owner could establish standard costs for direct labor, direct materials and overhead per unit of output. Train each baker and sales person to build in quality in his or her work station and reduce costs.

6. **Question:** *A number of standards have been discussed as measures of investment profitability. These measures include the payback period, the rate of*

return, and the discounted rate of return. Illustrate cases in which each of these profitability measures may be considered superior to the others.

Answer: They all exist because they're used to evaluate investment proposals. Each method emphasizes a particular aspect of an investment and its own advantages and disadvantages.

7. Question: *How might an organization utilize control procedures to help ensure that employees adhere to high ethical standards?*

Answer: Organizational leaders could measure and maintain inventory figures to guard against employee theft. The could an assessment of employees' ethical behavior as part of the evaluation. They could ask establish procedures and practices for employees to sign out equipment they use.

8. Question: *Under which circumstances would the use of feedback control procedures be inappropriate?*

Answer: Feedback methods are inappropriate if output can't be measured or goals operational.

9. Question: *Why might managers have to make trade-offs between adherence to various types of control mechanisms (e.g. between cost and quality controls)?*

Answer: When quality is viewed as occurring at the end of a production process. When productivity and quality are not viewed as conflicting but are the concern of all members of the organization.

10. Question: *If employee performance evaluations have to be based on subjective criteria, should they be utilized at all? What is the reasoning behind your answer?*

Answer: Subjective information can be very valuable in that employees are provided with feedback and information on one person's reaction to their behavior, quality of work, etc. This data, along with other, more quantifiable information, establish a more complete picture, than quantifiable data alone would provide.

11. Question: *Directing is a crucial aspect of control; and information received (the perceived performance of subordinates) and information sent (orders and instructions) are key elements of directing. What abilities and traits do you believe are associated with effective directing?*

Answer: If directing is conceptualized in terms of communicating, then the traits associated with effective communication are equivalent to those associated with effective direction. The student should not attempt to equate directing with managing. Managing includes more than directing—one can direct effectively, yet manage ineffectively.

181

CASE 10-1: BENCHMARKING PRACTICES AT XEROX

CASE SUMMARY: This case describes the importance of benchmarking as companies are striving to remain competitive in the global marketplace. To benchmark effectively, a company needs to secure support from top management, as well as integrate the process throughout the company. The case define benchmarking as: "the continuous process of measuring products, services, and business practices against those of the toughest competitors or companies renowned as leader" in that industry.

There are four major types of benchmarking activities typically used. These include internal, functional, generic and competitive. Internal benchmarking is the development of a process to transfer information regarding the best internal practices among divisions. Functional benchmarking focusses on determining and subsequently implementing best practices, regardless of their industry of origin. Generic benchmarking, the third type, identifies individuals within the company who are responsible for documenting specific means of improving process, overseeing their implementation and resolving cross-functional disputes. The final approach, competitive benchmarking implementing competitors' practices which improve the company's work.

ANSWERS TO QUESTIONS FOR ANALYSIS:

1. **Question:** *Can benchmarking be used successfully by all businesses, both large and small? Why or why not?*

   Answer: Yes, even if the company provides a single good or service, they still can make comparison functionally or generically. Initial costs may seem prohibitive, however, savings over time make benchmarking a worthwhile investment.

2. **Question:** *A critical component of functional benchmarking is identification of companies which employ best practices. How would an organization go about finding such companies?*

   Answer: Companies could identify other organizations that are implementing best practices through various means. Some of these include: studying financial figures of other companies, researching market share of competitors to determine which companies are going better according to that indicator, analyzing stock costs and increases, and researching customer satisfaction rates of other companies.

3. **Question:** *What incentives exist for an organization like L.L. Bean to share the secret of its "best practice" with Xerox?*

   Answer: Since these two companies are not direct competitors with each other, improving one is not going to result in a market decline of the other. Improvement in one domestic company helps overall national economy. Lay offs at Xerox results in their former employees being less likely to spend money at L.L. Bean, for example.

4.   **Question:**   *Provide examples of how one or several actual companies (besides those mentioned in the case) could employ each of the four types of benchmarking activities to improve operating results.*

        Answer: Within a hospital, for example, the four types of benchmarking could occur.

1. Internal Benchmarking: Due to overlap in departments as care to patients is provided, and research is completed, departments could share information and ideas regarding best internal practices.
2. Functional Benchmarking: The hospital could compare their services to other health care organizations and providers, such as HMOs, private doctors, clinics, or other research facilities, such as universities or private research organizations.
3. Generic Benchmarking: This approach would have efforts focused within divisions. For example, physical therapists could be observed and methods discovered and implemented to improve quality of care throughout the other units.
4. Competitive Benchmarking: The hospital could compare itself to other hospitals and make appropriate improvements.

CASE 10-2: DEVELOPING A NEW PRODUCT

CASE SUMMARY: The discussion of this case can center on any number of issues. For example, the decision to make the product has extended over a period of time with checkpoints along the way. Securing Underwriter's Laboratory approval, setting up a pilot line, and obtaining marketing projections indicate sequential gathering of data and experience. At this point, the issues seem to focus on the validity of the standard—a 14 percent markup and the appropriateness of the cost data. The manager's decision is to accept or reject the judgments of functional experts who, with the exception of the accountant, have a vested interest in producing the thermostat.

ANSWERS TO QUESTIONS FOR ANALYSIS:

1.   **Question:**   *If you were the plant manager, what would be your decision regarding the MT?*

        Answer: Student responses will likely differ. Some will argue for producing the thermostat, given the investment already made in the product and manager's estimates that production costs will probably be reduced substantially in the near future. However, others will probably be more cautious and argue that the decision should be put on hold until more cost analysis is conducted and until it's determined whether the new method for welding contacts will succeed. In the case (based on an actual incident), the plant manager went ahead with production, reasoning that the plant had made too great a commitment to back off.

2.   **Question:**   *If you decided to manufacture the MT, would your decision indicate that the standard of 14 percent markup is not valid?*

        Answer: Not necessarily. The decision could indicate that the 14 percent markup is feasible if expected reductions in costs occur and thus a 14 percent markup does not price the company's thermostat out of the market.

ADDITIONAL QUESTIONS AND ANSWERS

1. **Question:** *Briefly describe the three necessary conditions for an effective controlling function.*

   Answer: For an organization's controlling function to be effective: 1) standards must be established to be used as criteria against which future, current, or past actions are measured; 2) information indicating deviations between actual and standard results must be available; and 3) action to correct deviations between actual and standard must be possible.

2. **Question:** *Explain how the payback method of investment control works. What are its major shortcomings?*

   Answer: The simplest and most widely used capital control technique, payback calculates the number of years needed for a proposed acquisition to repay its original cost out of future cash earnings. The method has two shortcomings: it does not produce a measurement of profitability and it does not account for the time value of money (i.e., a dollar in the hand today is worth more than one received tomorrow).

3. **Question:** *Explain the difference between current and acid-test ratios.*

   Answer: The most often used measure of liquidity, the current ratio is the ratio of current assets to current liabilities. The acid-test ratio differs from the current ratio in that inventory and prepaid expenses are not included in the calculation of current assets in computing the ratio. The latter ratio is considered to be a stronger indicator of a firm's ability to meet its current obligations.

4. **Question:** *Briefly describe the four most widely used methods of feedback control.*

   Answer: The four methods are: 1) financial statement analysis which includes a detailed analysis of a firm's balance sheet, income statement, and sources-and-uses-of-funds statement; 2) financial ratios (such as current, inventory turnover, and debt to equity ratios); 3) quality control analysis which involves analyzing finished products to ensure they meet quality standards; and 4) standard cost analysis which compares actual costs to predetermined standard costs in manufacturing via the establishment of a standard cost accounting system.

5. **Question:** *Differentiate between preliminary, concurrent, and feedback control.*

   Answer: Preliminary control involves managerial actions taken to increase the probability that actual results will compare favorably with planned results. It is control before the fact. Concurrent control are actions taken by managers that direct the work of subordinates. It is control of the activity while it occurs. Feedback control focuses on historical outcomes as the bases for correcting future actions.

6.   **Question:** *In your opinion, what are the shortcomings of using statistical quality control for monitoring the quality of goods produced?*

      Answer: The major shortcoming is that the technique is not flawless and can result in error. For instance, the technique involves inspecting only a sample of a lot of goods. If mistakes are made in obtaining samples to inspect, the sample might not reflect the quality of the overall lot. However, statistical sampling is by far the most effective technique for the amount of time and effort required as it is usually impossible to inspect every product off the production line.

7.   **Question:** *Why is employee performance evaluation considered the most important and most difficult feedback control technique ?*

      Answer: It is the most important because the technique involves the evaluation of an organization's most important asset-—people. It is the most difficult because employee performance evaluation is the most subjective technique. It essentially involves one individual judging another and this situation presents the potential for a variety of problems (e.g., rater and ratee defensiveness, rater bias).

8.   **Question:** *What is the primary purpose of the preliminary control of cash?*

      Answer: The major purpose is to ensure that cash is available during the period of inventory buildup and is used wisely during periods of cash abundance. Typically, as inventories build up, cash decreases to pay debts incurred in producing the inventory. However, cash is most needed at this point. Preliminary control of cash attempts to resolves this dilemma.

9.   **Question:** *Explain why the standards which chief executive offices (top management) must consider are more subjective and ambiguous than those which subordinates (first-level management) must consider.*

      Answer: The chief executive must achieve goals that are long-run and relatively unstructured. First-level managers relate more closely to the basic output of the organization and consequently standards are more objective and straightforward.

10.   **Question:** *Explain how the college or university you attend controls the teaching performance of the faculty. Organize your answer in terms of the three types of control.*

      Answer: This is an excellent classroom exercise and can be assigned as a group project. Ordinarily, students will find that preliminary control is the dominant types with some use of concurrent control such as student evaluation.

11.   **Question:** *Discuss the Japanese term kieretsu. What effect does this have on U.S. business?*

      Answer: Translated to English, kieretsu means business society. These societies or clusterings of businesses are composed of several layers of contractors and thus, provide Japanese companies the ultimate means of preliminary control. There is a 100% probability that suppliers and vendors conform to the manufacturer's plans and objectives.

Use of a kieretsu effectively dictates that U.S. nationals will never be integrated into mainstream management positions in Japanese companies.

LEARNING OBJECTIVES

After completing Chapter 11, students should be able to:

Define	the meaning of motivation.
Describe	the difference between content, process, and reinforcement theories of motivation.
Discuss	why most behavior is thought to be goal directed.
Identify	the five core motivational dimensions used in job enrichment.
Compare	the distinguishing characteristics of the reinforcement and expectancy theories of motivation.

CHAPTER SYNOPSIS

This chapter addresses motivation by centering on three subjects: the nature and overall process of motivation, significant motivation theories, and management programs designed to increase employee motivation. Motivation is defined as an inner state that activates or moves. Attention is given to the difficult managerial challenge of motivating employees, since motivation is a factor which cannot be observed, only inferred from employee behavior, and since people are motivated by different things.

The bulk of the chapter focuses on the major motivation theories. The authors present the theories in two groups—**content** theories (Maslow's need hierarchy and Herzberg's two-factor theory) and **process** theories (equity theory, expectancy theory, and reinforcement theory). Each theory is discussed in terms of its major principles, findings of empirical tests of the theory, strengths and shortcomings of each theory, and its contributions to management. The section concludes with the Porter-Lawler motivation model which integrates elements of all of the theories described in the chapter.

Job enrichment and pay incentive programs are presented as two ways management can increase employee motivation. Discussion of money as a motivator focuses on the requirements and drawbacks of relating pay to performance. Programs at Nucor and DuPont are described. Two other major strategies to motivate employees, **Employee Stock Ownership Plans** and **flexible working hours**, are also presented.

The chapter opens with a **Management In Action** section which examines the effects of a cultures work ethics and fairy tales on the motivational level of its people. The chapter's **Management Focus** segments discuss the changes in motivation many managers experience around age 40, the extrinsic and intrinsic rewards that are motivators at Mary Kay Cosmetics, and the pay levels and other motivational factors at employee-owned Publix supermarkets.

TEACHING TIPS

LECTURE & DISCUSSION IDEAS

1. One effective way to generate student interest in motivation theory is to have them assess each theory in terms of their own motivational makeup. Ask your students to determine which model best depicts the motivation process and to explain why. Also, have them discuss each model's value to managers.

2. To illustrate the applied implications of expectancy theory, have your students 1) identify a management situation from their work experience; 2) assume the manager's role; and 3) prepare an action plan to motivate subordinates, based on expectancy theory. Of course, the plan should focus on boosting a subordinate's expectancy, instrumentality, and valences. For example, a subordinate's expectancy (perceived relationship between effort and performance) can be strengthened by such managerial actions as providing the subordinate with all needed materials to perform the tasks, sufficiently training the employee in the task's procedures, and clearing any barriers (e.g. red tape, etc.) that hinder employee task performance. The most challenging managerial task is boosting employee valences, specifically, the subordinate's desire for outcomes which the organization can realistically provide.

3. If there are students in your class who are native to countries other than the United States, ask them to confirm (or disagree with) Holfstede's Dimensions as reported for their native region or country. Have the class as a whole discuss the similarities and differences among motivating factors in different countries around the world.

4. Students should have their own opinions on the relationship between the age of forty and the motivational wall. If there are students near or over age 40 in the class, ask them to discuss their experiences with motivational inspiration, and to compare and contrast their experience today with their experience of 15 or 20 years ago. Draw up a list of the key work motivators for the older and younger students in the class, and look for commonalities and differences.

PROJECT / EXERCISE IDEAS

1. Have your students develop their own theory of motivation. They should be allowed to incorporate into their theory perspectives from the theories presented in the chapter; however, the final product should largely be based on their own experiences and opinions. In developing their theory, students should:
   a. Explain the theory's principles (using a diagram, if preferred).
   b. Support the theory with logic and examples from their own work experience and examples in business.
   c. Discuss the theory's application to management.
   This assignment can be used as an individual or group project. It is particularly interesting when students present their theories in class; a lively debate typically results among students with widely different theories.

What motivates subordinates? Everyone has a different answer, as illustrated by the different motivation theories and by opinions in the media of managers in different businesses and in different managerial levels within businesses. Have your students develop a profile of what motivates subordinates based on interviews with a particular group of managers or subordinates. For instance, the following groups could be interviewed:
—Top executives of a small business firm
—Middle-level managers of a business firm
—First—line supervisors in an assembly line production firm
—First-line supervisors in a service firm
—Local union officials
—Assembly line workers
—Secretaries
—Nurses

LECTURE OUTLINE NOTES

I. Chapter Introduction

    A. Motivation is important to management because:

        1. Employees must be motivated to perform at an acceptable level.

        2. Managers must be motivated to do a good job.

        3. Employees must be motivated to join the organization in the first place.

II. What is Motivation?

    A. Definition—an inner state that activates or moves.

        1. From a manager's perspective, a motivated employee:

            a. Works hard.

            b. Sustains a pace of hard work.

            c. Has self-directed behavior toward important goals.

        2. Involves a person's desire to perform.

        3. Performance is evaluated to indirectly determine desire.

        4. Performance difficulties are not necessarily motivation problems.

    B. The process of motivation (see Figure 11-1).

        1. It contains three steps:

            a. An unsatisfied need—the process' starting point. Causes tension within the individual.

            b. Goal-directed behavior—toward satisfying the need and eliminating the tension caused by need frustration.

            c. Need satisfaction—accomplished by achieving the goal.

    C. Is everyone goal oriented?

        1. No, but most people are.

            a. Programs such as those at Pecos River Learning Center

emonstrate ways to channel goal-directed behavior.
1) Humans are wanting animals whose needs depend on what we already have. Only unsatisfied need influences behavior; satisfied needs are not motivators.

III. Motivation Theories

    A. Categorized in two groups:
        1. Content theories—attempt to identify the elements within the employee and work environment which energize and sustain behavior.
        2. Process theories—attempt to explain and describe the motivation process—how behavior is energized, directed, sustained, and stopped.
    B. Content theories:
        1. Maslow's Hierarchy of Needs
            a. Stresses two premises:
                1) Humans are wanting animals whose needs depend on what we already have. Only unsatisfied needs influence behavior—satisfied needs are not motivators.
                2) A person's needs exist in a hierarchy of importance (see Figure 11-2). Once a more important need is satisfied, the need "next in line" in importance emerges and motivates a person to seek satisfaction. The five levels of needs, in priority of importance are:
                    a) Physiological needs—the human body's primary needs, such as food, water, and sex. Dominate over all other needs when they are unsatisfied.
                    b) Safety needs—for example, protection from physical harm, sickness, financial disaster. Job security is a safety need which is being challenged for many as organizations downsize.
                    c) Social needs—need for love, affection, belongingness in interpersonal and group relationships.
                    d) Esteem needs—need for awareness of importance to others (self-esteem) and for actual esteem from others.
                    e) Self-actualization—need to fulfill one's potential to grow and develop talents and abilities completely. Satisfaction of this need is possible only after all other needs are satisfied.
            b. Applying Maslow's Theory in Management
                1) Widely accepted and used by practicing managers.
                2) Some areas of management influence in each of the five levels of hierarchy are shown in Table 11-1.
            c. Criticisms of Maslow's Theory
                1) There are individual differences in people's needs.
                2) Needs overlap and may fit in many or all of the categories.
                3) Depicts need hierarchy as static instead of recognizing

190

that people's needs change over time.

2.   Herzberg's Two-Factor Theory—advanced by Frederick Herzberg in 1959, based on a study of engineers' and accountants' good and bad feelings about their jobs.

    a.   Proposes two types of factors pertinent to employee motivation:

        1)   "Maintenance factors"—employees are dissatisfied when they are absent but aren't strongly motivated by their presence in the work environment.

            a)   Essential to maintain an adequate level of employee satisfaction.

            b)   Herzberg's ten maintenance factors: salary, job security, status, work conditions, satisfying interpersonal relationships with peers, subordinates, and supervisor, technical supervision, company policy and administration, and personal life.

        2)   "Motivational factors" (also called "satisfiers")—conditions which motivate employees when present but don't result in a high level of dissatisfaction when absent from the workplace.

            a)   Herzberg's six satisfiers: achievement, recognition, advancement, responsibility, possibility of personal growth, and the work itself.

        3)   Maintenance factors are peripheral to the job itself, and more related to the work environment; motivational factors relate directly to the job itself.

        4)   When employees are highly motivated, they have a high tolerance for dissatisfaction arising from the maintenance factors. However, the reverse is not true.

    b.   Motivational factors are similar to what psychologists call intrinsic motivators (the work itself as rewarding); maintenance factors are similar to extrinsic motivators (rewards with meaning outside the workplace).

    c.   Applying Herzberg's Theory in Management

        1)   Extends Maslow's ideas and makes them more applicable in the workplace.

        2)   Has resulted in a focus on job enrichment efforts.

        3)   Explains why increased salaries, fringe benefits, and better working conditions may not result in greater effort to work hard, since a focus only on maintenance factors won't improve motivation.

    d.   Criticisms of Herzberg's Theory

        1)   Theory's tenets are based on research using a limited subject sample (accountants and engineers). Maintenance and motivational factors for those professional workers may differ for blue collar and other types of workers.

        2)   Defensive processes within study subjects may have influenced responses concerning satisfaction and

191

dissatisfaction. (People tend to attribute sources of satisfaction to themselves and sources of dissatisfaction to factors outside themselves.)

3) The theory may oversimplify the relationship between the motivation/dissatisfaction relationship and true sources of job satisfaction and dissatisfaction.

4) Research only examined satisfaction, not productivity. They may in fact not be highly and positively related.

5) Research testing the theory has produced mixed results.

3. Comparison of Maslow's and Herzberg's models.

a. Herzberg's maintenance factors satisfy Maslow's lower level needs (physiological, security, social); the motivational factors satisfy Maslow's high level needs (esteem, self-actualization).

b. Herzberg adds to Maslow's hierarchy by grouping the five need levels into the two job-oriented categories of motivational and maintenance factors.

c. Key similarities and differences in the models are shown in Figure 11-4 (similarities) and Table 11-2 (differences).

D. Process theories—focus on how motivation occurs.

1. Equity Theory—popularized by J. Stacy Adams

a. Proposes that perceived inequity is a motivational force. People who believe them have been treated inequitably will attempt to remove the inequity (see Figure 11-5.)

1) Equity is evaluated as a ratio of inputs (experience, effort, ability) to outputs (pay, recognition, promotions, benefits.)

2) Efforts to reduce inequity may include quitting, changing inputs, requesting and receiving a change in outputs, or changing the perceived value of existing outcomes.

b. Applying Equity Theory in Management.

1) Since feelings of equity and inequity are based on perceptions, mangers must understand the importance of those perceptions.

2) Reward systems must be very carefully administered.

c. Criticisms of Equity Theory

1) It fails to provide specific methods for restoring equity.

2) Managers may face difficulties if the referent person is a friend, a family member, or an imaginary person.

3) The focus of research into theory has been on pay; other rewards must be investigated as well.

2. Expectancy model—proposed in 1964 by Victor Vroom.

a. Defines motivation as a process governing choices. Asserts that motivation (work effort) will occur if the individual values the respective reward, and if the person believes that his/her effort will achieve a performance level which in turn will result in obtaining the reward (see Figure 11-6 for an illustration of the model).

b. The theory's key terms:

Choice—individual's freedom to select from a number of alternative behaviors (levels of work effort).

Expectancy—person's belief that a particular behavior will or won't be successful.

Preferences (valences)—the values a person attaches to various outcomes (rewards or punishment).

Instrumentality—the probability a person assigns to the performance-outcome link.

   c.   In equation form: Motivation = Expectancy x Instrumentality x Preference ($M = E \times I \times P$). Generally, the higher these three variables, the greater the individual's motivation and resulting work effort. (Note that if any one of the factors approaches zero, the multiplicative product will also approach zero.)

   d.   Managers must understand the values employees assign to expectancy, instrumentality, and preferences. Table 11-3 shows a rank ordering of 10 work-related factors for different employee groups.

   e.   Applying the Expectancy Theory in Management.

      1)   Managers can influence expectancy by hiring people with needed skills, providing training and leadership support.

      2)   Managers can influence instrumentality by being supportive, realistic, and offering advice.

      3)   Managers can influence preference by listening to and guiding employees, and providing proper resources.

   f.   Critical assessment of Expectancy Theory

      1)   Complexity—by far the most complex motivation theory, which presents problems in testing the theory.

      2)   Measurement of variables—problems in measuring preferences, expectancy, and effort.

3.   Reinforcement theory based largely on the work of B.F. Skinner.

   a.   Based on the idea that behavior results from consequences.

      1)   Work behavior can be controlled by manipulating the consequences which follow the behavior (called **operant conditioning**).

      2)   Thorndike's Law of Effect—workers are likely to repeat behavior that results in a pleasing outcome (for example, a reward) and not repeat behavior that results in an unpleasant outcome (for example, punishment).

   b.   Applying Reinforcement Theory in Management

      1)   Managers can use four types of reinforcement (see Figure 11-7).

         a)   Positive reinforcement—rewards (for example, pay raise, praise or promotion).

         b)   Negative reinforcement—avoiding an unpleasant consequence by exhibiting a desired behavior (for example, being on time to avoid a punishment).

         c)   Extinction—withholding positive reinforcement.

         d)   Punishment—implementing an unpleasant

193

consequence (for example, demotion or reprimand).

    2)   Managers can apply different schedules of positive reinforcement:

        a)   Continuous reinforcement schedule—administering a reward every time a desired behavior occurs (usually results in the fastest learning).

        b)   Intermittent reinforcement schedule—periodically rewarding desired behavior (results in slower learning but stronger retention of what is learned).

    c.   Criticisms of Reinforcement theory

        1)   Ethical questions—the theory has been criticized as bribery and manipulating a subordinate to fit a manager's concept of the ideal employee.

        2)   Relies solely on extrinsic rewards; ignores the motivational impact of intrinsic rewards.

        3)   Leaves unanswered questions such as: What reinforcers should be used? How long will a reinforcer be successful?

III.   **The Porter-Lawler Model**—An Integrative Model of Motivation, developed by psychologists Lyman Porter and Edward Lawler.

    A.   Integrates ideas, variables, and relationships presented in other models (such as the need hierarchy, two-factor theory, expectancy theory, and reinforcement theory).

    B.   The model's key points (see Figure 11-8).

        1.   Performance must be measured accurately and systematically so rewards can be distributed equitably.

        2.   Employee motivation depends on a perceived direct-relationship between effort and performance, performance and rewards, and rewards and satisfaction.

            a)   The effort-performance relationship depends on a strong understanding by the employee of what is expected of him or her.

            b)   The performance-reward relationship requires a perception of equitability in intrinsic and extrinsic rewards.

            c)   The use of reinforcing and satisfying rewards can lead to future encouragement of goal-directed behavior.

    C.   Using the model

        1.   Managers must ask:

            a.   What are the needs of the subordinate?

            b.   Can I help this subordinate satisfy those needs?

            c.   Do I administer rewards that are based on performance and sufficient to induce the effort needed to do the job?

            d.   Does the employee have the appropriate characteristics to do the job?

            e.   Am I accurately measuring performance?

            f.   How can I sustain the subordinate's motivation?

IV. Motivation, Cultural Diversity, and Cross-Cultural Issues
    A. Do motivation theories work the same for employees from various cultures?
        1. Assessing needs, preferred rewards, and work patterns is an important aspect of managing a diverse workforce.
            a. Effective managers may need to study the fundamentals of various cultures.
            b. It may be impossible to adapt to every culture represented in the workplace.
        2. The minority share of the workforce is growing rapidly.
            a. By 2005, California's population will be greater than 50% people of color, speaking more than 80 languages.
        3. There are primary and secondary dimensions to diversity (see Figure 11-9).
    B. A new management approach
        1. To optimize performance, managers need to learn more about the motivational needs, goals, and reward preferences of employees.
    C. Cross-cultural motivation—research by G. Hofstede
        1. Hofstede's research goes beyond American-based motivation theories, discussing four dimensions
            a) Power distance—the society's acceptance of unequal distribution of power in organizations.
            b) Uncertainty avoidance—the society's comfort with ambiguity.
            c) Individualism—the society's focus on immediate family vs. overall society needs.
            d) Masculinity—the society's degree of achievement preference, assertiveness, and materialism.
        2. Similarities and differences discerned by Hofstede's research in regions and countries around the world are summarized in Table 11-4.
        3. Research suggests that contents, process, and reinforcement explanations for motivation may not hold up universally.
            a) The theories are individually-focused, while many cultures have a group focus.

V. Management Strategies for Increasing Motivation

    A. **Job Enrichment**
        1. Involves "enriching" a job (making the job more motivational) by incorporating Herzberg's motivational factors and providing employees with the opportunity to grow psychologically and mature in a job.
        2. Directly includes greater scope for achievement and recognition, more challenge and responsibility, and opportunity for advancement and growth. Incidental inclusion of such factors as pay, working conditions, organizational structure, communications, and training.
        3. Herzberg emphasizes the distinction between job enrichment and job enlargement (increasing the number of tasks in a job).
        4. Job enrichment increases a job's range (the number of activities performed) and depth (the autonomy, responsibility, and discretion or control over the job).

195

5. Five core dimensions have been suggested by Hackman and other researchers to enrich jobs:
    a. Variety—tasks requiring different operations, procedures and equipment. Challenging as they require use of a range of skills.
    b. Task identity—enables employees to perform a complete piece of work.
    c. Task significance—amount of impact that the work has on others within the organization or in the community.
    d. Autonomy—employee's control over job duties and work area.
    e. Feedback—information employees receive concerning their job performance.
6. Organizational Approaches
    a. Volkswagon combined use of automation and robots with job enrichment on the assembly line. They have increased loyalty and reduced absenteeism and turnover.
    b. A General Foods plant using work teams of 7 to 14 employees with a high degree of autonomy and frequent feedback, and with high job variety, has improved productivity and decreased absenteeism and turnover. Proctor & Gamble and Saturn have had similar results.
    c. Non-Linear Systems replaced an assembly line with teams having minimal supervision. However, because of low team structure and cohesiveness, productivity and quality gradually diminished.
7. Job enrichment may be successful in some instances but not others, and is not universally desirable.
B. Relating Pay to Job Performance
    1. Each of the content and process theories of motivation suggests that money can have an influence on effort and persistence.
    2. Research studies suggest that pay can motivate if the pay plan:
        a. Creates a belief that good performance leads to high levels of pay.
        b. Minimizes negative consequences of good performance.
        c. Creates conditions so that desired rewards other than pay are viewed by employees to be related to good performance.
    3. However, many companies do a poor job of relating pay to performance (see Figure 11-11 for a chart depicting the negative consequences of pay dissatisfaction).
    4. Money as a motivator
        a. Nucor Manufacturing Corp.—maintains four compensation plans (all designed around groups of 25 to 30 employees)
            1) Production incentive plan—employees' earnings are based on their group production performance.
            2) Department head level program—incentive compensation is based on the division contribution to the company as a whole.
            3) Incentive plan for non-production employees who are not at the department manager level—monies are based on the division's or the corporation's return on assets.

196

4) Senior officer programs—bases over half of each officer's compensation on company earnings.
        b. Nucor also uses other innovative approaches such as
            1) A profit-sharing plan with a deferred trust, in place of an actuarially-based retirement plan.
            2) A service award program which gives company stock, rather than plaques or gifts.
        c. DuPont's fibers department in Wilmington, Delaware has implemented a new bonus system. For 3 years, employees who qualify for substantial merit raises have foregone them for the opportunity to earn bonuses as high as 18%. Bonuses are based on measurable performance.
C. Employee Stock Ownership Plans (ESOPs)
    1. Approximately 10 million employees in more than 10,000 organizations own about $150 billion of stock in their companies. Of this, 40% is in ESOPs, with the remainder in profit sharing, 401(k) plans, and stock purchase plans.
    2. Employee ownership may increase motivation, commitment, and loyalty.
    3. ESOPs also give employees the right to vote their ownership shares, which can defend against hostile takeovers.
    4. Downsides of ESOPs include the financial risks to employees (which may be negative in terms of motivation) and the fact that employee participation in decision-making is handled by trustees (who are often executives of the company).
D. Flexible Working Hours (Flextime)
    1. A work schedule that allows employees some choice as to their working hours (see Figure 11-12 for a sample).
    2. Allows employees greater autonomy in scheduling work and personal time.
    3. Can be motivational, reducing absenteeism and tardiness and increasing job satisfaction.

ADDITIONAL QUESTIONS AND ANSWERS

1. **Question:** *How is reinforcement theory used by the instructor in the course you are now taking?*

   Answer: The students' answers to this question will of course depend on the particular instructor's methods and policies, and each student's perceptions of them. Students should be encouraged to think in terms of positive and negative reinforcement, extinction, and punishment. Praise and encouragement, peer pressure, grades, etc., should be discussed.

2. **Question:** *The Protestant work ethic is used to describe societal values. Is it still applicable to the increasingly culturally diverse workforce?*

   Answer: As is discussed in the **Management In Action** section at the beginning of the chapter, many national groups and cultures do not share the Protestant work ethic which has been seen as an integral part of American society. Japan, for instance, has a strong reputation for hard work, but certainly has no Protestant work ethic. In the increasingly complex and diverse societies of the '90's, simple notions like the Protestant work ethic may become less relevant, supplanted by more broadly defined indicators of motivational factors.

3. **Question:** *The manager of a team of engineers in a manufacturing plant was overheard saying, "I believe that money is the best of all possible motivators. You can say what you please about all that other nonsense; but when it comes right down to it, if you give a guy a raise, you'll motivate him. That's all there is to it. In light of what we have discussed in this chapter, advise this manager.*

   Answer: Students' advice may differ; however, in discussing this question, it is important to point out that individuals differ in their motivational makeup. No two individuals are alike concerning what motivates them. Thus, money will indeed significantly motivate some individuals; however, others may find aspects such as the job's challenge and level of interest and responsibility to be just as motivating as money, if not more so. The manager's blanket generalizations misses a key point about managers and motivation: the essential key to successfully motivating employees is first determining what motivates each individual and then following through by triggering those motivators as much as is feasibly possible. This manager would be well advised to become familiar with the Herzberg theory and with the Porter-Lawler model.

4. **Question:** *Whom do you make school, job, or friendship comparisons with on a regular basis? Have you ever perceived inequity when making comparisons? If so, how do you handle the inequity?*

   Answer: This question is intended to assist students in understanding Equity Theory, and the Equity component (in considering intrinsic and extrinsic rewards) of the Porter-Lawler Integrative model. Students may discuss whether perceived inequity is a motivational force for them, and whether the methods to reduce inequity on the job that are cited in the chapter (quit, change inputs, change outcomes, or change the perception of outcomes) are in accordance with their own experience.

5. **Question:** *Flextime has gained popularity in recent years. Is this type of schedule motivational? Why?*

   Answer: Flextime decreases absenteeism and tardiness, and increases job satisfaction. These results suggest flextime's motivational effectiveness. Flextime would be considered a maintenance factor, rather than a motivational factor, under Herzberg's Two-Factor theory; it addresses safety and social needs in Maslow's Hierarchy. Regardless of the culture(s) of the employees to whom flextime is offered, it allows them the ability to meet personal needs (for child or elder care, access to public transportation, and meeting personal responsibilities) and preferences (sleeping late, avoiding rush hour, getting home early). Flextime can also be motivational if it is offered as a reward or withdrawn as a punishment. It is, however, rarely implemented in this fashion.

6. **Question:** *What events have occurred in the United States in the past few years that suggests that job security is now more uncertain?*

   Answer: Job cutbacks and employee lay offs have become a serious concern. Companies are "flattening" their hierarchies, eliminating middle management jobs. Increased global competition in every industry and service has made it imperative that each job and employee is productive. Job security is very uncertain in today's economy.

7. **Question:** *This chapter emphasized that managers must be familiar with the fundamental needs of people to motivate employees successfully. Select two individuals you know well. Do they differ with respect to the strength of various needs? Discuss these differences and indicate how they could affect behavior. If you were attempting to motivate those persons, would you use different approaches for each? Why?*

   Answer: This question is designed to attempt to make the text material more relevant to students by having them relate it to their personal situations. For example, the student might believe that two friends are relatively insecure but are motivated in completely different ways to satisfy their needs. One might drive a big expensive car while another may choose an elaborate wardrobe or attempt to impress his or her professors in class. Endless numbers of examples could be provided. This question has shown quite favorable results in the way of class participation and meaningful discussion.

8. **Question:** *Can a student's "job" be enriched? Assume that you are to consult with your professor about applying the two-factor motivation model in your class. You are to answer these questions: Can you apply this approach to the classroom? Why?*

> *If you can, differentiate between maintenance and motivational factors and develop a list of motivational factors your professor can use to enrich the student's job.*

Answer: This question is designed to enable students to relate the "two-factor" theory of motivation to a situation they should be familiar with: the classroom. Arriving at a list of maintenance factors and motivational factors for the classroom situation should increase student participation and discussion. Common examples of maintenance factors are a good textbook and prescheduled examinations. Common examples of motivational factors are a dynamic lecturer and guest speakers, and interesting course content.

9. **Question:** *Assume that you have just read Vroom's thoughts on how the "goals" of individuals influence their "effort" and how the behavior the individual selects depends on an assessment of the probability that the behavior will successfully lead to the goal. What is your goal in this management course? Is it influencing your effort? Do you suppose another person in your class might have a different goal? Is that person's effort (behavior) different from yours? If your professor was aware of this, could it be of any value?*

Answer: Here students must think of Vroom's model in terms of their own situation. Relate the notion of goals (grades, knowledge, preparation for the future) to effort in the course. Also, discuss different types of effort (e.g., studying versus good attendance versus participating in class discussion versus visiting the professor in his/her office) as a means to achieve different goals.

10. **Question:** **Evaluate the pay system used at Nucor Corporation. What do you like about the system?**

Answer: The question is designed to influence students to think about money as a motivator. Several positive outcomes are demonstrated by the Nucor example. Likewise, students may identify several limitations. The intent is to get students to reflect about their own perspective of money and its influence.

END OF CHAPTER CASES

CASE 11-1: EXECUTIVE PAY: WORTH IT OR A DISGRACE?————————
CASE SUMMARY: U.S. executives take home far more in cash compensation (salary plus bonus) than their counterparts in Japan and Germany. (1992 salaries for the best paid U.S.

executives averaged $4.8 million, versus $1.8 million in Germany and $530,000 in Japan). However, this comparison may be misleading. U.S. executives tend to receive salaries fully exposed to income and social security taxes. Executives in other countries may receive a great deal of nontaxable compensation. One often-used approach is based on the fact that all major industrial countries other than the U.S. tax only income earned within the country's borders. Compensation may thus be paid to those executives, tax free, into foreign bank accounts. Also, non-U.S. executives may receive housing allowances, household help, fees for outside directorships, vacation tickets, country club memberships, cars, and other perks. A 1992 study showed that, based on the net purchasing power of the total compensation package, Mexican and Brazilian chief executives were the best paid in the world.

ANSWERS TO QUESTIONS FOR ANALYSIS:

1. **Question:** *Do you think that any executive is worth the kind of pay and perks provided to American chief executives presented in the case?*

   Answer: This is strictly an opinion question, designed to stimulate student discussion of the role of pay and perks as motivators to attract and retain individuals with the highest level managerial skills and expertise. Student discussion may be guided to an exploration of the role of equity theory in determining their own feelings and motivation levels.

2. **Question:** *The federal government has made some statements that they might intervene to control or cap what executives are paid for performance. Do you think that the government should play a role? Why?*

   Answer: Again, this is an opinion question. Student discussion will probably address the appropriate roles of government in a free enterprise economy. However, students may be encouraged to explore the impact of this type of governmental intervention on the motivation of senior level executives, and whether such regulation might encourage the best executives to leave the country to achieve higher levels of compensation elsewhere.

3. **Question:** *Do you believe that chief executives make comparisons of their pay with other chief executives similar to what we discussed in our discussion of equity theory? Why?*

   Answer: The business pages of local and national newspapers and magazines report on executive compensation packages virtually every day, and often carry reports of executive dissatisfaction based on precisely the kinds of comparisons under discussion. This question encourages an exploration of the broad applicability of equity theory. It also, however, provides an opportunity to discuss a major drawback of equity theory. Pay is only one of a range of benefits that can be assigned to employees, including chief executives. Comparisons are most likely to be made on the basis of the total compensation package, rather than just pay alone.

CASE 11-2: WORTHINGTON INDUSTRIES MOTIVATIONAL PACKAGE

CASE SUMMARY: Worthington Industries is the largest processed steel finisher in the U.S. The company's motivational philosophy is summed up as "Pay workers well, treat them like people and expect them to work a bit harder than people who regard the boss as an antagonist." John H. McConnell, founder of Worthington, eliminated time clocks and plant supervisors; allowed workers to refuse to ship product if they feel it is substandard; paid workers a salary (plus bonus and profit sharing)as opposed to an hourly wage; and promised not to lay employees off in bad times. Absenteeism is low at Worthington, productivity is high, and McConnell's successor as chief executive—his son, John P.—is continuing this entrepreneurial approach at running the business.

ANSWERS TO QUESTIONS FOR ANALYSIS:

1. **Question:** *Which theory of motivation does John H. McConnell apply to Worthington Industries?*

    Answer: McConnell's approach follows the five content and process theories discussed in the chapter. He addresses all of Maslow's Hierarchy of Needs as well as Herzberg's motivational and maintenance factors and provides for equity, expectancy, and reinforcement through company-wide profit sharing. Individual performance measures are not discussed in the case. However, group performance is certainly measured, through the performance of the company as a whole, and is a key determinant of the bonuses and profit sharing issued as rewards at the end of the year.

2. **Question:** *Why would unions support or reject McConnell's ideas about motivating employees?*

    Answer: Student responses will depend largely on their own viewpoints of unions, as well as the degree and types of management/labor collaborations they have encountered in their own experience. Historically, unions have tended to seek rigid wage and benefit structures, independent of the performance of the company as a whole, and to seek to strictly define job duties by job title. These union efforts are counter to McConnell's approach. Unions in the 1990s, however, have often worked more collaboratively with management (and *vice versa*) in seeking ways to encourage employee ownership of organizations. McConnell would be likely to encounter far more union support today than in the past.

3. **Question:** *What does McConnell mean that it is necessary to be totally committed to the motivation program to be successful?*

    Answer: McConnell's approach requires a strong commitment on the part of both management and labor. Management must be lean, affording and encouraging line employees the opportunity to make crucial decisions traditionally reserved to management. And employees must be willing to take on that extra responsibility, and to risk some of their own economic well-being for the sake of the strength of the company (especially in lean times). An organization cannot adopt this approach while maintaining its old management structure and adversarial manager-employee relationships. The collaborative relationship McConnell advocates represents a fundamental shift in the hierarchical structure of most organizations—not an undertaking to be embarked upon lightly.

ADDITIONAL CHAPTER QUESTIONS AND ANSWERS

1. **Question:** *Discuss the major difference between the content theories and process theories of motivation.*

   Answer: The major difference is the focus of concern. The content theories (Maslow and Herzberg) are concerned with identifying the elements within the individual and the work environment which energize and sustain behavior. Process theories (equity, expectancy and reinforcement) focus on the process of how behavior is energized, and how it is directed, sustained, and stopped.

2. **Question:** *Although Maslow's need hierarchy is recognized as a major contribution to our understanding of motivation, the theory has also been substantially criticized. In your opinion, what are the major shortcomings present in Maslow's theory?*

   Answer: Students may offer several criticisms. They may question the theory's consistency, noting that some people sacrifice lower level needs for higher ones (e.g., a "starving artist" or martyr). Though the theory has much common sense appeal, it has little empirical support. In testing the theory, problems occur in measuring Maslow's different needs. Maslow's theory also assumes that we consciously know what motivates us, thus ignoring the subconscious aspect of motivation.

3. **Question:** *Among your friends and acquaintances, have you known someone whom you believe is self-actualized? In terms of individual characteristics, how does this person differ from other people you know?*

   Answer: This question is designed to spur students to think about the concept of self-actualization and how it affects a person's personality when present within the individual. Students may suggest several characteristics of a self-actualized person such as self assurance, openness, and a high level of energy. (Some students may assert that they have never known a self-actualized person, which raises the question: Can a person ever become truly self-actualized?)

4. **Question:** *Suppose you are the president of a manufacturing company. You want to provide your managers with opportunities to fulfill their esteem and self-actualization needs. What steps could you take to do so?*

   Answer: To help satisfy subordinates' esteem needs, the president could provide them with significant job activities and responsibilities, assign them high job titles, and recognize and publicize their good job performance. Concerning self-actualization, the president could encourage high achievement and creativity and provide subordinates with challenging responsibilities and advancement opportunities.

5. **Question:** *Briefly discuss the major criticisms of Herzberg's "two-factor" theory of motivation. In your opinion, which shortcoming is the most serious? Explain.*

   Answer: Among the theory's shortcomings: 1) the theory's principles are based on research using a sample of accountants and engineers, thereby raising the possibility that motivational and maintenance factors may differ for other types of workers; 2) research findings have not consistently supported the theory; 3) subjects' responses concerning their sources of satisfaction and dissatisfaction may have been influenced by defensiveness; and 4) the theory may oversimplify the relationship between motivation and satisfaction/dissatisfaction and the true sources of job satisfaction and dissatisfaction. Which is the most serious of these shortcomings is subject to individual student opinion.

6. **Question:** *Commented a chief executive officer of a Fortune 500 company: "Motivating employees is the most difficult and challenging task the manager faces. What do you think?*

   Answer: Motivating employees is a difficult task for two primary reasons. First, to effectively motivate an employee, the manager must understand the employee's motivational makeup—the ingredients that activate the person to perform. However, the motivational makeup is different for each individual, so any single managerial effort to motivate (e.g., a pay plan, profit sharing, job enrichment) won't be effective for all workers. And attempting to understand the motivational makeup of each worker individually is an exceptionally difficult, if not impossible, task, especially in the increasingly multi-cultural workforce. Second, motivation is not directly observable; a manager can only make inferences about an employee's level of motivation from observing his/her behavior. Inaccurate assumptions based on observations are occasionally made.

7. **Question:** *Differentiate among positive reinforcement, negative reinforcement, extinction, and punishment. In your opinion, which type of reinforcement is most motivational? Explain.*

   Answer: Positive reinforcement involves rewarding desired behavior (either intermittently or every time it occurs). Extinction involves withholding positive reinforcement. With negative reinforcement, desired behavior is rewarded by withholding an undesirable consequence (such as scolding or demotion). Punishment involves implementing an unpleasant consequence in response to undesirable behavior. Students' opinions will differ concerning the most motivational reinforcer. However, many are likely to assert that positive reinforcement is the most effective, pointing to its dominant use in organizations as evidence.

8. **Question:** *Said one first-level supervisor: "I would never use operant conditioning with my subordinates. It is bribery, pure and simple." Do you agree?*

   Answer: Students will likely be sharply divided on this question. Some students typically resent the manipulative implications of operant conditioning. However, others will argue that in a general sense, all motivational programs in organizations (e.g., compensation, promotion, job enrichment, recognition) involve operant conditioning where desired behavior is rewarded and undesired behavior is not, in one way or another.

9. **Question:** *Why would a professional athlete earning over $1 million not be satisfied with this amount of reward for performing?*

   Answer: Students should recognize that the issue here is not the absolute amount of pay but rather the perception of the amount relative to that of other players and how they perform. If this amount is lower than other players' salaries with whom the athlete favorably compares his or her own performance, then he or she may feel a reward inequity, and be demotivated to the point of either seeking another position or reducing performance to the level at which he or she perceives the other players to be.

10. **Question:** *Why isn't job enrichment a universally desirable program? Provide examples of work situations and environments where job enrichment probably would not succeed.*

    Answer: Job enrichment may not be desirable because some employees are satisfied with their jobs and don't want them to be enriched. Some people don't want the added responsibility and demands that job enrichment can place upon the employee. Further, job enrichment may not be feasible because of the job's technological constraints. For example, enriching an assembly line worker's job can be difficult because enrichment could require major changes in the line's technology. In this situation, management must weigh the benefits of job enrichment against the costs of implementation.

12   MANAGING WORK GROUPS

LEARNING OBJECTIVES

After completing Chapter 12, students should be able to:

Define   such terms as group think, group development acculturation, and group conflict.

Describe   the important characteristics of groups in organizations.

Discuss   how cohesiveness can influence a group's overall performance.

Compare   the causes of and solutions to intragroup and intergroup conflict.

Identify   the key reasons why informal groups appear in organizations.

CHAPTER SYNOPSIS

This chapter examines the issue of managing work groups and group processes in organizations. Work groups are collections of employees who share certain norms, and who strive to satisfy their needs by attaining group goals. The chapter divides work groups into two classifications—**formal groups** and **informal groups,** and discusses the types of groups **(command, task, interest, friendship)** within the two categories. Special attention is focused on **committees,** a special form of task group, and their uses and the roles of the committee chair and members. **Self-managed groups** are discussed and a highly successful use of these groups at Johnsonville Foods is profiled. **Quality circles** are also discussed in terms of functions, structure, processes, and contributions. QCs at Southern Pacific Railroad are profiled as an example of a QC program at work in a large organization, and research studies in U.S. companies are described indicating mixed results in the long run. The special issues that arise in multicultural work groups are also explored.

The development of work groups is presented in terms of a four-phase progression from the initial mutual acceptance phase to the final control phase where the work group exercises control over members most effectively, becoming a "mature" team. The makeup of work groups is discussed by describing primary group characteristics: **group structure and roles, group goals** (including **achievement goals** and **maintenance goals**), **group leadership, group norms** (focusing on factors which affect member conformity), **group cohesiveness** (focusing on influential factors), and **intragroup** and **intergroup conflict.** Major attention is focused on management strategies for resolving conflict between groups in terms of indirect approaches **(avoidance, bargaining, persuasion,** and **problem solving)** and direct approaches (**domination, removing key figures in the conflict,** and **superordinate goals**). The chapter concludes with a discussion of membership satisfaction and the pros and cons of group decision making.

The chapter's **Management In Action** describes efforts at Bell Labs since the breakup of AT&T to blend the strengths of individualism and teamwork through nine distinct work strategies. **The Management Focus** sections discuss the success of the ten million emigrants from India around the world, and tie their acculturation to the diversity they experienced in their life experiences in India; the balance of roles between teams and individuals in organizations, and the importance of specific purpose and goals-setting for effective teams; and labor-management collaborations as a method for reducing conflict.

TEACHING TIPS

LECTURE & DISCUSSION IDEAS

1. Often during the course of discussing this chapter, students will ask why so much research has focused on the study of informal groups. In your discussion of this question, it's useful to note that we study groups because of their substantial importance to organizational performance and because of their unpredictability. The dynamics of a group are always complex and often uncertain. There are examples of groups where a certain "chemistry" resulted in accomplishments normally beyond the group's capabilities (witness the 1980 Olympic Gold Medal Hockey Team, and the phenomenon of the Beatles). There are also examples of groups composed of brilliantly capable members who as a group produced abysmal failure (e.g., J.F. Kennedy's Bay of Pigs advisory group).

2. One rich source of illustrations of many of the chapter's concepts is your students' own experiences with groups. As almost everyone has been and are members of numerous groups (e.g., family, church, social clubs, sports teams, work groups), students should be able to draw upon their own group experiences to extend their own understanding of group dynamics and processes and contribute, via class discussion, to others' understanding. Use your students' experiences provided in class discussion to illustrate such topics/issues as: 1) why individuals join groups; 2) the stages of group development; 3) group cohesiveness; and 4) group norm conformity and the functions of norms. Concerning the first above-mentioned lecture idea, have students consider whether they have ever been a part of a group that achieved beyond its means or failed when it shouldn't have (given the quality of the group members). Have them describe the dynamics at work in each instance.

3. Students may also have experience with instances of groupthink, or may be able to provide clear examples from historical and current geopolitical events. Ask students to describe how the groupthink process evolved, and try to pinpoint opportunities to avoid or break out of the groupthink mode that arose but were not taken advantage of in the examples given.

PROJECT / EXERCISE IDEAS

1. Instead of drawing upon students' experiences with groups in class discussion, have your students prepare a written profile of a group in which they've been a member. In their reports, students can outline the four stages of group development, discuss the

characteristics that the group demonstrated in each phase, and include the estimated time length of each phase. In particular, students can profile an incident of intergroup conflict, discussing its causes and consequences and how the conflict was resolved. They can also address basic group characteristics (such as norms and cohesiveness) and discuss each as it appeared in their group.

2.   One of the fascinating aspects of group dynamics is a group's ability on occasion to perform well beyond or well short of its capabilities. To further develop this point, have your students identify a group which has experienced such a phenomenon and write a brief group profile, focusing on the group's makeup, performance, and reasons for its performance. The subject group should be sufficiently prominent so that published information is available. Some examples: the 1980 U.S. Olympic Hockey team, the Beatles, and J.F.K.'s Bay of Pigs and Cuban Missile Crisis advisory groups. Rather than focusing on groups that have performed extraordinarily well or badly, you can have students focus on quite prominent groups *per se* for their profiles. In this regard some possible group subjects are the New York Yankees in the 1950s and 1960s, the "brat pack" of actors from the 1980s, or the cabinet and White House Staff in Richard Nixon's second term as President.

3.   Have your students (in groups of three to five members each) interview a successful business manager concerning the manager's strategies for resolving intergroup conflict.

LECTURE OUTLINE NOTES

I.   Chapter Introduction

   A.   **Work groups** and **teams** are interchangeable terms.
   B.   A work group is a **collection of employees (managerial or nonmanagerial) who share certain norms and strive to satisfy their needs by attaining group goals.**
   C.   Work groups are studied in a management text because:
      1.   They are inevitable in organizations, so it's in management's interest to understand the dynamics of work groups.
      2.   They strongly influence members' behavior and job performance.
      3.   Group membership can have positive and negative organizational consequences.
   D.   Managing individuals in groups is emerging as a key theoretical and practical field.

II.   Classification of Work Groups

   A.   Two broad classifications: Formal and Informal. See Table 12-1 for a comparison.
      1.   **Formal groups**—groups formed by management to perform the organization's work (for example, departments, production teams).

2.	**Informal groups**—natural groups of people which form in the work situation to meet members' social needs.

III.	Why Groups Form

    A.	To sustain and satisfy needs of individuals:

        1.	**Physical reasons**—When individuals are placed in close physical proximity to each other, they tend to interact and communicate with each other, facilitating group formation.

        2.	**Economic reasons**—Individuals form groups because they believe they can derive more economic benefits in their jobs (for example, workers obtaining group incentive pay).

        3.	**Sociopsychological reasons**

            a.	**Safety needs**—work groups insulate members from outside pressures, alleviate an individual's sense of "aloneness" in an organization, and help members learn a different job which alleviates feelings of job insecurity.

            b.	**Social needs**—groups fulfill members' needs for affiliation.

            c.	**Esteem needs**—groups help fulfill esteem needs by prestige gained from membership.

            d.	**Self-actualization**—groups help workers self-actualize by helping workers develop job-related skills.

IV.	Types of Groups

    A.	**Command group**—the subordinates who report directly to a given supervisor. A formal groups shown on the organizational chart.

    B.	**Task group**—employees who work together to complete a project or task (for example, a quality control project group). A formal group.

    C.	**Interest group**—formed by employees to present a united front on an issue (e.g., a group of women employees who form a women's interest group). An informal group, typically of shorter duration than other group types.

    D.	**Friendship group**—formed because of members' common characteristics (for example, age, ethnic background, interests in sports). Often interacts outside job activities. An informal group.

    E.	**Committee**—though criticized by many as dysfunctional, committees are frequently used in organizations to exchange views and information, recommend action, generate ideas, and make decisions.

        1.	Generally, committees should be kept small as large groups hinder communication and are more likely to generate stress and conflict.

        2.	Committee chairperson—individual charged with providing the committee with proper direction toward meeting objectives, keeping the committee moving, and minimizing needless delays and conflicts. He/she must:

            a.	Balance control and freedom so members can contribute.

            b.	Be a careful, open-minded listener, allow members to voice opinions, involve all members in committee activities, display an active interest in committee's purpose and members' ideas, and help members focus on the task at hand.

        3.	Committee members—must be cooperative rather than competitive.

Cooperative groups have more ideas, are more productive, have more member satisfaction, generate more effective communication, and are more strongly motivated to perform the group task.

4. To avoid committee paralysis and other problems that can afflict committees:
    a. Hold meetings only when they really are needed.
    b. Establish an overall purpose and objectives to be covered.
    c. Invite only those who are needed and who can contribute.
    d. Distribute an agenda and necessary handouts before the meeting.

    e. Make all room/layout arrangements ahead of time.
    f. Be punctual in beginning and ending the meeting.

F. **Quality circles (QCs)**—groups which meet regularly to solve quality control and productivity improvement techniques and to identify and solve work-related problems.
1. History of QCs
    a. W. Edwards Deming, an American engineer, introduced statistical quality control to Japan.
    b. The Japanese adapted the techniques and disseminated them widely.
    c. The term Quality Circle was coined, and processes were formalized, in Japan in the 1960s.
2. Specific features of QCs
    a. Have from four to 15 members (usually eight or nine) and are usually led by the work area supervisor and composed of workers from that area.
    b. Members meet weekly on company time with pay.
    c. Members are trained in what quality circles are and in problem-solving techniques.
    d. Members select problems/projects for the circle.
    e. Participation is voluntary; circles exist as long as the members wish to meet.
3. The QC problem-solving process (see Figure 12-1):
    a. Identifying problems and developing solutions.
    b. Managerial review of solutions and decision to accept or reject.
    c. Organizational implementation of solution.
    d. Circle's and organization's evaluation of success.
4. Quality Circles at Southern Pacific Railroad
    a. Southern Pacific, when purchased by Philip Anschuty, was not making money, had no effective strategic plan, was not competitive, had a high degree of customer hostility, and had antagonistic unions.
    b. Anschuty implemented a three phase plan
        1) Hire a Vice President for Quality
        2) Involve the unions in quality
        3) Establish QCs (called quality improvement teams).
    c. The quality circles are about 75% intra-unit and 25% inter-unit.
    d. QCs have been accompanied by an extensive training program.

e.   There have been improvements in quality and profitability-whether they are sufficient remains to be seen.

5.   Some experts caution that circle successes in Japan may be largely due to Japanese cultural factors. Thus, U.S. circle effectiveness should be evaluated over an extended period (four to six years).

    a.   Quality circles may experience a "group decline" over time, where the QCs meet less often, become less productive, and fewer resources are committed to the program.

    b.   QCs may raise expectations that cannot be met. Ideas suggested may be unworkable in the daily workflow, or may meet management resistance.

    c.   Many organizations are replacing QCs with *ad hoc* task forces or improvement teams.

        1)   Managers may feel they have more control over the group.

G.   **Self-managed groups**—groups where members exercise control in meeting performance objectives; members manage the group.

1.   Groups are given some autonomy, with administrative review, to complete jobs and accomplish goals.

2.   Typically consists of 3-30 members.

3.   Can arrange schedules, set profit targets, hire and fire members, order materials, improve quality, and devise strategy.

4.   In a survey of 476 Fortune 1000 firms, only 7 percent of the work forces are organized into self-managed teams. But 50% will project that they be using self-managed teams this decade.

5.   Self-managed teams are applicable when a job has a high interdependence between 3 or more workers.

H.   Multicultural Work Groups

1.   Managing multicultural work groups requires that managers create a work atmosphere of respect for employees from different cultures.

    a.   Organizations must re-evaluate their training, recruitment, advancement, and motivation programs.

    b.   Wang has established diversity training for managers that calls for

        1)   An awareness of one's own behavior.

        2)   A recognition of one's biases and stereotypes.

        3)   A focus on job performance.

        4)   An avoidance of assumptions.

2.   **Acculturation** is the transfer of culture from one group to another. There are several degrees of acculturation.

    a.   **Assimilation**—everyone conforms to the values and norms of the dominant culture.

    b.   **Separation**—a minority group is unwilling or unable to adapt to the dominant culture.

    c.   **Pluralism**—groups attempt to accommodate to each others' cultures.

3.   About 35% of U.S. population growth in the 1980s was due to immigration.

212

4.   To integrate groups, organizations may
       a.   Communicate in as many languages as is necessary.
       b.   Use multilingual testing and advertising.
       c.   Offer cross-cultural mentoring.

V.   Work Group Development

   A.   Groups develop along two dimensions:
      1.   Relationships among members.
      2.   Task and problem-solving activities.

   B.   Development proceeds in four phases (see Figure 12-2 for the four stages in terms of relationships and task function maturity).
      1.   **Mutual acceptance**—after an initial period of uneasiness and insecurity, members learn about and begin to accept each other.
      2.   **Decision making**—open communication, problem solving, and decision making occur as group develops strategies to make the job easier and to help members perform more effectively.
      3.   **Motivation**—group solidarity is emphasized. The group is reaching maturity, and members realize cooperating is more productive than competing.
      4.   **Control**—group is successfully organized and exercises sanctions when necessary to pressure members to obey group norms. This stage reflects a "mature" group.

   C.   Management needs to determine each group's active stage of development, and to blend the talents of individuals and the group.

   D.   Eastman Chemical has replaced a number of senior vice presidents with self-managed cross-functional teams.

VI.   Characteristics of Work Group—similar to those of formal organizations, including standards of conduct, communication systems, and reward and sanction mechanisms.

   A.   **Group structure and roles**
      1.   Structures emerge as groups move through developmental phases, and group members take on roles or sets of activities.
      2.   **Group role**—behaviors that a member exhibits in a social context. **Role differentiation** involves a member taking on different roles (e.g., task-oriented roles are those that involve initiating action, stimulating task-oriented discussions, and using facts to solve a group problem). See Table 12-1 for a summary of 3 main roles that emerge in groups (task-oriented, relations-oriented, and self-oriented).

   B.   **Group goals**—two types:
      1.   **Manager-assigned goals**—the reason for group formation.
      2.   Group goals
         a.   **Achievement goals**—provide groups with direction and an end-target result.
         b.   **Maintenance goals**—sustain the group and maintain its existence.
      3.   Four factors increase member's commitment to group goals:
         a.   Member's participation in group activities.
         b.   Management's tying incentives to goal attainment.
         c.   Management's providing feedback on goal accomplishment.

d.   Management's training members in the goal-setting process.

C.   **Leadership**
  1.   Within formal groups, leaders are appointed. They are followed because they are perceived as having power and influence to reward and punish members.
  2.   In informal groups, leaders emerge from within. Their roles include:
    a.   Initiate action and provide direction, and settle group differences.

    b.   Communicates the group's beliefs about policies, the job, organization, supervision and other job-related matters to nonmembers.

D.   **Work group norms**—shared attitudes which give rise to agreements among group members as to how members should behave (for example, members shouldn't perform above a certain job level, members should help each other when they have the time).
  1.   Social pressures that facilitate member conformity to norms:
    a.   Group pressure—applied to members who aren't conforming. Pressure is optimal when it results in conformity that yields cooperation, efficiency, and the accomplishment of group goals.
      1)   Member conformity to group norms is affected by:
        a)   **Task characteristics**—the more difficult, unfamiliar, and ambiguous the task, the more inclined a member is to obey a norm.
        b)   Member's **personality**—an individual with low levels of self-esteem and intelligence will more likely conform than one with opposite characteristics.
        c)   Group characteristics—as group size increases, pressure to conform increases. Also, conformity is more likely if a member is alone in his or her views, or if deviance results in social isolation.
    b.   **Group review and enforcement**—the group reviews a member's degree of compliance. If found lacking, the group can implement corrective action ranging from talking with the member, to scolding the member privately and publicly, to ostracizing the member which is the ultimate enforcement action.

E.   **Group cohesiveness**—the attraction of members to the group and the strength of forces on individual members to remain active in the group and resist leaving it (see Figure 12-3 for some factors that influence cohesiveness).
  1.   All of the characteristics of groups are influenced by the group cohesiveness.
  2.   Highly cohesive groups tend to show more member communication, and to have greater member satisfaction, than low cohesiveness groups.
  3.   Groupthink—a phenomenon described by psychologist Irving Janis, in which highly cohesive groups lose their ability to critically evaluate situations or information.
    a.   Symptoms include:
      1)   Illusion of invulnerability-arising from overconfidence.

214

2) Illusion of mortality—the group sets its own morality.
3) Stereotypes of outsiders—those outside the group become targets.
4) Pressure for conformity—pressure within the group to maintain group norms.
5) Self-censorship—avoidance of public expressions contrary to the group's views
6) Illusion of unanimity-perceived, rather than actual, unanimity of support for an action.

b. To avoid inappropriate decisions resulting from groupthink, leaders must encourage expression of alternate viewpoints and careful consideration of consensus views.

F. Size—impacts on group cohesiveness and member effort levels
1. Research indicates an inverse relationship between group size and cohesiveness.
2. **Social loafing**—individuals in a group tend not to work hard, because there are others to handle the workload. More common in large groups.

G. **Intragroup conflict**—occurs among a group's members when there are incompatible goals, cognitions, or emotions between individuals in a group that lead to opposition or antagonistic interaction. Always exists to some extent. Members having interpersonal conflict tend to refrain from most group activities. Intragroup conflict can produce an ineffective and fragmented group. Management's goal: minimize the conflict.

H. **Intergroup conflict**—occurs between groups.
1. Some of the more important reasons conflict develops>
a. Limited resources—groups compete for limited funds, personnel, and other organizational resources.
b. Communication problems—groups miscommunicate because of a lack of understanding of the other's vocabulary or jargon.
c. Different interests and goals—conflict is intensified when management sides with one group's goals, leaving another group feeling ignored.
d. Different perceptions and attitudes—the perceptions and attitudes of a group affect how the group perceives and responds to other groups. Groups tend to overvalue themselves and undervalue other groups.
e. Lack of clarity—Confusion over who is responsible for certain tasks. Leads to groups competing for control over activities which are recognized.
2. Management strategies to deal with intergroup conflict:
a. Indirect approaches:
1) **Avoidance**—ignoring the problem. This can work, or it can intensify the problem if groups become more hostile.
2) **Bargaining**—involves groups agreeing about what each will give and get from the other. Can be successful if both groups are better or at least no worse off after an agreement is reached.
3) **Persuasion**—groups find common areas of interest,

finding points of agreement and realizing their importance to each group in attaining organizational goals. Possible if clashes between group leaders do not exist.

    4)   **Problem solving**—effective when the conflict is over ways to accomplish a goal on which the groups agree. Involves discussing alternative solutions and selecting one acceptable to both groups.

  b.   Direct approaches:

    1)   **Domination**—management exercises its authority and requires that the problem be solved by a certain deadline. However, groups may join ranks to resist the domination.

    2)   **Remove the key figures in the conflict**—effective if conflict is due to personality differences between some members. However, the members may be respected leaders. Also, this strategy can create martyrs to whom members will maintain allegiance. Also, it's often difficult to determine whether conflict between members is due to personality clashes or because they're representing their groups.

    3)   **Finding superordinate goals**—establishing goals desired by both groups that can only be accomplished when the groups work together. When cooperation is required, conflict is usually reduced. (Optimal profits to increase profit-sharing payouts may be an effective superordinate goal.)

VII.   Consequences of Group Membership

   A.   Member satisfaction—according to research, member satisfaction is positively affected by three factors:

    1.   Members' **perceived freedom to participate** in group activities—can increase members' perceptions of being a valued group member.

    2.   Perceived **goal attainment**—the greater the level of perceived goal attainment, the greater the member's satisfaction.

    3.   **Status consensus**—the members' agreement about the relative status of all group members (the group's status hierarchy).

    4.   Members are much less satisfied if their goals and needs conflict with the group's overall goals and needs.

   B.   Group decision-making effectiveness—key question: are decisions made by groups superior, inferior, or equal to those made by individuals?

    1.   Group assets

      a.   A group has a greater body of knowledge and information.

      b.   More members accept and support a decision when the group solves a problem than when one person solves it.

      c.   Communication breakdown between decision maker and implementers is minimized when implementers participate in making the decision.

    2.   Group liabilities

      a.   Group pressure can silence individual disagreement and favor

216

too-easily reached agreement.

b.   The group can be dominated by an individual due to characteristics unrelated to decision-making skill.

c.   "Stand taking" can occur where members are more concerned with winning than with reaching the best decision.

ANSWERS TO DISCUSSION AND REVIEW QUESTIONS

1.   **Question:**   *What did Lewin mean when he stated that "it's easier to affect the personality of ten people if they can be melted into a group than to affect the personality of any one individual separately"?*

       Answer: Lewin meant that a group is more manageable than ten individual personalities. Each group forms, develops, and encourages a personality with norms, values and procedures. As groups mature, they develop shared relationships. The group itself polices attitudes and behaviors of group members through the group pressure and group review and enforcement processes. On the other hand, individuals each go their separate ways and can be more difficult to control, supervise, and coordinate.

2.   **Question:**   *This chapter focuses on groups and the crucial role they play in organizations. Is it possible for managers to use both the advantages of teamwork and individualism to accomplish goals? Explain.*

       Answer: The answer is an unqualified yes. Through the material already covered in the text (especially Chapter 11, *Motivation*), and the chapters to follow (especially Chapter 13, *Leading People In Organizations*), this course covers both group and individual processes that managers can use toward achieving the organization's goals. While no job can be completed in isolation in today's interconnected world, *all* jobs have components requiring individual effort. Effective managers take advantage of the strengths of both teamwork and individualism as appropriate to achieve desired ends.

3.   **Question:**   *Informal groups exist in organizations and are very important to their members. If an organization has a number of informal groups, is this an indication that the company is being poorly managed? Why or why not?*

       Answer: Individuals working in an organization naturally form informal groups through interpersonal interaction. Even the most successful organizations (using any criteria such as profits, morale, or loyalty to distinguish success) have informal groups. In some cases these informal units serve a positive organizational purpose, while in some instances

217

they resist management and are a negative force. They will, however, continue to exist regardless of the management strategies used; truly effective managers will put effort into achieving the organization's goals by harnessing the energy of the informal groups.

4.   **Question:** *What should a manager look for in determining whether a group is beginning to use a groupthink process in analyzing situations?*

       Answer: Unanimity of opinion is unusual in any group, on almost any topic with the potential for controversy. Repeated unanimity, or unanimity on an emotional or non-routine issue, is *de facto* cause for consideration of the possibility of groupthink. The other five symptoms proposed by Janis (illusion of invulnerability, illusion of morality, stereotypes of outsiders, pressure or conformity, and self-censorship) are all signs managers should look for closely; and they should work with group leaders (if the managers are not in fact the leaders themselves) to point out these symptoms to the group as they occur.

5.   **Question:** *How is the concept of group norms and control used by weight-reduction clinics and stop-smoking clinics?*

       Answer: In these groups, pressures are so strong that they sway behavior. This is possible because the members value group opinion and norms. Because of their feelings about the group, they comply. The group is able to shape and control the individual. These groups use both group pressure and group review and enforcement strategies to encourage members to conform.

6.   **Question:** *Why is role differentiation likely to occur in groups?*

       Answer: As groups develop, roles for each member within the group will evolve to give structure to the group. The roles individuals self-select, whether they be task-oriented, relations-oriented, or self-oriented, are likely to reflect their needs and expectations from the group. Each person has strengths, weaknesses, and individual interests; the role differentiation that occurs will reflect those individual differences.

7.   **Question:** *How would a group's structure influence the members' behavior and attitudes?*

       Answer: Students may cite several examples of how a group structure can affect individual members. As one example, research has shown that group members who aren't central members of a group's communication network (comprised of stable patterns of communication within the group) are much less satisfied with the group than are members who assume more central positions in the network. Research has also shown that group dissatisfaction is high when the group's communication structure is not conducive to the group task. Also, if the group's structure does not facilitate member participation in the group's activities, the member is likely to feel a much lower level of satisfaction with the group.

218

8. **Question:** *Explain how synergy in a group can be positive or negative.*

   Answer: Synergy in a group usually has positive effects when the group maximizes the use of the combined skills, experience, energy, ideas, etc. of its members. However, when some group members do not contribute in terms of work or ideas, which tends to happen more in large groups, this "social loafing" has a detrimental effect on the group's processes and outcomes, with "negative synergy" as a result.

9. **Question:** *How can managers improve their understanding and ability to deal with the acculturation process among a culturally diverse work group?*

   Answer: It is important that students consider their own options in learning to manage in an increasingly diverse workforce. Such mechanisms as participation in special seminars or training courses on multi-cultural issues, reading about the native cultures of the organization's employees, learning new languages or seeking translator services, or creating special opportunities for employees to share their cultural norms and values with each other should all be discussed.

10. **Question:** *How can one individual dominate the discussion or activities of a group attempting to reach decisions ?*

    Answer: An individual with status, power, or a dominating personality can literally take over a group. This person can dominate through his or her ideas, or through the expression of those ideas, and actually manipulate a group of people. Dominating individuals may gain their influence through individual characteristics in an informal group, or through assignments in a formal group.

END OF CHAPTER CASES

CASE 12-1: SAN DIEGO'S ZOO TEAM APPROACH

CASE SUMMARY: Until four years ago, employees at the San Diego Zoo had narrowly-defined job responsibilities. With the zoo's development of bioclimatic zones, in which animals and plants are grouped together in cageless enclosures by habitat type, the zoo also reorganized its staff. Self-directed groups, including animal and plant specialists, construction and maintenance workers, were formed to manage each zone. Members of the groups received extensive cross training, and each group is now responsible for its own work plan, budget, and overall management. Team members report greater job satisfaction, and zoo attendance is up.

The adoption of the self-directed team approach is rapidly gaining in popularity throughout business organizations in the U.S. Many believe that self-directed teams may be one of the most productive forms of employee involvement.

Self-directed teams are *not* teams of co-workers from the same functional department who join together to foster team spirit, nor are they short-term multidisciplinary groups formed to solve a specific problem. Rather, they are cross-trained teams who are organized to carry out the business' functions over the long term. Implementation of self-directed teams requires changes in attitudes, organizational structures, information systems, compensation and rewards, and career pathing in an organization.

ANSWERS TO QUESTIONS FOR ANALYSIS:

1. **Question:** *Should leaders at the San Diego Zoo have feared loss of power when the self-directed teams were established? Why?*

    Answer: Instructors may wish to use this question to explore the meaning of "power" in organizations. They may see "power" as the direct day-to-day control over individuals' specific work activities, focusing on the technical and operating levels, or as the exercise of managerial problem-solving and setting of strategic directions for an organization, focusing on strategic-level managerial responsibilities. Working with self-directed teams certainly implies a loss of the former, with a corresponding increase in importance of the letter. This in turn implies a move "up" the organization level, with managers acting less at the traditional first or middle level and more at the top level of management.

2. **Question:** *Was the San Diego Zoo move to self-directed teams automatically self-directing?*

    Answer: A move to self-directed teams is *never* automatically self-directing. Management at the zoo made the determination to utilize bioclimatic zones, determined the composition of the teams, provided for the needed cross-training, and facilitated group formation. Management must also play a continuing role in such areas as information flow, compensation, evaluation, and strategic direction.

3. **Question:** *Why is management of change so much a part of the transition to self-directed teams?*

    Answer: Change is a difficult process in organizations, and fundamental change is far more likely to meet with resistance than incremental change. Chapter 16 of the text discusses the impacts of change and the mechanisms for managing change in organizations; these considerations are critical in the establishment of self-directed teams because few aspects of an employee's work experience are untouched in this type of transition.

CASE 12-2: LAKELAND POLICE DEPARTMENT

CASE SUMMARY: This case identifies two major needs of police departments: to improve the relationships with the public and to recruit quality personnel. The Lakeland Police Department is facing problems in both areas. The department is suffering poor relations with the community which have lately escalated due to charges of police brutality and discrimination. The personnel and training departments are involved in intense conflict over recruiting practices. The bickering has been publicized by the local media and the chief has scheduled a meeting with the two department heads to deal with the problem.

ANSWERS TO QUESTIONS FOR ANALYSIS:

1. **Question:** *Which solution do you consider to be the best for improving community-police relations?*

   Answer: While both of the proposed solutions are worthwhile, the second (forming a neighborhood committee) has advantages that the first (training officers who work in the neighborhood) does not, and so should be implemented more quickly. By forming a formal group (with some informal group characteristics) to address the issue, the police department affords neighborhood residents the opportunity to become part of the solution. As that group matures, the solutions it devises will be seen by its own members and other members of the community as having credibility, based on their own input. They may also identify group goals, beyond the manager-assigned goals that are the initial reason for the group's existence, to help foster increasingly positive relations between the police and the community. One likely recommendation of the committee is training for the officers; when implemented as a result of the committee's deliberation as opposed to unilaterally by the police department, this action may gain in credibility among both police officers and the community.

2. **Question:** *Why has the conflict between Tandy and Rossano become disruptive?*

   Answer: Conflict has emerged because there appear to be limited resources—recruits. The personnel director and training director have not coordinated the changes in requirements. This has led to a reduced number of potential recruits. They experience limited resources, along with communication problems and a difference in opinion about what the quality of recruits should be. These problems when combined are disruptive. In addition, negative press is another force irritating the parties.

3. **Question:** *What are some feasible solutions to the conflict between Personnel and Training?*

   Answer: One feasible solution is for the units to work together in developing superordinate goals. The chief could insist that these directors work together and provide him with a copy of superordinate goals. Another solution would be for the Chief to serve as moderator. He could hear both sides and present his viewpoint. A more authoritarian solution would be for the Chief to enforce a gag rule, with neither Tandy nor Rossano discussing problems with the press. This would also apply to personnel in their units. Then the Chief could insist that they reach a mutual agreement in solving the problem by some specified date. Each solution is feasible, but each has some potential side effects. The Chief, by intervening, could force a solution. This could solve the situation but create long-run negative feelings. The behavioral approach that could have the fewest negative side effects might involve a meeting in which the Chief communicates his feelings about how this problem is hurting the department. He could ask for Rossano and Tandy's help to develop a solution so that the department image does not continue to suffer. The Chief could stress pride, image, attitude, dedication, and professionalism in this meeting. This might help the two directors get together to reach a compromise solution.

ADDITIONAL QUESTIONS AND ANSWERS

1. **Question:** *Why is proximity a factor that can encourage the formation of groups?*
   Answer: An employee tends to communicate with workers in close proximity simply because they are most accessible to the employee. This accessibility provides the opportunity for workers to talk, exchange ideas, and become friends, all of which facilitates group formation.

2. **Question:** *Differentiate between formal and informal groups.*
   Answer: Formal groups are formed by management to perform the organization's work. Informal groups are groups in the work environment which develop to meet members' social needs or their particular interests.

3. **Question:** *Why do most people comply with group norms?*
   Answer: Students may offer several reasons. Those covered in the text are pressure exercised by the group for conformity, and group review and enforcement whereby group members can take a variety of corrective actions when norms are not obeyed.

4. **Question:** *Why is being a good listener an important requirement for serving as the chairperson of a committee?*
   Answer: Being a good listener affords four important advantages to the chairperson. First, being attentive enables the chairperson to better "pick up on" the comments and ideas of committee members. Second, a good listener encourages member contributions; people are more apt to speak if they believe the chairperson is sincerely interested in what they have to say. Third, relationships between members and the chairperson are enhanced in the sense that members feel the chairperson respects and values their contribution. Fourth, a good listener may be able to detect and forestall the development of groupthink.

5. **Question:** *How would social loafing be handled within a highly cohesive group?*

Answer: In a highly cohesive group, once social loafing was identified, the group would likely not tolerate the situation. Such is particularly the case if the group is small and has established high group performance goals. However, if the highly cohesive group is large and/or has set low performance goals, the attitude toward social loafing would probably be more permissive.

6. **Question:** *Have you been a member of a group where groupthink was present in the group's decision-making process? What symptoms of group think did you witness? How would you have alleviated the problem?*

Answer: This question is intended to spur students to consider the symptoms indicative of groupthink and to evaluate a past experience with respect to groupthink. You may want to ask students how they personally reacted to the situation as a member of the group before the consequences of the group's decision were known, and afterward.

7. **Question:** *A manager stated that if he were doing a good job of managing, no informal groups would be formed by subordinates. Do you agree? Explain.*

Answer: Good management can reduce employees' tendency to form groups for such reasons as the worker's need for safety and self-actualization. However, informal groups develop for reasons that are unrelated to the quality of management. Workers can form groups because of the desire to interact socially on and off the job, because of the esteem provided by membership in a particular group, or simply because of common interests among members or close proximity. They can also form informal groups that actually supplement the work of good management, such as quality of work life groups to explore wellness issues or employee skill exchange groups. It would be counterproductive for good management to attempt to forestall the formation of such groups.

8. **Question:** *Why does a manager need to know how groups can influence the behavior of subordinates?*

Answer: Managing effectively requires knowing as much as possible about why subordinates behave as they do. Managers need such knowledge to better understand and manage individual employees and the groups that substantially influence subordinates. Groups influence every person. Have your students consider this: Why do they dress like they do? Why are they studying in college? Why do most people eat three meals? Group forces like these affect everyone's behavior, on the job as well as off.

9. **Question:** *Discuss the factors which affect a group's cohesiveness.*

Answer: Six factors affect cohesiveness: 1) group size (typically the larger the group, the less cohesive it is); 2) the dependence of members on the group (to fulfill needs); 3) goal agreement (membership agreement on

223

the group's goals); 4) the achievement of group goals (the more successful the group in this respect, the greater the group's cohesiveness); 5) group status (status and cohesiveness are positively related); and 6) management demands and pressures (a high level tends to increase cohesiveness). These are shown in Figure 12-3.

10. **Question:** *Which of the reasons mentioned in the text do you believe is most influential as to the formation of informal groups? Why?*

Answer: This question is intended to spur students to consider the relative importance of the factors that promote informal group formation.

13

LEADING PEOPLE IN ORGANIZATIONS

LEARNING OBJECTIVES

After completing Chapter 13, students should be able to:

Define	what is meant by the term leadership.
Describe	the importance of being able to lead an increasingly multicultural workforce.
Discuss	the power bases that leaders can use to influence the work behavior of followers.
Compare	the similarities and differences in the University of Michigan, Ohio State, and Managerial Grid personal-behavioral explanations of leadership.
Identify	important differences among situational theories of leadership.

CHAPTER SYNOPSIS

This chapter presents the major theories on leadership, and focuses on current issues concerning leadership in business today. The chapter is presented in four topic sections—the concept and definition of leadership, selected leadership theories, leadership effectiveness factors, and multicultural leadership.

The concept of leadership is addressed by examining the key differences between **leading** and **managing**. Leadership is a process of exerting influence; one component of influence is power. In this regard, the **five bases of power** developed by French and Raven (**coercive, legitimate, reward, expert**, and **referent**) are discussed. Leadership as a reciprocal process between leaders and subordinates is also explained, and the mutual benefits gained by viewing leadership from this perspective are discussed. McGregor's concept of the **Theory X and Theory Y** manager is also described to illustrate the important influence of leader attitudes on leader behavior.

The bulk of the chapter centers on describing and evaluating three categories of leadership theories: 1) **trait theories**; 2) **personal-behavioral theories** (the leadership continuum, University of Michigan's job-centered/employee-centered theory, Ohio State University's two-dimensional theory, and the leadership grid); and 3) **situational theories** (Fiedler's contingency theory, House's path-goal theory, Vroom-Yetton-Jago's leader-style theory, Hersey and Blanchard's tridimensional theory, and transformational leadership.) In presenting each theory, the text explains the theory's underlying principles, discusses findings of major research which have tested the theory, and provides a critical assessment (focusing on the theory's strengths, shortcomings, and its applicability to managers).

An important part of understanding the dynamics of leadership is realizing that several factors which strongly influence leadership effectiveness aren't directly addressed by the major theories. Six **leadership effectiveness factors** are discussed—the leader's perceptual accuracy concerning subordinates, the leader's and subordinates' background, experience, and personality, the expectations and style of the leader's superior, the leader's understanding of subordinates' tasks, and the leader's peer expectations. Each factor is discussed in terms of its impact on leader effectiveness. In accommodating the increasingly diverse workforce, difficulties in applying leadership styles in a multicultural environment are discussed, along with the influence of national origin on managers' views of effective leadership.

The chapter's **Management In Action** looks at the management styles of three successful business leaders, who differ in their approaches but who all are good listeners, possess great drive, have integrity, and want to be leaders. The chapter's **Management Focus** sections explore employee empowerment and Hampton Inn's 100% satisfaction guarantee; gender bias as exemplified by the small number of top level women executives and as perpetuated through performance appraisal, salary assignment, management development, benefits, promotion, and informal culture practices; and the successes of Glaxo in managing cultural diversity in its worldwide operations.

TEACHING TIPS

LECTURE & DISCUSSION IDEAS

1.   At some time during your discussion of leadership, students will likely ask: of what use is leadership theory to practicing managers? Of what real world value are the theories provided in the chapter? One way to spur students to answer their own question is to select two or three theories and have students examine each theory's usefulness to the practicing manager. From such assessment should come some interesting insights into the contributions which leadership theory provides to management.

2.   As the chapter notes, one critical shortcoming of the trait theories and personal-behavior theories of leadership is that no single set of traits or behaviors is optimally effective in all situations. Moreover, few people will agree on one set of traits or behaviors as the most effective. To illustrate this point (and spur class discussion), have each of your students first identify the most effective leader he or she has encountered (whether in real-life experience, or in television/film/theatrical productions) and then jot down on paper a list of the three traits and three behaviors which most accounted for that leader's effectiveness. Then, have the students compare lists. Undoubtedly, much disagreement will occur concerning the "best" leader traits and behaviors (in fact, a few blatant contradictions should emerge). It might be insightful to compare the lists by the leader's gender and age to see if cited traits/behaviors differ according to these factors.

3.   Employee empowerment is a concept many organizations discuss but few actually implement. Students can be encouraged to discuss in more detail the organizational and managerial implications of the empowerment program at Hampton Inn as described in the Management Focus. Have students discuss ways in which empowerment

programs could be implemented in other organizations with which they're familiar, and explore what the impacts would be on the organizations.

PROJECT / EXERCISE IDEAS————————————————————————————————

1. Have your students scan recent issues of major business periodicals (e.g., *The Wall Street Journal, Business Week, Fortune, Forbes, Inc.)* and select a reported example of poor or excellent business leadership. The students can report on their selected examples, explain in what ways the leaders exhibited poor or excellent leadership, and relate the leaders' approaches to leadership theory.

2. To facilitate a more in-depth understanding of the leadership theories covered in the chapter, have each of your students select one theory, research the theory (by reading three studies that test the theory), and draw up a brief report which:
   1. addresses the theory's major strengths and shortcomings (based on research); and
   2. discusses the theory's practical relevance to practicing managers (based on the student's own opinion).
   Then, select three of the theories covered in the chapter and have the students who have researched those theories present their lists of strengths and weaknesses in class. Class discussion should focus on major agreements and disagreements concerning students' critical assessment of each theory and, in particular, the theories' relevance to managers.

3. Attempts to define transformational leadership characteristics have met with little formal success, although Burns, Bennis, and Bass have attempted to identify the skills transformational leaders employ. Students may select individuals whom they consider to be transformational leaders, and carry out research to try to identify whether those skills are sufficient in making them transformational leaders. If they are not sufficient, have them try to identify what other factors are involved. (This project may be carried out in conjunction with the Experiential Exercise at the end of the chapter.)

LECTURE OUTLINE NOTES

I. **Leadership** is:

   A. The ability to persuade people to work toward meeting organizational goals enthusiastically. (See Figure 13-1 which illustrates that managers are not always leaders.)
   B. The human factor that binds a group together.
   C. A process wherein one person exerts influence over others.
      1. Managerial influence is greatly affected by the amount of **power** which subordinates believe their manager possesses. French and Raven propose that five bases of power exist:

227

a. **Coercive power**—based on subordinates' fear that the superior will punish noncompliance.

b. **Reward power**—based on subordinates' perception that compliance with the wishes of a superior will lead to rewards (monetary or nonmonetary).

c. **Legitimate power**—derived from the supervisor's position in the organizational hierarchy.

d. **Expert power**—based on the leader's expertise, special skill, or knowledge which peers and subordinates perceive as exceeding their own.

e. **Referent power**—based on a follower's identification with a leader.

f. Critics say there is little distinction between the five power bases (for example, a manager's reward and coercive power are correlated with his/her legitimate power).

D. Influence should be viewed as a mutual exercise. Influence can be shared and both leader and follower can gain:

1. The leader gains better interaction and more respect from followers.

2. Followers learn more about the leader.

3. The greater the total influence leaders and followers have in the organization, the better the performance of the total system.

4. **Empowering** subordinates is growing in popularity.

a. Defined as providing employees at all levels the authority and responsibility to make decisions on their own.

b. Empowered employees believe they have a say in how their jobs are done.

c. Empowerment is challenging to implement.

II. Leader Attitudes: Important Assumptions

A. Leader attitudes greatly affect leader behavior because of the leader attitude-behavior link ("**the self-fulfilling prophecy**")—if, for instance, a manager views subordinates as lazy and inept, he/she will treat them accordingly.

B. McGregor categorized managerial attitudes into two sets of assumptions about employees:

1. **Theory X** manager—assumes that employees dislike work, lack ambition, avoid responsibility, prefer job security the most, and must be coerced and closely supervised to work adequately. Uses an authoritarian and directive leadership style.

2. **Theory Y** manager—assumes that employees want self-direction and self-control in their work, and want to be creative and assume responsibility. Believes that physical and metal effort at work is as natural as play or rest. Uses a more democratic leadership style.

C. Women versus Men as Leaders

1. Empirical evidence shows no clear pattern of difference in styles of female and male leaders. However, a study for the International Women's Forum found that:

a. Women are more likely to use power based on charisma, work experience, and contacts; while men use power based on organizational position.

           b.   Women are more likely than men to use transformational leadership.

           c.   Women who self-describe as predominantly "feminine" or "gender-neutral" have a higher following among their female subordinates than do self-described "masculine" women.

           d.   Women executives earn the same pay as their male counterparts.

      2.   Some men and some women are great as leaders, and some are disastrous.

III.   Trait Theories

    A.   There has been much research to identify characteristics of leaders that predict success.

      1.   Little agreement has been reached among researchers.

    B.   Desirable characteristics include:

      1.   Drive—willingness to take initiative.

      2.   Motivation—desire to lead others.

      3.   Integrity

      4.   Self-confidence

      5.   Intelligence—ability to process complex information.

      6.   Knowledge-of the job, organization, and industry.

IV.   **Personal-Behavioral Theories**—Contend that leaders are best classified by behavioral styles as opposed to personality traits. Focus on what the leader does when performing managerial tasks.

    A.   **Leadership continuum theory**—Tannenbaum and Schmidt

      1.   Depicts a range of leader behavior from boss-centered to subordinate-centered leadership. Contends that effective leaders are adaptable, delegating authority effectively depending on situational factors. Leaders should not be strictly autocratic or democratic, but flexible. (See Figure 13-2, showing the continuum.)

    B.   **University of Michigan** research—Likert and others

      1.   Researchers established two leader style dimensions:

           a.   **Job-centered leader**—structures subordinate jobs, supervises closely, uses incentives to spur production, and determines standard rates of production.

           b.   **Employee-centered leader**—focuses on human aspects of subordinate problems, and on building effective work groups. Specifies objectives, communicates them to subordinates, and provides latitude to accomplish the job.

      2.   Research concluded that employee-centered leadership is more effective in increasing group productivity.

    C.   **Two-dimensional theory-Ohio State University** researchers (late 1940s)

      1.   Proposed two leadership behavior dimensions:

           a.   **Consideration**—developing a work atmosphere of mutual trust, respect for ideas of subordinates, and consideration of feelings of subordinates.

           b.   **Initiating structure**—structures leader and subordinate roles,

229

plans work activities, schedules work, communicates pertinent information.

2. Among research results:
   a. In a production environment, initiating structure behavior was positively related and consideration behavior was negatively related to subordinate group proficiency. Relationships were reversed in nonproduction divisions.
   b. Overall, high structure and low consideration were related to more absenteeism, accidents, grievances, and turnover.

D. **Managerial/Leadership**—Blake and Mouton, Blake and McCanse
   1. Plots leadership styles on a two-dimensional grid which serves as a framework to diagnose a leader's style and track the leader's movement to the "ideal" style.
   2. Grid scales are Concern for People and Concern for Production (see Figure 13-3).
   3. Focuses on five core styles
      a. Impoverished leader (1,1)—exerts only enough effort to get work done.
      b. Task leader (9,1)—primary focus on task efficiency; little concern for development and morale of subordinates.
      c. Country club leader (1,9)—focuses on being supportive and considerate of employees; little concern for task completion.
      d. Middle of the road leader (5,5)—seeks adequate task efficiency and satisfactory morale.
      e. Team leader (9,9)—high concern for production and subordinates. Ideal leader style.
   4. Asserts that leaders can move from their initial leader style to the (9,9) style via a six-phase managerial development program.
      a. Prior to the program, 65% of managers rate themselves as (9,9) leaders; after the program, only 16% really believe they fit the bill.
   5. Program is unique in that:
      a. Line managers run the program.
      b. A conceptual framework of management is used.
      c. The entire managerial hierarchy undergoes development, not just one level.

E. Synopsis of the Personal-Behavioral Approach
   1. The theories present two overall types of leadership (see Table 13-2):
      a. Boss-centered/job-centered/initiating structure/concern for production.
      b. Subordinate-centered/employee-centered/consideration/concern for people.
   2. A major question: is one leadership style best in all situations? Many argue not. Some of the theories (e.g., Leadership Grid, leadership continuum) have not been substantially tested by research.

V. **Situational Theories**—these theories assume that no single leadership style is effective in all situations: situational factors influence the effectiveness of leader behavior.

230

A. Contingency theory—Fred Fiedler
   1. Proposes that there is no one best way to lead; that leader effectiveness depends upon leader style and **situational favorableness** which is the result of three dimensions:
      a. Leader-member relations—degree of confidence subordinates have in the leader, subordinates' loyalty, and leader's attractiveness.
      b. Task structure—the degree to which subordinate tasks are routine.
      c. Position power—power inherent in the leadership position.
   2. Leadership style is measured using the Least-Preferred Co-worker (LPC) Questionnaire. High LPCs (those who rate their LPC in more positive terms) are assumed to be people-oriented. Low LPCs are task-oriented.
   3. Fiedler asserts that low LPCs are most effective in situations that are either highly favorable (good leader-member relations, structured tasks and strong position power) or unfavorable (poor leader-member relations, unstructured tasks, and weak position power). High LPC leaders are most effective in situations of moderate favorability. (See Table 13-3 for the range of possible situations).
   4. If the leader style-leadership situation is a poor match, the situation should be engineered to fit the leader's style. For instance:
      a. Leader-member relations can be improved by restructuring the leader's group of subordinates to make the group more compatible (in terms of background, education, etc.) with the leader.
      b. Task structure can be increased or decreased.
      c. Leader position power can be increased or decreased (via changing the leader's rank, providing the leader authority in performance evaluation of subordinates).
   5. Fiedler opposes leadership training because he believes it is ineffective. However, in many organizations, real world factors (such as unions, technology, time, and costs) may prohibit situation engineering.
   6. Critical assessment
      a. Strengths—One of the first models to consider situational factors in leadership and to view leader effectiveness as being contingent on leader style and situational factors.
      b. Weaknesses:
         1) The methodology of the LPC measure—no one is certain what LPC actually measures.
         2) Only high and low LPC scores are considered. What about the middle LPC leader?
         3) Many subjects used in Fiedler's studies (for example, basketball players) aren't representative of subordinates in business organizations in general.
B. **Path-goal theory**—Robert House
   1. Asserts that a leader can increase subordinate motivation, satisfaction, and performance by using four leadership styles:
      a. Directive—no subordinate participation in decision making.

231

        b.   Supportive—leader is friendly toward and interested in subordinates.

        c.   Participative—leader takes suggestions from subordinates.

        d.   Achievement oriented—leader sets challenging goals for subordinates and demonstrates confidence in their ability to achieve those goals.

2. Suggests that different styles can be used by the same leader in different situations (unlike Fiedler).

3. Managers influence the paths between subordinate behaviors and goals by:

        a.   Recognizing and stimulating subordinates' need for rewards over which the manager has control.

        b.   Rewarding goal achievement.

        c.   Supporting subordinates' efforts to achieve goals.

        d.   Helping to remove barriers to goal achievement.

        e.   Increasing subordinates' opportunities for personal satisfaction.

4. A limited number of studies have tested the theory. Studies have found that:

        a.   Moderators such as subordinates' preference for structure and need for achievement had significant effects on which leadership style produced positive subordinate outcomes.

        b.   Supportive leadership has its most positive effect on satisfaction when subordinates work in stressful, frustrating jobs.

        c.   In three organizations, subordinates with non-routine jobs working with achievement-oriented leaders were more confident that their efforts would produce better performance.

5. A comprehensive path-goal theory suggests that:

        a.   Managers stimulate subordinate efforts by offering valid rewards and linking them to effort and performance.

        b.   Whether effort results in performance depends on subordinate knowledge, skills, and abilities and on lack of obstacles in performing the job.

        c.   If rewards are valued and fair, subordinates will be satisfied and less likely to quit.

C. **Leader-Style theory**—Vroom and Yetton, Vroom and Jago

1. Attempts to identify the effective leadership style for a given set of circumstances or situations.

2. Uses five leadership styles ranging from A-I (where the leader solves the problem using available information) to G-II (where subordinates generate ideas and reach a consensus solution with the leader acting as chairperson).

        a.   A=Autocratic
               B=Consultative
               G=Group

3. Appropriate leadership style depends on the attributes of the problem along with seven specific diagnostic questions.

        a.   A decision tree is used to determine the best leadership style for a given problem situation (see Figure 13-4).

4. Tests of the theory have found that:
   a. Managers at upper levels tend to use more participative styles than those at lower levels.
   b. Managers of retail franchises who more closely conformed to the decision tree's recommended style were more successful and had employees who were more satisfied with their job.
5. The revised model appears to be more valid than the original model. Responses to diagnostic questions are now based on 5-point ratings rather than yes/no responses.

D. **Tridimensional leader effectiveness theory**—Hersey and Blanchard
   1. Identifies two leader styles, similar to those of the Two-Dimensional Theory:
      a. **Task behavior**—organize and define the roles of followers, explain what must be done, and direct flow of work.
      b. **Relationship behavior**—maintain personal relationships with followers by being supportive, sensitive, and facilitative.
   2. A LEAD (Leaders Effectiveness and Adaptability Description) questionnaire is used to determine the leader's preferred style.
      a. Contains 12 leadership situations in which respondents select an alternative action for each situation that they believes most closely describes how they would behave in that situation.
      b. A LEAD-other survey is completed by the leader's subordinates, peers and/or boss.
   3. Asserts that leader flexibility (ability to vary style in different situations) is important in unstructured, non-routine, fluid work situations with significant environmental change.
      a. Effectiveness is situational; an effective leadership style in one situation may be ineffective in another.
   4. A quite popular theory among managers, since it is simple, interesting, and relevant. However, few studies have tested the theory, and results are unclear.

E. Comparison of Situational Theories
   1. See Table 13-4 for comparisons by theme, leadership styles, relationship base, and application value for managers.

F. Transformational leadership—J.M. Burns, Bernard Bass
   1. A transformational leader displays or creates:
      a. charismatic leadership.
      b. inspirational leadership.
      c. intellectual stimulation.
      d. a feeling that each individual follower counts.
   2. Transformational leaders stimulate, shift, and use the values, beliefs, and needs of their followers in a rapidly-changing crisis-laden situation.
      a. Personal-Behavior and Situational Theories focus on transactional leadership.
   3. The transformational leader is viewed by subordinates as more charismatic and intellectually stimulating than a transactional leader.
   4. An area of concern is that the attempt to define charisma is analogous to the trait theories of leadership—the qualities are elusive and difficult

to define.

5.   Questions yet to be answered by the theory:
   a.   Is charisma a rare attribute that few understand and possess?
   b.   Can a leader's charisma be strengthened/improved?
6.   Skills used and sharpened by transformational leaders:
   a.   A vision that can be articulated.
   b.   Clear communication of that vision.
   c.   Trust building, through fairness, decisiveness, and consistency.
   d.   Positive self-regard.

VI.   Selected factors influencing leadership effectiveness

A.   The ability to accurately perceive subordinates. Important in each of the situational models.

B.   Leader's background, experience, and personality—strongly affect leadership style; but styles can generally be altered.

C.   Follower's background, experience, and personalities are important because leadership is a mutual-sharing process.
1.   **Maturity** of followers is the willingness and ability to take responsibility for directing their own behavior.
   a.   Job maturity—knowledge, skills, and experience.
   b.   Leaders may attempt to determine background and maturity of followers, and adapt their leadership style appropriately.

D.   A leader's style is strongly influenced by his/her superior's own style and expectations.

E.   The leader who understands the nature, makeup and demands of subordinates' tasks can more accurately select the appropriate leadership style to fit the task.

F.   A leader's peers (particularly their expectations and stated judgment of the leader's performance) can heavily influence the leader's style.

G.   Integrating Influence Factors
1.   See Figure 13-6 for the reciprocal interactions between these factors and leadership effectiveness.
2.   Leaders must diagnose themselves and their total leadership environment.
3.   Training in diagnosing work situations and applying appropriate leadership approaches is difficult and time-consuming.
4.   Managers in the U.S. must make the effort to learn positive leadership examples today; consumers throughout the world are seeking quality, price, design, value, and appeal first, and new manufacturing, marketing, and competitive practices are required.

VII.   Multicultural Leadership

A.   Leadership activities are difficult when the workforce is multicultural.
1.   Trait, Personal-Behavioral, and situational theories ignore multicultural differences.

B.   National origin of leaders influences their views of leadership (see Figure 13-7 for some specific comparisons.)

C.   Simply transporting a leadership style from one country or culture to another is the wrong way to achieve success.

234

1. **Question:** *How would a leader assess the maturity of his followers?*

   Answer: If the employees are using the knowledge, skills, and experience necessary to successfully perform their tasks without close supervision, then they have sufficient job maturity. Implicit in those actions is that they also have psychological maturity—i.e. the willingness to do the job and take initiative, and the desire for greater responsibility. If followers are not performing tasks on their own, the leader must first assess knowledge, skills, and abilities, either through an interview, a test, or direct observation. Assessment of psychological maturity may be carried out through assignment of successively more difficult unsupervised tasks.

2. **Question:** *Does the Vroom-Yetton-Jago approach to leadership suggest that leaders can or cannot be trained to improve their effectiveness? Explain.*

   Answer: Leadership training is certainly a part of the Vroom-Yetton-Jago approach. The leader is trained to recognize the situation and then to adapt his or her style to fit the situation. A key part of the training is to apply the diagnostic questions and consider the answers in implementing a particular style.

3. **Question:** *Which role is the leader expected to play in the path-goal leadership theory?*

   Answer: Using one or more of four leadership styles, the leader assumes a coaching role, motivating the subordinate by helping him or her set challenging goals, determining the best path to those goals, and removing stressful obstacles that block the path to goal attainment. It is particularly important that the leader chart realistic paths for the subordinate.

4. **Question:** *Why is the diagnostic skill of the leader so vital to the situational approach to leadership?*

   Answer: In the situational approach, the leadership role is dynamic—by definition, situational leaders adapt their leadership style in response to the specific situation encountered. Unless the situation is diagnosed correctly—in terms of the needs of the subordinates and the organization, as well as the nature of the task—the leader may choose an inappropriate approach.

5. **Question:** *Women can lead just as effectively and as ineffectively as men. Comment.*

   Answer: The validity of the statement is evident on its face, and is verified by the research cited in the chapter. Students may be encouraged to think about the most effective and ineffective male and female leaders they have encountered, and to attempt to identify the work or personality characteristics which made them effective or ineffective. The majority of the factors identified will be unrelated to gender.

6. **Question:** *Why is it inappropriate to assume that the leadership style that works best in a manufacturing company in Marietta, Georgia, will be just as effective in Lagos, Nigeria?*

   Answer: Gerbert and Steinkamp's study of leadership in Nigeria and Taiwan, as cited in the chapter, demonstrates that the types of leadership strategies favored today in the United States, with a heavy emphasis on employee empowerment and an employee-centered approach, would not be effective in Nigeria. Cultural norms and values (see also text Chapter 3) impact on individuals' expectations in both the leader and follower roles.

7. **Question:** *Can charisma be enhanced or increased? Why?*

   Answer: Weber's introduction of charisma into the study of leadership defined it as involving the possession of a divine grace. Although the skills used by transformational leaders have been articulated to a degree, and transformational leaders have been extensively studied, the specific knowledge of the definition of charisma has not increased appreciably. Since it is impossible to specify what charisma is, it is also impossible to say whether it can be increased. Students should conclude that the study of transformational leadership is indeed still in its infancy.

8. **Question:** *What other factors not included in Figure 13-6 are important in the achievement of leadership effectiveness?*

   Answer: This is an opinion question, and students will differ in their responses. They may suggest such items as factors in the external environment (e.g., the state of the economy, availability of able subordinates, federal regulations) or levels of available organizational resources (e.g., money, information, technology, people).

9. **Question:** *The four skills of a transformational leader involve vision, communication, building trust, and a positive self-regard. Can individuals be trained to improve these leadership skills?*

   Answer: Although vision is probably the most difficult of the four skills to develop, all of the skills can indeed be ingrained and enhanced through training and development opportunities. Student discussion should incorporate an awareness that these four skills are necessary to transformational leaders but do not *define* transformational leadership. The intangibles that constitute charisma are impossible to quantify. We thus cannot know if they can be trained, or how to do so.

236

10. **Question:** *Why would American leadership techniques probably have to be modified to be somewhat applicable in Poland?*

    Answer: The business culture of the U.S. is very different from that of Poland, which has relatively recently emerged from more than four decades of Communist rule. The cultures of the two societies are very different. Cultural diversity necessitates adaptation to achieve leadership success. American managers must therefore be open to new styles of managing and leading people.

END OF CHAPTER CASES

CASE 13-1: THE TROUBLED HOSPITAL SUPERINTENDENT

CASE SUMMARY: Tyler Medical Center is a large (1850 employees), well-respected institution. The hospital superintendent has six functional areas in direct report. Two of those, Medical Services and Nursing Services, are difficult to work with. Medical Services includes MDs and laboratory technicians. Nursing Services, with 42 supervisors and 975 total employees, includes nursing staff for bedside care, operating rooms, delivery rooms, and nurseries. The superintendent has found that a direct, frank communication style works better with Medical Services than with Nursing Services. In fact, the Nursing Services administrators are hostile toward the superintendent and toward Medical Services, and have been rude to patients. The nursing administrators believe that no standards for assessing their performance have been set, and that they are being scrutinized more closely than Medical Services.

ANSWERS TO QUESTIONS FOR ANALYSIS:

1. **Question:** *What are some of the causes of Don's problem with the nursing administrators?*

   Answer: The superintendent's assessment at monthly meetings involves someone from outside the profession judging the work of professionals. The nurses felt that they were being held to a different standard from that applied to other professionals in the hospital, and that they weren't given an opportunity to work in the setting of that standard. The superintendent used an initiating-structure approach with the nurses, while they felt he used more of a consideration approach with the doctors.

2. **Question:** *As a superintendent in Tyler Medical Center, would it be necessary to consider situational leadership theories? Why?*

   Answer: A situational approach should indeed be used in deciding how to cope with and manage the areas for which the superintendent has administrative responsibility. Each of the functional areas has unique characteristics and needs. To facilitate communication and effective management, it is necessary to assess those characteristics and utilize appropriate leadership approaches.

3.   **Question:**   *What kind of modification in the three situational dimensions—leader-member relations, task structure, and position power—could aid Don in improving his relationship with Nursing Services?*

      Answer: **Leader-member relations:** Don could ask for the nursing leaders' opinions on how to improve his relationships with the nurses. If reasonable recommendations are made, he should accept and implement them immediately.

      Task structure: Don could inform the nurses how important their job is to the patients and the hospital. He should then discuss at the monthly meeting his reason for more closely supervising the nursing operation. If he cannot justify this closeness of supervision, he should modify his practice and allow the nursing administrators more latitude in setting and achieving goals.

      Position power: Don could develop a presentation for the supervisors which indicates how he is balancing the desires and requests of many potentially conflicting groups. The key thrust of this approach would be to convince the nurses of his extremely difficult role as administrator, why he must use control, and how knowledgeable and expert he is on the total hospital system. Alternatively, he could select a chief administrator in each of his functional reporting areas, and make that person more directly responsible for the day-to-day review of activities and performance.

CASE 13-2: HARLEY - DAVIDSON: A LEADER ON A MOTORCYCLE ─────

CASE SUMMARY: Richard F. Teerlink, president and CEO of Harley-Davidson Inc., describes the dramatic turn-around his company has exhibited since the mid 1980s. He believes that management is the core of the problem for companies today. Leaders, in his view, are responsible for defining reality, being a servant, and saying thank you. The Harley values today are: 1) tell the truth, 2) keep your promises, 3) be fair, 4) respect the individual, 5) encourage intellectual curiosity. If all companies had those values, according to Teerlink, they could throw away many of their procedures manuals.

Empowerment of employees at Harley means giving employees permission to make decisions, but also building "fences". Teerlink doesn't believe in elaborate definitions of productivity; rather, he focuses on doing the right thing and doing the thing right.

Harley is flexible in its management approach. It has recently moved to a more formal corporate organization, and is becoming more directly involved in foreign markets.

ANSWERS TO QUESTIONS FOR ANALYSIS: ──────────────────────────

1.   **Question:**   *Discuss Richard Teerlink's critique of management. Why do you think he doesn't receive praise for his critique from corporate managers?*

      Answer: Students will certainly have opinions about Teerlink's views of managers. Many may disagree that managers are the main problems with organizations—but his ideas are a good stimulus for discussion and exploration. The reason he doesn't receive praise from managers (except probably from the bravest and most iconoclastic) are obvious.

2. **Question:** *What aspects of empowerment does Teerlink practice?*

    Answer: Empowerment is defined as providing employees at all levels the authority and responsibility to make decisions on their own. Although specific examples are not addressed in the case study, Teerlink's approach seems to give employees a great deal of latitude. They are, however, kept from having free reign via a clear understanding of their levels of authority. And the empowerment extends to not only allowing employees to make correct decisions, but also allowing them to make incorrect decisions, and still continuing to support them.

3. **Question:** *Teerlink emphasizes quality at Harley-Davidson. Do you think that the culture of the firm has really changed to embrace the CEO's vision of quality?*

    Answer: From the reading, it seems clear that the culture at Harley-Davidson has changed enormously under Teerlink. All of the changes enumerated have at their foundation the problems Teerlink cited in examining quality at the "old" Harley-Davidson. While the changes have been far-reaching and have had many ramifications for the organization, Teerlink's basic premise seems to have been a restoration of quality in all aspects of the organization. (Quality is defined and discussed in detail in Chapter 17 of the text.)

ADDITIONAL QUESTIONS AND ANSWERS

1. **Question:** *Some critics claim that to be an effective leader by Leadership Grid standards, a manager must be "all things to all people." Do you agree? Explain.*

    Answer: This question is designed to spur students to consider the demands which a (9,9) style places on a leader and whether meeting these demands (maintaining a flexible leadership style which emphasizes people and production) is feasible.

2. **Question:** *As French and Flaven assert, leaders draw their influence from several different bases of power. Which bases of power have you seen exercised in organizations? Which do you believe are most effective in influencing subordinate behavior?*

    Answer: The purpose of this question is to encourage students to differentiate between the types of leadership power which they've observed in organizations and to evaluate their relative effectiveness in leading subordinates. Legitimate and reward powers are most often observed; referent is the least observed.

3. **Question:** *What are the significant differences between leaders and managers?*
    Answer: Leaders in organizations can be managers in that they plan, organize, and make decisions to manage the ongoing activities of the organization. However, the key ingredient of leadership is the ability to unite a group of people and influence them to achieve particular organizational goals. In this respect, all managers aren't leaders because some lack the ability to influence.

4. **Question:** *Discuss the contribution(s) the trait theory has made to our understanding of leadership. Why have researchers dismissed trait theory as a viable perspective on leadership?*
    Answer: Through research, trait theory has added to our understanding of the substantial importance of particular traits (e.g., self-assurance, intelligence, decisiveness) and insignificance of other traits (e.g., masculinity-femininity) in management success. However, trait theory also presents several shortcomings. For instance, it ignores the role of subordinates, and does not specify the relative importance of various traits. Moreover, the number of potential traits is endless, and some are difficult or impossible to define. Research findings to date are also inconsistent.

5. **Question:** *Max DePree of Herman Miller suggests that empowerment is challenging to organizations. Do you agree? Why?*
    Answer: This question allows students to examine more closely the assertion that it is difficult for leaders to share responsibility for decision-making, problem-solving, and job design. In fact, it may also be difficult for non-managers to share in those duties. The controversy cited in the chapter over the use of tropical wood in Herman Miller furniture is a relatively minor example of the kinds of issues which may arise in organizations when highly empowered employees make far-reaching decisions. Students may refer to the "fences" alluded to by Harley-Davidson's Richard Teerlink in Case 13-2.

6. **Question:** *"Because of their cultural conditioning to be assertive and competitive, men make better leaders in organizations than women." Respond to this statement.*
    Answer: This question is designed to open a lively student debate concerning whether assertiveness and competitiveness are: 1) necessary ingredients to successful leadership; and 2) exclusively masculine characteristics. If assertiveness and competitiveness are essential to success, can women assert themselves, compete and lead successfully? If they are not essential to success, what characteristics are essential? Opinion should differ if students are candid with their feelings.

240

7. **Question:** *Some scholars believe that leaders actually exert limited influence on the organization because of such constraining factors as pressure from peers, subordinates and supervisors, the limits of the leader's own abilities, organizational policies, and numerous factors (e.g., social, economic, political) outside the organization which are beyond the leader's control. Do you agree? Explain.*

   Answer: This question is designed to spur students to consider that other factors beyond the leader affect and often impinge on leader effectiveness. Students will likely agree that other factors affect leader influence; however, opinion should differ concerning the degree of influence of the mentioned factors on an effective leader.

8. **Question:** *Evaluate Fiedler's leadership theory in terms of its strength and shortcomings.*

   Answer: Fiedler's theory was one of the first models to view leader effectiveness as contingent on situational factors. However, the theory presents some shortcomings which include exclusion of leaders with middle LPC scores, the methodology and meaning of the LPC measure, and the fact that many subjects used in Fiedler's studies aren't representative of subordinates in organizations.

9. **Question:** *Of the leadership theories presented in the chapter, which theory, in your opinion, contributes most to our understanding of leadership? Why?*

   Answer: This question is designed to spur students to evaluate the strengths and shortcomings of the theories presented in this chapter and to assess, in part, each theory's applicability in organizations.

10. **Question:** *What contribution(s) did the personal-behavioral theories make to our understanding of leadership? Why have researchers dismissed them as a viable perspective on understanding leadership effectiveness?*

   Answer: The theories added to our understanding of the role of behavioral styles in leadership. However, many researchers have dismissed these theories because they advocate a "one best" leadership style which is presumably superior in all situations. Much research has shown that effective leadership style depends on the respective situation; utilizing a particular style in all cases is generally not successful.

COMMUNICATION AND NEGOTIATION

LEARNING OBJECTIVES

After completing Chapter 14, students should be able to:

Define	each element in the process of communication.
Describe	communication and negotiation in organizations.
Discuss	nonverbal communication and its importance in organizations.
Compare	situations in which informal and formal channels of communication would be utilized.
Identify	the major reasons why communications break down.

CHAPTER SYNOPSIS

The chapter's treatment of the issue of interpersonal and organizational communication focuses on six topics of importance: the communications process and its components, directional flows of organizational communication, the dynamics of interpersonal communication, the barriers to effective communication, managerial strategies to improve the communication process between managers and subordinates, and the negotiation process. The chapter begins by presenting a model of the communication process. The model's components **(communicator, perception and interpretation, encoding, message, channel, receiver, decoding, noise, and feedback)** are explained with examples provided to clarify each concept. The importance of nonverbal communication is discussed and international differences are highlighted.

Concerning the directional flows of organizational communication, **downward, upward, lateral, and diagonal** communications are discussed, with examples provided that illustrate how organizations utilize each directional channel. The chapter's discussion of interpersonal communication focuses on four managerial communicative styles **(Types A, B, C, and D)** and four "regions" where interpersonal communications occur (the **arena, blindspot, facade,** and **unknown**).

Nine common communication barriers **(differing frames of reference, selective perception, poor listening skills, value judgments, source credibility, semantic problems, filtering, time pressures,** and **communication overload)** are explained, with examples provided to illustrate the impact on organizations.

The chapter then gives an overview of managerial strategies to improve the manager's communicative abilities **(following up, regulating information flow, utilizing feedback, empathy, simplifying language, effective listening,** and **using the grapevine).** It then defines the negotiation process, and presents the components of effective negotiations **(prenegotiation tasks, negotiation tactics,** and **the roles of personalities and trust in negotiations.)**

The chapter's **Management In Action** describes programs in place at Avon, Apple Computer, Digital, and Prudential Insurance to increase communication regarding employee diversity. The **Management Focus** sections describe Hanna Anderson's proactive solicitation of customer comments during the order-taking process; the rapidly changing advances in information technology and telecommunications technology today; and Reflexite Corporation's innovative upward feedback program, allowing employees to notify management of problems and assist in their solution.

TEACHING TIPS

LECTURE & DISCUSSION IDEAS

1. One way to illustrate the nature and consequences of communications barriers is to have your students recount a past situation where they experienced a substantial breakdown in communications with another individual(s). Ask students to identify the communications barrier(s) at work. Why did they occur? What were the consequences of the breakdown? Was the problem resolved and if so, how? Then ask one or two students to share their experiences and explanations in class discussion.

2. Have your students ever participated in a negotiation? If they have ever purchased a car or a house, rented an apartment, or acquired any other big-ticket item, they probably have. Explore the negotiation tactics described in this chapter. Did the other party use any of the tactics described? Did the student?

PROJECT / EXERCISE IDEAS

1. Have your students prepare a profile of someone they know well who is a type A, B, C or D communicator. Their profile should focus on the individual's communication style, personality characteristics and the student's assessment of why the person uses that particular communication style. Is the style effective? What problem(s) does it present?

2. As a group project, have your students interview the director of corporate communications for a local business. In their written report, students should focus on the department's communication functions, particular challenges in effectively communicating with employees, and on the director's perspectives on the uses of informal communication channels (in particular, the grapevine).

3. Have your students, on an individual basis, interview a first line, middle, or top-level manager concerning his/her use of formal and informal communication channels in management. The written report should focus on the manager's communication style, use of communication channels, perspective on communication barriers, strategies for alleviating barriers, and the manager's advice in developing effective communication

skills. In discussing students' reports, focus on any differences in communication styles and use of communication channels that differ according to the manager's position in the organizational hierarchy. Some differences should emerge.

LECTURE OUTLINE NOTES

I. Chapter Introduction

    A.   Communication is one of the most vital skills for managers.
        1.   Managers rarely work with "things". Rather, they work with "information about things".
        2.   Communicating involves the emotional, psychological, and mental characteristics of individuals, as well as the technical characteristics of the medium of communication.
        3.   Organizations are increasingly assessing managerial communications skills and providing training to overcome deficiencies.

II. The Process of Communication

    A.   **Communication is the transmission of common understanding through the use of symbols.**
    B.   The communications process involves important stages and elements (see Figure 14-1 for a diagram of the communication process):
        1.   **The communicator**—whether a manager, a non-manager, a department, or the organization itself, the communicator initiates the process with the need to transmit an idea, message, or information to another party.
        2.   **Perception and Interpretation**—how the receiver views or perceives the communicator's message.
        3.   **Encoding**—the communicator translates the communication into a language or some other systematic set of symbols which the receiver can understand.
        4.   **The message**—the result of the encoding process; what the communicator hopes to communicate to the receiver, either verbally or nonverbally.
        5.   **The channel**—the carrier of the message; that is, the means by which the message travels (for example, telephone, telegram, memo, tone of voice, reward systems, computers).
            a.   **Unintended** messages—sent by silence or inaction on an issue.
            b.   **Nonverbal communication**—communication without words—e.g., a smile, a frown, even the seating arrangements at a committee meeting.
            c.   **Body language**—a prominent type of nonverbal communication.
                1)   Open body positions that suggest acceptance or openness to what is being said—leaning forward, uncrossed arms and legs.

              2)   Closed positions that suggest being uncomfortable (physically or psychologically)—leaning back with crossed arms and legs.

              3)   Meanings are culturally derived.

      d.   Paul Ekman's Facial Affect Scoring Technique (FAST) proposes that emotions can be found in the following parts of the face:

              1)   Fear—in the eyes

              2)   Sadness—in the brows, forehead, eyes

              3)   Disgust—nose, cheeks, mouth

              4)   Happiness—cheeks, mouth, eyes

              5)   Surprise—any area of the face

              6)   Anger—forehead, brows

6.   **Decoding**—the message's receiver translates the message into a meaningful "language." Involves interpretation—that is, the receiver translating the message in light of his or her previous experiences and frame of reference. A common problem—important parts of the message are lost in the decoding process.

      a.   Staff specialists and technical employees may employ language and symbols in their communication that other employees cannot understand.

7.   **Receiver**—the recipient of the message. Effective communication is "receiver-oriented" and requires that the communicator understand the receiver's decoding ability.

8.   **Feedback**—occurs when the receiver responds to the message, enabling the communicator to determine whether the message has been received and has produced the intended response. Feedback forms are:

      a.   **Direct** (for example, verbal exchanges, facial expressions).

      b.   **Indirect** (for example, declines in productivity, increased absenteeism).

9.   **Noise** factors which can distort the intended message. Noise can be present in any of the elements of communication.

III.   Communications in Organizations

    A.   Organizational communication flows in four directions (see Figure 14-2 for a visual depiction of the four directions of organizational communications flow):

      1.   **Downward**—from individuals at higher levels to those at lower levels of the organization.

        a.   The five most common types are job instructions; job descriptions; organization policies; procedures, and practices; employee performance feedback; and indoctrination of company goals.

        b.   Often inadequate and inaccurate in many companies. ("We have no idea what's happening.")

        c.   In large organizations, communication with employees is typically undertaken by a trained staff of communication experts who produce a publication ("house organ", e.g., a newsletter) that:

            1)   Explains the organization's plans and programs.

            2)   Answers complaints and criticisms.

               3)   Defends the status quo and those responsible for it.

    2.   **Upward**—from individuals in the lower levels to those in the organization's higher levels. Often difficult to achieve, especially in larger organizations, but vital in providing top management with organizational information essential for effective decision making. Common mediums: suggestion boxes, group meetings, grievance procedures.

        a.   The Japanese place a strong emphasis on face-to-face communications between top-level managers and rank-and-file employees.

    3.   **Lateral**—horizontal communication in an organization (for example, a telephone conversation between the vice president of marketing and the vice president of finance).

    4.   **Diagonal**—the least used channel of communication. Occurs when individuals sidestep formal channels (for example, a financial vice president communicating directly with members of the organization's sales force).

IV.   Interpersonal Communication

    A.   Flows from individual to individual in face-to-face and group settings, varying in form from direct orders to facial expressions.

    B.   There are four regions of information known and unknown by the self (communicator) and others (see Figure 14-3):

        1.   The **arena**—the region most conducive for effective interpersonal communication; where all the information necessary for carrying on effective communication is known to the communicator and the message receiver(s). The area of common understanding.

        2.   The **blind spot** where relevant information is known to others (receivers), but not the communicator. Places the communicator at a disadvantage, and diminishes the arena.

        3.   The **facade**—where information is known to the communicator but not to the receiver(s). The communicator presents a "false front" to the receiver(s) which diminishes the arena.

        4.   The **unknown**—where neither communicator nor receiver knows the relevant feelings, sentiments, and information of the other (e.g., "I don't understand them and they don't understand me").

    C.   Strategies for improving interpersonal communications.

        1.   **Exposure**—occurs when the communicator is open and honest with receivers. Enlarges the arena and reduces the facade. Often involves risks, increasing the communicator's vulnerability.

        2.   **Feedback**—occurs when the communicator seeks information and opinions from others. Enlarges the arena and reduces the blindspot. Less under the control of the communicator than is the provision of exposure.

    D.   Management styles—the way in which an individual prefers to relate to others. A manager's style can substantially affect his or her ability and willingness to use feedback and exposure to improve interpersonal communication. There are four basic managerial styles:

        1.   **Type A**—often autocratic, Type A managers refuse to use either

feedback or exposure and often appear anxious, cold, aloof, and even hostile with subordinates.

2. **Type B**—managers desire some type of satisfying relationship with subordinates but they are unable to open up and express themselves. Using only feedback but no exposure, they primarily resort to facades.

3. **Type C**—managers overuse exposure and are primarily interested in telling, not communicating. This style enlarges the blindspot.

4. **Type D**—the most effective style, balancing the use of feedback and exposure and enlarging the arena.

V. Why Communications Break Down

    A. Communications breakdowns occur when a defect arises in any one of the components in the communication process. Nine major barriers to effective communication frequently arise:

        1. **Differing frames of reference**—people can encode and decode messages differently because of different frames of reference which are a product of different individual backgrounds and experiences. The result is distorted communication. Individuals with responsibilities in different areas of the organization, or at different organizational levels, can use different frames of reference which are partly a product of their organizational position (for example, a first-line supervisor's frame of reference can substantially differ from that of a vice president).

        2. **Selective perception**—occurs when people block out information that conflicts with their beliefs, attitudes and values, and perceive only information that is consistent with these elements.

            a. Results in **stereotyping** because individuals hear only information which confirms their perceived notions.

        3. **Poor listening skills**—not listening to the communicator. Many people have poor listening habits.

        4. **Value judgments**—are used when a receiver assigns an overall worth to a message before receiving the entire communication. The value judgment may be based on such factors as evaluation of the communicator and the receiver's previous experiences with the communicator.

        5. **Source credibility**—the trust, confidence, and faith that the receiver has in the communicator's words and actions. Directly affects the receiver's interpretation of the message.

        6. **Semantic problems**—arise when words and terms used to communicate the message are not understood in the same way by the communicator and the receiver. In particular, international semantic differences need to be understood by managers dealing globally, and in-group language can be problematic when communicating outside the group.

        7. **Filtering**—manipulating information so it is perceived as positive to the message receiver (analogous to "telling the boss what he/she wants to hear"). Generally, the larger the number of managerial levels in an organization, the greater the degree of information filtering that occurs.

        8. **Time pressures**—hinder communication because managers lack the time to communicate with each subordinate. **Short—circuiting** often results,

247

in which someone normally included in the communication channel is excluded because of time pressures.

9. **Communication overload**—occurs when managers "screen out" many messages (never decoding them) because they are deluged with information.

B. All these barriers are within individuals or within organizations.

1. Attempts to improve communications must focus on changing people and/or the organizational structure.

VI. Improving Communications in Organizations

A. Managers can employ seven strategies to improve their ability to both encode and decode information:

1. **Following up**—on messages sent to ensure that receivers correctly decoded the message.

2. **Regulating information flow**—by implementing the "exception principle" of management whereby only significant deviations from policies and procedures should be brought to the manager's attention. (More useful for classical organizations than neoclassical organizations with free-flowing information.)

3. **Utilizing feedback**—a channel for receiver response, allowing the communicator to determine whether the message has been received and has produced the desired response. Table 14-1 gives the characteristics of effective and ineffective managerial feedback.

   a. Managers often give too little feedback to their subordinates.

4. **Empathy**—the ability to put oneself in the other person's role and assume the person's viewpoints and emotions. This ability is vital to anticipating how messages will be decoded by receivers.

   a. Decoding is done through the perceptions of the receiver.

5. **Simplifying language**—focusing on transmitting understanding.

6. **Effective listening**—making the decision to listen with understanding.

   a. The Ten Commandments for good listening—stop talking, put the speaker at ease, show the speaker you want to listen, remove distractions, empathize with the speaker, be patient, hold your temper, go easy on argument and criticism, ask questions, and stop talking.

7. **Use the grapevine**—often a fast, efficient, and accurate communication medium. Capable of transmitting information quickly because it is flexible and involves face-to-face communication and is often used to spread rumors. The grapevine will always exist in organizations.

VII. Improving Group Communication through Negotiation

A. The effective negotiation process is a collaborative pursuit of joint gains and a collaborative effort to create value where none previously existed.

1. Two people or groups attempt to make joint decisions regarding the allocation of scarce resources.

2. Managers negotiate with subordinates, superiors, vendors, and customers daily.

B. Group negotiations

1. Occur when the work of one group is dependent on the cooperation and actions of another group over which the first group's manager has no control.
2. The only really successful negotiations are those in which all affected parties feel like they have won.

C. Prenegotiation tasks
   1. Understanding the other side.
      a. Managers should thoroughly understand the other side's needs and positions regarding the issues to be resolved.
         1) Managers must ask questions to gain the needed information.
         2) Surprise only hinders and delays the negotiation process.
   2. Knowing all the options
      a. Information must be used to develop, understand, and evaluate options. The greater the number of options that can be identified, the greater the likelihood that both groups can benefit from the negotiation process.

D. Negotiation Tactics
   1. There are many tactics. The appropriate tactic depends on the situation. Some of the most common tactics:
      a. Good-person/bad-person—the bad-person advocates positions so out of line that whatever the good-person says sounds reasonable by comparison.
      b. The nibble—getting an additional concession after an agreement is reached.
      c. Joint problem solving—jointly coming up with ways both sides can win.
      d. Power of competition—using competition to make opponents think they're not needed.
      e. Splitting the difference—used when the negotiations are at an impasse.
      f. Lowballing—using low offers and concessions to lower the other group's expectations.

E. The Impact of Personalities on the Negotiation Process
   1. Negotiators come from different backgrounds, and with different perspectives.
      a. They have different propensities to take risks.
   2. Managers should look for what really motivates the individuals on the other side.

F. The Role of Trust in Negotiations
   1. There is a greater likelihood of beneficial outcome if the groups in a negotiation have a degree of trust for each other.
      a. There is generally some chicanery in the negotiating process. Negotiators will bluff about the firmness of their position when they are in fact flexible.
   2. A good negotiator will never place the other party in a position where he/she can't move without losing face.
   3. Negotiations can improve communication between groups.

ANSWERS TO DISCUSSION AND REVIEW QUESTIONS

1. **Question:** *What types of barriers to communication exist in a class setting? How can they be overcome?*

    Answer: All of the nine barriers to communication described in the text can occur in a class setting, whether we consider the instructor to be the manager and the students to be subordinates or *vice versa*. For instance, a long-time manager as the instructor in an Intro to Management class has a very different frame of reference than do the students, and may exhibit poor listening skills in taking students' questions. Students likewise may have semantic problems if they haven't done their homework and are unfamiliar with the terminology, or may face communication overload at midterms time. Overcoming these barriers in the classroom is similar to overcoming them in other settings; students may discuss the uses of following up, utilizing feedback, empathy, simplifying language, and effective listening in resolving communication problems in the classroom. (Note that regulating information flow and using the grapevine are less likely to be effective in the classroom environment.)

2. **Question:** *As American corporations hire increasing numbers of immigrants, what role will the assessment of nonverbal communication play in interviewing job candidates?*

    Answer: The use of nonverbal communication assessment will be more difficult because of a lack of comparative experience of the assessor. A reduced role should result until an effective experience base is built up. Meanwhile, interviewers should seek guidance on how to interpret nonverbal cues of people from different cultures.

3. **Question:** *Based on your own experience, which element of communication has most often been the cause of your failure to communicate? How can you improve your communication effectiveness?*

    Answer: Responses are specific to each student's experiences. Concerning steps to improve communication ability, students may mention such alternatives as following up on a message sent to ensure the message was correctly decoded, obtaining and using feedback from message receivers, simplifying language, and developing empathy and effective listening techniques.

4. **Question:** *Are you a Type A, B, C, or D person when you engage in interpersonal communications? Are you satisfied to be what you think you are? Why? If not, how could you change?*

    Answer: Responses are specific to each student's experience and opinion, although most students will probably claim to be type D communicators. The instructor may wish to challenge students to a more in-depth

250

appraisal of their true style. Regarding ways to change interpersonal communication style, students may mention such approaches as developing effective listening skills and empathy, actively seeking feedback from others, and attempting to be more open with feelings and opinions. All of these approaches are applicable to altering Types A, B, and C.

5. **Question:**   *How would you feed back information to employees about their performance?*

    Answer: Performance feedback is best provided to employees on a continual basis, but is difficult for many managers and supervisors to deliver effectively. Performance feedback is different from the feedback described in the chapter for improving communications—performance feedback is a *type* of communication, while communications feedback is a *strategy* for improving overall information encoding and decoding. Six of the seven strategies (all except the grapevine) are effective means for providing performance feedback; the grapevine as a mechanism may be a devastatingly inappropriate approach.

6. **Question:**   *Why is source credibility such an important trait for a manager to possess? How can one increase his own source credibility?*

    Answer: There is unlikely to be a great deal of disagreement among students that subordinates, peers, supervisors, and the general public all must have trust, confidence, and faith in a manager for that manager's communications to be received straightforwardly. Discussing students' feelings about communications attempts from business or political leaders who they don't trust may assist in focusing the discussion. Mechanisms for increasing one's source credibility are as complex as the human personalities of the managers themselves; exploration of the topic will generate lively debate.

7. **Question:**   *Describe a situation where you heard a rumor through a grapevine. Did the rumor turn out to be true?*

    Answer: It is helpful to try to steer this discussion toward rumors in business or school (as opposed to social) situations. As students discuss their experiences, they may wish to consider whether some of those rumors may have been deliberately started by other managers or executives in the organization.

8. **Question:**   *Why is accuracy of lateral information so important to employees working in different units?*

    Answer: Lateral communication is the principal mechanism whereby various organizational departments can gain a clear understanding of other areas and their functions. The accuracy of lateral information is critical in effective strategic decision making, planning, and coordinating among the departments.

9. **Question:** *Describe a situation where you, as an individual or member of a group, were involved in a negotiation process. Did you consider the outcome of the process as being satisfactory to both sides? Why or why not?*

   Answer: This question provides an opportunity to reinforce the notion that truly successful negotiations are those in which both sides feel as though they have won. The discussion should focus on the collaborative efforts used and joint gains realized, as well as on the prenegotiation and negotiation strategies used. The point can also be made that in both very successful and very unsuccessful negotiations, personalities and trust between the parties may be key.

10. **Question:** *How could a lack of trust between two departments in an organization lead to a breakdown in negotiations? Provide an example to back up your answer.*

    Answer: If departments don't trust each other with vital information about themselves, it is much more difficult to arrive at truly beneficial outcomes. Examples of negotiations which have broken down over lack of trust are plentiful; political negotiations in countries with internal warring factions (such as Bosnia and Herzegovina in the 1990s, or Lebanon in the 1980s) demonstrate the impact of lack of trust on negotiations.

END OF CHAPTER CASES

CASE 14-1: QUALITY COMMUNICATION AT FEDERAL EXPRESS

CASE SUMMARY: The success of Federal Express in the international air-freight business arena is attributable in part to its extensive efforts at continuing communications with employees and customers. When Federal Express purchased Flying Tiger Line (an organization with a long history and a largely unionized employee base), top executives of both groups immediately gave a company-wide presentation over the company's satellite television network emphasizing that the move was a merger, not an acquisition. For months thereafter, extensive in-house communications strategies were used to talk with and listen to employees; FedEx management believes this communications effort has spurred corporate growth. FedEx also uses technology to insure a high level of customer access between themselves and their customers at all times. As a result of its efforts, FedEx has won the Baldrige Award and been named in "The 100 Best Companies to Work for in America".

ANSWERS TO QUESTIONS FOR ANALYSIS:

1. **Question:** *What is your opinion of the employee communication strategy that FedEx employed at the time of the merger?*

   Answer: The information presented in the case indicates that FedEx used multiple channels to allow for information flow in multiple directions, and to facilitate accurate decoding of management's messages. Students should discuss how the communications described were effective in terms of the concepts discussed in the chapter.

2. **Question:** *How does FedEx's communication strategy influence the effectiveness of the organization?*

   Answer: FedEx's communications strategies center on its customers and its human resources, the most critical direct forces impacting on any business organization. It may be instructive to ask students to compare what they know of FedEx's communications with what they know of the U.S. Postal Service, or other large organizations with both domestic and international focus, to try to assess the degree to which effective communications are a key competitive factor.

3. **Question:** *Suggest other means by which companies such as FedEx could further their communications activities, both with employees and customers.*

   Answer: This is an exercise in creativity, in which students may suggest a broad variety of communications messages and channels. A key point to make is that *communication* is not the same as *effective communication*. In utilizing multiple means for communicating, organizations must incorporate mechanisms from among the strategies to facilitate accurate encoding and decoding of messages.

CASE 14-2: "DO YOU KNOW WHAT I LIKE ABOUT YOU?"————————

CASE SUMMARY: This case profiles Jim McCabe, a successful, self-made bloodstock agent in the thoroughbred horse industry. Evidently, Mr. McCabe is experiencing some communications problems with his subordinates which seem to be a product of his own Type A communications style. This case provides an excellent opportunity for students to assess and discuss the costs which an ineffective interpersonal communications style can incur.

ANSWERS TO QUESTIONS FOR ANALYSIS: ————————————

1. **Question:** *What is your impression of McCabe?*

   Answer: McCabe is a highly ambitious, fast-moving individual who evidently employs a Type A style of interpersonal communication. He tends to be impatient and wants results fast.

2. **Question:** *What is your opinion of his communications to the other employees of the firm?*

   Answer: His communications are often ineffective because of his Type A style. McCabe obviously has little time or interest in two-way communications with employees. He is interested only in the "bottom line" in communicating with employees and is not interested in "details" and employees' opinions and perspectives. However, he is likely ignoring pertinent information from subordinates. It is clear that he also is not effectively encoding his messages because employees have misunderstood his requests in the past. Evidently, McCabe is not clearly specifying what he wants from his subordinates. This may be due to his work overload or to his assumption that his subordinates know what he wants. However, often they do not.

3. **Question:** *What might be the reasons for his demands on employees?*
   Answer: His demands are likely the result of a misassumption that his employees know what he wants.

4. **Question:** *Could this influence the effectiveness of the organization? In what ways?*
   Answer: It certainly does. Much time is wasted in subordinates correcting their "mistakes" because they didn't understand what McCabe wanted. Obviously, morale is adversely affected as subordinates can't seem to satisfy the boss and likely become discouraged and dissatisfied.

ADDITIONAL QUESTIONS AND ANSWERS

1. **Question:** *During disagreements, we often hear someone say, "That's not what I said." Discuss what this statement means in terms of the elements of communication presented in the chapter.*
   Answer: This statement illustrates a breakdown in the communication process. As a result, communication has not occurred. The breakdown may be due to one or more of a variety of factors—including encoding or decoding of the message, or communication barriers such as selective perception, differing frames of reference, filtering, or communication overload. The key point is that in this situation, communication has not occurred because the intended message was not received.

2. **Question:** *Briefly review the elements of the communications process.*
   Answer: The elements are: 1) the communicator who sends the message; 2) encoding, which is the process of translating the communication into a language which the receiver can understand; 3) the message which results from the encoding process; 4) the medium which is the means by which the message travels; 5) decoding which occurs when the message's recipient translates the message into a meaningful language; 6) the receiver who is the message's recipient; 7) feedback which occurs when the receiver responds to the message; 8) noise which includes factors that can distort the intended message; and 9) the perception and interpretation which occur on the part of both the communicator and the receiver.

3. **Question:** *Explain how differing frames of reference can act as a communicators barrier.*

   Answer: Because of differing frames of reference (a product of different individual backgrounds and experiences), the recipient may receive a different message in the decoding process than what the communicator intended in the encoding process.

4. **Question:** *What, if anything, can managers do to remove barriers to communication that are beyond their control?*

   Answer: Managerial actions in this regard are limited in effectiveness. For instance, there is little managers can do to substantially influence different subordinate frames of reference which have developed over years of individual experience. However, it can be argued that (within limits) effective listening and open communication by managers can ease problems caused by different barriers.

5. **Question:** *Do you believe you are an effective listener? What steps could you take to improve your listening skills?*

   Answer: This question is intended to encourage students to evaluate their own listening abilities and to consider whether they subscribe to some of the poor habits (e.g., faking attention, avoiding difficult listening) that result in poor listening. Making the "decision to listen" is probably the key element here; students can be encouraged to discuss the obstacles to making that decision.

6. **Question:** *If a manager does not achieve the purpose or effect that he or she desired as a consequence of sending a message, has communication occurred?*

   Answer: Effective communication is transmitting a "mutual understanding" by using symbols, whether the symbols be facial expressions, language, or some other means. Reaching a mutual understanding between the message sender and receiver is the essence of communication. If the message's intended effect isn't realized, no effective communication has occurred because the mutual understanding—the key to effective communication—wasn't achieved.

7. **Question:** *How often do you experience communications overload? What approaches do you use to manage the problem?*

   Answer: This question is intended for students to assess situations in which they've experienced communications overload and the steps they've taken to alleviate the problem. Another question to ponder: How effective are their strategies? Are others potentially more effective?

8.   **Question:** *Can you think of a situation when you've "selectively perceived" new information? What do you think caused the "block-out"? Was the selective perception justified?*

        Answer: In answering this question, students should consider the circumstances that might lead to selective perceptions in a business setting, and the costs versus benefits of selective perception.

9.   **Question:** *Differentiate between a blindspot a facade.*

        Answer: The blindspot is the region of information where relevant information is known to others (receivers) but not to the communicator, placing the communicator at a disadvantage. The facade is where information is known to the communicator but not to the receiver, placing the receiver at a disadvantage. Here, the communicator presents a "false front" to the receiver.

10.   **Question:** *Of the communication barriers discussed, which barrier do you believe is the most difficult to alleviate? Explain.*

        Answer: Students will likely provide different views on this question. Arguably, conflicting frames of references and selective perception are the most difficult barriers to alleviate. Conflicting frames of reference will always exist in communication between two or more people simply because each individual differs in his/her background and experiences from which frames of reference are developed. Selective perception is a defensive mechanism used to protect one's own sense of the world and is very difficult to eliminate from cognitive processes.

HUMAN RESOURCE MANAGEMENT

LEARNING OBJECTIVES

After completing Chapter 15, students should be able to:

Define   human resource management (HRM).

Describe   the activities conducted by various divisions of a human resource department: employment, training and development, wage and salary management, employee benefits and services, and labor relations.

Discuss   what is meant by sexual harassment.

Compare   HRM activities in large and small business organizations.

Identify   the impact that laws and executive orders have had on the management of human resources.

CHAPTER SYNOPSIS

This chapter addresses the multi-faceted functions of human resources management by focusing on seven topics: The **HRM function, recruitment of employees, employee selection and placement, training and development, performance appraisal, wage and salary management,** and **labor relations.**

Termed both a line and staff function, HRM is defined as the process of accomplishing organizational objectives by acquiring, retaining, terminating, developing and properly using an organization's human resources. The major laws affecting HRM in the U.S. today—**the Civil Rights Act of 1964, including Title VII and the EEOC amendment, the Civil Rights Act of 1991, the Americans with Disabilities Act of 1990,** and **the Family and Medical Leave Act of 1993**—are discussed in detail, as are definitions of and mechanisms to combat sexual harassment in the workplace. The **recruitment** function of HRM is discussed in terms of its major objective—acquiring the most qualified candidates for vacant positions. Much of the discussion focuses on **job analysis** including the two primary approaches to job analysis (functional job analysis and the position analysis questionnaire) and the analysis' end products, the **job description** and **job specification.** Concerning employee selection and placement, the chapter presents a eight-step model of the selection and placement process which serves as the framework of discussion. The eight steps (**preliminary screening, application completion, interviews, testing, background check, hiring decision, job offer,** and **employment orientation**) are presented with emphasis on interviews and testing (the advantages and disadvantages of testing are explored). **Alcohol and drug testing** are discussed, along with the promising new area called **performance testing.** Following implementation of the Employee Polygraph Protection Act of 1988, pen-and-paper **honesty testing** is also examined. Employee **training and development** is addressed by summarizing the objectives and types of training programs and major managerial development methods. Discussion of **Performance appraisal** focuses on the three requirements of performance appraisal (standards, information, and corrective action), major decisions to make in setting up a system, and two popular performance appraisal techniques (graphic rating scales and BARS) with sample formats provided to illustrate each technique. Concerning **wage and salary management**, the chapter discusses the three major types of compensation: wages (discussion focuses on the ways in which wage levels are determined), salaries, and benefits and services.

The chapter's final section focuses on **labor relations** in organizations. A brief overview of the roles of **unions** in the U.S. is presented along with the reasons people do and don't join unions. The process of **collective bargaining** is also presented, focusing on the different types of collective bargaining and bargaining relationships, bargaining issues, the different approaches to resolving a negotiating impasse between management and labor (e.g., **strike, lockout, work slowdown, mediation,** and **arbitration**), and the existence and use of **grievance procedures** in organizations.

The chapter's **Management in Action** describes efforts at four organizations (Colgate-Palmolive, Corning, Quaker Oats, and Monsanto) to move beyond diversity training, incorporating diversity management effectiveness into managers' performance appraisal and/or compensation, and creating mentoring programs. The **Management Focus** sections examine the highly-regarded employee benefits programs at Hallmark Cards; the use of daily performance testing as an alternative to drug testing at San Diego's Old Town Trolley; and two cases in which fired employees successfully sued their employers in firing and defamation cases in which facts were not certain or fired employees were made a public example.

TEACHING TIPS

LECTURE & DISCUSSION IDEAS

1.   One way to further explore the process of employee selection is to obtain a number of job application forms from a variety of businesses (large and small companies from different industries) and duplicate two or three forms as class handouts. Have the students read the forms in class and compare and contrast the applications in class discussion, evaluating the information value of the questions and the overall quality of the applications.

2.   To demonstrate the difficulty in developing effective performance criteria, suggest two or three occupations (e.g., pediatrician, Congressmember, production manager) in class and have students, as an in-class assignment, develop a list of criteria for each position.

3.   One way to encourage students to more closely evaluate the two performance appraisal techniques covered in the chapter is to ask them to offer strengths and shortcomings for graphic rating scales and the BARS technique beyond those noted in the text. You could also obtain sample appraisal forms from local businesses and have students evaluate them as a basis for class discussion.

4. Although there are formal, legal definitions for sexual harassment in Title VII, many managers and employees are uncertain as to what does and does not constitute sexual harassment in the workplace. If the dynamics of the classroom situation allow, students can be encouraged to discuss and debate their opinions as to what actually constitutes sexual harassment. In this discussion, the instructor's role is as both a facilitator (to keep the flow of information focused) and a resource (keeping the definition of sexual harassment handy and answering students' questions).

PROJECT / EXERCISE IDEAS

1. As an individual or group project, have your students interview a recruiter from a local business (or one from a major company on campus to recruit students) concerning his or her approach to recruiting. The interview can cover several topics including:
    a. The specific qualities the interviewer looks for when interviewing candidates.
    b. The importance of personality, appearance, and resume in evaluating a candidate.
    c. Favorite questions used by the interviewer that are particularly revealing concerning the candidate's characteristics.
    d. The best and worst things to do in an interview.

2. Few issues are more controversial in business today than Affirmative Action, with proponents asserting that the program is necessary to ensure equal treatment in hiring and promotion decisions while critics assert that the program discriminates against qualified non-minorities. Put the issue before your class by conducting a class debate on the question: Should Affirmative Action programs be maintained in businesses? Establish two debate teams (of five to seven members each) with each team assuming one side of the question. Each team should thoroughly research the issue and use information as a basis for its position. The students who are not on a team should also research the issue, write a paper that presents both sides of the issue, and assume responsibility for asking pertinent questions to both teams during the debate conducted in class. The team winner can be determined by class vote.

3. Instead of obtaining performance appraisal forms yourself, have your students, as a group assignment, obtain an example of a performance appraisal from a local business and critique the form in terms of its strengths and weaknesses.

4. Are unions diminishing in influence in the U.S. today? Students can be encouraged to interview local managers and executives, union leaders, and unionized and non-unionized workers, asking the importance of unions in American business. Although the viewpoints expressed will range widely, students can look for common threads and attempt to discern for themselves the values of unions in the 1990s.

LECTURE OUTLINE NOTES

I.   Human Resource Management

    A.   Involves the securing, retaining, and developing of an organization's human resources.

    B.   Is both a line management responsibility and a staff function.

    C.   Is handled by an HRM department in larger organizations.

    D.   Plays an important role in strategic planning as organizations seek to compete effectively at home and internationally.

        1.   Executives believe service and product quality and productivity are critical; and prefer human resource methods over technology methods to improve quality and productivity.

    E.   A formal definition: HRM is the process of accomplishing organizational objectives by acquiring, retaining, terminating, developing, and properly using human resources in an organization.

        1.   **Acquisition**—involves recruiting, screening, selecting, and properly placing personnel.

        2.   **Retaining**—important, as losing good people incurs costs in seeking and hiring new people.

        3.   **Termination**—procedures are usually specified by an HRM staff expert or a labor contract.

        4.   **Developing**—involves training, educating, appraising, and preparing personnel for present and future jobs, to meet employees' need for personal growth.

        5.   **Proper use of people**—involves understanding both individual and organizational needs.

    F.   The Personnel/HRM Department

        1.   Organized according to the needs, objectives, and size of the organization.

        2.   A typical HRM department in a large organization is shown in Fig. 15-1.

            a.   Includes Employment, Wage and Salary, Labor Relations, Training and Development, and Employee Benefits and Services divisions.

    G.   Laws and Regulations

        1.   **The Civil Rights Act of 1964**

            a.   **Title VII** prohibits discrimination in hiring, compensation, terms and conditions, or privileges of employment based on race, religion, color, sex, or national origin.

                1)   Any employer with 25 or more employees is covered.

            b.   **Equal Employment Opportunity Commission (EEOC)**

                1)   Created in 1972 as an amendment to Title VII, to investigate discrimination charges and file civil suits if necessary.

            c.   Title VII today specifies that firms actively recruit and give preference to minority group members in employment decisions

260

(affirmative action).

2. **The Civil Rights Act of 1991**
   a. Prohibits discrimination on the basis of race and prohibits racial harassment.
   b. Burden of proof that discrimination did not occur is on the employer.
   c. Reinforces the illegality of hiring, firing, or promoting decisions on the basis of race, ethnicity, sex, or religion.

3. **Americans with Disabilities Act of 1990 (ADA)**
   a. Expands the Vocational Rehabilitation Act of 1973.
   b. Employers must make reasonable accommodations to provide qualified individuals access to a job, including providing needed technology.
   c. Post-job-offer medical examinations are not allowed.
   d. All companies with 15 or more employees are covered.
   e. People with AIDS are included in the disability category.
   f. Language is ambiguous, and many EEOC cases have been filed.

4. **The Family and Medical Leave Act of 1993 (FMLA)**
   a. Guarantees 12 weeks of unpaid leave per year for family-related matters:
      1) Childbirth or adoption
      2) Personal or family illness
   b. Covers companies with 50 or more employees.

H. **Sexual Harassment**
   1. Covered by Title VII.
   2. EEOC definition: *unwelcome sexual advances, requests for sexual favors, or other verbal or physical conduct of a sexual nature constitute sexual harassment when:*
      a. *submitting to or rejecting such conduct is an explicit or implicit term or condition of employment*
      b. *submitting to or rejecting the conduct is a basis for employment decisions affecting the individual*
      c. *the conduct unreasonably interferes with an individual's work performance or creates an intimidating, hostile, or offensive working environment.*
   3. **Meritor Savings Bank v. Vinson**—1986
      a. A Supreme Court case which asserted the right of women to a harassment-free workplace.
   4. Sexual harassment behavior is subtle and difficult to prove.
      a. Only 34% of harassed women tell the harasser to stop, and only 2% file a formal complaint.
   5. To control and eliminate harassment, organizations may follow steps such as:
      a. develop a clear written policy defining and prohibiting sexual harassment.
      b. institute training for all employees.
      c. institute a clear filing and investigative process.
      d. thoroughly and immediately investigate claims.

        e.   take corrective actions.

        f.   follow up on corrective action.

        g.   Periodically survey employees and terminating employees about sexual harassment.

        h.   Assure commitment from the top levels of the organization.

II.   **Employment Activity**

    A.   The Employment Division carries out an organization's HRM functions.

        1.   **Human resource planning**—estimating the size and makeup of the future workforce. This helps the organization acquire the right individuals when they are needed.

            a.   The longer the period predicted, the less accurate the prediction.

            b.   Complicated by economic, political, and labor supply changes.

            c.   **Formal approaches**

                1)   Mathematical projections

            d.   **Informal approaches**

                1)   Estimating from experience

            e.   In the 1990s, HRP has included approaches to layoffs, reductions in work hours, and early retirements.

    B.   **Recruitment**

        1.   Recruitment's major objective—acquire the best qualified candidates to fill vacancies.

        2.   Requires an understanding about the jobs to be filled.

            a.   **Job analysis**—the process of determining the tasks that comprise the job, and the skills, abilities, and responsibilities required.

                1)   Data about the job is collected via many means (e.g., interviews, surveys, expert observers, etc.)

                2)   Job analysis data is used to produce:

                    a)   **Job description**—specifies the job title, duties, machines and materials used, type/degree of supervision, working conditions and hazards.

                    b)   **Job specification**—specifies jobholder qualifications required (e.g., education, work experience, judgement, responsibility, etc.).

                    c)   See Figure 15-2 for an illustration of the relationship of job analysis, job description, and job specifications.

            b.   Two widely used approaches to job analysis:

                1)   **Functional job analysis**—most widely used method. Focuses on four individual job dimensions:

                    a)   What the worker does in relation to data, people, and jobs.

                    b)   Methods and techniques the worker uses.

                    c)   Machines, tools, and equipment the worker uses.

                    d)   Materials, products, subject matter, and services the worker produces.

                    e)   FJA can be used to classify jobs or to define performance standards.

2) **Position Analysis Questionnaire**—focuses on individual's behavior in performing the job. Attempts to identify six dimensions:
    a) Information sources critical to job performance.
    b) Information processing and decision-making critical to job performance.
    c) Required physical activity and dexterity.
    d) Required interpersonal relationships.
    e) Physical working conditions, and the individual's response to them.
    f) Other job characteristics (e.g., work schedule and responsibilities).
3) Though FJA and PAQ overlap considerably, PAQ additionally considers the employee's psychological responses to the job demands and context.
  c. Performing an accurate job analysis is often a complex task because the job functions are difficult to quantify (e.g., managing, organizing, controlling).
3. Recruiting actions—sources of candidates include:
  a. Reviewing files on previous applicants.
  b. Working with college placement centers.
  c. Using private employment agencies, executive search firms, and state employment agencies. In no-fee agencies, employers pay the finder's fee, not the applicant.
  d. See Table 15-2 for a listing of organizational recruitment sources and methods by occupation.

C. Employee **Selection and Placement**
1. The selection process includes eight steps (see Figure 15-3).
  a. **Preliminary screening** to screen out unqualified applicants.
  b. Completion of **application**—questions must predict job success.
    1) HRM personnel develop questions after a job analysis.
  c. **Interviews**—there are three basic interviewing steps. Interviewers:
    1) Must acquaint themselves with the job analysis.
    2) Must analyze the information on the applications.
    3) Must ask questions that can add to what is included on the application.
  d. **Testing**—installing a good testing program costs time and money and must be done by experts.
    1) Testing provides three advantages:
      a) Provides improved accuracy in selecting employees—if important differences among applicants can be measured via tests.
      b) Provides an objective means for evaluating applicants.
      c) Provides information about training, development and counseling needs.
    2) Testing is subject to several criticisms:

263

        a)   They're not infallible.

        b)   They're often given too much weight in the selection decision.

        c)   They can discriminate against minorities.

        d)   They cannot substitute for judgement.

    3)   **Alcohol and drug testing** is increasing.

        a)   Abuse of these substances costs U.S. industry more than $100 billion per year.

        b)   Companies also use drug education programs, supervisory awareness training, and employee assistance programs. See Figure 15-4 for workplace initiatives to combat drug abuse.

        c)   **Performance testing**—measures the ability of a person to do the job on the day she or he is tested. May be more accurate than drug testing.

    4)   **Employee Polygraph Protection Act of 1988**

        a)   Prohibits polygraph tests on applicants or employees, with few exceptions.

        b)   Organizations are now using paper-and-pencil **honesty tests**. Research on the results of honesty tests has been mixed in its conclusions regarding the effectiveness and fairness of the tests.

  e.   Checking applicant's **background information**—verifying information by consulting references (especially previous employers).

  f.   **Hiring decision**.

  g.   **Job offer**, contingent on a medical exam.

    1)   The exam is used to screen out people with physical disabilities that might create undue expense, and to insure that people are placed in jobs they can physically handle.

  h.   **Employment orientation**.

D.   Training and Development

  1.   Includes several activities including informing employees of policies and procedures, educating them in job skills, and developing them for future advancement.

  2.   **Training** is designed to improve a person's skills to do the current job.

  3.   Training programs—must meet four objectives to be effective. Training programs must:

    a.   Be based on organizational and individual needs.

    b.   Specify problems that will be solved.

    c.   Be based on sound learning theories.

    d.   Be evaluated to determine if they are working and cost-effective.

  4.   **Development**

    a.   Associated with managerial personnel.

    b.   **Managerial Development**—educating and developing selected personnel so they have the knowledge and skills needed to manage in future positions.

1) Objectives:
  a) to ensure the long-range success of the organization.
  b) to furnish competent replacements.
  c) to create an efficient team that works well together.
  d) to enable each manager to use his or her full potential.
2) Necessary because of:
  a) high executive turnover.
  b) shortage of managerial talent.
  c) society's emphasis on lifelong education and development.

c. Management development methods include:
  1) Formal development programs
    a) conducted by training units or consultants in universities and specialized training centers.
  2) On-the-job development via:
    a) Understudy programs—where a manager works as a subordinate partner with a boss, to eventually assume the boss' position responsibilities.
    b) Job rotation—each assignment is generally about six months.
    c) Coaching—a supervisor teaches knowledge and skills to a subordinate.

E. **Performance Appraisal**
1. Involves the formal evaluation of an employee's performance.
  a. Includes feedback to the individual and determination of whether and how performance can be improved.
2. Requires:
  a. **Standards**—prior specification of acceptable levels of job performance.
  b. **Information**—to measure actual job performance against standards.
  c. **Corrective action**—to restore any deviation of actual performance from standards.
3. Is an inherently emotion-laden process, involving an individual judging another's performance.
4. Has the characteristics of all feedback control methods (see Figure 15-5).
5. The first step is to determine standards ("criteria") that indicate successful performance.
6. Performance appraisal information enables managers to judge subordinate's performance. Managers must decide three issues:
  a. **Sources of appraisal information**—there are five sources:
    1) The appraise's supervisor(s)—usually, the subordinate is appraised by the immediate supervisor, who should be most familiar with the subordinate's performance.

265

2) Peers—often problematic as peers need mutual cooperation to perform work which this method can undermine.

3) The appraisee (self)—can improve the employee's understanding of job performance, increase commitment, and reduce hostility between superiors and subordinates over ratings. However, ratings may be unjustifiably high and not sufficiently critical.

4) Appraisee's subordinates.

5) Individuals outside the work environment.

b. Schedule of appraisal—older or tenured employees are usually appraised yearly; recent hirees are appraised more frequently. The schedule depends on the situation and on appraisal purposes.

1) The appraisal form should focus on task accomplishment, personal development, and the organization's objectives.

c. Appraisal methods—procedures/techniques used to appraise employees.

1) One or more of several performance appraisal techniques can be used.

2) **Graphic ratings scales**—the oldest and most widely used appraisal procedure (see Figure 15-6 for some samples of rating formats).

a) Rater usually uses one form per subordinate.

b) Form contains several performance criteria to be rated.

c) Rating scales are distinguished by how the criteria are defined, the degree to which the person interpreting the ratings can tell what response was intended by the rater, and how carefully the performance criteria are defined by the rater.

3) **Behaviorally Anchored Rating Scales** (BARS)

a) In developing a BARS, employees are involved in identifying and defining important areas of performance. **Critical incident statements** are developed and used as criteria to discriminate among performance levels (see Figure 15-7 for a BARS performance dimension form).

b) A BARS contains six to ten behaviors, each uniquely described as shown in Figure 15-7. Levels of performance are anchored by numbers and critical incident statements.

c) Participation of the jobholder and superiors in the development of the BARS should reduce defensiveness toward evaluation.

d) The rating form should be valued, meaningful, and cover all aspects of the job.

266

F.   Wage and Salary Management

    1.   **Employee compensation**—the primary types of compensation are:

        a.   **Wages**—workers are paid by time period (e.g., a daily or weekly wage) or by number of units produced (piecework system).

            1)   Piece rate is calculated by dividing the hourly rate for the job by the number of units an average employee is expected to produce in an hour.

            2)   A daily rate of pay is easier to understand and is generally preferred by unions over piece rate, because unions believe piece rates tend to reduce group cohesion.

            3)   **Job evaluation** systems are used by some firms to determine the relative worth of a job and to make wage adjustments. In the system, all of the firm's jobs are ranked, from highest to lowest, on the basis of skill, difficulty, working conditions, contributions to goods or services and other characteristics.

            4)   Laws regulate wages and salaries (e.g., the minimum wage, which since 1991 has been $4.25 per hour; the prohibition of minors working in dangerous jobs; and the forbidding of different wages on the basis of worker sex.)

            5)   **Comparable worth** - a concept that asserts that wages should be comparable for jobs of similar true worth. Often in these cases, jobs generally held by women pay less than jobs of comparable worth which are held by men.

                a)   In the last 10 years, full-time women employees have made about 67% of what full-time men earn. The earnings gap across occupations is shown in Figure 15-8.

                b)   Redress for comparable worth inequities has usually involved Title VII of the Civil Rights Act; the affirmative defenses for pay differentials are seniority, merit, quality or quantity of work, or any condition other than sex.

                c)   Comparable worth is likely to remain an emotional issue until the earning gap is reduced or until courts are more sympathetic to comparable worth cases.

        b.   **Salaries**—typically paid to managers; compensation on a weekly or longer schedule.

            1)   The Hay Associates consulting firm has developed a system to determine salaries for middle and top management positions.

                a)   The position is analyzed using the job description. Three factors are assessed (job know-how, problem solving, accountability).

                b)   Through a statistical procedure, job evaluations in a company are converted to Hay control standards, a special ranking system.

    c)   Hay publishes annual management salary surveys for similar jobs.

2.   **Benefits and services**—forms of supplementary compensation, monetary and nonmonetary payments over and above wage and salary rates.

    a.   **Benefits** are financial in nature; **services** are employer-supplied programs, facilities, or activities.

    b.   Elder care and day care services/benefits are becoming more popular.

        1)   The Internal Revenue Code permits exclusion of up to $5000 of employer payments for dependent care expenses from an employee's annual taxable income.

        2)   Some companies are working cooperatively to offer elder care services.

        3)   90% of working women will become pregnant during their working lives.

            a)   Many employers provide child care assistance, ranging from on-site child care facilities to the arrangement of part-time work schedules to work-at-home programs.

    c.   A family-friendly index has been developed, rating company programs and benefits (see Figure 15-9).

G.   **Labor Relations**

    1.   **Unions**

        a.   Employees have the right to form unions for the purpose of improving wages, hours of work, benefits, working conditions, and management practices of dealing with workers.

        b.   Unions are recognized as a certified representative of employees when they vote in the union.

        c.   Unions were very strong in the U.S. in the 1950s, when 36% of the workforce was unionized. Today, union strength is about 16% of the workforce.

        d.   Union membership in the transportation and communications industries is high, while in the service and finance industries it is low.

        e.   Non-unionized employers often copy the HRM practices of unions today.

        f.   Many people don't join unions because:

            1)   they must pay union dues.

            2)   they dislike the union's reputation.

            3)   they believe management's HRM practices are sound and fair.

            4)   management programs have been successful in keeping unions out.

        g.   **Collective bargaining**—a process used when a union is present and certified in the organization.

            1)   Management and labor negotiate a contract for employees who are union members.

2) Four types of **collective bargaining** dominate discussions about contracts and issues:
   a) **Distributive**—parties are in conflict over an issue. Usually involves a fixed amount of resources. If one party wins, the other loses.
   b) **Integrative**—more than one issue is involved. Usually give and take exists so both parties can benefit.
   c) **Concessionary**—unions give concessions or givebacks to management, usually to survive and so employees can keep their jobs.
   d) **Continuous**—a joint labor-management committee meets on a regular basis to explore and resolve problems and issues.

h. **Bargaining issues**
   1) According to the Labor-Management Relations Act of 1947 (the Taft-Hartley Act), wages, work hours, conditions of employment and safety are **mandatory issues** for bargaining.
   2) **Permissive issues**—matters that the parties may negotiate if they both agree to do so.
   3) **Prohibited issues**—not allowed in negotiations (e.g., that the employer only use union-produced supplies).

i. **Conflict resolution**
   1) If an agreement can't be reached via collective bargaining, the union may **strike** the firm (employees refuse to come to work).
   2) Management may not permit employees to work and resort to a **lockout**.
   3) Employees may implement a work **slowdown**.
   4) **Mediation** - a neutral third party helps the two parties resolve the impasse.
   5) **Arbitration** - a third party listens to both parties, analyzes the arguments, and makes the decision that both parties must accept. The decision is final.
   6) Collective bargaining provides a **grievance procedure** for resolving conflicts concerning an established contract. See Table 15-3 for a typical grievance step-by-step approach.
   7) Unions and management today are attempting to work more on a cooperative and less on an adversarial basis.

269

ANSWERS TO DISCUSSION AND REVIEW QUESTIONS

1. **Question:** *Discuss with a small business owner the types of human resource management in which the owner engages. What did you find out?*

   Answer: This individual project idea provides students the opportunity to extend their textbook knowledge of the different HRM functions to a real-world understanding of how these functions (e.g., recruiting, selection and placement, training, etc.) are conducted in an organization. When students report their findings, compare and contrast in class discussion the different ways that HRM activities are organized and performed in the different companies (and relate these differences to such variables as company size, industry, and characteristics of the company's workforce).

2. **Question:** *Why has honesty testing grown in popularity?*

   Answer: The Employee Polygraph Protection Act of 1988 has outlawed polygraph use in all but a few hiring or employee evaluation decisions. Organizations with a need to insure honesty have had to turn to other mechanisms—paper-and-pencil honesty tests are an available and accessible tool for employers. In student discussion, the question of why honesty testing is necessary or desirable—in which industries, and among what employee groups—can be raised.

3. **Question:** *Does the Family and Medical Leave Act of 1993 seem fair? Can small businesses afford this type of law? Why?*

   Answer: All of these questions were hotly debated in Congress when the law was first considered. After insuring that students are aware of the law's specific requirements (especially regarding organization size and employee length of service), a debate in-class may be embarked upon to explore the benefits and liabilities of this aspect of social responsibility by businesses.

4. **Question:** *Some persons refer to comparable worth as an emotional issue. What do they mean when referring to it as emotional?*

   Answer: Emotional issues arouse feelings such as anger, frustration, hate, resentment, etc. When (in the case of comparable worth) a woman feels she has contributed just as much as a man to an organization's bottom line, but is paid much less, all the above feelings are bound to surface. (Remember the Equity Theory of Motivation in Chapter 11.) Comparable worth today is more than just an emotional issue—it is also a legal and moral issue, and one all organizations must address.

5. **Question:** *Is drug testing an invasion of a person's right to privacy? Discuss.*

   Answer: Employees' rights in the workplace is an emerging issue. Drug testing is a controversial issue. The class may be split on whether it is an invasion of a person's rights. Students should identify the pros and cons associated with drug testing, exploring whether it is appropriate for some occupations and employees, all occupations and employees, or none.

6. **Question:** *Why is job analysis such a vital step in the development of a performance appraisal technique or method?*

   Answer: Job analysis is important because it identifies the specific job dimensions that can be used to distinguish one job from another. From a job analysis, managers can write job descriptions, develop performance criteria, and perform job evaluation. Each of these features result in a performance appraisal system or form. Without job analysis, management can't pinpoint the dimensions that are important and needed to perform a job. Unless employees and employers know and agree to what the dimensions of a job are, it is impossible to appraise the employee's performance in that job.

7. **Question:** *An engineer stated, "My job is so complex and dynamic that it is virtually impossible to find criteria for assessing job performance." What do you think about this claim? Why?*

   Answer: This claim is an exaggeration and is misleading. Peter Drucker has stated that unless a person can identify criteria for his or her job, we must ask if the job is really needed. There are few jobs for which criteria don't exist. Of course, for some jobs, careful, tedious work is needed to determine these criteria. However, unless the engineer is able to point to criteria, how would it be possible to reward, promote, or coordinate his or her performance? How would even he or she know if the job was being done effectively?

8. **Question:** *It seems as though every action in a firm is referred to as a strategy. Why is the management of human resources referred to as a strategic requirement of an organization?*

   Answer: It is strategic in nature because of the HRM implications. The recruitment, selection, development, and proper use of employees in an organization is the defining activity around which the organization revolves. Without effectively-used staff, there would be no organization, especially in today's highly competitive global marketplace.

9. **Question:** *Why has union membership declined in the past 20 years in the United States?*

   Answer: A number of reasons are cited for the decline in union membership. Employees may resent paying union dues, union reputations may be poor, employees may perceive fair HRM practices in the work environment (perhaps because management follows union practices even without a union actually in place), and/or there may be active management programs in organizations designed to keep unions out.

10. **Question:** *It is stated that in most situations sexual harassment is subtle. What does this mean?*

    Answer: The definition of sexual harassment includes such terms as "unwelcome", "physical contact of a sexual nature", "explicit or implicit term or condition of employment", "basis for employment decisions", "unreasonably interferes". For most people, these do not seem like solid, thoroughly-defined terms. In some instances, harassment behavior is blatant and clear-cut. In many circumstances, though, the victim of sexual harassment is made to feel uncomfortable, rather than having to fend off overt attempts at sexual contact or being directly told that the job depends on submitting to sexual behaviors. It is largely for this reason—the subtlety of sexual harassment—that such a large percentage of harassment cases go unreported and unchallenged.

END OF CHAPTER CASES

CASE 14-1: PINKERTON: A SCREENING LESSON

CASE SUMMARY: Pinkerton Security is one of the oldest and largest security agencies in the world. In hiring its own staff, Pinkerton employs careful security measures, including thorough background investigations and in-depth pre-employment testing to corroborate skills, experience, and integrity. The first step in Pinkerton's screening process involves having candidates fill out applications and go through initial interviews—a standard process for business organizations. But then Pinkerton has candidates complete a pencil-and-paper honesty test that has been screened for compliance with the ADA and the Civil Rights Act of 1991. Applicants then interact with a telephone-based system called IntelliView. Using this system, they respond via push buttons to questions offered in a consistent, neutral tone by a computerized voice. The results of this "interview", which is not scored, are immediately available to the Pinkerton recruiter, and can help pinpoint areas with undesirable responses for follow-up in a face-to-face interview.

Pinkerton also completes an extensive background check on prospective employees, by checking social security numbers, court records, credit histories, and even motor vehicle records. Civil checks may even be carried out if warranted. Pinkerton believes that this thoroughness has helped it hire the best people—and they now provide their screening services for outside clients as well.

ANSWERS TO QUESTIONS FOR ANALYSIS:

1. **Question:** *What lessons should a student of management learn about background checking from reviewing the Pinkerton case?*

   Answer: There are several lessons that should be learned, the most prominent of which is that such extensive background checking is *not* necessary or desirable in most employment decisions. Pinkerton provides an excellent example of an organization with very specific HRM needs, which has devised a procedural approach that precisely meets those needs. As was discussed in the chapter, each company must organize its HR department and functions according to its own set of needs, objectives, and size.

2. **Question:** *What should a pre-employment check provide a company?*

   Answer: All the information that is necessary to insure that the applicant has accurately represented his or her qualifications, and has the appropriate skills and experience for the job.

3. **Question:** *Is the cost of the type of screening conducted by Pinkerton too prohibitive? Why?*

   Answer: For most organizations, the answer would be a resounding yes for most of their employees. However, given the special needs Pinkerton has for its own staff, the cost of the checking is an investment to ensure that the most appropriate candidates are selected, and so the costs are not too prohibitive. The costs of not doing the extensive checking would likely be much higher in the long run.

CASE 14-2: GOAL SETTING AT TENNECO

CASE SUMMARY: This case profiles a new performance planning, evaluation and goal setting program implemented at Tenneco, a large, diversified company. The program is designed to create an atmosphere of self-motivation and personal satisfaction among employees. Work performance and personal development objectives are emphasized. Another major emphasis is on attaining a balance between work performance and personal development objectives.

ANSWERS TO QUESTIONS FOR ANALYSIS:

1. **Question:** *What advantages were there in using a task force with representatives from each divisional company to develop performance planning and evaluation (PP&E) at Tenneco?*

   Answer: One advantage is that each divisional company provides input in the program's development. These firsthand inputs add accuracy and depth to the final product. The task force, by participating, can also display commitment to others in the divisional companies. They participated and are committed to what was developed. This helps increase the credibility of the process for employees from throughout the corporation.

2. **Question:** *Does Tenneco's president seem concerned about the development of people? How did you reach this conclusion?*

   Answer: He shows a great deal of concern for people. His quoted statement provides this evidence. In addition, the overall emphasis of PP&E is people-based. Many businesses' goal setting programs place a primary focus on organizational end results. At Tenneco the picture is more balanced. People and organizations are included in plans, procedures, and results. In fact, if the program has a fault, it is that it seems to side primarily with people over organizational concerns. Whether this one-sidedness can be sustained indefinitely is debatable.

3. **Question:** *What would be the value of Tenneco's top management supporting the PP&E program?*

   Answer: The value would be to set an example. If top management supports PP&E, it is given legitimacy and credibility. Others will view this support as an example to be followed. In hierarchical organizations, there is a strong inclination to follow the leaders. In Tenneco's case the leaders want and support PP&E. Thus, subordinates are inclined to follow suit.

ADDITIONAL QUESTIONS AND ANSWERS

1. **Question:** *Describe how a performance evaluation method can be a source of demotivation for those being evaluated.*

   Answer: A performance evaluation method can be demotivational if the method is flawed and results in an unjust appraisal of the subordinate's performance. For example, a poorly constructed graphics rating scale or the critical incident method inadequately applied by a supervisor can result in an unfair performance evaluation. The employee might then understandably question whether he should try to perform well. Also, in an environment in which no differential rewards (in terms of compensation or recognition) are offered in response to positive appraisals, employees may feel that their hard work is counter to their own best interests.

2. **Question:** *Is it better to have a personnel specialist recruit or have the job's operating manager recruit?*

   Answer: Students may differ in their opinions; however, most will likely assert that the personnel specialist should do the recruiting. The specialist is more knowledgeable concerning the overall company, its policies, employee benefits and services and on other topics of importance to the potential job candidate. The specialist is also schooled in effective recruitment techniques and the overall do's and don'ts. However, the specialist should fully understand the demands of the job that he or she is recruiting for, and should consult with the operating manager if he/she has any questions.

274

3. **Question:** *Recruiting is a mutual process. The organization and the individual are both involved in recruiting. How would you look for a job if you were interested in working for a bank within a 100-mile radius of your college?*

Answer: This question provides an opportunity for students to share their own job-hunting strategies. Compare and contrast their ideas in class discussion, and compile a list of the best job-hunting strategies to use when looking for a job.

4. **Question:** **Why are organizations so interested in benefits and services for employees?**

Answer: Organizational interest in benefits and services can be due to several factors, including the increasing role that benefits and services play in attracting and retaining top-notch employees, especially those in areas where the demand for personnel exceeds market supply. This question provides an opportunity for students to discuss which benefits and services they would most value as entry-level or top-level employees.

5. **Question:** *What action decisions can be made when there is a shortage of qualified candidates for job positions?*

Answer: Shortages can be alleviated by increasing recruitment, providing more training, and lowering selection standards (which can present problems). Some shortages will result in expanded jobs for present employees because additional human resources can't be found.

6. **Question:** *Are equal employment opportunities and affirmative action programs the same concept or activity? Explain.*

Answer: They are linked in that affirmative action programs exist to ensure equal employment opportunity for minority and female job applicants and employees. However, equal employment opportunity programs simply insure that no individuals will be discriminated against because of status in any of the categories enumerated in the Civil Rights Laws, while affirmative actions programs actively recruit and give preference to minority group members in employment decisions.

7. **Question:** *Why do organizations conduct employee training?*

Answer: Training is conducted to meet several objectives that include improving the quantity and quality of worker output, lowering the number and costs of accidents and waste in job performance, reducing absenteeism and turnover, and increasing job satisfaction (since training can boost an employee's self esteem). In general, training is designed to help employees perform their current job better.

8. **Question:** *Define training.*

Answer: Training is a systematic process of altering the behavior and/or attitudes of employees in a direction that increases organizational performance. A formal training program is the organization's effort to provide opportunities for the employee to acquire job-related skills, attitudes, and knowledge.

9. Question: *What is the difference between a job description and a job specification?*

    Answer: A job description specifies the job title, duties, and machines used, type and degree of supervision, working conditions and hazards of the respective job. A job specification specifies the requirements of the jobholder to effectively perform the job; these requirements include such factors as education, work experience, and physical capabilities.

10. Question: *What is the value in using more than one appraiser of an employee's performance?*

    Answer: The value is that multiple observations can provide a more complete picture of an employee's performance. One person may have only a partial or even biased viewpoint. By combining a number of views, a more complex and accurate picture of the person's performance may be available.

ORGANIZATIONAL CHANGE, DEVELOPMENT, AND INNOVATION

LEARNING OBJECTIVES

After completing Chapter 16, students should be able to:

Define the term organization development.

Describe a five-step model or framework that displays the organization change process.

Discuss four major reasons why people resist change.

Compare specific techniques that are used to bring about structural, people, and technological changes.

Identify some of the productivity and human resource advantages and disadvantages associated with robotics in work settings.

CHAPTER SYNOPSIS

This chapter addresses the issues and techniques of organizational change and development by focusing on a five-step model of the organizational change process and its components. Before presenting the model, the chapter defines **organizational development** as a method that facilitates change and development in organizational structures and processes, people, and technology. Resistance to change, a key problem confronting any change effort, is discussed by explaining four common reasons for employee resistance (parochial self-interest, misunderstanding of the change and mistrust of management's motives, different assessments of the change, and a low tolerance for change). Six suggestions for minimizing resistance are described.

The organizational change model consists of five steps: the stimuli (forces for change) which spur the organizational change process, diagnosis of the problem, identifying and selecting alternative change techniques while considering conditions which limit change effectiveness, selection of a change strategy, and finally, implementing the change program and evaluating its outcome. Concerning the first phase, **forces for change,** three external forces (**changes in the marketplace, technology,** and **the environment)** and two internal forces **(people** and **processes)** are discussed. **Problem diagnosis,** the model's second step, is discussed in terms of three questions that must be asked: What is the problem, what must be changed, and what outcomes are expected.

The chapter addresses the third step by presenting **change techniques** in three categories: **structural changes** (changes in the nature of job content, such as job enrichment and job enlargement, and changes in sociotechnical systems), **people change** (supervisory training, including sensitivity training; team building; life and career planning; and Total Quality Management), and **technological change** (robots). The need to recognize the limiting conditions which affect change outcomes is addressed by describing three major limiting factors: **leadership climate, the formal organization, and organizational culture.**

Selecting the **change strategy** (step 4) is addressed by describing three approaches (**unilateral, shared, and delegated)** for implementing change. Two dimensions of **change**

implementation—timing and scope—are discussed as are three criteria for evaluating **program effectiveness.**

Figure 16-7 provides an excellent overview of the issues, questions, and data collection methods for evaluating a planned organizational change effort.

The chapter's **Management in Action** provides guidelines for Managing Diversity (MD), which is the process of creating and maintaining an environment that naturally enables all organizational members to reach their full potential in pursuit of the enterprise's objectives. The **Management Focus** sections describe bibliometrics, a statistical method used by organizations to scan patents and scientific papers for potential innovations that will have an impact on the way they do business in the future; the failure of a quality improvement program in the machine-building sector in the former Soviet Union; the strategies undertaken by BankAmerica Corporation and Continental Bank Corp. to recover from large losses in the middle 1980s; the role of Raymond Smith, CEO of Bell Atlantic, as a change agent within the organization; the use of sensitivity training as an organizational development strategy for dealing with diversity in large U.S. organizations; the benefits of team-building meetings among executives in a large manufacturing firm to address conflict issues; and the results of an Ernst and Young study of TQM implementation in North American, German, and Japanese companies, showing that while companies must follow their own path to TQM, they must go through three stages of quality implementation: novice, journeyman, and master.

TEACHING TIPS

LECTURE & DISCUSSION IDEAS

1. To supplement your discussion of sensitivity training, ask your students whether they have ever participated in a **T-group experience (some might have).** Ask those who have to describe their experiences, and whether, in **their opinion, T-group learning outcomes can be** transferred to the work environment and contribute to organizational performance.

2. Do people really resist change? Can that resistance be effectively turned around? The chapter presents a number of reasons why change makes people uncomfortable, and suggests management strategies to overcome resistance to change. Ask students what their own perception is of change in their own lives, and in the organizations with which they are affiliated. For instance, the class might explore how they would feel if the name of the college or university they are attending were to be changed. How could the administration get a buy-in from the college community for such a change? Would the strategies suggested in this chapter be of help?

1. To enhance your students' understanding of the impact of technological change, as a group project, have your students identify a local business that has recently undergone substantial technological change (e.g., computerization or other new production technologies). Have the students prepare a written report on the effects of the change on the organization. The students can gather the information by interviewing a representative of the organization who was involved in implementing the change. As an alternative, students can research an organization reported in the business media that has recently undergone substantial technological change and report on its effects using published articles.

2. Mergers are a very substantial and unsettling experience for employees of most businesses. Have students identify a business in your community which has been acquired by or merged with another corporation in the past few years. (Banks, department stores, and movie theaters are all likely candidates.) They can interview managers in those businesses to determine what went right and what went wrong with the process, from the perspective of managing change. How did the new organization encourage acceptance of the change among its employees?

LECTURE OUTLINE NOTES

I. Chapter Introduction

    A. Changes in organizations in the 1980s and 1990s have been significant and irreversible. Managers are responding to:
        1. Global competition.
        2. Diversity in the workplace.
        3. The drive for quality and competitiveness.
        4. Ethical Dilemmas.
    B. Contemporary business organizations must deal with changing circumstances far more substantial that anything since the start of the Industrial Revolution.
    C. Change management is an integral responsibility of managers, not a peripheral one.
    D. **Organizational development (OD)** is a method for facilitating change and development in structures and processes (e.g., relationships, roles), people (e.g., styles, skills) and technology (e.g., more routineness, more challenge).

II. Resistance to Change

    A. Most OD efforts eventually encounter resistance from employees who resist change for several reasons. Four prominent reasons why people resist change in general are:
        1. **Parochial self-interest**—fear of losing something they value (for example, loss of power, resources, freedom to make decisions, friendships, and prestige).

2. **Misunderstanding and lack of trust**—lack of understanding of the reasons for and implications of the change. Most likely occurs when they don't trust those initiating the change.
3. **Different assessments**—those affected by the change view the change differently than the change initiators, largely because they don't have all relevant information.
4. **Low tolerance for change**—emotional inability to make the change transition (for example, people fear they lack the necessary new skills, or they believe that accepting the change is tacit agreement that their previous behavior and actions were wrong).

III. Minimizing Resistance to Change

    A. Kotter and Schlesinger offer six ways for managers to minimize change resistance.
        1. Communicate and educate employees before the change occurs.
        2. Involve those who will be affected by the change in the change's design and implementation.
        3. Be supportive of employees when change is occurring to help alleviate fear and anxiety.
        4. Negotiate with opposing employees—give something to reduce change resistance (e.g., getting a worker to move to a less desirable location by increasing his or her monthly salary).
        5. Use manipulation and co-optation—use devious tactics to convince others that change is in their best interests, or co-opt individuals by giving them a major role in the design or implementation of the change. Ethical questions arise with this tactic and preclude its widespread use.
        6. Use explicit and implicit coercion—apply threatening behavior (threatening the employees with job loss, poor job assignments, etc., to gain agreement). A risky alternative.

IV. **A Model for Managing Change**

    A. See Figure 16-1 for a process model of managing organizational change. Each of the chapter's following sections addresses one of the model's five steps.
        1. Forces for change continually act on organizations.
        2. Managers must:
            a. Sort out information on change forces.
            b. Diagnose the problem.
            c. Identify alternative change techniques.
            d. Identify limiting conditions.
            e. Choose change strategies and techniques.
            f. Implement change, and monitor its impact.

V. Step 1: **Stimuli—Forces for Change**

    A. The stimuli (forces for change) are classified into two groups:
        1. **External forces:**
          a. Changes in the marketplace—changes can occur in:
              1) Competitor's actions (e.g., introducing new products, increasing advertising, reducing prices, or improving

customer service).
- 2) Customer tastes and incomes.
- 3) Changes in resources (e.g., changes in the numbers and quality of the labor force, changes in the materials and energy supply).
- b. Changes in technology—(e.g., the advent of business computers).
  - 1) Information technology is transforming organizations like never before.
    - a) Effective implementation of information technology can yield competitive advantages due to lowered costs, time reduction, increased output quality, improved learning, and enhanced quality of work life.
- c. Changes in the environment—movements over which manages have no control but which may affect the organization's fate (e.g., the increased internationalization of business in the 1990s).
  - 1) Organizations in the former U.S.S.R. are struggling to accommodate to the marketplace.
- 2. **Internal forces:**
  - a. Changes in **processes**—decision-making, communications, and interpersonal relations.
  - b. Changes in people—evidenced by low morale and high absenteeism and turnover.

VI. Step 1: **Reaction—Recognition of the need for change**

A. Recognition stems from signs of problems which require change. The most important sources of information are present in the company's preliminary, concurrent, and feedback control data. In this respect, the change process can be viewed as the corrective-action requirement aspect of the control function.

VII. Step 2: **Reaction—Diagnosis of the Problem**

A. This step involves answering three questions:
- 1. What is the problem, as distinct from the symptoms of the problem?
- 2. What must be changed to resolve the problem?
- 3. What outcomes (objectives) are expected from the change, and how will such objectives be measured?

B. Necessary information may be readily available (for example, in financial statements or departmental reports) or it may need to be generated through committees and task forces.
- 1. One information-generating method is the **attitude survey** (see Figure 16-2) which enables employees to evaluate management, pay and pay-related items, working conditions, equipment, and other job-related items. The data is usually collected by questionnaire, thoroughly analyzed, and fed back to organizational members.
- 2. The objective of an attitude survey is to pinpoint the problems as perceived by members of the organization.

VIII.   Step 3a: **Stimuli—Alternative Change Techniques**

    A.   Change techniques are classified according to the major focus of the technique—changing structure, people, or technology.

        1.   The three are *not* distinct from each other; interrelationships must be acknowledged and anticipated.

    B.   **Structural change** involves managerial action that attempts to improve performance by altering the formal structure of task and authority relationships. This can involve:

        1.   Changes in the nature of jobs, including:

            a.   **Job enrichment**—involves despecialization of jobs (see Chapter 11 for a discussion of job enrichment and motivation).

                1)   One attempted application of job enrichment in the stock transfer department of a large metropolitan bank showed no perceived impact on the employees of the changes of job characteristics. However, structural changes did not go far enough in the organization—delegation of authority and increased autonomy were not provided for in the implementation.

            b.   **Job enlargement**—involves increasing the number of tasks in the job. Saab Company in Sweden enlarged workers' jobs at an auto engine assembly plant by having each worker follow an engine from start to finish, increasing the time a worker spends on the assembly of an engine from 1.8 minutes to 30 minutes. Here, the intent is to make the job more interesting and challenging. (See Figures 16-3 and 16-4 for a comparison of before and after tasks). Adding meaningless tasks to a job is also enlargement, but it can produce the opposite effect.

            c.   **Changes In line-staff relationships**—usually involve creating staff assistance as either an ad hoc or permanent solution.

        2.   Changes in **sociotechnical systems**—involve efforts to develop a better fit between the technology, structure, and social interaction patterns of a unit, department or office.

            a.   An outgrowth of research originally done at the Tavistock Institute in Great Britain.

            b.   Groups of employees at all levels examine all aspects of the work operation, and share responsibilities for change initiation.

            c.   An example: at Rushton Coal Mine in Phillipsburg, PA, a management-union steering committee established a program which trained workers in all jobs in a section, trained members in group problem solving and in mine laws, and made crew members responsible for coal production and handling of grievances. The results included better performance, lower absenteeism, and higher job satisfaction.

            d.   Changes can present problems:

                1)   Sociotechnical system change has often ignored individual differences in how people react to various changes.

                2)   Union officials may believe that management-worker

cooperation undermines union influence.

         3)   Managers may claim that such efforts undermine management's right to manage.

C. **People change**—involves efforts to redirect and improve employee attitudes, skills, and knowledge bases. Prominent approaches:

    1.   Training and development programs

        a.   **Supervisory training**—attempt to provide supervisors with basic technical and human relations skills.

            1)   Emphasize people skills—how to handle malcontents, loafers, troublemakers, or complainers.

            2)   Include communications, leadership styles, and organizational relationships.

        b.   **Sensitivity training**—a training technique which attempts to make a participant more aware of himself/herself and of his/her impact on others.

            1)   Sensitivity training assumes that poor task performance is due to emotional problems of people who must collectively achieve a goal.

            2)   Stresses the process rather than the content of training, and emotional rather than conceptual training.

            3)   The participant training group of managers (also called a T group) usually meets at a place away from work. The group engages in a dialogue with no agenda or focus. The emphasis is on self-discovery, with motives and feelings revealed through behavior toward others and through the behavior of others in the group.

            4)   The trainer's role is to observe and lead unobtrusively, interpreting the roles of participants and encouraging them to analyze their contributions without being perceived as a threat.

            5)   The critical test: whether the experience itself is a factor leading to improvement in task performance. Difficulties:

                a)   Session behavior may not be possible or allowed in the workplace.

                b)   The session's supportive environment is not likely to be found on the job.

                c)   Training may hinder participants' ability to perform job tasks.

                d)   The training itself can induce stress and anxiety.

            6)   Research evidence on the technique's effectiveness has produced mixed results. One review of research studies found that sensitivity training:

                a)   Is most effective at the personal level.

                b)   Stimulated short-term improvement in communication skills.

                c)   Encouraged trainees to believe that they controlled their behavior more than others.

                d)   Is likely to increase the participative orientation of trainees in leadership positions.

e)   Improved perceptions of others toward the trainee.

7)   In deciding whether to use the technique, managers must determine if changes induced by sensitivity training are instrumental for organizational purposes, and if the prospective participants are able to tolerate the potential anxiety of the training.

8)   A major shortcoming of sensitivity training is its assumption that when a person becomes self-aware through the technique, positive changes will occur. Such is not always so.

2.   **Team building**—a change technique involving a group that works on a problem facing the members.

    a.   Involves five steps (see Figure 16-5 for the sequence of events in team building):

        1)   The problem is identified.

        2)   The full group diagnoses the problem.

        3)   The main contributing reasons to the problem are identified.

        4)   Alternative solutions are identified and their positive and negative features are discussed.

        5)   A solution is selected and implemented.

    b.   A key benefit—the group members, through interaction, become more familiar with one another and the solution.

    c.   To be successful, four requirements must be met:

        1)   The group must have a natural reason for existing.

        2)   Group members must be mutually dependent on one another.

        3)   Group members must have similar status.

        4)   Group communications must be open and trusting.

    d.   Results of team-building at the GM-Toyota joint venture (NUMMI) are good after four years, but team building does not entirely eliminate dissension, disappointment, or jealousy within organizations.

3.   **Life and career planning**—through company-sponsored programs. Involves having individuals assess their life and career plans in a systematic and thorough manner.

    a.   The sequence of steps in many programs is:

        1)   The individual assesses life and career paths up to the present.

        2)   Formulates career and lifestyle objectives, and forecasts the future.

        3)   Develops an action plan to meet objectives.

    b.   Life and career planning are generally done concurrently.

4.   **Total Quality Management (TQM)**—one of the most important and widespread approaches to change in the 1990s, involving a near-total transformation of an organization's structural and people components.

    a.   Employee involvement is critical to success.

<ul>
<li>b. TQM has many meanings and definitions. In large, though, it endorses fact-based decision-making, quality products and services, and employee-centered management through empowerment and participation.</li>
<li>c. On a formal level, TQM requires complete job redesign to include self-directed work teams, organic organization structure, and cross-functional coordinative groups.</li>
<li>d. On an informal level, TQM requires trust and commitment to the organization and its mission, cooperativeness rather than competition among individuals and groups, and honesty in the reconciliation of differences.</li>
</ul>

D. **Technological change**—involves applications of new ways to transform resources into goods or services.
1. **Robots**—a "reprogrammable multifunctional manipulator designed to move material, parts, tools, or specialized devices through programmed motions for the performance of variety of tasks."
   a. More sophisticated robots are called intelligent; less sophisticated ones are called dumb, slaves, grasshopper (in the automobile industry), or CAM (Computer-Aided Manufacturing).
   b. A technological force creating fear and resistance among many people.
   c. Growth in robot use will continue, because of decreasing costs for use and the development of the microprocessor.
   d. Japan uses most of the world's robots, and is developing microbots—motors, sensors, and other devices as small as a human hair.
2. Technology is a key determinant of structure. Organizations with simple and stable technology should adopt a structure that tends toward classical organization, while those with dynamic technology should move toward neoclassical structure.
   a. Organizations must be willing to use technology to change their systems rather than just mechanizing the old ways of doing businesses.
3. According to Floyd Mann, adopting new machines in the factory involves changes in job content, division of labor, social relations among workers, working conditions (improved), supervisory skills, career patterns, promotion procedures, job security, wages (higher), job prestige, and around-the-clock operations.

E. Figure 16-6 which portrays the structural, people, and technology approaches to organizational change, the types of programs in each approach, and the anticipated outcomes.

IX. Step 3b: **Reaction—Recognition of Limiting Conditions**
A. Three sources influence the outcome of management change efforts:
1. **Leadership climate**—the nature of the work environment resulting from the leadership style and administrative practices of superiors. Success requires management commitment to the effort, and the organization's leadership style can itself be the objective of change.
2. The **formal organization**—must be compatible with the proposed change.

3. **Organizational culture**—the impact on the work environment resulting from group norms, values, philosophy, and informal activities. The culture must be conducive to the planned change, and the change strategist must anticipate the resistance that can evolve from the affected work groups.

X. **Step 4: Reaction—The Strategy for Change**

A. Selecting the strategy for change influences the final outcome. There are three approaches:
   1. **Unilateral approach**—usually involves an edict from top management describing the change and the responsibilities of subordinates in implementing it.
   2. **Shared approach**—involves lower-level groups in the process of either defining the problem and alternative solutions or defining solutions only after higher-level management has defined the problem.
   3. **Delegated approach**—complete authority is relinquished to subordinate groups, which are responsible for analysis of the problem and proposed solutions.

B. The selected strategy's objective is to minimize resistance and maximize cooperation and support.
   1. Strategies that tend toward a shared approach are relatively more successful.

XI. **Step 5: Reaction—Implementation and Evaluation**

A. Change implementation has two dimensions:
   1. **Timing**—selecting the appropriate time to initiate the change. Change is best implemented during a slack period so the effort does not compete with ordinary business operations. On the other hand, if the problem is critical, immediate implementation may be necessary.
   2. **Scope**—selecting the appropriate scale of change. Implementing throughout the organization simultaneously accomplishes implementation in a short period of time; a level-by-level, phased-in implementation requires more time.
      a. Successful implementations often use a phased approach, limiting the scope but providing feedback for each subsequent implementation.

B. Evaluation involves comparing the results with the objectives of the change program. Three types of criteria can be used:
   1. **Internal criteria**—directly associated with the basis of the program (for example, did the employees in the job enrichment seminar learn the core dimensions of the job?)
   2. **External criteria**—related to the effectiveness of employees before and after the change is implemented (for example, increased number of units produced per work hour, increased sales volume).
   3. **Participant reaction criteria**—attempt to determine how the individuals affected by the change feel about it.

C. It is useful to use multiple and systematic assessment of the outcome of a change program. See Figure 16-7 for a matrix which summarizes what to measure and how to collect information in a program evaluation.

286

ANSWERS TO DISCUSSION AND REVIEW QUESTIONS

1. **Question:** *How could team building enhance commitment to a structural change in an organization?*

   Answer: Since in the team building process, the full team is involved in diagnosing the problem and selecting the solution, team members are much more likely to feel ownership of the process and have a stake in the success of the change. They can then influence their co-workers who are not part of the team, and spread the ownership of the process to others.

2. **Question:** *In which situations might change be undesirable? Utilize examples in answering this question.*

   Answer: Change is least desirable when it is unplanned, or when it is poorly planned, or when the organization is not prepared to deal with the ramifications of the change even if they have planned for it. Forces external and internal to the organization can create undesirable results. Students should identify several examples. Coca-Cola's introduction of New Coke, and its subsequent need to "re-introduce" Coca-Cola Classic, is a good example showing the emergence of undesirable results..

3. **Question:** *Why is it important to focus on problems versus focusing on symptoms of problems?*

   Answer: Correctly identifying the problem(s) is an essential part of the total strategy for change. Separating problems from the symptoms is necessary to define objectives to guide proposed changes. Incorrectly focusing on symptoms will not resolve critical problems, which may continue evolving to a catastrophic stage.

4. **Question:** *Can you present an example that you are familiar with in which a job can be enlarged? Use the Saab example to help you think through the necessary features for job enlargement.*

   Answer: The reader must use personal knowledge and experience to come up with a job that can be enlarged. Most jobs can be enlarged by adding activities. However, knowledge about such activities is needed to present a comprehensive and feasible enlargement plan.

5. **Question:** *It has been claimed that as the tasks performed by humans become more complex, the probability of robots replacing human labor increases. Do you agree?*

   Answer: There are two perspectives to this issue. First, it can be argued that as tasks increase in complexity, the tendency for robots to replace human labor increases because the robots can better perform the complex tasks which are more prone to human error. However, complex tasks often require human reasoning and decision-making as the task is being performed. Robots cannot fulfill this aspect of a complex task. Thus, whether robots replace humans in complex tasks depends on the nature of the tasks's complexity.

6. **Question:** *Using an organization that you are familiar with, present an example of a situation where change was resisted. Looking back, what possible solutions could have been pursued to overcome the resistance to change?*

   Answer: Students should identify examples of resistance to change. In doing so, they should understand that resistance is high when individuals believe that the *status quo* is desirable, or when they fear the unknown pain that will accompany the change more than they fear the pain of the known problems they are currently dealing with. The mechanisms for overcoming resistance that are mentioned in the chapter should be of use to them in hindsight.

7. **Question:** *As an individual or group project, interview academic officers in the university or college you attend. These officers can be chairs, deans, presidents or their representatives. Obtain from these interviews an understanding of what forces are acting on the institution to bring about change and what responses the institution is undertaking to meet these forces.*

   Answer: This exercise should encourage the students' understanding of how managers explicitly or implicitly apply the change model shown in this chapter. In particular, students should look for evidence of the managers' ability to recognize a need to change, to diagnose the problem, to select an appropriate change strategy, and to implement and evaluate change at the school.

8. **Question:** *Why has Total Quality Management (TQM) become such a popular response to change in the 1990's? What forces have created the importance of quality in goods and services as a necessity for becoming and remaining competitive?*

   Answer: TQM is popular because of the success of major organizations throughout the country that have adopted it, and because it has been encouraged by not only business leaders but also the U.S. government (through the Baldrige Award and other avenues). TQM provides a synthesis of the motivation, communication, and work group concepts covered in this section of the text; recognition that "business as usual" just won't work in this age of global economies requires different approaches with as solid a grounding as TQM.

9. **Question:** *What particular factors which cause people to resist change generally would cause them to resist TQM? Explain your answer.*

   Answer: All four of the factors cited in the chapter to explain why people resist change figure prominently in the answer to this question. Parochial self-interest might come into play if current workers, supervisors, or managers believe that the work of functional coordinative groups will erode their own current power base in the organization. Since trust and commitment is a key element of TQM implementation, misunderstanding and lack of trust are antithetical to TQM and would lead to resistance to TQM approaches. Different assessments of the situation from those of the advocates of TQM come into play among employees who are happy with the way things are right now, and see no need for change. And for employees with a low tolerance of change, TQM represents just about the biggest change that can be incorporated in an organization.

10.   **Question:**   *Explain why the strategy for implementing change can have such a significant impact on the potential success of organizational change.*

   Answer: As the chapter discusses, resistance to change is pretty much a given among human beings. The best strategy to use in implementing a change is certainly situational; some changes, such as changes to meet legislative or Board of Director mandates, suggest a unilateral strategy. Others, such as a change in the structure or administration of benefits, might be better handled using a shared strategy. Choosing an inappropriate strategy for the situation or the limiting conditions (leadership climate, formal organization, and organizational culture) creates additional tension, and might doom the change to failure.

END OF CHAPTER CASES

CASE 16-1: IMPLEMENTING TOTAL QUALITY MANAGEMENT AT THIOKOL CORPORATION

CASE SUMMARY: This case describes the implementation of a TQM program at Thiokol/Huntsville Division (THD) in northern Alabama. With approximately 700 employees, the division carries out research, engineering, and production of small to mid-sized rocket motor propulsion systems.

THD embarked on implementation of a Total Quality/Continuous Improvement (TQ/CI) process in mid-1989. The working definition they use is: *Doing the right things right, the first and every time, in a mode of continuous improvement, focused on customer satisfaction.* To define measures of success, they developed an attitude and opinion survey, covering approximately 50 business practices/philosophy areas plus traditional human resource "climate" questions, and administered it to all employees. The results allowed for prioritization and publicity of the first improvement targets for the business. To establish structure for the TQ/CI program, an Executive Steering Council was established, and the five-year strategic business plan was modified (and is updated annually) to incorporate strategy, objectives, timeframes, and goals. On the training front, all employees received specific training in TQ/CI sessions (with a kickoff by the supervisor of each session for his or her subordinates) targeted to their specific business areas and responsibilities, to learn tools necessary for total quality implementation in the process they work on.

THD established two types of teams: departmental teams and critical process improvement teams. The departmental teams include every member of each department or group (unlike Quality Circles, in which participation is voluntary). The task of the departmental teams is to determine supplier-customer relationships, define customer expectations, map and review departmental processes, establish improvement opportunities, provide internal and external feedback and measurement to monitor for continuous improvement, and report status to management. The critical process improvement teams consider multiorganizational, high impact processes, and are charged with evaluating the processes for restructure and improvement opportunities.

Under the belief that *what gets measured gets improved*, each business unit manager is required to work with his or her staff to establish improvement measures for their key activities and to keep progress charts clearly visible in the work area.
THD has been very successful to date, with double digit improvement in all areas. While it traditionally takes five years to change a company culture, management at THD has changed the way people *act*, and has achieved significant results. Further, the team-generated improvements of processes are most often low- or no-cost solutions through streamlining and restructure.

THD has also involved customers in their TQ/CI process, through "concurrent engineering" of new products. Suppliers are brought in during the preliminary design phase to ensure producibility of the final requirements. Frequent communication with external customers insures that integration and performance requirements will meet their expectations. Also on the supplier end, a cost-based supplier rating and certification system has been developed to allow buying decisions to be made based on the historical true cost of doing business with a supplier.

The next areas for change at THD include integration across functional systems; compensation and reward systems; recruitment and selection; individual job structure; training and skill development; organization structure; and evaluation and recognition.

ANSWERS TO QUESTIONS FOR ANALYSIS: ─────────────────────────────

1. **Question:** *What are the factors for success in the Thiokol case? What did the firm do that led to improvements in performance?*

   Answer: There are many factors for success at Thiokol; students may examine the case and find that Thiokol has taken seriously all the critical factors in TQM implementation: a total transformation of the organization, with complete job redesign; functional coordinative groups; trust and commitment fostered from the highest levels; and an environment of cooperation rather than competition among employees. Among the key activities that have led to performance improvement have been employee attitudinal surveys leading to determination of improvement targets; direction from a high-level Executive Steering Committee; continuous updating of the five-year strategic business plan; extensive, relevant employee training; assignment of responsibility to both departmental and cross-departmental critical process improvement teams; measurement of improvement on a departmental basis; and involvement of customers and suppliers.

2. **Question:**   *What strategy for change did the company use? Did the strategy for change have anything to do with the program's success?*

    Answer: THD's strategy for change is clearly shared. High-level executives are involved not only in the Steering Council, but also directly in the classroom with their subordinates. Workers at all levels participate in departmental teams. Each employee has specific responsibilities for making TQ/CI work. It is difficult to imagine that the program could have been as successful as it has with a unilateral or a delegated approach, by the very nature of the type of change involved in the program.

3. **Question:**   *Can the increases in performance be sustained if the culture does not change? Explain your answer.*

    Answer: The culture at THD has already changed dramatically. The improvements seen are not just cosmetic, but are rather an indication that communication among employees, managers, customers, and suppliers is highly focused and is in itself highly productive. If the culture were to revert to its former characteristics, performance would also likely revert quickly. To sustain continuing improvements, the culture will indeed have to keep changing to match the new needs of the organization.

CASE 16-2: ORGANIZATIONAL CHANGE: THE GLOBAL ARENA———————————

CASE SUMMARY: This case discusses the job enrichment and job enlargement that is occurring as a result of the development of large multinational institutions, specifically in the banking industry. Just 500 MNCs today control more than half of the world's exchange of manufactured goods and services. Bankers must be knowledgeable in the details of worldwide financial markets. Several scenarios are presented to illustrate the business manager's need to understand foreign exchange rates, hedging, futures, options, and risk assessment. Emphasis is placed on the powerful external forces requiring managers to change the way they think, conduct business, organize the workforce, and view opportunities.

ANSWERS TO QUESTIONS FOR ANALYSIS: ———————————————————

1. **Question:**   *How could the change model in Figure 16-1 be used to emphasize why American managers must learn to deal with foreign exchange rate changes?*

    Answer: The world of business is changing at an increasingly rapid pace with the rapid growth and improvements in communications and other technologies. To cope with this change, it is helpful for all managers to have systematic mechanisms with which to consider the change around them. The model can help American managers by clarifying the change process for them, and by providing them with ways to organize their work and the work of their subordinates. Given the external and internal forces in the world's financial markets, American managers must seek appropriate change mechanisms; working with foreign exchange rates is one of those mechanisms.

2. **Question:** *What type of people-change approaches could be used to help managers, such as the treasurer prepare for a changing international world ?*

    Answer: Among those mentioned in the chapter, supervisory training might be used to insure that supervisors themselves have the skills needed, as well as the people-skills to bring their subordinates along with them. Life and career planning might be important because there are many more options for work in large MNCs with worldwide operations. And team building might help the treasurer and his/her managers by assisting them in getting a buy-in from the people they work with and providing them with a meaningful opportunity for input as to the direction of the organization.

3. **Question:** *Why is it likely that some managers will resist learning about international market conditions, requirements, and opportunities?*

    Answer: Internationalization is simply another example of a major change in business, along with changing technology, communications, and economies. Some managers will resist learning about international markets because people in general resist change, regardless of where it occurs.

ADDITIONAL QUESTIONS AND ANSWERS

1. **Question:** *Some experts believe that resistance to change is a natural human tendency that is based primarily on the fear of the unknown. Why do people resist structural, behavioral, and technological change?*

    Answer: People resist change because of fear of the unknown and because change can upset their physical, mental, emotional, and social balance at the workplace. For instance, a technological change on an assembly line can affect not only how an employee physically does the job, but also his social relationships with his peers, and his mental and emotional perspective of his job and his place in the organization. All change initially creates instability as workers slowly adjust to all the effects of change and restore their "balance." By nature, most people don't welcome such instability, even if it is temporary.

2. **Question:** *Do you believe that planned change is more effective and generally successful than unplanned change? Why?*

   Answer: Yes. Implementing change is like tossing a pebble in a pond. Its ramifications can become substantial and extensive. Any effective planning that predicts and prepares for those ramifications (especially resistance to change) will ease the difficulties of change implementation.

3. **Question:** *Why is it important for a manager to recognize the need for change?*

   Answer: Effectively recognizing the need for change (and taking action) usually solves a problem before it becomes costly to the organization. If managers ignore signals of the need for change, they later often pay the price of dealing with a crisis that occurred because managers did "too little, too late."

4. **Question:** *How does a manager become attuned to the internal and external forces of change in an organization?*

   Answer: Managers can increase their awareness by implementing such approaches as establishing and maintaining effective upward and downward communication channels with peers and subordinates and with key external contacts such as competitors and government officials. Information is the key; any action which increases the quality of information supplied from within and outside the organization is beneficial to the manager.

5. **Question:** *The following comment was overheard: "Structural, behavioral, and technical changes are all geared toward one major outcome—improved productivity. Thus, the best way to improve production output is to use the optimal mix of strategies, and this means everything available." Why is this statement incorrect?*

   Answer: Throwing every strategy in but the "kitchen sink" can make any change effort—by its nature already complex—unmanageably complex, and ultimately lead it to become out of hand. Change requires a careful rather than haphazard selection of strategies that will minimize adverse reaction and effects of change. Caution and careful planning are in order.

6. **Question:** *Timing is the selection of an appropriate moment to initiate a change. Why is timing so important in implementing change ?*

   Answer: Timing can determine the success or failure of a change effort. For instance, poor timing can sabotage a change program by creating a situation where the program competes with the organization's ordinary operations. Delayed implementation of a critically needed change can also diminish the effectiveness of the change effort.

7. **Question:** *A model can serve as a guideline for someone actually managing employees. The model used can alert managers to various constraints or issues that may appear. Would there be any value for a manager in understanding the parts of the model represented in Figure 16-1? Explain.*

   Answer: This model stresses a planned change orientation. Knowledge of the model would stress the importance of diagnosis, recognizing limitations, and evaluation. These factors are important for the success of any planned change program. Without paying attention to these kinds of factors, a manager cannot analyze and properly utilize changes that should be or are actually occurring.

8. **Question:** *The initiator of change may be a manager or an outside consultant. Does it matter whether the initiator is an employee of the organization or an outside consultant?*

   Answer: Yes, it does. An important requirement of successful change implementation is that the initiator of change be accepted and respected by key people in the organization. The drawback of using outside consultants is the tendency of some managers to resent and mistrust the consultant as someone who does not truly understand the organization and its problems.

9. **Question:** *"Technology should be used as a means to aid, not replace humans." Evaluate this statement as it applies to a service company you are familiar with.*

   Answer: The banking industry is a good example of how technology has aided humans. Such devices as automated teller machines can perform laborious tasks more efficiently and accurately than humans can, and can stay in service continuously, providing customers with better access to their money. The humans who formerly handled the duties now taken on by the machines are available to solve more complex problems, or to deal with problems that require interpersonal interaction. Students should be able to identify other services industries where technology has had a positive impact.

10. **Question:** *Why should organizational change be monitored?*

    Answer: Implementation of change does not guarantee its success. Change must be continually monitored to smooth out problems that can occur and to make necessary adjustments when unforeseen circumstances arise as a result of change.

17
PRODUCTION AND OPERATIONS MANAGEMENT

LEARNING OBJECTIVES

After completing Chapter 17, students should be able to:

Define the term product (service) quality.

Describe why the production process at Burger King is a worker-paced system.

Discuss the area of influence of production and operations management.

Compare some of the main factors that affect quality.

Identify the four specific production/operations management functions: design, scheduling, operation, and transformation control.

CHAPTER SYNOPSIS

This chapter addresses production and operations management by presenting an overview of the P/OM systems perspective of organizations. The quality concern of P/OM, the process of establishing a quality control program, and the production and operations management systems are also explained. In regard to the systems perspective, the chapter discusses the system's five major components - main inputs, the transformation process, random events, output, and feedback. Three exhibits, Figures 17-1 and 17-2, and Table 17-1 clarify the systems concept and its components. Four specific functions of the transformation process (design, scheduling, operations and transformation control) are defined.

The chapter addresses P/OM's quality concern by defining quality and discussing the costs of quality (preventive, appraisal, and failure costs), the funnel principle and the seven primary factors which affect quality: policy, Information, engineering/design, materials, equipment, people, and field support. The development of quality control programs is discussed in terms of the five-step development process (develop quality characteristics, establish quality standards, develop the quality review program, build quality commitment, and design and use quality measurements and the reporting system). The chapter concludes with a profile on P/OM operations at Corning focusing on the company's production processes and management system.

The **Management in Action** describes the five areas in which Malcolm Baldrige Award contenders must demonstrate commitment, and the three positive results most often reported. These three are: attainment of lower costs and improved quality, increased customer satisfaction, and increased employee satisfaction. In addition some general information about the Malcolm Baldrige is given.

The **first Management Focus** illustrates that the perception of quality if different in different countries. The **second Management Focus** discusses how the Japanese have taken quality one step further. Having reached excellent levels of quality of the product, they are now considering the "personality of the product." These subtle changes seem to be making a difference an can even be noticed in advertising. The **final Management Focus** highlights the side effects encountered as manufacturing firms in the United Kingdom have implemented Japanese-style manufacturing methods. Some of these include: 1) flattening of the organizational structure, resulting in middle management lay-offs; 2) increased dependency on suppliers and assemblers; 3) confrontation of the existing organization culture; and 4) discovery that the implementation process is never complete.

TEACHING TIPS

LECTURE & DISCUSSION IDEAS

1. One way to spur class discussion on the topic of quality is to pose the question: Why are people more quality conscious today than ever before? In discussing this question, have students assess their own expectations of quality in the products and services they buy. What factors account for an individual's different expectations. Why are expectations high for some products and not so high for others?

2. An effective way to illustrate the relationship of quality to business success is to present examples of firms that have paid dearly for a poor quality product and of firms that have reaped substantial benefits for high quality products and success. The Ford Edsel is an excellent example of the price a company can pay for producing a "lemon" automobile. Examples of successful high quality firms are Mercedes Benz, IBM, and Mitsubishi, Ben and Jerry's Ice Cream.

3. To supplement your discussion of the factors that influence product/service quality, ask your students to recall their own work experiences in an organization. Was the quality level of the product/service the company produced high or low? What factors contributed to the quality level? Have students present their diagnoses in class discussion and their ideas on how quality could have been improved in their respective organizations.

PROJECT / EXERCISE IDEAS

1. Have your students identify a local firm that has developed a reputation for quality products or services. As a group assignment, they can interview a high-ranking manager on the company's philosophy on product or service quality, the quality control program applied in the company's production processes, and how the product/service quality is communicated in the company's marketing efforts. This project should provide students with a better understanding of the benefits and costs of producing a high quality product or service.

2. A guided tour of a large manufacturing plant can provide students with considerable insight into how the transformation process of a large goods producing company

works. If possible, it would be helpful to arrange for the students to meet P/OM managers, product designers, schedulers and other employees who direct the various aspects of the company's transformation process.

LECTURE OUTLINE NOTES

I.   Production and Operation Management:
     A.   Terms manufacturing management, production management and operations management are interchangeable.
     B.   Is concerned with the efficient management of the producing function whether it be manufacturing or service, public or private, large or small, profit or non-profit.
     C.   Is highly applications-oriented and has borrowed principles and techniques from scientific management, behavioral scientists, and management science.
     D.   Table 17-1 illustrates various productive systems.
     E.   Systems Approach
          1.   A collection of objects united by some form of regular interaction and interdependence.
          2.   Figure 17-1 illustrates the organization as a system.
          3.   The transformation aspect of an organization, where input is changed to output, is where P/OM activities are conducted.
          4.   Focuses on the supply side of business.
          5.   Affected the behavior and performance of other major functions.
     F.   Good and Services
          1.   Product is a generic label for output of a production system; goods or services.
               a.   Goods are defined as movable personal property.
               b.   Service is an activity required by a customer or work done by another person.
          2.   Production function is the transformation of inputs into goods or services.
          3.   Affected frequently by unpredictable or random events.
               a.   weather
               b.   government regulations
               c.   equipment failure

II. Managing the Transformation Process

     A.   Design - first function
          1.   Involves making decisions on equipment selection, types of production process, and work flow patterns.
          2.   Transformation Processes are divided according to the type of project or work.
               a.   Continuous Process

        1)   very specialized

        2)   producing one type of product

   b.   Intermittent Process

        1)   more general

        2)   utilize a variety of equipment

   c.   One Shot Projects

        1)   Produce a single outcome

        2)   Example: bridges, highways, building construction

3.   The decision on which process to utilize is based on four considerations.

   a.   economic considerations

   b.   volume required

   c.   labor resources

   d.   skills available

B.   Scheduling - covers both long and short runs.

1.   Long-range scheduling forecasts and estimates of product and service demand.

2.   Can involve management of projects over time.

3.   Short-range scheduling involves employees' daily or weekly work activities.

C.   Operation - actual implementation of P/OM procedures.

D.   Control

1.   Requires some method of measuring the product or service before being sold or used.

2.   Inspection is one means of control.

III.   Effective Management of the Transformation Process

A.   *Fortune* magazine examined 10 factories in America for their records of high productivity, high product quality, or both.

B.   Many of these top companies did things the same way.

1.   Make us of most current production management methods for planing and controlling the transformation process.

2.   Reduce the barriers between product design and manufacturing.

3.   Create working conditions that allow employees to make quality products.

   a.   Allow workers to stop the production process to correct defects.

   b.   Can continue to hold the line until source of the defect is discovered.

4.   Help employees understand that the enemy is competition, not management.

5.   Get managers and nonmanagers to think off themselves as teams.

IV.   The Management of Quality

A.   Quality is often ignore due to emphasis on quantity because quality is more difficult to evaluate.

B.   Quality is defined as the "totality of features and characteristics of a product or service that near on its ability to satisfy stated or implied needs,"

1.   Customers are the key perceivers of quality.

2.   With the increase in global markets, managers must recognize the effect of cultural differences on the meaning of quality.
3.   Management Focus looks at this.

C.   *Fortune* established stringent criteria to qualify a company's product as a world champ.
1.   General Dynamics for aerospace
2.   John Deere for agricultural equipment
3.   Apple for personal computers
4.   Genetek for pharmaceutical
5.   Medtronic for medical instruments

D.   American quality leaders commit to exceeding standards of excellence through several means.
1.   Surpass customer expectations.
2.   Provide produce that suits the function.
3.   Improve their products continuously.
4.   Listen to anyone who has something to say about their products.

E.   Consumers' perceptions of "excellence" based on degree to which product of service meets her or his individual specifications and requirements.
1.   Table 17-2 summarizes the dimensions of quality.
2.   Important to consider two points regarding these perceptions.
      a.   Different consumers emphasize different dimensions of quality.
      b.   Perceiving "excellence" can be highly subjective, such as aesthetics.

F.   The importance of market information concerning consumers' views is explained in Management Focus.

G.   Important relationship between quality and price.
1.   Concept of cost of quality and its component parts.
      a.   Prevention costs are the costs of preventing defects and are a precontrol aspect of quality control.
      b.   Appraisal costs involved in directly evaluating quality, such as the cost of inspections and testing.
      c.   Failure costs occur when a defect is produced and identified.
            1)   Internal failure cost - found before the item leaves the plant.
            2)   External failure cost - defect is found by the customer.

H.   Quality Funnel Principle - the nearer to the start of the production process, the lower the cost of quality.
1.   Prevention costs are incurred primarily at the beginning and are the least expensive.
2.   Appraisal costs incurred primarily during the production process and are more than prevention costs, but less than failure costs.
3.   Failure costs are incurred mostly at the end and are the most expensive.

I.   Current shift to prevention or precontrol efforts.
1.   Employee training and greater consideration of the design of the manufacturing process are some such efforts.
2.   With this shift overall quality costs decrease.
      a.   Appraisal costs are reduced.

b.   Failure costs are reduced.

V.   Factors That Affect Quality

    A.   Policy
        1.   Specify the standards or levels of quality to be achieved in a product or service.
        2.   Management considers three factors in determining quality policies.
            a.   Product or service's markets
            b.   Competition
            c.   Image - long-term interests can be damaged by making a product of quality inconsistent with firm's image.

    B.   Information
        1.   Accurate information must be obtained about customer preferences and expectations.
        2.   Also need accurate information about competitors' quality standards.
        3.   Competitive benchmarking is one effective method.
        4.   New computer technology assists with obtaining and analyzing information.

    C.   Engineering and Design - must translate the policy into an actual product or service.

    D.   Materials
        1.   Finished product only as good as raw or starting materials.
        2.   Precontrol strategies are being used to improve this aspect of production.
            a.   Reduces the number of suppliers.
            b.   Develops long-term relationships with best suppliers.

    E.   Equipment - ability to accurately and reliably produce desired outcomes is important.

    F.   People - vital contributors
        1.   Working individually or in teams.
        2.   Managers must provide training and enable people to develop attitudes that value quality.

    G.   Field Support - can have a positive impact on a product's quality image.

    H.   Japanese methods bring together in one system all elements of a quality management.
        1.   Just-in-time (JIT) production
        2.   Jit supply of purchased parts
        3.   Statistical process control (SPC)
        4.   Systems of production control, such as kanban.
        5.   A Management focus explores the experience of the UK with implementing some of these methods.

VI.   The Basic Elements of a Quality Management System

    A.   Develop Quality Characteristics - use the customer's definition of quality; they are the key perceiver of quality.
    B.   Establish Quality Standards.
        1.   Specific quality requirements for the organization's output.

2.   Couple these standards with objectives.
C.   Develop a Quality Review Program
  1.   Management must establish methods for quality review.
    a.   Decide where the reviews will be conducted.
    b.   Determine who will do the reviews.
    c.   Specify when they will occur.
    d.   Define how the review will be reported and analyzed by managers.
  2.   Representative Sampling could be used.
    a.   Less costly than inspecting all products manufactured.
    b.   Creates the following obstacles, however:
      1)   risk that more low quality products may get out because occasionally defective products will slip through;
      2)   customer goodwill may be tarnished because of this; and
      3)   need to make a previous determination about the acceptable number of defects or low-quality products.
    c.   Can take several forms.
      1)   Random spot check
      2)   Statistical analysis also available
      3)   Other methods.
D.   Build Quality Commitment
  1.   All employees must share this commitment.
  2.   Encourage this through five actions:
    a.   Communicate the need for quality.
    b.   Train employees in the skills and knowledge of quality.
    c.   Secure employee involvement in quality.
    d.   Reward for quality.
    e.   Design and use a quality measurement and reporting system.

VII.   Total Quality Management (TQM)

A.   Companies who use TQM philosophy usually follow three principles.
  1.   The objective of quality control is to achieve a constant and continual improvement in quality and provide more and better quality for customers.
  2.   The focus of quality improvement and quality control extends beyond the actual product or service that an organization provides to every process in the organization.
  3.   Employees bear a major responsibility for quality improvements.
B.   Involves the same five elements of a quality control system, however, the breadth of quality focus requires extra efforts.
  1.   Quality audit - a careful study of every factor that affects quality in an activity and all processes.
  2.   Employee training emphasized and focuses on problem-solving skills and specific techniques, such as data collection, etc.
  3.   Top management team are often the first to receive training in quality concepts and control.
  4.   A special staff of managers are often on hand to help implement and

maintain TQM.
   a.   direct employee training
   b.   conduct quality audits
   c.   assist in establishing standards
   d.   perform other functions in the TQM effort
5.   TQM councils or committees, which are often created, oversee organization-wide TQM effort.
C.   Total Quality Management at Corning - a thorough description of their work is included.
D.   Post-Total Quality Management at Xerox - description of the efforts involved in going beyond winning the Malcolm Baldrige Award to developing new initiative or "rugged groupism."

ANSWERS TO DISCUSSION AND REVIEW QUESTIONS

1.   **Question:**   *Explain how international events affect the inputs required for a production process. Provide examples from recent events that have appeared in the media.*

   Answer: There has been a change in customer attitudes and expectations, as well as a drastic change in the sorts and quality of materials available. Increased globalization has increased consumer awareness of quality potential. A potent example of the increase in expectations has come about in the media itself. Consumers/viewers now expect to see world events in their living at the very time they are occurring. And the quality of that media needs to be very consistent, crisp and accurate. The ability to provide this level of quality means that consumers now expect that level of quality all of the time.

2.   **Question:**   *Describe the transformation processes that are required in a large grocery chain such as Kroger Company of Safeway Supermarkets. Consider these organizations at both the store and corporate levels of the system.*

   Answer: The production activities are the production of service to the customer by making available food goods to the customer that are high quality, conveniently accessible, and reasonably prices. Specifically, the activities include cutting, packaging and pricing meat, fish, and poultry products, displaying and pricing produce, canned and other goods, and checking and bagging the groceries.

3. **Question:** *What does a city produce, and what are the elements of the system that a city uses to produce its output?*

   Answer: A city produces services for its citizens, such as police protection, entertainment (the local zoo, arts activities and other events sponsored by the city), and such services as a library, fire protection, and justice (via the municipal court system).

4. **Question:** *What inputs, transformation elements, and outputs does a university use to do its work? How does you university of college rate in your opinion as a production/operations management system?*

   Answer: There will be some differences among inputs, transformation elements and outputs depending upon the mission of the institution. However, there are many similar elements among all colleges or universities. For example, inputs would include students, funds from alumni, research knowledge already available to faculty and practitioners at the school, food for the food service, furniture, etc. The transformation elements would include the various offices and services provided, such as the classroom experiences, the processing of financial aid information, the living experiences in the residence halls. The outputs would include employable graduates, research findings from faculty, community services by members of the institution, involvement of the university in shaping local, state and federal policy, etc.

   An interesting exercise would be to have students develop a rating criteria for the transformation processes and the outputs, and to have then evaluate several schools. This comparative activity would provide greater depth to their understanding.

5. **Question:** *Explain why the assurance of quality involves not only the design of the product but also the design of the production process that will manufacture the product.*

   Answer: By instilling quality in each element of the production process, a sense of quality control is obtained. For instance, if quality is incorporated in a product's design, in the design of production process, in scheduling, and in operations, then the quality of the produced goods is being controlled indirectly. Further, if quality is considered in the initial activities of a good's production (e.g., its design, etc.), then the number of quality problems in the latter stages of the production process will be reduced as will the costs of the problems.

6. **Question:** *Why do organizations not inspect 100 percent of all inputs and outputs to assure quality at both these points in the production system?*

   Answer: Inspecting every product produced is a quite time-consuming and costly activity. Correctly using statistical sampling techniques can result in a 99 percent certainty that the quality of a portion of the goods produced (which are sampled) is representative of the quality of the entire lot of goods produced. Using sampling techniques thus requires considerably less time and costs and yet approaches 100 percent certainty that the sample's quality represents that of the entire lot from which the sample is drawn. Thus, almost all companies apply sampling techniques instead of 100 percent inspection. Most organizations also believe that the payoff of 100 percent inspection (assurance of a set quality level in every product) isn't worth the costs required to inspect every product. They consider that total certainty concerning quality isn't worth the price they must pay.

7. **Question:** *What is your understanding of total quality management (TQM)? Is it just another management fad that will be history by the time you finish this course or begin your own career in business?*

   Answer: Many management and business experts are predicting that the survival of any industry and America itself, when considered as a economic unit, will depend on their ability to engage actively in implementation of TQM. Our competitors around the globe will provide goods and services both cheaper and more effectively unless we continue our efforts.

   This significant differences between regular control systems and TQM are:
   1. Involves the same five elements of a quality control system, however, the breadth of quality focus requires extra efforts.
   2. Quality audit - a careful study of every factor that affects quality in an activity and all processes.
   3. Employee training emphasized and focuses on problem-solving skills and specific techniques, such as data collection, etc.
   4. Top management team are often the first to receive training in quality concepts and control.
   5. A special staff of managers are often on hand to help implement and maintain TQM and provide direct employee training, conduct quality audits, assist in establishing standards, and perform other functions in the TQM effort
   6. TQM councils or committees, which are often created, oversee organization-wide TQM effort.

8. **Question:** *Using the quality funnel principle as the basis for your discussion, explain how TQM minimizes quality assurance costs.*

   Answer: The quality funnel principle states that the nearer to the start of the production process the implementation of quality controls, the lower the cost of quality. Prevention costs are the least expensive since they are incurred primarily at the beginning of the manufacturing or service delivery process. Since TQM provides a great deal of attention to the prevention costs, building in quality along the way, and minimizes defects as a result the costs of quality control are greatly reduced.

9. **Question:** *What seems to be the bases for the success that Corning has achieve in its quality management efforts?*

    Answer: Corning has involved all of its employees in their quality improvement efforts, they have listened carefully to their customers, who are in fact the primary perceivers and definers of quality, and the commitment from top management to this process has been steady throughout.

10. **Question:** *Explain why the management of quality and productivity involve all functions of the business, not just the production/operations function.*

    Answer: P/OM is concerned with the efficient management of the production of the firm's goods and/or services. As such, it is a line activity. Other areas of the organization such as accounting and finance serve to support the P/OM function and are staff activities. P/OM produces the goods/services that marketing sells to customers; marketing is the other line activity of an organization.

    The groups are combined into a single unit to unitedly achieve their maximum potential. The objectives become uniform in their efforts to outperform competitors while producing quality products and services.

END OF CHAPTER CASES

CASE 17-1: A Visit to Burger King

CASE SUMMARY:

Briefly describes production at a typical Burger King. The layout of the store, a description of the typical worker (high school student, part-time), worker ratios, and schedules are provided. Particular emphasis is given to describing the manager's role in ensuring delivery of quality services and products, as well as monitoring costs, and the effective running of the business. Exhibits 1 and 2 illustrate the layout of the store and the work flow process.

ANSWERS TO QUESTIONS FOR ANALYSIS:

1. **Question:** *Describe how Burger King could implement a TQM management system including specific methods and procedures associates with the Baldrige Award criteria as described in the Management in Action.*

    Answer: Criteria for Malcolm Baldrige Award:
    1. Customers have final say.
       Burger King currently allows customers to customize their sandwiches. In addition, BK would need to secure additional feedback from customers as to their perception of the quality they receive, and their ideas for improvements.

2.   Commitment to quality throughout the organization.
Training, visits from top management and evaluations based on quality improvements could be instrumental in establishing this norm.

3.   Continuously improving quality.
Benchmarking, which is explained in a previous chapter, could be useful to this extent. Increasing standards could continue to be set for all employee to strive for. Additional and on-going training would also assist in meeting this criteria.

4.   Decision making reflects data, not habit.
BK could collect additional data about service times, waste produced, efficiency in preparing correct amount of food in anticipation of peak times and slow periods would be some areas in which to begin.

5.   Enable/empower employees.
The establishment of teams, creating work shifts who frequently work together, meetings which specifically focus on allowing the employees to determine how to continue to improve quality are three methods that could be used.

2. **Question:** *Describe how each of the factors that affect quality would apply in a typical Burger King.*

   Answer: Lower costs due to waste and defects, increase product reliability and consistency, provide greater on-time delivery, decrease errors, increase customer satisfaction and return rates, increase employee satisfaction and involvement in decision making, and focusing on efforts to decrease absenteeism and turnover.

3. **Question:** *What special problems, if any, does a typical Burger King face because it employees such a large number of part-time workers?*

   Answer: Part-time workers often tend to be less committed to the organization and the accomplishment of its objectives than full-time workers. There is higher turnover, so costs are increased for training. Also will the need for more employees, since so many are part-time, there are more challenges to developing a team, which is critical for implementing TQM.

CASE 17-2: Managing the Production of Cookies ————————
CASE SUMMARY:
This case profiles the computerized control system at Mrs. Field's Cookies, the leader in the retail cookie market. It is a network for management and operations control. The program tells what must be done each hour to meet the sales goal. The computer is also used for scheduling, interviewing, personnel administration, equipment maintenance, inventory supply orders, and communications between store managers and Mrs. Field's.

1. **Question:** *Aside from the advantages, do you see any shortcomings in the Fields' computerized approach to control? If so, what are they?*

    Answer: While the computer network for management and operations control may provide a highly consistent product and service, many of the managers may feel that the system is too confining. If the computer makes all the decisions the lack of autonomy may be detrimental.

2. **Question:** *Is one type of control emphasized in the computerized control system? Explain.*

    Answer: Each of the three types of control are used in the computerized system. Precontrol is exercised in activities such as production, inventory supply orders, and communications. Concurrent control is exercised in scheduling, interviewing, and personnel administration. Postcontrol occurs in equipment maintenance situations.

3. **Question:** *Would this approach to control be useful in all types of companies and industries? Explain.*

    Answer: Each company and each industry has its own specifics which must be addressed. No two can be considered as duplicates. While portions of the approach may be useful in various applications, the system must be adapted to each situation.

ADDITIONAL QUESTIONS AND ANSWERS

1. **Question:** *What are the important lessons to be learned from the Management in Action which describes the experience of UK firms that implemented Japanese manufacturing methods? How does the discussion of motivation, organizational change and development, and leadership relate to these lessons?*

    Answer: The Management in Action segment indicates the achievement of high productivity levels and quality depends on good management of people as well as techniques. Japanese methods are no solutions unless managers implement them with great care. A knowledge of how to motivate, lead, and organizational change is essential to implement Japanese methods effectively.

2. **Question:** *Pick a specific organization (other than a fast-food restaurant) and identify its inputs, transformation processes, and outputs.*

    Answer: This question is intended for students to apply these concepts to an actual organization. Selected organizations can include an automotive parts store, a hairdressing salon, an unemployment agency, and a hospital.

3.   **Question:** *How important is worker cohesiveness in a worker-paced service operation such as a Burger King restaurant?*

     Answer: It is very important, because production efficiency depends on smoothly flowing production activities performed by its teams of workers. In fact, to facilitate efficient production, Burger King encourages a sense of team spirit among its employees.

4.   **Question:** *How could international politics affect the inputs required for a production process? Provide some recent examples of this in American organizations.*

     Answer: Students will likely present several examples because international politics frequently affects the supply of imported materials needed by many U.S. companies. For instance, the oil embargo in the 1970s resulted in price increases for petroleum inputs for many companies in America. In short, poor relations between the U.S. and foreign countries can reduce the flow of needed raw materials into the U.S. which are needed for good production. As a result, prices on such materials that are available increase because of the material scarcity.

5.   **Question:** *Explain why a manufacturing firm cannot achieve perfect quality of output. If perfect quality is impossible, explain how a production manager could establish acceptable quality.*

     Answer: Perfect quality is impossible because of the inherent variability in material, machines, and people. The establishment of acceptable quality must take into account the best possible quality, the average quality, and the tolerances required and demanded by the customer.

6.   **Question:** *Organizations, particularly business firms, have taken a renewed interest in production-operations methods. What economic circumstances and events seem to account for this re-emphasis on productivity and efficiency?*

     Answer: Students may cite several factors. Among them: customers are becoming more quality conscious, demanding more for their money. Many industries are being more competitive requiring that competitors increase efficiency in order to maintain or increase profits. Also, a troubled economy can spur businesses to become more efficient in order to gain as much profit as possible for each item sold as product demand typically declines in financially bad times.

7.   **Question:** *Briefly define the four specific functions of the transformation process.*

     Answer: The four functions are: 1) design of the process which includes making decisions on equipment selection, the type of production process, and work flow patterns; 2) scheduling the transformation process to produce the goods or services on time; 3) operation of the process which involves implementing P/OM procedures; and 4) transformation control which are those activities that ensure that the goods and/or services produced meet quality standards.

8. **Question:** *Differentiate between intermittent, continuous, and "one-shot" transformation processes.*

    Answer: A continuous transformation process is very specialized and produces one product or service. An intermittent process is more general and uses a variety of equipment. A "one-shot" process is used in building a "one-shot" product such as a highway or ship.

9. **Question:** *How should quality realistically be defined?*

    Answer: According to the chapter, quality should be defined in terms of accuracy (in matching specifications and consumer expectations) and timeliness (essentially producing the product when needed).

10. **Question:** *Explain the funnel principle.*

    Answer: The funnel principle states that the nearer to the start of the production process, the lower the cost of rejecting a sub-quality product. The highest rejection costs occur when the customer rejects the product (where the costs of processing resources, processing the complaint, and loss of goodwill are incurred).

11. **Question:** *Briefly state the five steps that comprise the establishment of quality control programs.*

    Answer: The five steps are: 1) the product's or service's quality characteristics are defined (which involves examining such factors as customer expectations, marketing department suggestions, and technical specifications); 2) quality standards are established which involves determining the desired quality levels; 3) the quality review program is developed which involves determining the methods for review, where and when reviews will be conducted and by whom, and how the review will be reported and analyzed by managers; 4) commitment to quality within the organization is developed; and 5) quality measurements and the reporting system is designed and implemented.

12. **Question:** *What are the requirements for building a commitment to quality within the organization?*

    Answer: Three conditions are essential. First, all employees must believe that quality output is an accepted and rewarded practice. Second, the employees must be aware of the quality standards and know how to meet them. Third, the employees must possess the skills to meet the quality standards.

13. **Question:** *Briefly identify the factors that affect product and service quality.*

    Answer: There are four primary factors:
    1. policy that determines the product's market and sales price and

the product image which the company wants to establish;

2.   the product/service design;

3.   production equipment that can meet the quality standards at reasonable costs;

4.   field support which essentially is service support provided by the company to the customer once the produce is purchased.

18   PRODUCTION AND INVENTORY PLANNING AND CONTROL

LEARNING OBJECTIVES
After completing Chapter 18, students should be able to:

Define   the terms production planning and inventory control.

Describe   the applications and limitations of linear programming, program evaluation and review technique, economic order quantity, material requirements planning, and just-in-time models.

Discuss   the importance of production and inventory planning and control in product and service providing organizations.

Compare   the circumstances which would determine whether linear programming or program evaluation review technique is the appropriate production planning model.

Identify   the characteristics of inventory that enable a firm to use economic order quantity, material requirements planning, and just-in-time models for inventory control.

CHAPTER SYNOPSIS

The chapter addresses production planning by providing an in depth look at two prominent production planning techniques—linear programming (primarily used in planning repetitive production) and Production Evaluation and Review Technique (PERT), a most popular network model typically used in planning non-repetitive projects (for example, large, highly complex one-of-a-kind projects). The application of linear programming in the opening **Management in Action** segment shows how the Montreal Urban Transport System saved money and determined utilization and schedules of vehicles. In its treatment of linear programming, the chapter discusses the technique's characteristics and functions and presents a brief overview of the method's varied applications. A sample production planning problem is presented which is used to illustrate in depth the technique's key steps. These include translating the problem into mathematical equations, graphing the equations, and determining the optimal solution. The section concludes with a brief overview of the major benefits of linear programming. A **first Management Focus** segment looks at the use of LP in a small textile firm. The chapter examines PERT by presenting a sample problem and illustrating the steps for determining the critical path. The chapter also includes an overview of the benefits by PERT.

The **second Management Focus** describes the use of manufacturing resource planning (MRPII) in Canada's second largest pharmaceutical company. Encountered problems with the system, however, realized the flaws were with implementation of the system not the system itself. The **final Management Focus** discusses the use of Just-In-Time things with the implementation of, and specifically the training about TQM and were able to apply the best of JIT fundamentals to improve their training efforts.

This chapter also looks at the management task of inventory planning and control by examining four major topics: the types and purposes of inventory, and the three primary techniques of inventory control: the economic order quantity method (EOQ), material requirements planning (MRP), And just-in-time (JIT) inventory control. Concerning inventory types, the chapter discusses the four basic inventory categories (raw material, supplies, work-in-process inventory and finished goods) and provides examples to illustrate each type. The five primary purposes of inventory are also explained (the promotion of customer service, manufacturing flexibility, production/operation certainty, production smoothing, profits through speculation). The economic order quantity method of inventory control is presented by first defining the method's key concepts (ordering and carrying costs) and then presenting a step-by-step explanation of the model's use. The method's major limitations are also discussed. Material requirements planning is addressed by discussing the system's three basic elements (master production schedule, bill of materials, and inventory records) and the six basic management decisions which are necessary for system operation. The importance of adaptability for system effectiveness and just-In-time inventory, the present "state-of-the-art" in inventory control, are discussed. The chapter concludes with a brief comparison of the EOQ and MRP techniques.

The **Management Focus** segments highlight 1) the application of PERT to the Olympics, and 2) how computer developments have enhanced the applicability of PERT to organizations.

TEACHING TIPS

LECTURE & DISCUSSION IDEAS
1.   Typically, the best way to enhance students' understanding of the linear programming and PERT techniques is to focus on actual applications of the techniques in businesses. Three possible project ideas are presented in the Project/Exercise Ideas to help you in this regard.

PROJECT / EXERCISE IDEAS
1.   As a group assignment, have your students interview the inventory control manager of a local business and prepare a written or oral report on the company's inventory control system. The report can focus on such topics as the techniques used in inventory control and the company's approach to safety stock, work-in-process inventory and other elements of the inventory control system. This project idea has been tested in the classroom and one of its demonstrated benefits are the insights gained by students into unique problems in inventory control systems that are related to the specific nature of the respective business. Essentially, different businesses with different types of inventory and production processes experience different inventory problems. How businesses approach their inventory problems is another source of useful insights.

2.	Invite two inventory control managers from two businesses with different production processes to discuss the above mentioned topics in inventory control.

3.	To provide an indepth perspective on the chapter material, invite a member of the management science faculty who specializes in inventory control to discuss the subject and the latest developments in inventory control and MRP systems. The speaker may be able to provide more information and insights into Japan's just-in-time inventory control system.

4.	The best way to increase student understanding of the PERT and linear programming techniques is to focus on actual applications in business. Here are three ways to do so:

a.	As a group written or oral report, have your students identify a local business that has used or is using one of the two techniques and interview a member of the organization who is involved in managing its use. The interview should focus on the nature of the problem for which the technique is used, the steps involved in using the technique (e.g., gathering information, computer usage, etc.), special problems encountered and necessary revisions, and the benefits the technique has provided for production planning.

b.	Have your students select an article in a major management research publication (e.g., Interfaces, Decision Sciences) which describe an application of PERT or linear programming in solving an actual production problem. Students can prepare a written or oral report on the article, summarizing the respective problem, the technique's application, and results. Typically, reported applications address particular and usually unique problems encountered in using the respective technique, usually because of some unique feature of the problem. This aspect of the article can provide students with greater insight into the flexibility and limitations of the two techniques.

c.	Have students create their own problem which is appropriate for linear programming of PERT. This exercise has typically been used as a short paper assignment where students explain the nature of the problem, state the problem data and provide problem calculations, the solution, and an overall discussion of the exercise.

5.	Invite a P/OM manager from a local business that has used or uses linear programming or PERT in its production planning. He or she can address the same issues which would be covered in a student's written or oral report.

6.	For a more thorough perspective on these techniques, invite a member of the management science faculty at your school who has done research and consulting work in organizations using one or both of these techniques. The speaker can provide insights into the latest developments in their application, and particular problems in using the techniques to solve production planning problems. He or she should also be able to provide some interesting and varied examples of the uses of PERT and/or linear programming in organizations.

I. Production Planning
    A.   Presented in context of two situations
        1.   A manufacturer with multiple products.
            a.   demanded by large numbers of consumers
            b.   items such as, autos, home products, appliances, textiles
            c.   requires managers to determine the specific number of each products to produce given resources constraints and creative profitability of each item.
        2.   A firms that takes on few, but large scale projects
            a.   typically one of a kind project
            b.   construction, buildings, ships, dams
            c.   production planning requires determination of the combination and sequence of activities given the cost and time constraints.
    B.   Two of the more widely used techniques are linear programming and program evaluation review technique.
    C.   Planning Repetitive Production: Linear Programming
        1.   Determining which specific combination of products to manufacture, during a given time period becomes more complex as the number of products increases.
        2.   Programming methods assist with these decisions.
        3.   Linear Programming is the simplest method.
            a.   Linear because mathematical equations and the objective to be achieved are in the form of linear relations between variables.
            b.   Linear relationship between two or more variable is directly and precisely proportional.
        4.   Specific Applications of Linear Programming
            a.   Production Planning - a manager must determine the levels of a number of production activities for the planning period.
            b.   Feed Mix - linear programming used to allocate the various grains so that the result meets nutritional, dietary and cost requirements.
            c.   Fluid Blending - variation of feed mix, which requires the blending of fluids, such as chemicals, into a finished product.
            d.   Transportation - to select routes the minimize total shipping costs, given a number of supply sources and destinations, or the scheduling of ports of call.
            e.   Advertising Media Mix - enables the manager to determine how to allocate funds over various media to achieve maximum exposure.
            f.   Linear programming has also proven to be useful in other areas:
                1)   determining effective generation of electricity with regulation of a dam
                2)   allocation of tax dollars to public projects

    3) tree development
    4) credit to customers
    5) dollars to investments
    6) hospital resources to patients
5. The Value of Linear Programming
    a. Improved Planning
        1) expand the analytic and planning abilities of managers
        2) permits an exhaustive search of alternatives
        3) systematically searches for optimum solution
    b. Improved Decisions - quickly finds the best solution under a variety of conditions.
    c. Improved Understanding of Problems
        1) analyzing very complex problems
        2) improve manager's comprehension and appreciation of complex problems.
        3) comprehend more easily the effects of alternative assumptions

D. Planning Nonrepetitive Production: PERT
    1. Technique used to combine resources or to control activities.
    2. Called network models.
    3. Especially suited for projects that are not routine or repetitive, where coordination is needed to ensure the tasks are accomplished in the appropriate order.
    4. Program evaluation and review technique (PERT)
        a. minimizes conflicts, delays, and interruptions by coordination various aspects of entire job
        b. assists in completing work on schedule
        c. identifies both potential problems and solutions
    5. PERT especially useful when manager has not encountered particular problem before and unlikely to again.
        a. These projects have two common characteristics
            1) extremely complex with potentially thousands of interdependent tasks
            2) most tasks are single occurrence and not likely to be repeated
        b. Historical data not available for nonrepetitive projects.
        c. Management must still plan and control nonroutine operations.
        d. Allows the project to be considered in its entirety.
    6. Specific Applications of PERT
        a. One of the most widely used production planning models.
        b. Developed through cooperation with US Navy and consulting firm of Booz, Allen & Hamilton
            1) 1958 - Polaris missile project
            2) Credited with reducing by two years the completion time of the project.
            3) Spread rapidly throughout defense and space industries.
            4) Many government agencies require contractors to use PERT.

315

        c.   PERT also used successfully with:
- 1) Constructing new plants and hospitals
- 2) Designing new automobiles
- 3) Coordinating numerous activities in managing new projects
- 4) Planning and scheduling space probs
- 5) Managing accounts receivable
- 6) Installation of large-scale computer systems.
- 7) Ship construction and aircraft repair.
- 8) Mergers and acquisitions
- 9) Economic planning in new developing countries
- 10) Large conventions and meetings

        d.   Network models provide direct aid to managers in two areas:

            1)   Improved Planning

                a)   Shows manager interconnections of tasks and provides possible timeframes.

                b)   Increases ability to plan an optimum schedule before work even starts.

                c)   Time reductions brought about in several ways:
- i. Reduce expected time on the longest path through the network.
- ii. Eliminate some part of the project.
- iii. Adding more resources - people or machines.
- iv. Purchasing components.
- v. Changing some work to parallel activities.

            2)   Better Control

                a)   Completion of the plan itself forces manager to plan more thoroughly.

                b)   Computer graphics programs help considerably
- i. simply hand sketch a network
- ii. put information in proper form
- iii. submit data for processing
- iv. receive completed network within hours

                c)   Time consuming aspects of planning have been practically eliminated with computer assistance to planning via PERT.

                d)   Both an internal and external control.

                e)   Hospitals have found PERT useful in reducing costs.

II. Inventory Control

- A. Securing and maintaining optimal quantities and types of physical resources required by the organization's strategic plan.
- B. Manufacturing process as a flow of materials through a process that changes the form of those materials into finished goods.
- C. Inventory control at the heart of production control.
- D. Inventory Management as a Strategic Factor
  - 1. Black and Decker Manufacturing Company (BD)

  a. world's largest manufacturer of power tools

  b. located in Hampstead, Maryland

  c. assembles over 120 major product groups requiring 20,000 inventory items

  d. always alert to ways to control inventory

  e. PACE: planned action and constant evaluation - system which combines latest computer technology and control techniques

   1) Sound Material Plan - controls quantities ordered, dates of order and reorders and changes in specifications.

   2) Commitment to executing the plan - avoid unnecessary inventory costs.

   3) Constant evaluation of ways to reduce inventory levels.

   4) Insistence on maintaining accurate records

 E. Types of Inventory dependent on the nature of the particular business.

  1. Inventory is costly because of costs to store, move, safeguard and insure it.

  2. Raw Materials - ingredients that go into the final product.

  3. Supplies - materials that do not become part of the final product.

   a. MRO: maintenance, repair and operating

   b. usually small in number and expense

  4. Work in Process - raw materials moving through the stages of production.

  5. Finished Goods - consists of final, unsold products.

   a. Stored

   b. Amount depends on industry

   c. Exists in all industries

 F. Economic Order Quality (EOQ) Model - involves balancing costs of having too much inventory and the costs of having too little.

  1. Cost Factors in Inventory Control

   a. Ordering Costs of getting items

   b. Carrying Costs - usually expressed in annual figures

    1) Interest on money invested in inventory

    2) cost of storage

    3) rent

    4) obsolescence

    5) taxes

    6) insurance

   c. These two costs are related to each other as illustrated in Figure 18-1.

  2. Limitations of EOQ Model

   a. Conditions of certainty rarely exist

   b. estimating demand is difficult

   c. Many variable affect demand, such as competitor's prices, economic and social conditions

   d. Best for controlling inventory that has independent demand - demand unrelated to the sale or usage or other items.

III. Materials Requirements Planning

 A. Developed to control inventories with dependent demand.

B. Popularity increased significantly since the early 1970s; transportation industries have been the quickest to adopt method.
C. The Basics of MRP
   1. Involves breaking down a product into its components and subassemblies.
   2. Three basic tools:
      a. Master Production Schedule - details the planned quantities of finished goods to be produced during a particular period of time.
      b. Bill of Materials - defines the required components of inventory that have dependent demand.
         1) Figure 18-2 shows the relationship between Master Production Schedule and Bill of Materials - become increasingly more complex as the number of products increases.
      c. Inventory Records - a perpetual, current status of each component subassembly and finished good.
D. The Complete MRP System
   1. Illustrated in Figure 18 - 3, which seems simplistic, however system is very complex.
   2. Example of IPE-Cheston Company is included.
E. Manufacturing Resource Planning (MRPII)
   1. Integrates production planning, inventory control and strategic planning.
   2. Expands the concept of bill of materials to include all resources required of a product.
   3. Works best with lot and batch manufacturing, whereas mass producers must rely on forecasts of economic factors.
F. Just-in-Time Control - provides the raw material or component part just before it is needed, and thus attempts to eliminate the need for inventory.
   1. The Basic Elements of JIT
      a. Reason for inventory is the existence of uncertainty in the production process, cause by a number of factors:
         1) Faster-moving subsystems must have inventories of slower-moving subsystems.
         2) Unreliable deliveries of acceptable materials from vendors.
         3) Equipment breakdown
         4) Unskilled employees
         5) Flow of components is interrupted.
   2. American car manufacturers rely more on JIT now than ever before.
   3. Japanese and American firms have successfully implemented JIT, thus, eliminating both the human and technical reasons for inventory.
   4. Developing effective supplier relationship under JIT is often the most challenging aspect of this model.
   5. Successful managers follow three steps:
      a. Communicate benefits of JIT of firm and suppliers to suppliers
      b. Train the suppliers in JIT.
      c. Help the supplier in finding ways to simply processes.
   6. The Management Focus highlights how JIT principles were applies to training.

G.   Some Problems and Limitations of JIT:
     1.   Coordinating the buyers delivery requirements.
     2.   Maintaining the agreed upon level of quality.
     3.   Convincing suppliers of benefits.
     4.   Coordinating information flow between buyer and supplier.
H.   Managers can overcome some difficulties by:
     1.   Acknowledging the need for a level of safety stock.
     2.   Building that level into inventory strategy.
     3.   Recognize the JIT is not a substitute for management.
     4.   By remembering the JIT is merely a way to control costs and inventory; nothing more.

ANSWERS TO DISCUSSION AND REVIEW QUESTIONS

1.   **Question:**   *Explain the two general types of production systems and give examples of each one.*

     Answer: The two types are: repetitive production systems that produce large numbers of multiple products (i.e., producing 5,000 Toyota Tercels and 2,000 Toyota Corollas each week in one Toyota plant) and nonrepetitive production where a large-scale, highly complex product (in a one-of-a-kind production activity) is produced (i.e., a ship, shopping center, or spare shuttle construction project).

2.   **Question:**   *Why is it useful to think of production planning as a problem that involves the allocation of scare resources to alternative products or services?*

     Answer: Because such is production planning's primary activity. The chief objective is to do so in such a way that makes the most effective use of the scarce resources (time, labor, materials, and overhead).

3.   **Question:**   *The text discusses a number of different production planning problems for which linear programming solutions are available. Describe what each of these problems has in common which makes them amenable to linear programming.*

     Answer: In each problem, an objective is specified (minimize costs or maximize profits). Constraints exist and can be specified and the problem characteristics are such that a linear relationship can be assumed to exist between the variables in the equations used to solve the problem. In sum, the problem characteristics meet the assumptions necessary for the LP technique to be effectively use.

4.   **Question:**   *Illustrate the practical value of linear programming by relating the benefits to the planning and controlling functions of management.*

      Answer: Linear programming typically provides management with specific amounts to be allocated in performing a certain activity (e.g., the amount of advertising funds to be allocated across various media in promoting a product, the specific mix of grains to produce a nutritional feed mix). These amounts provide content for the management's plans in these areas. The amounts also serve a controlling function because they are standards of sorts, and management must ensure that the specific amounts have been allocated and take correction actions if they have not.

5. **Question:** *Helene Manufacturers, Inc. produces two different models of professional hair dryers. Dryer A contributes $20 profit, and dryer B contributes $10. Each dryer must do through three manufacturing processes: X, Y, and Z. Dryer A requires four hours in department X, five hours in department Y, and five hours in department Z. Dryer B requires nine hours in department X, six hours in department Y, and 14 hours in department Z. The available time in departments X, Y and Z are 180 hours, 150 hours, and 175 hours respectively. Using the graphic method, find the optimum combination of the products.*

Hair Dryers' Manufacturing Processes: Time Requirements

Department	Time Required Dryer A	Dryer B	Available Time
Department X	4	9	180
Department Y	5	6	150
Department Z	5	14	175
Profit	$20	$10	

Contribution

Answer: Using the graphic method, find the optimum combination of the products that would maximize total profit. Suppose the company could concentrate all its efforts on one model. Would this change the solution?

Maximize P = $20A + $10B
Subject to:
4A + 9B $\leq$ 180 Dept. X
5A + 6B $\leq$ 150 Dept. Y
5A + 14B $\leq$ 175 Dept. Z

Mathematical solution:

5A + 14B = 175
-(5A + 6B = 150)
‾‾‾‾‾‾‾‾‾‾‾‾‾
   8B = 25
    B = 3.125 or 3

Substituting:
5A + 6(3.125) = 150
5A + 18.75 = 150
5A = 131.225
A = 26.25 or 26

P = $20(26) + $10(3)
 = $520 + $30
 = $550

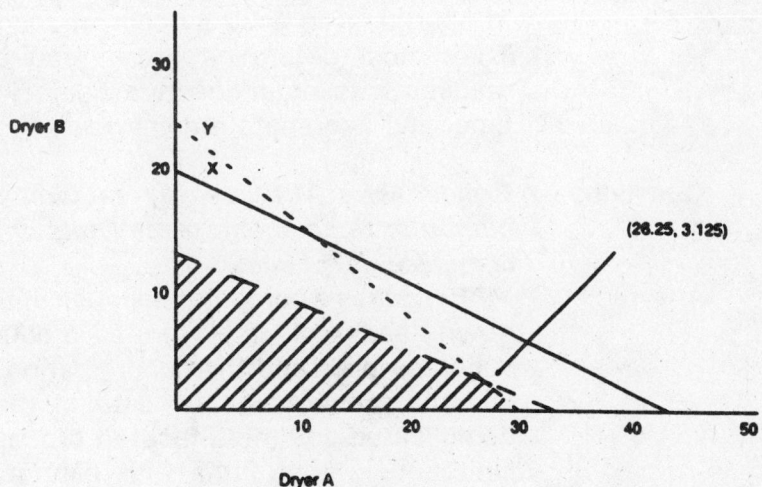

Note: If the company would concentrate all efforts on one model, they would only produce 30 units of Dryer A, which would bring $600 in profit.

6. **Question:** *What are the specific characteristics of production problems for which PERT is an applicable technique?*

   Answer: PERT is useful for nonrepetitive production projects which pose the special problem of how to manage work which is performed only once. PERT provides a method for keeping track of all events and activities in a project and to help ensure that the project is completed in time.

7. **Question:** *Under what circumstances is MRP preferable to EOQ as an inventory control method? Are EOQ and MRP mutually exclusive? That is, must a firm use one or the other for all inventory items? Explain.*

   Answer: MRP is preferable to EOQ for firms with job-lot or batch-processing technology and where production is discontinuous, varied, and dependent on relatively uncertain customer demand. The two methods are typically mutually exclusive; however, they can be used together in firms with job-lot/batch-process and continuous process manufacturing technologies.

8. **Question:** *Define the basic tools and decisions comprising an MRP system. Which decisions are pivotal for determining the relative effectiveness of an MRP system?*

   Answer: Four basic tools comprise an MRP system:

   1) the master production schedule which details the planned number of finished goods to be produced during a particular time period;
   2) the bill of materials which defines the required components for each sub-assembly and finished good;
   3) inventory records which list the current status of each component subassembly and finished good; and
   4) the computer.

   In operating an MRP system, management must make six decisions. They must determine gross requirements (a pivotal decision), net requirements, order quantities, safety stock and lead times, order release time, and aggregate requirements.

9. **Question:** *Explain why MRP usually requires computer utilization. Does the computer requirement place limits on the kinds of firms for which MRP is applicable? Explain.*

   Answer: MRP requires a computer because of the complexity involved in breaking down each of the firm's products into its components and subassemblies and then coordinating component ordering and delivery and the production-start date of the subassemblies. In sum, it's a complicated and multi-faceted process. Computer requirements are a limitation in that firms that cannot afford the necessary computer hardware and software cannot effectively use MRP.

10. **Question:** *What are the important economic and ethical issues associated with obtaining the necessary supplier relationships to make JIT a successful method for controlling inventory costs?*

   Answer: There are essentially three steps in developing supplier relationships. First, communicate the benefits for both parties. Second, train the suppliers in JIT concepts. Third, help the suppliers simplify their own production processes to make frequent deliveries easier.

END OF CHAPTER CASES

CASE 18-1: CONTROL IN FURNITURE PRODUCTION

CASE SUMMARY: The production of furniture offers many opportunities for applying management science models. This exercise emphasizes the use of linear programming to determine optimal cutting patterns. As the exercise unfolds, the student is brought to the realization that management science models are not always preferable to more traditional ways of making decisions. The article on which this exercise is based presents two additional examples of unsuccessful applications of linear programming.

ANSWERS TO QUESTIONS FOR ANALYSIS:

1. **Question:** *What general principles, if any, regarding the application of linear programming models are suggested by this case?*

   Answer: There have been too few published reports of unsuccessful applications of linear programming to draw any general principles. However, this exercise suggests that traditional ways should not be dismissed out of hand, especially when these ways have evolved in the context of tightly structured problems.

2. **Question:** *How would you, as production manager, explain to the veteran employee, your decision to engage the college professors? How would you avoid giving the impression that your decision expressed lack of confidence in the employee's work?*

   Answer: It is virtually impossible to avoid the impression that the decision to hire the professors reflects no confidence in the veteran employee's work. In fact, the decision reflects exactly that position. It's better to recognize and acknowledge that point at the beginning.

3. **Question:** *In addition to the problem of defining efficient cutting patterns, what are some of the other problems to which linear programming can be applied in furniture manufacturing?*

   Answer: Certainly, linear programming could be used to determine production runs, to allocate materials to product lines, to assign employees to products, and to determine efficient shipping and warehousing routes.

CASE 18-2: JUST-IN-TIME INVENTORY CONTROL AT THE TOYOTA TRUCK PLANT

CASE SUMMARY: This case discusses the use of JIT in the manufacturing processes of a Toyota flat bed manufacturing plant in Long Beach, California. What is unique about the situation is that U.S. workers and managers implemented, operate, and manage the JIT system. The case also makes the important point that successful JIT implementation and management requires focusing on all elements of the manufacturing system, not just inventory control. The case provides an excellent opportunity for students to identify and discuss the challenges of making JIT a success.

ANSWERS TO QUESTIONS FOR ANALYSIS:

1. **Question:** *Do you believe that JIT can be applied in plants that do not have a "Japanese connection?" What, if anything, is there about JIT that is peculiarly Japanese?*

   Answer: Implementation without a "Japanese connection" can be accomplished; however, the task is quite difficult and requires careful consideration of all changes in the manufacturing process required for JIT to be a success. Many have argued that the peculiarly Japanese element of JIT is the Japanese penchant for eternal improvement, always striving for perfection. In a sense, JIT is perfection in inventory control. The traditionally American perspective on inventory control (e.g. reliance on buffer stocks as protection against uncertainty) is quite different.

2. **Question:** *Why is it necessary to consider the entire manufacturing process in order to make improvements in inventory control?*

   Answer: It's necessary because inventory management affects and is affected by all elements of the manufacturing process. Have your students think about this point and provide examples to support the statement.

3. **Question:** *What features of the JIT approach can apply in organizations that do not have inventories such as banks, professional firms, and the like?*

   Answer: Perhaps the primary feature is the objective of providing a smooth production process whether the output be making loans, handling checking account deposits or performing the array of services provided by service companies.

ADDITIONAL QUESTIONS AND ANSWERS

1. **Question:** *Describe and illustrate the application of MRP in managing the university cafeterias. Assume that the menu plan for the semester is the master production schedule. What then are the bills of materials? The inventory records? How would order points and lead times be determined? How would aggregate requirements be determined?*

Answer: The bills of materials lists all of the menu's components—individual food items and ingredients that are necessary to produce some menu items (e.g., spices, flour, sugar, etc.). The inventory records list the current status of each component, subassembly, and finished good (food ingredients and finished food items). Order points and lead times would be determined by assessing the current inventory stock levels, demand, and points of demand. A particular order point would be calculated by subtracting lead time from the date the item is required for production. Aggregate requirements would be determined by incorporating planned orders for food ingredients and release dates for all food components in the master schedule.

2. **Question:** *Cite some nonrepetitive problems, other than those discussed in the chapter, for which PERT would be useful as a planning and control tool. Use your personal experiences if necessary. Which of these problems would cause you the greatest difficulty in determining expected times of completion?*

 Answer: PERT has found wide use in marketing in the area of new product planning and product development, in management in such areas as production, personnel, and research and development. In fact, it is widely used in most all areas of business and government in which a process in nonrepetitive and requires the coordination of many activities.

3. **Question:** *Assume that you have been assigned a term project in one of your management courses. It is your task to collect data for the report from both library sources and personal interviews with local business people. You have a total of ten weeks in which to complete the assignment. List the activities and their optimistic, most likely, and pessimistic times and construct a PERT network for the project.*

 Answer: This question is designed to allow the student to attempt to apply some basic PERT principles to a familiar situation. It will involve the four basic phases in constructing a simple network:

 a. Define each task that must be done.
 b. Estimate how long each task will take.
 c. Construct a network.
 d. Find the critical path.

4. **Question:** *Place the following activities in the form of a PERT network: a) Remove carburetor; b) Rotate tires; c) Put on snow tires; d) Tune motor; e) Clean and replace air filter; f) Test drive car; g) Remove air filter; h) Complete tune-up.*

 Answer: This question is strictly designed to get the students involved in constructing a network for a project. There is no correct answer since it will vary depending upon which activity is done first. It usually results in a great deal of class participation.

5.   Question: *The Lisa Ann Company makes two products. Product A contributes $20 profit and Product B contributes $12 profit. Each product must go through two manufacturing processes in order to be completed. Product A requires 12 hours in Department X and 4 hours in Department Y. Product B requires 4 hours in Department X and 8 hours in Department Y. There is a total of 60 hours available in Department X and 40 hours in Department Y. Find the optimum combination of the two products which would maximize total profit. Use the graphic method.*

Answer: Answer: Maximize $P = 20A + 12B$
Subject to: $12A + 4B \leq 60$ Dept. X
$4A + 8B \leq 40$ Dept. Y

Mathematical solution:
$3(4A + 8B = 40)$
$= 12A + 24B = 120$
$\underline{-(12A + 4B = 60)}$
$20B = 60, B = 3$

Substituting:
$4A + 8(3) = 40$
$4A + 24 = 40$
$4A = 16, A = 4$
$P = \$20(4) + \$12(3)$
$= \$80 + \$36 = \$116$

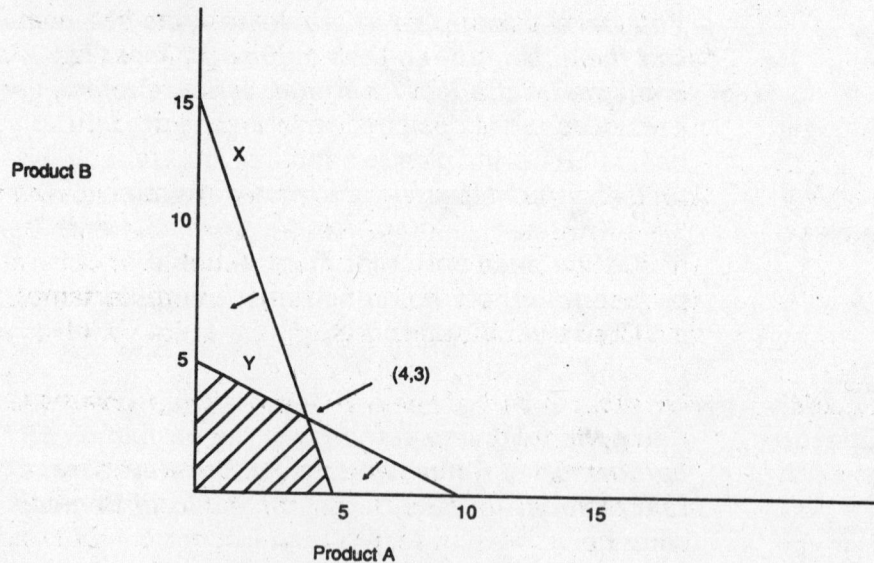

Axis Intercepts:
Dept. X: (5,0) (15,0)
Dept. Y: (10,0) (0, 5)

326

6. Question: *Answer each of the following questions: I) Can there be slack time on the critical path? 2) Can there be slack time on a noncritical path? 3) Can there be any such thing as negative slack? 4) Of what value are the slack time calculations?*

Answer:

1) Yes. There can be slack time on the critical path when more time has been allotted to the path than is actually needed.

2) Yes, but the critical path will always have less slack time than the noncritical path.

3) Yes. Negative slack occurs when the project has been allocated less time than it is expected to take to complete the project.

4) The most important value of the slack time computation is that it may enable the manager to shift resources to the critical path, thereby perhaps shortening the time of the entire project.

7. Question: *Can you think of an allocation problem, other than those discussed in this chapter, where linear programming might possibly be of some help? Describe it in a short paragraph indicating the objective and the various constraints.*

Answer: This question is designed to allow students to relate allocation problems from their own experiences to linear programming. While all examples may not lend themselves to linear programming solutions, they will nevertheless force students to identify allocation problems. Then the simplifying assumption of linear relations between variables can also be discussed to the end that they will realize that most real world problems, in fact, do not have linear relations among variables. This realization should lead into the next question

8. Question: *Describe the characteristics of the linear programming model.*

Answer: The LP model is normative because it selects the best alternative to meet a specified objective. The model's variables are deterministic; that is, they are assumed to be known with certainty. Overall, the model assumes certainty and assumes that its variables are linearly related.

9. Question: *For what types of linear programming problems is the graphic method not applicable?*

Answer: The method can't be used for problems with more than two variables in the objective function (e.g., three products when the objective is, for instance, to minimize production costs). Only two variables can be graphed. However, LP problems with almost unlimited number of variables in the objective function and constraint equations can be solved using a computer.

327

10. **Question:** *Briefly identify the benefits of linear programming.*
    Answer: The technique:
    1) improves planning by enabling a thorough search of alternative solutions and a systematic search for the optimal solution;

    2) improves decisions by quickly finding the optimal solution under a variety of conditions; and

    3) improves the manager's understanding of problems via its highly efficient way of analyzing quite complex problems and its structuring of problems.

11. **Question:** *What is the key variable of interest in any PERT problem?*
    Answer: Time.

12. **Question:** *Why can PERT be used for effective concurrent control?*
    Answer: A major advantage of PERT and other network models is that the tremendous planning involved in constructing the network contributes significantly to the definition and ultimate concurrent control of the project. For internal control, it provides time schedules for each activity, and networks can therefore be revised if unforeseen difficulties arise. Resources can be shifted and activities can be rescheduled with a minimum of delay on the outcome of the project. For external control, in projects where subcontractors are used, the necessity for meeting scheduled dates can be stressed by showing the subcontractor the negative effects of a delay on the entire project. When subcontractors are involved, it is usually vital that they meet their scheduled delivery date.

13. **Question:** *Briefly summarize the benefits provided by the PERT technique.*
    Answer: The technique affords two overall advantages. It improves planning by increasing the manager's ability to plan an optimal schedule while the project is still in the planning schedule. This is done by showing the manager the interconnections of tasks and estimated activity times for each task. Second, PERT improves control both internally (by providing time schedules for each activity which enable managers to revise networks if problems arise) and externally by demonstrating to subcontractors the importance of meeting deadlines. This is accomplished by using the PERT network chart to show the negative effects of a delay on the entire project.

14. **Question:** *What are the limitations of linear programming?*
    Answer: This question is intended for students to identify and evaluate the technique's shortcomings. Responses will differ; however, it can be argued that the chief shortcoming is the technique's assumption of a linear relationship among variables. Such does not often exist in the real world.

15. **Question:** *Is the EOQ model able to adjust to changes in demand over a period of time? Why?*

    Answer: Yes, the model can adjust by changing the D value in the formula. For instance, if demand is different for the January-April period, then the demand value in the formula will reflect this.

16. **Question:** *If you knew at what point on a graph ordering costs and carrying costs intersect, what would you also know about the economic cost size ?*

    Answer: The point where ordering costs and carrying costs intersect represents the minimum total inventory cost.

17. **Question:** *What is your opinion regarding the argument that JIT will never take hold in America as it did in Japan because of the cultural differences between the two countries?*

    Answer: There is little doubt that JIT is compatible with certain Japanese cultural values. Whether American manufacturers can adopt JIT with the ease of their Japanese competitors remains in doubt. Whether cultural values are either necessary or sufficient for JIT success remains an open question.

18. **Question:** *Under which circumstances can a firm consider the feasibility of implementing a JIT inventory control system? List firms for which JIT might be feasible.*

    Answer: JIT is a way to control inventory costs. It works best in companies where inventory and product demand can be accurately forecast, the production processes are repetitive, and high quality suppliers are located nearby. Examples of firms where JIT might be feasible include: GE, Goodyear Tire, Ford, and General Motors Corp.

19. **Question:** *Differentiate between four types of inventories.*

    Answer: Raw materials are those ingredients that comprise the final product (e.g., paper, ink, and binding that make up books). Supplies are maintenance, repair and operating items that aren't part of the final product but that indirectly support the production of goods. Work-in process is comprised of raw materials moving through the production process. Finished goods are the final, unsold goods stored at the manufacturing facility.

20. **Question:** *Distinguish between ordering costs and carrying costs.*

    Answer: Ordering costs are the costs of getting a particular item into actual inventory. The costs are essentially the clerical and administrative expense of ordering, receiving and placing goods in inventory. Carrying costs are the various expenses incurred as a result of carrying items in inventory such as the interest on money invested in inventory, the cost of storage space, and rent.

21. **Question:** *What is the difference between independent and dependent demand?*
Answer: Independent demand occurs when a product's demand is unrelated to the sale of other items such as finished goods and supplies. With dependent demand, a product's demand is related to the sale of other items. Many products such as raw materials and components have dependent demand in that their demand depends on demand for finished goods.

22. **Question:** *What are the major limitations of the EOQ inventory control model?*
Answer: There are three major limitations. First, the model's assumptions of certainty are rarely realistic. Second, estimating demand is often difficult and it usually can only be roughly estimated. Third, the model is most applicable to control inventory with independent demand. Independent demand rarely occurs.

23. **Question:** *Define safety stocks.*
Answer: Safety stocks are reserves of raw materials, components, and finished goods that are held in inventory to be used when production problems (e.g., equipment breakdowns, supply shortages) occur. Safety stocks enable the provision of finished goods to continue when these types of problems would otherwise cut short the supply of finished goods to the consumer.

24. **Question:** *Briefly identify the five primary purposes of inventories.*
Answer: Inventories serve to promote customer service by providing products when customers demand them. Inventories also promote manufacturing flexibility and certainty in production/operations. Inventories serve as a hedge against uncertainty via a reserve of safety stock. Inventories also promote production smoothing and provide potential for profits through speculation wherein, during inflationary periods, a firm can profit by purchasing inventory at a low price, holding it until prices increase, and then selling it at a profit.

25. **Question:** *Reread the section on MRP systems in the chapter. Then consider the question: in your opinion, what potential challenges face a company attempting to implement MRP in its manufacturing system?*

Answer: This question makes an excellent project idea where students can interview individuals involved in MRP to determine some of the most challenge problems that can occur (and how the respective company solved them). Or students can research the question by referring to journals such as Inventory and Production Management which publish numerous articles on the dynamics of MRP implementation.

26. Question: *The chapter notes that in most firms, inventory and production planning and scheduling has not been used as a strategic tool and integrated into the company's strategy plan. Why?*

Answer: A chapter notes that one reason is that sophisticated, computerized techniques for these activities are being developed faster than companies can implement them. This situation also relates to the gap between the development of management science techniques and their application which was discussed in the Foundations Chapter. An individual's natural resistance to change is also relevant here.

27. Question: *What overriding characteristic must an MRP system possess in order to be effective?*

Answer: A system must be adaptive to unexpected changes in elements of the system such as changes in lead-times and safety-stock levels due to changing supplier capabilities. A system's adaptability depends on speedy access to needed information and input of the information into the system.

28. Question: *Why it is necessary for firms to carry inventories of finished goods? What purposes are served by such inventories?*

Answer: Students may suggest several reasons; the two primary reasons are to:

1) be prepared for unexpected and sudden increases in consumer demand for the finished goods; and

2) be prepared for unexpected manufacturing problems that prohibit finished goods from being produced for some time. The finished goods inventory serves as a buffer or safety stock between uncertainty in the market and in the production process.

19

MANAGING INFORMATION FOR DECISION MAKING

LEARNING OBJECTIVES

After completing Chapter 5, students should be able to:

Define	decision support systems
Describe	the different sources of information
Discuss	the functions of decision support systems
Compare	the advantages of the central bank with those of an information center
Identify	the important issues associated with managing information

CHAPTER SYNOPSIS

The chapter addresses decision support systems by focusing on five topics: the emerging need for decision support systems, the relationship between decision support systems (DSS,) the relationships between a manager's level in the organization and his or her particular information needs, and designing and organizing a decision support system.

Concerning the need for decision support systems, the chapter discusses three factors which have contributed to this emerging need: the recognized importance of information in decision making, the mismanagement of information, and the advent of personal computers in business. An important segment of the chapter is the discussed distinction between decision support systems and management information systems. Table 19-1 compares the two systems in four different organizations. The chapter discusses information needs for the different levels of management by focusing on the decision types relevant to each management level and the kinds of information relevant to these decision types. The design of a decision support system is discussed in terms of external information flows (intelligence information and organizational communications) and intraorganizational informational flows and the four functions of a decision support system (determination of management's information needs, gathering and processing information, and information utilization). The chapter concludes with a discussion of the systems perspective and the steps involved in designing a decision support system.

Two important DSS components, the central data bank and Information center, are presented and each component's respective functions are explained. This final chapter segment emphasizes the importance of viewing information as a resource and the need to use information efficiently.

The **Management in Action** focuses on the steps being taken in Australia to develop a large-scale data collection program regarding health care. This data will help to establish benchmarks through comparisons. The **first Management Focus** provides an example of how one industry has been able to use computerized information to assist its salespeople with the information overload they encounter. The **second Management Focus** describes how Bell Canada developed a single integrated financial information system based on DSS software. And the **final Management Focus** explains a recent study finding that many corporate information systems are moving toward recentralization.

LECTURE & DISCUSSION IDEAS

1. The introduction of planned change in an organization can, along with the intended results, present some unexpected outcomes. The implementation of decision support systems is no exception. There is an increasingly common situation in organizations with decision support systems—the CEO using his or her DSS to bypass middle managers for information and, in some cases, to check up on managers. As a result, some observers believe that the DSS is upsetting the balance of power in many organizations. Is such activity by the CEO supportable (when does managing become meddling?)

2. One way to expand upon the chapter's coverage of decision support systems is to ask students to consider how the systems are affecting the manager's everyday job. What aspects of the job should be most affected? DSS is becoming a particularly useful tool for strategic analysis. You may want to have students consider the usefulness of DSS in this regard.

3. DSS can be a powerful managerial decision-making tool. However, it can also hinder decision making. For example, some DSS users note that managers can become so entranced by the touch-of-a-finger availability of massive amounts of once unavailable information that, even with an effective DSS, they become bogged down by too many details. Thus, a "can't-see-the-forest-for-the-trees" dilemma emerges. It's insightful to have students discuss the potential pitfalls using a DSS. What adjustments in their decision-making processes might managers have to make?

PROJECT / EXERCISE IDEAS

1. You may want to further develop the question (offered in Lecture Idea #2) on how decision support systems are changing manager's jobs by having your students interview a manager who regularly uses a DSS in his or her work. Have students prepare a written or oral report on how the system's use has altered the manager's job in terms of time, activities and responsibilities. As a DSS user, the manager can provide some insights into the adjustments necessary to accustom oneself to working with the system.

2. Invite a DSS manager to speak to the class on the topics that would be covered in the exercise interview. The manager could also discuss the nature of his or her work focusing on relationships with management and the particular challenges the job presents. Considering the feelings of many MIS managers that they're being excluded from top management it could be insightful to ask the manager to address this issue.

I.   Sources of Information - develop a clear understanding of the various information flows that managers must manage.

    A.   External Information Flows - proceed from the organization to its environment and/or from the environments to the organization.
        1.   Illustrated in Figure 19-1.
        2.   Intelligence Information
            a.   Elements of the organization's operating environment
            b.   From clients, patients, customers, competitors, suppliers, etc.
            c.   Use in evaluating short-run, strategic planning information on the economic environment.
            d.   Has long-run significance to the organization and aids in long-range strategic planning.
            e.   Example from Frito-Lay is provided.
    B.   Intraorganization Flows - Information flowing within an organization

II.   Managing Information for Better Decision Making

    A.   An effective decision support system integrates decision making throughout the organization and provides means or managing rivalry among the unity.
    B.   The Importance of Information in Decision Making
        1.   A major purpose of a manager is to convert information into action.
        2.   Information-decision systems should be considered in conjunction with the fundamental managerial functions of planning, organizing and controlling.
        3.   The effectiveness of an organization is more often than not tat the mercy of the information available to its managers.
    C.   Mismanagement of Current Information
        1.   The ability to generate information is really not the problem.
        2.   Typically massive amounts of information is produced.
        3.   Complaints are:
            a.   Too much of the wrong information and not enough of right information.
            b.   Information is too scattered throughout the organization.
            c.   Vital information is sometimes suppressed.
            d.   Vital information arrives too late.
        4.   Historically managers did not have to deal with so much information.
    D.   The Increased use of Personal Computers
        1.   The capacity to extract, process and analyze data accurately is amazing.
        2.   Computers have become smaller, faster and smarter
        3.   More technological advancement faster than any other innovation in history.
        4.   Computers have changed the way information is utilized through computer networks.
        5.   Example of enormous changes at Westinghouse Electric Corporation due

to their use of electronic mail.

    a.   Can communicate from home to anyone in the 38-country network.

    b.   Has created a permanent record of communications.

    c.   Less expensive than a personal call.

    d.   Less costly than a telex letter.

    e.   More effective means of communication than others used.

III.   The Need for Decision Support Systems

    A.   The Need of Managers

        1.   DSS is a specialized information system designed to support a manager's skills at all stages of decision making.

        2.   DSS shapes information to management's needs.

        3.   Effective DSS will do the following:

            a.   support but not replace management decision making

            b.   assist management throughout the organization, but primarily at middle- and top-levels

            c.   enable decision maker to interact with the computer to examine the effects of alternative decisions.

            d.   gather, store, and make available data and models relevant to specific types of decisions

            e.   invite usage

    B.   Need for Specific Information for Specific Decisions - types of information needed are classified by types of decisions being made:

        1.   Planning Decisions - involve formulating objectives for the organization, the amounts and kinds of resources needed, and the policies.

            a.   Comes from external sources.

            b.   Relates to present and predicted state of the economy.

            c.   Complicated by the size and complexity of the organization.

        2.   Control Decisions - ensure the organization's performance is consistent with objectives.

            a.   Internal Sources.

            b.   Budgets and measuring performance.

            c.   Takes many forms.

            d.   In some cases provides data to customers.

        3.   Operations Decisions -focus on the daily activities of the organization and how effectively its resources are being used.

            a.   routine and necessary sources

            b.   generated internally, often from one designated source

            c.   primarily used by first-line supervisors.

IV.   The Function of a Decision Support System

    A.   Should provide four services:

        1.   Determination of Information Needs

            a.   Questions helpful for identifying manager's information needs are presented in Table 19-1.

            b.   Managers who are expected to use the system should be involved in implementing it.

        c.   Recognize different information is needed for formulating organizational objectives than form scheduling production.

        d.   Must distinguish between "need-to-know" and "nice-to-know" information.

  B.   Information Gathering and Processing - to improve overall quality of information there are five components.

      1.   Evaluation involves determining how much confidence can be placed in information.

      2.   Abstraction involves editing and reducing incoming information.

      3.   Indexing provides classification for storage and retrieval.

      4.   Dissemination entails getting right information to right people.

      5.   Storage is necessary since organization has no memory of its own.

  C.   Information Utilization - major goal of a DSS is to provide the right information to the right decision maker at the right time.

V.   Designing a Decision Support System

  A.   Requires a systems perspective.

  B.   The Central Data Bank - centralizing information so data can be accessed by any decision maker as needed.

  C.   The Information Center - which is essentially the same as the Central Data Bank, however, with this there is a central entity for gathering and processing of information.

      1.   Dispersed information must be identified throughout the organization.

      2.   Activities must be viewed as parts of a whole.

      3.   Activities must be brought under the management of a separate, centralized information center.

  D.   Information as an Organizational Resource

      1.   Frequent problem is that much data is generated for no real purpose and should be eliminated.

      2.   To promote effectiveness DSS should be viewed as a resource.

          a.   Vital to the survival of the organization.

          b.   Can only be used at a cost.

          c.   Must be at the right place at the right time.

          d.   Must be used efficiently for an optimal return on its costs.

ANSWERS TO DISCUSSION AND REVIEW QUESTIONS

1. **Question:** *What reasons account for the growing importance of information in management decision making? Can a manager make a decision without information? Explain.*

Answer: Some of the increased importance of information in decision making id being driven by the fact that is simply is available, and thus the effective decision makers are actually those who can determine which information is necessary. The changing external environment precipitated by the global economy is creating new demands for managers to utilize all information available prior to making any decisions.

From one perspective a manager is simply unable to make any type of decision without information; the manager will always have some data available, even if only in the form of intuition and values, which are gaining in significance as important tools in effective managing. However, a wise manager includes other types of information whenever possible.

2. **Question:** *Explain how a DSS can be designed to provide information for each step in the decision-making process. For which steps would the development of information be most difficult?*

Answer: Student responses, of course, will vary. Several may cite the determination of management's information needs while others will note that finding relevant information and organizing it into a useful form is the most challenging task. The point of this question is for students to consider the tasks involved in establishing a DSS and the challenges that each task presents.

3. **Question:** *Explain how the use of person computers and laptop computers can ease the sense of information overload.*

Answer: The use of these two tools allows the manager to access information when and where they chose. They are not longer at the mercy of someone else providing them with data or an analysis, thereof. On the other hand, some individuals claim the feeling of greater overload since they at tempted to access data more often and in places before which were considered "out-of-touch," such as vacations.

337

4. **Question:** *What kinds of information would a manager need to make the following decisions?* a) Hiring a new employee.
b) Promoting an employee.
c) Purchasing a computer system.
d) Assigning salespersons to regions.
e) Assigning shelf space to a product.

Answer: This is a student involvement question that typically generates a lively class discussion. In answering the question, students will likely use a process similar to Figure 19-2. They will determine information needs, sources, and to what use the gathered information would be put.

5. **Question:** *Provide examples of decisions other than the ones listed in question 4 to illustrate the difference between planning, control, and operations decisions.*

Answer: Students will likely present a wide variety of examples.

Some examples are:
selecting the market for a new product and determining corporate objectives (planning),
developing a quality control system (controlling),
and determining the span of control for an accounting department (operating).

6. **Question:** *Interview a member of the college admissions office and determine the kinds of decisions made in the office and the kinds of information required for each decision. Design the basic elements of a DSS that could provide the appropriate information.*

Answer: One of the most difficult aspects of the work of the admissions office is to manage incoming enrollment numbers. Students must be recruited and attracted to the school; selections must be made from among those students who are interested in attending, and offers given. One of the difficult balancing aspects of this work is ensuring that enough quality students are interesting in attending who fit with the mission of the school. Since most students will be accepted than will eventually attend, due to competition from other schools, careful analysis must be done to determine how may students to accept in order to achieve the desired numbers at the school.

There are many approaches to creating a DSS system to manage this work. Students should be encouraged to explore thoroughly all of the aspects of this area of decision making. Many will have personal information to share regarding their involvement with this system as an external customer.

7. **Question:** *What are the different functions of a decision support system? How do these functions differ in manufacturing as compared to service organizations?*

Answer: A DSS provides four functions: identifying managerial information needs, gathering and processing the information, and information utilization. In an overall sense, the functions do not differ in manufacturing and service organizations. Regardless of the type of organization, managers have information needs and a DSS seeks to fulfill them by obtaining, processing, and making available decision-relevant information when it's needed.

8. **Question:** *Explain how a manager could make sure that the centralized information center does not become overly powerful in the organization by virtue of its position as monopolist of information.*

Answer: An important and potent source of power in organizations is the control of a valuable resource; as controller of information (a critically valuable resource when it's timely and relevant), the information center can potentially become quite powerful. This potential problem is a top management issue and should be addressed by periodically evaluating the center's activities to ensure that the center acts in the best interests of management (e.g., providing information when requested and working to serve all managers rather than a favored few) and not in the interests of building and exploiting its power.

9. **Question:** *If information is a resource, as suggested by the chapter discussion, should it be valued in the balance sheet like other assets? Why or why not?*

Answer: It should be valued in the balance sheet like other assets; however, this is an ideal that will likely never be realized.

The reason: the exceptional difficulty in valuating information. For example, the value of information is greatly affected by unique ownership. If the information is highly relevant and is possessed by only one company, it's much more valuable than relevant information shared by all competitors. However, how does management determine if other competitors have the information? If competitors don't have the information today, they may obtain it tomorrow which greatly lowers the information value (causing much fluctuations in the balance sheet figures). In sum, valuating information is a very diffiCUlt task.

10. **Question:** *In the modem age of information, is the study of information little more than the study of computer technology, including hardware and software? Explain your answer.*

Answer: No. Computer technology is an essential element of the study of information; however, a thorough study of information also requires understanding information flows in an organization, in the external environment, and the ways to gather and evaluate information, and many other factors.

CASE 19-1: INFORMATION SYSTEMS DEVELOPMENT TO COMPETE FOR THE BALDRIGE AWARD

CASE SUMMARY: This case describes one entrepreneur's initial encounter with the requirements for applying for the Malcolm Baldrige Award. Joseph Arthur had been successfully running 12 sit-down, family-style restaurants in Kentucky and Tennessee utilizing the production and control mechanisms of fast food restaurants. He sought advice from his dataprocessing staff as to whether he would have the information available to complete the application.

ANSWERS TO QUESTIONS FOR ANALYSIS:

1. **Question:** *Where in the organization would the data processing staff likely find the answers to each of the questions posed in the category?*

    Answer: Although only limited information is provided in the case about the specifics of the data processing systems within his restaurants, students will be able to explore the various pieces of information necessary for completion of the application. This case question also provides the opportunity to explore the Malcolm Baldrige specifics.

2. **Question:** *Which of the specific areas of concern would be the most difficult to develop answer? Explain and indicate what you would be to get the answer.*

    Answer: Given the history of effectiveness of the stores, data about competitors and benchmarking from comparative systems seems to be more readily available. Information about customers may be the more challenging to gather.

3. **Question:** *In your personal opinion, what do you think of amount of detail required to document this category of the Baldrige Award? Could a firm likely spend a lot of time completing the applications and get little in the way of return? What could be the reasons to go through the exercise even if the chances of winning are very low?*

    Answer: Students will certainly have a variety of responses to this question. Many companies have reported that the mere completion of the application, while extremely time-consuming and draining on resources, has greatly improved the quality of the company and their increased ability to fulfill their strategic plan.

CASE 19-2: HOW DO WE EVER MAKE A DECISION?

CASE SUMMARY: This case concerns the initial steps in the development of a DSS for Lobo-Enterprises, a poorly performing business in substantial need of an information system. The case focuses on the report by the Purchasing Department manager on the department's information needs and sources. This list is quite lengthy, leading one purchasing agent to reply, "How do we ever make a decision?

1. **Question:**   *What would be your answer to Scott Reed's question?*
    Answer: Such a question is understandable given the department's complex information needs and lengthy list of information sources. However, the purpose of a DSS is to make such complexity manageable by gathering and processing the department's requested information and rendering it accessible and useful to the department members when needed.

    So the answer should be: You make a decision by correctly using an effective DSS and the information it provides.

2. **Question:**   *Could Figure 19-3 be of use to Lobo Enterprises? How?*
    Answer: The figure could be used to better manage the information needed to make purchasing decisions. Reeves has, in fact, taken the first step by detailing the information needs and sources for purchasing decisions. This exercise can be used to clearly illustrate the need for and basic purpose of DDS.

3. **Question:**   *Could the concept of a central data bank be of use to Lobo Enterprises? Why? Illustrate, using specific examples.*
    Answer: The central data bank is essential for Lobo Enterprises because the bank stores all information and enables members from each department to easily obtain information provided by other departments and stored in the bank. For instance, the central data bank would enable the purchasing department to quickly and easily obtain needed information provided by the engineering department and the R&D department which are two of its key information sources.

ADDITIONAL QUESTIONS AND ANSWERS

1. **Question:**   *What are the key differences between management information systems and decision support systems?*
    Answer: The primary difference between a DSS and a MIS is that a MIS is a computerized system that provides managers with information. A DSS is an MIS that is designed with the primary objective of managerial decision support, i.e., shaping information to meet manager's decision needs.

2. **Question:**   *What are the different external and internal information flows that the college ar university you attend must deal with? If possible, interview campus administrators and determine which of these flows they*

consider most critical for the effectiveness of their decisions.

Answer: External information flows can include information from competitors' actions (other colleges and universities), from the state government (which provides public schools with funding), and from the parents of students. Internal information flows include information transmitted internally and usually reciprocally among departments, divisions and colleges (e.g., student admissions figures from the registrar's office to specific academic departments).

3. **Question:** *How does planning information differ from control information?*
   Answer: Planning information relates to the top management tasks of formulating objectives, the amounts and kinds of resources necessary to attain the objectives, and the policies that govern their use. It forms the input for the nonprogrammed types of decisions made at this level in the organization. Control information aids managers in making decisions which are consistent with the achievement of organizational objectives as well as seeing how efficiently resources are being used. Its primary users are middle managers and the information serves as input into the programmed and nonprogrammed types of decisions made at this level. It enables middle managers to determine if "actual results" are meeting "planned-for-results" (objectives).

4. **Question:** *Discuss what is meant by the statement: "In the area of organizational information, more is not always better.*
   Answer: Today, many managers often feel buried by the deluge of information and data that come across their desks. Much of it is useless or too old to be of value. This "information overload" is one reason why the concept of DSS developed. Managing existing information in the "Age of Information" is a critical task of a DSS.

5. **Question:** *Question: Briefly describe the reasons why the need for decision support systems has emerged in recent years.*
   Answer: This need results from three factors. First, managers are increasingly recognizing the importance of quality information as a prerequisite to quality decision making. Second, information is often mismanaged and misused because there has been no systematic way to gather relevant information and organize it effectively as a tool for managers. A third factor is the advent of the personal computer. It's predicted that most managers will have a personal computer at their desks by 1990 which will provide quick and easy access to volumes of information. This easy access requires that information be effectively managed.

6. **Question:** *Does the organization level of managers affect their information needs? How? Explain, using examples.*
   Answer: Yes. Top level managers need information for planning decisions. This type of information usually comes from the external environment and relates to factors such as the economy, resource availability, and the

political and regulatory environments. Middle-level managers need information for controlling decisions which comes mostly from internal (often interdepartmental) sources. First-level managers need information for operations decisions which is generated internally, usually from one designated department.

7. **Question:** *Why must information be viewed as a resource for a DSS to operate effectively?*

   Answer: Information must be viewed as a resource because it is an essential prerequisite for effective decision making. As a resource, it must be efficiently used, that is, organizing information so that only what is needed by managers is provided at the right time.

8. **Question:** *When is a DSS an MIS?*

   Answer: By its nature, a DSS is a specialized MIS designed to support a manager's skills at all stages of decision making. An MIS is a DSS only if it is designed with the primary objective of managerial decision support.

9. **Question:** *Differentiate between the two broad types of information flows in an organization.*

   Answer: External information flows are comprised of information that flows from the organization to the external environment and vice versa. Intelligence information flows from the environment into the organization (e.g., data on clients, competitors, suppliers, the government). Organizational communications flow from the organization into the external environment and are controlled by the organization. Intraorganizational flows refer to information that flows vertically and horizontally within the organization.

10. **Question:** *What is the role of an integrated DSS in an organization. Are there potential disadvantages?*

    Answer: Student should understand an integrated DSS facilitates planning, budgeting, and controlling across departments to achieve uniform objectives. Also, intelligence information is effectively gathered and utilized. Some pitfalls are evident: CEO's using the DSS access to the point of intrusion, inefficiencies, and detail oriented.

11. **Question:** *Briefly identify the three tasks that must be performed for an information center to be developed.*

    Answer: First, the organization's dispersed information activities must be identified throughout the organization. Then, these activities must be viewed as parts of the whole, which is the organization's overall information system. Lastly, the activities must be managed by a separate, centralized information center.

12. **Question:** *In your view, what types of organizations would best benefit from a DSS? What kinds would least benefit? Explain your reasoning.*

Answer: Responses, of course, will vary; however, most should agree that a DSS would be most beneficial for organizations operating in a highly complex external environment where change is turbulent. Here, the quality of decision making is particularly important and the need for the least environmental information is particularly acute.

344

20 ENTREPRENEURSHIP

LEARNING OBJECTIVES

After completing Chapter 20, students should be able to:

Define the term entrepreneur.

Describe the characteristics and motivations of entrepreneurs.

Discuss why entrepreneurship is a concept that fits people from around the world.

Compare the managerial tasks of the entrepreneur with those of the nonfounder CEO of a large, ongoing corporation.

Identify the benefits that result from developing a business plan.

CHAPTER SYNOPSIS

This chapter addresses the issue of entrepreneurship and management by focusing on three major topics: the entrepreneur, entrepreneurship and the functions of management, and the special challenges of entrepreneurship. The chapter begins with a brief discussion of the importance of small business to the U.S. economy and the unique differences between the entrepreneur and his or her counterpart: the large-company CEO.

Concerning the entrepreneur, a definition of the entrepreneur is presented, and the risks that the entrepreneur faces in launching a new business (business, financial, career, psychological, and family and social risks) are discussed. The entrepreneur's different motivations for creating a company are also discussed as are common individual characteristics of entrepreneurs.

Entrepreneurial success requires effectively applying the four management functions; thus much of the chapter focuses on how each function applies to creating a business. The discussion of planning focuses on start-up planning and the five questions which planning must answer: what product or service will the new business provide, what market will be served, and how will the business be established, operated, and financed. In discussing each of these questions, several topics are presented including the differences, strengths and weaknesses of the approaches to starting a business (buyout, start-up and franchise), and the different sources of new venture funding. Discussion of the organizing function and entrepreneurship centers on many entrepreneurs' tendency to be very flexible in their development of the company's initial organizational chart and job descriptions. Concerning the leading function, the entrepreneur's unique advantages an disadvantages in providing effective leadership are discussed. Discussion of the controlling function in new businesses focuses on the types of control that entrepreneurs emphasize and the increasing use of computer systems to achieve effective control. The chapter concludes with a discussion of three major challenges that confront many entrepreneurs at some point in their careers:

1) adapting their management style to the needs of a large business;
2) handling especially high levels of stress; and
3) achieving a satisfactory sale of their company.

345

The chapter's **Management In Action** segment describes the increasing numbers and importance of women as entrepreneurs. The **first Management Focus** explains how many large companies are taking the best of entrepreneurship and small business thinking inside of their corporate walls. Going global with small businesses is the main topic of the **second Management Focus**. The **final Management Focus** describes incubation as a possible funding method for the development of small businesses.

TEACHING TIPS

LECTURE & DISCUSSION IDEAS

1. To encourage some budding entrepreneurs in your class, ask your students what ideas and goals they might have for starting a new business venture. This may then be followed through with a discussion of entrepreneurial characteristics and potential by having them refer to Figure 20-1 and assess themselves. Using this, take several students and their ideas and have an open discussion of just what is needed for each kind of business venture, what kinds of demands are likely to be place on the student as manager, how they can be resolved, etc. What motivations are involved?

2. An effective way to personalize the discussion of the risk factors involved in launching a new business would be to follow the previous discussion theme and have some students put their plans into perspective regarding the role they would play in career options, effects on family and social life, and financial plans. Using a question and answer format, and open discussion with the class, this can help consider such risks on a personal level.

3. As preparation for this class and to provide the basis for interesting discussion, have students interview a local franchisee and find out what was entailed in starting the franchise and how the manager feels it is affecting her career, finances, social and family life, etc.

4. An interesting way to demonstrate many factors in this chapter is to use the Business Plan (Table 20-4) to work through one student's ideas into focus and reality and illustrate factors which need to be considered regarding financial and marketing plans and the managerial functions.

PROJECT / EXERCISE IDEAS

1. To extend student understanding of the work involved in determining what product to provide and market to serve in launching a new business, have your students, as a group project, select an industry and research the industry as a possible market for starting a new business. In analyzing the industry, they should focus on such factors as the market's size, the competition (determining the bases of competition e.g., price, quality, reputation), and customers. From their research, students should provide a list

of the most important challenges facing an entrepreneur in establishing a new business in the respective industry.

2. Have your students select an acquisition that is widely reported in the business literature and as a group project, research the acquisition. There is a very large number of publicized acquisitions to select from (over 30,000 full acquisitions have occurred in the U.S. since 1980). Their reports should focus on identifying from their research, the benefit and pitfalls of using an acquisition strategy to enter an industry.

3. Invite an entrepreneur who has established a successful business in the community to speak to your class. He or she can address a number of topics including:
    — the special challenges of launching a business
    — the approach used to determine the type of business to establish and product/service to provide
    — the personal sacrifices that entrepreneurship often entails
    — the rewards of entrepreneurship

4. Invite an entrepreneur who has operated a franchise. He or she could provide much insight into the dynamics, advantages and shortcomings of franchising as a strategy for establishing a business.

5. If someone on your faculty has conducted research on entrepreneurs, invite him or her to talk to your class about the latest research on the characteristics and motivations of entrepreneurs. One question to pose: do men and women entrepreneurs differ in their motivations, management styles and other management-related characteristics?

LECTURE OUTLINE NOTES

I. Introduction
    A. Small business substantially contributes to the economic well being of the U.S.
        1. The 14 million-plus small businesses provide over 80 percent of the new jobs in the U.S.
        2. U.S. small business community is the world's fourth greatest economic power.
    B. The entrepreneur:
        1. Establishes and manages a new enterprise.
        2. Faces challenges that differ from those of the large-company CEO. The entrepreneur:
            a. Is deeply involved in every aspect of the business.
            b. Copes with greater personal and professional risk
                1) Usually, his or her personal financial resources will be lost if the business fails.

        c.   Is singularly accountable for the business' performance.

C.   Each year, about 1.3 million individuals become entrepreneurs in the U.S.

D.   Conferences are being held around the world to bring entrepreneurs together from different countries.

E.   Eastern European governments want to encourage entrepreneurs as their respective economies become capitalistic.

        1.   One example: 24-year old Mikhail Gulyaev launched a medical equipment company in the Soviet Union. He has joint ventured with a California medical equipment firm to make magnetic resonance image systems. He will sell the MRI machines for $400,000 - $500,000 each in Eastern Europe (General Electric sells their own machines for $1.7 million each).

II. The Entrepreneur

A.   Though many definitions of entrepreneur exist, we define the entrepreneur as the creator and manager of a business.

B.   Initially the entrepreneur manages a small business.

        1.   According to the SBA and Committee for Economic Development, the small business:

            a.   Is privately owned (usually by top management).

            b.   Maintains local operations.

            c.   Employs less than 500 people.

C.   The entrepreneur faces several risks:

        1.   Business risk—from 25 to 33 percent of all independent small businesses fail during the first 2 years of operation; 8 of every 10 fail within 10 years, primarily due to poor management.

        2.   Financial risk—the entrepreneur invests most if not all of his or her financial resources in the business.

        3.   Career risk—leaving a secure job for an uncertain future.

        4.   Family and social risk—A new business leaves little time for family and friends.

        5.   Psychological risk—the risk of personal failure if the business does not succeed.

D.   Entrepreneurs create businesses for:

        1.   Independence—to be their own boss.

        2.   Personal and professional growth.

        3.   A better alternative to a dissatisfying job—according to a survey of CEOs of the Inc. 500 (the 500 fastest-growing private companies in the U.S.), frustration with working in a large company was a primary motivator for starting a new business.

            a.   Many female entrepreneurs cite the inability to advance in big companies, frustration with the corporate grind, and the need for flexibility in having a career and family as reasons for starting a business.

        4.   Income—for the sizeable profits that a successful business can bring and/or the enjoyment of making their own money.

        5.   Security—in the middle and latter stages of their careers, many feel that

managing their own business is more secure than facing the possibility of being laid off.

E. According to research, entrepreneurs:
1. Have a greater need for independence and autonomy compared to managers.
2. Have a high tolerance of ambiguity.
3. Have high energy, endurance, self-esteem, and a need to take charge. See Figure 20-1 which shows some differences in the personal characteristics of Inc 500 CEOs and Fortune 500 CEOs and senior executives.

III. The Tasks of the Entrepreneur

A. Entrepreneurial success requires effectively applying the management functions, and before doing so, taking the first step-deciding whether to become an entrepreneur (the entrepreneurial decision).
1. Making the right decision requires a:
a. Clear understanding of entrepreneurship and the requirements for success.
b. An accurate self-appraisal of skills and shortcomings. See Table 20-3 which provides students an opportunity to assess their entrepreneurial potential.

B. Planning—likely contributes the most to new venture performance. Provides a blueprint for action for the first critical months of the business.
1. The entrepreneur performs:
a. Ongoing planning—for the established business (discussed in earlier chapters).
b. Start-up planning—done before the new venture opens for business.
2. Start-up planning involves answering five questions:
3. What product or service will the new business provide? And what market will be served?
a. A product/service can be selected by conducting an information search to identify opportunities.
1) The list of prospective businesses is reduced by considering each business' feasibility and compatibility with the entrepreneur's goals and strengths.
2) Each business' market must be analyzed, assessing:
—the market's size
—competition
—determining competition bases (price, image, quality).
—customers
—assessing demographics, especially purchasing power.
—market share
—determining share the business can reasonably attain.
3) Market analysis for a totally new product/service is more challenging because no data exist on pricing and demand.
4. How will the business be established?

a. Buyout—via buying an existing company.
    1) Affords speedy market entry.
    2) Company may have hidden problems.
    3) All aspects of the business can't be developed as the entrepreneur prefers; he/she must deal with what is there.
b. Start-up—creating the business from scratch.
    1) Freedom to define and build the business as desired.
    2) Risks, time demands, and effort are high.
c. Franchise the entrepreneur provides a product/service under a legal contract with the franchise owner (franchisor).
    1) The entrepreneur pays an initial fee and a percentage royalty on sales.
    2) The franchisor provides the distinctive elements of the business (e.g., name, image, signs, facility design).
    3) A very popular form of business with a lower failure rate than start-ups due largely to franchisor support.
    4) Entrepreneur's creative freedom is inhibited by the franchise contract; problems arise when franchisors don't provide needed support.

5. How will the business be operated?
a. Determined by conducting planning in production, marketing, personnel, R&D and other aspects of the business.

6. How will the business be financed?
a. Requires conducting financial planning which involves:
    1) Estimating the business' projected income and expenses.
    2) Estimating the required initial investment.
    3) Locating sources of funding.
b. In locating funding, many entrepreneurs rely substantially on their own personal savings.
    1) Other sources of funding include commercial and investment banks, savings and loan associations, the SBA, and venture capitalists.
c. Chances of obtaining funding are enhanced by preparing a business plan which:
    1) Presents an overall analysis of the proposed business and contains answers to the five questions of start-up planning.
    2) Considered by many to be the most important document the entrepreneur will write. Is presented to prospective investors.
d. See Figure 20-2 for sources of funding a new venture.

C. Organizing
1. This function is often neglected in the early start-up stages.
2. When established, job descriptions and the organizational chart are often kept flexible.
a. Many entrepreneurs avoid developing written job descriptions in the early stages of the business so employee potential and

growth isn't constrained when the company is small.

        b.   The organizational chart is often viewed as a dynamic, continually changing picture of the company structure. It is a tool for continually assessing and re-evaluating the company.

D.   Controlling

    1.   Controlling activities are especially important in the new business. Mistakes are bound to be made given the newness of every operation, and resources are limited. Errors must be identified and quickly corrected.

    2.   Initially control systems are basic and collect information on sales, production rates, inventory, accounts receivable and payable, and cash flow.

        a.   Maintaining adequate cash flow is a common problem according to a survey of entrepreneurs. Survey results are graphed in Figure 20-3.

    3.   Many new companies are installing computerized control information systems to monitor aspects of company performance and conduct financial and production analysis.

        a.   Control systems aid growth by providing information about the company's abilities and limits.

E.   Managing People in the Small Business

    1.   Some important differences exist between the small company entrepreneur and the bigger-company CEO in managing employees:

        a.   The entrepreneur is solely responsible for effective leadership; no cadre of managers share leadership responsibilities.

        b.   Quality of leadership is even more vital in the new business because there are no slack resources to compensate for the effects of poor leadership.

        c.   The entrepreneur has one major disadvantage - he or she usually cannot offer the salary and benefits that bigger companies can provide.

        d.   He/she has two major advantages:

            1)   He/she does not have to deal with already established traditions and policies that may hinder employee motivation and performance.

            2)   The small group environment of a young business with strong leadership can produce a highly cohesive and motivated group of employees.

IV. Special Challenges of Entrepreneurship

    A.   Growth of the enterprise—the company's transition from a small shop to a larger, complex company requires changes in the entrepreneur's tasks and management style.

        1.   A hands-on involvement in all operations is no longer effective; some work and responsibilities must be delegated. The entrepreneur must focus more on long-term planning and coordinate the work of other

        managers.

2.   Some entrepreneurs like Mitch Kapor don't make the transition. They resign and start-up another company. Some learn to delegate by doing so gradually and to those equipped to handle the responsibility.

B.   Entrepreneurial stress

1.   Entrepreneurs of small businesses experience much stress given the risks of entrepreneurship and singular accountability for the business.

2.   According to one study, entrepreneurial stress is also caused by loneliness, total immersion in the business, frustration with employee problems, and an overly high need for achievement that results in frustration when unreasonably high goals aren't met.

3.   To alleviate stress, some entrepreneurs make changes in their business routine, set time aside for social activities and interact more with employees and other entrepreneurs.

C.   Selling the company

1.   Many entrepreneurs eventually sell their companies and approach the sale with three objectives:

a.   Locate the right buyer—one with objectives for the firm that are compatible with those of the entrepreneur.

b.   Secure satisfactory terms of the sale—e.g., the right price, terms of payment, and special conditions.

c.   Obtain satisfactory autonomy—if the entrepreneur stays on to run the company, he or she wants as much autonomy as possible.

2.   Many entrepreneurs who remain as head of the acquired firm have problems coping with the changes (reduced autonomy, often lesser salary). Many end up leaving sooner than intended.

ANSWERS TO DISCUSSION AND REVIEW QUESTIONS

1.   **Question:**   *Why is so little attention paid to small business even though these businesses constitute a significant portion of the US economy?*

       Answer: The answers to this are quite broad. A significant understanding to this quandary can be gained by closely examining the political decision-makers in this country. A significant number of them have either been involved with large corporations, or their families have been. In addition, a great deal of influence is exercised by big business on national decision making in ways that small business professionals are not organized yet to accomplish.

2. **Question:** *Do all individuals have the ability to someday become entrepreneurs? Why or why not?*

   Answer: The real question is not regarding ability, but rather inclination or preference to become. The following of entrepreneurial dreams and avenue is as much about personal choice as anything else. Any individual could work to overcome any shortcomings they may initially have. In addition, with the increasing role of consultants entrepreneurs could receive necessary advice in any area. The more significant determination is probably not ability but aptitude.

3. **Question:** *Do you consider yourself to possess an entrepreneurial orientation? Frame your answer in the context of the entrepreneurial quiz?*

   Answer: Obviously, students responses to this question will differ greatly. Be certain to explore the various aspects of the entrepreneurial orientation. Who has what portions? How do they know? Have they received information from others confirming or supporting their own perceptions?

4. **Question:** *Hewlett-Packard, Lands' End, David's Cookies, and Cuisinart are all highly successful businesses that had no formal business plan when they were established. Does their success diminish the importance of a formal plan? Discuss.*

   Answer: Not really. Many experts in business start-ups would likely assert that these cases are exceptions to the rule. A formal business plan is important because preparing the plan forces the entrepreneur to carefully develop in his or her mind every important element of the business and to articulate each element in writing. Plan development is an effective way to discover important weaknesses in the prospective business, things that the entrepreneur had not identified and that need to be resolved.

5. **Question:** *Many managers, especially women, voluntarily leave large organizations to start their own business. Do you think this trend will continue? Why or why not?*

   Answer: Individuals who do future forecasting suggest that one out of three employed individuals will be working for small business by the year 2000. If this is the case, this trend will certainly continue. Also, will the continual right-sizing of large corporations fewer individuals are finding the security they once experienced in large companies. As a result many people are taking into their own hands their ability to develop a secure professional future and are beginning their own businesses.

6. **Question:** *What are the drawbacks of maintaining orally communicated and flexible job descriptions in the early stages of a new business?*

   Answer: Job descriptions that are orally communicated rather than stated in writing create confusion and role ambiguity for the job holder. The entrepreneur must be sure that although flexibility exists in the individual's job, he or she also has a clear understanding of the job's core responsibilities and requirements.

7. **Question:** *Suppose you are the head of a young, fast-growing company (you pick the specific industry depending on personal interests). How would you go about the process of beginning to delegate decision-making and other authority to employees within your organizations? At what stage of growth should this delegation begin?*

   Answer: While some entrepreneurs will find themselves struggling to truly involve others in their companies, research indicates that people are most committed to decisions which they have helped to make. Thus, in order to increase employee's loyalty to the continued welfare of the organization, all managers are strongly encouraged to involve others in decision-making as soon as, and as often as possible.

8. **Question:** *Beyond those in the chapter, identify other strengths and shortcomings of the franchising strategy for starting a new business. In your view, which strength is the most valuable; which shortcoming is the most costly for a franchisee?*

   Answer: Quick entry to the market and potential instant success and riches are the usual attractions on which students will focus. They will probably think that "getting rich quick" is the most valuable, but should be encouraged to consider importance of training and experience with little risk involved as being greater long term benefit. Locking one's career into that company, and reducing the opportunity for one's own innovative ideas and control will probably be viewed as the most costly shortcomings of the franchising strategy.

9. **Question:** *What special problems face the entrepreneur who needs highly skilled employees but lacks the financial resources to fund a strongly competitive compensation program? How can an entrepreneur deal with this problem?*

   Answer: A financially-limited entrepreneur faces the problem of securing talented employees with little to offer in the way of salary and benefits. In these cases, some entrepreneurs offer profit sharing or stock ownership as tools for securing skilled personnel. Thus, if the employees believe in the future of the new company, they may be willing to settle for lower salaries/benefits but with the possibility of major income if the business takes off.

10. **Question:** *Many entrepreneurs ultimately decide to sell their business even though it is highly successful, so that they can start another one. What factors might influence this decision?*

    Answer: The text outline several considerations when the decision of whether or not to sell a company is being made. One of the most important, however, is the acknowledgement of the attitudes of the entrepreneur him or herself. Many of these individuals find the start up and initial challenges to be the most enjoyable, and are not particularly interested in running an on-going organization. Thus, even if other factors are not perfect for selling the organization, the entrepreneur simply may not be happy to continue with the initial organization.

END OF CHAPTER CASES

CASE 20 -1: THE TROUBLE AT ITS

CASE SUMMARY: This case tells of the downfall and eventual rebuilding of an entrepreneurial enterprise. ITS provided security personnel to airports around the country and was enjoying tremendous success until an audit discovered tremendous mis-handling of funds by several employees. Eventually forced into bankruptcy, the originator of the company, decided to again focus on his main business and re-grew his interest into a corporate stronghold.

ANSWERS TO QUESTIONS FOR ANALYSIS:

1. **Question:** *What type of controls could Weitzel have implemented to prevent the above incidents from occurring?*

   Answer: Effective implementation of control processes, such as accounting information reviews, costs analyses, etc. may have alerted Weitzel to some of these problem earlier.

2. **Question:** *How do you think Weitzel was able to make amends with the three clients who were overcharged, as well as regain other lost business?*

   Answer: Perhaps his greatest strength was his believe in himself. He knew he has not intentionally harmed these clients, except as he is responsible for his lack of management of information. Thus, he was able to approach these clients in an honest and forthright manner. He probable made financial restitution and requested their continued support of the company.

3. **Question:** *What disadvantages do small businesses and their owners face (versus large businesses) when incidents such as the above occur?*

   Answer: There are two major disadvantages. First, due to the limited number of individuals working in small companies, many people are the only employee in their role within the organization, therefore, there can be greater possibility of keeping information from others. However, once the company has already encountered problems, the concern for a small business owner is that their individual funds and personal resources are often tied up in the company.

4. **Question:** *Describe three other employee-related problems that a small business could encounter as it is enjoying rapid growth. How would you solve these problems?*

   Answer: Students will be able to provide a wide range of responses to this question. Encourage them to consider the challenges raised due to limited professional resources, limited resources, etc.

CASE 20-2: WILL THIS BUSINESS SUCCEED

CASE SUMMARY: This case profiles a new business idea developed by Todd LeRoy and Michael Atkinson that is just beginning to be realized. The idea is to franchise video cassette drive-through rental outlets. Each outlet is a small Fotomat-type kiosk which a franchise owner buys and can place in a high-traffic area. The two partners are sure their idea can't miss. The market for videocassette rentals is growing, and the outlets maintain low overhead costs because they specialize in highly popular tapes and forego the high inventory costs of a large inventory of less popular tapes. The entrepreneurs also plan to provide franchisees with substantial franchise support (e.g., promotion materials). Projected profits per franchise are high.

However, some new venture experts are less optimistic about the future of "Video 1 st." Here are excerpted comments from a panel of experts, from "What the Experts Say," (Inc., February 1988, pp. 48-49). "The (videocassette rental) market has peaked. There is already a lot of shakeout. There is less and less of an aftermarket for used tapes, which Video 1st is counting on being able to sell."

(About pricing): "It's a cutthroat market. One dollar (per tape) is not uncommon, compared to Video 1st's $2.95. It sounds nice people would pay premium for convenience or mystique, but people have tried it, and it hasn't worked."

. . .video traffic comes in bunches: 70 percent of your business takes place on Friday, Saturday, and Sunday, and even that 70 percent is generally crammed into a few peak hours during each of those days. If you have long lines of cars during these peak periods, you're going to discourage people from even lining up."

"what's not clear. . .is what they're going to do for potential franchisees that an individual entrepreneur couldn't do for himself. What does Associated Video Hut propose to do to add value to Video's 1st's name— which is the main thing they can do for franchisees? Anyone can put up a kiosk and stock it with tapes."

ANSWERS TO QUESTIONS FOR ANALYSIS:

1. **Question:** *Identify and assess the strengths and shortcomings of the concept behind Associated Video Hut.*

   Answer: Clearly, the concept of carrying only high-volume titles is a major plus as it reduces burdensome and very costly inventories of cassettes that often sit unrented. The highly mobile kiosk concept is also a plus. However, as the above comments suggest, the overall concept has problems. The founders' projections are a bit optimistic. To meet proforma profit projections, they must renew their entire inventory per kiosk every three months. Reinvestment in inventories is much higher than they project.

2. **Question:** *Would you buy a "Video's 1st" franchise? Why or why not?*

   Answer: After a careful analysis of the business idea, most students would decline the offer. However, a franchisee could be successful if he or she could locate in an area where the market is not saturated and could handle the peak periods of demand by, for example, locating 2 or 3 kiosks in an area. Imaginative advertising would also help.

3. **Question:** *What suggestions can you provide to improve the business concept and operations?*

   Answer: Students may offer such advice as focusing on a regional market first. Going national is very risky in such a mature market. Pick franchise sites carefully, boost the unique visibility of Video 1st kiosks via imaginative promotion and kiosk design, and provide franchisees with substantial support.

ADDITIONAL QUESTIONS AND ANSWERS

1. **Question:** *Why do most people believe incorrectly that large firms stimulate and create most job growth in the United States?*

   Answer: Most of the media sources (business journals, television, and newspapers) focus on huge corporations and their impact on the economy. The truth is small businesses produce over half of the nation's GNP.

2. **Question:** *Can an individual acquire, via training, the talents and skills essential for entrepreneurial success? Discuss.*

   Answer: As faculty in schools of business, no doubt we should support a "yes" answer to this! Many students will no doubt offer examples of small business owners they know who have not been to college or had any formal training and are very successful. However, one might ask H they learned it from a family member through OJT, as is often the case. The opposite case can be made by referring to the high proportion of failures attributable to poor management and by the fact that many of those pitfalls could no doubt have been avoided through the study of management, in particular the planning stage. Refer to management focus for other perspectives.

3. **Question:** *What do your answers to the entrepreneurial quiz say about you? Do you agree?*

   Answer: Students' interest should be high and they should be eager to respond. Students should understand some answers can give an indication of their entrepreneurial potential.

4. **Question:** *Do you think that entrepreneurs are born or are special individuals who become proficient through a mix of genes, training, and education? Explain.*

   Answer: This is classic case of "nature or nurture" - which as a social science has never been solved. Nontechnical abilities are essential and generally are individualized. Technical skills can be acquired through training and skills to achieve entrepreneurial success. Entrepreneurs are not born an instant success.

5. **Question:** *Suppose you are the head of a young, fast-growing computer software manufacturer. You are experiencing considerable stress from your job. What changes would you make to alleviate the problem?*

   Answer: The entrepreneur could delegate some tasks to his or her subordinate managers to help lighten the workload. He or she could make time for social activities perhaps setting one day a week aside for family and friends with no work interruptions. An exercise program would also help relieve stress.

6. **Question:** *Many acquisition observers assert that one reason so many acquisitions fail is that the acquired company is so much smaller than the buyer and the practices of the two firms are so distinctly different. Explain.*

   Answer: When the parent company is huge and the acquired firm very small, the parent's control systems are much more complex and sophisticated than the systems used by the small company. Management of the acquired firm sometimes has difficulty in adjusting to these systems; some managers also feel intimidated by them. When the parent is more bureaucratic (i.e., utilizing a System-I design), its slow-moving processes can stifle a smaller company, eliminating its innovativeness and creativity. In some cases where the acquired firm provides a very small percentage of the parent's revenues, the acquisition fails from lack of attention by corporate headquarters.

7. **Question:** *Discuss the ways in which the entrepreneur's challenges differ from those of the CEO of an established, much larger organization.*

   Answer: The entrepreneur CEO copes with greater personal and professional risk given that his or her personal financial resources will usually be lost if the business fails. The entrepreneur is also solely accountable for the business' performance. There is no board of directors to share the responsibility. There is also no excess resources to cover the impact of managerial mistakes and oversights or unforeseen developments. The entrepreneur also often lacks the financial resources to attract highly qualified personnel.

8. **Question:** *Of the different individual characteristics that facilitate effective entrepreneurship, which characteristic, in your opinion, is most important? Justify your selection.*

   Answer: Students will likely differ in their responses; however, expect several to assert that energy and leadership skills are especially important as is the ability to deal with risk and uncertainty.

9. **Question:** *Discuss the strengths and shortcomings of a buyout approach to establishing a business.*

   Answer: A buyout enables an entrepreneur to quickly enter a market. He or she has a ready-made business and thus doesn't have to spend the many months and even years in building such aspects of a business as a distribution network, efficient manufacturing facilities, a reputation and satisfactory market share. However, almost every business on the selling block has problems, some of which the entrepreneur may be unaware. He or she is also limited to his freedom to define and build the business just as he or she desires.

10. Question: *Identify a successful entrepreneur beyond those discussed in the chapter's entrepreneur profiles. What are the major ingredients in their success?*

Answer: There are many publicized entrepreneurs whom students may cite such as Mary Kay of Mary Kay Cosmetics, Ted Turner of the Turner Broadcasting System, Ray Kroc of McDonald's and Tom Watson of IBM. Success can be attributed to such factors as identifying a latent consumer demand and thus a market that was untapped, and the ability to, as Peter Drucker says, "create a customer." This factor certainly applies to Ms. Kay and Mr. Turner.

11. Question: *As the chapter notes, many entrepreneurs eventually sell their business. In your opinion, why is turnover high among those who initially remain to manage the now-acquired company?*

Answer: Certainly problems in coping with reduced managerial autonomy is a problem. Among other problems are coping with a reduction in compensation. Many entrepreneurs earn lower compensation after the sale because as owners of their firms, they expensed many personal costs to the business. Many also make a substantial sum from the sale and decide to retire early or start another business.

12. Question: *What are the strengths and shortcomings of franchising?*

Answer: Those who franchise often benefit from strong support from franchisors. That's one reason why the survival rate is much higher for franchises than for start-ups. However, such support sometimes isn't provided which can create major problems. The entrepreneur also has limited authority over such decisions as product/service pricing, company name, and facility design.

13. Question: *Discuss the various risks that an entrepreneur faces in launching a business.*

Answer: The entrepreneur incurs substantial business risk given the high failure rate of new ventures, financial risk, career risk given that he or she often leaves a secure job to start a business. The entrepreneur also incurs family and social risk because a new business leaves precious little time for spending time with family and friends. There is also the psychological risk, the risk of personal failure if the business fails.

14. Question: *What are the different reasons why individuals become entrepreneurs?*

Answer: The decision to become an entrepreneur may be due to several motivations. These include the desire to be one's own boss, the desire for personal and professional growth, to achieve a more satisfying alternative to a dissatisfying job, to earn a hefty income, and to attain job security.

15. Question: *Differentiate between start-up planning and ongoing planning.*

Answer: Start-up planning is done before a new venture opens for business. It consists of making five primary decisions: the business' product /service and market, the means of the business' establishment, how the business will be operated, and how the business will be financed. Ongoing planning involves planning activities for the established business.

16. **Question:** *Many students are often surprised to learn that America's small business community is the world's fourth greatest economic power. Why?*

Answer: In their management studies, students read and learn much about the country's major and most powerful corporations—IBM, AT&T, Apple Computer, General Motors, Honeywell, for example. Scan current business periodicals and you'll find that these companies also dominate the content of these publications. In the midst of all this publicity, the power of the corner grocery and other small businesses, on a national scale, often goes little noticed.

21 MANAGEMENT CAREERS

LEARNING OBJECTIVES

After completing Chapter 21, students should be able to:

Define   the concept of career effectiveness and the criteria that determine career effectiveness.

Describe   the relationship between career stages and career paths.

Discuss   the positions supporting and opposing the creation of "mommy track" career paths in organizations.

Compare   the needs of individuals and organizations in career planning.

Identify   the potential benefits and pitfalls of mentoring relationships.

CHAPTER SYNOPSIS

This chapter looks at management careers by focusing on seven topics: the distinction between the terms "career in management" and "management careers," career effectiveness, career stages, career paths, the nature of management as a career, characteristics of effective managers, and career planning.

The chapter addresses career effectiveness by discussing the four major criteria for its assessment—career performance, career attitudes, career adaptability, and career identity.

Three perspectives of career stages are presented: the most basic perspective which applies to all employees, and perspectives which apply to managers and professionals. Career paths, the means to career goals, are discussed in terms of prevailing attitudes about career path success, the more recent approach to basing career progression on individual preferences and real-world experiences, and the "mommy track" as one alternative for balancing career and family demands.

The chapter discusses the nature of management as a career through the three tasks of the modem manager (managing work and organizations, people, and production/operations). Concerning characteristics of effective managers, the chapter discusses three primary requirements—the will to manage, supervisory abilities, and the ability to assess one's own potential for an effective managerial career. The chapter concludes with a look at career planning via informal and formal career counseling and personnel practices (job posting and tuition aid programs) which facilitate employee development.

The **Management in Action** for this chapter briefly discusses the recent large number of dismissals and layoffs of middle managers. The **first Management Focus** describes career development in a global corporation, while the **second Management Focus** mentions the changing attitudes of the younger workers or "YIFFies." A **third Management Focus** outlines the benefits and challenges for women in mentoring relationships. The lengthening of time spent per job between promotions and the increase in lateral moves are the topics covered the **fourth Management Focus**. And the chapter concludes with a **final Management Focus** on counseling employees in a downsized organization.

LECTURE & DISCUSSION IDEAS

1. In discussing management careers in class, students almost always express a need for advice on how to go about finding that all-important first job that launches their careers in business. We've found that most students are ill-prepared for conducting an effective job search. If this is the case in your class, you may want to include in your lecture some information on how to conduct a job search (and on such topics as how to write a resume and perform effectively in job interviews). It is useful to obtain a book on resume writing and provide students with some examples of effectively written and organized resumes. Many books on resume writing include samples. Some excellent sources should be available at the school library or in the school book store. If your school has a career planning and placement center, you can invite a member of the center's staff to speak to your class about these job search topics.

2. An increasingly relevant topic related to management careers is the dual-career couple. No doubt many of your students will face this situation in the coming years and its problems and challenges. One effective exercise can help you address this issue: divide the class by sex into two groups. Have the male group and female group each consider the advantages of being a member of a two-career marriage. Each group should also prepare a list of the problems it can produce and list proposed ways of dealing with the problems. Then, have each group present its list in class discussion and discuss the proposed solutions. This exercise is guaranteed to provoke some interesting class discussion and insights into the advantages and problems of the two-career situation.

PROJECT / EXERCISE IDEAS

1. As an individual or group assignment, have your students interview a male and female high-level executive in a local business and prepare a written or oral report on the executives' career path. The report should address each step of the career path, the barriers encountered and how the executive dealt with each career obstacle.

2. Students could prepare a written or oral report on the nature of a major mid-life career change. The report can be based on an interview with an individual who changed careers after several years of work in an occupation. This report can address such issues as the motivation for such change, the psychological adjustments needed for the transition to a new career, and the rewards and problems which such a move can provide.

3. Students could also prepare a report on an actual career counseling/development program at a local business. The report can be based on an interview with the program director and can focus on the program's goals, content, and impact on employees and the company.

4. Invite a high-ranking executive to talk about his or her career paths. The executive should be able to provide students with some valuable advice concerning how to

launch and develop an effective management career. You may want to ask the executive whether he or she encountered the career dilemmas noted in lecturette 22-1.

5.   Invite a married dual-career couple to speak to your class (ideally one where both individuals are managers in local businesses). The couple could provide some interesting insights into the problems they've encountered, the ways they've dealt with them, and the benefits (and pressures) which two careers can present to a married couple.

6.   Today, more and more high-ranking executives are "dropping out"—leaving high-paying and high-pressure jobs for low-keyed occupations. One effective way to address this issue is to locate a "drop-out" and invite him or her to speak to your class about the phenomenon and the reasons why he or she dropped out, how the move changed his or her life, and the problems and rewards which resulted from the move.

LECTURE OUTLINE NOTES

I.   Introduction

   A.   There is a key distinction between "careers in management" and management as a career"
      1.   "Careers in management" implies description of what constitutes management careers and where they're acted out.
      2.   "Management as a Career" implies more personal issues:
         a.   Why one should pursue a management career.
         b.   Who should attempt a management career.
         c.   How an individual can have a successful and fulfilling managerial career.

II.   Careers in Management

   A.   A career is the individually-perceived sequence of attitudes and behaviors associated with work-related experiences and activities over the span of a person's life.
      1.   A career consists of attitudes and behaviors.
      2.   It is an ongoing sequence of work-related activities.
      3.   It is clearly work-related.
   B.   Career effectiveness—is judged by the individual and the organization. Can be based on four often cited criteria:
      1.   Career performance—usually indicated by an individual's salary and position.
         a.   The more quickly salary and position advancements are made, the more successful is career performance.

         b.   Career performance indicates an individual's degree of contribution to organizational objectives.
         c.   Two obstacles can hinder appraisal of career effectiveness:

          1)   An organization can fail to fully recognize performance.

          2)   Organizational expectations may not match an individual's goals or abilities. The individual may have high potential but may place higher priority on activities outside the job.

  2.   Career attitudes—involve how individuals perceive and evaluate their careers. The more positive the attitudes, the more effective the career.

  3.   Career adaptability—involves an individual's application of the latest knowledge, skills, and technology in his or her career. Requires the ability to adapt to change. Often occurs in professional careers (for example, law, medicine).

  4.   Career Identity—encompasses two components:

      a.   The extent to which individuals are aware of their interests, values, and expectations.

      b.   How individuals view their lives (the extent to which they see themselves as extensions of their pasts).

      c.   Key questions: "What do I want to be and what do I have to do to become what I want to be?"

C.   Career stages—Every employee proceeds through distinct though interrelated career stages. Several versions have been developed.

  1.   Establishing a Career

      a.   Occurs at the onset of a career.

      b.   During this stage individuals require and seek support from others, particularly their managers.

  2.   Advancing a Career

      a.   Period of moving from job to job, both inside and outside the organization.

      b.   Promotions and advancements, and opportunities to exercise independent judgement are critical.

  3.   Maintaining a Career

      a.   When limits of a career are reached.

      b.   Focus on job currently doing.

      c.   Managers at this stage often become mentors.

      d.   Enhancement of peer relationships.

          1)   Information Peer - to learn the ropes on how to get the job done.

          2)   Collegial Peers - help define professional roles

          3)   Special Peers - are used to acquire a sense of competence and to help manage stress and anxieties.

  4.   Withdrawing from a Career

      a.   Individual has completed one career and may move on to another.

      b.   Others may experience self-actualization through activities that were impossible to pursue while working.

D.   Career paths—from an individual's perspective, the sequence of jobs which can lead to achieving personal and career goals. Important for an organization's manpower planning.

  1.   Prevailing attitude is that failure results when an individual does not move up in the organization. Such make it difficult for managers to accept lateral or downward transfers when they no longer want to pay the price of upward promotion.

364

2.	An alternative is basing career progression on real-world experiences and individual preferences. These paths:
   a.	Include lateral, downward, and upward possibilities not tied to normal rates of progress.
   b.	Should be tentative and responsive to changing organizational needs.
   c.	Should be flexible and consider an individual's qualities.
   d.	Each job along the path is specified in terms of acquirable skills, knowledge, and other specific attributes, not merely educational credentials, age, or work experience.
3.	There is no single correct path to a successful managerial career. Not everyone advances up each rung of the career ladder.
4.	Career plateauing—the point in a career when movement further up the ladder is very unlikely. The final point of ascension in a career. Individuals differ in their likelihood of future promotion.
   a.	Major causes of career limitations in the 1980s are mergers and restructurings, vastly reducing the number of managerial jobs.
   b.	Responses to maintain career advancement include "zig-zagging" from company to company, lateral transfers, further education and dual career paths to resume professional status.
5.	The "mommy track"—Proposed by Felice Schwartz in 1989 as one way to provide women with greater flexibility in managing career and family.
   a.	Schwartz' proposed that organizations:
      1)	Identify two separate groups of women employees: "career-primary" women who have made careers their top priority and plan to have no children; "career and family" women— who want to combine career with family and need flexibility in working hours and demands.
      2)	Provide "career primary" women with the same career paths, opportunities, and demands as their male counterparts.
      3)	Create a separate path for "career and family" women which enables them to take time off or work part-time during critical child rearing years. Their pay and advancement rates would be lower while on this track; a "mommy tracker" would later resume her full speed ahead managerial career.
   b.	The proposal is very controversial.
      1)	Proponents—organizations can keep talented women who would otherwise leave; women can more easily handle career and child-rearing demands.

      2)	Critics—Legitimizes the view that women should bear the bulk of child- rearing responsibilities which contradicts the growing trend of fathers assuming a larger child-rearing role. Legitimizes women's status as second-class employees and the track may permanently derail a mommy tracker's career.
6.	A related issue: dual-income couples (29.4 million such couples in the U.S.)

a. Confusion exists over a man's role in an executive marriage. Men can feel threatened by wives who are also providers.

b. These marriages work best when no one keeps score concerning earnings, promotions, and other job-related factors.

III. Management as a Career

A. As a career, management involves:

1. Managing work and organizations—the focus of the Classical Approach and planning, organizing and controlling subjects.

2. Managing people to achieve effective individual and group performance. Requires knowledge of individual differences, motivation, leadership, group dynamics. The most difficult and challenging aspect of the manager's job.

3. Production/operations—managing the production and operations functions using math, statistics, models, computers as decision aids.

IV. Who Should Pursue Management as a Career?

A. No one set of factors or traits can predict a successful career in management. Education and career planning can be offset by factors beyond the manager's control.

B. Characteristics of effective managers—Three abilities are essential:

1. The will to manage the individual must want and need to influence the performance of others and gain satisfaction from it.

a. The will to manage is positively correlated with a favorable attitude toward authority, assertiveness, sense of responsibility, and the desire to compete, exercise power, and stand out from others in a group.

b. Studies by Miner show that the will to manage among students has declined in the 1970s compared to the 1960s, which if true, should give a competitive edge to those with the will to manage in the 1980s.

c. Studies show that the will to manage can be developed through training.

2. Supervisory ability—the ability to effectively utilize the correct supervisory tactics required in a particular situation.

3. Ability to assess one's potential for an effective management career—an individual's ability to discern whether he or she wants and is able to have a career in management.

V. Career Planning

A. Involves matching an individual's aspirations with available opportunities in the organization. Intertwined with career pathing, the sequencing of specific jobs associated with those opportunities. See the career planning and pathing process in Figure 22-2.

1. Career planning identifies means to a desired end.

2. Many organizations are using career planning to proact, not react, to problems of ineffective managerial careers.

3. Effective career planning requires that individuals have information about career paths, expected vacancies, and position requirements.

B. Matching individual and organizational needs is often done by:

1. Informal counseling—provided by the personnel department. Not considered a primary service by the organization.
    a. Counseling by supervisors is usually included in performance appraisals; however, since supervisors' knowledge about the overall organization is limited, more formal career counseling methods are often adopted.
2. Formal counseling—workshops, assessment centers, and career development centers designed to serve specific employee groups (for example, management trainees, 'fast-track' management candidates).
    a. An example: Syntex Corporation's Career Development Center. The staff first identifies an individual's strengths and weaknesses along eight skills determined to be most critical to effective management: problem analysis; communication; setting objectives; decision making and handling conflict; selecting, training, and motivating employees; controlling employees; interpersonal competence; and use of time.
        1) Each manager attends a week-long seminar where he/she completes management simulations requiring the use of these eight skills. Afterwards, the individual meets with his/her immediate supervisor and develops a career plan.
3. Personnel practices—organizations:
    a. Offer tuition aid programs to encourage employee development.
    b. Post jobs (job posting) which publicizes job openings and provides substantial information and time for those interested to apply.
4. The success of any career counseling approach depends on the extent to which individual and organizational needs are met.
5. Studies show that career planning is most effective for people with relatively high growth and achievement needs, a past history of career successes, and the ability to carry out their career plans. However, more research is necessary before any definite conclusions can be drawn.

ANSWERS TO DISCUSSION AND REVIEW QUESTIONS

1. **Question:** *How has the emergence of diversity in the workplace and the global market effected career planning?*

   Answer: Difference cultures approach all aspects of career planning differently. In some culture the role of the supervisor is clearly defined in terms of the advancing of subordinates. In other cultures individuals do not have clear expectations about any sort of advancement. In addition, with the increased number of global organizations, the ability of an employee to respond in various settings is now considered normal evaluation material for promotion and advancement.

Also with the diversification of the workplaces, the role of the old networks to promote and support only certain individuals in a organization are slowly being eroded.

2. **Question:** *Rank the relative importance of the four characteristics of effective careers from the perspective of the individual, and the organization. Explain your answer.*

    Answer: These four characteristics are: performance, attitudes, adaptability, and identity.

    Perhaps identity is the most critical to the individual. This includes two important components. The first is the extent to which the individual has clear and consistent awareness of their interests, values and expectations for the future. The second is the extent to which individuals view their lives as consistent through time, and the extent to which they see themselves as extensions of their pasts.

    Some students would probably state that organizations would perhaps view performance as the most important. Interestingly, much recent work is finding that attitudes and adaptability are more critical than outcomes or performance.

3. **Question:** *What has been your experience with job interviews and previews? Have they accurately described the job as you subsequently experienced it? What could the organization have done to more accurately depict the job as you experienced it?*

    Answer: Students will undoubtedly have a wide variety of responses to this question. Assist them in exploring why these differences exist? How much does their own involvement in the job shape the work of the job after they are in it?

4. **Question:** *Why has career counseling for pre-retireers emerged as an important issue in organizations? How does career counseling for pre-entry employees differ from pre-retirement employees?*

    Answer: As the "baby boomers" are aging there are more and more individuals entering this age group and thus the attention being given to this group is increasing. Additionally, since individuals are living longer, the post-retirement years are becoming more important in terms of life planning.

    Career counseling for pre-entry and pre-retirement stages will be both substantially different and similar. For both groups there are issues of exploring new, as-of-yet, undiscovered opportunities and potentials. Both group are embracing the notions of "what if" and options. However, the pre-retirement individual will most likely have clearer information about her or his values, interests and desires which can both assist and challenge the future career planning for that individual.

368

5.	**Question:**	*Of what value to an organization is the mentor relationship?*
	Answer:	The primary value of mentor relationships to an organization is their ability to provide effective, quality development of junior-level managers. When developed and managed well, mentoring relationships can serve as a very valuable management development tool.

6.	**Question:**	*How can you discover career paths in a particular organization? Is this the kind of information you would want to receive when you interview for a job? What questions would you ask to get this information?*
	Answer:	Career paths are most often learned from veteran employees who "made it." The question should certainly be raised in job interviews and should be asked in a straightforward manner.

7.	**Question:**	*As the CEO of a large company, would you implement a "mommy track" program in your firm? Why or why not? As a young female executive who plans to have a family, would you support a mommy track? Explain.*
	Answer:	This subject should stir some lively debate among your students, and perhaps some strong disagreement between males and females about perceived special treatment of women under such a program. Perhaps it should be called a "person track". Opinions, of course, are personal, but among the many trade-offs, students should realize the difficulty in implementing such a program company-wide.

8.	**Question:**	*Many individuals leave their first jobs within the first two years. Why do you think this situation occurs?*
	Answer:	Very simply, the individual's needs and expectations have changed. It is part of progressing through the stages of an individual's career.

9.	**Question:**	*How would you know that your career had plateaued in an organization? If you were frustrated by being plateaued, what actions would you take to alleviate your dissatisfaction?*
	Answer:	Students may cite several indicators, which can include several performance appraisals which did not result in promotions, subtle changes in the person's relationship with his/her supervisor, and the promotions of the person's peers. Responses to career plateau can include "zig-zagging" from company to company, lateral transfers, further education, or perhaps resumption of professional career path. Students should be aware that, while these represent constructive options, many managers in such situations simply resign themselves to a stagnant situation, hoping that something will change, even though they do nothing about it. By the way, they should also be alerted to the reality of such situations relative to typical organization structures. Since these are usually a pyramidal shape, most organizations of any kind need only a small proportion of "chiefs" compares to that of "indians"—i.e. promotion naturally gets harder as one moves up the career ladder.

10.	**Question:**	*In your opinion, what personal characteristic is most important for achieving success as a manager? Explain.*

    Answer:	This question is intended to prompt enough discussion to bring forth a number of different opinions about which personal characteristic is most important to make the students realize that no one trait can be consistently associated as the most important. Students should also be helped to understand that what is important is what a manager does—i.e. the on-the-job behaviors—not personal characteristics.

END OF CHAPTER CASES

CASE 21-1: CAREER DEVELOPMENT AS A PERSONAL RESPONSIBILITY—————

CASE SUMMARY: This case explores in some depth how one organization uses more effective career planning with their employees to increase commitment among employees. By assisting individuals in determining how the fit into the long-term planning of the organization, each individual is better able to know how to make optimal contributions to the organization.

ANSWERS TO QUESTIONS FOR ANALYSIS: ——————————————————

1.	**Question:**	*Explain how the R& D unit integrated the unit's objectives with its employees' objectives through the career development program.*

    Answer:	Moved both employees and managers from a view of the worker as being present in the organization merely to complete certain necessary tasks. Eventually the program became a catalyst for improving employee-supervisor relationships because career development of individuals was closely linked to the ongoing needs of the organization.

2.	**Question:**	*What can you identify as potential sources of conflict among employees and their supervisors who participate in the process?*

    Answer:	Both employees and their supervisors may perceive the career planning process as a waste of time and yet feel unable to articulate this concern since there appears to be such an organizational culture toward this activity. They may both feel, that while important, the task can be distracting from the "real" work of the organization. Some employees may perceive themselves as ready for career advancement that their supervisor may not support either due to their real belief that the individual is not yet ready or their own desire to keep that particular employee within their own department. On a contrary note, some supervisors may perceive that an employee is ready for advancement which the employee may not want or feel capable of.

3.	**Question:**	*In what ways could the IDP concept be used in the context of classrooms, students and teachers?*

    Answer:	This would be a very stimulating discussion for involving students in designing their classroom experience, as well as determination of how they will be evaluated. In many ways, this is similar to outcome-based education, which is gaining a stronghold in many school at both the secondary and higher education levels.

CASE 21-2: CAREER DEVELOPMENT IN THE GOVERNMENT————————

CASE SUMMARY: This case profiles GAO's new career development program and provides an indepth look at the program's components. The program is comprised of three parts:

1. philosophy, concepts, and overview, which emphasizes the philosophy of career development at GAO (rather than dealing with issues at an abstract level)

2. individual career planning process where employees participate in a number of exercises designed to develop a better understanding of oneself and the environment and to facilitate future career planning and life management

3. organizational career development process, which emphasizes GAO's stake in career development.

ANSWERS TO QUESTIONS FOR ANALYSIS: ————————————————

1. **Question:** *Evaluate the GAO career development program.*
    Answer: Student evaluation will likely differ; however, most will probably give the program high marks, especially for its assessment of managers' needs as the initial step in implementing the program. The program's organization into three components is also a strong point because due attention is given to both individual and organizational needs.

2. **Question:** *What would be your answers to the five questions raised in part 1 of their training program?*
    Answer: Student answers will vary; discussion of this question should focus on the issues which two of the five questions raise—whether careers development should address (or emphasize) individual or organization needs and whether the programs raise false expectations. The latter issue is a major concern in many organizations with career development programs because often individuals come to expect more from their employers (in terms of career advancement) simply by virtue of participating in the program.

3. **Question:** *What should be the policy of organizations in mature and declining industries be toward career development?*
    Answer: This is an opinion question; however, it can be argued that such organizations should offer career development programs for employees. However, the organizations should take care not to raise false expectations and to provide employees with a clear and realistic picture of future career opportunities in the company.

ADDITIONAL QUESTIONS AND ANSWERS

1. **Question:** *Define and explain your personal concept of career. Is the concept, as you define it, applicable only to those who are gainfully employed? In the explanation, compare your concept of career with the one used in the chapter discussion.*

   Answer: This question is intended to spur students to develop and assess their own concept of career. Many students will likely assert that one need not be gainfully employed to have a career as a career can encompass any continual series of work efforts (e.g., volunteer work, the career of housewife or househusband) regardless of whether an individual is employed or not.

2. **Question:** *Illustrate, using examples, a situation in which you or a person you know experienced difficulty in achieving both personal and career goals.*

   Answer: The instructor's personal experience will be valuable. If the class has some students who have previous work experience perhaps they can share some examples. Students should understand often personal and career goals may not match.

3. **Question:** *Which organizational characteristics are most important to you in selecting your next job?*

   Answer: Have students identify key organizational characteristics which are important to them personally. The list may vary from ethical philosophy to advancement to compensation packages. It is important to highlight trade-offs among some of the characteristics. For example, status and advancement with the company will require long hours at the office away from family and other more pleasurable activities.

4. **Question:** *In your opinion, what are the advantages and shortcomings of being a mobile manager (changing jobs frequently throughout a managerial career)? Discuss.*

   Answer: Students will no doubt put varying emphasis on different factors depending on their personal priorities. However, they should recognize that mobility - the flexibility to change jobs, usually involving relocation - tends to facilitate a more rapid career advancement than lack of mobility. If a manager is offered a promotion which means moving and she or he turns it down, that offer will probably not be made again. Other disadvantages associated with the lack of flexibility in assignments are reduced experience, and impact on personal and family life. More and more managers are becoming disinclined to move as often as managers did in the past, reflecting an increased emphasis on the quality of life and leisure.

5. **Question:** *Select a contemporary public figure—Donald Trump, Mike Eisner, George Bush for example—and evaluate their careers in terms of your criteria for career success.*

    Answer: This question is intended for students to apply their own criteria for success to notable careers. It typically provides some useful insights for students in evaluating their own success criteria.

6. **Question:** *What is your career plan? How many of your friends seem to know what they want from their future careers? For what reasons do young people typically have difficulty with the question of "What do I want to do?"*

    Answer: This exercise is a very personal one for each individual. The likely results are that neither students nor their peers have very explicit career plans. They will likely have aspirations, but not plans. The responses to why students do not have career plans will reflect on one of two explanations:

    1)   lack of information about opportunities; or
    2)   lack of understanding of their own needs and abilities.

7. **Question:** *What conflicts do you think you will have when you take your first job upon graduation? Which of these conflicts are ones that you can now plan for and anticipate coping responses?*

    Answer: Student responses will differ. Some probable cited problems will include inner conflict over whether they made the right occupational choice and insecurities over their abilities to do their jobs.

8. **Question:** *Do you believe that you can cope with the personal and career problems of a dual-career situation? If so, what experiences in life have prepared you to cope with the problems? If not, why not?*

    Answer: This question is excellent for class discussion because it raises an issue that is an increasing reality for married couples as more women are seeking professional careers. In terms of experiences that have prepared students for this situation, many will likely cite family experiences (working mothers and fathers). Issues of feminism, economics and family should also emerge in the discussion.

9. **Question:** *As the text defines "career," who is the sole judge for career success? Why is this proper and yet unrealistic?*

    Answer: The individual pursuing the career is the sole judge. Since each of us must bear the costs of our career decisions (and reap the benefits), it is proper that we decide for ourselves. The unrealistic aspect of this point of view is that the economic and status rewards of careers are bestowed by others—bosses, clients, customers, etc. In a sense, they determine career success by providing society's designated symbols of success.

10. **Question:** *Is it possible that some managers are satisfied with experience of mid-career plateaus? Explain.*

    Answer: Yes. These individuals no longer wish to pay the price for further advancement; they are "burned out" psychologically and/or physically. They have discovered nonwork related sources of personal satisfaction. Other explanations could be enumerated.

11. **Question:** *University colleges and departments typically employ secretaries to assist professors. Visit the personnel department of the university you attend and determine whether career paths have been developed for these secretaries. If none exist, how would you go about preparing them?*

    Answer: This exercise can be assigned as a group project. Chances are that formally devised career paths do not exist. To prepare them would involve documenting the careers of existing secretaries who have had sufficient years of experience to establish patterns. The "typical" career path can then be identified.

12. **Question:** *Briefly discuss four criteria of career effectiveness.*

    Answer: The four criteria are:

    1. career performance (which is usually indicated by an individual's salary and position);

    2. career attitudes (which involve how individuals perceive and evaluate their careers);

    3. career adaptability (involving an individual's application of the latest knowledge, skills and technology in his or her career); and

    4. career identity (which encompasses the extent to which individuals are aware of their interests, values, and expectations, and how individuals view their lives).

13. **Question:** *Provide a brief overview of the characteristics of an effective manager.*

    Answer: Successful managers possess three characteristics:

    1. the will to manage which is the desire and need to influence the performance of others and to gain satisfaction from it;

    2. supervisor ability; and

    3. the ability to assess their future potential for an effective management career.

14. **Question:** *In your own words, define "career."*

    Answer: Student definitions will vary; however, they should be similar to the text definitions: the individually-perceived sequence of attitudes and behaviors associated with work-related experiences and activities over the span of a person's life.

374

SECTION III

ANALYSIS OF COMPREHENSIVE CASES

THE USE OF CASES AS SUPPLEMENTS

The cases and exercises you will find in various chapters in the book require students to take an active and participative role in the learning process rather than a passive one. These learning activities are used to provide more realism in the learning experience. We have found that teaching students is made more insightful, challenging, and interesting by studying both active personal experiences, as well as general concepts and theories. The general concepts and theories will furnish you with many principles to guide action and the cases and exercises will enable students to test concepts and theories in actions.

CASE METHOD

The "real world" cases in the book place the student in a simulated organizational climate as a manager, leader, or nonmanager who must make decisions. A case is...a story of organizational issues which actually have been faced by people, together with facts, opinions, and prejudices upon which decisions must be made. A key feature of a case is that decisions which require action must be made.[1]

With the case method, the process of arriving at an answer is more important than the answer itself. It is anticipated that by working through cases the student will develop an understanding of the process of reaching decisions and be able to convincingly support and communicate these decisions to others. Instead of sitting back and reacting to the comments made by an instructor, a student in analyzing cases is asked to make decisions typically with incomplete information and in a limited time period, which is usually the situation faced by most managers.

There are no ideal solutions to any of the cases used in this book. Searching for the perfect answer will be futile. Instead, the student should learn to critically and thoroughly think through the issues, problems, facts, and other information presented in the cases. Critical thinking is required to make better decisions. Thorough thinking is needed so that decisions reached can be communicated and intelligently discussed in classroom discussions. Classroom discussions about the cases should clearly illustrate the thinking processes used by the students.

The preparation of classroom discussion of the cases in this book could follow a set pattern. One suggested pattern would be:
1. Read the case rather quickly to get a fell of what is involved.
2. Reread the case and sort out the assumptions, hunches, and facts.

---

[1]Kenneth L. Bernhardt and Thomas C. Kinnear, *Cases in Marketing Management* (Plano: Business Publications, Inc., 1978), p.3.

Since all the cases are rather incomplete, the student will need to make plausible assumptions about the situation. List them and be able to support the plausibility of your assumptions.

These assumptions will enable your to "fill in the blanks" that exist in the cases. Remember that in organizations decisions are generally made with incomplete information and some uncertainty.

3.   Identify the major problems and subproblems which must be considered in the case.

4.   List the problems in order of importance or priority. That is, what problems have to be solved first.

5.   Develop a list of alternative courses of action that would minimize or eliminate the problems. If possible, have at least two fully developed alternatives which are feasible solutions.

6.   In developing the alternative courses of action, outline the constraints (e.g., resources, historical precedent, competition, skill limitations, attitudes) which will limit success.

7.   Select the course of action that is best for the problems identified in step #3. Show how the course of action would work and be able to discuss why it would be the most successful alternative to solve the problems.

The instructor's role can vary from observer to active participant, depending on his or her preference. Whatever role the instructor uses, the steps outlined above will permit the student to integrate book material, personal experiences, and the case information in reaching decisions. In evaluating a student's case analysis, instructors can evaluate many different factors. It has been suggested that a good case analysis will:

1.   Be complete.
2.   Avoid rehashing what is in the case.
3.   Make feasible and sound assumptions.
4.   Accurately identify the main problems.
5.   Create good alternative courses of action.
6.   Pinpoint potential constraints which could limit the solution selected.
7.   Communicate clearly the decision.
8.   Illustrate to others how the decision reached can solve the problems presented in the case.

Good case analysis requires time and a systematic plan of action. The payoff is that the student will be able to communicate her or his thinking process. Another benefit will be applying the content discussed in the chapters to the case. This application and active involvement are why cases can be insightful, challenging and interesting.

MANAGING WORK AND ORGANIZATIONS PP. 297-300

CASE SUMMARY:

This case does an excellent job of explaining how individuals within the same organization can experience situations very differently depending on their involvement in the decision making and how changes affect them. The first portion of the case outlines the historical growth and then stagnation of High-Tech Incorporated. A need for action is clearly made.

The arrival of Stan Kuntz in his new position of vice president of planning, information and control brought many possibilities for organizational improvement. Clearly Kuntz had the skills and expertise necessary to address the concerns facing the company. However, he made decisions, while apparently effective in the short-term, created a great deal of concern throughout the organization.

The remainder of the case explains the responses to Kuntz' actions from various individuals within the organization. Each major are of High-Tech Incorporated presents their perspective in short notations which were collected during Nancy Bowman's consultation. She had been brought in my David Franklin, High-Tech current president and CEO.

Precise data and facts are presented which illustrate how Kuntz' actions have created a wide variety of responses. The case also demonstrates how merely using short-term financial measurements do not provide the entire picture. Information from all chapters of Part II is integrated into the presenting concerns in the case.

Answers to Questions for Analysis

1. **Question:**   *Evaluate Stan Kuntz' overall approach to solving the problems at High-Tech Incorporated.*

    Answer: Kuntz has clearly responded to the charged presented to him upon his promotion. He was to get the organization back on steady feet financially. And when viewed only in terms of that aspect of his work he has, in fact, been able to work some miracles.

    What this case so articulately illustrates, however, is the short-term financial indicators are not enough to measure an organization's well-being. Employee morale has plummeted, customers are being to express concern about quality, new customers are not being secured at the same rate as in the past.

2. **Question:** *Evaluate Kuntz' four objectives. What other types of objectives should be added to his list?*

    Answer: Currently Kuntz' list reads:

    1. Cut costs of doing business. Methods would include evaluation of all projects and, if their returns were below the expected rate, they would be eliminated.
    2. To ensure that all new investments would provide at least 20 percent return within their first two years.
    3. To improve the profit margin.
    4. To help the company stock price regain its past peak.

    Unfortunately, what was not on this original list was the continuation of positive aspects of the organization. There was excellent performance already going on in many areas of High-Tech which should have been safeguarded. An important part of organization improvement is understanding what is already going well.

3. **Question:** *Explain why top management and division managers have different opinions regarding the effects of Kuntz' efforts.*

    Answer: As is often the case in organizations, individuals give the most attention to the aspects of the work and outcomes that most closely affect them. Thus, each individual perceives the result of Kuntz' work in light of their area of concern.

4. **Question:** *Do you feel that appropriate performance standards have been set for evaluating division performance? What additional standards, if any, should be utilized?*

    Answer: The aspects of performance regarding interpersonal relationship, measurement of customer satisfaction, and employee retention and morale have not been included at all.

5. **Question:** *How should Kuntz' performance be evaluated?*

    Answer: Given the objective given to him upon his promotion, Kuntz is delivering very well. However, there are many feedback and control mechanisms that need to be utilized to determine what steps need to be taken next.

6. **Question:** *What is your evaluation of both the short-term and strategic planning processes taking place at High-Tech?*

    Answer: Several of the necessary short-term processes are already in place and Kuntz is actually doing an excellent job of implementing them. However, the strategic or large picture perspective of planning is missing almost entirely.

7. **Question:** *What role, if any, should social responsibility play in the control process at High-Tech Incorporated?*

   Answer: In the past employees were encouraged to do volunteer work within the community, and were in fact provided time from work to do that. This certainly provided many positive outcomes, including positive feelings within the employees themselves about their particular volunteer efforts and High-Tech. In addition, community members were given a positive impression of High-Tech.

8. **Question:** *Have President Franklin and the vice presidents (excluding Kuntz) been remiss in attending to their duties? Explain why or why not?*

   Answer: Apparently the focus in the organization took a sharp shift toward improving the short-term financial measurements. Each top manager actually needed to assume responsibility for ensuring that a long-term, big picture perspective was maintained.

9. **Question:** *What recommendations should Bowman make to President Franklin? Based on these recommendations, what actions should Franking take?*

   Answer: There are some indicators which suggest that some immediate actions must be taken. Additional outcomes must be identified which will get High-Tech back to some of their previous positive work. In addition, there is an urgency about reopening lines of communications and in getting the information flowing throughout the company in all directions. There is all the needed information available within the organization to determine how to proceed. This information must be accessed by actively involving all employees in rectifying this situation. The success and secure future of High-Tech is not Kuntz' objective along. All members need to work to solve the current concern.

   What is very clear is that Franklin does not have the luxury of taking no action. He need to involve himself more at this point with the daily management. As things improve, he can again strive to delegate more authority, perhaps this time with some limitations.

MANAGING PP. 530-533—————————————————————————————

CASE SUMMARY:

This case tells a highly interesting story that requires students to apply their knowledge of leadership styles, group characteristics, group dynamics, and the interaction of these three variables in affecting group performance. The case is organized as a prediction case composed of four parts, in which students answer questions relevant to a part before preceding on to the next section of the case. The case works particularly well as an oral classroom exercise. Have students read the first part and cover the text page when finished. Then read the part I prediction question to the students and have them discuss the question. Proceed in this format for parts II, III and IV.

Part I Summary: A young college student describes his job as a landscape worker for a small private landscaping company in a New Jersey town. The company's five-man crew is supervised by Joe Brewster, the company owner, who works along with the crew and maintains a flexible, "consideration"-oriented leadership style. Far from an authoritative taskmaster, Joe allows the crew plenty of flexibility in their tasks, compliments their work when it is done well, and doesn't show his authority. He shares in the tasks and is well regarded by his employees.

Answer to Prediction Question

1. **Question:** *What will be the productivity in terms of quantity and quality of the work crew? Why?*

    Answer: Many students will assert that the quality of work will be high because of the crew's enriched jobs. (They determine task assignments and the order in which the tasks in a given project are performed; the crew members also interact with customers and determine when they'll eat lunch.) However, quantity may not be high because as job enrichment research indicates, enriched jobs tend to boost the quality but not quantity of work output. (Another factor supporting high quality is the unhurried pace of the job.) Some students may argue that group task performance may not be substantial because Joe is lacking in the task-oriented, "initiating structure" style of leadership. These students will likely predict that performance quantity will be less than impressive because the work tempo seems so relaxed. In directing discussion on this question, it's useful, once the comparison of the task characteristics to job enrichment arises, to have the students discuss the job in terms of the five core dimensions of enriched jobs.

Part II Summary: The work crew's productivity is high, exceeding typical summer crew productivity levels by 15 percent. A major factor in the productivity is the crew's positive attitudes toward their work, their high sense of job responsibility, and their pride in their work.

Answer to Case Question

1. **Question:** ***What elements in the situation contributed to these positive results? Can you think of things that, if present, might have led to very different results? Explain how.***

    Answer: Productivity is high because of the above-mentioned factors (pride, strong sense of job responsibility, and a high level of job satisfaction). These feelings are likely the result of the job's characteristics, a highly cohesive group composed of people who sincerely enjoy working with each other, and a supervisor who allows them freedom in performing their work. The group's cohesiveness is likely due to several factors: common background (all live in the same geographic area and attended the same high school), similar educational level, seemingly similar abilities, good group performance (highly cohesive groups usually perform well), shared enjoyment of the task (they all like the outdoors), and small group size. Good pay is also a factor. However, very different results could have occurred if other factors were present. Students will likely suggest several which could include low pay, an autocratic boss, group members who dislike the task, and a strong low-productivity group norm.

Part III Summary: The case narrator has returned to the company for a second summer's work, but much has changed. Joe no longer works with the crew; rather he has organized two crews (one staffed by the old crew members and the other by newcomers). Two young college graduates (with degrees in agricultural management) now supervise the crews. Given a free hand to supervise the crews, the new bosses are more authoritative, deciding when the crews will eat lunch, making job assignments, and eliminating some of the crew's other freedoms.

Answers to Prediction Questions

1. **Question:** ***What kind of issues or problems are likely to develop during the second summer? Why?***

    Answer: The supervisors have created a situation that's headed for major problems. They've disrupted the work environment of the "old-timer" crew by changing the nature of the job and the workers' flexibility in performing the work. The close-knit, secure, and positive culture created in the previous summer has largely been eliminated. The likely result: lower morale, less job satisfaction, and ultimately less effective group performance.

2. **Question:** *How will productivity compare with that of the previous summer in terms of quantity and quality? Why?*

Answer: Both levels will probably decline. The men previously achieved in both areas because they felt a pride in and ownership of their work (due largely to their freedom to perform their jobs their own way) and because they felt comfortable in their group work environment. Now the freedom and comfort have been eliminated by the supervisors' changes.

3. **Question:** *What would have been your advice to the two supervisors about how they could best approach their new role?*

Answer: Many students will suggest that the supervisors should have talked to Joe Brewster at length about the nature of the "old-timer" crew, particularly focusing on their performance and their work style last summer. Given the group's high productivity last summer, the supervisors should have followed the "if it's not broke, don't fix it" truism and not instituted major changes in how the workers are supervised or how the work is performed.

Part IV Summary: Morale and productivity declined in the "old-timer" group; as the situation worsened, crew members complained to Joe Brewster. However, no changes were made; rather, the supervisors seemed to push the workers harder. Meanwhile, the new crew's productivity also declined largely because they were not sufficiently trained to perform their jobs (a task the supervisors ignored). By mid summer, overall productivity across the two groups was 20 percent below the previous summer's rate.

Answers to Questions for Analysis

1. **Question:** *What caused the poor production condition during the second summer?*

Answer: Factors already discussed (essentially a mismatch between leadership style and work situation) played a major role. Insufficient training of new workers was also a major factor.

2. **Question:** *How might this situation have been avoided from the beginning?*

Answer: Students will offer several suggestions. For example, the problems likely could have been avoided by the appointment of members of the "old-timer" crew as supervisors. Joe Brewster may have detected the problem much earlier if he had kept in closer contact with the crew operations (occasionally visiting the work sites and observing how the supervisors interacted with the crew members).

3. **Question:** *What should Joe do now?*

Answer: There are several options including: 1) Joe could fire the new supervisors, or fire the head of the "old timer" crew while retaining one new supervisor for the new crew. However, such an approach is appropriate only if he determines that the situation cannot be corrected while retaining the new supervisors. 2) Joe could identify needed changes in the supervisors' management style and inform the

384

supervisors that they must make the needed changes (and help them to do so where feasible). 3) Joe could instruct the new crew supervisor to train the new crew members (and possibly transfer an "old-timer" to the new crew to help train the members).

Regardless of the strategy selected, the "old timers" must be given back their job-enriched freedoms and responsibilities. They performed exceptionally well under those conditions, and there is no reason to believe that the results would be different during the second summer with enriched jobs.

4. **Question:** *Do you think the supervisors could have effectively adopted Joe's style of leadership? What kind of problems might they have had if they did? How should they have conducted themselves?*

   Answer: It's unlikely that the supervisors could have effectively managed the workers using Joe's style of leadership. They are different individuals with different backgrounds and a different leadership perspective. Supervising "just like Joe" would have probably been perceived as phony by the workers. However, the supervisors could have adopted a more flexible leadership style, respecting the crew's previous performance and affording them the freedom to do the job as they saw fit. Concerning the new crew, the supervisors should have recognized the workers' lack of experience and their insecurity about their work. In this situation, a more authoritative style might have been in order, but it should be coupled with effectively teaching the new workers how to perform the job.

MANAGING PRODUCTION AND OPERATION   PP.612-617——

CASE SUMMARY:

This case about First National Bank of Chicago and their commitment to quality. This case is an excellent summary of the kinds of effects organizations undergo as they look to deliver quality services and products to their customers.

Much of the case outlines specifics that tie very closely to the requirements of application for the Malcolm Baldrige Award. The organizational framework was investigated to determine is the previous structure and design were assisting in the delivery of quality work to their customers. Along those same lines, customers were embraced as a main element in their quality improvement efforts. First National realized that the customer's definition and perspective of quality is what is really important as these efforts are begun.

A thorough understanding of measurement techniques was developed among First National employees so actual data, and not just anecdotal incidents were used to establish goals and measure outcomes. Individuals employees were also integrated as a vital part of the process through quality circles, their evaluations, the timely performance awards.

Clearly First National underwent tremendous efforts to make the improvement they did. Their efforts have really been well worth it. Errors have dropped significantly, costs were reduced and perhaps most importantly, customers were the recipient of the improvement in quality.

Answers to Questions for Analysis

1.   Question: *Compare First National Bank's quality improvement program with what your have learned to be essential steps of a successful quality improvement program.*

    Answer: Students could be encouraged to create comparison charts which illustrate the numerous similarities among the bank efforts and the "textbook" answers. In addition, provide to students information about the Malcolm Baldrige Award presented in the chapter case. They would then determine how the bank would respond to the questions raised on the application.

2.   Question: *Would you consider what First National Bank has done to be an illustration of total quality management? Explain.*

    Answer: Given that TQM is an ongoing, continuous improvement, there are

386

certainly always other avenues of improvement that can be explored. However, in terms of their present efforts, First National Bank appears to have embraced TQM thoroughly.

3. **Question:**   *In what ways, if any, would the linear programming, PERT, MRP, and economic order quantity techniques be useful in assisting First Chicago to achieve its operations and quality goals?*

    Answer: While typically concerned for use in manufacturing, these tools could in fact provide excellent information and guidelines for their continued efforts.

4. **Question:**   Evaluate the information system that is in place to evaluate progress toward quality-improvement goals.

    Answer: To improve quality within any organization, having access to information before improvements efforts are made, as well as on an on-going process is critical. First National Bank of Chicago seems to be well on their way of ascertaining and utilizing the necessary information.

SECTION IV

ANALYSIS OF EXPERIENTIAL EXERCISES

THE USE OF
EXPERIENTIAL EXERCISES
AS SUPPLEMENTS

In various chapters, we have presented exercises that focus on individual self-assessment and group analysis. Again, the reason for the inclusion of these exercises is to have the student become an active participant in the learning process. We believe that some amount of active involvement will permit the student to acquire a better feel for the concepts and theories discussed in the book. Using the exercises can be a rewarding experience for each student. The student must, however, become involved if he/she is to be rewarded. A few suggestions would be to:

Complete the exercise in an honest way.
By participating honestly, a student will be able to determine how similar and different his or her approach or attitude is from others.

Allow others to comment on your responses to the exercise
Receiving feedback f rom others participating in an exercise can provide valuable insights about your opinions and preferences.

Relate the exercise to the book material
Integration practice is a sound learning device. Each exercise can be related to the content found in the chapters.

Reexamine the exercises at the end of the course
Determine if you have changed preferences, opinions, and attitudes.

An important feature of using exercises is that learning for each student from the same exercise varies. By using exercises we expect students to learn different things from the individual self-assessment and group discussions.

We hope that by becoming involved with the exercises each student can improve his or her
1. self-awareness
2. communication skills
3. understanding of group processes and structure
4 knowledge about such topics as motivation, leadership, group conflict and organizational change.

If these objectives can be accomplished, the exercises will be considered a successful part of this book. There were many exercises that could have been included in the book. We carefully selected exercises that were tested with different student groups and proved to be successful.

We selected exercises that are:
1.   Realistic.
2.   Possible to cover in one or no more than two class periods.
3.   Interesting to students.
4.   Relevant and related to the material covered in the book.
5.   Involvement oriented.

1

ATTITUDES ABOUT BUSINESS ORGANIZATIONS

PAGES IN TEXT: 27 - 28

PURPOSE

The purpose of this exercise is to identify attitudes that students have about business and various industries.

THE EXERCISE IN CLASS

Student responses will definitely differ according to age, work experience, and political orientation. Each student's major course of study will also influence ratings. The business students rate business generally higher in all areas covered in the survey.

Two sets of mean ratings are presented. Rating A is based on a full-time day student group of undergraduates—average age 26.1 years, 3.2 years of business experience, 42 males, 25 females. Rating B is based on an evening class of part-time students—average ages 31.4 years, 9.1 years of business experience, 35 males, 21 females.

AREA OF CONCERN	RATING A MEAN	RATING B MEAN
Energy Conservation	2.7	3.3
Quality of Worklife	3.8	3.2
Pollution	2.4	2.7
Inflation	1.9	2.1
Higher Education	2.2	2.7
Obsolete Employees	2.8	2.4
Urban Areas	2.2	3.1
Handicapped	3.1	3.8
Minorities	3.0	3 7
Ethical Behavior	3.2	3.3
Technological Advancement	3.7	3.5
Rewarding Performance	3.1	2.4
Profit Margin	3.8	2.9
Strong Government	3.2	2.7

The industry ratings are also interesting and are influenced by a number of factors including knowledge of and experience in the industry, age, political orientation, and college major. The Rating A and Rating B groups are the same as those doing the rating of the business support areas.

INDUSTRY	RATING A MEAN	RATING B MEAN
Automobile	2.8	2.7
Steel	2.7	2.5
Tobacco	2.2	2.0
Food Processing	3.6	3.5
Banking	3.7	3.3
Publishing	3.0	2.5
Religion	2.7	3.2
Oil	2.6	2.5
Chemicals	1.9	1.7
Electronics	3.7	3.4
Tire and Rubber	3.1	3.2
Television	2.7	2.2
Aerospace	3.2	3.0
Health Care	3.1	3.2
Education	3.3	3.1
Fast Food	2.7	2.8
Computer	3.7	3.6
Paper	3.1	3.0
Insurance	2.0	1.6
Car Repair	1.4	1.3
Prescription Drugs	1.9	2.4

Have your students compare their mean scores with those of the two rating groups (A and B). Remember that the location of the country and its dominance and recent events in the press will also influence the ratings. Our classes attempted to analyze the three lowest rated industries and the three highest rated industries. Why are they rated like this? This created a lively class discussion.

RATING A HIGHEST THREE		RATING B HIGHEST THREE	
Banking	3.7	Computer	3.6
Electronics	3.7	Food Processing	3.5
Computer	3.7	Electronics	3.4

LOWEST THREE		LOWEST THREE	
Prescription Drugs	1.9	Chemicals	1.7
Chemicals	1.9	Insurance	1.6
Car Repairs	1.4	Car Repairs	1.3

SOME QUESTIONS TO ASK THE GROUP:

1. What factors influenced your ratings of the industries?

2. In the last ten to 15 years, have the levels of support for the stated areas of concern changed in some industries? If so, identify the industries.

3. Identify and discuss the factors that influenced such change.

4. Overall, which three areas of concern have received the least support from the listed industries? Why?

5. Overall, which three areas of concern have received the most support from industries? Why?

393

PROFILE OF AN EXTERNAL ENVIRONMENT

PAGES IN TEXT   57 - 58

PURPOSE

To enhance students' understanding of the importance, dynamics, and challenges of the external environments in which organizations operate.

THE EXERCISE IN CLASS

This exercise should bring home to the students the differential impact that various external forces have on companies within different industries, and how companies attempt to deal with such forces, frequently with a very different approach. Also, by having to predict the level of influence such forces may continue to have, students should recognize the sometimes static, but often dynamic nature of such forces and the need for continued environmental scanning and a proactive planning stance. The exercise calls for a written report. However, it's a good idea to set aside some class time for each team to give a summary of their findings, so that others may gain a broader understanding than would be allowed by limiting them to their own research.

SOME QUESTIONS TO ASK THE GROUP:

1. To what extent do you think the forces affecting this company are typical of those affecting the entire industry?
2. What do you think of the strategy this company is using to control the effects of these forces? Do you think other companies in this industry are adopting the same stance?
3. What strategy do you think the company should use in the future?
4. Under what level of risk do you think this company is operating relative to these environmental forces?
5. What are the alternative potential outcomes this company may experience by responding to such threats and opportunities in this manner?

3

LAUNCHING AN INTERNATIONAL BUSINESS

PAGES IN TEXT: 91

PURPOSE
The activity is designed to enhance students' understanding of the key elements of the international environment and their impact on expanding a business internationally.

SOME QUESTIONS TO ASK THE GROUP:
This exercise is an excellent opportunity for demonstrating to students the complexities of international business and the many factors which must be considered in developing an international strategy. If you are conducting the "Create A Company" exercise, this activity is very similar to the exercise's fifth part, "Expansion Abroad." In conducting this exercise, you must want to have students focus on one aspect of their prospective host country's environment (e.g., the political climate) and have an equal number of groups focus on each of the three primary environmental aspects.

SOME QUESTIONS TO ASK THE GROUP:

1.   Which environmental elements poses the greatest challenge for successfully doing business in the country?

2.   Based on your research, would you hire local citizens to assume your facility~s management positions or rely on expatriates? What facts support your strategy?

3.   If you plan to use expatriates, what type of training program would you conduct to prepare them for their assignments?

4.   If political instability is a potential problem, what actions would you take to reduce your political risk?

ETHICAL DILEMMAS

PAGES IN TEXT: 120

PURPOSE
This activity is designed to illustrate the complexity of ethical decision making and how people can differ in their views of what is and is not ethical behavior.

THE EXERCISE IN CLASS
This activity provides an excellent opportunity to demonstrate to students the "difficult calls" that they can encounter as managers in organizations concerning ethical and unethical behavior. We've used this exercise several times in class and have found a considerable disagreement across students concerning what should be doing in each of the ethical dilemmas. Here is a summary of the responses of 1,500 adults and 400 middle-level managers to each of these dilemmas. The individuals completed the exercise as part of the Wall Street Journal/Gallup poll on ethics in America.

The Roundabout Raise:
Turn down the raise, said 65 percent of the general public and 91 percent of the executives. About 25 percent of the general public and seven percent of the executives disagreed, believing Joe should take the "authorization."

The Faked Degree:
More executives would dismiss Bill (50 percent) than overlook the claim (43 percent). On this issue, the public was much more lenient. About 66 percent would overlook the false claim; 22 percent would dismiss Bill.

Sneaking Phone Calls:
Generally, both the executives and the public believe Helen should report the employee (64 percent of the public and 76 percent of the executives). Twenty-six percent of the public and 19 percent of the executives recommend disregarding the calls. However, change the financial amount of calls made and opinions substantially change. When told that the indiscretion amounted to $10 a month rather than $100, only 47 percent of the general public and 48 percent of the executives recommended turning in the employee (38 percent of the public and 47 percent of the executives favored disregarding the calls).

Cover-Up Temptation:
Both the public and the executives took the hard line: 63 percent of the general public and 70 percent of the executives say Bill should report the problem and fix it. Some 25 percent of the

396

public and 24 percent of the executives recommend disregarding the problem. This problem was the only one where younger respondents took the tougher ethical stand than did their elders.

SOME QUESTIONS TO ASK THE GROUP:

1. What factors account for your differing views on what is and isn't ethical in each of these dilemmas?

2. Generally, the polled executives took a harder line on ethics than did the public. Why?

3. You could argue that the survey's findings don't support the public's view that managers are often unethical. Why does the public hold this view?

5

LOST-AT-SEA DECISION MAKING

PAGES IN TEXT: 149 - 150

PURPOSE

The purpose of this exercise is to offer students the opportunity lo compare individual versus group decision making.

THE EXERCISE IN CLASS

The following are the rankings of the 15 items provided by the officers of the U.S. Merchant Marines:

	EXPERT RANKINGS
Sextant	15
Shaving mirror	1
Five-gallon can of water	3
Mosquito netting	14
One case of U.S. Army C rations	4
Maps of the Pacific Ocean	13
Seat cushion (flotation device approved by the Coast Guard)	9
Two-gallon can of oil-gas mixture	2
Small transistor radio	12
Shark repellent	10
Twenty square feet of opaque plastic	5
One quart of 160-proof Puerto Rican rum	11
Fifteen feet of nylon rope	8
Two boxes of chocolate bars	6
Fishing kit	7

Typically, for most groups the group accuracy score will exceed each member's individual score in terms of accuracy. Sometimes this does not occur and in these cases, it's interesting to examine why. You might want to discuss why—overall—that decision making by groups is superior to decision making by individuals, emphasizing the tasks's characteristics. The section on group decision making in Chapter 12 is helpful in this regard.

398

SOME QUESTIONS TO ASK THE GROUP:

1. To the most accurate and least accurate groups): Explain the approach your group used in ranking the items. (Instructor: It's useful to compare and contrast the two approaches.)

2. (To all groups): What decision-making strategies did you use that were most effective? Looking back on your group activity, how would you change your decision making approach?

3. What advantage(s) does group decision making provide over individual decision making in this exercise?

4. Would group performance in this exercise increase with increasing group size? Explain.

5. Did a member of your group exercise substantial influence? What was the source of his/her influence?

6

USING THE ELEMENTS OF PLANNING IN YOUR OWN LIFE

PAGES IN TEXT: 179

PURPOSE
The purpose of this exercise is to apply the elements of planning to your own life.

THE EXERCISE IN CLASS
This activity requires each student to focus on a personal situation from the perspective of using professional planning steps, from determining a major objective, deciding on the actions necessary to achieve that objective, what resources will be required and how to actually implement those decisions. The result should be a realization that formal planning can be applied to any situation resulting in a greater potential for controlling outcomes.

SOME QUESTIONS TO ASK THE GROUP:

1. Was this a situation from your past? If so, what kind of planning steps did you use and what were the results?

2. What would you do differently now?

3. What results would you expect after using the above planning steps?

7

THE IMPORTANCE OF
THE PLANNING FUNCTION

PAGES IN TEXT: 205

PURPOSE
The purpose of this exercise, which requires some out-of-class homework to prepare the answers, is to emphasize the importance of planning in organizations in various industries.

THE EXERCISE IN CLASS
The environmental forces that impact any organization are numerous. This exercise forces the student to carefully look at the government, technology, competition, economy, and other forces that impact the organization's plans and policies.

Each of the organizations listed are faced with environmental forces that are each slightly different. For example, General Motors is faced with government regulations and so is General Mills, Del Taco, Honeywell, and each of the others. However, the GM concerns are different than the others because they are in a different business. Each of these organizations must monitor the main environmental forces so that effective plans ban be developed. Have the students place the environmental forces on a flip chart and then compare each organization' list.

This will reveal some common and some dissimilar factors. It will also illustrate that although many of the forces emanate from the same general group, they affect an organization differently.

SOME QUESTIONS TO ASK THE GROUP:
1.   Identify the most positive and most negative environmental force for each organization. Explain the reason for your selections.

2.   How can an organization effectively monitor the environmental developments?

3.   In your opinion, which of the organizations operates in the most turbulent environment? The most stable environment? Explain

4.   Does the nature of an organization's external environment (turbulent, stable, etc.) affect the dynamics and structure of its strategic planning system (and strategy implementation. How?

5.   Del Taco is the smallest organization on the exercise list. Does organizational size affect the organization's strategic planning processes and system? How? Does size affect the company's vulnerability in the external environment? Explain.

8

DESIGNING THE
NEW ORGANIZATION

PAGES IN TEXT: 241

PURPOSE
The purpose of this exercise is to provide students with first-hand experience in organizing a new business venture.

THE EXERCISE IN CLASS

The George Ballas portion of the exercise is actually true. He was an entrepreneur who struck it rich with the Weed Eater. The Gammons are not going to compete with the big distributors of Weed Eater "look-a-like" products such as Sears, Wards, Penneys, etc. but they may be able to carve out their market niche. This exercise should point out that even relatively small operations (although sales expectations could be in the $500,000 range) needs some form of organization. The students need to include in their design some concern for production, marketing, personnel, and finance issues. These probably should not be separate departments (the firm is too small) but someone needs to handle these aspects of the business.

SOME QUESTIONS TO ASK THE GROUP:

1. What design issues were considered in the group in organizing the venture?
2. What design features are needed to attract the retail establishments?
3. How did your group view the competition and what the Gammons had to do to compete?
4. What is the advantage of establishing a design at the start of a new venture?
5. How could a classical design arrangement work?
6. Are some matrix or project design features needed?
7. What would be a test for assessing the success of your (the group) design?
8. What environmental factors should be considered by small business owners like the Gammons when entering a new venture?

Ventures of all kinds are available to even students: money, ideas, energy to work, good luck, and risk taking are all important in making a venture successful. However, even H all of these ingredients are present, it is necessary to put a design (structure) together. How the pieces fit together is extremely important to the success of the venture. If the firm is not well designed, it will generally be inefficient, slow reacting, and suppressive.

9
ORGANIZATIONAL DESIGN IN THE CAMPUS SETTING

PAGES IN TEXT: 268

PURPOSE
The exercise enables students to use certain theories of organization design to describe the organizational design of units that make up their college or university. **The Exercise In Class** This exercise enables students to use certain theories of organization design to describe the design of organizations that make up their college or university. It is very effective for reinforcing student understanding of the purposes, strengths, and limitations of theory in the context of management.

SOME QUESTIONS TO ASK THE GROUP:
1. What should be going on with this department according to the theory you are applying?
2. How is the department actually structured now?
3. How do you account for any differences in the design between theory and actual?
4. How do you assess the effectiveness of the department?
5. How do you think the design could be made more effective? What specific changes would you make?

10

PAPER PLANE CORPORATION

PAGES IN TEXT: 292 - 294

PURPOSE
The purpose of this exercise is to work on a task that requires planning, organizing, and controlling.

THE EXERCISE IN CLASS
This is a simulation of a total managerial and organizational experience. The students have to plan, organize, control, and direct to be profitable. The student quickly finds out how important the managerial functions are in completing this exercise. Those groups that have no plan, are not organized, and have no quality control function do not perform well on this exercise. If you use a number of rounds for this exercise, point out how the group either improves or makes no progress. A group that is disorganized in the first round and doesn't change in later rounds makes no progress. The organized groups seem to make steady progress.

SOME QUESTIONS TO ASK THE GROUP:
1.   Did your group plan, organize, control? Explain.
2.   Why was your group successful? Not successful?
3.   Is this a realistic view of managerial functions in action? Why?
4.   Did your group have a leader(s)? Was he or she effective? Why?
5.   How was control applied in this exercise?

YOUR JOB PREFERENCES COMPARED TO OTHERS

PAGES IN TEXT: *338 - 339*

PURPOSE

The exercise is designed to identify what makes a job attractive or unattractive to you. Preferences of employees, if known, could be used as information by managers to develop and restructure jobs that are most attractive, rewarding, and generally more fulfilling. It is this type of information that would permit a manager to create a positive motivational atmosphere for subordinates.

This exercise will display major differences in opinion. We have used the exercise in the classroom and in training programs and found some interesting rankings. Recently, three groups of trainees—engineers, nurses, and district sales managers, ranked the factors. The top three ranked factors for each group were
the following:

Nurses	**Engineers**	**Managers**
1. Pay	1. Challenge	1. Advancement
2. Schedule	2. Advancement	2. Pay
3. Advancement	3. Feedback	3. Challenge

Student groups in most cases rank advancement, challenge, responsibility, feedback, and pay as the most preferred. It seems that in ranking what others prefer, pay is ranked higher than in the personal preference rankings. Why? Perhaps ranking pay high makes people feel uncomfortable about themselves. They do not want to appear monetarily oriented so they place pay in the middle of their rankings. As your class about this
tendency after they have completed the exercise.

The rankings of ten full-time management classes for their preferences were tabulated to provide an example of student preferences. There are 418 full-time students, 285 males, 133 females.

	Aggregate Mean Values of Student Rankings		Rankings of Others	
Advancement	4.3		5.2	
Pay	3.8	3	2.9	1
Fringe Benefits	5.1		4.7	
Schedule	8.7		8.6	
Location	7.8		7.0	
Supervisor	13.1		12.4	
Feedback	3.7	2	4.9	
Security	4.6		3.9	2
Challenge	3.4	1	4.3	3
Working Conditions	8.1		7.8	
Co-Workers	9.7		7.6	
The Organization	12.8		11.4	
Responsibility	8.9		8.0	
Training and Development Opportunities	10.1		9.8	

SOME QUESTIONS TO ASK THE GROUP:

1. How does your group's rankings compare with those presented? What factors could account for differences?

2. Will your rankings change over time? If you believe so, project a set of rankings (the top three job factors) for yourself at: 1) age 30; 2) age 45; and 3) age 55. Generally, how do you believe the rankings will change?

3. Do men and women differ according to the importance of job factors? If so, for which factors are differences the most substantial? Why?

4. Which preferences is most important to you now? Least important? What reasons account for these two rankings?

5. Does society's culture influence individual job preferences? If so, how? Provide an example to support your view.

12
GROUP BRAINSTORMING IN ACTION

PAGES IN TEXT: 372

PURPOSE
The purpose of this exercise is to provide experience in group brainstorming—to learn to use and pool the ideas, good and bad, of group members.

THE EXERCISE IN CLASS
It's important to note that this exercise has two phases which the groups should clearly understand:

1)   phase 1—where all group members independently develop at least two ideas as solutions for the problem; and

2)   phase 2—when the group leader records all ideas presented independently by the group members.

During this phase, group members should "piggyback"—develop additional ideas which are triggered by the ideas presented by individual members. Piggybacking is a major advantage of group brainstorming as it essentially involves members building upon presented ideas. No evaluation is allowed.

Once the groups have finished brainstorming, you may want to have each group tally the number of ideas generated and then select the three ideas which the group believes are its best. Then write on the board, the top three ideas presented by each group, and the total number of ideas generated by each group. In post-exercise discussion, it is useful to point out that the outcomes of group brainstorming are often disappointing because: —Individuals are often inhibited by the group—they are reluctant to offer all of their ideas due to a fear that their ideas will be viewed as poor ones or even silly sometimes the group brainstorming session will be dominated by a member who is not the most skilled in brainstorming, or in encouraging others to be comfortable and open with their ideas. —Idea evaluation typically creeps into the group process which hinders the group's creativity.

SOME QUESTIONS TO ASK THE GROUP:
1.   How easy (or difficult) was it to refrain from openly evaluating the ideas presented? Why?
2.   Did your group piggyback? Did the group's best ideas come from individual brainstorming or piggybacking?
3.   What steps would you suggest be taken to make any group's brainstorming efforts more effective?

13

THE TRANSPORTATION LEADER

PAGES IN TEXT: 489 - 410

PURPOSE
The purpose of this exercise is to have each individual assess their leadership orientation between transformational and transactional leadership style.

THE EXERCISE IN CLASS
This exercise assigns points among 10 pair of statements that characterizes leadership orientation. Students divide 5 points between the two statements of leadership. For each question a vote is taken among class members to determine leadership orientation. Students can compare their leadership orientation with others in the class. The scoring sheet identifies the Hems associated with each leadership orientation respectively, transformational versus transactional. The higher column total indicates a stronger agreement with the leadership orientation by the student.

SOME QUESTIONS TO ASK THE GROUP:
1.   How do your results compare with the leadership orientation suggested by the class?

2.   Which leadership orientation is most effective in a typical organization?

3.   What work environment is most conducive to a transformational leadership orientation? transactional leadership orientation?

4.   How does one change from a transformational leader to a transactional leader or vice versa?

PERCEPTUAL DIFFERENCES

PURPOSE

The purpose of this exercise is to illustrate how people perceive the same situation differently through the process of selective perception.

THE EXERCISE IN CLASS

This exercise demonstrates the wide variety of perceptual differences among people when considering a situation where little factual information is provided. The exercise should also indicate that most people selectively perceive the information they are comfortable with in analyzing the situation. Many will also subconsciously fill in gaps of information with assumptions they suppose are facts. The answers to the 15 questions are:

1.	?	Do you *know that* the "businessman" and the "owner" are one and the same?
2.	?	Was there *necessarily* a robbery involved here? Perhaps the man was the rent collector—or the owner's son—they sometimes demand money.
3.	F	An easy one to keep up the test-taker's morale.
4.	?	Was the owner a *man?*
5.	?	May seem unlikely, but the story does not definitely preclude it.
6.	T	The story says that the owner opened the cash register.
7.	?	We don't know who scooped up the contents of the cash register or that the man necessarily *ran* away.
8.	?	The dependent clause is doubtful. The cash register may or may not have contained money.
9.	?	Again, a robber?
10.	?	Could the man merely have appeared *at* a door or a window without actually entering the store?
11.	?	Stores generally keep lights on during the day.
12.	?	Could not the man who appeared have been the owner?
13.	F	The story says that the man who appeared demanded money.
14.	?	Are the businessman and the owner one and the same—or two different people? The same goes for the owner and the man who appeared.
15.	?	"Dashed?" Could he not have "sped away" on roller skates or in a car? And do we know that he actually left the store? We don't even know that he entered it.

SOME QUESTIONS TO ASK THE GROUP:

1. How many "wrong" answers did you have?

2. To what do you attribute these differences? What is there about you, your environment, your background which you believe affected your perception in this way?

3. What do you think you can do to attempt to make your assessment of such situations more accurate in the future?

15

A CONTROL PROCEDURE: YOUR PERSONAL PERFORMANCE APPRAISAL

PAGES IN TEXT: 447

PURPOSE

The purpose of this exercise is to apply performance appraisal guidelines to your own activities and objective.

THE EXERCISE IN CLASS

There is no set pattern in responses to this exercise. The reference points selected are usually school, career, current job, future life, and occasionally, family. The interesting feature of this exercise is the difficulty many people have in developing measures to evaluate their accomplishments. Some believe that measures can't be developed for the areas they selected. Others have problems in even specifying the objectives they hope to accomplish.

SOME QUESTIONS TO ASK THE GROUP:

1. Do you believe that your objectives will change over a lifetime? In what ways and to what extent? Will the ranking of your objectives change over time? Explain.

2. The group interactions clearly show that some differences exist across the objectives selected by individuals. Why?

3. Are objective or subjective measures predominant in regard to your major areas of concern?

4. What reference point did you select for the exercise? What factors influenced your choice? If you consider the reference point to be the most important element of your life, what factors influence its level of importance?

5. Select two subjective measures which you've identified for your major areas of concern. What steps could you take to boost the validity of these measures?

16

ARE YOU RECEPTIVE TO CHANGE?

PAGES IN TEXT: 517 - 519

PURPOSE

The purpose of this exercise is to help students to determine how open- or closed-minded they are to change.

THE EXERCISE IN CLASS

Students complete a series of questions, self score and compare with others. The message is that resisting change is almost an inevitable fact of life. The way a person thinks indicates how resistant to change he or she will be when faced with changes in structure, technology, and personnel. This exercise will provide some insight to students into their relative openness toward change.

SOME QUESTIONS TO ASK THE GROUP:

1.   How do your results match your personal image of how willing you are to accept change?

2.   As a future manager, what implications can you draw from this exercise to help you to understand the impact of change on employees? What can you do to minimize that impact and encourage acceptance?

18

APPLICATION OF
INVENTORY CONTROL

PAGES IN TEXT: 577-578

PURPOSE

The exercise reinforces students' understanding of the technical aspects of inventory control, as well as their appreciation of information and assumptions as vital parts of inventory control.

THE EXERCISE IN CLASS

This exercise sets up a basis for comparisons among student groups of their evaluation of the applicability of inventory control in a hypothetical firm in a specific industry. It serves to point out that inventory systems depend upon the knowledge base of those who develop them.

SOME QUESTIONS TO ASK THE GROUP:

1. What are the implications of your findings for applying theory to specific situations?

2. What variables in each company tend to affect the workability of such techniques as EOQ, MRP and JIT?

DSS DESIGN IN A CAMPUS BOOKSTORE

PAGES IN TEXT: 609

PURPOSE
The exercise enables students to experience the difficulty of developing an information system that provides pertinent and timely data for decision making.

THE EXERCISE IN CLASS
Student groups have to prepare and present a tentative design for a decision support system for the campus bookstore, taking certain factors and parameters into account in the design. The exercise helps to reinforce the students' understanding of decision making and decision support systems in the context of an organization that they know very well since they all will likely have bought and sold books at the local bookstore.

SOME QUESTIONS TO ASK THE GROUP:
1.   To what extent do you feel your recommended system will solve the problems of the bookstore and the students?

2.   What basic objectives underlie the system you have designed?

3.   What other applications could such a system have?

4.   What is the relationship between the information system you have designed and the objectives of management control in an organization. What types of control would result?

20
PORTRAIT OF
AN ENTREPRENEUR

PAGES IN TEXT: 647

PURPOSE
This activity is designed to enhance students' understanding of the entrepreneurial personality, and the motivations, challenges, and rewards of entrepreneurship.

THE EXERCISE IN CLASS
This exercise provides an opportunity for students to extend their understanding of the entrepreneur—what drives the individual, the nature of his or her business, and the challenges that entrepreneurs face in their jobs. In discussing the groups' findings, it is useful to focus on identifying the common individual characteristics and business challenges that the interviewed entrepreneurs share and to identify unique differences.

SOME QUESTIONS TO ASK THE GROUP:
1.   In addition to the findings regarding common entrepreneurial characteristics, what are some common managerial behaviors—i.e., specific activities, which can ??been seen across group findings?

2.   What commonalities, if any, can be seen in their backgrounds? What about leadership style?

3.   Considering what you've learned, would you like to take the plunge and become an entrepreneur?

21

CAREER PLANNING
THE TQM WAY

PAGES IN TEXT: 675

PURPOSE
The purpose of this exercise is to provide students with experience in thinking about what is important in their lives and careers.

This exercise is useful in that it provides students with a systematic approach to begin thinking about future career goals and planning stemming from their objectives. Many students will have difficulty with the exercise (especially part d) because most have previously given little thought to specifying what they want from their future careers. It's useful to approach the exercise with the intent of providing students with some insights into self-assessment in terms of personal need for satisfaction and career goals. One way to help students in this regard is to encourage class discussion of the types of personal satisfaction which students seek and the sources of such satisfaction in a career.

SOME QUESTIONS TO ASK THE GROUP:
1. Your cited desired future career events are fulfilling/satisfying because they meet specific personal needs. What are those needs? Try to identify and describe them.

2. Concerning your rankings of future career events in terms of fulfillment and satisfaction, will your rankings change as you get older? What future situational factors might change your rankings?

3. Concerning a future career in management, what are the advantages and disadvantages of such a career?

4. In your opinion, what are the skills that are most important in achieving success as a manager? Why?

5. In your opinion, what factor does luck play in career outcomes?

SECTION V

THE VIDEO
RESOURCE GUIDE

This Video Resource Guide is intended to provide the instructor with resources that can serve as a supplement to ideas, topics, and concerns presented in *Fundamentals of Management,* ninth edition. Videos can stimulate student participation and enhance the learning experience. They can be a dynamic real-life learning tool that can be adapted to the course material.

More than 100 new video titles have been added in this edition of the Instructor's Manual, and are indicated in bold type.

Organization of Materials

The Video Resource Guide is divided into six sections. Five sections parallel the text's five divisions; the sixth section is composed of additional supplementary topics. Within each section, videos are grouped by topic and are listed in alphabetical order. Videos are listed by topic rather than chapter because video titles are often applicable for more than one chapter. For instance, videos on Total Quality Management are relevant to chapters on motivation, managing work groups, leadership, and the controlling function.

Each video is abstracted; and the release date, approximate running time and distributor are noted where available. In some cases the film producer is included and precedes the distributor's listing (e.g., "producer name/distributor(s) name(s)"). The listing abstracts were developed from the most current catalogue descriptions available.

Even though brief video abstracts are available, it's useful to preview videos before using them, to aid in integrating the video into the class. The addresses of distributors are included in the guide along with telephone numbers where available. Most distributors provide support materials for the videos, ranging from a brief synopsis and/or preview guide to extensive "how to use" kits." Note: Though one distributor is usually listed for each video, many videos are carried by multiple distributors. So if you're not satisfied with one distributor's rental price or other arrangements, try another distributor in the directory of distributors. Also, many colleges and universities have individual or consortium-type arrangements with state or regional university distribution centers or library systems for the use of video material. Often such arrangements provide lower rental rates than what is typically listed in video catalogues. Instructors, by working with media/library centers, can often receive the lowest rates available. Catalogues can be obtained by writing or calling the sources listed. Video source representatives are generally helpful and willing to provide materials that are necessary to make final selection decisions.

TABLE OF CONTENTS

PART 1: MANAGEMENT AND THE ENVIRONMENT (Chapters 1-4)———————

1.A. ENVIRONMENTS OF MANAGEMENT—————————————————————

An Act of Congress (1979; 58 min.; Charles Guggenheim-Learning Corporation of America /AFL-CIO Film Division) A behind-the-scenes look at how Congress passes legislation. Follows the progress of a controversial bill, the Clean Air Amendment, as it moves through the committee structure onto the floor of the House and finally becomes a law. Shows how legislative conflicts between environmental and automotive interests are resolved.

Bankrupt (The Enterprise Series) (1981; 30 min.; WGBH/Learning Corporation of America) The workings of the bankruptcy laws are illustrated graphically by tracing the rise and subsequent failure of Inforex, a $70 million-a-year computer firm. Initially high successful with its product, a data entry machine, the company was soon in financial trouble because it was unable to come up with a second profitable product. The film traces the course of events as Inforex filed for protection under the Federal Bankruptcy Act, which allowed it to keep its creditors form taking over the assets and selling them. Shows that bankruptcy laws five businesses a second chance, which may not always be successful.

T*he Business of America* (1983; 43 min.; California Newsreel/Penn State Audio Visual Services) Confronts a critical issue of the 1980s: Can the traditional American business system reverse the decline in industry and provide for the economic and social needs of all Americans? Contends that pressure on mature industries to move into more immediately profitable ventures has discouraged long-term investment in manufacturing technology and research. Focuses on U.S. Steel in Homestead, Pennsylvania, to show how disillusioned, unemployed steelworkers are exploring self-reliant alternatives to corporate control over investment.

Buy-Out (1983; 28 min., GBH-Learning Corporation of America/Penn State Audio Visual Services) Examines the problems of one of the largest experiments in employee ownership; Hyatt Clark Industries of New Jersey, an automobile support industry purchased from General Motors by company workers led by Jimmy Zarrello and Jimmy May. Lack of profits and deep-seated labor-management strife made the first year difficult, but with productivity levels higher, Hyatt Clark hoped to break even in the second year. From the Enterprise 2 series. Host: Eric Sevareid.

Case for competition: Money talks series #5 (1962;30 min.; Carousel Films) Competition begets lower prices, provides greater variety; favorable to consumers. Views how government and business see four subjects outside the area of competition-labor, monopoly, profits, subsidies.

A Coal Operator's Turn (1981; 29 min.; WPSX/Penn State Audio Visual Services) Profile of Alan Walker, president of Bradford Coal Company, one of the ten largest coal businesses in Pennsylvania and one of the few that remains family owned and operated. Walker voices his frustrations over governmental regulations that he claims are making H more and more difficult to conduct his business efficiently and economically. Follows Walker's efforts to compromise with Pennsylvania's Department of Environmental Resources on such issues as permits, citizen complaints, and pollution. On video cassette only.

Consumer Power: Whistleblowing (1973; 24 min.; CBS/University of Illinois Film Center) Consumer advocate Ralph Nader and Robert Townsend, author of "Up the Organization", make a case for ethical whistleblowing as a form of individual action against public abuses by large organizations. Two whistleblowers relate their stories: Edward Gregory persisted in his warnings of defects until General Motors finally recalled millions of cars for correction; Dale Hagedorn and his wife protested until Union Carbide's plant in Anmoore, West Virginia, took steps to control air pollution.

Drucker, A Day with Peter F.: Econ. Devil; Triumph, Fail (1988; 73 min.; George Washinghton University) There has been no period in economic history in which more people have pulled themselves out of poverty and into productivity and economic competence than that of the last 30 years.

Ethics of Bankruptcy, The: Dialogue, Putnam, Guthrie #7 (1987; 20 min.; Harvard Business School) A Harvard MBA class discussion on the Braniff case.

Eye on the Media: Business and the Press (1984; 49 min.; CBS News/Carousel Films) The press has come under close scrutiny in recent times and big business is constantly concerned about being subjected to journalistic "hatchet jobs." This issue and others are examined in an edited version of a three hour seminar, Harvard law professor Charles R. Nesson is the moderator and he is joined by a number of prominent participants representing the broadcast industry, the press and the business community. The issues are addressed in a lively, artful and intelligent manner. On video (VHS and Beta) only.

The Fed—Our Central Bank (1978; 20 min.; Federal Reserve Board of Governors) Provides an overview of the structure, goals, and operations of the Federal Reserve System. The central theme is how the value of money is determined and maintained. Emphasizes the impact of America's central bank on the individual citizens.

Who Protects the Consumer? (1979; 29 min.; WQLN/Instructional Media Services-University of Utah) Milton Friedman presents evidence to support his view that most government consumer-protection activity hurts consumers and the nation. Describes how closely regulated industries lose their right, and their will, to innovate and seek new ways of competing for the consumer's money, thus denying the consumer improved products, services, and lower prices. Shows the enormous amounts of paperwork generated by consumer protection rules and the difficulties of getting new products onto the market.

Gibbons vs. Ogden (1979; 36 min.; WQED/University of Iowa Media Library) Explores the far-reaching consequences of Chief Justice Marshall's historic, precedent-setting decision in this case early in the 19th century, by which his interpretation of the interstate commerce clause of the Constitution extended federal power over the regulation of commerce at the expense of states' rights, thereby laying the foundation for an American "common market" long before Europe adopted it.

The Incredible Bread Machine Film (1975; 32 min.; World Research, Inc./University of Illinois Film Center) Series of fast-paced vignettes portrays effects of excessive government intervention. The producers state that the goal of the film is to motivate thought and to challenge preconceived concepts of the market system and its interlocking relationship with individual freedom.

Inflation File (1978; 25 min.; World Research, Inc./University of Illinois Film Center) Explains basic economic principles comparing a free market system with other forms. Through case histories, dramatizations, group discussions and animation, the film examines the role of government in personal freedom, inflation, supply/demand cycles, and other basic economic concepts.

The Lady and the Stock Exchange (1975; 28 min.; New York Stock Exchange/University of Wisconsin-Madison) Tells the story of a family's first investment experience in order to illustrate how the stock exchange works, what brokers do, and how to make sensible investments.

Mad River—Hard Times In Humboldt County (1982; 54 min.; KCSM/Penn State Audio Visual Services) A portrait of a rural northern California community facing environmental and economic disaster when 300 workers lose their jobs at the Mad River Plywood Mill. Examines the conflict between environmentalists who want to regulate the timber industry and lumber corporations who want to protect their business interests, and points out the heartaches and hardships of the workers and families caught in the middle.

Money Story (1977;17 min.; Federal Reserve Board of Governors) Explains the daily operation of the Federal Reserve Bank. Discusses currency and coin circulation, check collecting and clearing, and the role of the individual Federal Reserve Bank president, his staff and directors. System policies and decisions are also discussed, particularly

OSHA (1981; 25 min.; U.S. Department of Labor/AFL-CIO Film Division) Explains how OSHA was set up to stem the tide of disease, injury and death, and what worker rights are under the law. Explains how NIOSH conducts tests, how standards are set, how OSHA inspectors come into the workplace to interview workers and investigate complaints. Workers talk about specific health hazards in textile mills and foundries, and how their plants are forced to comply with the law.

Scarcity and Planning (The People on Market Street Series) (1980;17 min.; Walt Disney Productions/UCLA) Explores the concept of labor as a marketable item. Discusses the influence of wages on the number of workers an employer will hire and the factors that cause wages for a particular occupation to rise or fall. Examines the economic problem of organizing and coordinating the work of many people to produce desired goods.

Search for Stability: Money talks series #2 (1962; 30 min.;Carousel Films) Seeking means by which wild fluctuations in prices, employment and production can be alleviated. Explains how money can play a part, and how the federal reserve bank can influence stability.

The Wall Street Connection (1985; 40 min.; WCBS/California Newsreel) A fast-paced, highly interesting look at Wall Street—the frenetic high-stakes culture of New York's stock and commodity traders. Examines the dynamics and implications of how 98 percent of the nation's capital is bought and sold via speculation. Focuses on concern by some experts that the "casino-like" trading by large institutional investors will lead the nation to "economic suicide." A highly acclaimed film.

You'll never shop alone (1983; 30 min.; KSTP-TV Mpls./St. Paul) Short news pieces on consumerism.

1.B. APPROACHES TO MANAGEMENT

Animal Crackers (1989;15 mins; Cally Custis Committee) This film helps managers remember basic management fundamentals when they are on the firing line and do not have time to review their seminar notes or management books.

Managers with Impact: Versatile and Inconsistence (1988; 32 min.; MTI Film & Video) Effective leaders are those who can and do change their management styles to meet new challenges. Case study analyzes what qualities define a manager with impact. Includes instructor manual.

Profile of a Manager (1989; National Educational Media; Britannica Films) This program depicts the people problems that can come with increasing responsibilities. Emphasizing the need for continuing training in basic management skills, this video presents critical incidents in the life of a manager.

So You Want To Be A Manager: An Historical Perspective (1986; 35 min.; Salenger Educational Media) How can productivity be increased? That has been the major question facing managers since the first person hired someone to help perform a task. And with that question, management theory was born. This film traces the history of management theory from its early exclusive concern with the task, through Hawthorne and its emphasis on people, to today's more sophisticated and eclectic concerns with task, people motivation, and leadership styles.

Theory Z: An Alternative Management Style (1980; 95 min.; Chrysler Learning, Inc./University Film & Video) Explores the success of Japanese business in terms of the increasing rate of productivity. Among the major ideas presented are: gaps in productivity between Japanese and American organizations; characteristics of Japanese and American organizations, including lifestyles and career paths; and Theory Z management style, its evolution, implications and applications for the manager of the future.

1.C. ENVIRONMENT

Asbestos: The Way to Dusty Death (1978; 51 min.; ABC-TV/University of Illinois Film Center) As little as one-half day of exposure to asbestos dust can lead to irreversible lung damage and to several types of cancer. One of the patients interviewed in this film was exposed to the dust only when she, as a child, embraced her father on his return from work. Now, a young mother of three, she is dying of asbestos-caused disease. Asserts that these dangers were known and deliberately ignored by people in responsible positions in government and industry, and that this practice continues even now.

Corporate America and the Environment (1990; 2 hrs; Governors State University; Oklahoma State University) A two-hour version of the original satellite videoconference. Segments include national leaders from corporate, environmental and political sectors, positive examples and case studies of corporate responses to pressing environmental concerns. Includes: increasing regulation on all government levels; proposals for environmental audits; the growth of consumer demand for "green" products; a movement in the investment community toward environmentally conscious investing; and enhancing profits through conservation policies.

Energy: What About Tomorrow? (1978; 21 min.; United Nations/Barr Films) Explains how shortages of oil and natural gas, rising costs of power, and world population growth have combined to stimulate an intensive search for alternate energy sources for the next century.

Energy Crunch: The Best Way Out (1980; 52 min.; CBS News/Carousel) Host Dan Rather shows how the U.S. can eliminate 98 percent of its foreign oil imports by 1990 by applying existing technologies and common sense to improve efficiency. Details what can be done: insulation and leak-plugging in homes; computer-run energy management systems for business and industry; improved building design; more efficient lighting; cogeneration; auto improvement; and use of solar energy. Looks at Portland, Oregon's successes in cutting energy consumption city-wide.

The Global Energy Game (1978; 34 min.; University of Illinois Film Center) Clarifies the complex economic tactics of international oil producers and consumers. The impact of multinational oil maneuvering on jobs and the standard of living in the U.S. is emphasized as a group of six players at a simulated "game" of international economic survival reveal how the motives and positions of each affect all the others. Host Adam Smith presents the narration in three parts: Petroleum Power Politics; Solving the Import-Export Dilemma; and Inflation and the Declining Dollar.

Greenhouse Crisis: The American Response (1989; 11 min.; Union of Concerned Science) An introductory video on the link between energy use and global warming. Explains why carbon dioxide emissions from the burning of fossil fuels is believed to be the principal cause of global warming.

Hazardous Waste: The Search for Solutions (1984; 30 min.; AFL-CIO Film Division) Focuses on what people can do to protect communities from the effect of toxic chemicals that have been dumped in some 14,000 known waste sites around the nation. In the absence of strong government action to protect the environment, citizen groups have emerged to organize for action. Focuses on different approaches which citizens of five states have developed and created the background for a discussion of lobbying, coalition building and right to know laws.

Man and His Environment (1978; 28 min.; National Audio Visual Center) Man's efforts to stabilize the delicate balances of the ecosphere are illustrated here in segments featuring architecture, industrial and urban conservation, solar energy, and working models of small-scale rural self-sufficiency. Mixing lyrical photography and scientific fact, this program points to several areas of conservation research that have far-reaching implications.

PCB (1979; 57 min.; WGBM-TV/University of Illinois Film Center) Explains the mechanism of chemical pollution of the environment by nonbiodegradable substances which have been proven to cause cancer and birth defects. Ninety percent of toxic waste containing such elements is not illegally dumped. Covers the problems involved in identifying legal dumping sites, recounting known cases. Commentary by Barry Commoner.

Plastics Recycling Today: A growing Resource (1988; 12 min.; Society/Plastic Industry) Deals with the industry of recycling plastics in today's world as a resource for better waste management.

Race to save the Planet - Parts 5 & 6 (1990; 120 min.; WGBH-TV, Boston) Part 5: Remnants of Eden - Protecting the diversity of living organisms while addressing the needs of growing human populations. Part 6: More for Less - Search for new way to use energy efficiently.

A Short Film on Solar Energy (1979;10 min.; University of Illinois Film Center) Roles of the sun—past, present and future—in relation to the earth and its inhabitants, are filmed and commented on. First, the sun's contribution, through the water cycle and the nourishment of plants, to evolution and the build-up of fossil fuels is delineated. An animated sequence follows, in which the problem of the unbridled consumption of fossil fuel energy is graphically pinpointed in an indirect (but not subtle) plea for conservation. A third section presents brief facts about solar collectors, photovoltaic cells, the advantages of solar over other types of energy sources, and the potential for future applications of solar energy. Academy Award nominee.

Technology and Values: The Energy Connection (1979;19 min.; University of Illinois Film Center) An animated parable concerning the almost frivolous use of natural resources to fuel production of—in this case—propeller-topped beanies. Stresses the need to reevaluate the worth of our products and activities, particularly in view of the growing population and energy demands of future generations. Points out that the development of new technologies using water, wind, solar, tidal geothermal, and nuclear power have not been perfected and will require political and economic incentives to do so.

Thine Is the Power: A Citizen's Guide to the Nuclear Energy Debate (1977; 52 min.; University of Illinois Film Center) A Canadian study of the pros and cons, a summary of the statistics and a hint at some of the implications of the proliferation of nuclear power plants. Shows the problem of nuclear waste and the results of one known accident in which the victims were so radioactive that the ambulance, as well as the bodies, became nuclear waste. Recommends alternatives in the renewable energy area: sun, wind, and tide, as decentralized and less socially vulnerable.

Business Ethics (1988; 30 mins; MTI; Coronet/MTI Film & Video) An exploration of creative ways to handle business dilemmas. Designed to help managers develop skills needed to effectively identify and deal with ethical dilemmas when they arise. Pt 1 - Out on a Limb. Pt 2 - The Whistleblower. Pt 3 - A Question of Loyalty.

Can a Corporation have a Conscience? (1990; 116 min.; CST) Leaders from business, education and the law meet on the St. Thomas campus to discuss the ethical issues often confronted by a corporation and their responses to these ethical challenges.

Corporations and Conscience: "The Business File" #10 (1987; 25 min.; Harvard Business School) Explores the topic of business social responsibility and ethics.

Decision Making: A Matter of Values and Ethics (1986; 25 mins Salenger Films) An in-office scenario illustrates the roles values do, or should, play in business decision-making.

Decision Making (1980; 20 min.; International Cinemedia, Ltd./University Film & Video) Ethical questions and obligations of the employer-employee relationship are explored with on-the-job decisions affecting attitude and environment of a working situation. Problems of employee theft, waste reduction and time loss are considered.

Ethical Analysis in Management: Some Tools #1 (1987; 27 min.; Harvard Business School) Discusses ethical analysis and trends in management. Includes instructor manual.

Ethics In American Business (1988; PBS;Coronet/MTI Film & Video) This video provides suggestions for formulating a legal code of business ethics.

The Environment: Business and Social Responsibility (1985; 30 mins; Dallas County community College and Kent Publishing) One segment of a 28 part program to introduce the viewer to the fundamentals of business.

Human Experimentation: Process of Ethical Decisionmaking (120 min.; Georgetown University) Lecture by Dr. Veatch. With Jack W. Provonsha, M.D.

Marketplace Ethics: Issues in Sales and Marketing (1990; 29 min.; Ethics Resource Center) Designed to aid commercial businesses in understanding their ethical responsibilities.

Matter of Judgement, A: Ethics at Work Series (1986; 30 min.; Ethics Resource Center) First of the "Ethics at Work" series deals with conflicts of interest.

Values and Decisions: The Roger Berg Story (1977;16 mins; Salenger Educational Media) Explores a possible conflict of interest situation. Through the dilemmas faced by Roger Berg, a young executive, it illustrates the role values play in the decision-making process and shows how values, in turn, influence the way people deal with the consequences of their decisions.

1.E. INTERNATIONALMANAGEMENT

The Age of Uncertainty: The Big Corporation (1976; 59 min.; BBC/University of Illinois Film Center) Galbraith creates a fictional multinational corporation, "U.G.E." to illustrate the typical origin and growth, development and repercussions, of the Western big corporation, presenting it as "the institution that most changes our lives." Compared and contrasted with actual footage of operations at Philips, and by interviews with businessmen at Esalen Institute.

An American Valley (1979;12 min.; U.S. Dept. of Labor/AFL-CIO Film Division) Discusses what happens to workers who lose their jobs because of the flood of imports coming into the United States. Explains the Trade Adjustment Assistance program that provides financial benefits for workers whose jobs have been destroyed or hours of work reduced, and how they qualify for benefits under the Trade Act of 1974.

The Colonel Comes to Japan (The Enterprise Series) (1981; 30 min.; WGBH/Learning Corporation of America) Looks at Japan and one outfit that has been able to penetrate its fierce, competitive restaurant market. Kentucky Fried Chicken was asked by the Japanese conglomerate Mitsubishi to participate in a joint fast-food venture. Mitsubishi provided Kentucky Fried Chicken with the poultry and led the Colonel through the maze of Japanese bureaucracy, and ever since, Kentucky Fried Chicken has been netting a solid profit. Shows one Tokyo outlet and the difference between the restaurants in Japan and the United States.

Controlling Interest: The World of the Multinational Corporation (1978; 45 min.; California Newsreel/University of Illinois Film Center) Using examples of Brazil, Chile, and United States, this film reveals the connections among such phenomena as economic development, runaway shops, world hunger, human rights violations, U.S. foreign policy, and the growing power of the multinational corporation. Includes interviews with major corporate figures. Raises questions about the compatibility of their pursuit of profit and pressing social needs.

Doing Business In the Pacific Rim (1990; 3 hrs; 2 tapes; National University Teleconference Network; Oklahoma State University) Intended to sharpen understanding of emerging U.S. commercial opportunities in Japan, Republic of Korea and Taiwan, plus provide a forum for identifying possible competitive linkages throughout the region.

Enterprise: The Buck stops in Brazil (1983; 30 min.; WGBH-TV, Boston) A surprising look at international banking and the specter of default.

Enterprise: Hong Kong dresses up (1983; 30 min.; WGBH-TV, Boston) S. T. King's strategy of offering fewer goods at higher quality to deal with the quota restrictions given an incisive look into economic planning within the freest of free-market economics.

European Integration 1992: Implications for American Business (1988; 31/2 hrs; 2 tapes; National University Teleconference Network; Oklahoma State University) Leading officials from business and government discuss the impending economic integration of Europe from both the U.S. and the European points of view, with emphasis on how American business can prepare for this event.

Europe 1992: A new American Challenge (1990; 120 min.; Oklahoma State University) What challenges will be faced by businesses producing in Europe after European integration? How will the business climate change? Will we see "Fortress Europe?"

Europe 1992: Making the European Market: Threatening for U.S. Exports? (1989; 120 min.; Oklahoma State University) Purpose of teleconference: to provide an introduction to the european community as a political and economic entity.

Managing Cultural Differences (1984; 30 mins; 6 progs; Gulf Publishing Company; International Training Company) This program gives an in depth look at how cultural differences can affect business and management practices.

Managing the Overseas Assignment (1988; 30 mins; Encyclopedia Britannica Educational Corp.; Britannica Films) Trying to complete a business deal and figure out foreign customs can be a tricky maneuver to pull off. This program deals with these issues.

One Man's Multinational (The Enterprise Series) (1981; 30 min.; WGBH/Learning Corporation of America, UCLA) Traces the story of Thomas Bata and his multi-national shoe manufacturing empire. One out of every three pairs of shoes sold in the non-Communist world bears the Bata name. Bata has 100 subsidiaries in every part of the globe and is the largest private employer in Kenya. Also takes a look at his philanthropic activities.

Career Escalator: Education and Job Competition (1982; 28 min.; LCA/Instructional Media Services, University of Utah) Examines the pressure that exists for the Japanese to graduate from an elite university to ensure a life of security with a top corporation. Explains this phenomenon through the lives of a student cramming for his University of Tokyo entrance exams and a senior executive of Mitsubishi Corporation.

Doing Business in Japan (1990; 62 min.; KCTS-TV, Seattle) Kan looks at the business climate in Japan.

Doing Business In Japan: Negotiating a Contract (1976; 34 min.; Vision Associates, Inc.) Provides a careful analysis of the negotiation process, exploring such complex elements as language and communication, culture and pragmatic disparities of background, social setting and entertainment, use of the interpreter, and a variety of other critical points essential to successfully doing business in Japan.

Inside Japan: Industry and Management (1990; 25 mins; Centre Productions Inc.) A behind the scenes look at Japanese industry is provided.

The Japan They Don't Talk About (1986; 52 min.; NBC/Films, Inc.) This special NBC White Paper documentary examines the little-known aspects of modern Japan that are a far cry from the popular perceptions about the country held today. Among the factors explored are the networks of "sweat shops" that support the country's top companies, Japan's housing problems, and the lack of care of Japan's elderly. An excellent, especially insightful look into the "dark" side of the Japanese miracle.

Japan 2000: Global Perspectives (1989; 27 min.; Nebraskans for Public TV) An engaging view of the Japanese people as they work to define and deal with their country's leadership role in the global community of the 21st century.

Japan 2000: The View from within (1989; 27 min.; Nebraskans for Public TV) A look at Japan's changing roles for women, at its aging population, and at economic restructuring and regional development from the perspective of the Japanese people.

The Kyocera Experiment (The Enterprise Serles) (1981; 30 min.; WGBH/Learning Corporation of America) Examines the Kyocera Company, a Japanese firm located in San Diego that employs American workers. Details such Japanese management techniques as consensus, permanent employment, "quality circles," and worker responsibility and their application at this plant. Also focuses on tension between Japanese managers and American salesmen, caused by management's misunderstanding of American sales approaches.

Lifetime Employment Conditions of Industrial Work Life (1982; 28 min.; LCA/Instructional Media Services, University of Utah) Examines through the work-life of an assembly line employee at Mazda Automobiles, Japan's famous "Theory Z" methods used to ensure a consistently high level of quality and productivity. On VHS video only.

Lifetime employment: Human Face of Japan Series (1982; 28 min.; Learning Corp. of America) Dependent on importation of natural resources for 120 million population, Japan must rely on manufactured imports for economic survival. Focuses on "Theory Z" to ensure high quality and productivity.

Loosing the War with Japan (1992; 88 min.; Public Broadcasting) Examines the successful strategies Japan is using to win American markets and the reason U. S. Companies seem unable to compete.

Made In Japan, Part 2: Business Practices and Changing Lifestyles (1981; 22 min.; University of Illinois Film Center) Identifies elements in business philosophy and in business-government interaction which Japanese managers feel contribute to their success. Japanese industrialists do not understand government as an adversary, but as a joint venture and a research and development resource. Since neither the individual nor the firm is as heavily taxed as in America, more capital is available for reinvestment in improving equipment and procedures. Americans living and working in Japan comment.

On The Line (1981; 37 min.; King Arthur Productions/University Film & Video) Follows the actual experiences of four American workers who visited a Japanese factory, immersed themselves in its day-to-day life, and intensively examined its methods and operations. It portrays their reactions and discoveries, showing in powerful and compelling terms why they returned to their jobs in the U.S. determined to work smarter and with greater pride.

100 Million Varied Consumers (1979; 20 min.; Japan Trade Center/Association Films) This film offers an insightful educational tour of Japanese tastes and modes of life through everyday activities of the Japanese consumer. Scenes include department stores and supermarkets, fashion, housing, food, numerous consumer products, leisure and recreational facilities, all illustrating how East and West live in harmony in Japan. Shows the great market potential in Japan with its 100 million consumers and their insatiable desires for something new and different.

People and Productivity: We learn from the Japanese (1987; 28 min.; Encyclopaedia Britannica) Key ideas from the Japanese business philosophy on how attitudes improve productivity and employee relations. Business leaders, both Japanese and American express views on this approach to industrial production.

The "Salary Man": Japan's White-Collar Worker (198?; 28 min.; University of Illinois Film Center) Documents a typical day in the life of the average Japanese office worker. There are six million of them in Tokyo, many of whom commute by bicycle to the suburbs. Discusses the several styles of lunch-hour and after-hour activity, and shows preferred family amusements for weekends.

Tokyo in Tennessee (1982;15 min.; Carousel Films) At a time when the U. S. auto industry laid off 300,000 workers and suffered record-low sales figures, and the quality of American-made cars was in question, the Nissan Motor Corporation of Japan built a truck plant in Tennessee. Focuses on a group of American autoworkers sent by Nissan to Japan for special training in the Japanese work ethic, which emphasizes teamwork instead of a boss-worker relationship that often results in mistrust. Produced for CBS "60 minutes."

Tomorrow & Yesterday: Modern Technology & Ancient Culture (1982; LCA/ Instructional Media Services, University of Utah) Demonstrates that even as they play a leading role in the technological age, the Japanese continue to observe the traditions of their ancient civilization. Shows through the daily events in the lives of the Kimuras, a modern family headed by a design engineer in a large construction company, how the two roles of old and new meet.

Working Couple Urban Family (1983; 28 min.; Instructional Media Services, University of Utah) Shows that Japanese workers are subject to the strains of urban life as illustrated in this story of two Tokyo residents; pharmaceutical clerk, Mr. Yokoyama and his wife, a shopkeeper. Demonstrates urban living also has its rewards in the richness of leisure and community activities.

Yen for Harmony: Japanese Managers Try Their Style in North America (1978; 26 min.; Cinema Guild) Participatory management, consensus decision making, and lifetime employment are the basis of the Japanese system. Panasonic plant in Japan shows the system in action. Will these management methods work in a Western society? The film answers this question with sequences filmed in operations set up in the YKK Zipper and Japan Airlines companies.

Note: For additional films on Japan, see the "Managing Productivity" section in Part 4.

Can You Have It All? Do You Want It All? (1980; 43 min.; Penn State UniversityDependent on importation of natural resources for 120 million population, Japan must Audio Visual Services) A two-part videotape designed to help young people think concurrently about their career and family plans. In part one, fourrely on manufactured imports for economic survival. Focuses on "Theory Z" to ensure women, each of whom has made different choices, discuss how to combine andhigh quality and productivity. manage career, marriage, and family. In part two, four men, each representing a different situation, discuss the new roles they are finding themselves in as women increasingly choose to pursue careers. Only on 3/4" VHS

Moore Report: You've come a long Way, maybe? (1981; 60 min.; WCCO-TV, Minneapolis) A profile of the world of the working woman with a special emphasis on the controversial subject of "comparable worth."

The Power Pinch: Sexual Harassment In the Workplace (1980; 26 min.; University ofExamines the successful strategies Japan is using to win American markets and the Iowa Media Library) When sexual harassment invades the workplace, womenreason U. S. Companies seem unable to compete. employees become targets for a serious and illegal power play. This film explores this problem and illustrates behavior which is defined as sexually harassing, including more subtle forms. It explains the underlying causes for such behavior and shows what all involved parties—management and employees—can do to prevent its occurrence. Three victims of work-related sexual harassment incidents discuss the emotional and economic repercussions. Interviews with prominent business executives and EEOC trainers emphasize the legal and economic ramifications.

Pregnant But Equal: The Fight for Maternity Benefits (1982; 24 min.; Penn State University Audio Visual Services) The Pregnancy Discrimination Act, passed by Congress in 1978, made it illegal for employers to discriminate against pregnant workers. This film states that some companies are failing to comply with the law and that many workers have inadequate benefits and are not aware of their rights. Focuses on one group of factory workers and their fight for maternity benefits.

Protection of Equality? Women's Rights In the Workplace (1983; 35 min.; Penn State University Audio Visual Services) An historical documentary about protective labor legislation and its impact on women from 1850 to the early 1980s. Illustrates the need for protective legislation throughout the history of labor in America, but also suggests that by making protection a women's issue, women were deprived of occupational opportunity. Commentary by Eleanor Smeal, president of the National Organization for Women.

Sexual Harassment - Taking new Aim at an old Problem (1985; 16 min.; Oklahoma State University) Sexual harassment is any unwanted attention of a sexual nature from someone in the workplace or classroom that creates discomfort or interferes with the job or academic performance.

That's Not In My Job Description. Sexual Harassment Serles (1981; 19 min.; American Media Inc./University Film & Video) Demonstrates what sexual harassment is and explores the many serious consequences (declining morale, loss of civil rights and sexual integrity, declining productivity, etc.) This shorter format covers a broader range of harassment than other films, including name-sex and older women-younger man situations. The program also demonstrates individuals taking action to fight harassment problems.

A Threat to Your Profits. Sexual Harassment Serles (1981; 19 min.; American Media Inc./University Film & Video) Focuses on corporate manager and supervisor responsibilities. Sexual harassment can cost a great deal in lost profits, low productivity, employee turnover, and litigation fees. The film emphasize prevention as the key to eliminating sexual harassment on the job. The program is designed to create an awareness of potential problems.

Turning Point - The Willmar 8...A Follow-Up (1983; 60 min.; Public Broadcasting Sys.) A follow-up on the eight women who filed discrimination charges against a bank and got fired.

Why Not a Woman (1976; 26 min.; Pennsylvania Commission for Women/Penn State Audio Visual Services) Documentary about women in blue-collar jobs — welding, carpentry, appliance repair, mechanics. Shows attitudes of their male coworkers, teachers, and supervisors.

Women at Work: Change, Choice, Challenge (1978;19 min.; University of Iowa Media Library) A dialogue with seven women, expressed in counterpoint with actual on-the-job scenes, reveals their attitudes about their work, training and personal roles. An oil worker, nurse, jockey, locomotive engineer, surgeon, judge and candidate for Congress all have strong reasons for their career choices and different views of their work-family-community relationships.

Women In Management: Threat or Opportunity? (1976; 26 min.; CRM/McGraw-Hill Films/University of Illinois Film Center) Using the Weyerhauser Company as a model, this film examines the issues as aspiring women in management roles. Stereotypes, pay scales, potential for advancement and other issues are discussed.

Women in the Corporation: On a Par, Not a Pedestal (1977; 26 min.; Cinema Guild) Over 60 percent of the home office employees of Connecticut General Insurance Company were women, holding clerical positions. They felt they were not appreciated by management and that opportunities for advancement were limited. Faced with this pressing situation, management instituted a program emphasizing affirmative action. Today, Connecticut General's program of in-house workshops and training sessions is considered by many experts in the field to be one of the most extensive and effective.

Women In the Workplace (1984; 18 min.; Penn State University Audio Visual Services) Filmed lecture by Carole Keller explains the twelve basic behaviors of the troubled female employee, pointing out employee and employer barriers in discussions about problems. Emphasizes identification of alcohol and drug abuse indicators among working women and discusses the subtle differences between troubled male and female workers.

Women of Steel (1985; 30 min.; Mon Valley Media/AFL-CIO Film Division) Tells the story of four women who escaped low-paying dead end jobs through an affirmative action program in the steel mills in the 70's. Just as their lives begin to improve, the women lose their jobs in the 1980 recession. To support their families they are forced to return to the low-paying pink collar jobs they thought they had left behind.

The Workplace Hustle (1980; 30 min.; University of Iowa Media Library) A film about the sexual harassment of working women that is designed to inform, motivate and sensitize. Ed Asner is spokesperson, exploring the issues in a direct and candid manner. Features Lin Farley, an expert in the field and author of the book, *Sexual Shakedown.*

Very Enterprising Women (1980; 15 min.; Small Business Administration/ National Audio Visual Center) The chances of any new business surviving more than five years are one in four—but the five women featured in this motivational documentary have succeeded against these odds. Their energy, imagination, and hard work have led to accomplishments in enterprises as varied as market research and truck farming.

2.A. SCIENTIFIC MANAGEMENT————————————————————————————————

Clockwork (1982; 25 min.; Eric Brietbart/California Newsreel, Penn State Audio Visual
Services, University of Iow Media Library)
Excellent documentary on Frederick Taylor and the development of scientific
management. Includes rare original footage of Frank Gilbreth's use of cinematography
in time-motion studies, reducing complex tasks into frame-by-frame elements.
Documents and discusses present day manifestations of scientific management such
as assembly-line production.

Frederlck Taylor & Scientific Management (1984; 10 min.; Salenger Educational Media)
Although many organizations adopted Frederick Taylor's methods, organized labor
strongly objected to Taylor's proposals. Because of labor's reactions, a congressional
investigation attempted to determine whether Taylor's Scientific Management was a
valid contribution to labor-management relations or just another fancy name for work
speed-up. This film explains Taylor's principles of scientific management and
dramatizes the main issues of the congressional hearing. The film also explores the
relevance of Taylor's concepts for today's managers.

Original Films of Frank B. Gilbreth (1968; B&W; 26 min.; University of Connecticut
Erickson Memorial Film Library) This film is essentially a summary of work analysis
films which were taken by Frank B. Gilbreth between 1910 and 1924 showing a
number of industrial operations from which the time motion study technique was
developed.

Time Study for Union Members (1977; 30 min.; Pennsylvania State University
Television/Penn State Audio Visual Services) Outlines the basic steps required in
establishing job standards by means of stopwatch time study. The steps are illustrated
when a radial drill press operator tells the shop steward that he can't make the rate
set for the job and the steward reviews the stopwatch time study procedure.

A Worker's Introduction To Time Study (1976; 31 min.; Pennsylvania State University
Television/Penn State Audio Visual Services) Shows the basic steps used in
stopwatch time-motion study. Example of a radial drill press operator who feels that
the standard for his operation does not allow for sufficient earnings. Standard is
reevaluated, with explanations of every step.

2.B. DECISION MAKING

Abilene Paradox (1984; 27 min.; CRM/Instructional Media Services, University of Utah) Uses a series of four vignettes to describe the symptom of the Abilene Paradox, probe the reasons behind the participant's behaviors, and offers strategies for eliminating this form of collective decision-making confusion. Points out the paradox occurs when participants in a group decision agree without communicating their reservations to others in the group.

Creative Problem Solving: How to Get Better Ideas (1979; 28 min.; University of Nebraska, IMS, University of low) Creativity is often viewed as an endowment of the elite few. This film shows how the act of creative problem solving can be developed in each individual, but is often inhibited by criticism, or lack of self-confidence. Animated sequences explore the psychological underpinnings of creativity according to Freud, and then to the "split brain theory." Professor James Adams suggests ways of implementing the dictum "the best way to have a good idea is to have lots of ideas."

Creativity: The Only Way To Fly (1983; B&W; 7 min.; Salenger/Instructional Media Services, University of Utah) Helps recognize some of the characteristics of the creative individual and identifies the characteristics of the environment needed to nurture creativity. Uses humorous newsreel film clips of airplane inventions to point out the need for organizations to draw upon and encourage what may be their most valuable resource: the creative person.

Dealing with Decisions, Part 1: Self-awareness (1982;13 min.; UCLA) Stresses the importance and significance of decisions in determining the quality of life. Because of the pressures society exerts, self-knowledge is a critical factor in the decision-making process. Underscores the importance of accurately defining goals to be reached or problems to be solved in terms of personal priorities. Slide presentation.

Dealing with Decisions, Part 2: Information and Alternatives (1982;15 min.; UCLA) Discusses the four essential elements of the decision-making process—imagination in considering alternatives, careful assessment of possible outcomes (rewards vs. risks), systematic acquisition of information, and critical judgment of what is and is not truthful. Points out the pitfalls of "either-or" decision making. Slide presentation.

Dealing with Decisions, Part 3: Risks and Pressures (1982; 14 min.; UCLA) Depicts realistic and typical problems which require decision. Dramatizes the weight of peer pressure as an influence on decision-making. Emphasizes that while every decision carries a degree of risk, bypassing the decision making process by letting others make the final choice is an unsatisfactory solution. Slide presentation.

Decision Analysis (1988; 20 programs; MIT; Massachusetts Institute of Technology) Business managers are told how they can make the decisions that will be best for their company.

Decision Making (1982; 20 min.; Instructional Media Services, University of Utah) Explores the moral and ethical questions and obligations of the employer-employee relationship together with many of the on-the-job decisions that can affect the attitude and environment of a working situation. Discusses openly the problems of pilfering and theft, reducing waste, losing time, setting priorities and personal conflict versus job requirements.

Decision Making: Alternatives and Information (1982;17 min.; University of Illinois Film Center) Uses the dramatic/satiric format of a "crisis intervention team" to whisk newly promoted supervisor Frank Webster off to "Decisions, Unlimited" to be taught skills which will enable him to make up his mind. Set up as a sort of laboratory, Decisions Unlimited puts people through listing and prioritizing alternatives, collecting information, and predicting outcomes, to the point where they are ready to take action to get out of their dilemmas.

Decision Making: Outcomes and Action (1982;18 min.; University of Illinois Film Center) Decisions Unlimited's 'crisis intervention team' focuses on David Stanley, who has been asked to recommend someone to fill the job out of which he has been promoted. David learns, with their coaching, how to use information in predicting outcomes and assessing probabilities. Assists viewers in grasping techniques for establishing and narrowing alternatives to the point of action.

Decision Making Skills Part 1,2,3 (1979, Guidance Associates, Inc.) Part 1: Values. Part 2: Information. Part 3: Strategies.

Decision Making: Values and Goals (1982;17 min.; University of Illinois Film Center) Teaches initial steps in decision making (articulating and prioritizing values, choosing a goal). Uses the format of an unorthodox counseling center set up as a lab, to which a 'crisis invention team' brings a young lady who is having trouble deciding between two jobs. Viewers learn methods with her as she sorts through the possibilities.

Decisions (1981; 28 min.; McGraw-Hill Films/University of low Media Library) Examines the decision-making process from both a practical and psychological point of view, analyzing the reasons why decisions can be difficult to make. By making viewers aware of the emotions that can be involved in important decisions, this film prepares them for the anxiety that may be ahead and teaches the self-confidence that is necessary for making decisions in a rational, orderly way.

Decisions! Decisions! Decisions! (1984;18 min.; University of Illinois Film Center) Enumerates effective steps toward intelligent decision making, and illustrates with vignettes wherein the young person's decision is of increasing complexity. Ranges from a decision of whether to babysit or go to a party, to a decision regarding which parent the child should choose to live with in a divorce situation.

Effective Decisions - Effective Executive Series #4 (1968; 22 min.; BNA Communications) Stresses the importance of postponing decision-making until dissent, opinions and facts have been presented and both sides of the problem analyzed. No case against a decision is no case for one.

How to Take the Right Risk - Manager & Org. Series # 5 (1977; 21 min.; BNA Communications) Drucker outlines the steps you should take before making a decision, discusses how to determine if a decision is needed at all, describes the importance of feedback and defines the goals to be achieved.

Problem Solving - A Process for Managers (1989; 20 mins; National Educational Media; Britannica Films) This program introduces managers to a practical, efficient six-step problem solving method applicable to most management problems.

Problem Solving Strategies: The Synectics Approach (1979; 27 min.; McGraw-Hill Films/low State University) A documentary distillation of an actual Problem Solving Laboratory conducted at Synectics Incorporated, in which viewers are given a simple set of innovative strategies that can be used to stimulate organizational creativity and streamline problem solving. The techniques used in Synectics are applicable to both individual and group idea-generating sessions in a variety of business, industrial and organizational areas.

ZEA: A Study in Perception (1990; 5 min.; National Film Board Canada) Illustrates that each person sees reality from a slightly different perspective. Relates perceptual insights to managerial problem solving in work situations. Includes instructor manual.

2.C. PLANNING

Applied Strategic Planning: Executive Briefing (1986; 45 mins; University Associates Inc.) From an executive point of view, an instructional tape about Pfeiffer's ASP model as it pertains to business organization.

Competitive Strategy - Tape 1 (1988; 20 min.; Harvard Business School) Segment 1 - Industry analysis. Discusses the five forces that determine the nature of competition and profitability in an industry. Includes instructor manuals.

Focus the Future (1989; 27 mins; BNA Communications) Through vignettes and commentary, this video illustrates why long-term objectives are needed, what they should consist of, who should handle them and the importance of getting answers to the question, "What will we be doing five years from now?"

Managing Discontinuity (1989; BNA Communications) The social, political, and economic upheavals we are encountering today, such as energy and environmental situations, confirm Peter's Drucker's contention that management must anticipate, prepare for and look beyond sharp breaks in trends.

Michael Porter on Competitive Strategy (1989; 50 mins; Harvard Business School) The professor at HBS gives a few tips that will keep your business on top of its competition.

Planning (1971; 10 mins; Resources for Education and Management) Short and long-range planning are discussed. Keys to participative planning are presented.

Planning & Goal Setting - Manager and Org. Series #4 (1977; 22 min.; BNA Communications) Drucker proves that planning and goal setting are as important for individual managers and small organizations as for large ones.

Planning and Policy Making (1978; 60 mins; Columbia Pictures; Exec-U-Service Associates) A look at what a manager can do to improve his or her contribution to the planning and policy making process. A concept of structuring boss and subordinate relationships to achieve goals is established.

Planning, Organizing and Controlling, Part 1(1975; 21 min.; BNA/UCLA) Points out common sources of contingencies in business planning and tells how to identify them before they happen, what patterns to look for and how to distinguish between general and specific contingencies. Gives tips on budgeting time, including the scheduling of dull, uninteresting work.

Planning, Organizing and Controlling, Part 2 (1975; 21 min.; BNA/UCLA) Looks at the actions supervisors must take to prepare employees to handle all sorts of contingencies. Shows how to reinforce fundamentals, prevent the erosion of training and discusses ways to motivate employees to perform dull, tedious jobs correctly.

Planning, Organizing, and Controlling, Part 3 (1975; 21 min.; BNA/UCLA) Centers on the critical decision of whether or not a supervisor should intervene in a contingency and, if so, when. Outlines active steps a supervisor can take to prevent a contingency from getting out of hand.

After all, You're the Supervisor (1979; 20 min.; Rondtable Productions) Illustrates the typical problems encountered by some first-time supervisors who have been promoted from the ranks.

Building a Working Team - Two Person Communication #3 (29 min.; BNA Communications) Talks about being organized, how to build a winning team, and about control and relationships. Explains the use of different forms of control.

Changing Organizations: Designing for People and Purpose (1978; 26 min.; Hobel-Leiterman Productions/Penn State University Audio Visual Services) Professor Jay Lorsch of Harvard University illustrates the theories of organizational structure and, in particular, his own contingency theory of task-organization-people "fit." Contrast between those organizations involved in highly specific tasks with immediate feedback and those involved in ambiguous tasks with long-term feedback is shown in scenes at Manufacturers Hanover Trust and General Foods.

Participative Management: We learn from the Japanese (1984; 28 min.; Encyclopaedia Britannica) Video Tape exemplifying the Japanese and the way they conduct business/management. Case study examines Nissan's small truck plant in Smyrna, Tenn. and workers exchange. Includes instructor manual.

Managing Projects (1988; 24 mins; British Broadcasting Corporation; Films Inc.) Managers are shown how to break down one large assignment into several smaller ones so it will be more manageable.

Participative Management (1984; 28 min.; Brigham Young University, Audiovisual Services) Using Nissan as a real-life example, this film shows how participative management works to create a family spirit based on cooperation and the vested interest of all employees in the company's success.

Staffing for Strength - Effective Executive Series #5 (1968; 30 min.; BNA Communications) The effective organization is one that can make common people achieve uncommon performance. Drucker considers the problems of demands on subordinates, and how they may better achieve these demands.

Through the Hoop: Corporate Team Building (1989; 20 mins; National Educational Media; Britannica Films) This program focuses on the principles of corporate team building.

2.E. DELEGATING AUTHORITY

A Case of Working Smarter, Not Harder (1982;16 min.; CRM-McGraw Hill Films/University Film & Video) This true-life case study provides a practical role-model, how-to-lesson for supervisors and managers who are uncertain about how to delegate, and it makes clear the difference between delegating and dumping.

Delegating (1981; 30 min.; McGraw-Hill Films/University of low Media Library) Examines the issue of delegating authority through a variety of entertaining scenarios, making viewers aware of some of the hidden traps in delegation, and provides basic steps for the manager to ease his or her workload, improve the finished product and build a stronger, more efficient department.

Delegating Work (1959; 8 min.; McGraw-Hill Films) Methods for improving supervision through better delegation. Demonstrates that failure to delegate part of his work load has a very serious personal effect upon a supervisor.

The Handoff: A Film About Delegation (1979;11 min.; Salenger Educations Media) Dr. Warren H. Schmidt, business consultant and professor of organizational behavior at the University of Southern California, uses the football analogy to propose guidelines for the art of delegating authority. These guidelines are demonstrated in vignettes played within a corporate setting.

No-Nonsense Delegation (1978; 26 min.; University of Illinois Film Center) Four keys to effective delegation, as outlined in the original book by Dale McConkey, professor of management at the University of Wisconsin, are presented and dramatized. Deciding how and when to delegate is perhaps the most important skill of management. Overcoming obstacles to these decisions is illustrated, with the result of a better distributed work load and a more satisfied group of work participants.

2.F. CONTROLLING

Case of Working Smarter, Not Harder (1982;16 min.; University of California, Extension Media Center, Berkeley) A reporter uncovers a true story about a successful manager who never solves operating problems nor makes operating decisions; yet he runs the most effective plant in the company. This film unlocks the secret of effective management by delegation and a control system which spawns incentive and promotes training.

Gathering Good Information - Two Person Communication # 1 (27 min.; BNA Communications)Describes the use of control between employees, how to make decisions between them, and talks about scouting out business prospects.

Managerial Control (1989; 20 mins; National Educational Media; Britannica Films) This presentation of three real-life vignettes reveals how simple control procedures help managers keep their operations within budget and on schedule without losing sight of their goals.

The Peter Hill Puzzle (1989; 32 mins; National Educational Media; Britannica) This program illustrates the close interrelationship of cost management with every other aspect of keeping an organization viable - leadership, innovation, motivation, problem solving, communication, conflict resolution and human interactions.

Stepping up to Supervisor (1985; 23 min.; University of California, Extension Media Center, Berkeley) Illustrates the changes employees face when they first become managers. In a dramatized situation, two new supervisors learn to handle their responsibilities and understand the skills of controlling, communicating and delegating.

2.G. GENERAL MANAGEMENT TOPICS

After All, You're The Supervisor (1979; 20 min.; Roundtable Films) A new supervisor discusses what it's like to be a new manager. Flashbacks illustrate how the new manager performs his job (handling the wide variety of skills necessary to cope with the day-to-day problems of a firstline supervisor) and how he deals with the normal fears and feelings most people have when embarking on a new career.

Excellence in the Public Sector (1989; 52 min.; Northern Light Production) Peters proves that the management revolution is also brewing in the public sector - in such places as city government, the forest service and even the Department of Defense.

Fergl Meets the Challenge (Fergl Builds a Business Series) (1978; 22 min.; Walt Disney Productions/University of Wisconsin-Madison) The importance of risk-taking and creative problem-solving are explored as Fergi, Inc. continues to expand. Shows how businesses avoid duplications of effort and how management delegates authority. Test-marketing is explored as a creative step toward mass-marketing. Also illustrates that business needs creative people and detail-oriented people, organizers and decision makers.

How to Fail in Managing Without Really Trying (1974; color; 32 min.; Salenger Educational Media) This well-known lecture by Dr. Harold Koontz, leading management consultant, lecturer, educator, and author pinpoints 20 ways managers may fail in their managerial functions without really trying.

How to Manage: The Process Approach and Henrl Fayol (1981; 14 min.; Salenger Educational Media) Explains the five distinct functions, or processes of managing: planning, organizing, directing, coordinating, and controlling. Illustrates how today's manager can use his/her "process approach" to aid them in becoming more effective in their jobs.

Middle Manager as Innovator (1984; color; 33 min.; Harvard Business School-Learning Corporation of America/University Film & Video) What is the key to the return of American business leadership? What can give a business "the leading edge?" It is the ability to innovate; the process of bringing any new problem-solving idea into use. Dr. Rosabeth Moss Kanter, author of *The Change Masters,* profiles two companies, one traditional (New England Bell), the other non-traditional (Data General) and focuses on two innovators and how they brought their ideas to fruition.

The New Supervisor: Making the Transition (1984; color; 24 min.; Sandler Institutional Films/Bar Films, University Film & Video) Three experienced supervisors explore the differences between being an individual worker and a supervisor. In a series of on-the-job vignettes, they discuss: the importance of thinking like a manager—not a worker, delegating versus doing the work yourself, employee training and development, communicating your expectations, using feedback and employee ideas, handling behavior problems, and the need to admit and learn from your mistakes.

Project Management - Vol. 1 (1990; 58 min.; Careertrack Publications) Examines seven traits of a successful project manager and explains how to identify a project's real objectives, ensure tasks are completed in a timely manner and negotiate for necessary resources.

Two good Business Ideas that Failed (1981; 30 min.; University of Wisconsin) Two entrepreneurs who had good ideas, ambition and energy still didn't make it. Done with humor and humanity, they tell their stories)

3.A. MOTIVATION——

Business, Behaviorism, and the Bottom Line (B.F. Skinner Film Series) (1972; 22 min.; Creative Media-McGraw-Hill/low State University) Dr. B.F. Skinner defines the terms behaviorism, operant conditioning, reinforcement, and shaping as they apply in the business world. Also presents Edward Feeney, vice-president of Emery Air Freight Corporation, systematically applying and interpreting these behavioristic concepts in an industrial setting. Illustrates how millions of dollars have been saved through a performance system based on accurate feedback and positive reinforcement.

Common Sense Motivation (1981;12 min.; Guild Sound and Vision/Roundtable Films) Defines the sources of job satisfaction that motivate employees through one manager's attempts to motivate an employee whose job performance is deteriorating. The film provides a checklist of management skills required to motivate employees and discusses the application and value of motivation as a supervisory skill.

The Go-Giver (1981; 30 min.; Iowa State University) A dramatic story of a manager in a publishing company. It describes the problems he has in managing and motivating his people. It is also the story of a father raising his son along. He finds that motivation at home also applies at work. The film points out techniques which managers can utilize to make themselves more effective.

Human Nature & Organizational Realities: Motivation & Production # 3 (1967; 25 min.; BNA Communications) Chris Argyris analyzes need for change in management's attitude toward motivation and productivity of rank and file worker. Apathy and lack of effort in the work force reflects unhealthy work environment.

The Human Problems of Management: Approaches to Organizational Behavior Modification (1978; 26 min.; University of Illinois Film Center) Edward Feeney, a leading industrial consultant, discusses operant conditioning and the five-step structure of behavior modification. Scenes at the Johns Mansville plant, the Purolator plant, and General Motors illustrate significant behavior patterns that influence a company's productivity.

I Call It Work (1979; 22 min.; University of Illinois Film Center) Examines cases in which people have made radical changes from highly remunerative jobs because such jobs provided them no sense of inner satisfaction. Interviews a former lawyer who now works as a publisher. Questions a system which has caused widespread discontent with its absence of human values.

If You Snooze, You Lose (198?; The Film Library) When a manager acts upon his employee's safety suggestions, he discovers an upward swing in productivity and profits.

It's a Matter of Pride (1977;17 min.; Salenger Educational Media) Introduces the concept of motivation via dramatized vignettes of several typical job situations which are humorously portrayed to reveal the rewards of having pride in one's work and to illustrate how a lack of pride can be harmful.

Helping People to Perform - Manager & Organization #5 (1977; 23 min.; BNA Communications) Drucker's view on training as well a new insight into motivation as he ends the argument of performance vs. potential and stresses the removal of obstacles to performance.

Job Enrichment: Managerial Milestone or Myth? (1977;14 min.; Salenger Educational Media) Focuses on job enrichment as a technique of job design. Defines job enlargement, and evaluates the impact of job enrichment, compares and contrasts it with job enrichment on organizational performance and employee satisfaction and motivation. Concludes that job enrichment works when it "fits," or is contingent on: 1) the nature of the technology it is being applied to; and 2) the nature of the person working on that technology.

KITA - or What have You done for Me lately? Motivation to Work #2 (1968; 30 min.; BNA Communications) Explains Herzberg's motivation-hygiene theory, what it is, why it doesn't motivate, and how to manage it. Illustrates management's effort to use hygiene as a motivator. Dr. Fred Herzberg discusses and illustrates his "Motivation-Hygiene Theory." Emphasizes that motivation is found only in job itself, in the opportunity to satisfy the human need for accomplishment.

Managing Motivation (1981; 10-1/2 min.; Salenger Educational Media) Discusses the manager's role in motivating employees and defines and illustrates three factors important to motivation: providing desirable rewards, creating expectations of success, and maintaining open communications.

Modern Meaning of Efficiency - Motivation to Work #1 (1969; 25 min.; BNA Communications) Poor attitudes can be the result of employee inefficiencies. Proper utilization of people requires fitting the abilities and aspirations of people to their jobs.

Motivation: The Classic Concepts (1985; 20 min.; CRM/Instructional Media Services, University of Utah) Identifies and explains the five classical theories of motivation: Douglas McGregor's Theory X and Y, Abraham Maslow's needs hierarchy, Frederick Herzberg's "hygienes" and "motivators", David McClelland's motivational profiles, and B.F. Skinner's behavior reinforcement. Illustrates applications of these theories by using dramatized scenes of a work force attempting to produce a new computer that will keep up with the competition.

Motivation: Making it Happen (1979;13 min.; Stephen Bosustow Productions/University Film & Video) Animated story of Ernie, who organizes the company band. He has no musical education or background and the problem becomes

446

a challenge when he adopts a positive attitude.

Motivating/Directing/Leading - The Basics of Winning with People (1989; 30 mins; RMI Media Productions Inc.) Find out how to get other people to do what you want them to do.

A New Look at Motivation (1980; 30 min.; CRM, McGraw-Hill/Instructional Media Services, University of Utah) Examines the obvious needs, such as the need for money, security, or advancement, which motivate people to work, as well as the underlying social motives, that is the need for power, affiliation, or achievement. Presents various management techniques and their effectiveness, suggesting that rewards, raises, and other bonuses are not as motivating as showing workers to find motivation from within themselves through increased participation, and such programs as flexitime and team production.

Passion for Excellence (1985; 50 min.; Brigham Young University) Discusses and illustrates how successful organizations create and sustain their competitive edge.

The Power of Positive Reinforcement (Behavior in Business Series) (1979; 28 min.; Creative Media, McGraw-Hill/Penn State University Audio Visual Services) An introduction to behavior modification as used in business organizations. Presents the main principles underlying behavior modification in order to help managers plan effective programs for their companies. Also looks at behavior modification programs implemented in an amusement park and with the Minnesota Vikings football team.

Productivity through People: Management Action Program #3 (1986, 29 MIN.; Nathan/Tyler Productions) Helping your employees feel like winners, giving employees the opportunity to manage themselves, and celebrating success, all encourage productive employees.

Profiles In Management/Part 2: On Motivation (1988;16 min.; Salenger Films) Three internationally known CEOs: (Jane Evans, Monet Jewelers; Sanford Sigoloff, Wickes Companies; Harold M. Williams, The J. Paul Getty Trust), discuss their motivational techniques.

Second Effort (1969; 28 min.; Dartnell Corporation) The Story centers around Lombardi, who upon meeting a salesman, suddenly becomes sales trainer par excellence. Shows five motivational principles which can be used to improve a salesman's performance.

Stop Procrastinating. . .Act Now! (1985; 23 min.; Callner Film Production/University Film & Video) Procrastination is the intentional and habitual postponement of something that should be done. It's one of the most universal of human failings. With the help of the narrator/host, six procrastinators take an honest look at themselves, their habits and excuses and begin to find concrete solutions to their problem.

Supervisor- Motivating Through Insight (1989;11 mins; National Educational Film Festival; Britannica Films, Inc.) This program uses a chess game metaphor to demonstrate motivation principles and counter old myths about job needs.

To Humanize the Assembly Line (Target the Impossible Series) (1974; 24 min.; Hobel-Leiterman/Cinema Guild) One successful experiment in counteracting the psychologically destructive side effects of boring, repetitious work is reviewed in a visit to the Volvo plant in Sweden. Examines the nature of the problems created by repetitive work, and the solutions tried in the Swedish environment.

Understanding Motivation: Motivation & Prod. #5 (1967; 26 min.; BNA Communications) Gellerman explains the scope of behavioral science as it applies to the field of management.

3.B. GROUPS

The Abilene Paradox (1984; 28 min.; Penn State University Audio Visual Services) Jerry Harvey, professor of management science at George Washington University, explains how to recognize the Abilene paradox, a phenomenon that occurs when groups continue with misguided activities because no member is willing to raise objectives. After illustrating the problem with vignettes placed in business, personal, and educational settings, Harvey discusses the psychological principles of the phenomenon and strategies for avoiding it.

Building More Effective Teams: The Organization Development Approach (1978; 26 min.; University of Illinois Film Center) Peter Block, consultant in organizational development, takes the forty members of a BOCES management team, and their supervisor, through steps designed to help deal with tension in organizations and to establish balance between the ideals of structure and flexibility. His goal is to solve particular problems and to impart skills for dealing with similar future problems.

Change Master I, The: Understanding the Theory (1986; 28 min.; Encyclopaedia Britannica) Turning into the environment, Kaleidoscopic thinking, communicating a clear vision, building coalitions, working through teams, persisting and persevering, making everyone a hero, 3 keys to embrace change.

Conformity - Candid Camera Segments (30 min.) Various candid camera clips dealing with conformity in the social environment. Very old but funny. In black & white.

448

Conformity and Independence (1975; 22 min.; University of Illinois Film Center) Dramatizations depicting actual experiments review the formation of group frames of reference, how people are influenced by other people's behavior. Makes an important distinction between true independence and the "anti-conformity" which is often taken for it. Defines and gives examples of the three different processes of group dependency: internalization, compliance, identification. Cites dangers. Reviews research results of Sherif, Asch, Milgram, Kelman, Crutchfield, and Moscovici.

The Crisis Management System (198?; 30 mins; MTI Teleprograms Inc.) This series presents a team approach to gather data that will be used to solve a crisis.

Do You Believe In Miracles? (1981; 24 min.; ABC-TV/University of Illinois Film Center) Interviews members of the U.S. Gold Medal Hockey team, winner of what was probably the greatest upset in sports history, the Lake Placid Winter Olympic victory of a group of college boys who had never played together before the Olympics. Tells how they think they were able to do this and recaps game highlights.

Group Dynamics: "Groupthink" (1973; 22 min.; McGraw-Hill Films/University of Illinois Film Center) Illustrates and analyzes eight symptoms of "groupthink": the illusion of invulnerability, shared stereotypes of the enemy, rationalization, the illusion of unanimity, direct pressure on the deviant member, and mindguarding—a device that protects the group from dissenting opinions. Includes examples from many kinds of organizations, and from decision-making processes that influenced many important recent events. Commentary by Dr. Irving L. Janis and Dr. David Kanouse.

How to Work with Fellow Managers - Manager & Org. Series.#2 (1977, 21 min.; BNA Communications) Drucker shows how to eliminate frictions with your peers, gain the cooperation needed to do your own work, and how to make yourself understood and respected by your fellow managers.

Team-Building: Making the Task the Boss (1983;18 min.; Penn State University Audio Visual Services) Presents a series of vignettes to show how groups function within an organization and how to avoid the pitfalls that are common in group situations. Recommends ways to build and maintain an organizational team, including creating an environment in which people feel it is safe to speak, obtaining a commitment from team members, and focusing on the task, not individual ambitions, as the team's goal.

Team Work and Team Work (1993; 75 min.; George Washington University) Teleconference of May 6, 1993 with Peter Drucker. Part of the "Business and Management" series.

We're on the Same Team, Remember? (1990; 21 mins; Rank Roundtable Training) Improving teamwork and individual responsibility: What else could possibly go wrong? Who's to blame? Everyone in the organization would benefit by: improving teamwork and cooperation; becoming more active in enhancing their organization's image and improving customer satisfaction; developing an awareness of the high cost of inadequate communication within their organization; and using the sales department as the primary link to the customer and a reference point in coordinating the team effort.

3.C. QUALITY CIRCLES

Call to Arms, A (1987; 45 min.; Mass. Institute Video Course) A look at products under the statistical control of quality. Quality, productivity and competitive position. William Conway, President of the Nashua Corporation.

Employee Involvement: Issues and Concerns (1982; 27 min.; LCA Video/Films, Inc) Many companies have implemented, or are considering implementing, employee involvement programs such as quality circles. Yet certain expectations and attitudes can bar the way to progress in such programs. This audio/visual package is designed to address such problems. It helps viewers examine the feelings— both management's and labor's—that impede employee involvement. It shows how real companies have trained supervisors to gain insights into workers' concerns and channel them into effective participation.

The Extra Care Story: A Quality Circle Case Study (1981; 34 min.; Johnson & Johnson/Films, Inc.) Details the quality circle program at a Johnson & Johnson facility in Tampa, Florida, from introduction to implementation, emphasizing the transformation from initial employee skepticism to a highly successful program.

Face to Face: Coaching for Improved Work Performance (1981; 24 min.; Cally Curtis Company) A step by step process to improve quantitative/qualitative work performance. Viewers are shown how to analyze real performance problems and told how to talk about such problems to subordinates. Manual.

Helping People Perform - Manager & Organization Series #3 (1977; 23 min.; BNA Communications) Drucker's view on training as well as a new insight into motivation as he ends the argument of performance vs. potential and stresses the removal of obstacles to performance.

Quality Circles (1983; 27 min.; University of Wisconsin Bureau of Audio Visual Instruction) Transforming staff and management suggestions to innovations is the goal of this film. Takes viewers around the globe to witness an American idea in action from conference tables of the world's largest steel manufacturer to the workbenches of a renowned name in elegant china.

Quality Circles: For My Own Cause (1988; 27 mins; Chuck Olin and Associates; Britannica Films) This film shows how quality circles, when properly applied, can increase productivity and provide a more rewarding work environment.

Quality: Whose Job Is It? (1989; 20 mins; Salenger Films Inc.) This presentation stresses the value of involving everyone in the process of improving quality: giving fast and courteous service to internal and external customers, meeting customer needs, searching for better ways to do things, encouraging teams to solve problems.

We Are Driven: Quality Circles in America (1984; 60 min.; PBS/University of low Media Library) A profile of Nissan Motors and their attempts to keep unions out of their new plant in Tennessee. Although the industrial might and management techniques of the Japanese have taken the United States by storm, some experts question the validity of the Eastern techniques as a miracle cure for ailing businesses, and in turn reveal the "darker side" of acclaimed Japanese management techniques.

3.D. LEADERSHIP

Building a Climate for Individual Growth - Motivation to Work #4 (1969; 25 min.; BNA Communications) Talks about being organized, how to build a winning team, and about control and relationships. Explains the use of different forms of control.

The Effective Uses of Power and Authority (Organizational Behavior Series) (1979; 32 min.; CRM, McGraw-Hill/University of Wisconsin-Madison) Illustrates the shapes and forms power takes and shows how misused power can lower the productivity and self-esteem of workers while power correctly utilized as a management tool can enable one to accomplish goals independently as well as organizing and motivating others to help solve specific corporate problems. Looks at legitimate, reward, coercive, expert, and information power. Presents methods of dealing with conflicts of power.

Everyone Can be a Leader (1989;15 mins; Salenger Films Inc.) This film stresses the importance of everyone's job and presents positive alternatives to job frustration and apathy. it also suggests appropriate ways to communicate with management, to sell ideas and to solve problems.

Helping: A Growing Dimension of Management (1978; 30 min.; CRM/Instructional Media Services) Illustrates the importance of giving an employee the opportunity to learn, and then allowing and expecting him to grow. Examines briefly the nature of helping behavior, why people help each other, what a mentoring relationship is, organizational environments that help or hinder this relationship. Gives two examples of ongoing monitoring programs. Uses interviews, true-life dramatizations and film clips from a seminar to demonstrate the points made.

Juran on Quality Leadership (1988; 45 min.; Juran Institute, Inc.)

The Leadership Alliance (1988; 65 mins; Video Publishing House; Blanchard Training and Development) Tom Peters shows how four present day leaders, including Pat Carrigan of General Motors and Ralph Stayer of Johnsonville Foods, overcame nearly insurmountable odds by empowering team leaders and members to think and perform in creative, new ways. An award winning program, it became an instant classic after its recent airing on PBS.

The Leadership Edge (1988;18 min.; Salenger Films) Effective leaders use three strategies: 1) they communicate a clear sense of purpose; 2) they involve others; 3) they demonstrate commitment. Leadership is a skill; it can be learned.

Leadership: Style or Circumstance? (1975; 27 min.; CRM, McGraw-Hill Films/University of low Media Library) Two styles of leadership, relationship-oriented and task-oriented, are examined. Shows through interviews with the presidents of Baskin-Robbins and Deluxe General, that the effectiveness of each style of leadership depends upon the specific situation. While showing that the same individual or group may receive different styles of leadership at different times, the film also points out ways of developing leadership and insuring the effectiveness and longevity of such leaders when they are on the job.

The Managerial Grid in Action (1974; 30 min.; BNA Communications/University Film & Video) The Managerial Grid approach to management is explained by its originators, Robert R. Blake and Jane S. Mouton.

New Leadership Styles: Towards Human and Economic Development (1978; 26 min.; Andy Olenyik/Cinema Guild) Discusses the role of the manager in modern organizations, qualities essential for effective leadership, and the impact of flexible leadership by showing the leadership styles of two successful executives who have humanized their companies' work environment by giving more "power to the people." Shows how employees like the responsibility and rise to the challenge as they are allowed to make decisions, share in profits, and chart the course for the future.

Seeking Understanding & Acceptance - Two Person Communication #1 (30 min.; BNA Communications) Meanings are in people. Zeros in on problems of appraisal, gibing instructions and evaluation to help people understand what you want them to accomplish.

Situational Leadership (1977;16 min.; University of Illinois Film Center) Dr. Paul Hersey presents his tested theory of leadership, which involves assessment of the maturity level of the employee prior to a decision as to whether the best style for the occasion is telling, selling, participating or delegating. Takes into account leadership's two dimensions: task behavior and relationship behavior.

You Gotta Believe (1978; 25 min.; BFA/Florida State University) Tommy Lasorda, manager of the Los Angeles Dodgers, has the magic to inspire the team to reach its full potential by making each player believe in himself and his abilities. This film reveals a winning philosophy and applies it to managers.

3.E. COMMUNICATING

Bob Knowlton Story, The (1967; 28 min.; Roundtable Productions) Raises questions about managing a subordinate when he is the authority in his field. Importance of managers and subordinates keeping channels of communication mutual.

Body Business (1983; 60 min.; Instructional Media Services, University of Utah) Presents Dr. Ken Cooper, a noted business training consultant, as he regales an audience of trainers with a dynamic presentation laced with humor and startling truths about the impact of body language.

Bottom Line Communicating: Get To The Point (1982;19 min.; University of Iow Media Library) A how-to study of communication strategy which causes behavior changes because the communicator knows how to use the main point—the bottom line—and when it will do the most good. Shows how to know what to say, how to say it, and where to put the bottom line which results in a positive system of communication that works.

Burying the Hatchets (1989; 21 mins; National Educational Media; Britannica Films) This program explores real situations full of emotional tension which can cause feuding parties to ruin their working relationship.

Business Courtesy (1989;12 mins; National Educational Media; Britannica Films) This program presents some principles of non-verbal communications with special emphasis on smiling, avoiding distracting gestures, practicing eye contact, and maintaining good personal appearance.

Call For Success (1982;14 min.; Instructional Media Services, University of Utah)
Presents the message: What you say and how you say it tells a lot about you and your company. Offers a practical detailed guide to effective verbal communication and comprehensive analysis of do's and don'ts of telephone contact. Uses brief dramatization to point out need of organization, clear speech patterns, knowledge of subject matter and written messages. Discusses and illustrates good telephone manners.

Communication (1981; 48 min.; CRM-McGraw-Hill Films/University Film & Video) Stresses the skill of perception as a foundation of effective management. Stereotyping as a factor in perception as well as the personal backgrounds of employees can influence inter-personal dynamics at work. Everyday interaction with peers and employees is a focus of this multi-media program.

The Communication Connection (1990; 27 mins; American Media Inc.;)
Effective employee communication cuts down on conflicts and increases productivity.Communicating Effectively—An Essential Skill for Job Success (1977; 21 min.; Barr Films/University of Nebraska) Good communication skills, attitudes, and personal success go hand in hand. How you appear to others is a form of communication. Do you establish and maintain eye contact during a conversation? Do you attempt to speak up and avoid mumbling? When you ask a question, do you expect to listen for an answer? Are you secure enough to admit it if you make a mistake? Do you actively attempt to improve your ability to follow directions? As these and other elements of communication improve, interpersonal relations and success in general seem to flourish as well.

Communicating Non-Defensively: Don't Take It Personally (1983; 25 min.; Instructional Media Services, University of Utah) Explains when and why defensive communication is likely to take place. Defines a step-by-step plan of counteraction that works. Details the attitudes and behavior necessary to cultivate non-defensive communication.

Communication: Barriers and Pathways (1979; 16 min.; IMS/University of Wisconsin Bureau of Audio Visual Instruction) Identifies a number of communication barriers, including poor oral and written organization, distractions, and differences in perception. Defines ways managers can develop effective communication skills. Roles of both verbal and nonverbal communication are examined as well as that of feedback.

Communication: The Company Grapevine (1983; 26 min.; University of Wisconsin-Madison Bureau of Audio Visual Instruction, University Associates) Employees who are expected to be loyal and hardworking need to know management's goals, objectives, and strategies—especially at times of extensive change. When management allows an information vacuum to develop, the space will be filled by gossip and speculation. This case-study film shows just how the grapevine works, and what damage it can do. It makes clear that employees' natural concerns and curiosity are resources to be used wisely.

Communication: Getting In Touch (1979;14 min., University of Illinois Film Center) Animated study of sales psychology with emphasis on communicating: when "Clumps," furry aliens, are discovered to have settled in the area next to Belleview, many clumsy attempts to communicate with them fail. Only Henderson of the Bell Factory reads all he can find about Clumps, and learns the Clump language. Seeking out the Clump point of view before he ever reveals that he has anything to sell makes him a success.

Communication: The Message (1977;14 min.; University of Nebraska) The information shared by the sender and receiver can be seen, heard, or both. Certain elements can make this message understandable or incomprehensible—it can be garbled, incomplete, muddled or clear. The point of the message, whether vital or routine, should not be missed. This film message about messages makes its points abundantly clear.

Communication: The Receiver (1977;14 min.; University of Nebraska) The target of the sender's message may shut H out by not listening, watching or reading attentively. The film points up the need for the receiver to be sensitive to incoming messages, how to evaluate the message and send feedback to the sender.

Communication Roadblock (1977;15 min.; BFA/Florida State University) Frustration, anger, even open conflict can emerge from imprecise or manipulative use of language. This film deals with defining terms, understanding biases, and distinguishing fact from opinion.

Communication: The Sender (1977;12 min.; University of Nebraska) Communication begins with the sender using verbal or visual media, or both. Skills involved with being effective and ways in which the sender creates barriers to good communication are explored in several original sequences. The film itself is an audio-visual message sent with sparkle and originality which students can understand.

Communications or Confrontations—A Film About Interpersonal Relations (1977;18 min.; University of Nebraska) Three vignettes are presented to demonstrate how one's point of view can get in the way of meaningful communication: two students attempt to cooperate on a class report, a mother and daughter engage in all the cliches of putting each other down, a woman customer tries unsuccessfully to make a purchase from a young salesman during his first day on the job. The open-ended nature of this film encourages the audience to discuss the effects that different vantage points have on communication.

Helping People develop - Two Person Communications #5 (28 min.; BNA Communications) Rational for effective counseling, plus practical, how-to-do-it steps. Discover what you can and cannot accomplish, limitations of reward and reinforcement, and the effect of rule changes on workers.

Listen to Communicate (1980; 60 min.; CRM-McGraw-Hill Films/University Film & Video) Begins by describing the physiology of hearing as well as interferences that can affect hearing. Cultural and personal attitudes that affect listening are pursued including biases and personal "sets." The program emphasizes basic mental skills of indexing, sequencing, comparing and effects of non-verbal communication.

Listening Leaders (1989; 30 mins; Video Arts Inc.) An informative video that shows business managers how to best gather and keep their valuable information. Listening:

Matt and the Missing Parts (8 min.) Demonstrates the importance of communication between management and workers.

Manager of the Year (1988; 22 mins; Salenger Films, Inc.) This film presents to its audience the managerial skills necessary for effective listening.

Meetings, Bloddy Meetings (1993; 30 min.; Video Arts) New 1993 version. An indepth demonstration of the disciplines, techniques and attitudes required to make meetings shorter and more productive. John Cleese stars.

Meeting: The State of the Art (1980; 24 min.; University of low Media Library) Defines meetings as a process of communication, and stresses the importance of visualization of ideas in order to be most effective. Identifies language barriers and audience resistance, while recommending the overhead projector as the most versatile method of visualization in a meeting. Demonstrates methods of preparing overhead transparencies, as well as various methods of utilization.

Perception (1979; 30 min.; McGraw-Hill Films/University of low Media Library) Shows how perception is an individual and subjective means of viewing reality influenced by social upbringing and culture, as well as media. Several vignettes in business as well as social settings depict the consequences of individuals perceiving situations differently. Points out that diverse opinions can be normal and enriching, and a means by which to evaluate our own judgments and decisions. Perception: Key to Effective Management

The Power of Listening (1978; 27 min.; CRM-McGraw Hill Films/University of Illinois Film Center) Points out the deterrents to good listening and probes the many-faceted question of why we are so reluctant to listen, why we are so eager to talk. Against a backdrop of a college lecture, some of the major blocks to good listening are visualized. Students are shown to have pre-set ideas about the level and value of what will be said. Interviews take place with two experts in the field of listening. Dr. Stainbrook, a psychologist, and Dr. Anthony Alessandra, an organizational specialist who conducts listening awareness workshops for companies. Demonstrates ways that people can learn to break bad listening habits.

The Problem Solver (1981; 20 min.; University of Illinois Film Center) Lists and dramatizes humorously the six bad habits which prevent good listening. Bad habits dramatized are distraction, closed mind, non-stop talking, jumping to conclusions, prejudice, and thinking speed. Good types of listening include critical, sympathetic, and creative, whose techniques and characteristics are carefully presented.

Production '5118' (1955; 30 min.; Champion Paper and Fiber) A mature, thought provoking story of an adventure in communications -a man's ability to make himself understood. Received 6 National citations for outstanding accomplishments in communications and human relations.

Speaking Effectively. . .To One or One Thousand (1979; 23 min., CRM/University of Illinois Film Center) Points out that public speaking shouldn't be separated from other kinds of speaking—that the common denominator in all communication is that statement: "This is me, this is who I really am." Cautions that the nonverbal self can say more than words. Practice on delivery and participation in opportunities such as speakers' workshops are suggested for gaining confidence and self-esteem. Offers a look at some professional speakers who have come to feel comfortable in front of an audience and now find public speaking a source of confidence instead of dread.

Supervisory Communication Skills (1981; 23 min.; University of Illinois Film Center) Discusses the problems of communication between supervisors and employees, and presents seven basic tenets for successful communication: consider the message and its impact, look for a reaction, criticize constructively, praise the employee, remain tactful and sensitive, present alternatives, and anticipate and interpret change. Includes reenactments of potential problem situations which illustrate these guidelines. From the Supervising for Results series.

Transactional Analysis: Better Communication for Organizations (1978; 26 min.; Hobel-Leiterman Productions/Penn State University Audio Visual Services) Examines the applicability of transactional analysis for improving communications in organizations. Shows how American Airlines implemented T.A. for its own training purposes. Two employees talk about the success of T.A. in improving customer service. Discusses the growing need for organizations to train personnel in the elements of communication and advent of T.A. techniques.

Verbal Communication, The Power of Words (1981; 25 min.; CRM-McGraw-Hill Films/University of Illinois Film Center) Analyses the four stages at which communication may break down, and ways it happens, making suggestions about how to avoid such breakdowns. Warns against cliche, double-talk, jargon and qualifiers; recommends setting a good climate, using clear and direct language, monitoring the communication (getting verification that you have been understood).

You're Not Communicating (1980; 20 min.; Callner Film Productions/University Film & Video) Focuses on five vital elements of effective communication in sharply etched vignettes that identify common communication problems and how to remedy them. Humor and realism help viewers understand how the principles of communication can be put to work in their own lives—for increased success at school, at work and at home.

3.F. HUMAN RESOURCES MANAGEMENT

Discipline - A Matter of Judgement (1989;11 mins; National Educational Media; Britannica Films) This video teaches that discipline must educate, not humiliate, and urges fair, prompt and consistent disciplinary action.

Discipline Without Punishment (1982; 22 min.; CRM-McGraw Hill Films/University Firm & Video, Penn State Audio Visual Services) Presents a step-by-step method for discipline, beginning with initial stage of helping an individual recognize that there is an attitude of behavior that needs changing. It continues with the steps outlined until the behavior or attitude has changed, or the problem has been resolved. Uses several slice-of-life examples interspersed with analysis by experts including Dick Grote, author of *Positive Discipline.*

Fired (1983; 28 min.; WGBH-Learning Corporation of America/Penn State University Audio Visual Services) When Biff Wilson was fired, his company hired an executive outplacement firm to help him rebuild his confidence and learn job-finding skills. After following his counselor's advice to "use people," Wilson honed in on a medium-sized company; chatted with suppliers, buyers, and employees; and eventually landed an interview. Wilson was offered the job, replacing another executive about to be fired. From the Enterprise 2 series. Host: Eric Sevareid.

Firing Isn't Fun: A Guide to Effective Termination Meetings (1983; 31 min.; Penn State University Audio Visual Services) A series of vignettes demonstrates ways of handling termination interviews on the basis of poor performance and on the basis of company reorganization. Looks at the different reactions displayed by employees, including grief, anger, and indifference, as well as the manager's feelings of guilt, apprehension, and stress, and offers ways to deal with them. On 3/4" VHS video only.

How to Get the Most Out of Marginal Employees (1979; 25 min.; University of Illinois Film Center) Reviews methods for identifying, handling for improved performance and, if necessary, firing, marginal employees. Reasons for marginality include lack of ability, boredom, and personal problems. Methods include identifying the cause, making initial recommendations to the employee with new chances for reassignments within reason.

Managing People (1989;15 mins; Security pacific Bank Production; Britannica Films) This program uses brief dramatizations to show the interaction between a supervisor and an employee engaged in an evaluation session.

Managing People Problem Series (1989; 20 mins; National Educational Media; Britannica Films) This is a dramatization of real workplace situations. More Than A Gut Feeling (1984; 28 min.; University of low Media Library) Designed to provide supervisors and managers with the interviewing skills required for effective selection of new employees. Based on Dr. Paul Green's theory of "behavioral interviewing", a series of factual vignettes illustrates the elements of an effective interview, followed by the conduct of a complete and successful interview of a job applicant.

Recruitment, Selection, and Placement (1979;19 min.; BNA Communications) Illustrates the case of the supervisor who, needing several welders to complete a rush job, asks his people to pass the word among their friends, and ends up with a discrimination complaint. Considers the difficulties of word-of-mouth recruiting, the criteria for job tests, the do's and don'ts of interviewing, how to avoid charges of discrimination based on race, ethnic origin or sex, and four key points to remember when hiring.

Supervisors and People Problems Series: Supervising for Results (1981; 21 min.; International Cinemedia Ltd./Phoenix Films, University Film & Video) Addresses the problems of personal conflicts intruding on the workplace. Trained specialists discuss the difficulties in balancing personal problems and work, and suggest four approaches that can help a supervisor resolve such difficulties: know when to intervene, empathize with the employee's problem; listen carefully; and maintain a balance between personal and professional involvement.

Take the Time (1988; 20 mins; Creative Media) Managers are taught how they can use their workers' strengths and avoid their weaknesses. Taking Charge (1981; 28 min.; E.G.S. Film Partnership-Southerby Productions/University Film & Video) Provides managers with a dynamic approach to the detection and confrontation of the troubled employee. The film develops four major points: 1) In the area of declining performance, the manager has the opportunity to be a front line observer. Through the use of this simple on-the job behavioral checklist, the manager can trace a pattern of on-the-job problems; 2) A myriad of negative reactions are aroused in other employees when the manager does not face up to dealing with the troubled employee; 3) The manager, through avoidance, actually enables the employee to continue with his negative job pattern. There is really no such thing as doing nothing; and 4) When the manager gives the employee a clear-cut, documented message concerning his declining job performance, the employee gets an opportunity to take responsibility for changing this behavior. Substance abuse is costing business and industry over $40 billion per year in lost productivity. The film shows the effect of the abuse on one's health, career, lifestyle, and relationship; and shows the effect on the organization's functioning. It explains the role of the supervisor in identifying the problem, the role of "enabling" co-workers, how friends can help bring the abuse to the surface; and points out the key role played by the Employee Assistance Program.

3.G. LABOR UNIONS

Beyond the Workplace (1980; 30 min.; Ohio State University/AFL-CIO Film Division) Illustrates how unions meet the needs of union families and their communities through education, social welfare and community programs. Using early newsreel footage and photographs, the film traces labor's involvement in meeting workers' needs through alcohol/drug treatment programs, disaster relief, day care centers and retirement programs.

Dimensions of Bargaining (Out of Conflict. . . Accord Series) (1978; 29 min.; U.S. Department of Labor/AFL-CIO Film Division) Explains four dimensions of collective bargaining: horizontal (between teams); internal (within teams); vertical (between team and its contingency); and external (between each team and the community). Suggests some of the factors that make up collective bargaining, and discusses how each team attempts to reach agreement on priorities, how much they can give and what can be traded off, depending on its constituency and the community in which it operates.

The Faces of a Union (1980; 28 min.; United Steelworkers of America/AFL-CIO Film Division) Answers the questions: What does a union do? How does it function? Provides a perspective on how a democratic union functions. Cuts across the many activities of union members: on the job, processing grievances, investigating safety violations, bargaining a contract, and walking the picket line. Some footage of the early history of the union.

Fight For My Union? Damn Right I Would (1978;10 min.; AFL-CIO Committee on Political Education) Workers talk about what their union means to them and what conditions were like before the union represented them. The attack on unions is described in this film showing how corporate and right wing groups are intensifying their campaign to break unions and elect anti-union candidates. The film describes the growth of corporate pollical action committees and the implications of the Supreme Court decision allowing the use of corporate treasury funds for political purposes.

The Harmonics of Conflict (1978; 25 min.; U.S. Department of Labor/AFL-CIO Film Division) Designed as an introduction to the concept of collective bargaining. Concentrates on labor-management conflict and the collective bargaining process, briefly outlining the differences between bargaining in the private sector compared with bargaining in the public sector.

If You Don't Come In Sunday Don't Come In Monday: Parts 1 and 2 (1976; 58 min.; Manpower Education Institute of American Foundation on Automation and Employees/AFL-CIO Film Division) History of the American worker and growth of the union movement traced through historical film footage, photographs, and documents.

Labor's Turning Point (1982; 44 min.; KTCA-TV, Minneapolis) Documentary on labor and unionization.

Labor Unions: A Question of Violence (1976;15 min.; CBS News/Carousel Films) Documents the confrontation between a successful, independent, non-union building contractor in Philadelphia and the construction union. His fight to preserve his open shop precipitates violent union action. American Film Festival Blue Ribbon Award: Business and Industry.

Proud to be a Teamster; We're America's Teamsters (1987; 28 min.; Ralph Graves Productions) Story of who the Teamsters are, what they have to offer America's workers and what they accomplished in the world of labor. Outlines the diversity of the union and highlights programs, services, bens.

Seniority vs. Ability (1977; 30 min.; American Arbitration Association) An employee files a grievance because he was denied a promotion on the grounds that he lacks advanced education. He denies that the job requires more than high school and contends that his seniority rights were violated when management selected a woman with less seniority. The film shows the actual arbitration hearing and provides the background for discussion on mistakes in presenting a case.

Strike Call (1982; 20 min.; World Research, Inc.) Profiles a contract negotiations meeting between labor and management and the frustrations that result when management refuses to accept workers' demands for wage increases when productivity is down.

A Time of Challenge (1981; 27 min.; AFL-CIO Film Division) Commemorates the 100th anniversary of the founding of the labor federation, combines a look at the past with a look at unions today. Photographs and historic film footage portray the founding of the AFL in 1881 and 1886, early union leaders, and strikes which played a part in the development of unions in the U.S. Interviews with union members today reveal how they feel about their unions and the problems they face in the 1980s.

Voices of A Union (1982; 20 min.; AFL-CIO Film Division) Presents a colorful profile of a union showing the many kinds of work union members do and the various services that the union performs for its membership. Can be used in schools to give students information on the world of work and the role the union plays in representing its members through grievance procedures, bargaining, education, and other activities.

Waldenville I (Out of Conflict. . .Accord Serles) (1978; 38 min.; U.S. Department of Labor/AFL-CIO Film Division) Follows a collective bargaining negotiation between a public employees union and city officials to the point of deadlock and the realization that some form of neutral third-party intervention is required. Shows behind-the-scene compromises, trade-offs, and planning. Topics covered include: what compels the parties to negotiate; how negotiations are initiated; the attitudinal conditions for negotiate; how negotiations are initiated; the attitudinal conditions for negotiations; how proposals and counter-proposals are made and responded to; the mechanics of negotiations; how the momentum to deadlock develops; and how the parties come to realize that a mediator is needed.

Waldenville II (Out of Conflict. . .Accord Series) (1978; 31 min.; U.S. Department of Labor/AFL-CIO Film Division) This sequel to Waldenville I shows the mediation process itself and how the mediator works to assist the parties in reaching agreement by studying the issue, then talking with each side. From the first deadlock in negotiations, the dynamics of mediation are graphically illustrated—with the film ending short of total agreement between the parties to enable the viewing audience to forecast the final outcome of the mediator's intervention.

Waldenville III (1980; 36 min.; U.S. Department of Labor/National Audio Visual Center, Reference Section) Recommended for use with Waldenville I and Waldenville 11, this film explores the process of fact finding, contrasts it with arbitration, and considers its use as another means of reaching accord. Fact finding is presented as a process in which a third neutral party intercedes and recommends a settlement that considers the position of each of the negotiating parties.

The Waldenville Jogger (1980; 39 min.; U.S. Department of Labor/National Audio Visual Center, Reference Section) Dramatizes the grievance hearing between an employer and a union, following the case from just after an employee's suspension to the closing remarks at the hearing. Delves into the preparation each side makes before meeting at the table, the attitudes of the participants, how a grievance hearing is conducted, and how the arbitrator referees the proceedings.

Who Wants Unions? (1983; 27 min.; University of Iowa Media Library) Uses historic newsreel footage to illustrate its discussion of unions. . .the pros and cons. Juxtaposes the viewpoints of labor and management as it reflects on the subtle psychological approaches that have, for the most part, replaced violent altercations. While the film touches on the key arguments for and against unions, its strength lies in its open-ended conclusion—a perfect opportunity to elicit animated classroom discussion.

Conflict Management (1983; 57 min.; Instructional Media Services-University of Utah) Introduces Dr. Ken Cooper, an internationally respected business training consultant, as he shows how to manage conflict to create a positive work environment, to encourage productive people to come to you with their ideas, and to open your mind to new ideas.

Conflict on the Line: A Case Study (1982;15 min.; CRM-McGraw-Hill Films/University Film & Video) Conflict arises on the line between Dan and his supervisor, Shirley. Manager Arnold Mott attributes the conflict to their difference in goals: Shirley must produce so many units to meet the team's quota, while Dan needs more time to ensure the perfection of each unit. Shirley feels Dan is deliberately creating a bottleneck to make her look bad while Dan feels Shirley's new methods are only causing him to make mistakes. Later, Mon surprises the two when they renew the battle. A carefully designed freeze-frame ending allows maximum creativity in presentation.

Coping With Conflict (1979; 22 min.; Millbank Films Ltd./University Film & Video) Problems come up on the factory line and the production supervisor is given the "brush off" by his supervisor. Eventually, all problems are discussed and resolved. The film closes with a brief, but very concise statement on how to deal with such conflicts: segment the conflict in order to deal with one problem at a time; deal with emotions first, facts next; and make offers which cannot be refused.

The Engineering of Agreement (1978; 23 min.; Roundtable Films) Demonstrates successful directive and non-directive questioning techniques that are basic to obtaining cooperation and winning acceptance. Explains how to create an atmosphere for agreement.

Managing Conflict: How to Make Conflict Work for You (1978;15 mins; Salenger Educational Media) Identifies and illustrates several strategies for dealing with conflict. Introduces the concept that conflict, when managed properly, can be productive. Analyzes these strategies in terms of their advantages and disadvantages.

Resolving Conflict (1982; 22 min.; CRM-McGraw-Hill Films/University Films & Video) Three major conflict situations thread their way through the film. One involves two tennis professionals who have different views about scheduling and pricing for their tennis lessons. In another, apartment managers need to resolve a tenant dispute, and the third is a classic organizational conflict between marketing and graphics. Presents the conflict resolution tactics of imposing a solution, compromise and settling on a collaborative basis. Reasons for the intense feelings that conflict can generate: fear, anxiety, annoyance and avoidance, are also examined.

Supervisors and People Problems (1981; 21 min.; University of Illinois Film Center) Addresses the problems of personal conflicts intruding on the workplace. Trained specialists discuss the difficulties in balancing personal problems and work, and suggest four approaches that can help supervisors resolve such difficulties: know when to intervene, empathize with the employee's problem, listen carefully, and maintain a balance between personal and professional involvement. From the Supervising for Results series.

3.I. PERFORMANCE APPRAISAL

Conducting a Performance Appraisal (1985; 12 min.; MTI Teleprograms, Inc.) How to conduct a proper performance appraisal for the benefit of both the individual and the organization. Includes instructor manual.

Conflict: Causes and Resolutions (34 min.; Roundtable Productions) Peer managers can exert lateral leadership in managing conflicts. #1-Inept leadership add fuel to the fire. #2-Three ways of taking the lead to resolution; win/lose confrontation; negotiations; problem solving.

How Supervisors Should Appraise Employee Performance (1979; 23 min.; Bureau of Business Practice; University Associates) Shows supervisors how to conduct their appraisals to reduce turnover, discover talent and uncover employee discontent. The film slows how typical supervisors interview, analyze and evaluate—to see how they spot employees who need additional training, pick out those with supervisory potential, find those with the skills and attitudes to fill more demanding jobs.

Human Touch: Performance Appraisal (1983; 30 min.; AMI/University of Utah Instructional Media Services) Presents a variety of vignettes that reveal the tools and techniques of effective performance appraisal. Shows that performance appraisal is more than just filling out forms at an annual review session. Stresses that in a "High Tech" society "the human touch" is needed to motivate employees.

Judging People (1962; 23 min.; Roundtable Productions) Realistically shows your supervisor and interviewers how they can learn to avoid mistakes in sizing up people. Clearly explains how to make more reliable and accurate estimates of ability and performance.

Performance Appraisal (1985; 20 mins; Barr Films) Managers and supervisors learn how to conduct effective and productive performance evaluation interviews.

Performance Appraisal: The Human Dynamics (Behavior in Business Series) (1978; 25 min.; Creative Media-McGraw-Hill/Churchill Films, Instructional Media Services) In many organizations, performance appraisals have become nothing more than devices for grading employees. This film explains why a people-oriented approach, one of a mutual exchange of ideas, might improve communication and ultimately motivate employees to work harder toward management goals. Focuses on the Mattel Toy Company as an example of how a participatory, goal-setting performance appraisal system can work.

So Who's Perfect or How to Give and Receive Criticism (1984; 12 min.; Salenger/ University of Utah Instructional Media Services) Explores some of the common mistakes most of us make in giving and receiving criticism. Offers a simple step-by-step method for giving and receiving it productively. Illustrates what to do before giving criticism, what to do when giving it, what to do after giving it, and describes what to do when receiving criticism.

Where Are You? Where Are You Going? (1976; 24 min.; Roundtable Films) Illustrates a model performance appraisal from the preparatory stage right through the conclusion of the interview. The story focuses on the anxiety of a younger manager as she approaches her first appraisal interview several months after receiving her new assignment and the techniques her superior uses to put her at ease and probe the problem areas of her work.

Who Wants to Play God? (1979; 29 min.; American Media Inc./University of Iow Media Library, University Film & Video) Describes the performance analysis method of conducting employee evaluations. Looks at the rules of proper scheduling, checking the supervisor's performance first; analyzing performance, not personality; good listening; and talking straight. Presents the steps of the interview process along with examples of correct and incorrect methods. Stresses subordinate participation and positive reinforcement.

3.J. ORGANIZATIONAL CHANGE

Changes! Coping with Difficult Changes (1990;14 mins; American Media, Inc.) confusion, depression, and fear often accompany change. Whether it's change at work or at home, people often feel alone in their situation. This video was produced to help your staff better understand their feelings during change. It will show them the ACT principle—a step-by-step method for dealing positively with change.

Changemaster: Understanding The Theory (1987; 29 min.; Brigham Young University) Dr. Rosabeth Moss Kanter describes the seven ingredients that are essential to successful changemasters and explains how you and your company can create the kind of environment that builds innovation and promotes acceptance of change.

Changemaster Companies: Putting the Theory Into Action (1987; 42 min.; Brigham Young University) Three case studies of organizations on the cutting edge of innovation.

Managing Change, The Human Dimension (1983; 33 mins; Goodmeasure Inc.) This video was originally made for one of the world's largest corporations as an aid to managers experiencing a major divestiture. This presentation helps managers understand why people resist change and how to manage it more effectively.

3.K. GENERAL MANAGEMENT TOPICS

Case of the Missing Person (1983;16 min.; CRM/Instructional Media Services, University of Utah) Investigates a serious problem—a manager's negative expectations sabotaging a prize employee's self-confidence and performance. Shows that negative expectations are just as easily fulfilled as positive ones. Unfolds as a detective story with the personnel manager cast as the detective. Uses flashbacks to show how the employee was changed from a highly motivated person into an insecure and unproductive worker—a missing person. Suggests a solution to the problem.

Case of the Snarled Parking Lot (1981; 22 min.; CRM/Instructional Media Services) A fast-moving, entertaining dramatization of common management problems. Focuses on four errors of management traps—1) the trap of clouded communication, 2) the puppet trap—organizational dynamics, 3) the trap of tangled priorities—priorities management, and 4) the trap of the snap decision—decision making.

Coaching (1983; 25 min.; CRM/Penn State University Audio Visual Services) Describes coaching, the management skill that allows organizations to train, develop, and improve the job performance of their employees. Utilizes three vignettes in business and industrial settings to demonstrate both effective coaching techniques and some of the barriers that can hamper successful coaching.

Creative Management: A Key to the Kingdom (1979; 23 min.; AIMS/University of Iow Media Library) Emphasizes the benefits of creative management and steps to aid in its fulfillment. Demonstrates how managers can develop their own creative potential, as well as build a climate that enhances the creative potential of others within an enterprise. Uses both the real world and a fairy tale parable to point out the problems of noncreative management and paths toward greater creativity.

Dealing with Difficult People: The Manager's Guide to Dangerous Animals (1983;17 min.; Phoenix Films/Penn State University Audio Visual Services) Identifies particular types of problem employee personalities whose traits can be likened to those of certain animals—the defensive lamb, the defeatist mule, the dominant lion. Humorous dramatizations and graphics are used to portray each type and to show diplomatic approaches to these difficult people that will remove their potentially disruptive effects on an organization.

Drucker, A Day with Peter F.: Organization in Transition (1988; 76 min.; George Washington University) Organizational concepts and organizational structures are in rapid transition, their first major change since decentralization in the early 1950's.

Everything You Always Wanted to Know About Supervision (1980; 28 min.; American Media Inc./Iow State University) Demonstrates the skills and techniques necessary to manage for positive results. Dramatizes the story of a young woman who has become supervisor and thinks she "knows it all." After finding out differently, she learns how to organize, delegate, communicate, and motivate. Describes the results of positive reinforcement and feedback, effective listening, planning, and discipline, and of being direct and factual.

The Hawthorne Studies for Today's Managers: The People Factor (1984;11 min.; Salenger Educational Media) Illustrates the significance of one of the most important events in the history of management theory—the Hawthorne Studies. Using original footage from the 1920's, the film shows some of the experiments conducted by Western Electric which were designed to increase productivity by improving the work environment.

Human Resources and Organizational Behavior (1978; 26 min.; Document Associates/Cinema Guild) This thirteen part film series examines important issues in the behavioral sciences with an emphasis on management techniques. The films feature leading authorities, both academicians and professional practitioners, in the management, behavioral and social sciences who present new theoretical concepts and practical models on how to develop stronger organizations, more satisfied individuals and greater productivity.

Learning to Think Like A Manager (1983; 25 min., CRM-McGraw-Hill Films/Penn State University Audio Visual Services, Instructional Media Services—University of Utah) Dramatization highlights the crucial areas of effective management and cautions against the mistakes most often made by people in leadership roles, including mistaken attitudes toward power, one-way communication, and halfway delegation. Defines the "management experience" and explains how successful leaders use it to overcome hurdles.

Manager Under Pressure (1977;15 min.; Churchill Films) A manager confronted with intense personal and professional conflicts must analyze the alternatives and solutions available to him. Points out that times of puzzlement and pain, if explored properly, are times for gaining perspective and learning about ourselves.

Managing In a Crisis (1978; 28 min.; BNA Communications, Inc.) Richard Beckhard shows how to dig out the facts in a crisis, tone down emotions and convert antagonism into positive, constructive action. Though the dramatized situation deals with a small group, Beckhard also shows how to set up and conduct fact-finding or planning sessions involving dozens of people.

The One Minute Manager (1982; 50 min.; CBS-Fox/University of Nebraska Division of Continuing Studies) Kenneth Blanchard reveals the three secrets of the *One Minute Manager:* Minute Goal Setting which starts the whole management process, One Minute Praising, and One Minute Reprimand.

Organizational Climate (1985; 27 min.; CRM-McGraw Hill Films) Using a work group set within the television station, the film illustrates factors which contribute to negative climate-inconsistent expectations, inequitable workload distribution, overlapping responsibilities and underutilization of employees' real skills—and points out their outcomes—tension, hostility, frustration and sluggish performance. Offers strategies for assessing the climate with an organization and suggests techniques which can be used for improving the climate of any business environment. Touches briefly on successful experiments in job redesign undertaken by Volvo and the City of New York.

Rules of the Game (1982;19 min.; Instructional Media Services, University of Utah) Dramatizes the critical areas of work habits, deadlines, loyalty, business etiquette and recognition of the power structure. Uses a variety of job situations to effectively demonstrate these concepts and the responsibilities of both employer and employee. Presents a positive approach to the idea of the work ethic and the role each person must play so that everyone may benefit from improved productivity.

Stepping Up To Supervisor (1985; 20 min.; CRM/Instructional Media Services, University of Utah) Illustrates through dramatization, examples of problems and pitfalls faced new supervisors. Demonstrates possible methods that may be used to avoid these pitfalls. Points out that thinking like a supervisor is a learned process of seeing the workplace in a new way.

Supervising and People Problems (1982; 21 min.; Phoenix Films/University of low Media Library) Takes a realistic look at the balance between personal lives and work, providing employers, managers and supervisors with some common sense guidelines for dealing with human problems when they interfere with work. Analysis from various human resource experts and timely narration are interwoven effectively with real life reenactments of actual work situations, illustrating how the general principles discussed can positively affect an actual problem situation. (Supervising For Results series)

Supervision Prescription (1983; 30 min.; University of low Media Library) A dramatic story of a nurse who has just been promoted to supervisor of her area. At first Diane, the supervisor, feels since she's had a lot of working experience and knows her area "inside and out", supervision should be easy. As the story progresses, Diane realizes she knows less about supervising than she originally thought. Through several varied hospital situations, the fundamentals of supervision are covered— planning, delegation, communication, discipline, and motivation. Diane learns that when she executes management skills well, she can motivate her employees. In addition to these skills, trainees will receive valuable information on positive reinforcement and feedback, active listening, questioning and counseling skills, and ways to build better relationships for improved communication.

Thank God It's Friday (1981; 25 min.; Millbank Films Ltd./University Film & Video) Dramatizes the current managerial development problems of two brothers in their respective companies. Jerry, the younger, is brooding over his manager's recent annual appraisal of his work—that he is not reaching his full potential. He feels he spends all his time "spoon-feeding" those who work under him; therefore he doesn't have the time to develop his own potential. Richard, the elder brother, a plant manager, discusses with Alex, the training supervisor, the unfulfilled potential of Mike, one of Richard's managers. Alex is ready to begin another of his three-day self-development training sessions. Jerry and Mike attend the self-development sessions to the benefit of their companies.

Working With Difficult People (1984; 26 min.; CRM/Instructional Media Services, University of Utah) Focuses on three characters, each of them work with a person who exhibits difficult behavior. Uses vignettes to dramatize specific problems and possible working solutions. Offers a general strategy for dealing with difficult behavior: pin-point the problem, examine the relationships, determine the costs, and search for a solution and get an agreement and commitment to that solution.

Valuing Diversity: Part 1 - Managing Differences (1987; 30 min.; Copeland Griggs Production) Shows how to evaluate, develop and motivate diverse employees. Powerfully illustrates how assumptions, real differences and organizational culture affect the performance of managers. Includes instructor manual.

Valuing Diversity: Part 2 - Diversity at Work (1987; 30 min.; Copeland Griggs Production) Re: upward mobility in the multi-cultural organization. Shows how stereotypes and actual differences affect the employee's ability to succeed. Diverse individuals present strategies. Includes instructor manual.

4.A. COMPUTERS

About Computers (1979;10 min,; Fleck, Inc./University Film & Video)
An animated film which offers an explanation of computers and how they work. Describes uses of computers in various applications, including simulation of different solutions to a problem.

Autofact '86: Implementing CIM: A strategic Challenge (1986; 25 min.; SME-Society Mfgr. Engrs.) A close-up look at computer-integrated manufacturing. Developed by the Computer and Automated Systems Association of SME. Depicts integration of manufacturing spectrum from design to assembly.

The Billion Dollar Bubble (1979; 60 min.; BBC Horizon/University of Illinois Film Center) The story of the Equity Funding Corporation, a financial giant built by computer fraud—forged bank certificates, doctored computer tapes, counterfeit bonds, and fraudulent policies. The climax—the arrest of the computer.

CIM: Focus on Small and Medium Size Companies (1987; 32 min.; Society Mfg. Engrs. SME) Examines why smaller firms in particular will benefit from implementing CIM, and how two smaller companies have already successfully introduces CIM into their operations.

The Company, Computers and the Unions (1981; 24 min.; University Media, University of Illinois Film Center) Analyzes the impact of computer technology within a business environment. Uses a case study on the introduction of microcomputers in the accounting department of an insurance company to illustrate the behavior and ambiguous attitudes of staff and management. Management is torn between improved productivity and the risk of failure. Staff members see work improvement opportunities tempered by the risks in the form of redefinition of status, responsibility, and the chance of unemployment.

Computer Applications: Manufacturing and Design (1982; 30 min.; Encyclopedia Britannica Films/University Associates) Investigates computer techniques which have helped five different business organizations boost productivity, improve quality, and reduce costs. A manufacturer streamlines his jewelry production with the help of computer-enhanced artists' designs; robots programmed to perform a variety of complex tasks help the automotive industry produce cars more efficiently; the accuracy of digital computers in drafting and computation makes paper and pencil work obsolete for designers and sails; today's winemakers use small computers to control the quality of their product; and manufacturers of log cabins use computers to mass-market a traditional hand-crafted product.

The Computer Programmer (8): Artificial Intelligence (1982; 25 min.; University of Illinois Film Center) Presents computers as puzzle solvers, as Mac is led out of a British maze garden by a robot dog, Chris plays Tic Tac Toe ("Noughts and Crosses") with a microcomputer, showing how a computer can be said to 'learn'. Demonstrates applications of this capacity to assist doctors in diagnostic medicine. Closes with two robots playing chess.

Computers, Spies and Private Lives (1981; 57 min.; Iowa State University) Reveals how computers, routinely gathering information on our finances, politics, and tastes and habits, may pose a threat to our individual privacy. Discussed in detail are nationwide computer banks, which store this information, and computer thieves, who can break computer codes to obtain data that may endanger both domestic and international financial institutions. Also examined are telecomputers, which may replace direct mail, and "smart cards" which look like ordinary credit cards but which contain a computer code known only to the owner and thought to be unbreakable.

How Does A DBMS Work? (Computer-Based Information Systems) (1978; 25 min.; University of Illinois Film Center) Focuses on a simplified model of data base management, based on CODASYL ideas involving components fairly common among systems. Covers schema, physical description, subschema, schema processing and internal storage, storage mechanism, links, retrieval.

Information Systems and Databases (1980; 25 min.; University Media) Filmed at the Southend headquarters of Access, the joint credit card company, it takes viewers through the information system as a whole, showing information flow, and highlighting the different rhythms of data processing. The film deals with the idea of data structure in the context of the Access operations, introducing the problem of supporting two different structures simultaneously. Charles Bachman, Senior Scientist at Honeywell, deals with the theoretical strand running through the film.

Keeping Track: Database Management and Microcomputers (1989; 29 mins; The Production Group; AIMS Media Inc.) the importance of keeping an electronic filing system is shown.

Managing Information Systems Series (1989; 180 mins; 5 progs.; National Educational Media; Britannica Films) This series illustrates the management realities of corporate computing, the need for an information systems strategy, and concerns for data security in the modern organization.

New Generation of Manufacturing Software, A (1986; 16 min.; Fourth Shift Corporation) Program introduces the Fourth Shift Manufacturing computer program and with it, offers companies through functionality, design, training and support.

Now the Chips are Down (1979; 50 min.; BBC Horizon/University of Illinois Film Center) Shows how the microprocessor is made, why it is invented, and its present uses. Filmed examples include a machine that can read aloud, a driverless tractor, a production line without humans, and a warehouse that needs no staffing. Examines the future societal changes that will likely occur.

4.B. PRODUCT/SERVICE QUALITY

Action Plans for Implementing Quality and Productivity (1988; 60 mins; 3 progs; Massachusetts Institute of Technology) Dr. Myron Tribus suggests that American companies start planning ahead for the future instead of just shooting for the "quick fix".

Challenge for the Deming Prize: Total Quality Control in the Service Industry (1988; 29 mins; Chuck Olin and Associates; Britannica Films) This program features ways of business to improve sales, quality of operations, and all members of the company cooperating in a participative work program.

The Gospel According to St. Michael (1976; 45 min.; University of Illinois Film Center) Examines the philosophy, policy, methods and history of Britain's chain of Marks and Spencer "St. Michael" shops, which make more money per square foot of floor space than any other retailer. Shows how they have set industry standards for quality and services, as well as staff relations.

Management's Five Deadly Diseases: A Conversation with Dr. W. Edwards Deming (1984; 16 min.; Chuck Olin-Encyclopedia Britannica Films/University Film & Video) Dr. Deming has identified five major elements, which he refers to as deadly diseases, in the American approach to management that inhibit productivity and that erode the ability to compete in the marketplace. Deming argues that what is needed in the United States today, and indeed in the Western world, is a transformation in management style that must begin with the recognition and elimination of these diseases.

The Mark of Quality (1979;18 min.; J. 1. Case Co./University of Wisconsin-Madison) A film that illustrates the manufacture of J. 1. Case Company products. Covers all phases of production from design through engineering, testing, and manufacturing. Stresses the important role of dealers and service.

Roadmap for Change: The Deming Approach (1984; 29 min.; University of Wisconsin Bureau of Audio Visual Instruction) One "secret" to Japan's phenomenal business success is that the Japanese learned to achieve it from an American, Dr. W. Edwards Deming. His teachings in Japan beginning in 1950, created a total transformation in Japanese business resulting in what is known today as the "Japanese Industrial Miracle"—or "The Deming Approach." The film uses a case study to examine how Dr. Deming's 14 obligations of management are being implemented in one American corporation. At the Pontiac Motor Division of General Motors, top managers to line workers react to Deming's management philosophy.

Quest for Excellence - 1991 (1991; 16 min.; U. S. Dept. of Commer.) 1991 Malcom Baldridge Award winners are featured (Zytec, Selectron and Marlow). Executives and employees talk about the importance of quality. Portions of the ceremony are shown.

Quest for Quality (1989; 44 min.; Tennant Company) Tennant's quality improvement process using the Crosby approach.

4.C. MANAGING PRODUCTIVITY

Autonomous Production Groups: Responsibility Shared (1989; 29 mins; National Educational Media; Britannica Films) This program shows us how alternative forms of job sharing can generate amazing results - from entire divisions to smaller groups being nun by employees.

If Japan Can, Why Can't We? (NBC White Paper Series) (1980; 80 min.; NBC Films, Inc./University of Illinois Film Center) Examines the reasons for the increasing quality of Japanese goods, while American productivity suffers in contrast. Compares the Japanese and American economy, productivity, and industrial growth. Improving

Improving Productivity Through Employee Involvement (1988; 18 mins; Chuck Olin and Associates; Britannica Films) This presentation introduces the five step approach to the process of change within business; problem identification, problem analysis, recommended solution, presentation, review and renewal.

Increasing Productivity (1989; 14 mins; National Educational Media; Britannica Films) This program discusses the manager's role in directing the use of resources and examines the responsibilities for improvement that managers must assume: initiating change, measuring accurately, involving others, and providing leadership for increasing productivity.

474

In Search of Excellence (1985; 90 min.; Public Br.Sy.-Nathan/Tyler) Documentary on successful business. Investigates management in large and small companies. Focuses on innovation, productivity through people and shared values, and how companies have benefitted.

The Japanese Approach to Productivity (Part I) (1983; B/W; 60 min.; University of Iowa Media Library) A comprehensive four-part presentation made by Len Ricard, Director of Materials Management, General Motors and Ken Wantuck Director of Advanced Facilities Planning, Bendix Corporation, on the success story of the Japanese manufacturing productivity methods. In the context of two categories, waste elimination and respect for people, the discussion presents eight (out of fourteen) key Japanese productivity elements, including: 1) Focused Factory, 2) Group Technology, 3) Lifetime Employment, 4) Company Unions, 5) Attitude Toward Workers, 6) Automation, 7) Quality Control and, 8) Bottom Round Management. On 1/2" VHS video only.

The Japanese Approach to Productivity (Part II) (1983; 60 min.; University of Iowa Media Library) Part 11 presents the four remaining key Japanese productivity methods. Each element is assigned either to the waste elimination or respect for people categories. Elements include: 9) Subcontractors Network, 10) Quality Circles, 11) Just-In-Time Production, 12) Uniform Plant Load, 13) Kanban System and, 14) Minimum Setup Times. Profiles General Motor's new Integrated Supply Approach and the example of Toyota's Production System and presents six selected key productivity elements which apply to U.S. industry without having to adapt to Japanese culture. Just-In-Time Production is also presented.

Manufacturing Automation: A Key to Productivity (1984; 60 mins; 5 progs.; Deltak: The Diebold Group; Deltak Inc.) This series of programs explains the changing environment of manufacturing of automated products and what the future will be like. Manufacturing In the 1990's (1988; 45 mins; 9 progs; Massachusetts Institute of Technology) These tapes contain segments of a conference held on the future of industry.

People and Productivity (1982; 28 min.; Encyclopedia Britannica Films/University Film & Video) Examines some of the key ideas from the Japanese business philosophy and how these attitudes help to improve productivity and employee relations. Leaders in business, industry, unions, and education, both Japanese and American, express their views on this new, profitable approach to industrial productivity. Viewers learn about U.S. companies that have applied these ideas.

Productivity: It's a Personal Matter (1984; 20 min.; Contrast Creative Services/Salenger Educational Media, University Film and Video) Explores the basic idea of "work" and our attitude towards it: what work used to mean to people. . . how its meaning has changed in the minds of many Americans, and how that change has hurt us. Suggests that we may need to rediscover the value of work, for our own individual benefit as well as for that of our company and our country. Examines some of the contemporary negative attitudes toward work which block productivity and make workers unhappy. It also examines positive, healthy attitudes toward work by portraying a series of people who like work, who do it proudly and well.

A Productivity Film (1982; 6 min.; Learning Corporation of America) With bright animated images and lively narration, this film quickly reviews the reasons for declining American productivity. It clarifies the relationship between productivity and quality of work life as two sides of a coin, equating "the productive life" with "the good life" in terms everyone can understand.

Productivity for the Knowledge Worker (1988; 45 mins; 7 progs; Massachusetts Institute of Technology) This course is designed to raise productivity levels among people who are knowledge workers.

Productivity through People: Management Action Program #3 (1986; 29 min.; Nathan/Tyler Productions) Helping your employees feel like winners, giving employees the opportunity to manage themselves, and celebrating success, all encourage productive employees.

Quality Function Deployment: Budd Company Case Study (1987; 40 min.; Budd Co./American Supplier In.) Three case studies demonstrate the power of QFD in three key areas: Product design, process design and achieving organizational optimization.

Supervising for Productivity (1981; 18 min.; University of Illinois Film Center) Describes four ways in which supervisors can encourage their employees to think creatively and raise their company's productivity. Reenactment of actual working situations demonstrate the four supervisory guidelines: conducting ideas, assuming the role of leader and coordinator, motivating employees, and encouraging employee participation in the decision-making process. From the Supervising for Results series.

What This Country Needs (1981; 30 min.; WTTW/University of Illinois Film Center) Examines the U.S. productivity problem and its human element. A panel of experts addresses the problem, focusing on worker-management relationships, the implications of changing worker attitudes, and the need for management to provide motivation.

World Class Computer Integrated Manufacturing at A-B (1987; 10 min.; Allen-Bradley/Rockwell in) At Allen-Bradley, computer integrated manufacturing is producing over 600 world class contractors an hour for industrial motor starters. Discover how their productivity pyramid has shaped this facility.

Your Attitude Is Showing: The Answer to Greater Productivity (1978; 18 min.; University of Illinois Film Center) Using seven comic and imaginative "historical" vignettes, shows how attitudinal problems and solutions function in all eras of time. Combining live action and animation, uses a conversation between an amoeba and a bored, discouraged research scientist as a framework for reviewing self-help techniques.

4.D. PRODUCTION PROCESSES——————————————————————

Business Logistics Series Produced and distributed by Penn State Audio Visual Services. Each film released in 1982; 29 min.; study guide available.

Business Logistics: 1—Introduction to Logistics: Presents an overview of logistical management, including definitions and rationale for interest.

Business Logistics: 2—Approaches to Logistical Analysis: Approaches to looking at logistics systems and total cost analysis.

Business Logistics: 3—Integrated Logistics Systems: Breaks logistics down into two main parts, materials management and physical distribution, with emphasis on integration of the activities and how to operationalize the integration.

Business Logistics: 4—Logistical Environments: Macro/Micro: Looks at logistics in the economy and in the firm: What is its role, contributions, and/or relationships?

Business Logistics: 5—Logistical Environments: Internal Analysis of the factors which affect logistical costs, such as spatial relationships, completion, and product characteristics.

Business Logistics: 6—Inventory Analysis, Part 1: Introduction to inventory management and control, and how inventory fits into logistics systems and in the overall organization.

Business Logistics: 7—Inventory Analysis, Part 2: Analysis of basic inventory questions, classifications, and model forms.

Business Logistics: 8—Basic EOQ Model: Explanation of the basic inventory model and the development of the mathematics necessary for the decision framework.

Business Logistics: 9—Adjustment In Basic EOQ Model: Inventory In Transit: Analysis of how the basic model can be adjusted to take account of certain decisions important to logistics, with particular emphasis on how to evaluate the cost of inventory in transit.

Business Logistics: 10—Adjustment In Basic EOQ Model: Volume Rates: Adjustment in the basic model to take into consideration the inventory trade-offs of shipping larger volumes to take advantage of lower transportation rates.

Business Logistics 11— Warehousing, Part 1: Introduction to basic warehousing considerations with an emphasis on warehousing's role in logistics functions.

Business Logistics: 12—Warehousing, Part 2: Discussion of important warehousing decisions, including ownership and number.

Business Logistics: 13—Materials Handling and Packaging: Analysis of logistical dimensions of materials handling and packaging.

Business Logistics: 25—Location Factors: Looks at the important factors that affect location decisions.

Business Logistics: 26—Location Techniques: Discussion of techniques used in locational analysis.

Business Logistics: 29—Logistics Strategy: An Overview: Examination of long-run planning and how it relates to their parts of the organization.

The Great Wine Revolution (1977; 60 min.; Time/Life Films/University of Iowa) Explores the revolutionary changes in the wine industry—whose traditional methods are inadequate to supply the ever-increasing demand for its products—in its efforts to produce the perfect grape and to modernize and mechanize production.

Inventory Control for Manufacturers (1983; 12 min.; University of Iowa Media Library) The film shows that inventory control can be reviewed as meeting three objectives: 1) the purchasing of sufficient raw materials to satisfy production needs and to meet sales; 2) the establishment of proper levels of inventory as to ensure stock on hand to meet increased demand or to compensate for delays in replenishing either raw materials or finished goods; and 3) ensure that the investment in inventory is not excessive so as to avoid cash flow shortages, unnecessary borrowing, and the costs of carrying too large an inventory. Examines the three types of inventory carried by the average manufacturer. (Running A Small Business series).

Just In Time/ Just In Case (1988; 30 mins; Encyclopedia Britannica Educ. Corp.; Britannica Films) This program explains how wasted time and space can be eliminated to create a higher quality product.

Just in Time, Implementing (1987; 27 min.; SME-Society Mfg. Engrs.) Lots of people talk about it, but how are these techniques being incorporated on the plant floor?

Just In Time/ Just In Case (1989; 30 mins; National Educational Media; Britannica Films) This film shows how businesses can increase productivity by eliminating "waste".

New Industrial Revolution (1979;12 min.; USNSF/National Audio Visual Center) Demonstrates newly discovered techniques that are making modem day assembly lines more efficient. Shows systems developed to speed up assembly processes and eliminate routine jobs.

Setup Reduction for Just in Time (1990; 22 min.; SME-Society Mfg. Engrs.) You will see how several companies have implemented setup changes such as pneumatic die lift systems, automatic clamping devices, die conveyance systems, and simple, foolproof, lockdown and adjustment technologies.

Stockless Production (29 min.; Hewlett-Packard) Hewlett-Packard Corporation's discussion of the production process from the 'Push' to the 'Pull' method.

Vision: The far reaching Technology (1985; 27 min.; SME-Society Mfg. Engrs.) Compares today's diverse machine vision equipment and its applications and capabilities. Shows advanced computer architectures capable of high speed production processing.

4.E. STATISTICS

Inferential Statistics (Part I): Sampling and Estimation (1978;19 min.; Media Guild) Provides an ideal introduction to the topics covered. Presents an introduction to the concept of population and sample, random sampling and sample bias, point estimation and confidence intervals. They are described in the context of an extended, humorous example in which a company saves money by field analysis of the boss' dream before launching into production. An emphasis is placed on understanding the concepts that underlie statistics, rather that on computation or formal procedures.

Inferential Statistics (Part II): Hypothesis Testing Rats, Robots and Rollerskates (1978; 25 min.; Media Guild) Uses four short sketches to illustrate some principles of hypothesis testing: the need for a control group and for random assignment of subjects to groups, the necessity for statistics as a means to overcome population variability, the formulation of a statistical hypothesis and the possible errors, and the way in which hypotheses about the mean are tested. Throughout, the emphasis is on underlying concepts rather than formulae or computational procedures. The examples are humorous, although not at the expense of statistical explanation.

Practical Statistics: Program 1 & 2 (1987; 60 min.; Films, Inc.) Program #1 - Statistics Overview. Introduces major themes, collecting data, organizing and picturing, drawing conclusions. Program #2 - Behind the Headlines. Deeper look at data collections, surveys.

Practical Statistics: Program 5 (1987; 30 min.; Films, Inc.) Program #5 - Confident Conclusions. Focuses on the concept of a confidence interval and describes precisely what opinion polls do and do not tell us.

Statistics at a Glance (1972; 27 min.; J. Wiley and Sons/UCLA) Elementary principles of descriptive statistics: Frequency distributions, measures of central tendency, variability, and correlation.

Statistics In Quality, Productivity, and Problem Solving (1988; 45 mins; 11 progs.; Massachusetts Institute of Technology) This series tells businesses how they can achieve goals such as zero defects and efficient production.

Statistics, Products Design, Quality Control (1986; 60 min.; University of Wisconsin, Madison) Review of Dr. W. Edward Deming's theories in a lecture by Professor William G. Hunter.

5.A. ENTREPRENEURSHIP————————————————————————————

Beyond Excellence: The Super Achievers (1989; 90 mins; Video Arts Inc.) This tape features profiles of five different people who have raised businesses up with their own intelligence and hard work.

Bianchi, Antonett: Guts, Fear and No Fear (1984; 65 min.; CST) Antonett Bianchi speaks in OEC on entrepreneurs and how minorities get started.

Cash on the Vine (1984; 28 min.; Learning Corporation of America/Penn State University Audio Visual Services) Observes Sandra and Bill MacIver and their winemaker, Merry Edwards, as they pursue their business in the affluent world of fine wine. Their company competes not with the industry giants, but with some 500 other boutique shops.

Chef's Special (1983; 28 min.; WGBH-Learning Corporation of American/Penn State University Audio Visual Services) Focuses on David Garo Sokitch as he gambles about $1 million to find that perfect "mix" for a successful restaurant in San Francisco. Sokitch attended carefully to location, food, service, interior design, and publicity in preparation for *Garos'* opening, but four months later its fate was still undetermined. Though Sokitch and his investors have lost $20,000, Sokitch continues working enthusiastically. From the Enterprise 2 series. Host: Eric Sevareid.

Crosswind Take-Off (1984; 29 min.; WGBH, BBC, Learning Corporation of America/Penn State University Audio Visual Services) Follows the attempts of Moya Lear to produce the Lear Fan, an innovative jet designed by her late husband William Lear. Her fiercest competition came from Starship, a plane developed by Lear Fan, Ltd.'s former chief executive, Linden Blue. Despite unsuccessful attempts by both companies to meet the requirements of the Federal Aviation Administration and the subsequent closing of Lear's Belfast plant and the resignation of Blue from Beech Aircraft, both Lear and Blue are determined to produce the planes. From the Enterprise 3 series. Host: Eric Sevareid.

Doing Business (1981; 15 min.; Howard Libov/Cinema Guild) Offers a behind-the-scenes look at the pleasures and the dmiculties of operating a small, self-managed business. Examines three small businesses and how the people who manage and work in them are striving to become good business people while trying to find personal meaning and satisfaction in their jobs. Explores some of the new ideas that young people are bringing to business today, including the creation of worker-owned and managed enterprises, arranging non-stressful working conditions, and paying employees on the basis of need rather than by the hour.

The Entrepreneurs: An American Adventure (1986; 60 mins; PBS Video) The opening program profiles common threads among entrepreneurs. Not only do they devise or invent products, they market them on a vast scale, sometimes to the point of altering the whole fabric of American life. They share the courage to face and overcome the threat of failure. Examples include Thomas Edison, King Gillette, Margaret Rudkin, Charles Darrow, John Johnson, Wally Amos, Robert Pittman, and Wilson Greatbatch. Hosted by Robert Mitchum.

Entrepreneurs: The Risk Takers (1989; 20 mins; 4 progs; RMI Media Productions, Inc.) Students gain a special understanding of small business from this series.

Small Business Keeps America Working (1978; 28 min.; Coe Communications/U.S. Chamber of Commerce) Highlights the entrepreneurial spirit of personal independence that lies behind small business in America. Explores the risks and rewards of owning a small business and the businessperson's drive for innovation, which is seen as the key to future economic growth.

Starting A Business 1: Are You An Entrepreneur? (1982; 15 min.; University of Iowa Media Library, University of Illinois Film Center) Presents information to help a beginner determine whether he or she is an entrepreneur. Deals with three questions: What is an entrepreneur? What role does this person play in starting a business? What are the personal qualities usually found in successful entrepreneurs? Uses graphics and interviews with people who have successfully answered the question in businesses of their own to provide background about this type of career choice.

Starting A Business 2: What's the Best Business For You? (1983; 15 min.; University of Illinois Film Center) Provides guidelines for would-be entrepreneurs in assessing various business ideas. Explains what personal considerations should be taken into account at the outset. The three most important points to assess when investigating an entrepreneurial role in any new venture are the potential for growth of the business, the likelihood of sufficient income to meet expectations, and the market share potential. Uses graphics and interviews with entrepreneurs to demonstrate the importance of correct choices.

Starting A Business 3: Who Will Your Customers Be? (1982; 15 min.; University of Illinois Film Center) Outlines the steps required of an entrepreneur in identifying the potential customers of a business. Explores the kinds of information needed to determine the needs and wants of a specific target market, the suggested methods to use in collecting market information, and in assessing its validity. Uses graphics and interviews with entrepreneurs to demonstrate the advantages of determining a target market.

Starting A Business 6: What Will Your New Venture Demand? (1983; 20 min.; University of Illinois Film Center) Provides role definitions against which a potential entrepreneur can measure his own strengths: entrepreneurial, inventive, innovative, managerial. Describes environments in which each thrives, lists personal characteristics appropriate to each role. Interviews successful business people in each type-of role.

Starting A Business 7: Who Will Help You Start Your Venture? (1983; 20 min.; University of Illinois Film Center) Enumerates legal and financial types of help that may be needed by a new entrepreneur, with location i which the best of such help is apt to be available. Counsels against failing to investigate advisors, to determine the level of their professional competence. Describes a procedure for budgeting for consulting services, and urges that every available source of information be tapped.

Starting A Business 8: Do You Need A Business Plan? (1983; 21 min.; University of Illinois Film Center) Defines the role of a business plan in starting any enterprise, and describes the four steps to formulating such a plan. Interviews successful entrepreneurs about their planning methods, what errors they were spared by planning, and why they view it as indispensable. Lists advantages and uses other than financial.

Starting A Business 9: What Should Your Business Plan Contain? (1983; 22 min.; University of Illinois Film Center) Lists uses of the business plan for each of three types of business, outlines the sections that should be in every plan, and details what each section should contain. Emphasizes the vital parts to spotlight when seeking investors.

Starting A Business 10: How Will You Find Capital? (1983; 21 min.; University of Illinois Film Center) Differentiates business types and types of capital, illustrating how the secret of locating potential capital begins with knowing these differences. Types of capital covered are equity, near equity and debt. Provides examples.

Starting A Business 11: How Do You Buy A Business? (1983; 21 min.; University of Illinois Film Center) Encourages potential venturers to spend the necessary time in information-gathering and planning, rather than to accept any opportunity too quickly. Identifies sources of information and steps in planning, ways to value a company, to judge return on investment, and to plan strategies for acquisition.

Starting A Business 12: How Do You Buy A Franchise? (1983; 21 min.; University of Illinois Film Center) Uses interviews with successful entrepreneurs and franchise owners to provide background against which to define "franchise", and to tell how it works and how it differs from other types of enterprise. As the film comments, "Basically, you are buying a risk reduction, so as a general rule, the better established the franchise, the higher the cost."

Starting A Business 13: How Can You Survive Business Crises? (1983; 21 min.; University of Illinois Film Center) Stresses that the appropriate solution to a business crisis depends on the correct diagnosis of the solvency and viability of the business. Uses entrepreneurs who have been through business failures and tried again and succeeded, to discuss the forces (internal and external, controllable and uncontrollable) that precipitate crisis. Explores problem areas and general pitfalls.

Starting your own Business (1984; 60 min.; CST) Lecture Series.

Workout (1984; 28 min.; WGBH-Learning Corporation of America/Penn State University Audio Visual Services) Looks at how the Gloria Stevens chain, one of the first entries into the health-club business in the early 1970's, attempts to attract new customers without alienating current members. New president Arthur Blasberg attempts to rescue the floundering company by upgrading exercise programs, creating a new ad campaign, and hiring high-energy sales personnel to recruit new members. From the Enterprise 3 series. Host: Eric Sevareid.

5.B. MANAGEMENT CAREERS

The Blank Page (1990; 26 mins; National Safety Council) Geared toward making people want to take charge of their own lives and career paths. The message of an individual's importance to an organization makes the film applicable to any training session.

Career Development (1990; 20 mins; National Safety Council) In order to retain employees with exceptional potential, managers must be able to combine the requirements of the organization with the individual's need for growth in a positive, constructive manner.

Career Development: A Plan for All Seasons (Business and Management Series) (1978; 27 min.; CRM-McGraw-Hill/University of Iowa Media Library) Highlights how continual employee turnover, midcareer changes, and financial instability adversely affect productivity. Describes the philosophy behind implementation and positive results of career development programs which are considered to offer one of the best means of analyzing an employee's work goals and coordinating them with an organization's plans for positive, directed results. Presents one company's approach to helping its employees enrich their working lives through such a program.

Career Management: When Preparation Meets Opportunity (1990; 20 mins; National Safety Council) How employees can take control of their own careers through a process of self-assessment, research, and planning. Helps change employee attitudes, develop skills, and stimulate management support for the career management process.

Conducting an effective Job Interview (1988; 17 min.; Midi, Inc.) Behavior modeling exercises and action review techniques are combined to turn-key research results into a skill-building action plan to sharpen interviewing skills, focus abilities and increase success.

Doing Your Eight (1982; 20 min.; Instructional Media Services, University of Utah) Deals with the concepts of business routine, the individual's role in helping a company create a profit and the development of a business identity. Follows two young people through their initial job interviews, their training period and their first weeks at work. Illustrates that they learn the requirements of their positions, the importance of giving honest effort, and the interpersonal skills necessary to relate to their fellow employees.

Finding your first Job (1979; 60 min.) Process of preparing a resume' and seeking an interview.

Interview: Ready or Not? (1975; 24 min.; University of Illinois Film Center) In a job interview for the position of paramedic trainee, the interviewer's questions elicit inadequate responses from Vincent, a tense, seemingly unqualified, young man. It is suggested that the projector be stopped for discussion of the question, "Would you hire this person to work for you?" Later, it develops that the interview has taken place in a classroom and Vincent's classmates comment upon his presentation and encourage him to communicate his strong points, experience, capabilities, and personal qualities. The interviewer, a professional personnel officer from a large corporation, contributes by acting out her role as she would report the results of the interview to her supervisor.

The Interview Film: What To Know and What To Do (1977; 21 min.; University of Connecticut Erickson Memorial Film Library) Five young men and women apply for a single opening as cashier with a restaurant chain. Recruiting, screening, interviewing, and evaluation are seen from the employer's point of view. One of the five is hired, but viewers are left to determine the successful candidate based on their own personal observations and judgments.

Job Interview: I Guess I Got the Job (1985;13 min.; CRM-McGraw-Hill Films/Media Resources Center) Through flashbacks, the viewer observes the different approaches of two boys as they interview for the same job. The focus is on the subtle cues that can affect an interviewer's overall impression of an applicant —factors that may have nothing to do with actual qualifications.

Job Interview: Whom Would You Hire (Film A: Large Business) (1980; 20 min.; University of Illinois Film Center) Hidden camera films actual job interviews whose applicants later gave permission to use the footage. Employers state what they are looking for, and viewers are given the opportunity to judge where they would find it. Applicants represent both sexes, two races.

Job Interview: Whom Would You Hire? (Film B: Small Business) (1980; 22 min.; University of Illinois Film Center) Presents a montage of statements by managers as to what they are looking for in candidates for the positions they have open. Four vignette interviews between a manager and a candidate follow, covering a representative sample of applicants. Viewers are left to choose and give reasons.

The Job Interview Pro Bowl (Art of Communications Series) (1979; 20 min.; Centron Educational Films) In this dramatization, the job interview is treated as a spectator sport. Covers the job interview from the perspective of both applicant and interviewer. Uses "pre-game" interviews to describe how the applicant prepared for the interview and what skills and personal traits the interviewer will be looking for. Shows an actual interview and uses a "post-game wrap-up" to evaluate the entire interview process.

Lifelines: A Career Profile Study (1982; 26 min.; Cinema Guild) Using illustrations from three actual case histories, the film explores Dr. Edgar Schein's concept of "career anchors"—patterns by which individuals discover what they are good at and what they would like to do for the rest of their lives. Using the results of Schein's research into career formation, the film explores the five categories of career anchors: technical or functional; managerial competence; security; creativity; and autonomy. The close examination of the profiles of three careers reveals that people must define their life's work with a sense of who they are, what gives them satisfaction, and what they do best.

Packaging the Product (1979;15 min.; WCET-TV/University Film & Video) After a brief introduction identifying herself as a person who has conducted over 50,000 job interviews, Phyllis Martin suggests that a job seeker should strive for a "neat package." This entire series is concerned with those elements which a job candidate can control and one of these is appearance. The same model is shown in a variety of outfits to show that one person can project many "looks." The main idea in this sequence is that "the winning look" is the style of dress which is the most "businesslike" and not necessarily the "most attractive." By avoiding negative "distractions" and dressing and looking businesslike, the job seeker can score well on the first rating category of every interview. On 3/4" U-Matic.

The Resume (1979;15 min.; WCET-TV/University Film & Video) Those items which a resume must include are detailed and explained (work experience, education background, personal strengths, name and address, multiple phone numbers, job objective). Chronological, functional and original resumes are viewed and discussed. Covers the purpose and form which a successful resume should take.

6. ADDITIONAL TOPICS—————————————————————

6.A. TECHNOLOGY—————————————————————

Automated Material Handling: Manufacturing Insights (1986; 29 min.; SME-Society Mfg. Engrs.) Robotics and their uses in the manufacturing world.

The Business of Paradigms (198?; 30 mins; Charthouse Learning Corporation) Looking beyond the normal "way of doing business" might net you some fantastic innovations and opportunities.

Coping with Technology: Beyond Bureaucracy, Towards a New Democracy (1982; 26 min.; Cinema Guild) In this film, Dr. Warren Bennis provides a provocative analysis of the impact of technology on human life. He discusses the inability of rigid, bureaucratic organizations to cope with rapid technological growth, and suggests that new, more open and democratic forms must develop to keep pace with change. Robert Heilbroner, economist, and Buckminster Fuller, futurist, comment on the prospects of man and his organizations in the face of rapid technological progress.

The Future of Technology (1989; 28 mins; BNA Communications) Charles De Carlo of Sarah Lawrence College joins Drucker and Hall to discuss the role technology will play in solving present and future crises. Find out about the nature of technology, get an insight into the areas in which you can expect change, get ideas about technological issues than can affect your organization.

High Tech: Dream or Nightmare (1984; 49 min.; CBS-Carousel Films/Carousel, University of Iowa Media Library) Correspondent Walter Cronkite examines the impact of the high-tech revolution on the American blue collar workforce. Robots—steel collar workers—are taking over more and more jobs in factories throughout the country. The impact of this revolution is discussed by business and labor leaders, economists and workers, who suggest the need for programs to retain and relocate displaced workers.

Justification, Application & Predictions in Robotics (1986; 60 min.; SME-Society Mfg. Engrs.) Roundtable discussion of today's applications in robotics.

Risk - The Way to Grow (1988; 38 mins; Wade Maurice & Associates Inc.) Businesses that have innovative and imaginative employees have the edge over the competition and will make a greater profit.

All in the Game (1983; 28 min.; WGBH-LCOA/Penn State University Audio Visual Services) Traces the meteoric rise of Imagic, young home-video-game company, and its impact on a fiercely competitive market. Led by Founder William Gnubb, Imagic by September 1982 had soared to the number-two spot among its first product introduction, and was making plans for an initial public stock offering. But after industry leaders Atari and Mattel announced in December that fourth-quarter sales were less than expected, Grubb postponed the offering until the market regained bullishness on video stocks. From the Enterprise 2 series. Host: Eric Sevareid.

Billion Dollar League (10 min.; Honeywell Corporation) Honeywell's approach to employees in an attempt to reach the first billion dollar sales year.

Enterprise Series: All in the Game (1983; 30 min.; Learn Corp/Amer & WGBH-TV) A look at one of America's fastest growing home video game companies.

Henry Ford's America (1977; 57 min.; University of Illinois Film Center) Documents the turbulent history of the Ford dynasty, and the spawning and evolution of the automatic age. Henry Ford I introduced the Model T and the moving assembly line. He took the toy of the rich, made it the birthright of the American masses and changed the course of history. He left America free to move, and his grandson, Henry Ford II, makes sure it will move in the right direction.

Notes on an American Business: Part 1—Keep the Wheels Rolling (1977; 59 min.; Penn State University Television/Penn State Audio Visual Services) An overview of Sitkin Smelting and Refining, Inc. of Lewistown, Pennsylvania. Scenes at the company's Christmas party and inside the plant introduce employees whose perspectives are the focus of labor documentaries in the series. Features a "view from the top" by board chairman Lewis Sitkin, son of the company's founder. Sitkin reviews the history of the small business, its present and future status, and he is observed at work.

Notes on an American Business: Part 2—The Hot World (1977; 55 min.; Penn State University Television/Penn State Audio Visual Services) The world of work as seen be two employees of Sitkin Smelting and Refining, Inc. This documentary surveys the daily activity and explores the different perspectives of foundry manager Leon Grassmeyer and furnace foreman Bill Stimely.

Notes on an American Business: Part 3—Strike Up the Band (1977; 59 min.; Penn State University Television/Penn State Audio Visual Services) A profile of Jack Sitkin, vice-president of Sitkin Smelting and Refining. Examines the middle management problems facing Sitkin, how he responds to them, and the way his lively personality fits his goals as a small businessman.

Notes on an American Business: Part 4—The Alabama Connection (1977; 55 min.; Penn State University Television/Penn State Audio Visual Services) An account of the human and economic factors involved in making the decision whether or not to move part of Sitkin Smelting and Refining to Alabama. Focuses on vice-president Jack Sitkin surveying possible plant locations and dealing with government officials.

UW - Stout/Case - IH Project (International Harvester)(1988; 7 min.; University of Wisconsin) Program deals with J. I. Case Company, part of International Harvester, and its production and manufacturing strategy, and how UW-Stout assisted in the set-up of its program.

6.C. INDUSTRIAL DEMOCRACY

What About the Workers—Program 1: The Traditional Company (1978; 28 min.; Thames TV/Heritage Visual Sales, Inc./University of Illinois Film Center) Explores the concept of industrial democracy as a solution to Britain's management problems and the resulting industrial conflict and low productivity. Asks how workers should participate, and begins the answer by looking at a company which involves workers in the traditional way. Visits a company that gives workers the option to become shareholders in order to promote greater worker interest in management. Opinions are gathered from on-the-job sites, interviews, and board meetings.

What About the Workers: Program 3—Participation the CBI Way (1978; 28 min.; Thames TV/Heritage Visual Sales, Inc./University of Illinois Film Center) Observes the consultative system advocated by the CBI (Confederation of British Industries). Reports on two companies selected by the CBI, the Scottish and Newcastle Brewery and Cadbury Schweppes. The idea is that worker participation should start on the shop floor in order to avoid disputes before they arise. Follows the procedures used to allow employees to air their day-to-day grievances. Points out such problems as the temptation for shop stewards to cross over the line and become management men, and deciding at what stage in the decision-making process to involve the staff.

What About the Workers: Program 4—Industrial Democracy the Union Way (1978; 28 min.; Thames TV/Heritage Visual Sales, Inc./University of Illinois Film Center) A presentation of the role of "worker-director" in British industry, giving their view of their own role, to "project a shop floor view into the board room." Such representatives are in rather an awkward position, as they often have information it is better not to divulge. The idea met with much cynicism at its inception, but British Steel, which has had worker-directors since 1968, finds they have worked out well. A well-chosen worker-director with a good sense of morale can give an accurate assessment of the general employee reaction to projected changes, prepare employees for changes, and furnish feedback regarding actual effects of change. Interview technique, intercut with scenes of meetings and of activity in the manufacturing plants.

What About the Workers: Program 5—A visit to Germany and Sweden (1978; 28 min.; Thames TV/Heritage Visual Sales, Inc./University of Illinois Film Center) Because Sweden has a reputation of being a leader in the concept of "industrial democracy," the British team sends a union representative, a management representative, and program coordinator Hugh Macpherson on a visit to the Saab factory in Sweden and the Volkswagen plant in Germany. British representatives are asked what they expect to find, some of what they find is filmed, and their assessment of it is recorded.

What About the Workers: Program 6—A Discussion on the Government White Paper (1978; 28 min.; Thames TV/Heritage Visual Sales, Inc./University of Illinois Film Center) The government's white paper expressed the intent to pass a law requiring management to consult labor on decisions. Various potential effects on exiting companies, and their systems form the substance of a discussion moderated by Hugh Macpherson, and involving Sir John Mertram, Director General of the Confederation of British Industries, and Lynn Murray, General Secretary of T.U.C., which holds an opposing view. The white paper is variously criticized as "a straight-jacket on development," and seen as a threat to the various worker-director systems which are functioning to the satisfaction of the people involved.

6.D. STRESS

Burnout (1979; 26 min.; Gary Mitchell/University Film & Video) Identifies the symptoms of professional "burnout," providing a host of coping techniques for dealing with this work disease phenomenon.

Coping With Stress (1980;18 min.; Professional Research Inc./FilmFair) The film shows that everyone is subject to stress and stressful situations, whether at home, on the job or simply living day-to-day. Stress affects different people in different ways and can cause physical problems, psychological problems, or a combination of the two, all of which adds to the original stress problem, creating more tension. Focuses on effective ways to alleviate stress.

Managing Stress (1979; 33 min.; CRM-McGraw-Hill Films/Iowa State University) Examines aspects of stress which can be a healthy motivating force or build into unhealthy tension. Investigating both physiological and psychological effects, the film is designed to help viewers recognize common sources of stress, assess toleration capacity, and identify alternative means to cope with stress. A variety of film techniques, and a stress reduction technique used by Dr. James Manuso present the major issues of stress research.

Nature of Stress, The (1992; 60 min.; Alvin H. Perlmutter) Explores the long-term effects of stress and what is known about how to reduce them.

Stress: A Personal Challenge (1980; 30 min.; University of Illinois Film Center) Defines stress, its causes, and its results for the human mechanism, and prescribes ways of managing it and of defusing its harmful aspects. Stemming from tension caused by an alarm reaction that is seldom fully released, stress can be released in a combination of exercise and relaxation techniques that will enable a person to use its positive, energizing aspects.

Stress: Are We Killing Ourselves? (1979;15 min.; University of Illinois Film Center) Relates results of research on stress, giving symptoms and evaluating various ways of coping. The presented positive ways of dealing with stress include meditation and biofeedback.

The Stress Mess (1981; 25 min.; Barr Films/University Film & Video) A humorous yet hard-hitting training film that teaches how to reduce and manage stress, reveals many common signs of stress and shows how to identify the sources of stress in our lives. The film follows the Wilson family through a typical stress-filled day. Addresses many of the problems that cause stress in the modern business world and teaches time management techniques—setting priorities, delegating tasks, learning how to say no, and learning how to relax.

6.E. TIME MANAGEMENT

Finding Time (1980; 30 min.; Stephen Judson/CRM/McGraw-Hill/Iowa State University) Discusses the difficulties in scheduling personal and organizational time, demonstrating time problems created by overcommitment, procrastination, interruptions, preparations, meetings, day-dreaming and cramming. Suggests simple time management techniques for the worker and supervisor such as listing priorities, setting realistic goals, breaking overwhelming problems into management units, and taking "quiet hours" out from daily schedules.

Managing Time - Effective Executive Series (1968; 21 min.; BNA Communications) Dangers of mismanaged time and advantages of time logging are discussed. Emphasizes the need to delegate authority. Question "Am I giving right kind of time to the really important thing?" is asked.

Time of your Life (1985; 28 min.; Cally Curtis Company) Film is based upon the research of Alan Lakein who looks at time as it relates to life. The theme is: to waste time is to waste your life...to master your time is to master your life. With instructor manual.

The Time Trap (1981; 30 min.; American Media/University Film & Video) The objective of this time management film is to show participants how they can increase productivity by scheduling their time more effectively. Viewers will heighten their awareness of how they presently use their time and will learn specific techniques for more efficient use of their time in the future. Based on the book, *The Time Trap*, by Dr. Alec Mackenzie.

6.F. MISCELLANEOUS ISSUES

America Works: Industrial Policy (1983; 23 min.; Labor Institute of Public Affairs/AFL-CIO Film Division) This special edition introduces the debate over a coordinated policy to maintain the U.S. industrial base and develop new jobs. Senator Edward Kennedy, AFL-CIO President Lane Kirkland and investment banker Felix Rohatyn are joined by economists and other political and corporate leaders to present the argument.

Loose Bolts? (1972; 30 min.; Red Ball Films, Inc.) Filmed interviews of causes and results of worker dissatisfaction in auto assembly plant. Includes interviews of workers in 1972 Lordstown, Ohio dispute. Labor Dept. of Statistics emphasize meaning.

Pay Equity (1984; 28 min.; LIPA/AFL-CIO Film Division) Lynda Clendenning a librarian at the University of Maryland, leads a group of clerical workers in their fight to earn salaries equal to those of male workers in comparable jobs. A discussion of this issue takes place between Linda Chavez, Executive Director of the U.S. Commission on Civil Rights, Winn Newman, the attorney who successfully argued the landmark pay equity case in the state of Washington, and National Public Radio correspondent Nina Totenberg. An update features Mary Rose Oakar, (D-OH) discussing legislation now before Congress.

People at Work: A Right to Refuse? (1981; 13 min.; National Film Board of Canada/Penn State University Audio Visual Services) Open-ended dramatization examines the question: Do workers have the right to refuse a direct management order that they consider unsafe? Contends that this is one of the most controversial issues affecting the worker/supervisor relationship in postindustrial America, and one that is further complicated by a glut of federal and state regulations.

Teen Jobs and the Minimum Wage (1984; 28 min.; Labor Institute of Public Affairs/AFL-CIO Film Division) Milka Ruiz, Bronx New York teenager, leads a fight to protect decent paying jobs for herself and other young people. A panel discussion of the subminimum wage takes place between James O'Hara, former head of Minimum Wage Study Commission, Mark DeBernardo, Manager, Labor Law Unit, Chamber of Commerce and *Newsday* reporter Patrick Owens.

FILM DISTRIBUTORS DIRECTORY

AFL-CIO Film Division
Department of Education
Chicago, IL 60604
Washington, D.C. 20006
(202) 637-5153

American Arbitration Association
140 W. 51 St.
New York, NY 10020
(212) 484-4000

American Management Assoc., Inc.
135 W. 50th St.
NewYork, NY 10020
(212) 586-8100

American Media, Inc.
1454 30th Street
West Des Moines, IA50265
(1-800-262-2557)

Annenberg/CPB Project
P.O. Box 1922
Santa Barbara, CA 93116-1922
1-800-Learner

Argee Productions
114 King St. Suite 201
Madison, WI 53703
(608)255-8480

Arthur Mokin Productions, Inc.
P.O. Box 1866
Santa Rosa, CA 95402
(707)542-4868

Barr Films
12801 Schabanum Ave.
Irwindale, CA 91706-7878
1-800-243-7878

Beacon Films, Inc.
930 Pitner
Evanston, IL 60202
(708)328-6700

Blanchard Training & Development Inc.
125 State Place
Escondido, CA 92025
1-800-728-6000

BNA Communications, Inc.
9439 Key West
Rockville, MD 20850
Attention: Customer Relations Dept.
(301) 948-0540

Brigham Young University
Media Marketing
W-STAD
Provo, UT 84602

Britannica Films
310 S. Michigan Ave.
815 Sixteenth St., N.W.
1-800-554-9862

California Newsreel
149 9th St. #420
San Francisco, CA 94103
(415) 621-6196

Cally Curtis Co.
111 N. Las Palmas Ave.
Hollywood, CA 90038
(213)467-1101

Carousel Films, Inc
260 Fifth Ave. Rm. i05
New York, NY 10001
(212) 683-1660

CareerAids
20417 Nordhoff St. Dept. K
Chatsworth, CA 91311
(818)341-2535

Career Track Publications
3085 Center Green Dr.
P.O. Box 18778
Boulder, CO 80308-8778
1-800-334-7440

Centron Films
Centron Corporation
108 Wilmot Rd.
Deerfield, IL 60015
1-800-323-5343

Churchill Films
12210 Nebraska Ave
Los Angeles, CA90025
(213) 207-6600

Cinema Guild
1697 Broadway, Suite 802
New York, NY 10019
(212) 246-5522

CRM/McGraw Hill Films
2233 Faraday Ave.
Carlsbad, CA 92008-9829
1-800-421-0388

Dartnell Corporation
4660 N. Ravenswood Ave
Chicago, IL 60640
1-800-621-5463

Eastern New Mexico Univ.
Film Library
Portales, NM 88130
(505) 562-2622

Educational Video Network
1494 19th St.
Huntsville, TX 77340
(409)295-5767

Enterprise Media Inc.
374 Congress St. Suite 508
Boston, MA 02118
1-800-423-6021

Federal Reserve Board of Governors
Publications Services
Washington, D.C. 20551

FilmFair Communications
10621 Magnolia Blvd.
N. Hollywood, CA 91601
(818) 985-0244

Films, Inc. Education
5547 North Ravenswood
Chicago, IL 60640-1199
1-800-323-4222 (Ext. 43)

Florida State University
Instructional Support Center
Tallahassee, FL 32306
(904) 644-2820

General Motors Corp.
3044 W. Grand Blvd
Detroit, MI 48238

Goodmeasure Inc.
330 Broadway
Cambridge, MA 02139
(617) 491-7370

Instructional Media Services
128 E. Pittsburgh St
Greensburg, PA 15601

International Communications Agency
United States of America
Washington, DC 20547

Iowa State University
Media Resources Center
121 PearsonHall
Ames, Iowa 50011

LCA Video/Films
1350 Avenue of the Americas
NewYork, NY 10019

(212) 397-9330

Manpower Educational Institute of American
Foundation and Employees
127 East 35th St.
New York NY 10016
(212) 532-4747

Massachusetts Institute of Technol.
Dept. 99, Rm. 90-234
77 Massachusetts Ave.
Cambridge, MA 02139
(617)253-7444

Media Guild
(Also listed as University Media)
11722 Sorrento Valley Road
Suite E
San Diego, CA 92121
(619) 755-9191

National Audio-Visual Center
National Archives and Records Svce
8700 Edgeworth Dr.
Capitol Heights, MD 20743-3701
1-800-638-1300

National Safety Council
Greater Los Angeles Chapter
3450 Wilshire Blvd. Suite 700
Los Angeles CA 90010

Oklahoma State University
NUTN Central Office
332 Student Union
Stillwater, OK 74078-0635

PBS
1320 Braddock Place
Alexandria, VA 22314-1698

Pennsylvania State University
Audio Visual.Services
Special Service Building
University Park, PA 16802
(814) 863-3102

Pyramid Film Productions
P.O. Box 1048
Santa Monica, CA 90406
(213)828-7577

Rental Library Films, Inc.
8124 North Central Park Ave.
Skokie, IL 60076
(708) 256-4730

RMI Media Productions Inc.
2807 W. 47th Street
Shawnee Mission, KS 66205
1-800-821-5480

Roundtable Films, Inc.
113 North San Vicente Blvd
Beverly Hills, CA90211
(213) 657-1402

Salenger Educational Media
1 635 1 2th Street
Santa Monica, CA 90404
(213) 450-1300

Small Business Administration
81 1 Vermont Ave., N .W
Washington, D.C. 20416

Simon & Schuster
108 Wilmot Rd.
Deerfield, IL 60015
1-800-323-5343

Sperry-Univac
P.O. Box 500
Blue Bell, PA 19424

Thompson Mitchell & Associates
7 Piedmont Center
Atlanta, GA 30305
1-800-554-1389

Training Images International
7334 Topanga Canyon Blvd. Suite 117
Canoga Park CA 91303
1-800-882-9436

University Associates, Inc
8517 Production Avenue
San Diego, CA92121
(619) 578-5900

University Film & Video
University of Minnesota
3300 University Ave. S.E.
Minneapolis, MN 55414
(612) 373-3810

University of California
Extension Media Center
2176 Shattuck Avenue
Berkeley, CA 94704
(510) 642-5578

University of California-Los Angeles
Instructional Media Library
46 Powell Library
Los Angeles, CA 90024

University of Connecticut
Health Center Library
Farmington, CT 06032
(203)679-3272

University of Illinois Film Center
1325 S. Oak St.
Champaign, IL 61820
1-800-367-3456

University of Iowa
Media Library
C-5 East Hall
Iowa City, IA 52242
(319) 353-5885

University of Nebraska-Lincoln
Division of Continuing Studies
Instructional Media Center
421 Nebraska Hall
Lincoln, NE 68583-0900
(402) 472-1900

University of Utah
Instnuctional Media Services
207 Milton Bennion Hall
Salt Lake City, UT 84112

University of Wisconsin-Madison
Bureau of Audio-Visual Instruction
1327 University Avenue
Madison, WI 53706
(608)262-1644

Video Publishing House, Inc.
4 Woodfield Lake
930 N State Pkwy. Suite 505
Schaumburg 11 60173

Vision Associates, Inc.
665 Fifth Avenue
New York, NY 10022

World Research, Inc.
11722 Sorrento Valley Rd.
San Diego, CA92121

XICOM Video Arts
Sterling Forest
Tuxedo, NY 10987
1 800 431 2395

SPECIAL NOTE:

Many universities and colleges are willing to loan their videos. Also consider sharing rental dates with neighboring schools.

SECTION VI

ADDITIONAL TRANSPARENCIES

Exhibit 1.1 Fundamentals of Managing People: Two Approaches

Human relations approach

- Stimulated by the Hawthorne studies

- Concern for individual dignity

- Concern for developing human potential

- Concern for social environment

Behavioral science approach

- Involved in the scientific search for understanding behavior

- Use of psychology, sociology, and anthropology to understand behavior

- Use of research to gain knowledge

- Acceptance of total person

Exhibit 1.2 Managing Production and Operations

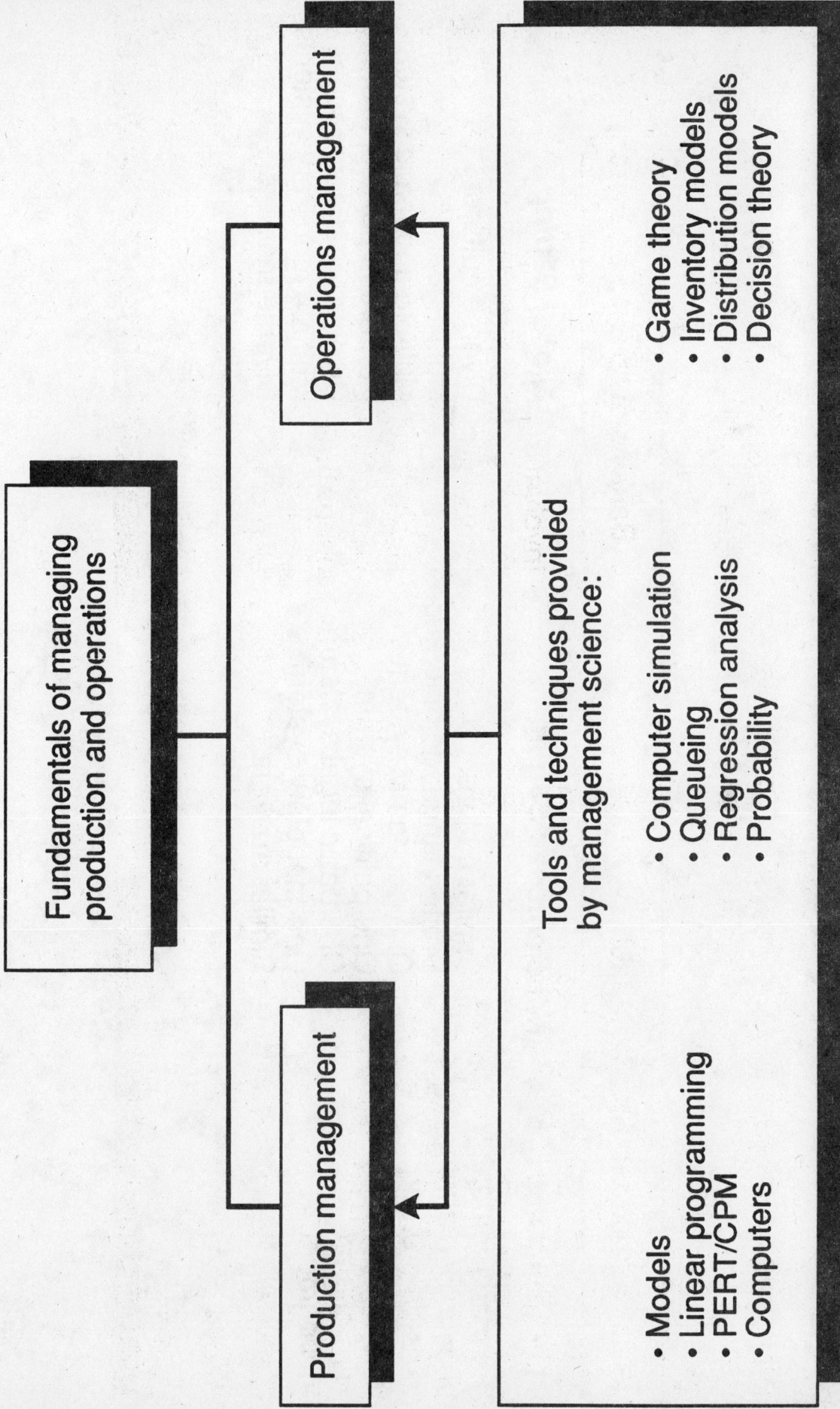

Fundamentals of managing production and operations

Operations management

Production management

Tools and techniques provided by management science:

- Models
- Linear programming
- PERT/CPM
- Computers

- Computer simulation
- Queueing
- Regression analysis
- Probability

- Game theory
- Inventory models
- Distribution models
- Decision theory

Exhibit 3.1   The Planning Environment in Domestic versus Global Settings

*The management
function of planning
takes on greater
complexity in an
international
environment.*

Domestic Setting

Similar culture.
Limited language differences.
One economic system.
One political system.
One basic legal system.
One monetary system.
Similar markets.

Global Setting

Diverse cultures.
Multilingual.
Multiple economic systems.
Numerous political systems.
Diverse legal approaches
Multiple monetary systems.
Diverse markets.

Exhibit 4.1 An Ethical Framework

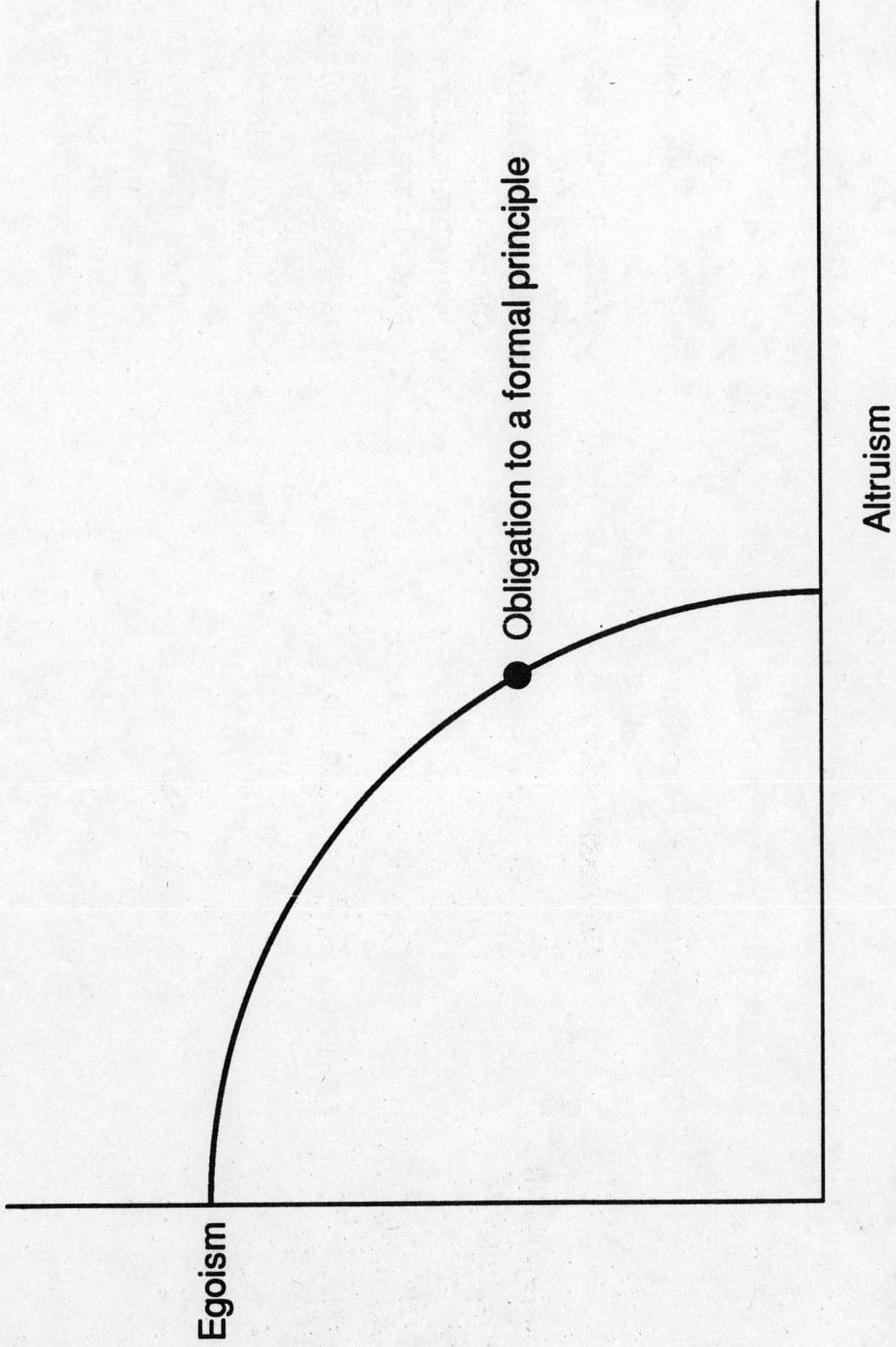

Egoism

● Obligation to a formal principle

Altruism

Exhibit 5.1 Types of Managerial Decisions

Type of Decision	Type of Problem	Procedures	Examples
Programmed	Repetitive, routine.	Rules. Standard operating procedures. Policies.	Business: Processing payroll vouchers. College: Processing admission applications. Hospital: Preparing patient for surgery. Government: Using state-owned motor vehicle.
Nonprogrammed	Complex, novel.	Creative problem solving.	Business: Introducing a new product. College: Constructing new classroom facilities. Hospital: Reacting to a regional disease epidemic. Government: Solving spiraling inflation problems

Programmed and nonprogrammed decisions result from different types of problems and use different types of procedures

Exhibit 7.1   Business Portfolio Matrix

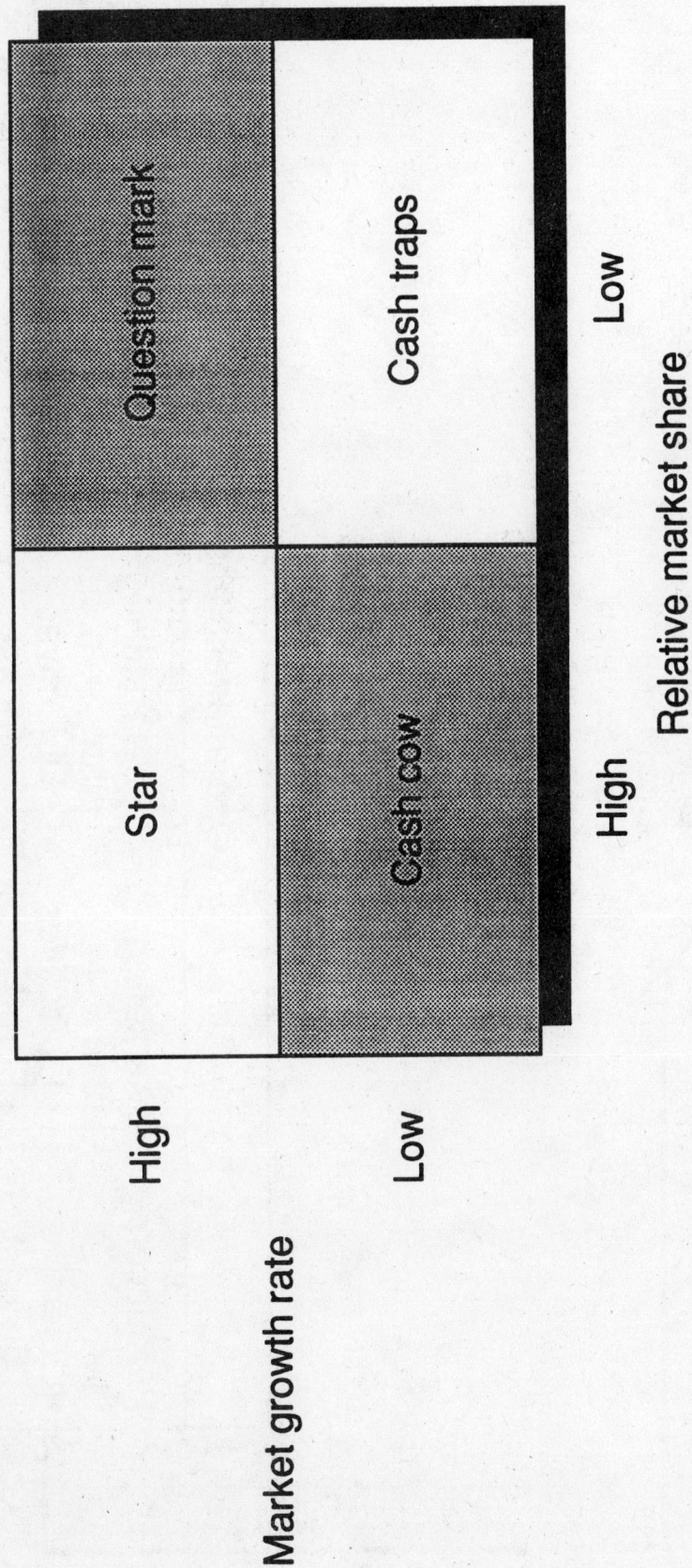

	High	Low
High	Star	Question mark
Low	Cash cow	Cash traps

Relative market share

Market growth rate

Exhibit 7.2   Relationship between the Organization's Strategic Plan and Operational Plans

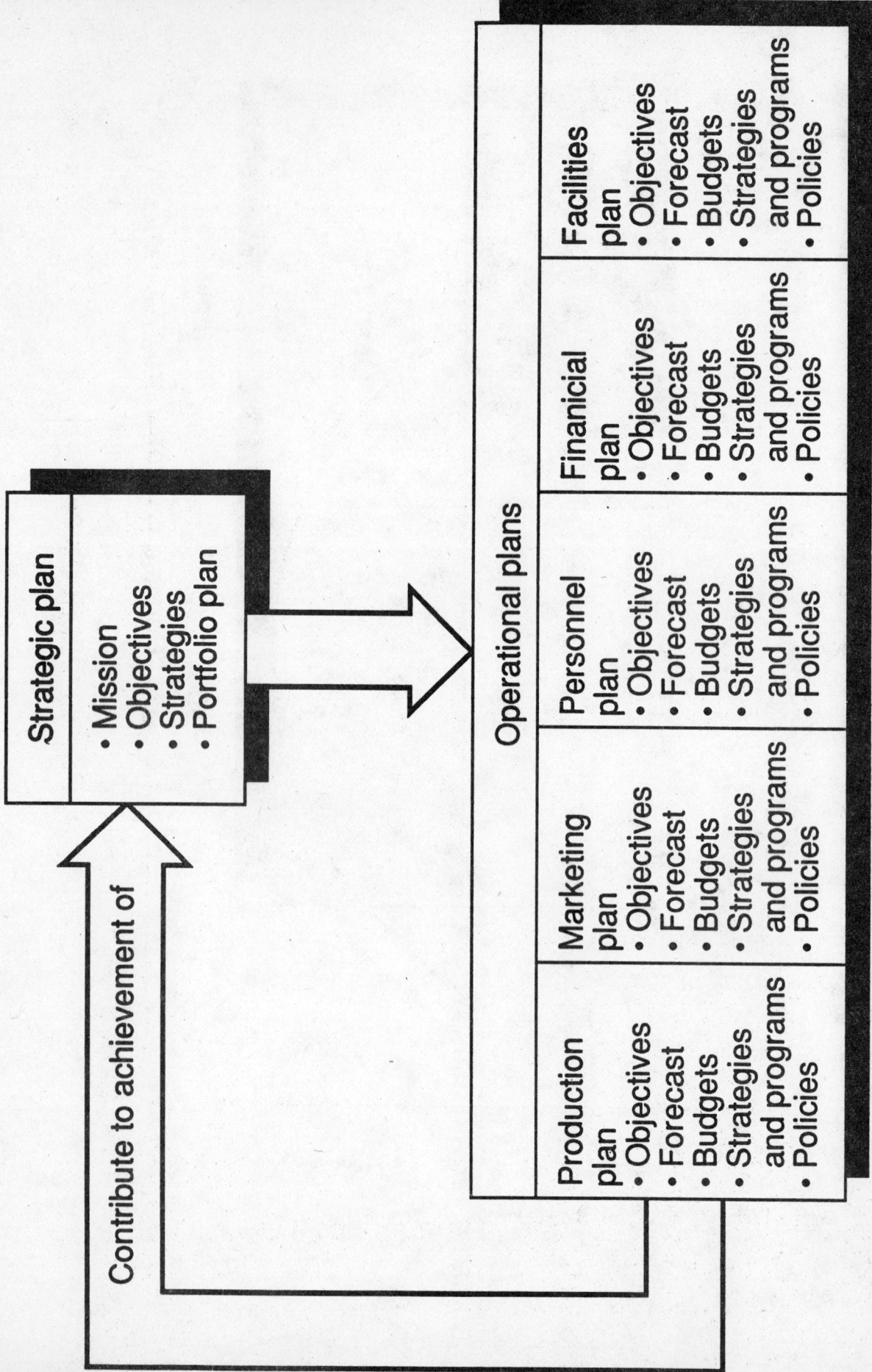

Strategic plan

- Mission
- Objectives
- Strategies
- Portfolio plan

Contribute to achievement of

Operational plans

Production plan	Marketing plan	Personnel plan	Financial plan	Facilities plan
• Objectives • Forecast • Budgets • Strategies and programs • Policies	• Objectives • Forecast • Budgets • Strategies and programs • Policies	• Objectives • Forecast • Budgets • Strategies and programs • Policies	• Objectives • Forecast • Budgets • Strategies and programs • Policies	• Objectives • Forecast • Budgets • Strategies and programs • Policies

Exhibit 8.1   The Economics of Specialization

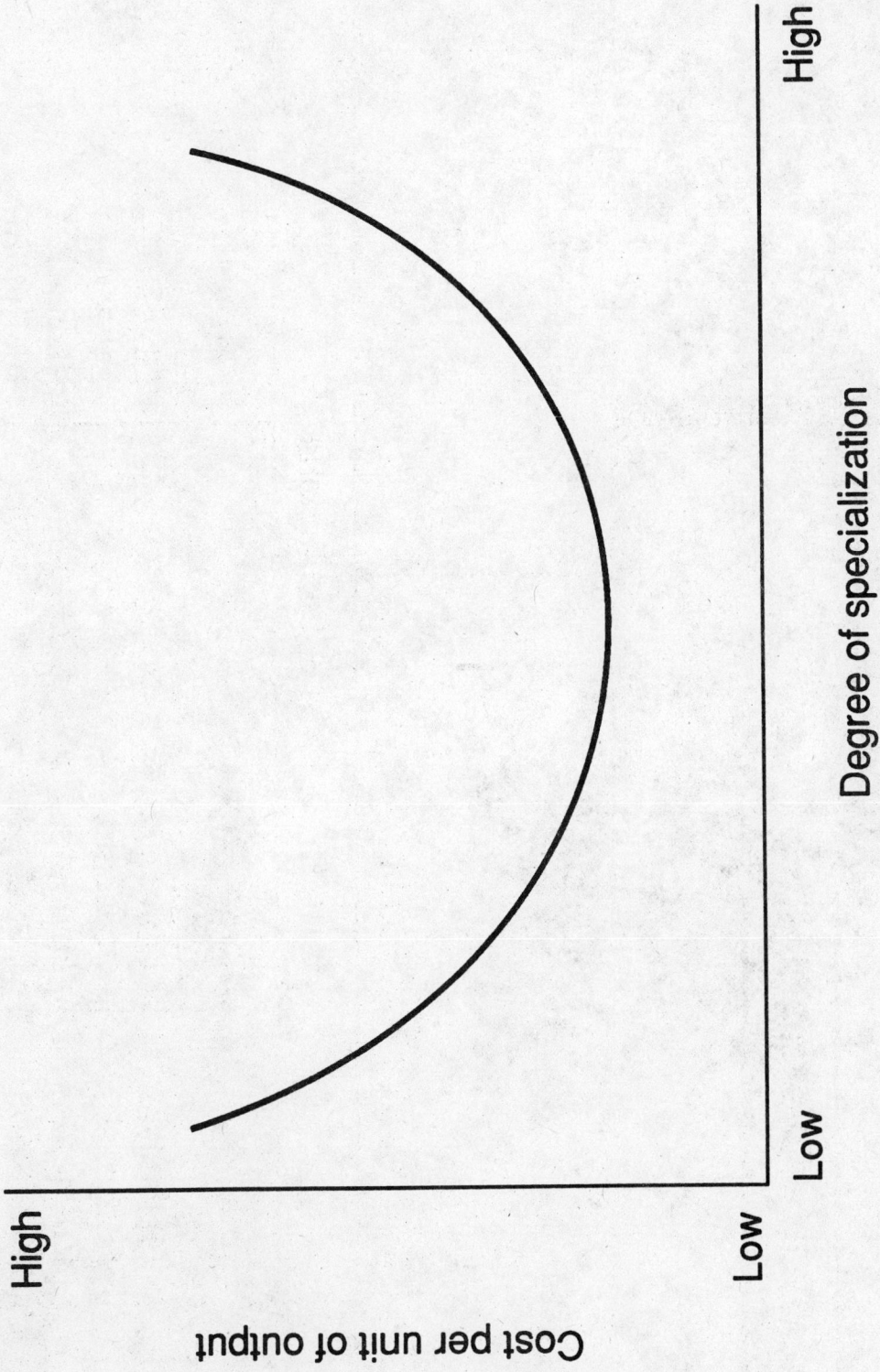

Cost per unit of output (vertical axis: Low to High)

Degree of specialization (horizontal axis: Low to High)

Exhibit 9.1   Technology and Organization Design

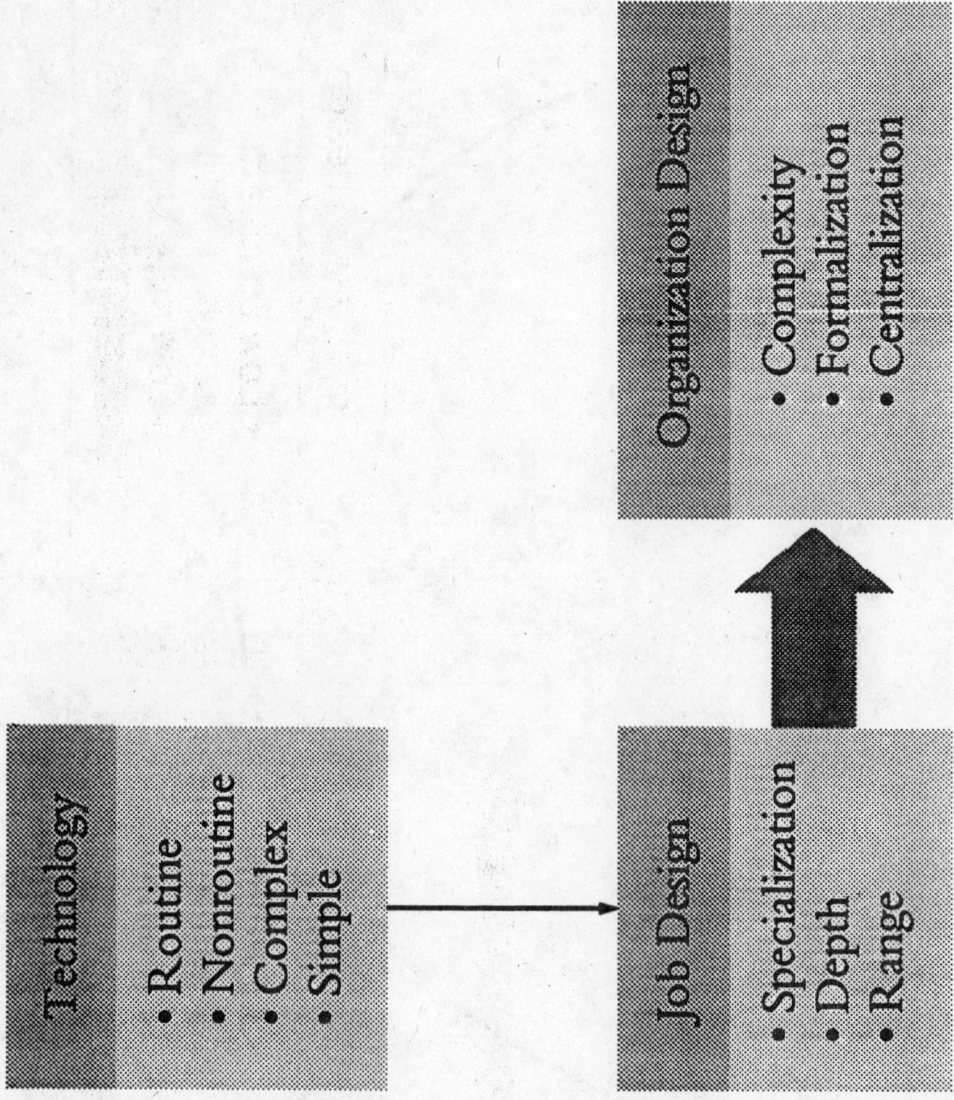

Technology
- Routine
- Nonroutine
- Complex
- Simple

Job Design
- Specialization
- Depth
- Range

Organization Design
- Complexity
- Formalization
- Centralization

Exhibit 9.2 Unit and Process Technology and Organization Design

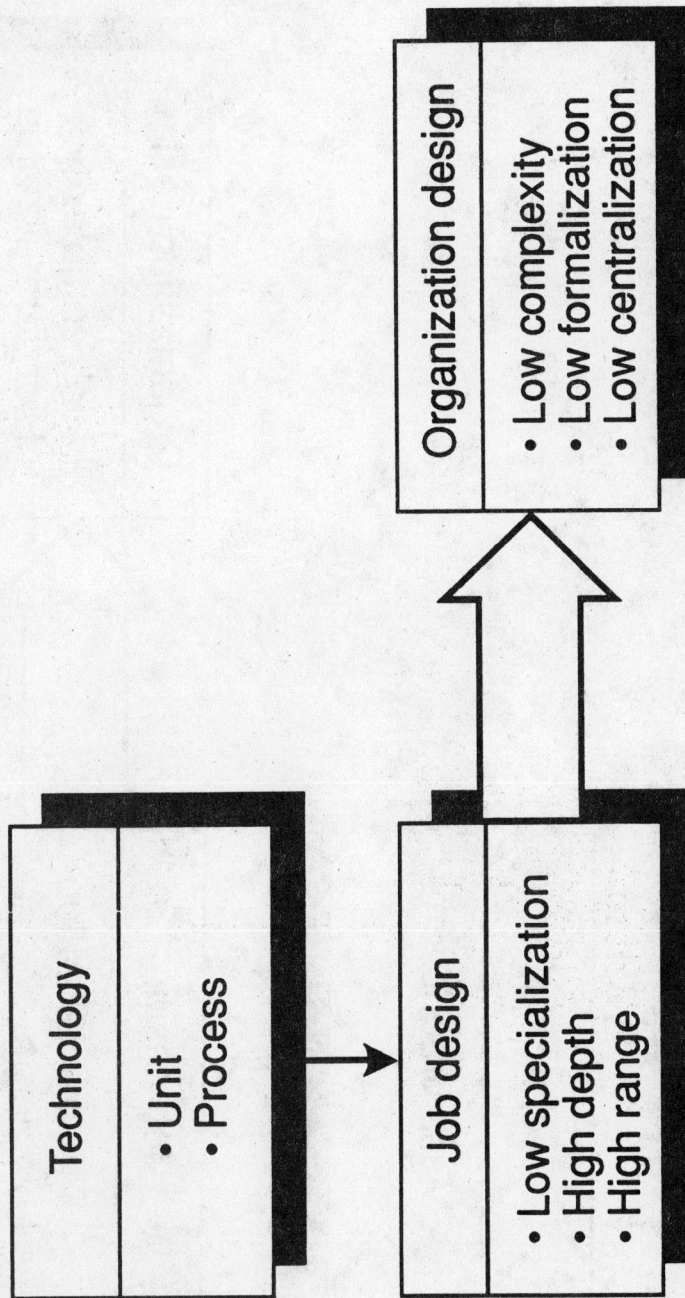

Technology
- Unit
- Process

Job design
- Low specialization
- High depth
- High range

Organization design
- Low complexity
- Low formalization
- Low centralization

Exhibit 9.3 Mass Production Technology and Organization Design

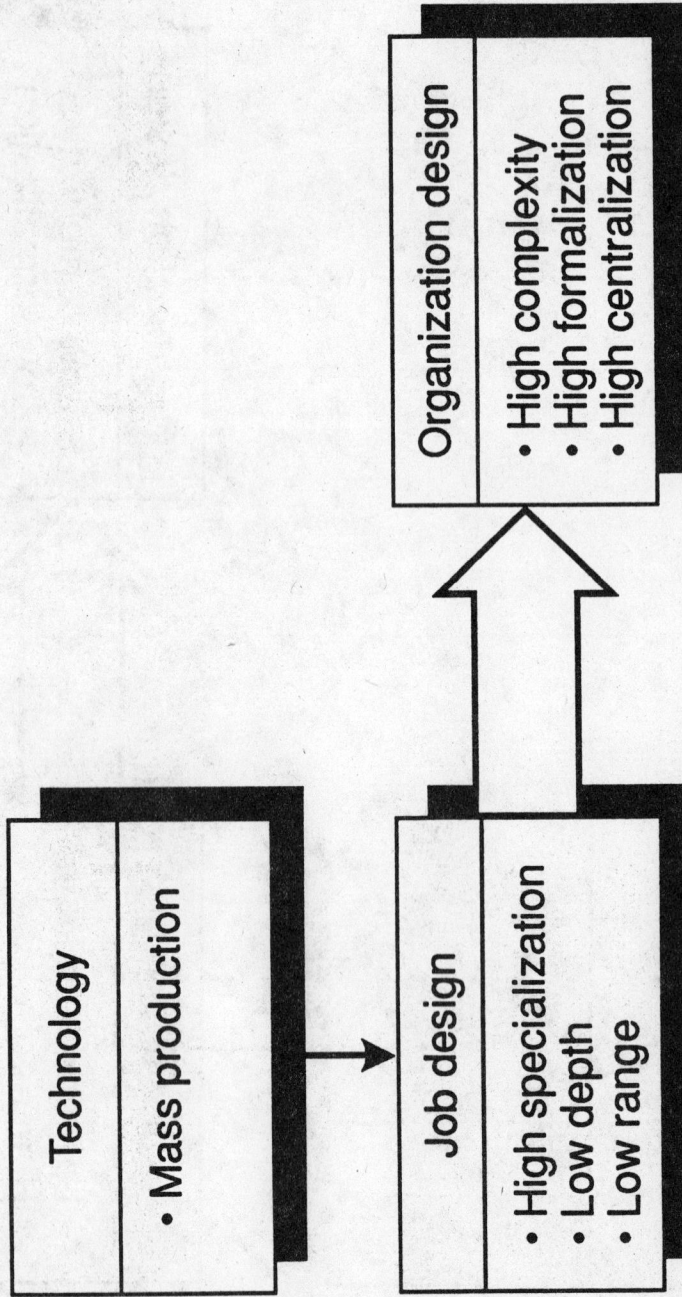

Technology

- Mass production

Job design

- High specialization
- Low depth
- Low range

Organization design

- High complexity
- High formalization
- High centralization

Exhibit 9.4   Strategic Choices and Organization Design

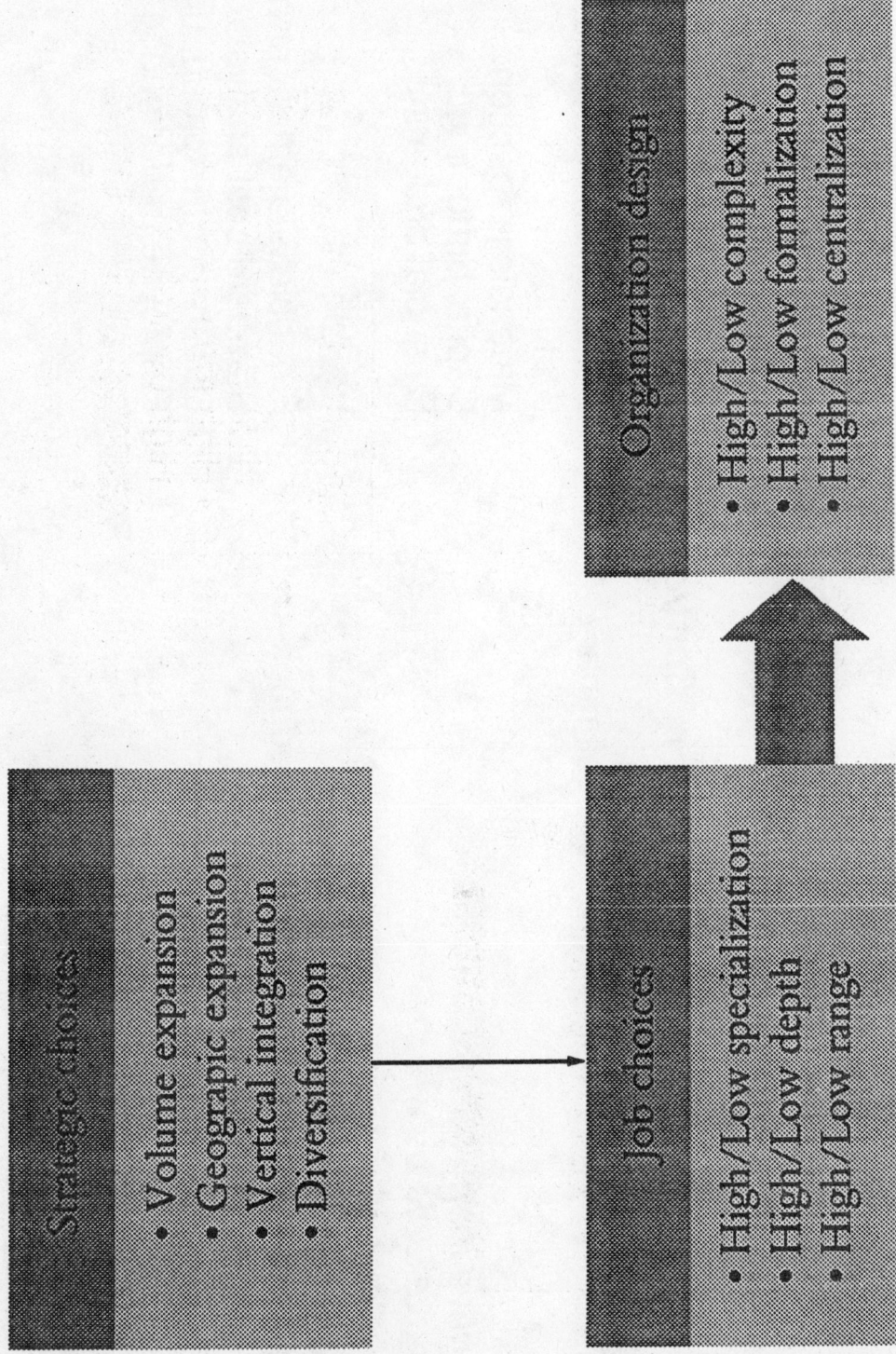

Strategic choices
- Volume expansion
- Geograpic expansion
- Vertical integration
- Diversification

Job choices
- High/Low specialization
- High/Low depth
- High/Low range

Organization design
- High/Low complexity
- High/Low formalization
- High/Low centralization

©Richard D. Irwin, Inc., 1995

Exhibit 10.1 Control Types and Techniques

Managers have many control techniques available by which to take corrective action.

Types of Control	Control Techniques
Preliminary	Selection and placement. Staffing. Materials inspection. Capital budgeting. Financial budgeting.
Concurrent	Direction.
Feedback	Financial statement analysis. Standard cost analysis. Quality control procedures. Employee performance evaluation.

Exhibit 10.2 Simple Relationship between Cash and Inventory

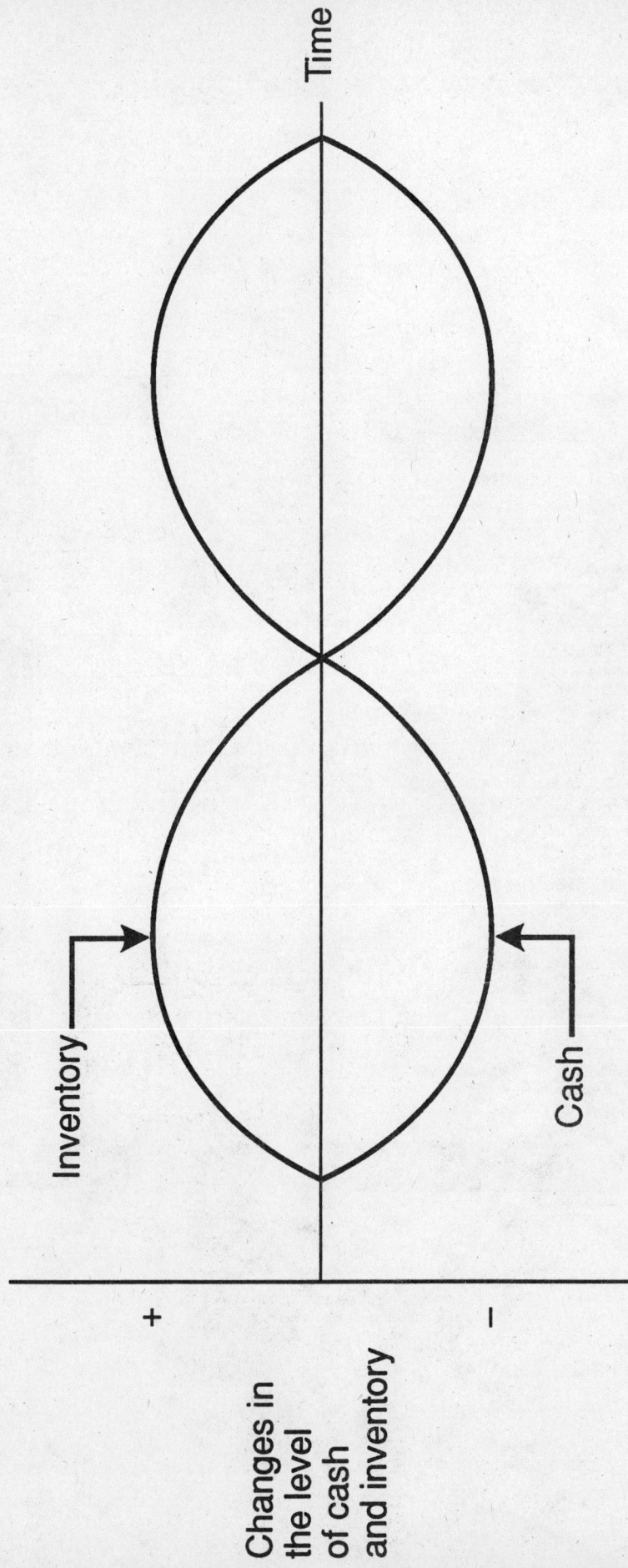

Time

Inventory

Cash

+

—

Changes in
the level
of cash
and inventory

Exhibit 11.1 The Process of Motivation

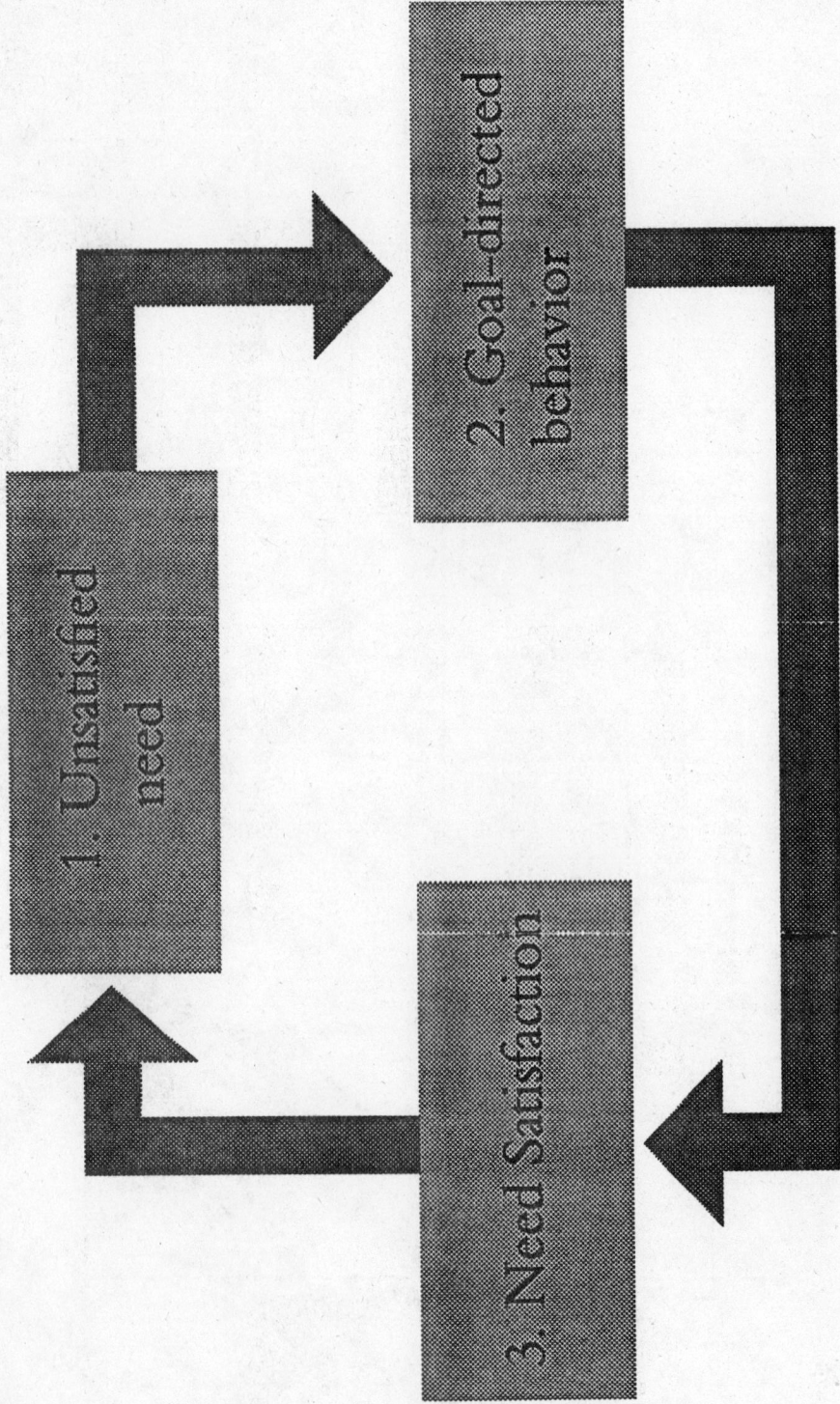

1. Unsatisfied need

2. Goal-directed behavior

3. Need Satisfaction

Exhibit 11.2 Consequences of Pay Dissatisfaction

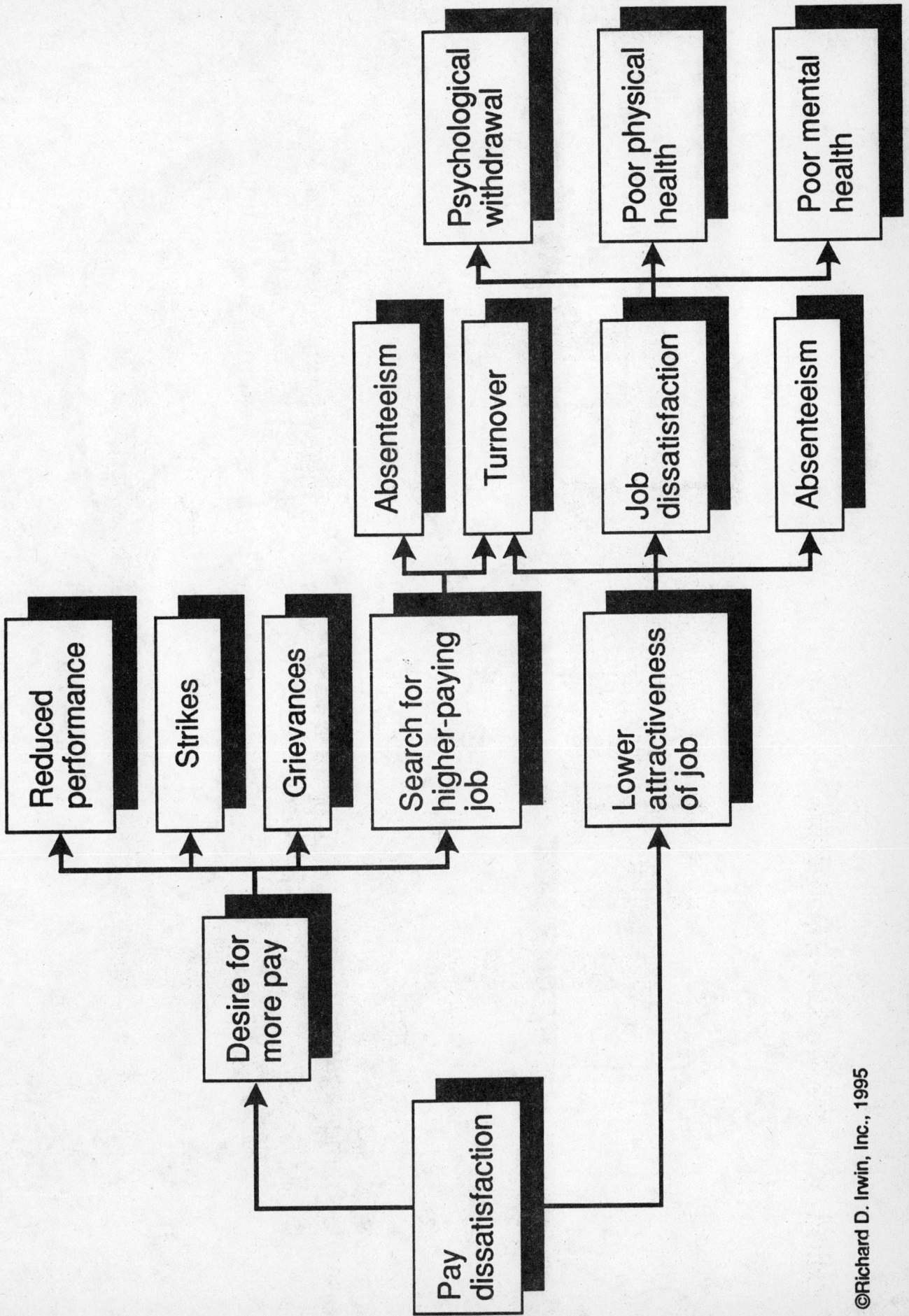

Exhibit 13.1 The Preferred Leader-Manager Mix

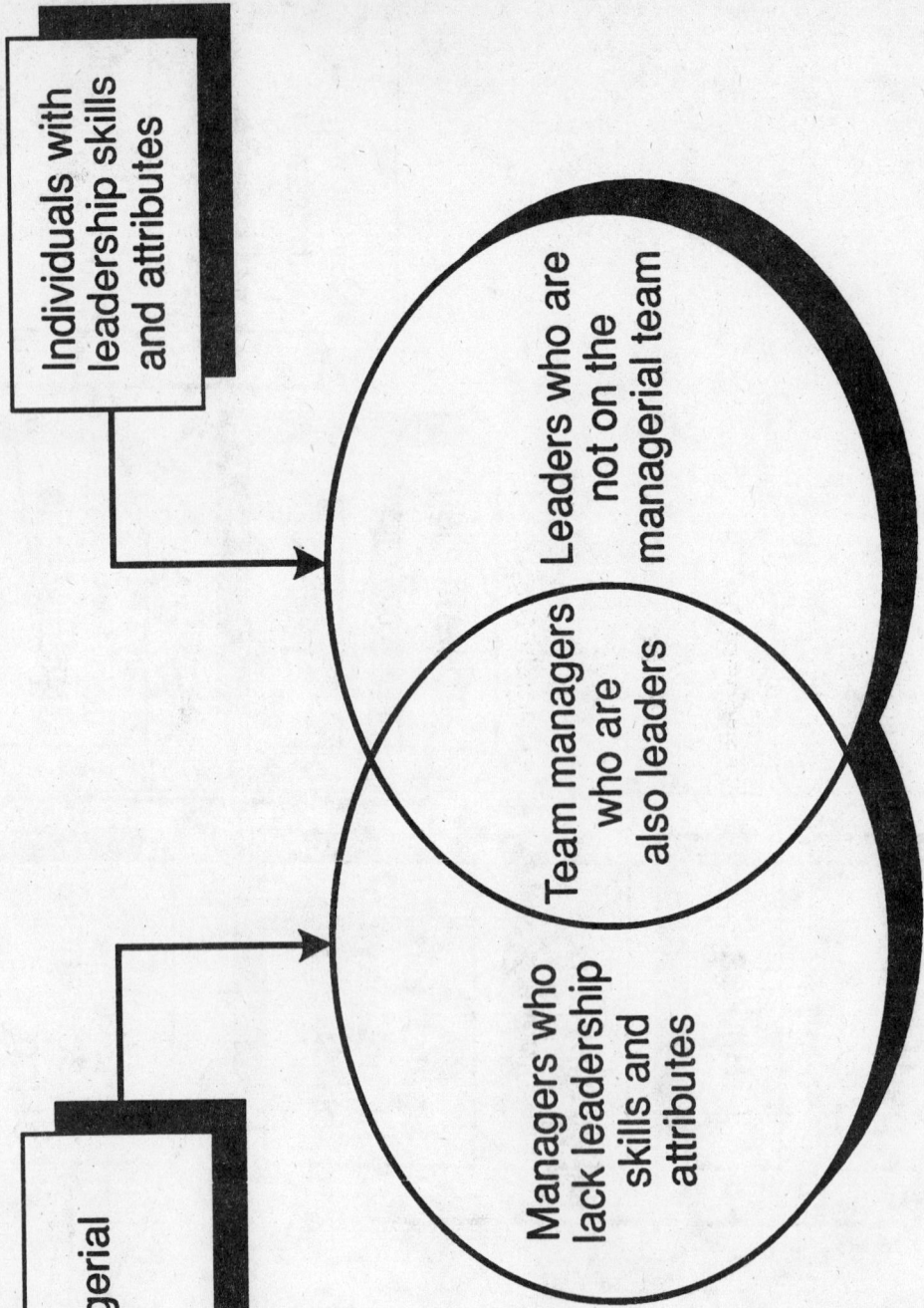

Individuals with leadership skills and attributes

Managerial team

Leaders who are not on the managerial team

Team managers who are also leaders

Managers who lack leadership skills and attributes

Leaders = Managers only in some cases, since leadership is only one part of management.

Exhibit 13.2   The Vroom-Yetton Decision Tree

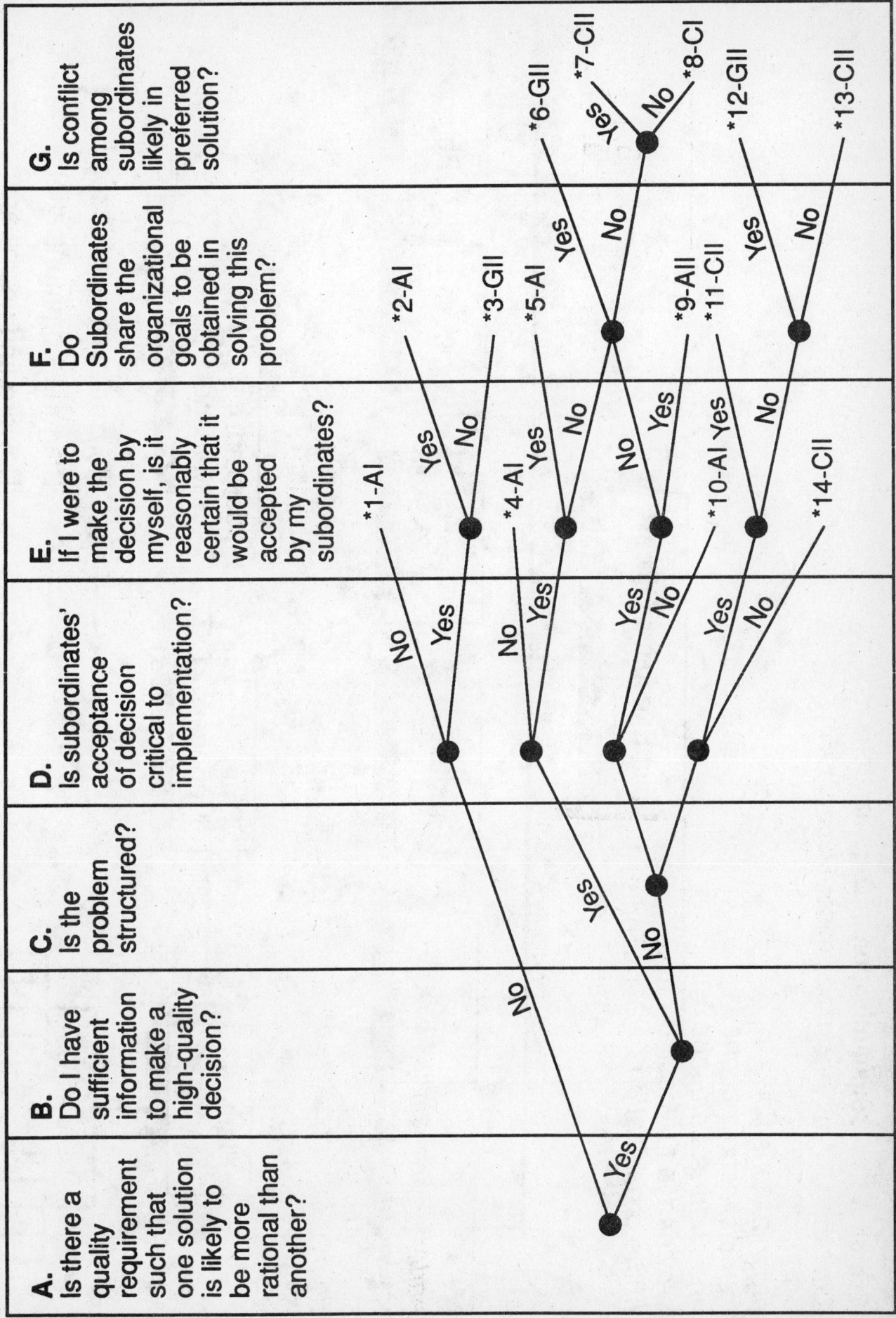

| A. Is there a quality requirement such that one solution is likely to be more rational than another? | B. Do I have sufficient information to make a high-quality decision? | C. Is the problem structured? | D. Is subordinates' acceptance of decision critical to implementation? | E. If I were to make the decision by myself, is it reasonably certain that it would be accepted by my subordinates? | F. Do Subordinates share the organizational goals to be obtained in solving this problem? | G. Is conflict among subordinates likely in preferred solution? |

Decision tree branches and terminal outcomes:

- *1-AI
- *2-AI
- *3-GII
- *4-AI
- *5-AI
- *6-GII
- *7-CII
- *8-CI
- *9-AII
- *10-AI
- *11-CII
- *12-GII
- *13-CII
- *14-CII

Branch labels: Yes / No at each node.

©Richard D. Irwin, Inc., 1995

Exhibit 14.1   Communication in Organizations

Communication in organizations flows in four distinct directions, and channels must be provided in the design of the organization.

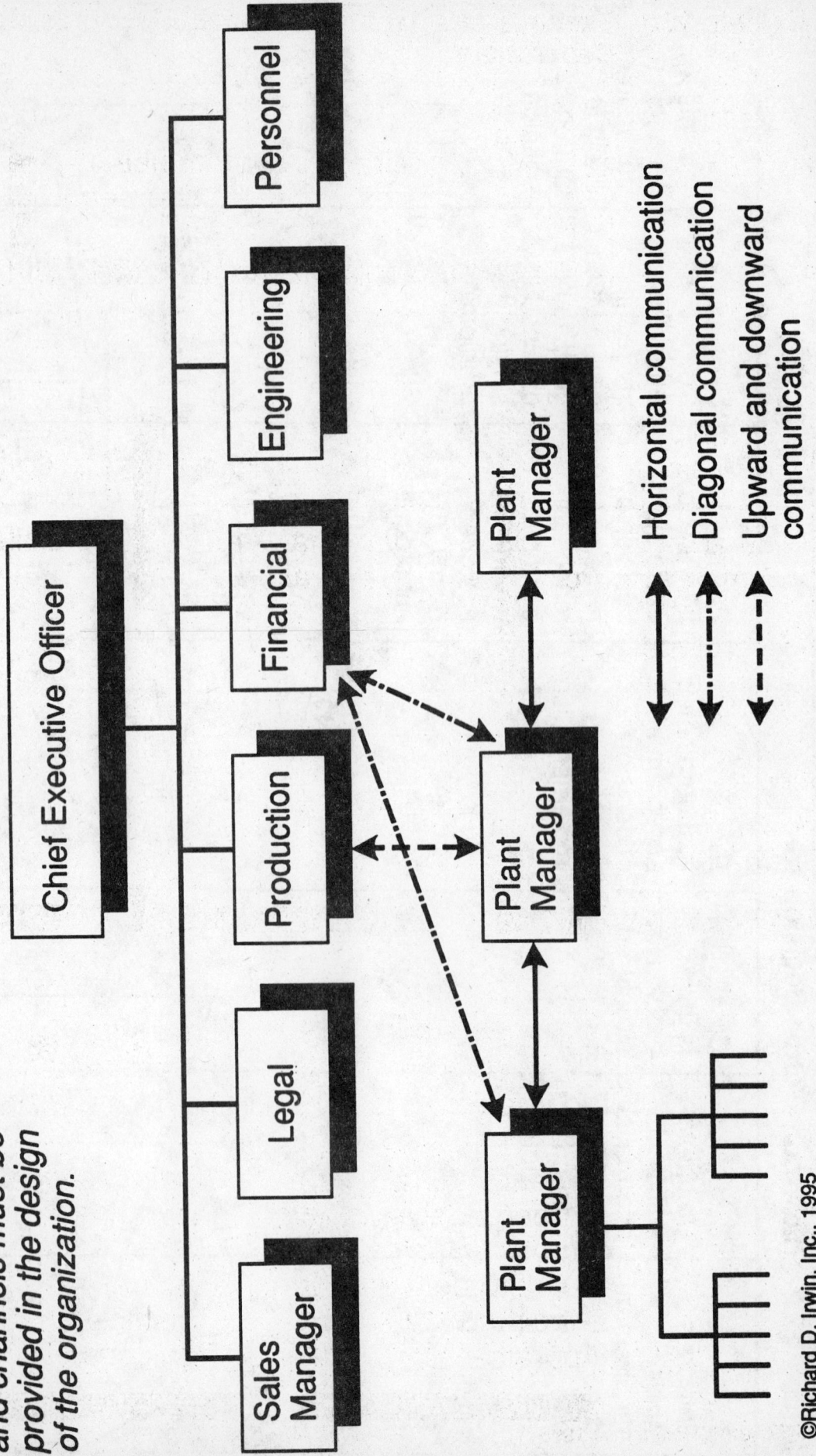

Horizontal communication

Diagonal communication

Upward and downward communication

©Richard D. Irwin, Inc., 1995

Exhibit 15.1 Example of a Personnel/Human Resource Management Department

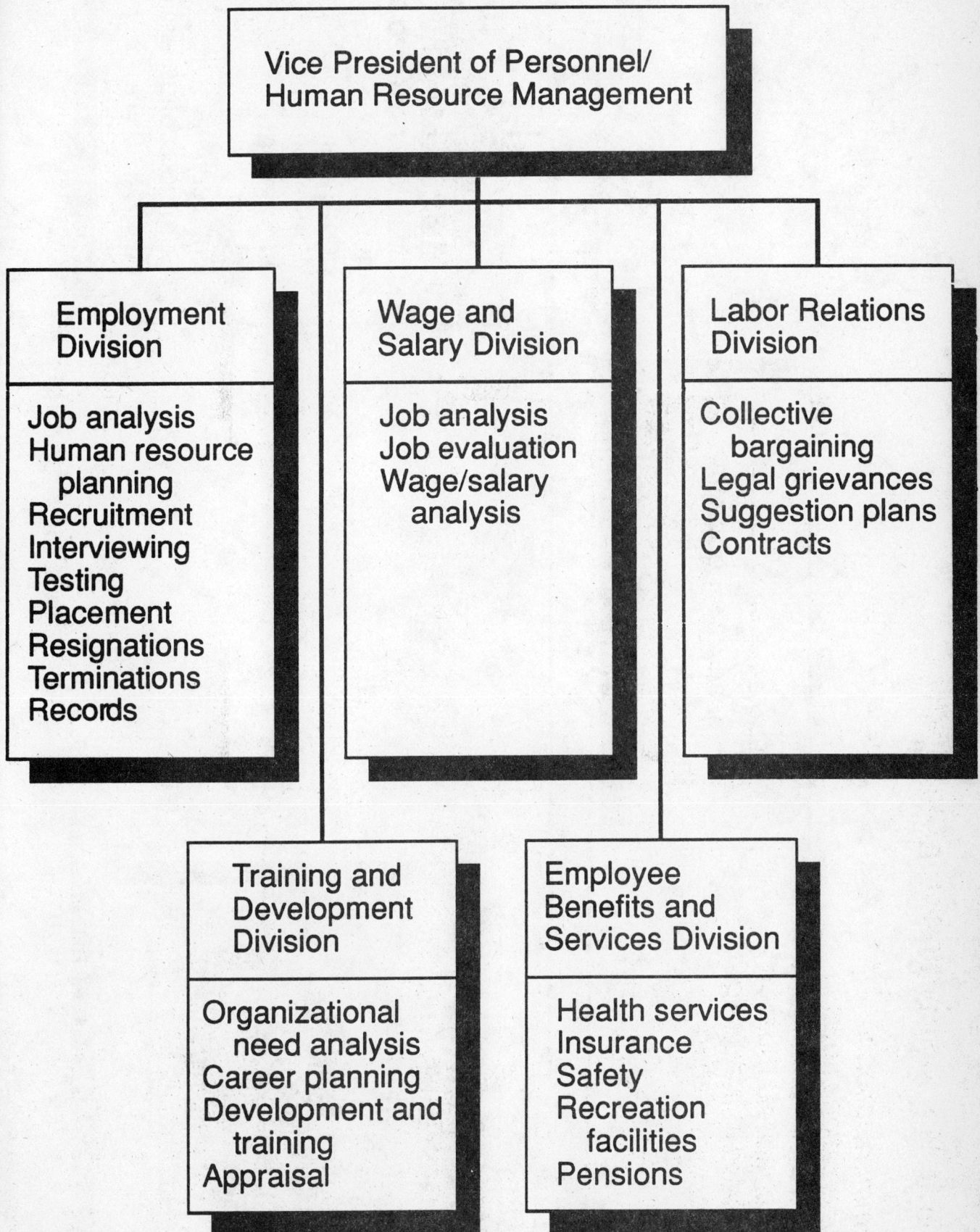

```
                    ┌─────────────────────────────┐
                    │  Vice President of Personnel/ │
                    │  Human Resource Management    │
                    └─────────────────────────────┘
```

Employment Division

Job analysis
Human resource
  planning
Recruitment
Interviewing
Testing
Placement
Resignations
Terminations
Records

Wage and Salary Division

Job analysis
Job evaluation
Wage/salary
  analysis

Labor Relations Division

Collective
  bargaining
Legal grievances
Suggestion plans
Contracts

Training and Development Division

Organizational
  need analysis
Career planning
Development and
  training
Appraisal

Employee Benefits and Services Division

Health services
Insurance
Safety
Recreation
  facilities
Pensions

Exhibit 15.2 Sources of Job Information

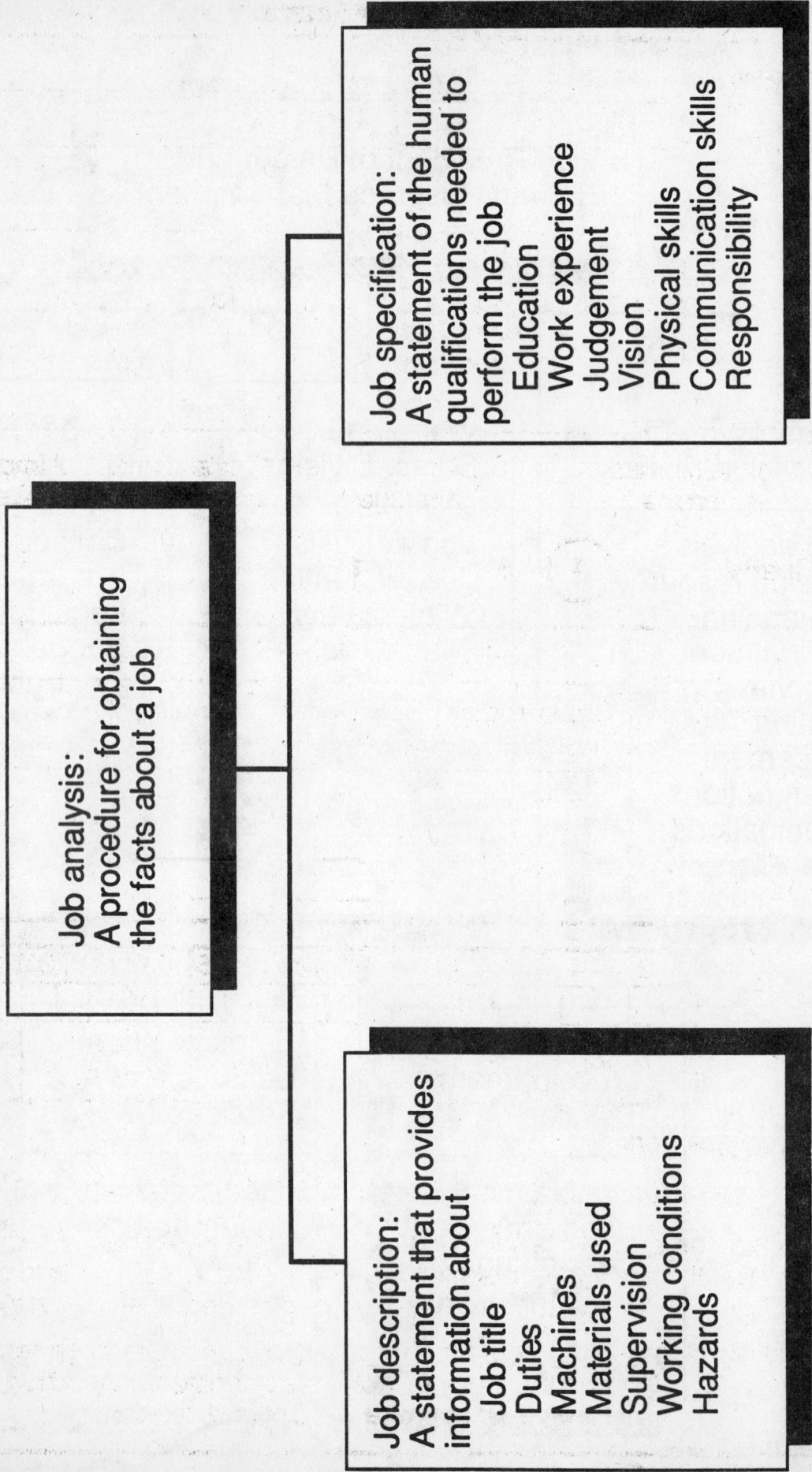

Job analysis:
A procedure for obtaining the facts about a job

Job specification:
A statement of the human qualifications needed to perform the job
  Education
  Work experience
  Judgement
  Vision
  Physical skills
  Communication skills
  Responsibility

Job description:
A statement that provides information about
  Job title
  Duties
  Machines
  Materials used
  Supervision
  Working conditions
  Hazards

Exhibit 15.3 Sample of Rating-Scale Formats

(a) Quality   High |___|___✓___|___|___| Low

(b) Quality   High |___|___✓___|___|___| Low
                 5   4   3   2   1

(c) Quality |___|___✓___|___|___|

| Exceptionally high-quality work | Work usually done in a superior way | Quality is average for this job | Work contains frequent flaws | Work is seldom satisfactory |

(d) Quality |___|___|___|___✓___|

| Too many errors | About average | Occassional errors | Almost never makes mistakes |

(e) Quality   5   ④   3   2   1

(f)

Performance factors	Performance grade			
	Consistently superior	Sometimes superior	Consistently average	Consistently unsatisfactory
Quality: Accuracy Economy Neatness	☐	☒	☐	☐

(g) Quality

1 2 3 4 5	6 7 8 9 10	11 12 13 14 15	16 17 18 19 20	21 22 23 24 25
			☒ (17)	
Poor	Below average	Average	Above average	Excellent

(h) Quality of work

15   13   ⑪   9   7   5   3   1

| Rejects and errors consistently rare | Work usually OK; errors seldom made | Work passable needs to be checked often | Frequent errors and scrap; careless |

(i) Quality of work   Judge the amount of scrap; consider the general care and accuracy of work, also consider inspection record. Poor, 1–6; average 7–18; good, 19–25.   __20__

Exhibit 16.1   Team Building: Sequence of Events

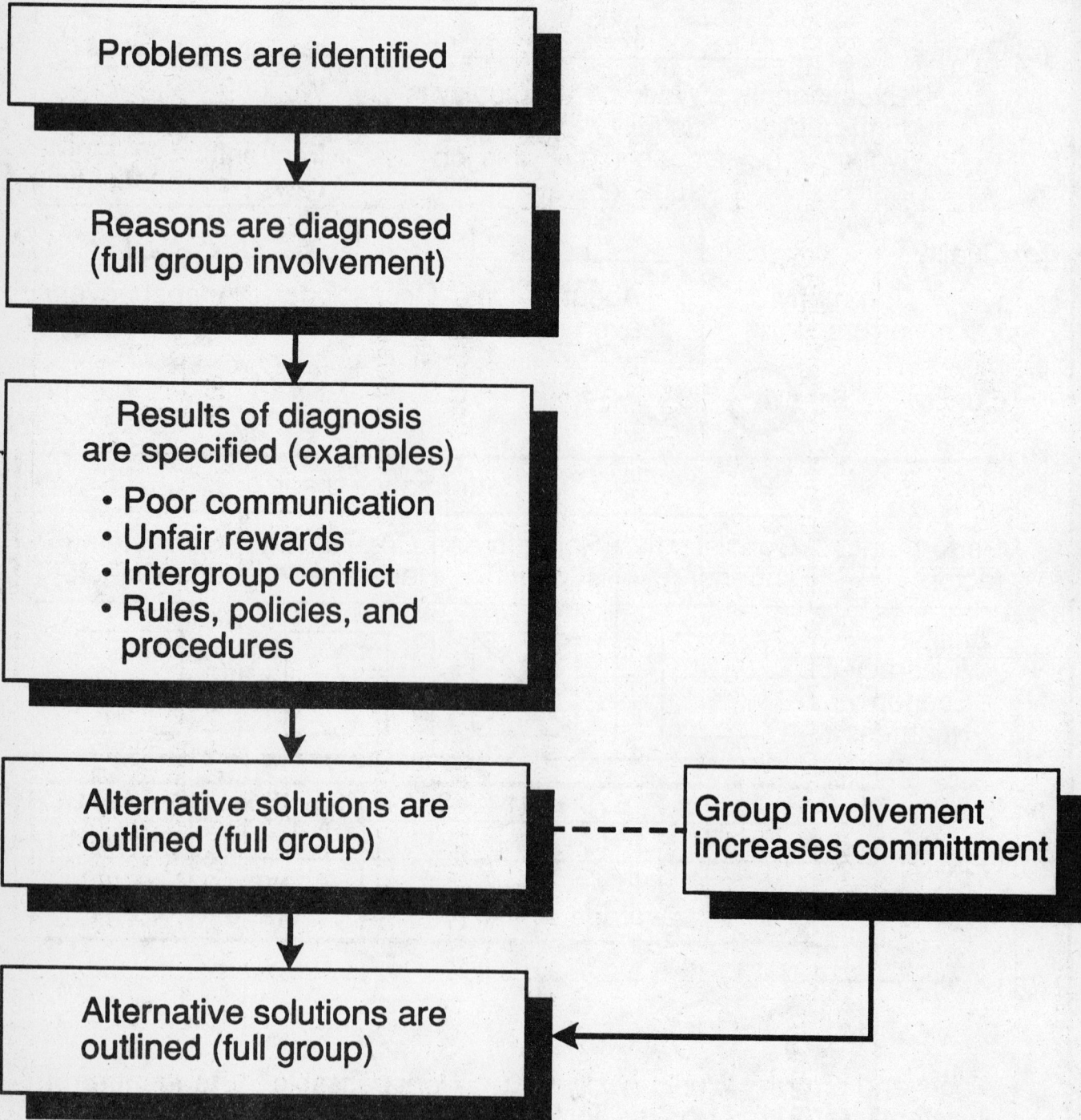

Problems are identified

↓

Reasons are diagnosed
(full group involvement)

↓

Results of diagnosis
are specified (examples)

- Poor communication
- Unfair rewards
- Intergroup conflict
- Rules, policies, and
  procedures

↓

Alternative solutions are
outlined (full group)

Group involvement
increases committment

↓

Alternative solutions are
outlined (full group)

Exhibit 16.2   An Evaluation Matrix: Issues to Consider

Relevant issues to Cover and Evaluate	Examples of What to Measure	Who or What to Examine for Answers	How to Collect Data to Answer issue Questions
1. Are the employees learning, changing attitudes, and/or improving skills?	Employees' attitudes and/ or skills before and after (even during) training or development sessions.	Comments. Method of participation Co-workers. Superiors.	Interviews. Questionnaires. Records. Observation.
2. Are organizational change materials used on the job?	Employees' on-the job performance, behavior, and style.	Subordinate performance, attitudes, and style.	Records. Interviews. Questionnaires. Critical incidents. Observations.
3. Are organizational change materials used on the job?	The fixed and variable costs of conducting the change programs.	Cost of consultants. Participant time. Travel expenses. Training aids. Rent. Utilities.	Budget Records.
4. Are organizational change materials used on the job?	Employees' on-the job performance, behavior, and style over an extended period of time.	Subordinate performance, attitudes, and style.	Records. Interviews. Questionnaires. Critical incidents. Observation (repeated).

Exhibit 17.1 Production Process Flow Diagram for a Burger King Restaurant (nonpeak period)

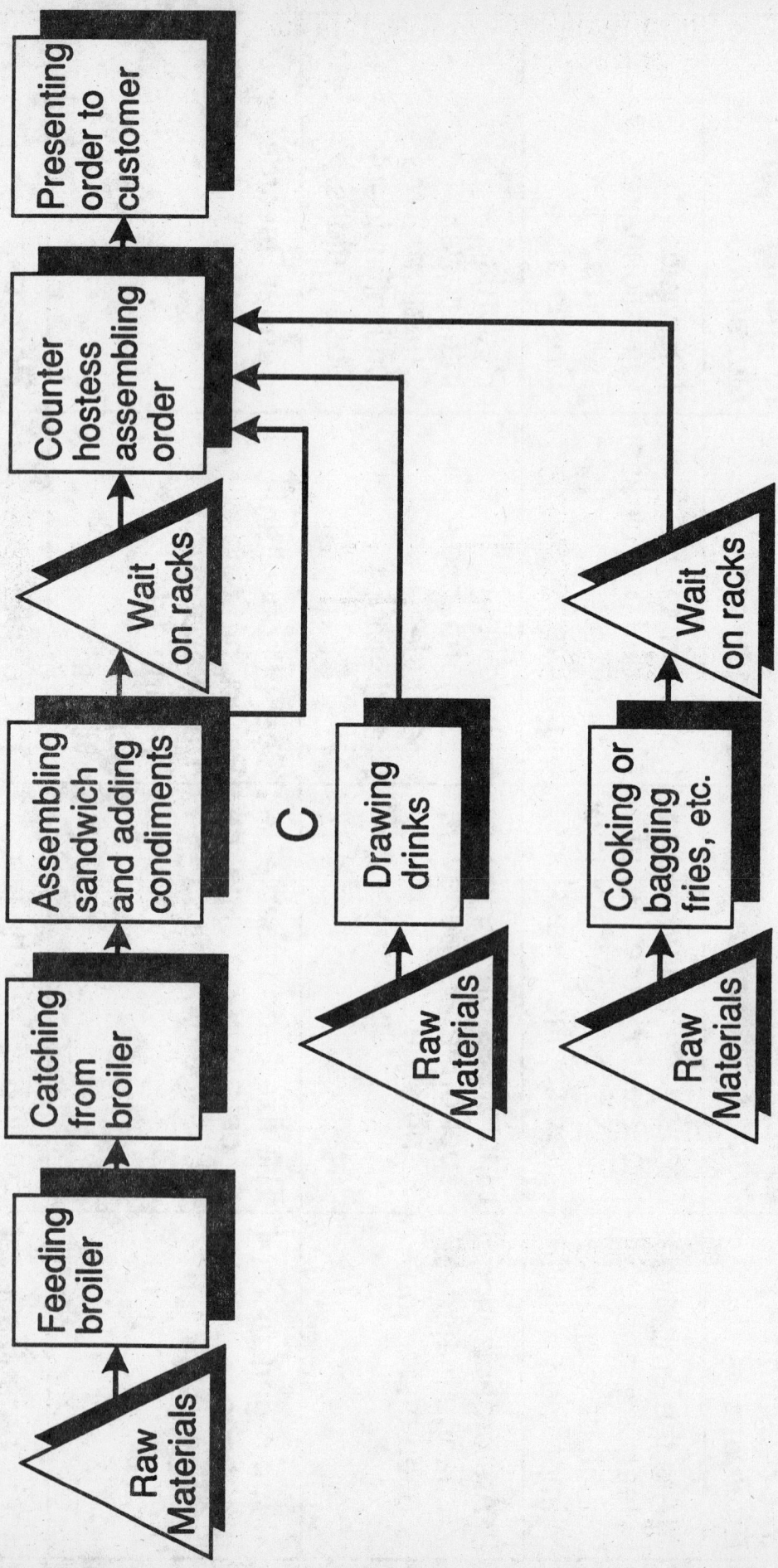

Exhibit 17.2   Information Flow Diagram for a Burger King Restaurant (nonpeak period)

Front counter

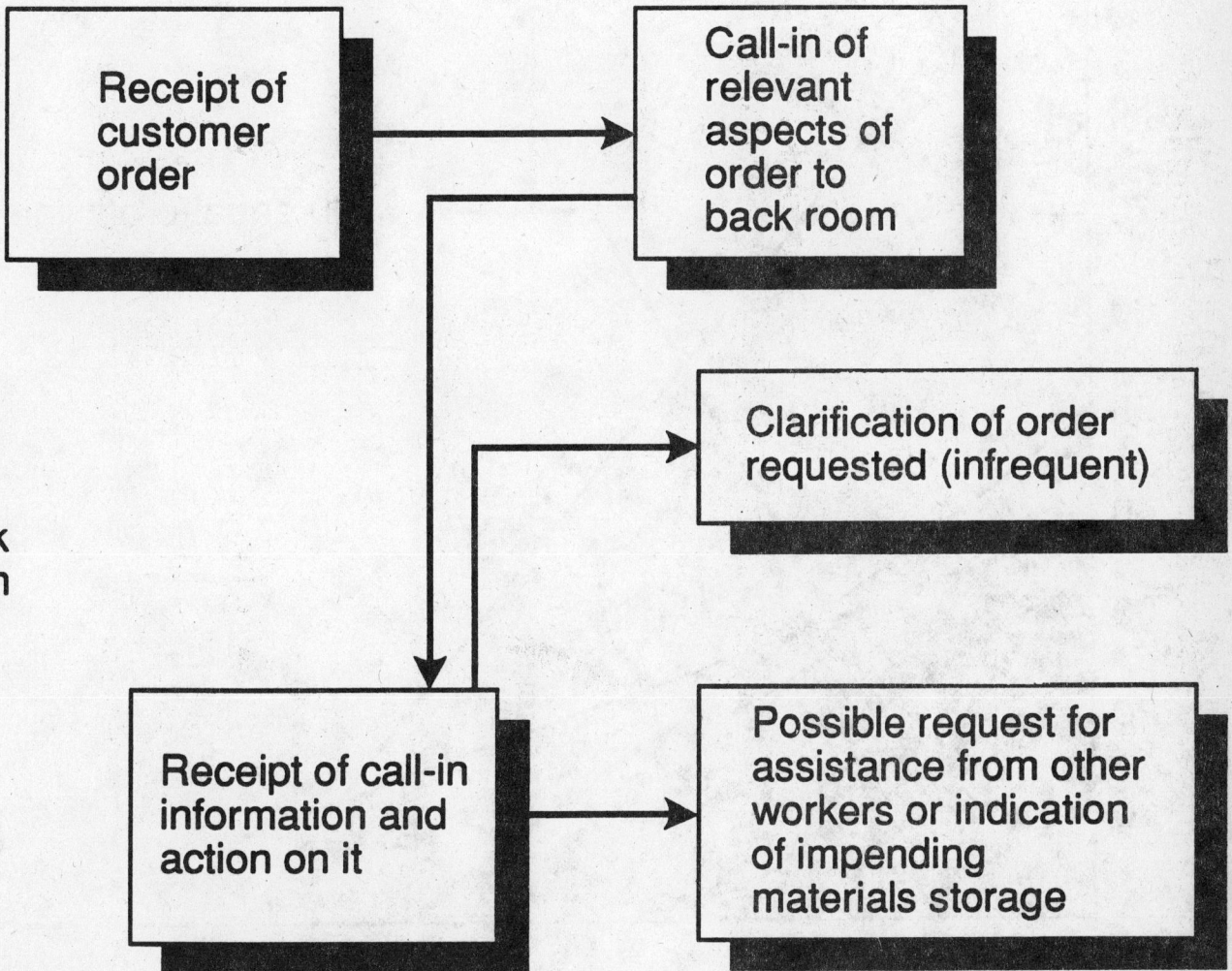

Receipt of customer order → Call-in of relevant aspects of order to back room

Clarification of order requested (infrequent)

Back room

Receipt of call-in information and action on it → Possible request for assistance from other workers or indication of impending materials storage

Exhibit 18.1 Equal-Profit Lines

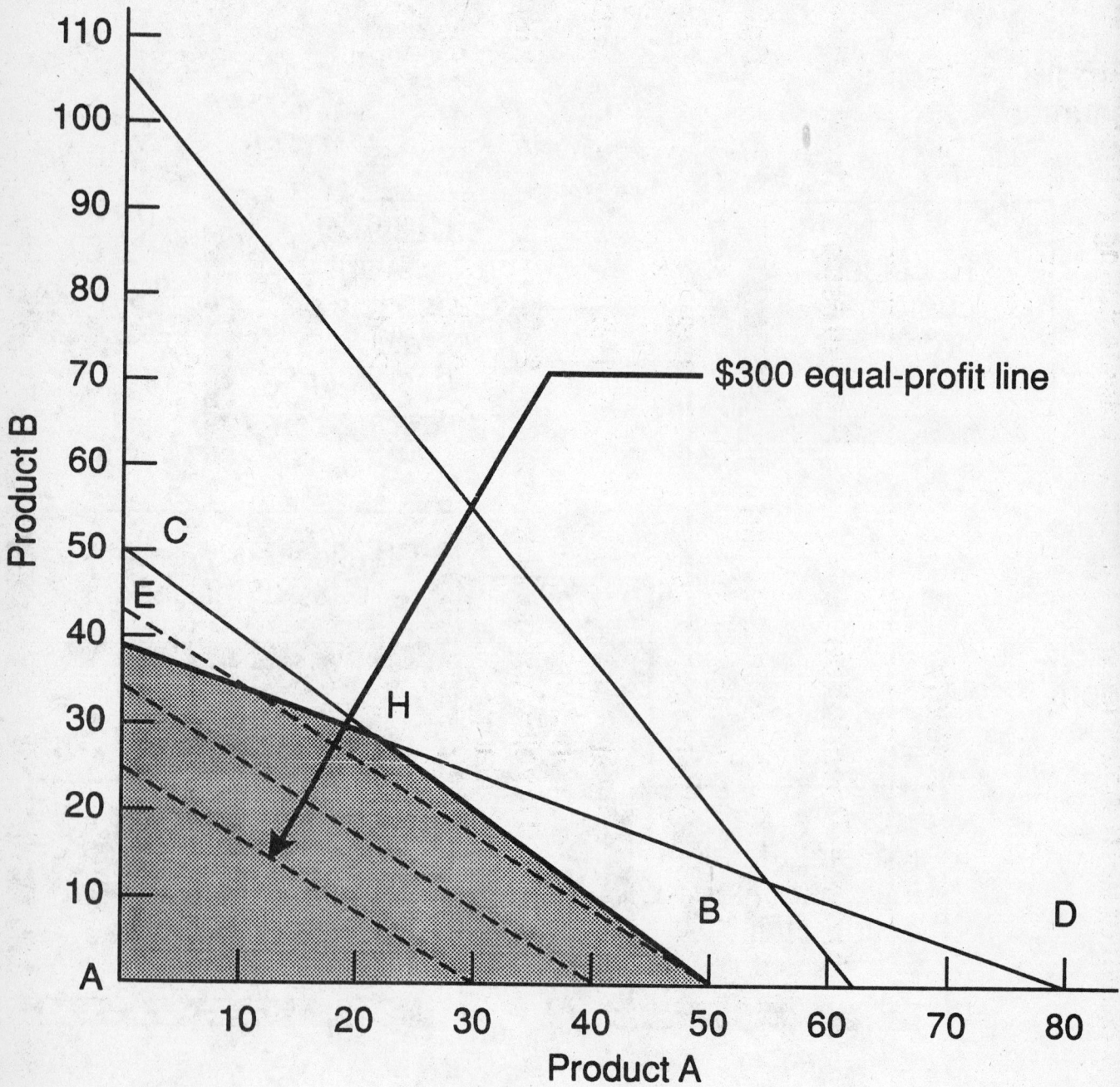

$300 equal-profit line

Product B

Product A

Exhibit 18.2 Description of PERT Activities and Events for Manufacturing of Prototype Aircraft Engine

Activity				Event		
Arrow	Description		Prerequisite	Circle	Description	
1–2	Develop engineering specifications.			2	Specifications completed.	
2–3	Obtain test models.		1–2	3	Test models obtained.	
2–4	Locate suppliers of component parts.		1–2	4	Suppliers located.	
3–5	Develop production plans.		2–3	5	Plans completed.	
5–6	Begin subassembly 1.		3–5	6	Subassembly 1 completed.	
4–6	Place orders for component parts and await receipt.		2–4	6	Component parts received.	
6–7	Begin subassembly 2.		5–6 and 4–6	7	Subassembly 2 completed.	
7–8	Begin final assembly.		6–7	8	Engine completed.	

*The effectiveness
of PERT depends
on accurate
determination of
all events
and activities*

©Richard D. Irwin, Inc., 1995

Exhibit 18.3 Typical PERT Network

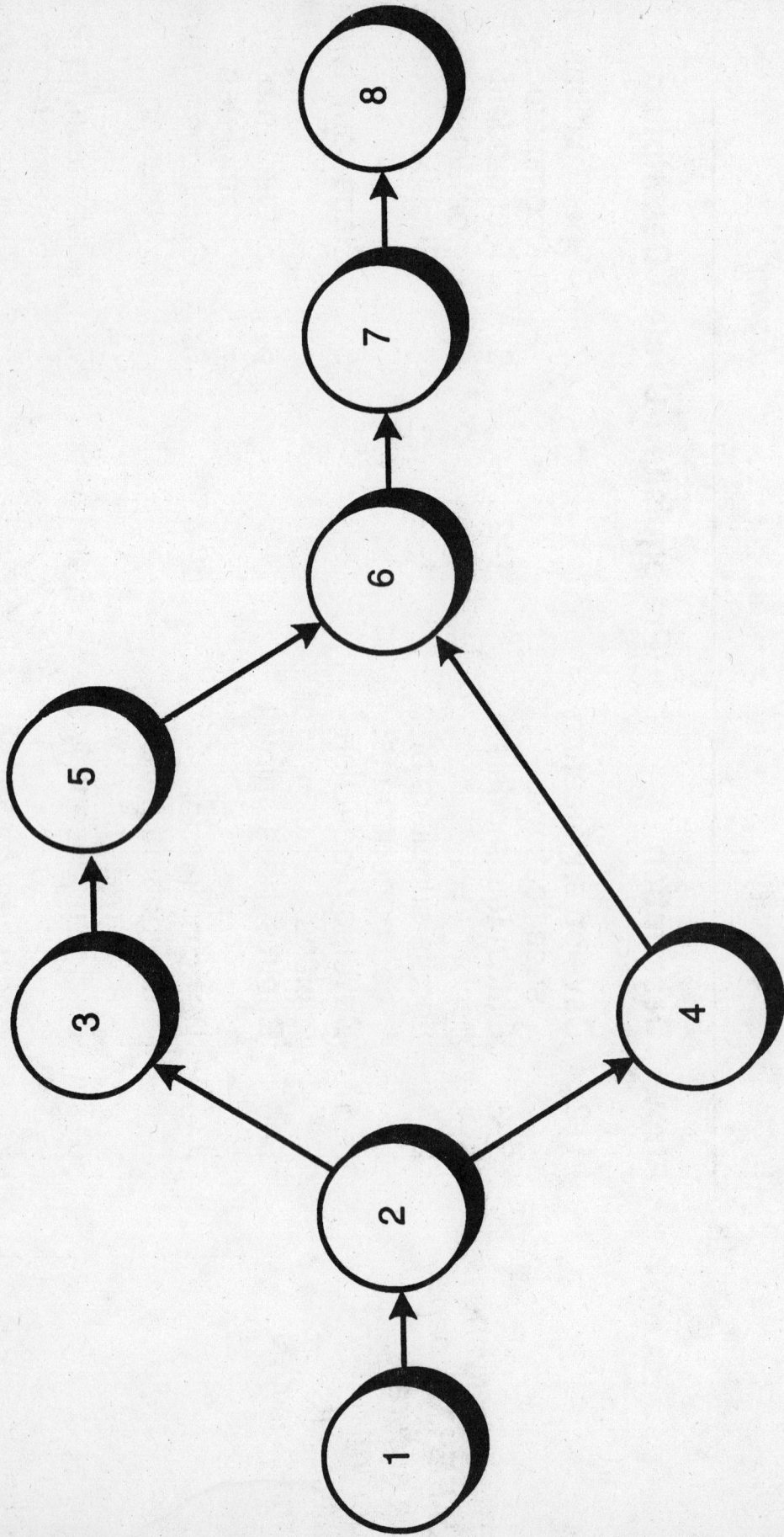

Exhibit 18.4 PERT Network: Time Estimates for Each Activity

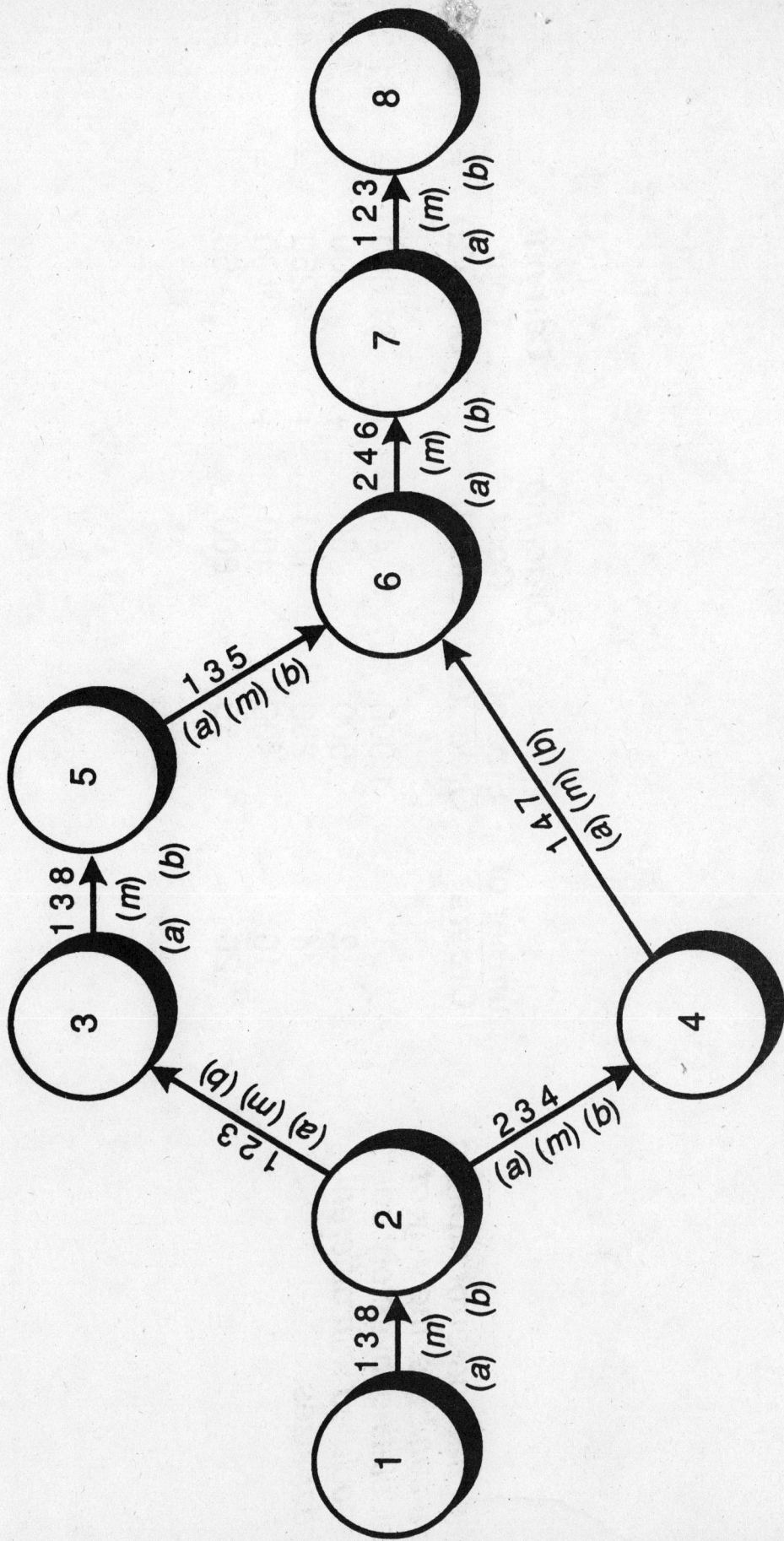

Exhibit 18.5 Trial-and-Error Method

The trial-and-error method is a cumbersome way of calculating inventory costs associated with different order sizes.

Number of Orders	Size of Order Q		Ordering Cost D/Q(J)		Carrying Cost Q/2 (VE)		Total Cost
1	1,000		$ 40	+	$1,000	=	$1,040
2	500		80	+	500	=	580
4	250		160	+	250	=	410
10	100		400	+	100	=	500
20	50		800	+	50	=	850

Exhibit 18.6 The Relationship between the Master Schedule and Bills of Materials

Master production schedule for week of November 20, 1991:

Product:	Bicycles	Baby carriages	Playpens
Quantity:	100	50	25

Bill of materials: Baby carriage:

Part Number	Description	Amount
1	Body assembly	1 each
2	Wheel assembly	2 each
3	Handle and frame assembly	1 each

Bill of materials: Wheel assembly:

Part Number	Description	Amount
2/A	Wheels	2 each
2/B	Axle	1 each

Bills of materials and master schedules enable managers to see the types and amounts of inventory required to produce a particular volume of output for a specified time period.

Inventory requirement for wheel, Part 2/A, for week is 50 (carriages) × 2(wheel assemblies) × 2(wheels) = 200 wheels.

Exhibit 18.7 Elements of MRP System

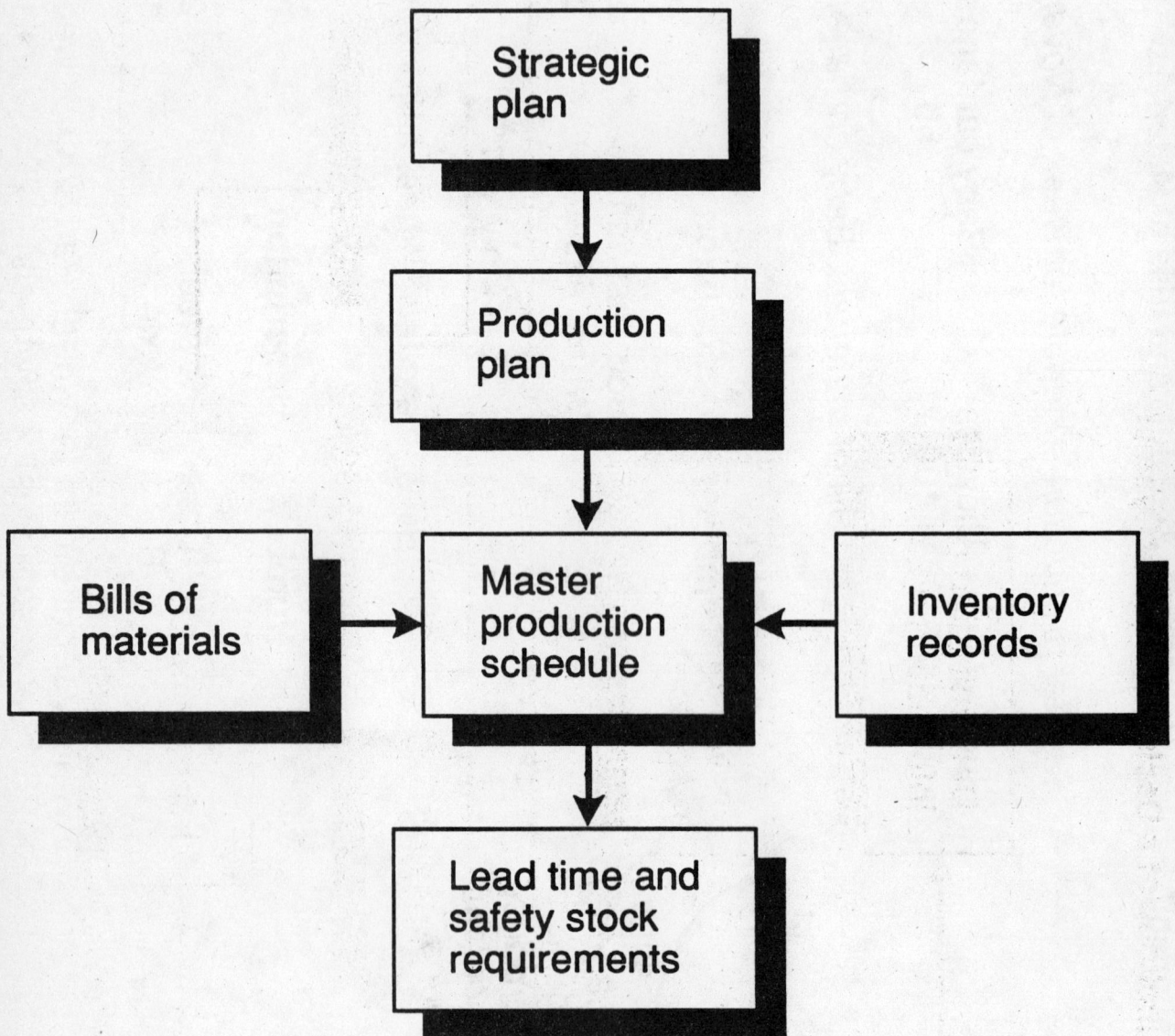

Strategic plan
→
Production plan
→
Bills of materials → Master production schedule ← Inventory records
↓
Lead time and safety stock requirements

Exhibit 19.1   The Functions of a Decision Support System

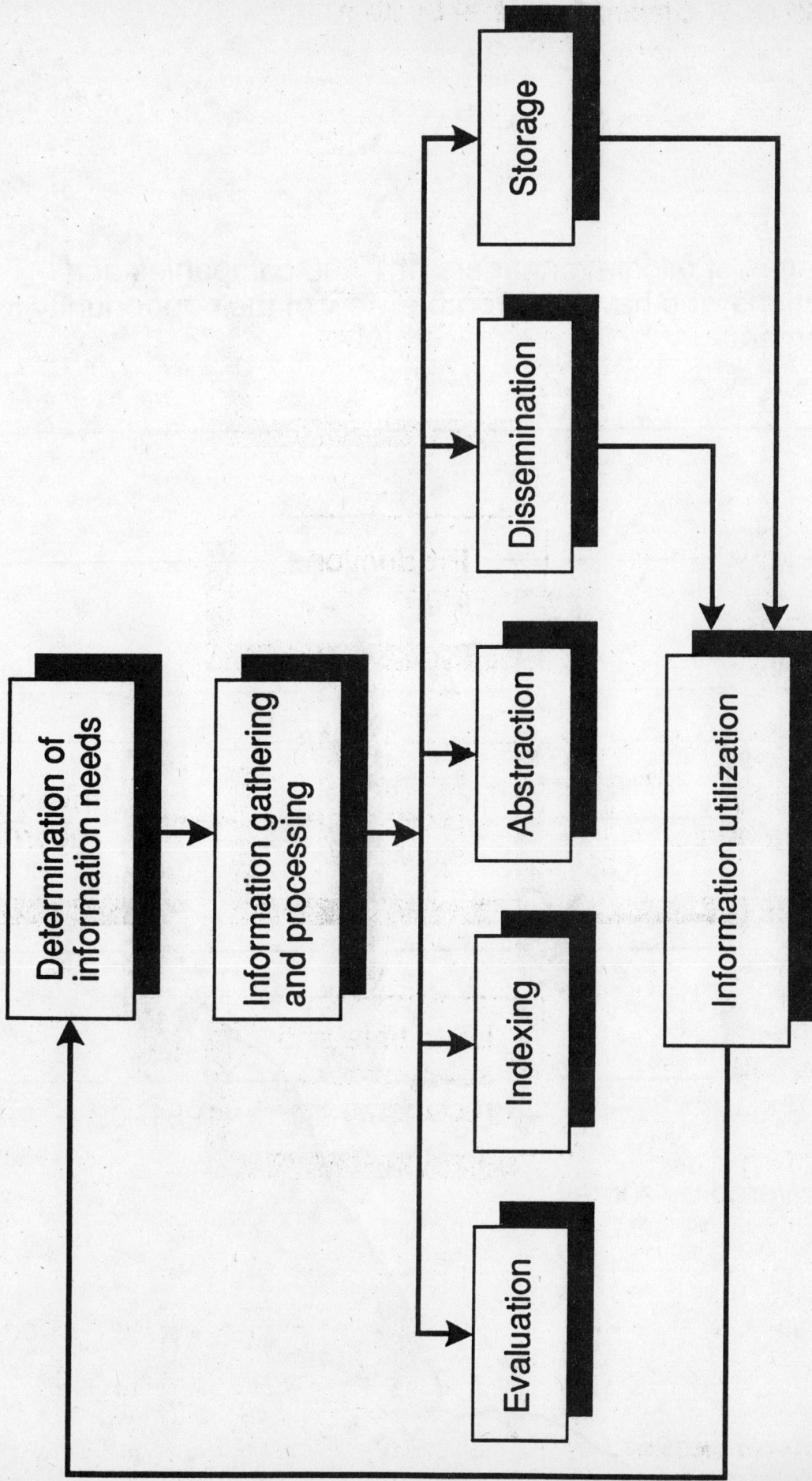

Exhibit 21.1   A Limited Future

Percentages of middle managers at 1,600 companies and organizations who have a favorable view of their opportunity for advancement:

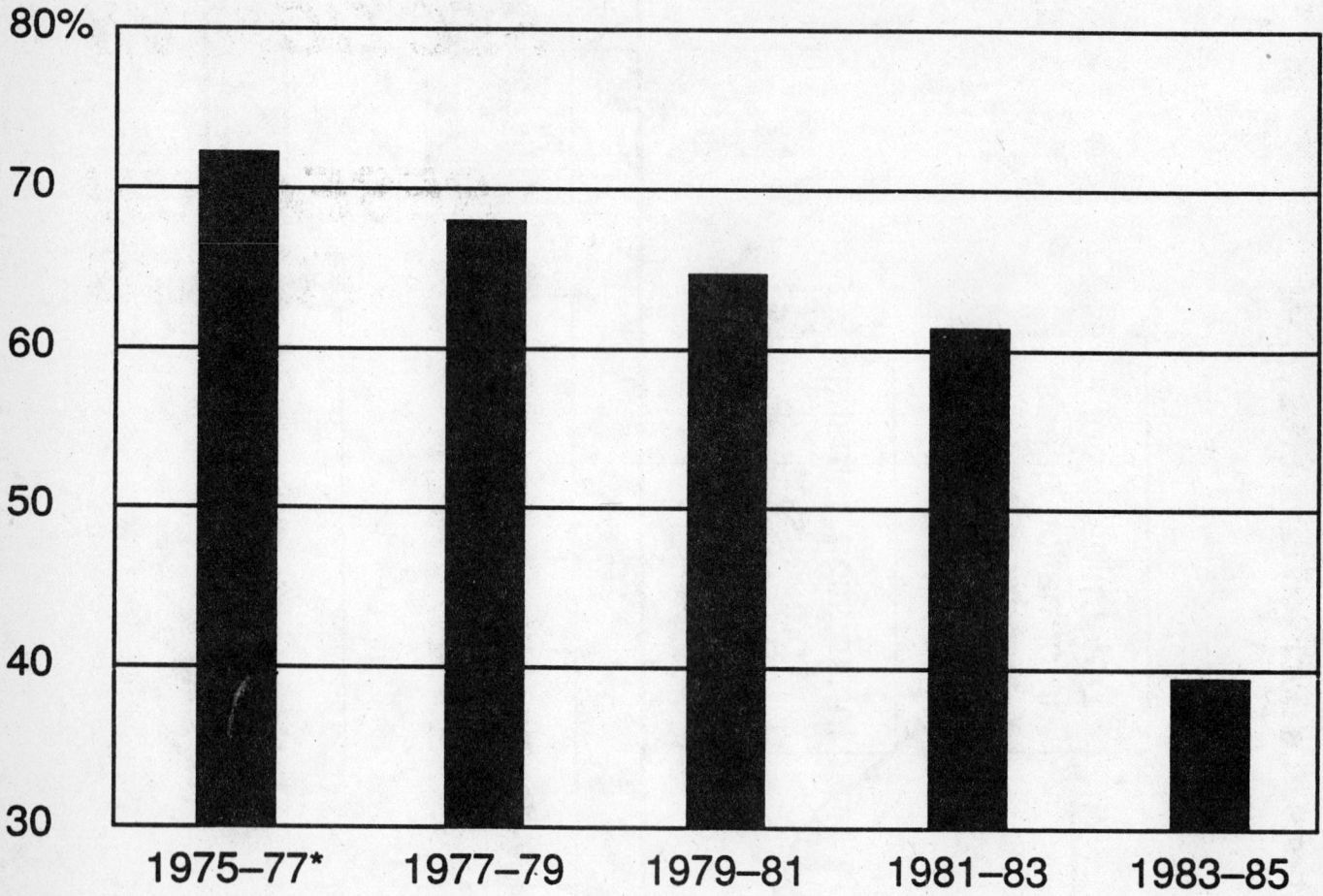

*Years covered by survey

SECTION VII

RESEARCH TOPICS

RESEARCH TOPICS

To assist students in promptly beginning their research, if papers are to be completed as a portion of their course requirements, the following lists of ideas have been included. The model syllabi indicates that a list similar to this will be provided for students information.

CHAPTER 1
Scientific Management: An Overview and Critical Assessment
The Contributions of Frederick Taylor to Scientific Management
The Classical Approach to Management: An Overview
The Future Outlook for the Use of Management Science Techniques in Organizations
A Review of Management Science Network Models
The Contingency Approach to Management in the 1990s
The "Art" of Being an Effective Manager
The Relationship Between Management Theory and Practice
Managing in a Culturally Diverse Organization
Changes in Management in Eastern Europe in the 1990s

CHAPTER 2
The Changing Demographics of the American Workforce
Profile of a Middle-Level Manager
Profile of a First-Level Manager
Women in Business: Managerial Accomplishments and Challenges
Managerial Skills and Effective Management
Coca-Cola Company: An Environmental Profile
How an Organization Monitors Its Competitors
America's Culture: Its Influence on Business
The Impact of Downsizing on the American Workforce
A Day in the Life of a Top-Level Manager: Do the Ten Managerial Roles Apply?

CHAPTER 3
Topic for Term Paper Debate: The Foreign Corrupt Practices Act—A Necessary Law?
The Growth of International Business in the U.S.: 1960-1989
_____: Profile of a Multinational Corporation
The Influence of Culture on MNC Operations
Strategies for Managing in a Politically Unstable Country
Profile of a Successful MNC Manager
The Leadership Function in Multinational Management
Ethics and Social Responsibility in Multinational Management
_____: Profile of a Major U.S. Exporter
Sourcing in North America under NAFTA

536

CHAPTER 8
How Organizational Structure Affects Performance
Innovative Structures in Organizations
The Uses of Multiple Structures
IBM: Profile of an Organizational Design
Product Structure: Its Benefits and Limitations
How Decentralization Works at General Electric
The Current Literature Relating to Job Design
The Pros and Cons of Job Enrichment
What the Organization Chart Doesn't Show
Functional Structure: Its Benefits and Limitations

CHAPTER 9
The Relationship Between Classical Organization Theory and Bureaucracy
New Theories of Organization Design
Designing the Organization from the Top Down or the Bottom Up: A comparison
The Benefits and Pitfalls of Matrix Organization Design
The Ideal Bureaucracy: A Critical Assessment
A Profile of the Woodward Studies
A History of the Development of Neoclassical Design
The Influence of Technology on Organization Design at General Motors
Topic for Term Paper Debate: Does Structure Follow Strategy?
Contingency Design: Myth or Reality?

CHAPTER 10
Profile of Two Successful Companies' Control Systems
The Response of Organization Members to Control Techniques
Standard Setting as a Collective Bargaining Issue
Techniques for Control of Capital Investments: An Overview
Techniques of Concurrent Controls
The Role of Budgeting in Financial Control
The Art of Establishing a Standard Cost Accounting System
Quality Control at Mercedes Benz
The Nuts and Bolts of Financial Statement Analysis
Techniques of Concurrent Control

CHAPTER 11
The Pros and Cons of Job Enrichment
The Role of Money in Motivating Workers
Equal Pay for Equal Worth—Motivational Issues of Male/Female Pay Differences
An Analysis of Maslow's Hierarchy of Needs
ESOPs: Benefits and Risks
The Strengths and Shortcomings of Expectancy Theory
Motivation in the Culturally Diverse Workplace
The Power and Risks of Using Punishment As a Motivator
Satisfaction in Herzberg's Two-Factor Theory
A Study of Organizations that Build Employee Pride and Self-Esteem

CHAPTER 12
Roles People Play in Groups
Acculturation in Groups
Minimize the Conflict: Managerial Approaches to Intragroup Conflict
The Bay of Pigs: The Domination of Groupthink
Watergate: Did Groupthink Exist?
The Rise of Self-Managed Work Groups
Quality Circles in U.S. Businesses Today
Why People Join Groups
The Dynamics of Intergroup Conflict
Managerial Strategies for Resolving Intergroup Conflict

CHAPTER 13
The Bases of Leadership Power
Path-Goal Theory: An Assessment
Leadership Traits of Women and Men
_____: A Charismatic Leader
The Role of the Self-Fulfilling Prophecy in Leadership
Transformational and Transactional Leadership: A Comparison
Can Leadership be Learned?
The Use of Tridimensional Leader Effectiveness Theory in Organizations Today
Training to Help Managers Move to Leadership Grid (9,9) Style
Applications of the Vroom-Yetton-Jago Leader-Style Theory

CHAPTER 14
The Importance of Effective Listening for Managers
A Survey of Effective Negotiation Tactics
Prescriptions for Alleviating Communications Barriers
The Organizational Grapevine: Its Value and Fallacies
The Relationship of Organizational Structure and Communication
Individual Personality and Communication
Techniques for Improving Upward Communication
The Benefits and Problems of Diagonal Communication
Body Language in the U.S. and Elsewhere
How Selective Perception Affects Communication

CHAPTER 15
Managerial Development: An Overview of Popular Methods
The Gender Gap in Earnings in U.S. Corporations
Day Care at the Company—Benefit or Necessity?
Appraising HRM at _____ (a large corporation)
A Critique of the Position Analysis Questionnaire
The ADA: A Current Status Report on Implementation in Business
An Historical View of the Evolution of Performance Appraisal in Organizations
The Pros and Cons of Testing in the Selection Process
The Psychological Barriers in Performance Appraisal
BARS: An Overview and Critical Assessment

CHAPTER 16

Why People Fear and Resist Change
The Impact of Robots on Industry in the 1990s
Internal and External Forces of Organizational Change
Does Sensitivity Training Affect Organizational Effectiveness?
Organizational Culture: Its Impact on the Effectiveness of Organizational Change
The Dynamics of the Team Building Process
Managerial Strategies for Overcoming Resistance to Change
TQM Implementation in U.S. Businesses
Techniques for Monitoring Organizational Change
How an Organization's Strategies for Change Influence its Outcome

CHAPTER 17

The P/OM Discipline: An Historical Overview
The Techniques of Transformation Control
Quality Assurance Efforts at Toyota
The Costs of Poor Product Quality
Steps Toward Effective Product Quality
Quality at McDonalds: A Profile
The Factors that Affect Product/Service Quality: An Overview
The Transformation Process at: A Profile
The Nuts and Bolts of Sening Quality Standards
Quality Improvement Efforts at Hewlett-Packard

CHAPTER 18

The Purposes of Inventories
Just-in-Time Inventory Control: Its Techniques, Benefits and Limitations
The Nuts and Bolts of Establishing an MRP System
Inventory Control: Criteria for Effectiveness
The EOQ Model: Uses and Limitations
The MRP at (a local business): A Profile
Techniques for Determining Safety Stock and Lead Times
Japan's Development of JIT Inventory Control: An Overview
Inventory Control in the Year 2000: Innovative Techniques on the Horizon
Pitfalls to Avoid in Establishing an MRP System

CHAPTER 19

The Nuts and Bolts of Developing and Implementing a DSS in an Organization
The Advent of Personal Computers and Their Impact on the Manager's Job
The Role of Information in Decision Making
The DSS at(a local business): A Profile
A Day on the Job of a DSS/MIS Manager
The Functions and Tasks of the Central Data Bank
The Uses and Misuses of Information
Techniques for Information Gathering and Processing in a DSS
The DSS Information Center: Tasks and Responsibilities
DSS in the Year 2000: New Functions and Responsibilities
The Advantages and Shortcomings of Linear Programming: A Review
An Actual Application of Linear Programming

540

CHAPTER 19 - continued

An Historical Look at the Development of PERT
A Review of Network Models
An Case Study of An Application of PERT
A Historical Overview of the Development of Linear Programming
The Use of Computers in Linear Programming
Special Problems in the Use of PERT
The Strengths and Limitations of the PERT Technique
Goal Programming: An Advanced Variation of Linear Programming.

CHAPTER 20

_____: Profile of an Entrepreneur
The Nuts and Bolts of Starting a Business
Franchising: An Overview
Topic for Term Paper Debate: Are Entrepreneurs Born, Not Made?
_____: Profile of a Business Buyout
The Risks of Starting a Business
Approaches to Financing a Start-Up
Behind the Boom in Women Entrepreneurship
The Nuts and Bolts of Writing a Business Plan
Start-Up Planning: Steps in Selecting a Product and Product Market.

CHAPTER 21

_____ (a local executive): Career Path Profile
Case Studies of Female Executives and their Career Plans
Dual-Career Couples: The Problems Encountered and Suggested Solutions
The Role of Work in an Individual's Life
The Meaning of Career Success from a Personal Perspective
The Role of Socialization in Managerial Development
The Mid-Career Crisis Phenomenon
Profile of a Career Counseling Program
The Nuts and Bolts of Career Planning
The "Art" of Getting that First Job